# Fracturing the Canon

An Interdisciplinary Humanities Reader

David Cann, Ph.D. I Julie Kubala, Ph.D. I Mary Twining, Ph.D. I Brenda Young, Ph.D.
Editors

CENGAGE
Learning

Australia • Brazil • Japan • Korea • Mexico • Singapore • Spain • United Kingdom • United States

CENGAGE
Learning™

**Fracturing the Canon**

**An Interdisciplinary Humanities Reader**

David Cann, Ph.D. I Julie Kubala, Ph.D. I
Mary Twining, Ph.D. I Brenda Young, Ph.D.
Editors

Executive Editor:
Michele Baird

Maureen Staudt

Michael Stranz

Project Development Editor:
Linda de Stefano

Senior Marketing Coordinators:
Sara Mercurio

Lindsay Shapiro

Production/Manufacturing Manager:
Donna M. Brown

PreMedia Services Supervisor:
Rebecca A. Walker

Rights & Permissions Specialist:
Kalina Hintz

Cover Image:
Getty Images*

ISBN-13: 978-0-759-30475-8

ISBN-10: 0-759-30475-0

**Cengage Learning**
5191 Natorp Boulevard
Mason, Ohio 45040
USA

Cengage Learning is a leading provider of customized learning solutions with
office locations around the globe, including Singapore, the United Kingdom,
Australia, Mexico, Brazil, and Japan. Locate your local office at:
**international.cengage.com/region**

Cengage Learning products are represented in Canada by Nelson Education, Ltd.

For your lifelong learning solutions, visit **custom.cengage.com**

Visit our corporate website at **cengage.com**

Printed at CLDPC, USA, 09-20

# ACKNOWLEDGMENTS

"How to Tame a Wild Tongue" from *Borderlands/La Frontera: The New Mestiza*. Copyright © 1987 by Gloria Anzaldua. Reprinted by permission of Aunt Lute Books.

"Black Athena" from *Black Athena: The Afroasiatic Roots of Classical Civilization* by Martin Bernal. Copyright ©1991 by Martin Bernal, reprinted by permission of Rutgers University Press.

"The Choking Doberman and its Ancestors" from *The Choking Doberman* and other "New Urban Legends" by Jan Harold Brunvand. Copyright © 1984 Jan Harold Brunvand, reprinted by permission of W.W. Norton & Co.

"The Black Manifesto" by James Forman from *National Black Economic Development Conference*, Detroit Mich., April 1969.

"Introduction to The Mismeasure of Man" from *The Mismeasure of Man* by Stephen Jay Gould. Copyright © 1981 Stephen Jay Gould. Reprinted by permission of W.W. Norton & Company.

"Who's Passing for Who?" from *Short Stories* by Langston Hughes. Copyright © 1996 by Ramona Bass and Arnold Rampersad. Reprinted by permission of Hill and Wang, a division of Farrar, Straus and Giroux, LLC.

"Nonviolence and Social Change" from *The Trumpet of Conscience* by Martin Luther King Jr. Copyright © 1968 the Estate of Martin Luther King Jr. and Writer's House. Reprinted by permission of Writer's House Inc.

"Clarence Thomas and the Crisis of Black Political Culture" from *Race-ing Justice, En-gendering Power* by Toni Morrison (editor) Copyright ©1992 by Manning Marable. Reprinted by permission of Pantheon Books, a division of Random House, Inc.

"Racial Formation" from *Racial Formations in the United States,* 2nd Edition, edited by Michael Omi and Howard Winant. Reproduced by permission of Routledge, Inc. Copyright ©1994.

"The Ideology of Machines: Computer Technology" from *Technopoly* by Neil Postman. Copyright © 1992 by Neil Postman. Reprinted by permission of Alfred A. Knopf Inc.

"La Guera" by Cherrie Moraga from *This Bridge Called My Back: Writings by Radical Women of Color*. Copyright © 1983 Cherrie Moraga and Gloria Anzaldua. Reprinted by permission of Kitchen Table/Women of Color Press.

"The Combahee River Collective Statement" from *Capitalist Patriarchy and the Case for Socialist Feminism* by The Combahee River Collective. Copyright © 1978 Zillah Eisenstein, reprinted by permission of Kitchen Table/Women of Color Press.

"Language and Literature from a Pueblo Indian Perspective" by Leslie Marmon Silko from *Yellow Woman and a Beauty of the Spirit*. Copyright © 1996 Leslie Marmon Silko, reprinted by permission of Simon & Schuster.

"The Epic of Sara" from unpublished work by Charles Bird; reproduced by permission of Charles Bird and Indiana University Press.

"Recitatif" by Toni Morrison. Copyright © 1991 Janklow & Nesbit Associates, Literary Agents, reprinted by permission of the author and the literary agents.

"Ain't I a Woman?" by Sojourner Truth. This speech is the record of Sojourner Truth's address at the 1851 Women's Rights convention in Akron, Ohio.

"Invisibility is an Unnatural Disaster" by Mitsuye Yamada from *This Bridge Called My Back: Writings* by Radical Women of Color. Copyright © 1983 Cherrie Moraga and Gloria Anzaldua. Reprinted by permission of Kitchen Table/Women of Color Press.

"No Name Woman" from *The Woman Warrior* by Maxine Hong Kingston. Copyright © 1975 Maxine Hong Kingston. Reprinted by permission of Alfred A. Knopf Inc.

"Three Thousand Dollar Death Song" by Wendy Rose from *Lost Copper*. Copyright © 1980 Wendy Rose, reprinted by permission from Malki Museum Press.

"We, the Dangerous" by Janice Mirikitani appeared in *Awake in the River, Poetry and Prose* from Isthmus Press. Copyright © 1978 Janice Mirikitani.

"The Only Traffic Signal on the Reservation Doesn't Flash Red Anymore" from *The Lone Ranger And Tonto Fistfight In Heaven* by Sherman Alexie reprinted by permission of Grove Press. Copyright © 1993 Sherman Alexie.

"Oedipus Rex, "Scene IV"" by Sophocles from *Oedipus Rex of Sophocles: An English Version* by Cornelia Fitts and Robert Fitzgerald (eds.) Copyright © 1949 Cornelia Fitts and Robert Fitzgerald, reprinted by permission of Harcourt, Brace and Company.

"Racism and Culture" by Frantz Fanon is reprinted by permission of The Monthly Review Press. Copyright © 1967 Frantz Fanon and Monthly Review Press.

"Chapter IV, The Rosetta Stone" from *The Rosetta Stone* by Ernest Alfred Wallis Budge . Copyright ©1989. Reprinted by permission of Dover Publications, Inc.

"Niani" from *Sundiata* is reprinted by permission of Pearson Education.

"Life of Hector" from *The Iliad* by Homer is reprinted by permission of Doubleday. Copyright © Robert Fitzgerald.

"On the Duty of Civil Disobedience" by Henry David Thoreau is reprinted from the Library of America.

"The Effects of Atomic Bombs on Hiroshima and Nagasaki" from U.S. Government Printing Office, 1946.

"When Heaven and Earth Changed Places" from *When Heaven and Earth Changed Places* by Le Ly Hayslip. Copyright © 1989 by Le Ly Hayslip and Charles Jay Wurts. Used by permission of Doubleday, a division of Random House Inc.

"Five Myths of Consumership" from The Nation, January 20, 1969 by Dallas Smythe. Copyright and reprinted by permission of The Nation.

"Gangsta Rap and American Culture" from *Between God and Gangsta Rap: Bearing Witness to Black Culture* by Michael Eric Dyson is reprinted by permission of the author and Oxford University Press. Copyright © 1996 Michael Eric Dyson.

"Dreams of an Insomniac: Jewish Feminist Essays, Speeches and Diatribes" by Irena Klepfisz is reprinted by permission of the author and Eighth Mountain Press. Copyright © 1990 Irena Klepfisz.

# CONTENTS

# Fracturing the Canon

## AN INTERDISCIPLINARY READER

*Julia Kubala, David Cann,*
*Mary Arnold Twining, and Keith E. Baird*

Terentius Afer, that is, Terence the African, (185-159 BCE) a Roman playwright, stated, Nothing human do I consider alien to me (Nihil humanum mihi alienum puto). This statement will serve as a fundamental principle for the study of human behavior and accomplishments which we know as humanities. The task we attempt in this book is an impossible one. We can only hope to partially achieve our goals. Even to attempt to introduce the achievements of one culture or civilization in a text is an impossible task. We cannot begin to hope that we can survey the cultures of all times and all places. Yet this book can begin to present the different flavors of human achievement throughout history. Even more importantly, it can begin to help us search for some of the right questions to ask about the humanities. This is not a new endeavor. Since the beginning of our search for knowledge, people have catalogued and evaluated the breadth and depth of human achievement in the arts and sciences. The development of the university system is, in effect, an answer to the questions of what is important in human history and culture.

## WHY INTERDISCIPLINARY?

The first question students may be asking themselves when they purchase their textbook is, what does interdisciplinary mean? First, we should back up and ask what disciplinary knowledge might mean. Academic disciplines refers to the divisions into subjects of knowledge, such as English, History, Philosophy, Anthropology, Fine Arts, Religion, Sociology, Psychology, and the Natural Sciences. Interdisciplinary studies, then, analyze both the connections among these disciplines as well as studies which may not fit neatly into any single category. An analogy might be useful here: think of the university as a symphony. To be a first-chair violinist, for instance,

one must try to be the best violinist and to know as much as possible about the violin. Similarly, if one is a disciplinary scholar, such as a professor of Philosophy, one must try to know everything there is to know about Philosophy. Interdisciplinary scholars, on the other hand, can be compared to the conductor of the symphony; we must know something about how each of the instruments works and how they all fit together to produce beautiful music. In order to explain this concept even more clearly, perhaps a brief history of interdisciplinary studies will be useful.

In recent years, many academic discussions have focused on the move toward interdisciplinarity within universities. This move has been, and still is, occurring because of an expansion of the traditional function of the university — to perpetuate an elite ruling class educated in the classics. Since the mid-twentieth century, the university has been opened up due to such programs as the GI bill and affirmative action. As the demographics of student populations changed, so did their needs from higher education. Consequently, the university has opened up, both to meet the demands of new technology, as well as to serve these emergent populations. For instance, student demands for African-American studies or Women s Studies contributed to this desire for information/course curricula outside traditional boundaries. These new departments not only criticized exclusions within traditional disciplines, but they also questioned the manner in which universities carve up knowledge into specific, oftentimes exclusive, categories. How can we, for example, expect students to understand Shakespearean literature without a consideration of British history, political climate, social systems, and other artworks? In The Structure of Scientific Revolutions, Thomas Kuhn states we want to describe that research as a strenuous and devoted attempt to force nature into the conceptual boxes supplied by professional education [and educators, Ed. Note] (5). Western thinkers have analyzed human knowledge into these boxes separating science from arts and philosophy when, in actuality, all belong under the rubric of Humanities particularly if we understand science to mean human knowledge.

One significant benefit of interdisciplinary thought, then, is that it has encouraged criticism of traditional ways of thinking, therefore opening up the university to new theoretical perspectives and international viewpoints. This twentieth-century expansion caused a virtual explosion of knowledge in the fields of theory and cultural criticism, due in part to the critique of the university as whitewashed, phallocentric, and elitist. A crucial part of questioning these institutionalized knowledges involves the idea that no knowledge can be separated from the person(s) who create it. In other words, the previously accepted notion that knowledge is acquired from an objective standpoint is only an illusion, or perhaps, a goal that we work toward. A central premise of this textbook, then, is that the way each individual perceives the world is fundamentally shaped by particular cultural biases and ideologies. While no one can escape these cultural institutions, it is also true that not everyone is affected in the same way by them. In this class, therefore, we will analyze the connections between individual experience and broader social structures in order to specifically describe both the institutions and their effects.

## DEBATES OVER "THE CANON"

The arguments over interdisciplinarity also parallel the arguments over the canon, which can be defined as the set of texts that comprise a standard of knowledge in a particular field. This, of course, leads to the very first set of questions we must ask: Where did this canon come from? What does it mean to propose a standard by which to measure knowledge and achievement?

By the term canon, most people really mean the Western canon. If one further unpacks this term, one finds that the Western canon really implies the canon of Western Europe and the successor countries that emerged from English settled colonies. Even the term Western Europe is a bit broad since the Western canon puts the most weight on the cultures of Germany, France, England, and the United States. The present definition of the canon further limits itself to the cultural productions of those in power. This means that the canon has an elitist and patriarchal bias. The cultural and human achievements of poor people, women, and/or subjugated races have been denigrated and often excluded from the high art and culture of the canon.

The analogy is often drawn between the bed of Procrustes and modern educational practice. Procrustes, according to the legend, was the inflexible owner of a bed to which his victims had to be sized; individuals would be stretched to fit if they were too small and cut down to size if they were too large. It is the ultimate metaphor of conformity to norms dictated by others. Western education has long had the reputation of changing very slowly from its established values and canons-nowhere more noticeably than in the humanities. It was these European-centered values that were forced upon Native Americans at the infamous boarding schools and imposed upon colonized African and Asians in India and the Far East, in short, wherever Western civilization spread to areas of the world which the Europeans had penetrated and imperialized. Little value was placed on the cultural traditions of subjugated peoples - their ability to represent and speak for themselves and their attachment to their ancestral belief systems - with the result that much was subsumed by the dominating culture or transmogrified to look as though it emanated from that Western source originally. Asian, Africa, and Slavic accomplishments in arts and literature have been minimally noted, but Native Americans have apparently achieved nothing at all according to the European-oriented canon.

At the present time, the intense debate over the notion of the Western canon and its content has spilled out of the halls of academia and entered the political arena. Some educational institutions have been profoundly shaken by the depths of this debate. Groups that have been historically excluded from the canon are demanding that the traditional notion of canon be questioned.

This text is an attempt to enter these debates and to further the process of changing the canon. We feel that the traditional canon reached its limit of usefulness in today s society and needs to be fractured. This is accomplished in part by the addition of material from cultures that have been previously excluded from the canon. Thus, we have included articles from the cultures of Asia, Africa, North and South America.

However, we are aware that more than just additional material of other cultures is needed. We need to question how and why the canon formed as it did. Thus, some of the material included in the text provides tools for critical thinking about culture and the politics of education. We stress the importance of critical thinking, not just for this one issue, but in all the areas of our social and personal lives. For example, one can not begin to understand the historic distortion and suppression of African cultures within the canon without examining the system of race that has developed in Western culture. This investigation implies a thorough critique of the notion of race and its implications for American society today.

Finally, we question the notion of objective, abstract, and disinterested knowledge and education. All knowledge and all educational systems have political ramifications. We agree with many of the authors included in the text and believe in education for social justice. This is an especially key emphasis for educational institutions that serve a population that has historically been oppressed or excluded from the centers of power in a society. Traditionally, universities have been the sites of both social control and of movements for social change. We hope that this text makes a contribution both to a fuller appreciation of all cultures and to a critique of our world that enables us to struggle towards more just, human communities.

## WHAT IS CRITICAL THINKING?

Students may now be asking themselves, what exactly is critical thinking? By critical thinking, we would like to encourage students to try to step outside of their own worldview and engage with their usual thought processes as if they were not so usual. One metaphor that students might keep in mind is to see themselves as anthropologists of their own culture. Students can move outside their own culture and try to look at it as if they were outsiders who are analyzing it. While we know that no one can ever completely separate themselves from their culture, the exercise of trying to de-familiarize ourselves from dominant ideologies can be extremely intellectually productive. In this textbook, we often compare different cultural perspectives on a single theme in order to facilitate this process; if other cultures, for instance, conceptualize race in a whole different way than we do, then that allows us to see how our conceptions reflect certain values within our culture. Two questions to keep in mind when engaging in this process are -- Who benefits from these ideological perspectives? And, who bears the brunt of the costs?

In this textbook, our interdisciplinary approach allows us to address subjects that students may be familiar with in ways that they might not have been exposed to. For instance, in our section State and Nationalism we will compare the Iroquois Constitution to the Declaration of Independence in order to investigate similarities between native cultures and the emergent United States. We will then examine uses of the Declaration in later liberation movements, such as the suffragists, as well as later changes in U.S. laws in terms of their effects on immigration. These comparisons will allow students to see that a document that they are probably knowledgeable about, the Declaration of Independence, is not simply a static, historical document, but it also has its own history and continuing effect on our national character. In order to facilitate these sorts of comparisons, we have chosen to structure the textbook thematically, taking as our topic many of the fundamental avenues by which dominant ideologies are reproduced: through notions of the individual and community, educational, economic and religious systems, popular culture, notions of statehood or history, as well as how these ideas change through war or non-violently, and so on.

As our knowledge of Asian, African, and Native American (South and North) cultures and attainments continue to increase, we can better understand that ideally all human groups should be represented in the humanities. Needless to say, we cannot honor them all by inclusion in this work. Nevertheless, we do hope to help students to become aware of the richness of global humanities from some of the selections contained in this volume and to introduce them to some significant writings which have not been brought to their notice.

## WHAT WILL WE DO IN THIS CLASS?

The development of critical thinking skills is fundamentally connected to other intellectual skills; in this course, we will focus on learning how to read and write analytically. While most of the articles themselves model critical thinking, we also encourage students to practice critical reading skills from the beginning of the course. Read with pen in hand so you can mark important or puzzling parts of the essay. That way, you will already be engaging with the text prior to class. During the class itself, we will focus on discussion; if you already have questions written in your text, you will be well-prepared for the class. The professors will also bring questions to the students, in order to provide more examples of textual interrogation. In terms of writing, we will emphasize the significance of writing itself as useful for learning, rather than focusing only on methods of writing. In other words, we believe that the act of writing is a tool for discovery, as well as a valuable skill in both academic and professional life.

The emphasis on critical thinking enables students to become active citizens, rather than merely passive consumers of knowledge, a skill which is necessary in order to have educated citizens in a democracy and productive members of the community. The rise of commercialism, capitalism, and the dominance of television have already taught students various ways to be passive, to buy information along with products. We believe it is the job of the university to counteract this teaching, to give students the tools with which to decipher manipulative strategies in order to have more control over the choices they can make.

**Study Questions**

1. What does "interdisciplinary" mean? why would we critique the practice of dividing knowledge into "disciplines"?

2. What is the significance of the title? what is the canon, and why would we want to "fracture" it?

3. Explain the arguments, pro and con, over the canon. How do these arguments relate to those over multiculturalism? Do we need a canon? If we do, what would you include in it?

4. Define subjective and objective thinking. how do the arguments against a canon involve a critique of objective thinking? Can knowledge be separate form the culture from which it derives? What do you think?

5. What is critical thinking? Why is it significant?

6. Pay attention to the last paragraph. What is th edifference between being an active citizen or passive consumer of knowledge? How is that relateed to the function of the university?

# I

# MYTH AND THE MAKING OF HISTORY

# EXCERPTS FROM BLACK ATHENA

## Martin Bernal (1937- )

*Martin Bernal grew up as the son of J. D. Bernal, a famous British crystallographer and Marxist historian of science. His maternal grandfather was Sir Alan Gardiner, millionaire and the greatest British Egyptologist of his generation. Bernal grew up in the Bohemian fringe of the British upper-class and was influenced by the emphasis on intellectual excellence found in this social strata. As a young man he lived for a year at the house of a leading Africanist anthropologist. He also spent some time living on the family's tea plantation in Malawi where he was introduced to African languages.*

*Bernal is currently a professor of Government Studies at Cornell University; he was formerly a Fellow of King's College, Cambridge. His specialization is the history of Chinese and Western cultural exchanges and Near Eastern Studies. Bernal spent more than a decade researching and writing his two-volume work Black Athena (1988, 1991). The first volume is an analysis of the history and sociology of European academic knowledge. It traces the historical awareness, among European scholars, of ancient Europe's cultural indebtedness to Africa and Asia, as well as the later repression of such awareness with the construction of the ancient Greek miracle. The second volume presents the historical, archaeological, linguistic and mythological evidence for Greek civilization's indebtedness to Africa and Asia. The title of the work comes from his claim that the Greek goddess,* Athena, *is derived from the Egyptian goddess Neith of Sais.*

*Reception of the two volumes of* Black Athena *has been mixed. Classicists, who read the work not so much as a critique of Eurocentic intellectual bias but as a denunciation of their discipline by an unqualified outsider, have often been dismissive. In the excerpts below, Bernal argues that the rise of slavery and colonialism during the 18th and 19th centuries prosduced a racist and Eurocentric viewpoint that has become dominant in the Humanities. He challenges us to revision the Humanities upon a non-Eurocentric and non-racist foundation.*

## INTRODUCTION

These volumes are concerned with two models of Greek history: one viewing Greece as essentially European and Aryan, and the other seeing it as Levantine on the periphery of the Egyptian and Semitic cultural area. I call them the "Aryan" and "Ancient" models. The "Ancient Model" was the conventional view among Greeks in the Classical and Hellenistic ages. According to it, Greek culture had arisen as the result of colonization, around 1500 BC, by Egyptians and Phoenicians who had civilized the native inhabitants. Furthermore, Greeks had continued to borrow heavily from Near Eastern cultures.

Most people are surprised to learn that the Aryan Model, which most of us have been brought up to believe, developed only during the first half of the 19th century. In its earlier or "Broad" form, the new model denied the truth of the Egyptian settlements and questioned those of the Phoenicians. What I call the "Extreme" Aryan Model, which flourished during the twin peaks of anti-Semitism in the 1890s and again in the 1920s and 30s, denied even the Phoenician cultural influence. According to the Aryan Model, there had been an invasion from the north—unreported in ancient tradition—which had overwhelmed the local "Aegean" or "Pre-Hellenic" culture. Greek civilization is seen as the result of the mixture of the Indo-European-speaking Hellenes and their indigenous subjects. It is from the construction of this Aryan Model that I call this volume *The Fabrication of Ancient Greece 1785–1985*.

I believe that we should return to the Ancient Model, but with some revisions; hence I call what I advocate in Volume 2 of *Black Athena* the "Revised Ancient Model." This accepts that there is a real basis to the stories of Egyptian and Phoenician colonization of Greece set out in the Ancient Model. . . .

*If I am right in urging the overthrow of the Aryan Model and its replacement by the Revised Ancient one, it will be necessary not only to rethink the fundamental bases of "Western Civilization" but also to recognize the penetration of racism and "continental chauvinism" into all our historiography, or philosophy of writing history. The ancient Model had no major "internal" deficiencies, or weaknesses in explanatory power. It was overthrown for external reasons. For 18th-and 19th-century Romantics and racists it was simply intolerable for Greece, which was seen not merely as the epitome of Europe but also as its pure childhood, to have been the result of the mixture of native Europeans and colonizing Africans and Semites. Therefore the Ancient model had to be overthrown and replaced by something more acceptable. . . .*

## BLACK ATHENA, VOLUME I: A SUMMARY OF THE ARGUMENT

The first volume of *Black Athena* is concerned with the development of the Ancient and Aryan Models, and the first chapter, "The Ancient Model in Antiquity," treats the attitudes of Greeks in the Classical and Hellenistic periods to their distant past. It considers the writings of authors who affirmed the Ancient Model, referred to Egyptian colonies in Thebes and Athens, and gave details of

the Egyptian conquest of the Argolid and the Phoenician foundation of Thebes. . . .

Chapter I goes on to discuss some of the equations made between specific Greek and Egyptian divinities and rituals, and the general belief that the Egyptian were the earlier forms and that Egyptian religion was the original one. Only in this way—the desire to return to the ancient and proper forms—can one explain why, starting in the 5th century at the latest, Egyptian deities began to be worshipped under Egyptian names—and following Egyptian ritual—throughout Greece, the East Mediterranean and later the whole Roman world. It was only after the collapse of Egyptian religion in the 2nd century A. D. that other Oriental cults, notably Christianity, began to replace it.

Chapter II, "Egyptian wisdom and Greek transmission from the Dark Ages to the Renaissance," considers the attitude of the Church Fathers towards Egypt. After the crushing of Neo-Platonism, the Hellenic, pagan descendant of Egyptian religion, and Gnosticism, its Judae-Christian counterpart, Christian thinkers tamed Egyptian religion by turning it into a philosophy. The process was identified with the figure of Hermes Trismegistos, a euhemerized or rationalized version of Thoth, the Egyptian god of wisdom; and a number of texts associated with Thoth, written in the last centuries of the Egyptian religion, were attributed to him. The Church Fathers . . . were united in the belief that the Greeks had learnt their philosophy from the Egyptians—though the Egyptians might have learnt some of theirs in turn from Mesopotamia and Persia. . . .

This belief continued through the Renaissance. The revival of Greek studies in the 15th century created a love of Greek literature and language and an identification with the Greeks, but no one questioned the fact that the Greeks had been the pupils of the Egyptians, in whom there was an equal, if not more passionate, interest. The Greeks were admired for having preserved and transmitted a small part of this ancient wisdom: to some extent the experimental techniques of men like Paracelsus and Newton were developed to retrieve this lost Egyptian or Hermetic knowledge. A few Hermetic texts had been available in Latin translation throughout the Dark and Middle Ages; many more were found in 1460 and were brought to the court of Cosimo di Medici in Florence, where they were translated by his leading scholar, Marsilio Ficino. These and the ideas contained in them became central to the Neo-Platonist movement started by Ficino, which was itself at the heart of Renaissance Humanism.

Although Copernicus' mathematics was derived from Islamic science, his heliocentricity seems to have come with the revival of the Egyptian notion of a divine sun in the new intellectual environment of Hermeticism in which he was formed. His champion Giordano Bruno, at the end of the 16th century, was more explicit on this and went beyond the respectable Christian Neo-Platonic Hermeticism of Ficino. Appalled by the Wars of Religion and Christian intolerance, he advocated a return to the original or natural religion, that of Egypt, for which he was burnt at the stake by the Inquisition in 1600.

This brings us to Chapter III, "The triumph of Egypt in the 17th and 18th centuries." . . . In general the 18th century was a period of Classicism and one with a desire for order and stability, and so Rome was usually preferred to Greece; at the same time—in order to break away from the feudalism and superstitious Christianity of the European past—there was great interest in other non-European civilizations. By far the most influential of these, for this century, were those of Egypt and China. Both were seen as having superior writing systems representing ideas, not sounds; and both had profound and ancient philosophies. Their most attractive feature, however, seems to have been that they were ruled rationally, without superstition, by a corps of men recruited for their morality and required to undergo rigorous initiation and training.

Egyptian priesthoods had in fact appealed to conservative thinkers at least since the time when Plato had modelled his Guardians on them. In the 18th century this line of thought was taken up by the Freemasons; but even in the Middle Ages, Freemasons appear to have been especially interested in Egypt because, following ancient tradition, they believed it to be the home of geometry or Masonry. With the formation of Speculative Masonry at the turn of the 18th century they drew on Rosicrucianism and Bruno to establish a "twofold philosophy." This entailed superstitious and limited religions for the masses but, for the illuminati, a return to the natural and pure original religion of Egypt, from the debris of which all the others had been created. Thus the Masons, who included almost every significant figure in the Enlightenment, saw their religion as Egyptian; their signs as hieroglyphs; their lodges as Egyptian temples; and themselves as an Egyptian priesthood. Indeed, the Masonic admiration for Egypt has survived the country's fall from grace among academics. With some degree of self-deprecation, Masons have maintained the cult until today, as an anomaly in a world where "true" history is seen to have begun with the Greeks.

The culmination of radical Masonry—and its most acute threat to Christian order—came during the period of the French Revolution. Here the political and military menace was accompanied by an intellectual challenge in the work of the great French scholar, anticlerical and revolutionary Charles Francois Dupuis. Dupuis's case was that Egyptian mythology—which, following Herodotus, he saw as the same as that of Greece—was essentially made up of allegories for the movements of the constellations, and that Christianity was merely a collection of misunderstood fragments of this grand tradition.

"Hostilities to Egypt in the 18th century" is the topic of Chapter IV. The Egyptian menace to Christianity naturally provoked response. . . . The threat posed by this "Radical Enlightenment" can explain the sharp change in Newton's attitudes towards Egypt. . . . Newton was concerned with a threat to his conception of physical order and its theological and political counterparts—a divinity, with regular habits and the Whig constitutional monarchy. The threat was of pantheism, implying an animate universe without need for a regulator or even a creator. . . .

Thus throughout the 18th and 19th centuries we find a *de facto* of Hellenism and textual criticism with the defence of Christianity. . . .

Newton had merely tried to demote Egypt in relation to Christianity; he did not try to raise Greece. By the middle of the 18th century, however, a number of Christian apologists were using the emerging paradigm of "progress," with its presupposition that "later is better," to promote the Greeks at the expense of the Egyptians. These strands of thought soon merged with two others that were becoming dominant at the same time: racism and Romanticism. Thus Chapter IV also outlines the development of racism based on skin colour in late-17th-century England, alongside the increasing importance of the American colonies, with their twin policies of extermination of the Native Americans and enslavement of African Blacks. This racism pervaded the thought of Locke, Hume and other English thinkers. Their influence—and that of the new European explorers of other continents—was important at the university of Göttingen, founded in 1734 by George II, Elector of Hanover and King of England, and forming a cultural bridge between Britain and Germany. It is not surprising, therefore, that the first "academic" work on human racial classification—which naturally put Whites, or to use his new term, "Caucasians," at the head of the hierarchy—was written in the 1770s by Johann Friedrich Blumenbach, a professor at Göttingen.

The university pioneered the establishment of modern disciplinary scholarship. In the same decade, other professors at Göttingen began to publish histories not of individuals, but of peoples and races and their institutions. These "modern" projects, combined with exhaustiveness and a critical approach to sources, can usefully be seen as an academic aspect of the new Romantic concern with ethnicity, current in German and British society at the time. 18th century Romanticism was not merely a faith in the primacy of emotion and a belief in the inadequacy of reason. Clustered around these were feelings for landscapes—especially wild, remote and cold ones—and admiration for the vigorous, virtuous and primitive folk who were somehow moulded by them. These sentiments were combined with the belief that as the landscape and climate of Europe were better than those of other continents. Europeans must be superior. They were championed by Montesquieu and Rousseau, but took firmest root in Britain and Germany.

By the end of the 18th century, "progress" had become a dominant paradigm, dynamism and change were valued more than stability, and the world began to be viewed through time rather than across space. Nevertheless, space remained important for the Romantics, because of their concern for the local formation of peoples or "races." Thus a race was believed to change its form as it passed through different ages, but always to retain an immutable individual essence. Real communication was no longer perceived as taking place through reason, which could reach any rational man. It was now seen as flowing through feeling, which could touch only those tied to each other by kinship or "blood" and sharing a common "heritage."

To return to the theme of racism. Many Ancient Greeks shared a feeling very like what would now be called nationalism: they despised other peoples and some, like Aristotle, even put this on a theoretical plane by claiming a Hellenic superiority based on the geographical situation of Greece. It was a feeling qualified by the very real respect many Greek writers had for foreign cultures, particularly those of Egypt, Phoenicia and Mesopotamia. But in any event, the strength of this Ancient Greek "nationalism" was negligible compared to the tidal wave of ethnicity and racialism, linked to cults of Christian Europe and the North, that engulfed Northern Europe with the Romantic movement at the end of the 18th century. The paradigm of "races" that were intrinsically unequal in physical and mental endowment was applied to all human studies, but especially to history. It was now considered undesirable, if not disastrous, for races to mix. To be creative, a civilization needed to be "racially pure." Thus it became increasingly intolerable that Greece—which was seen by the Romantics not merely as the epitome of Europe but also as its pure childhood—could be the result of the mixture of native Europeans and colonizing Africans and Semites.

Chapter V, "Romantic linguistics: the rise of India and the fall of Egypt, 1740-1880," begins with a sketch of the Romantic origins of historical linguistics and the passion at the turn of the 18th century for ancient India largely caused by the perception of a fundamental relationship between Sanskrit and the European languages. It also surveys the decline in the European estimation of China, as the balance of trade between the two turned in Europe's favour and the British and French carried out increasingly large scale attacks on China. I argue that these factors necessitated changing the image of China from one of a refined and enlightened civilization to one of a society filled with drugs, dirt, corruption and torture. Ancient Egypt, which in the 18th century had been seen as a very close parallel to China, suffered from the same effects of the need to justify the increasing European expansion into other continents and maltreatment of the indigenous peoples. Both were flung into prehistory to serve as a solid and inert basis for the dynamic development of the superior races, the Aryans and the Semites. . . .

In the late 18th and early 19th centuries, Romantic scholars saw the Egyptians as essentially morbid and lifeless. At the end of the 19th century a new contrary but equally disparaging image began to emerge. The Egyptians were now seen to conform to the contemporary European vision of Africans: gay, pleasure-loving, childishly boastful and essentially materialistic.

Another way of looking at these changes is to assume that *after the rise of black slavery and racism, European thinkers were concerned to keep black Africans as far as possible from European civilization.* Where men and women in the Middle Ages and the Renaissance were uncertain about the colour of the Egyptians, the Egyptophil Masons tended to see them as white. Next, the Hellenomaniacs of the early 19th century began to doubt their whiteness and to deny that the Egyptians had been civilized. It was only at the end of the 19th century, when Egypt had been entirely stripped of its philosophical reputation, that its African affinities could be re-established. *Notice that in each case the necessary divide between Blacks and civilization was clearly demarcated.* . . .

Chapter VI is entitled "Hellenomania, I: The fall of the Ancient Model, 1790–1830." Although racism was always a major source of hostility to the Ancient Model and became a mainstay of the Aryan one, it was matched in the 18th and early 19th centuries by an attack on the significance of Egypt from Christians alarmed at the threat of the religion or "wisdom" of Egypt. These Christian attacks challenged Greek statements about the importance of Egypt, and boosted the independent creativity of Greece in order to diminish that of Egypt. Indeed, it is deeply significant that the Ancient Model was first challenged between 1815 and 1830, for these were the years of intense reaction against the Masonic rationalism seen to be behind the French Revolution; and years of Romanticism and Christian revival. Further, as Christianity was identified with Europe, the two could come together with the notion of progress in a philhellenic movement which backed the struggle of the Christian, European and "young" Greeks against the "old" Asian infidel Turks. . . .

The title of Chapter VII is "Hellenomania 2: Transmission of the new scholarship to England and the rise of the Aryan Model, 1830–60." Unlike the Ancients, the proponents of the Aryan Model were firm believers in "progress." Victors were seen as more advanced, and hence "better," than the vanquished. Thus, despite apparent and short-term anomalies, history—now seen as the biographies of races—consisted of the triumphs of strong and vital peoples over weak and feeble ones. "Races," formed by the landscape and climates of their homelands, retained permanent essences, even though they took on new forms in every new age. For these scholars, in addition, it was self-evident that the greatest "race" in world history was the European or Aryan one. It alone had, and always would have, the capacity to conquer all other peoples and to create advanced, dynamic civilizations—as opposed to the static societies ruled by Asians or Africans. . . .

These paradigms of "race" and "progress" and their corollaries of "racial purity," and the notion that the only beneficial conquests were those of "master races" over subject ones, could not tolerate the Ancient Model. . . . The application of the model of northern conquest to Greece was thus obvious and very attractive: vigorous conquerors were supposed to have come from a suitably stimulating homeland to the north of Greece, while the "Pre-Hellenic" aborigines had been softened by the undemanding nature of their homeland. . . .

The question of "Semitic blood" leads us to Chapter VIII, "The rise and fall of the Phoenicians, 1830–85.". . . Consciously or unconsciously, all European thinkers saw the Phoenicians as the Jews of Antiquity—as clever "Semitic" traders. The predominant mid-19th-century view of world history was one of a dialogue between Aryan and Semite. The Semite had created religion and poetry; the Aryan conquest, science, philosophy, freedom and everything else worth having. This limited recognition of the "Semites" corresponded with what one might call a limited "window of opportunity" in Western Europe, between the disap-

pearance of religious hatred of the Jews and the rise of "racial" anti-Semitism. . . .

[Jules] Michelet's views on the Phoenicians were spread even more widely in [Gustave] Flaubert's immensely popular historical novel *Salammbô*, published in 1861. *Salammbô* contained vivid descriptions of Carthage at its most decadent which powerfully reinforced the already widespread anti-Semitic and anti-Oriental prejudices. Still more damning was his brilliant and gruesome description of the sacrifice of children to Moloch. The firm and public attachment of this ultimate biblical abomination to the Carthaginians and Phoenicians made it very difficult to champion them, and during the 1870s and 80s their reputation plummeted even faster than that of the Jews.

This leads us to Chapter IX, "The final solution of the Phoenician problem, 1880–1945." With this reputation and the rise of anti-Semitism in the 1880s, there was a sustained attack on the Phoenicians which was particularly fierce where it came to their legendary contacts with, and influence on, the Greeks—who had by now been given semi-divine status. . . .

The final elimination of the Phoenician influence on Greece—and its complete dismissal as a "mirage"—came only in the 1920s with the crescendo of anti-Semitism resulting from the imagined and real role of Jews in the Russian Revolution and the Communist 3rd International. In the 1920s and 30s all the legends of Phoenician colonization of Greece were discredited, as were reports of Phoenician presence in the Aegean and Italy in the 9th and 8th centuries B.C. The many previously proposed Semitic origins of Greek names and words were all denied. . . .

The 1930s were years in which positivism weakened in "hard" science but gained strength beyond its borders in such fringe subjects as logic and ancient history. Thus, in Classics, solution of the Phoenician problem seemed "scientific" and final: from now on the discipline could proceed scientifically or, as one would now put it, a paradigm had been established. Any scholar who denied it was outlawed as incompetent, unsound or a crank. The strength of this position is demonstrated by its survival for more than thirty years after the consequences of anti-Semitism were revealed in 1945. . . . In the long term, however, there has been a retreat from the Extreme Aryan Model, and this process is described in Chapter X, "The post-war situation: the return to the Broad Aryan Model, 1945-85."

It is probable that the foundation of Israel has been more influential than the Holocaust in the restoration of the Phoenicians. Since 1949, Jews—or at least Israelis, have been increasingly accepted as full Europeans. . . . Moreover, the 1950s also saw a sharp increase of Jewish confidence in their Semitic roots.

In the context of this process—and possibly because they were unable to accept the exclusiveness of either orthodox Judaism or Zionism—Cyrus Gordon and Michael Astour, two great Semitists, began to champion West Semitic Civilization as a whole and to attack the Extreme Aryan Model. . . .

[But] Gordon and Astour, for all their intellectual daring, have not challenged the Aryan Model itself. Neither of them has considered the possibility of a massive Semitic component in the Greek vocabulary; nor, given their Semitic preoccupations, have they investigated the possible Egyptian colonizations of Greece and the hypothesis that Egyptian language and culture played an equal or even more central role in the formation of Greek civilization.

## CHAPTER X—THE POST-WAR SITUATION: THE RETURN TO THE BROAD ARYAN MODEL, 1945-85

### THE RETURN OF THE EGYPTIANS?

. . . . While the—mainly Jewish—Semitists fought against the Extreme Aryan Model from the fringes of academia, the American champions of the Egyptians, who are largely Blacks, have challenged the Aryan Model from outside the system altogether.

A very small number of black academics, notably Frank Snowden . . . at . . . Howard, have been successful within Classics. They have concentrated on gleaning what little credit the Aryan model allows to Blacks while accepting both its prohibitions: the non-acceptance of a black component of Egyptian culture, and the denial of the Afroasiatic formative elements in Greek civilization. Other scholars, more keenly aware of the degree to which racism has pervaded every nook and cranny of 19th- and 20th-century European and North America culture, have been more sensitive. The pioneer in this effort was George G. M. James, a professor teaching at a small college in Arkansas. In 1954 he published a book entitled *Stolen Legacy: The Greeks were not the authors of Greek Philosophy, but the people of North Africa, commonly called the Egyptians*. . . . . I had to try twice to have a copy of *Stolen Legacy* accepted by the university library at Cornell before it was finally placed in a smaller branch library. It is not recognized as a *proper book*. Nor has it been read outside the black community. Within intellectual circles, however, it is highly praised and very influential.

*Stolen Legacy* is generally linked in people's minds to the school of thought pioneered by the late Senegalese nuclear physicist Cheikh Anta Diop. . . . [For] what most concerned him was the great achievements of Egyptian civilization; the systematic denigration of them by European scholars; and his faith that the Egyptians were, as Herodotos had specified, black. . . .

Thus, at the end of the 1980s, I see continued struggle among black scholars on the question of the "racial" nature of the Ancient Egyptians. On the other hand, there is no serious division among them on the question of the high quality of Egyptian civilization and of its central role in the formation of Greece. Furthermore, there is a general hostility among them to Semitic culture, especially when it is supposed to have affected Egypt. Meanwhile, where white scholars . . . are increasingly prepared to admit that West Semites played a substantial part in the creation of Greek culture, there is still a far greater reluctance to admit fundamental Egyptian influence upon it. One aspect of my work is an attempt to reconcile these two hostile approaches.

### THE REVISED ANCIENT MODEL

Interestingly, I find it easier to place myself and my promotion of the Revised Ancient Model in the spectrum of black scholarship than within the academic orthodoxy. . . . I am happy to be in the excellent company of Dubois, Mazrui and the others who, while they do not picture all Ancient Egyptians as resembling today's West Africans, do see Egypt as essentially African. . . .

### CONCLUSION

The main point I have been trying to make throughout this book is that the Ancient Model was destroyed and replaced by the Aryan Model not because of any internal deficiencies, nor because the Aryan Model explained anything better or more plausibly; what it did do, however, was make the history of Greece and its relations to Egypt and the Levant conform to the world-view of the 19th century and, specifically, to its systematic racism. Since then the concepts of "race" and categorical European superiority which formed the core of this *Weltanschauung* have been discredited both morally and heuristically, and it would be fair to say that the Aryan Model was conceived in what we should now call sin and error.

However, I insist that its conception in sin, or even error, does not necessarily invalidate it. Darwinism, which was created at very much the same time and for many of the same "disreputable" motives, has remained a very useful heuristic scheme. . . . All I claim for this volume is that is has provided a case to be answered. That is, if the dubious origin of the Aryan Model does not make it false, it does call into question its inherent superiority over the Ancient Model. . . .

**Study Questions**

1. Why did Bernal write Black Athena?

2. What are the Ancient and Aryan models of the origins of Greek civilization?

3. What evidence does Bernal give to support the Ancient model?

4. Explain how the rise of Romanticism and the paradigms of "progness" and "race" contributed to the rejection of the Ancient model?

5. Were the ancient Greeks racist? Did they "steal" the cultural heritage of Egypt? Where and when does the racism of today come from? Where do our modern notions of race come from?

6. Does the ethnicity or skin color of the ancient Egyptians have any bearing on Bernal's arguments? Why or why not?

7. Is Bernal's case weakened because he is a professor of Government and not a professor classics? What relevance is Bernal's own race to his claims?

8. What *should* be taught about ancient Greek civilization? Why are the origins of ancient Greece any more important than the origins of any other country?

# DISCOVERIES

## *Michael Dorris (1945-1997)*

*The late Michael Dorris tackles the question of the enhanced view we may have of Indians at Thanksgiving and the arrival of Columbus. In his novel, Guests, he presents a Native American perspective on the origins of our annual festival. In this selection from Discoveries, he helps us understand the invasion of the Europeans from a Native American viewpoint. He and his wife, Louise Erdrich, (Anishnabe) were prominent writers as well as advocates for Native Americans. He founded and taught in the Native American Studies Program at Dartmouth College. He has written novels such as Yellow Raft in Blue Water, essays as in Paper Trail which are concerned with Native American and family issues, and coauthored The Crown of Columbus with Louise Erdrich. He has also written childrens books.*

Who were, after all, the societies that greeted Europeans five, four, three hundred years ago? What were their motives, their important elements, their contrasts with the norms of Old World nations that attempted to dominate and destroy them?

Imagine the scene: it is an autumn day in the late fifteenth century. On a beach with rose-colored sand, some where in the Caribbean, two groups of people, the hosts and their visitors, are about to meet for the first time. Emerging from a long and frightening ocean voyage. They didn't trust where they were going and now they don't know where they've arrived - but it doesn't look at all like the India described by Marco Polo. They come from Spain and Portugal and Genoa, are Christian and Jewish. The more superstitious and uneducated among them feared that, by sailing west across the Atlantic, they would fall off the edge of the planet.

The men seek treasure and adventure, fame and glory but the people who greet them - if in fact they are "people" at all - seem, though handsome, quite poor. They are not dressed in fine brocade encrusted with precious jewels, as one would expect of subjects of the great Khan. They are, in fact, not dressed at all, except for a few woven shirts and dabs of ochre. Are they demons? Are they dangerous? Do they know where the gold is hidden?

Watching the boat draw near is a cluster of men, women, and children. They speak a dialect of the Arawak language and are delighted to receive new guests, especially ones who aren't painted white - signifying death. Strangers arrive often, anxious to barter parrot feathers or new foods or useful objects made of stone or shell. These particular visitors look rather strange, it's true: their bodies are covered with odd materials, not at all suited for the warm climate, and they communicate with each other in a tongue as indecipherable as Carib or Nahuatl.

Up close there are more surprises. The group includes no women and some among the hosts speculate why this may be the case. Have their clan mothers expelled these men, banned them to wander alone and orphaned? Has their tribe suffered some disaster? And another thing: they have the strong odor of people who have not had their daily bath. Are they from some simple and rude society that doesn't know how to comport itself?

But all this notwithstanding, guests are guests and should be treated with hospitality. They must be offered food and shelter, must be entertained with stories and music, before the serious business of trade begins.

The earth was much larger than Christopher Columbus imagined, its human population far more diverse. The land mass he encountered on his transatlantic voyages was thoroughly inhabited by more than one hundred million people, from the frigid steppes of Patagonia at the farthest extremity of South America to the dark arboreal forests of Newfoundland. In the inhospitable Artic, Inuits foraged for much of the year in small nuclear or extended family groups, assembling sporadically to carry on the necessary business of marriage, remembrance, or collective action, and only when the availability of food was at its peak. In the lush and verdant jungles of Yucatan and Guatemala, the Mayas had invented agriculture, writing, and an accurate calendar fifteen hundred years before the birth of Christ. Organized in complex, class-oriented societies, they subsisted on a nutritionally balanced diet based on maize, squashes, and beans. In the Andes of northwestern South America early Quechuas domesticated the potato, engineered an intricate system of roads and bridges, and formed a nation in which the state owned all property except houses and movable household goods, and taxes were collected in labor.

The Western Hemisphere was home to literally hundreds of cultures whose people spoke a multiplicity of dialects and languages derived from at least ten mutually exclusive linguistic families. Many societies had well-developed traditions of science and medicine - some 40 percent of the modern world's pharmacopoeia was utilized in America before 1492 - and literature, visual art, and philosophy flourished in a variety of contexts. Yet beyond a shared geography, there were few common denominators; due to the haphazard nature and long process by which in-migrating peoples distributed themselves throughout the continents, the Western Hemisphere thrived as living laboratory of disparate lifestyles, linguistic variety, and cultural pluralism.

Obviously, no single group was directly aware of more than a fraction of the other extant societies - and there was no conception of an overarching group identity. "We" was the family, the community, the tribe, and "they" were everyone else, known and unknown. The fact of cultural diversity, however, was manifest. Within a day's walk of virtually every indigenous population could be found at least one and probably more than one unrelated community whose inhabitants, relative to the visitor, spoke a totally foreign and incomprehensible language, adhered to a unique cosmology, dressed in unusual clothing, ate exotic foods, and had a dis-similar political organization with peculiar variations on age and gender roles.

A native person in most regions of precontact America could and undoubtedly did believe that he or she belonged to the smartest, most tasteful, most accomplished and most handsome human constellation in the universe, but clearly not the only one. Pluralism, in whichever way it was construed and explained, was inescapably the norm.

It is little wonder, therefore, that for Europeans of the fifteenth and sixteenth centuries, America proved to be much more than a single new world: it was an unimagined universe. The sheer heterogeneity of Western Hemisphere societies challenged every cherished medieval assumption about the orderly nature of human origin and destiny. It was as if a whole new set of potential operating rules were revealed - or, even more disconcerting, the cultural hodge-podge of America was an ego-threatening intimation that there were no dependable rules at all. Imagine the shock. To have believed for a thousand years that everything and everybody of consequence was known and neatly categorized and then suddenly to open a window and learn that all along one had been dwelling in a small house with no perspective on the teeming and chaotic city that surrounded one's accustomed neighborhood - no map or dictionary provided. How did Cain and Abel fit into this new, complicated schema? Which Old Testament patriarch begat the Lakota or the Chibcha? How did the Comanche get from the Tower of Babel to Oklahoma?

The contrasts between the Old World and the Americas were staggering. With only a few minor exceptions, virtually all Europeans spoke languages that sprang from a single linguistic family. Moreover, in the larger context, Europe's vaunted religious and philosophical divisions were basically variations on a concordant theme. Everyone from the Baltic to the Balkans to the British Isles professed belief in the same divinity or, in the case of the European Jewry, His father.

As side effects of this theological unity, Latin became a lingua franca for intellectuals from all sectors, and the Mosaic code formed the basis for practically every ethical or legal philosophy. The broad assumption of male dominance reigned uncontested, from individual marriage contracts to the leadership hierarchy of emergent nation-states. The Bible - in particular, the book of Genesis - was regarded as a literally true and factually accurate accounting of the origin of everything.

Significantly, in the Adam and Eve story, creation is intentional; a personalized, anthropomorphic God formed a man in His image and then threw in a woman, made out of a nonessential rib, for His company and pleasure. His word was law and His only token competition came from a fallen angel, also of His manufacture. After devising, in six days, a universe whose primary purpose was to exit as a backdrop and amusement park for man, the Divinity set up a test for the objects of his invention - a test that the Divinity, being omniscient as well as omnipotent, must have known all along man would fail.

Man did.

A nonbeliever attempting to analyze this saga might well find parts of it, while interesting, a bit bizarre. Why were men and women so disproportionately blessed? Why did God go to all the trouble? For all its paradox, however, the Genesis story did fulfill a function for the Hebraic culture to whom it was initially addressed. It authenticated divine sponsorship for the law of the land and proffered the explanation, so necessary for a poor, threatened minority population, that life was supposed to be pain, that man deserved what he got, and that the only true happiness and peace would come to the just after death.

The disparate creation stories Native Americans believed about themselves - be they emergence myths or earth-diver tales, divine births or great floods - are every bit as pregnant with particular meaning for their specific audiences as was Genesis for the Israelites. Take, for example, a tale found in several Northwest Coast repertoires: According to legend, one day Raven, the androgynous culture hero/Trickster, spies a bush containing a new kind of berry. They are purple and luscious, bursting with sweet juice, and Trickster can't resist. He/she begins to gobble them up and doesn't stop until every one is consumed. His/her breast feathers are stained and his/her belly is bloated, but Raven staggers to the side of a cliff, spreads his/her wings, and careens off into the air.

Suddenly Raven is seized by terrible stomach cramps and immediately experiences the worst case of diarrhea in history. It's terrible: everywhere Raven flies, his/her droppings land, until finally the attack is over, the pain subsides, and with a sigh of relief Raven looks down at the earth to see the mess he/she has made. And there we are, come to life: human beings! Raven beholds these ridiculous creatures, made out of his/her excrement, and laughs. And the ridiculous creatures squint up at Raven - and laugh back!

A society with this irreverent coda has a very different self-concept than one with solemn Genesis as its primary referent. The Raven tale is supposed to be funny, is aimed to entertain and thus be memorable. Creation itself, the story implies, was a totally random act - a fluke. Additionally, the first encounter between creator and createe is maddening for both. Theirs is a relationship without mutual culpability, without guilt, affection, or even clear purpose. As a matter of fact, subsequent chapters in the cycle demonstrate that the joking relationship between Raven and humanity persists and becomes even more perverse over time.

The universe based on such stories was conceived in large part as irrational, not a product of cause and effect, stimulus and response. Events occurred without great purpose and had to be dealt with on their own terms - pragmatically and intelligently. A plague of locusts, an earthquake, a misfortune did not take place because an individual or a people failed to satisfy a demanding and ambiguous Zeus or Jupiter or Jehovah, but rather were regarded as haphazard disruptions in the inevitable course of existence. Humor and fatalism, as opposed to responsibility and recrimination, were the appropriate attitudes toward misfortune. The gods, like everything else, were inscrutable. Harmony, in human communities or in nature as a whole, was best preserved through balance and established custom, and both people and divinities were but elements in a grand, interrelated panorama that encompassed all things.

Practically speaking, prior to the so-called Age of Discovery, Europeans had little contact with populations substantively dissimilar to themselves - certainly not enough to shake their entrenched ethnocentrism. Relations with central or eastern Asia, or sub-Saharan Africa, were rare, and usually filtered through the Islamic societies occupying the southern and eastern perimeters of the Mediterranean. Although Arabs were regarded in certain respects as exotic and the polar opposite of Christians, they were, nevertheless, comprehensible; generally similar in terms of skin pigmentation, patriarchal orientation, and even religious derivation, their customs fell within the range of at least plausible behavior. They were ideal "heathens" because they tended to embrace skewed versions of the values revered by Europeans: messianic and orthodox monotheism, territorial conquest, the accumulation of material wealth. In so doing, they provided a neat and precise contrast that, point by point, helped both groups define themselves (I.e., "this," not "that"). Throughout the Middle Ages, Europeans regarded rumored tales of a world beyond Granada or Cairo or Damascus, be they authored by Herodotus or Pliny, as odd to the point of science fiction and largely irrelevant to the daily lives of ordinary people.

This reassuring order suffered a severe blow when the first boatloads of Spanish and Portuguese sailors failed to topple off the edge of the world - pinpointed, predictably, just beyond the sight of Christendom's western shore - as they ventured far to the south and east. Verifying the immensity of Africa and the Orient, each continent bursting with undeniably non-European peoples and cultures, was traumatic enough news, yet not altogether a surprise. Alexander, after all, had been to India, and the spice route to Cathay was well worn. But with the dramatic materialization of the Western Hemisphere, the dazzling implications of global heterogeneity could no longer be avoided.

The argument for the centrality of Europe was forced to alter its traditional rationalizations in order to account for all else that turned out to exist. An initial solution, analogous to that of the ostrich sticking its head into the sand at the first sign of trouble, was abject denial. If new data didn't fit into old orthodoxy, then it couldn't be accurate. Later as the diversity of humanity became increasingly manifest, the working definition of "true human being" became more rigid, more narrow, and long theological debates took place on such esoterica as whether or not natives of America and Australia even had souls.

This condescending approach was hard to maintain in the face of the intelligence and industry evident in New World cities, bountiful agriculture, science, art, and, especially, wealth reported by conquistadors like Cortes and Pizarro. Indeed, the empire civilizations of Meso- and Latin America - those of the Aztec and Inca, especially - were probably easiest for Europeans to appreciate. Though the customs varied and the religions were unfamiliar to the early Spanish explorers, at least the motivating goals were recognizable: a thirst for conquest, the accumulation of wealth, a consolidation of political power in the hands of a single leader and his coterie. The large nation-states must have been reminiscent of Moorish analogs, with their swarthy looking populations, exploitable treasure, and grand capitals. Their wealth was obvious and marketable, their existing labor force was already organized and ready to be co-opted, and their belief systems posed familiar challenges for Christian conversion.

Smaller, tribally based cultures of North America, on the other hand, must have struck Europeans as utterly bizarre upon first encounter. By and large these groups maintained no standing armies, practiced a mind-boggling variety of inordinately flexible religions, were nonliterate, vague regarding the precise boundaries of their territory, and very often passed property and authority through a female line of descent. Few North American societies sought to impose ideology on neighboring cultures, insisting that the freedom of the individual predominated over the power of the state. Leadership tended to spring from expertise or proven ability rather than from dynastic heredity, and in any given tribe there might exist a multiplicity of "chiefs" - each a specialist in a limited arena of group life and none of them supreme over all others.

Furthermore, most native North American peoples considered land to be an abstract commodity similar in kind to air or water or fire - something necessary for human survival but above personal ownership. While the notion of a group or a person's rights to use a certain piece of property was widespread, there was almost no corresponding idea of "title," or land owned exclusively and permanently by those who didn't directly work it. Concepts of accumulation varied widely, from those who held all non personal items in common, to Northwest Coast "potlatch" societies like Kwakiutl and Nootka where family status depended on formal giveaways of property - to the point of temporary impoverishment.

Armed conflict could occur between tribes, parts of tribes, or individuals for a variety of reasons, but usually the hostilities lasted no longer than a single season or encounter, and loss of life was minimal. As a rule, there was no insistence upon "total victory" or the complete annihilation of an enemy. Battles were fought for personal reasons - revenge, honor, or greed - and once these limited objectives had been achieved, the reason for a prolonged hostile action no longer existed. Last year's antagonists might be next year's hunting partners.

As competition with European invaders became increasingly intense, few indigenous societies mounted effective resistance, and those that did were soon vanquished. Not only had most Native American cultures by and large failed to invent effective weaponry or support standing military forces, they were almost immediately devastated by an unseen foe that, according to some demographers, wiped out 95 percent of the precontact population. A pandemic of diseases that had long existed in the Old World but never previously in the New - influenza, smallpox, measles, tuberculosis, and cholera prime among them - was inadvertently carried to the Western Hemisphere by the first European visitors, and in a matter of several generations virulent bacteria spread throughout the indigenous population. Often by the time the first Spanish or British arrived in the interior of the continents, most Indians were already dead, the straggling survivors traumatized and in despair. The lands that, in their naïveté, some European Chroniclers called "empty," were in fact only recently depleted of their previous inhabitants.

Early European explorers in America, continually confronted with the unexpected, soon began to seek the miraculous, as well as the familiar, in their journeys. They sent home reports of the Seven Golden Cities of Cibola, of fountains whose waters restored eternal youth, of warrior queens who rode upon giants armadillos. Feudal-type agricultural societies, like those of the Cherokee or Creek, were labeled "civilized," and those whose dress, customs, and lifestyles seemed most foreign were "savage."

Rather, they were simply "different," part of the mosaic of human possibility and potential, the laboratory of cultural experiment, that characterized the America of 1491. Collectively, its tribes offered legacies of tremendous contribution to the contemporary world, from cultivated crops (corn, beans, squash, tomatoes, potatoes, manioc) to political structures (models of representatives government, gender equality) to philosophical approaches toward environmental conservation and peaceful coexistence. Many of the ideas and ideals first developed among its native peoples remain viable, sane options for a world that becomes, through technology, increasingly small, increasingly homogeneous. Diversity, that multifaceted reflection of human ingenuity, has become something of an endangered commodity - just when, perhaps, our stripped and exhausted planet needs it most.

Let us return, at last, to that hypothetical first meeting with which we began. In historical retrospect, is it unambiguously clear which group was "advanced," which was "primitive"? Barbarous - a term many Europeans and their Western Hemisphere descendants eventually used to describe Native American societies - is a relative, superficial designate, as it has been since the days when ancient Greeks judged the sophistication of foreigners on the basis of whether or not they grew beards. The Arawaks of the Caribbean never went to the moon or built a telephone, but they also never waged a war, never depleted the ozone layer with fluorocarbons. They were not saints, but neither were they devils. History remembers them most as beautiful, gentle, and impossible to enslave, not as conquerors or missionaries or industrialists.

Yes, the boys from the boat obviously fulfilled their ambitions: they "won." But in the long run, if we as species delimit our imaginations, forget or lose touch with the thesaurus of our marvelously diversified past, did *we*?

In conclusion, the plaster stereotypes must be abandoned, not only because they are simplistic and ill informed, but more so because they are far less intellectually engaging, less interesting, less stimulating, and less challenging than the living, breathing, often exasperating, and always complicated reality.

*Georgia Review*
*Fall 1992*

# COLUMBUS, THE INDIANS, AND HUMAN PROGRESS

*Howard Zinn*

Arawak men and women, naked and tawny, and full of wonder, emerged from their villages onto the island's beaches and swam out to get a closer look at the strange big boat. When Columbus and his sailors came ashore, carrying swords, speaking oddly, the Arawaks ran to greet them, brought them food, water, gifts. He later wrote of this in his log:

They...brought us parrots and balls of cotton and spears and many other things, which they exchanged for the glass beads and hawks' bells. They willingly traded everything they owned...They were well-built, with good bodies and handsome features...They do not bear arms, and do not know them, for I showed them a sword, they took it by the edge and cut themselves out of ignorance. They have no iron. Their spears are made of cane...They would make fine servants...With fifty men we could subjugate them all and make them do whatever we want.

These Arawaks of the Bahamian Islands were much like Indians on the mainland, who were remarkable (European observers were to say again and again) for their hospitality, their belief in sharing. These traits do not stand out in the Europe of the Renaissance, dominated as it was by the religion of popes, the government of kings, the frenzy for money that marked Western civilization and its first messenger to the Americas, Christopher Columbus.

Columbus wrote:

As soon as I arrived in the Indies, on the first Island which I found, I took some of the natives by force in order that they might learn and might give me information of whatever there is in these parts.

The information that Columbus wanted most was: Where is the gold? He had persuaded the king and queen of Spain to finance an expedition to the lands, the wealth, he expected would be on the other side of the Atlantic - the Indies and Asia, gold and spices. For, like other informed people of his time, he knew the world was round and he could sail west in order to get to the Far East.

Spain was recently unified, one of the new modern nation-states, like France, England, and Portugal. Its population, mostly poor peasants, worked for the nobility, who were 2 percent of the population and owned 95 percent of the land. Spain had tied itself to the Catholic Church, expelled all the Jews, driven out the Moors. Like other states of the modern world, Spain sought gold, which was becoming the new mark of wealth, more useful than land because it could buy anything.

There was gold in Asia, it was thought, and certainly silks and spices, for Marco Polo and others had brought back marvelous things from their overland expeditions centuries before. Now that the Turks had conquered Constantinople and the eastern Mediterranean, and controlled the land routes to Asia, a sea route was needed. Portuguese sailors were working their way around the southern tip of Africa. Spain decided to gamble on a long sail across an unknown ocean.

In return for bringing back gold and spices, they promised Columbus 10 percent of the profits, governorship over new-found lands, and the fame that would go with a new title: Admiral of the Ocean Sea. He was a merchant's clerk from the Italian city of Genoa, part-time weaver (the son of a skilled weaver), and expert sailor. He set out with three sailing ships, the largest of which was the Santa Maria, perhaps 100 feet long, and thirty-nine crew members.

Columbus would never have made it to Asia, which was thousands of miles farther away than he had calculated, imagining a smaller world. He would have been doomed by that great expanse of sea. But he was lucky. One-fourth of the way there he came upon an unknown, uncharted land that lay between Europe and Asia - the Americas. It was early October 1492, and thirty-three days since he and his crew had left the Canary Islands, off the Atlantic coast of Africa. Now they saw branches and sticks floating in the water. They saw flocks of birds. These were signs of land. Then, on October 12, a sailor called Rodrigo saw the early morning moon shining on white sands, and cried out. It was an island in the Bahamas, the Caribbean sea. The first man to sight land was supposed to get a yearly pension of 10,000 maravedis for life, but Rodrigo never got it. Columbus claimed he had seen a light the evening before. He got the reward.

So, approaching land, they were met by the Arawak Indians, who swam out to greet them. The Arawaks lived in villages communes, had a developed agriculture of corn, yams, cassava. They could spin and weave, but they had no horses or work animals. They had no iron, but they wore tiny gold ornaments in their ears.

This was to have enormous consequences: it led Columbus to take some of them aboard ship as prisoners because he insisted that they guide him to the source of the gold. He then sailed to what is now Cuba, then to Hispania (the island which today consists of Haiti and the Dominican Republic). There, bits of visible gold in the rivers, and a gold mask presented to Columbus by a local Indian chief, led to wild visions of gold fields.

On Hispaniola, out of timbers from the Santa Maria, which had run aground, Columbus built a fort, the first European military base in the Western Hemisphere. He called it Navidad (Christmas) and left thirty-nine crewmembers there, with instructions to find and store the gold. He took more Indian prisoners and put them aboard his two remaining ships. At one part of the island he got into a fight with Indians who refused to trade as many bows and arrows as he and his men wanted. Two were run through with swords and bled to death. Then the Nina and the Pinta set sail for the Azores and Spain. When the weather turned cold, the Indian prisoners began to die.

Columbus's report to the Court in Madrid was extravagant. He insisted he had reached Asia (it was Cuba) and an island off the coast of China (Hispaniola). His descriptions were part fact, part fiction:

Hispaniola is a miracle. Mountains and hills, plains and pastures, are both fertile and beautiful...the harbors are unbelievable good and there are many wide rivers of which the majority contain gold...There are many spices, and great mines of gold and other metals...

The Indians, Columbus reported, "are so naive and so free with their possessions that no one who has not witnessed them would believe it. When you ask for something they have, they never say no. To the contrary, they offer to share with anyone..." He concluded his report by asking for a little help from their Majesties, and in return he would bring them from his next voyage "as much gold as they need...and as many slaves as they ask." He was full of religious talk: "Thus the eternal God, our Lord, gives victory to those who follow His way over apparent impossibilities."

Because of Columbus's exaggerated report and promises, his second expedition was given seventeen ships and more than twelve hundred men. The aim was clear: slaves and gold. They went from island to island in the Caribbean, taking Indians as captives. But as word spread of the Europeans' intent they found more and more empty villages. On Haiti, they found that the sailors left behind at Fort Navidad had been killed in a battle with the Indians, after they had roamed the island in gangs looking for gold, taking women and children and slaves for sex and labor.

Now, from his base on Haiti, Columbus sent expedition after expedition into the interior. They found no gold fields, but had to fill up the ships returning to Spain with some kind of dividend. In the year 1495, they went on a great slave raid, rounded up fifteen hundred Arawak men, women, and children, put them in pens guarded by Spaniards and dogs, then picked the five hundred best specimens to load onto ships. Of those five hundred, two hundred died en route. The rest arrived alive in Spain and were put up for sale by the archdeacon of the town, who reported that, although the slaves were "naked as the day they were born," they showed "no more embarrassment than animals." Columbus later wrote: "Let us in the name of the Holy Trinity go on sending all the slaves that can be sold."

But too many of the slaves died in captivity. And so Columbus, desperate to pay back dividends to those who had invested, had to make good his promise to fill the ships with gold. In the providence of Cicao on Haiti, where he and his men imagined huge gold fields to exist, they ordered all persons fourteen years or older to collect a certain quantity of gold every three months. When they brought it, they were given copper tokens to hang around their necks. Indians found without a copper token had their hands cut off and bled to death.

The Indians had been given an impossible tasks. The only gold around was bits of dust garnered from the streams. So they fled, were hunted down with dogs, and were killed.

Trying to put together an army of resistance, the Arawaks faced Spaniards who had armor, muskets, swords, horses. When the Spaniards took prisoners they hanged them or burned them to death. Among the Arawaks, mass suicides began, with cassava poison. Infants were killed to save them from the Spaniards. In two years, through murder, mutilation, or suicide, half of the 250,000 Indians on Haiti were dead.

When it became clear that there was no gold left, the Indians were taken as slave labor on huge estates, known later as encomiendas. They were worked at a ferocious pace, and died by the thousands. By the year 1515, there were perhaps fifty thousand Indians left. By 1550, there were five hundred. A report of the year 1650 shows none of the original Arawaks or their descendants left on the island.

The chief source - and, on many matters the only source - of information about what happened on the islands after Columbus came is Bartolome de las Casas, who, as a young priest, participated in the conquest of Cuba. For a time he owned a plantation on which Indian slaves worked, but he gave that up and became a vehement critic of Spanish cruelty. Las Casas transcribed Columbus's journal and, in his fifties, began a multicolumn History of the Indies. In it, he describes the Indians. They are agile, he says, and can swim long distances, especially the women. They are not completely peaceful, because they do battle from time to time with other tribes, but their casualties seems small, and they fight when they are individually moved to do so because of some grievance, not on the orders of captains or kings.

Women in Indian society were treated so well as to startle the Spaniards. Las Casas describes sex relations:

Marriage laws are non-existent: men and women alike choose their mates and leave them as they please, without offense, jealousy or anger. They multiply in great abundance; pregnant women work to the last minute and give birth almost painlessly; up the next day, they bathe in the river and are as

clean and healthy as before giving birth. If they tire of their men, they give themselves abortions with herbs that force stillbirths, covering their shameful parts with leaves or cotton cloth; although on the whole, Indian men and women look upon total nakedness with as much casualness as we look upon a man's head or at his hands.

The Indians, Las Casas says, have no religion, at least no temples. They live in

Large communal bell-shaped buildings, housing up to 600 people at one time ...made of very strong wood and roofed with palm leaves...They prize bird feathers to various colors, beads made of fishbones, and green and white stones with which they adorn their ears and lips, but they put no value on gold and other precious things. They lack all manner of commerce, neither buying nor selling, and rely exclusively on their natural environment for maintenance. They are extremely generous with their possessions and by the same token covet the possessions of their friends and expect the same degree of liberality...

In Book Two of his History of the Indies, Las Casas (who at first urged replacing Indians by black slaves, thinking they were stronger and would survive, but later relented when he saw the effects on blacks) tells about the treatment of the Indians by the Spaniards. It is a unique account and deserves to be quoted at length:

Endless testimonies...prove the mild and pacific temperament of the natives...But our work was to exasperate, ravage, kill, mangle and destroy; small wonder, then, if they tried to kill one of us now and then...The admiral, it is true, was blind as those who came after him, and he was so anxious to please the King that he committed irreparable crimes against the Indians...

Las Casas tells how the Spaniards "grew more conceited every day" after a while refused to walk any distance. They "rode the backs of Indians if they were in a hurry" or were carried on hammocks by Indians running in relays. "In this case they also had Indians carry large leaves to shade them from the sun and others to fan them with goose wings."

Total control led to total cruelty. The Spaniards "thought nothing of knifing Indians by tens and twenties and of cutting slices off them to test the sharpness of their blades." Las Casas tells how "two of these so-called Christians met two Indian boys one day, each carrying a parrot; they took the parrots and for fun beheaded the boys."

The Indians' attempts to defend themselves failed. And when they ran off into the hills they were found and killed. So, Las Casas reports, "they suffered and died in the mines and other labors in desperate silence, knowing not a soul in the world to whom they could turn for help." He describes their work in the mines:

...mountains are stripped from top to bottom and bottom to top a thousand times; they dig, split rocks, move stones, and carry dirt on their backs to wash it in the rivers, while those who wash gold stay in the water all the time with their backs bent so constantly it breaks them; and when water invades the mines, the most arduous task of all is to dry the mines by scooping up pansful of water and throwing it up outside...

After each six or eight months' work in the mines, which was the time required of each crew to dig enough gold for melting, up to a third of the men died.

While the men were sent many miles away to the mines, the wives remained to work the soil, forced into the excruciating job of digging and making thousands of hills for cassava plants.

Thus husbands and wives were together only once every eight or ten months and when they met they were to exhausted and depressed on both sides...they ceased to procreate. As for the newly born, they died early because their mothers, over-worked and famished, had no milk to nurse them, and for this reason, while I was in Cuba, 7000 children died in three months. Some mothers even drowned their babies from sheet desperation...In this way, husbands died in the mines, wives died at work, and children died from lack of milk...and in a short time this land which was so great, so powerful, and fertile...was depopulated...My eyes have seen these acts so foreign to human nature, and now I tremble as I write...

When he arrived on Hispaniola in 1508, Las Casas says, "there were 60,000 people living on this island, including the Indians; so that from 1494 to 1508, over three million people had perished from war, slavery, and the mines. Who in future generations will believe this? I myself writing it as a knowledgeable eyewitness can hardly believe it..."

Thus began the history, five hundred years ago, of the European invasion of the Indian settlements in the Americas. That beginning, when you read Las Casas - even if his figures are exaggerations (were there 3 million Indians to begin with, as he says, or less than a million, as some historians have calculated, or 8 million as others now believe?) - is conquest, slavery, death. When we read the history books given to children in the United States, it all starts with heroic adventure - there is no bloodshed - and Columbus Day is a celebration.

Past the elementary and high schools, there are only occasional hints of something else. Samuel Eliot Morison, the Harvard historian, was the most distinguished writer on Columbus, the author of a multi-volume biography, and was himself a sailor who retraced Columbus's route across the Atlantic. In his popular book <u>Christopher Columbus, Mariner,</u> written in 1954, he tells about the enslavement and the killing: "The cruel policy initiated by Columbus and pursued by his successors resulted in complete genocide."

That is on one page, buried halfway into the telling of a grand romance. In the book's last paragraph, Morison sums up his view of Columbus:

He had his faults and his defects, but they were largely the defects of the qualities that made him great - his indomitable will, his superb faith in God and in his own mission as the Christ-bearer to lands beyond the seas, his stubborn persistence despite neglect, poverty and discouragement. But there was no flaw, no dark side to the most outstanding and essential of all his qualities - his seamanship.

One can lie outright about the past. Or one can omit facts which might lead to unacceptable conclusions. Morison does neither. He refused to lie about Columbus. He does not omit the story of mass murder; indeed he describes it with the harshest word one can use: genocide.

But he does something else - he mentions the truth quickly and goes on to other things more important to him. Outright lying or quiet omission takes the risk of discovery which, when made, might arouse the reader to rebel against the writer. To state the facts, however, and then to bury them in a mass of other information is to say to the reader with a certain infectious calm: yes, mass murder took place, but it's not that important - it should weigh very little in our final judgments; it should affect very little what we do in the world.

It is not that the historian can avoid emphasis of some facts and not of others. This is as natural to him as to the mapmaker, who, in order to produce a usable drawing for practical purposes, must first flatten and distort the shape of the earth, then choose out of the bewildering mass of geographic information those things needed for the purpose of this or that particular map.

My argument cannot be against selection, simplification, emphasis, which are inevitable for both cartographers and historians. But the mapmaker's distortion is a technical necessity for a common purpose shared by all people who need maps. The historian's distortion is more than technical, it is ideological; it is released into a world of contending interests, where any chosen emphasis supports (whether the historian means to or not) some kind of interest, whether economic or political or racial or national or sexual.

Furthermore, this ideological interest is not openly expressed in the way a mapmaker's technical interest is obvious ("This is a Mercator projection for long-range navigation - for short-range, you'd better use a different projection). No, it is presented as if all readers of history had a common interest which historians serve to the best of their ability. This is not intentional deception; the historian has been trained in a society in which education and knowledge are put forward as technical problems of excellence and not as tools for contending social classes, races, nations.

To emphasize the heroism of Columbus and his successors as navigators and discoverers, and to de-emphasize their genocide, is not a technical necessity but an ideological choice. It serves - unwittingly - to justify what was done.

My point is not that we must, in telling history, accuse, judge, condemn Columbus in absentia. It is too late for that; it would be a useless scholarly exercise in morality. But the easy acceptance of atrocities as a deplorable but necessary price to pay for progress (Hiroshima and Vietnam, to save Western civilization; Kronstadt and Hungary, to save socialism; nuclear proliferation, to save us all) - that is still with us. One reason these atrocities are still with us is that we have learned to bury them in a mass of other facts, as radioactive wastes are buried in containers in the earth. We have learned to give them exactly the same proportion of attention that teachers and writers often give them in the most respectable of classrooms and textbooks. This learned sense of moral proportion, coming from the apparent objectivity of the scholar, is accepted more easily than when it comes from politicians at press conferences. It is therefore more deadly.

The treatment of heroes (Columbus) and their victims (the Arawaks) - the quiet acceptance of conquest and murder in the name of progress - is only one aspect of a certain approach to history, in which the past is told from the point of view of governments, conquerors, diplomats, leaders. It is as if they, like Columbus, deserve universal acceptance, as if they - the Founding Fathers, Jackson, Lincoln, Wilson, Roosevelt, Kennedy, the leading members of Congress, the famous Justices of the Supreme Court - represent the nation as a whole. The pretense is that there really is such a thing as "the United States," subject to occasional conflicts and quarrels, but fundamentally a community of people with common interests. It is as if there really is a "national interest" represented in the Constitution, in territorial expansion, in the laws passed by Congress, the decisions of the courts, the devel-

opment of capitalism, the culture of education and the mass media.

"History is the memory of states, "wrote Henry Kissinger in his first book, A World Restored, in which he proceeded to tell the history of nineteenth-century Europe from the viewpoint of the leaders of Austria and England, ignoring the millions who suffered from those statesmen's policies. From his standpoint, the "peace" that Europe had before the French Revolution was "restored" by the diplomacy of a few national leaders. But for factory workers in England, farmers in France, colored people in Asia and Africa, women and children everywhere except in the upper classes, it was a world of conquest, violence, hunger, exploitation - a world not restored but disintegrated.

My viewpoint, in telling the history of the United States, is different: that we must not accept the memory of states as our own. Nations are not communities and never have been. The history of any country, presented as the history of a family, conceals fierce conflicts of interest (sometimes exploding, most often repressed) between conquerors and conquered, masters and slaves, capitalists and workers, dominators and dominated in race and sex. And in such a world of conflict, a world of victims and executioners, it is the job of thinking people, as Albert Camus suggested, not to be on the side of the executioners.

Thus, in that inevitable taking of sides which comes from selection and emphasis in history, I prefer to try to tell the story of the discovery of America from the viewpoint of the Arawaks, of the Constitution from the standpoint of the slaves, of Andrew Jackson as seen by the Cherokees, of the Civil War as seen by the New York Irish, of the Mexican war as seen by the young women in the Lowell textile mills, of the Spanish -American war as seen by the Cubans, the conquest of the Philippines as seen by black soldiers on Luzon, the Gilded Age as seen by southern farmers, the First World War as seen by socialists, the Second World War as seen by pacifists, the New Deal as seen by blacks in Harlem, the postwar American empire as seen by peons in Latin America. And so on, to the limited extent that any one person, however he or she strains, can "see" history from the standpoint of others.

My point is not to grieve for the victims and denounce the executioners. Those tears, that anger, cast into the past, deplete our moral energy for the present. And the lines are not always clear. In the long run, the oppressor is also a victim in the short run (and so far, human history has consisted only of short runs), the victims, themselves desperate and tainted with the culture that oppresses them, turn on other victims.

Still, understanding the complexities, this book will be skeptical of governments and their attempts, through politics and culture, to ensnare ordinary people in a giant web of nationhood pretending to a common interest. I will try not to overlook the cruelties that victims inflict on one another as they are jammed together in the boxcars of the system. I don't want to romanticize them. But I do remember (in rough paraphrase) a statement I once read: "The cry of the poor is not always just, but if you don't listen to it, you will never know what justice is."

I don't want to invent victories for people's movements. But to think that history-writing must aim simply to recapitulate the failures that dominate the past is to make historians collaborators in an endless cycle of defeat. If history is to be creative, to anticipate a possible future without denying the past, it should, I believe, emphasize new possibilities by disclosing those hidden episodes of the past when, even if in brief flashes, people showed their ability to resist, to join together, occasionally to win. I am supposing, or perhaps only hoping, that our future may be found in the past's fugitive moments of compassion rather than in its solid centuries of warfare.

That, being as blunt as I can, is my approach to the history of the United States. The reader may as well know that before going on.

# LANGUAGE AND LITERATURE FROM A PUEBLO INDIAN PERSPECTIVE

## *Leslie Marmon Silko (1948- )*

*Silko was born in Albuquerque, New Mexico, of Pueblo. Laguna, Mexican, and white descent. She grew up on the Laguna Pueblo reservation first attending an Indian school and later a high school in Albuquerque 50 miles away. Some of her poetry, prose, and fiction works include* Laguna Woman Poems, *(1974),* Ceremony *(1977),* Storyteller *(1981),* Almanac of the Dead *(1991) and* Yellow Woman *(1993).*

*Like this essay, much of her work has been concerned with the importance of storytelling and folk traditions in the Pueblo culture and how the dominant American society has tried to destroy these stories and ceremonies.*

Where I come from, the words most highly valued are those spoken from the heart, unpremeditated and unrehearsed. Among the Pueblo people, a written speech or statement is highly suspect because the true feelings of the speaker remain hidden as she reads words that are detached from the occasion and the audience. I have intentionally not written a formal paper because I want you to *hear* and to experience English in a structure that follows patterns from the oral tradition. For those of you accustomed to being taken from point A to point B to point C, this presentation may be somewhat difficult to follow. Pueblo expression resembles something like a spider's web—with many little threads radiating from the center, crisscrossing one another. As with the web, the structure emerges as it is made, and you must simply listen and trust, as the Pueblo people do, that meaning will be made.

My task is a formidable one: I ask you to set aside a number of basic approaches that you have been using and probably will continue to use, and, instead, to approach language from the Pueblo perspective, one that embraces the whole of creation and the whole of history and time.

What changes would Pueblo writers make to English as a language for literature? I have some examples of stories in English that I will use to address this question. At the same time, I would like to explain the importance of storytelling and how it relates to a Pueblo theory of language.

So I will begin, appropriately enough, with the Pueblo Creation story, an all-inclusive story of how life began. In this story, Tse'itsi'nako, Thought Woman, by thinking of her sisters, and together with her sisters, thought of everything that is. In this way, the world was created. Everything in this world was a part of the original Creation; the people at home understood that far away there were other human beings, also a part of this world. The Creation story even includes a prophecy that describes the origin of European and African peoples and also refers to Asians.

This story, I think, suggests something about why the Pueblo people are more concerned with story and communication and less concerned with a particular language. There are at least six, possibly seven, distinct languages among the twenty pueblos of the southwestern United States, for example, Zuñi and Hopi. And from mesa to mesa there are subtle differences in language. But the particular language being spoken isn't as important as what a speaker is trying to say, and this emphasis on the story itself stems, I believe, from a view of narrative particular to the Pueblo and other Native American peoples—that is, that language *is* story.

I will try to clarify this statement. At Laguna Pueblo, for example, many individual words have their own stories. So when one is telling a story and one is using words to tell the story, each word that one is speaking has a story of his own, too. Often the speakers, or tellers, will go into these words stories, creating an elaborate structure of stories within stories. This structure, which becomes very apparent in the actual telling of a story, informs contemporary Pueblo writing and storytelling as well as the traditional narratives. This perspective on narrative—of story within story, the idea that one story is only the beginning of many stories and the sense that stories never truly end—represents an important contribution of Native American cultures to the English language.

Many people think of storytelling as something that is done at bedtime, that it is something done for small children. But when I use the term *storytelling*, I'm talking about something much bigger than that. I'm talking about something that comes out of all experience and understanding of that original view of Creation—that we are all part of a whole; we do not differentiate or fragment stories and experiences. In the beginning, Tse'itsi'nako, Thought Woman, thought of all things, and all of these things are held together as one holds many things together in a single thought.

So in the telling (and you will hear a few of the dimensions of this telling), first of all, as mentioned earlier, the storytelling always includes the audience, the listeners. In fact, a great deal of the story is believed to be inside the listener, the storyteller's role is to draw the story out of the listeners. The story-telling continues from generation to generation.

Basically, the origin story constructs our identity —with this story, we know who we are. We are the Lagunas. This is where we come from. We came this way. We came by this place. And so from the time we are very young, we hear these stories, so that when we go out into the world, when one asks who we are or where we are from, we immediately know: we are the people who came from the north. We are the people of these stories.

In the Creation story, Antelope says that he will help knock a hole in the Earth so that the people can come up, out into the next world. Antelope tries and tries; he uses his hooves but is unable to break through. It is then that Badger says, "Let me help you." And Badger very patiently

uses his claws and digs a way through, bringing the people into the world. When the Badger clan people think of themselves, or when the Antelope people think of themselves, it is as people who are of *this* story, and this is *our* place, and we fit into the very beginning when the people first came, before we began our journey south.

Within the clans there are stories that identify the clan. One moves, then, from the idea of one's identity as a tribal person into clan identity, then to one's identity as a member of an extended family. And it is the notion of extended family that has produced a kind of story that some distinguish from other Pueblo stories, though Pueblo people do not. Anthropologists and ethnologists have, for a long time, differentiated the types of stories the Pueblos tell. They tended to elevate the old, sacred, and traditional stories and to brush aside family stories, the family's account of itself. But in Pueblo culture, these family stories are given equal recognition. There is no definite, preset pattern for the way one will hear the stories of one's own family, but it is a very critical part of one's childhood, and the story-telling continues throughout one's life. One will hear stories of importance to the family—sometimes wonderful stories—stories about the time a maternal uncle got the biggest deer that was ever seen and brought it back from the mountains. And so an indi-vidual's identity will extend from the identity constructed around the family—"I am from the family of my uncle who brought in this wonderful deer, and it was a wonderful hunt."

Family accounts include negative stories, too; perhaps an uncle did something unacceptable. It is very important that one keep track of all these stories—both positive and not so positive—about one's own family and other families. Because even when there is no way around it—old Uncle Pete *did* do a terrible thing—by knowing the stories that originate in other families, one is able to deal with terrible sorts of things that might happen within one's own family. If a member of the family does something that cannot be excused, one always knows stories about similarly inexcusable things done by a member of another family. But this knowledge is not communicated for malicious reasons. It is very important to understand this. Keeping track of all the stories within the community gives us all a certain distance, a useful perspective, that brings incidents down to a level we can deal with. If others have done it before, it cannot be so terrible. If others have endured, so can we.

The stories are always bringing us together, keeping this whole together, keeping this family together, keeping this clan together. "Don't go away, don't isolate yourself, but come here, because we have all had these kinds of experiences." And so there is this constant pulling together to resist the tendency to run or hide or separate oneself during a traumatic emotional experience. This separation not only endangers the group but the individual as well—one does not recover by oneself.

Because storytelling lies at the heart of Pueblo culture, it is absurd to attempt to fix the stories in time. "When did they tell the stories?" or "What time of day does the storytelling take place?"—these questions are nonsensical from a Pueblo perspective, because our storytelling goes on constantly: as some old grandmother puts on the shoes of a child and tells her the story of a little girl who didn't wear her shoes, for instance, or someone comes into the house for coffee to talk with a teenage boy who has just been in a lot of trouble, to reassure him that someone else's son has been in that kind of trouble, too. Storytelling is an ongoing process, working on many different levels.

Here's one story that is often told at a time of individual crisis (and I want to remind you that we make no distinctions between types of story—historical, sacred, plain gossip—because these distinctions are not useful when discussing the Pueblo *experience* of language). There was a young man who, when he came back from the war in Vietnam, had saved up his army pay and bought a beautiful red Volkswagen. He was very proud of it. One night he drove up to a place called the King's Bar, right across the reservation line. The bar is notorious for many reasons, particularly for the deep arroyo located behind it. The young man ran in to pick up a cold six-pack, but he forgot to put on his emergency brake. And his little red Volkswagen rolled back into the arroyo and was all smashed up. He felt very bad about it, but within a few days everybody had come to him with stories about other people who had lost cars and family members to that arroyo, for instance, George Day's station wagon, with his mother-in-law and kids inside. So everybody was saying, "Well, at least your mother-in-law and kids weren't in the car when it rolled in," and one can't argue with that kind of story. The story of the young man and his smashed-up Volkswagen was now joined with all the other stories of cars that fell into that arroyo.

Now I want to tell you a very beautiful little story. It is a very old story that is sometimes told to people who suffer great family or personal loss. This story was told by my Aunt Susie. She is one of the first generation of people at Laguna who began experimenting with English—who began working to make English speak for us, that is, to speak from the heart. (I come from a family intent on getting the stories told.) As you read the story, I think you will

hear that. And here and there, I think, you will also hear the influence of the Indian school at Carlisle, Pennsylvania, where my Aunt Susie was sent (like being sent to prison) for six years.

This scene is set partly in Acoma, partly in Laguna. Waithea was a little girl living in Acoma and one day she said, "Mother, I would like to have some *yashtoah* to eat." *Yashtoah* is the hardened crust of corn mush that curls up. *Yashtoah* literally means "curled up." She said, "I would like have some *Yashtoah*," and her mother said, "My dear little girl, I can't make you any *yashtoah* because we haven't any wood, but if you will go down off the mesa, down below and pick up some pieces of wood and bring them home I will make you some *yashtoah*." So Waithea was glad and ran down the precipitous cliff of Acoma mesa. Down below, just as her mother had told her, there were pieces of wood, some curled, some crooked in shape, that she was to pick up and take home. She found just such wood as these.

She brought them home in a little wicker basket. First she called to her mother as she got home, "*Nayah, deeni!* Mother, upstairs!" The Pueblo people always called "upstairs" because long ago their homes were two, three stories, and they entered from the top. She said, "*Deeni! Upstairs!*" and her mother came. The little girl said, "I have brought the wood you wanted me to bring." And she opened her little wicker basket to lay out the pieces of wood, but here they were snakes. They were snakes instead of the crooked sticks of wood. And her mother said, "Oh my dear child, you have brought snakes instead!" She said, "Go take them back and put them back just where you got them." And the little girl ran down the mesa again, down below to the flats. And she put those snakes back just where she got them. They were snakes instead, and she was very hurt about this, and so she said, "I'm not going home. I'm going to Kawaik, the beautiful lake place Kawaik, and drown myself in that lake, *byn'yah'nah* [the 'west lake'], I will go there and drown myself."

So she started off, and as she passed by the Enchanted Mesa near Acoma, she met an old man, very aged, and he saw her running, and he said, "My dear child, where are you going?" "I'm going to Kawaik and jump into the lake there."

"Why?" "Well, because," she said, "my mother didn't want to make any *yashtoah* for me." The old man said, "Oh, no! You must not go, my child. Come with me and I will take you home." He tried to catch her, but she was very light and skipped along. And every time he would try to grab her she would skip faster away from him.

The old man was coming home with some wood strapped to his back and tied with yucca. He just let that strap go and let the wood drop. He went as fast as he could up the cliff to the little girl's home. When he got to the place where she lived, he called to her mother. "*Deeni!*" "Come on up!" And he said, "I can't. I just came to bring you a message. Your little daughter is running away. She is going to Kawaik to drown herself in the lake there." "Oh my dear little girl!" the mother said. So she busied herself with making the *yashtoah* her little girl liked so much. Corn mush curled at the top. (She must have found enough wood to boil the corn meal and make the *yashtoah*.)

While the mush was cooling off, she got the little girl's clothing, her *manta* dress and buckskin moccasins and all her other garments, and put them in a bundle—probably a yucca bag. And she started down as fast as she could on the east side of Acoma. (There used to be a trail there, you know. It's gone now, but it was accessible in those days.) She saw her daughter was at a distance and she kept calling: "Stsamaku! My daughter! Come back! I've got your *yashtoah* for you." But little girl would not turn. She kept on ahead and she cried: "My mother, my mother, she didn't want me to have any *yashtoah*. So now I'm going to Kawaik and drown myself." Her mother heard her cry and said, "My little daughter, come back here!" "No," and she kept a distance away from her. And they came nearer and nearer to the lake. And she could see her daughter now, very plain. "Come back, my daughter! I have your *yashtoah*." But no, she kept on, and finally she reached the lake and she stood on the edge.

She had tied a little feather in her hair, which is traditional (in death they tie this feather on the head). She carried a feather, the little girl did, and she tied it in her hair with a piece of string; right on top of her head she put the feather. Just as her mother was about to reach her, she jumped into the lake. The little feather was whirling around and around in the depths below. Of course the mother was very sad. She went, grieved, back to Acoma and climbed her mesa home. She stood on the edge of the mesa and scattered her daughter's clothing, the little moccasins, the *yashtoah*. She scattered them to the east, to the west, to the north, to the south. And the pieces of clothing and the moccasins and *yashtoah* all turned into butterflies. And today they say that Acoma has more beautiful butterflies: red ones, white ones, blue ones, yellow ones. They came from this little girl's clothing.

Now this is a story anthropologists would consider very old. The version I have given you is just as Aunt Susie tells it. You can occasionally hear some English she picked up at Carlisle— words like

*precipitous*. You will also notice that there is a great deal of repetition, and a little reminder about *yashtoah* and how it is made. There is a remark about the cliff trail at Acoma—that it was once there but is there no longer. This story may be told at a time of sadness or loss, but within this story many other elements are brought together. Things are not separated out and categorized; all things are brought together, so that the reminder about the *yashtoah* is valuable information that is repeated—a recipe, if you will. The information about the old trail at Acoma reveals that stories are, in a sense, maps, since even to this day there is little information or material about trails that is passed around with writing. In the structure of this story the repetitions are, of course, designed to help you remember. It is repeated again and again, and then it moves on.

There are a great many parallels between Pueblo experiences and those of African and Caribbean peoples—one is that we have all had the conqueror's language imposed on us. But our experience with English has been somewhat different in that the Bureau of Indian Affairs schools were not interested in teaching us the canon of Western classics. For instance, we never heard of Shakespeare. We were given Dick and Jane, and I can remember reading that the robins were heading south for the winter. It took me a long time to figure out what was going on. I worried for quite a while about our robins in Laguna because they didn't leave in the winter, until I finally realized that all the big textbook companies are up in Boston and *their* robins do go south in the winter. But in a way, this dreadful formal education freed us by encouraging us to maintain our narratives. Whatever literature we were exposed to at school (which was damn little), at home the storytelling, the special regard for telling and bringing together through the telling, was going on constantly.

And as the old people say, "If you can remember the stories, you will be all right. Just remember the stories." When I returned to Laguna Pueblo after attending college, I wondered how the storytelling was continuing (anthropologists say that Laguna Pueblo is one of the more acculturated pueblos), so I visited an English class at Laguna Acoma High School. I knew the students had cassette tape recorders in their lockers and stereos at home, and that they listened to Kiss and Led Zeppelin and were well informed about culture in general. I had with me an anthology of short stories by Native American writers, *The Man to Send Rain Clouds*. One story in the book is about the killing of a state policeman in New Mexico by three Acoma Pueblo men in the early 1950s. I asked the students how many had heard this story and steeled myself for the possibility that the anthropologists were right, that the old traditions were indeed dying that and the students would be ignorant of the story. But instead, all but one or two raised their hands—they had heard the story, just as I had heard it when I was young, some in English, some in Laguna.

One of the other advantages that we Pueblos have enjoyed is that we have always been able to stay with the land. Our stories cannot be separated from their geographical locations, from actual physical places on the land. We were not relocated like so many Native American groups who were torn away front their ancestral land. And our stories are so much a part of these places that it is almost impossible for future generations to lose them—there is a story connected with every place, every object in the landscape.

Dennis Brutus has talked about the "yet unborn" as well as "those from the past," and how we are still *all* in *this* place, and language—the storytelling—is our way of passing through or being with them, of being together again. When Aunt Susie told her stories, she would tell a younger child to go open the door so that our esteemed predecessors might bring their gifts to us. "They are out there," Aunt Susie would say. "Let them come in. They're here, they're here with us *within* the stories."

A few years ago, when Aunt Susie was 106, I paid her a visit, and while I was there she said, "Well, I'll be leaving here soon. I think I'll be leaving here next week, and I will be going over to the Cliff House." She said, "It's going to be real good to get back over there." I was listening, and I was thinking that she must be talking about her house at Paguate village, just north of Laguna. And she went on, "Well, my mother's sister [and she gave her Indian name] will be there. She has been living there. She will be there and we will be over there, and I will get a chance to write down these stories I've been telling you." Now you must understand, of course, that Aunt Susie's mother's sister, a great storyteller herself, has long since passed over into the land of the dead. But then I realized, too, that Aunt Susie wasn't talking about death the way most of us do. She was talking about "going over" as a journey, a

journey that perhaps we can only begin to understand through an appreciation for the boundless capacity of language that, through storytelling, brings us together, despite great distances between cultures, despite great distances in time.

**Study Questions**

1. How does Silko feel about written speeches? How is the structure or logic of writing different from the spoken word (oral tradition)?

2. What does Silko mean by the phrase "language is story"?

3. How does storytelling function in Pueblo society?

4. Why are "negative" stories told and remembered?

5. How are stories connected to geography in the Pueblo culture?

6. How are stories and experiences related according to Silko?

# THE EPIC OF SARA

## Narrated by Sira Mori Jabaté

*Recorded in Kéla, Mali, in 1968 by Charles Bird. Transcribed and translated into English by Charles Bird and Kassim Kònè. This excerpt edited by Charles Bird.*

*Although The Epic of Sara was recorded in 1968, we can retrodict the presence of this and other epics earlier though it might be difficult to say exactly when. Clearly it takes place, like* Sundiata, *after the coming of Islam to West Africa in the eighth and ninth centuries.*

*Normally the humanities syllabus includes epics which feature male protagonists like the* Iliad *and the western influenced D. T. Niane* Sundiata *which includes women in necessary and supportive roles. In a more traditional transcription of the SonJara epic from oral sources in West Africa, we see jelimusow (plural of griotte) in significant roles such as announcing the royal births. These appearances in the transcribed oral sources document the presence of women as griottes in the society and, therefore, important figures in African literature. (Hale* Griotes and Griottes *221) not only is "The Epic of Sara" told by a female jeli, but it features a woman protagonist.*

Sira Mori Jabatè was one of Mali's Great Female Bards. She was especially renowned for *Sara*. For this version, she was accompanied by her brother, Yamuru Jabatè, and a chorus of adolescent females. Sira Mori passed away in 1989, and fifteen head of cattle were sacrificed at her funeral ceremony.

We include this as an example of epic for a number of reasons. Sira Mori uses the formal style of the traditional bards to deliver this story of the heroic behavior of Sara, whose promise would not be denied. The form she uses is more melodic than the typical Mande male bard's

narrative mode. As such it sounds more like praise song (*faasa*), of which Sira Mori was one of the great Mande masters. This is not, however, at all typical of praise song from the point of view of content. Praise songs do not tell stories. This is clearly poetic narrative, and heroic, and therefore, by any definition, it qualifies as epic. From the point of view of Maninka speakers, *Sara*, like the Sunjata epic, is called *maana*, the term they use when talking about poetic narratives.

The theme of *Sara* recurs in virtually all societies where marriages are arranged. In the Mande world marriages are officially arranged and sanctioned by the male authorities, often in conflict with the wishes of the bride and sometimes of the groom. In this story Sara has given the promise of her undying love to another, her "promise-sharer. "The story is about the importance of that promise and what Sara does to protect it. The poetic density of this text requires detailed explanation and commentary.

"Ah! Sara! Sara is sung for those of one voice. /Ah! Long-necked Sara!" 'Those of one Voice' translates *kankelentigi*, 'voice-one-master.' It means roughly 'someone who is true to his/her word.'

Mande poetry exploits polyphony. The word Sara itself is polyphonic. Sara is an Islamic woman's name probably borrowed very early with the introduction of Islam in West Africa in the eighth and ninth centuries. It is an Old Testament name, the wife of the patriarch Abraham. It is also a traditional Mande name given to the first-born girl. Sara is also the word for 'charm, grace,' and in this story, Sara's charm and grace constitute much of its understood content. *Sara* is also the word used to refer to 'payment, salary, reward.' This too is a subtheme of this story. Sara is rewarded for keeping her word.

> CHORUS: Ah! Sara is sung for those of one voice.
> Don't you see it?
> SIRA MORI: Sara! Sara is sung for those with promises.
> Long-necked Sara!
> CHORUS: Ah! Sara is sung for those of one voice.
> Don't you see it?
> SIRA MORI: Sara! Sara is sung for those with promises
> Long-necked Sara!
> Don't you see it?
> CHORUS: Sara is sung for those of one voice
> Don't you see it?
> SIRA MORI: Sara is not sung for "Money's in my pocket."
> Sara is not sung for "My name is gold."
> Sara is not sung for beauty.
> Sara is sung for a person's behavior, Allah!
> > (Yes! It's the truth! It's a matter of behavior. Sara was sung for the promise, for those who have seen tough days, for those who looked into fiery things.)

[The above paragraph presents Yamuru Jabatè's commentary on the story. It is not uncommon to have commentators who may from time to time contribute pieces to the performance. The phrase, *minw ye lon ye* translates literally as 'those who have seen the day,' which is used in Maninka to convey the sense of 'having met a challenge, having faced difficult times and come through them.' We used 'fiery things' to translate *ko wulen*, literally 'red thing.' *Wulen* has polyphonies extending from 'red' to 'hot, fiery, fierce.' As we read it, it refers to those who have suffered for a cause. An important theme introduced here is that the bards sing of a person's deeds. Their praise cannot be bought.]

> Sara is not sung for beauty.
> Sara is sung for a person's behavior.
> Sara is not sung for the charming.
> Sara is sung for a person's behavior
> Behaving is hard!
> > (Amazing! Amazing, Sira Mori!)
> Why union happens is that love is of paradise.
> Why union happens is that union is of paradise.
> No one should shame their sharer of secrets.
> Why union happens is that union is of paradise.
> Why union happens is that union is of paradise.

[We have translated *yomali kiyama* as 'paradise.' It could be translated as 'heaven, the hereafter.' It is not difficult to see that Sira Mori's story constructs a strong argument for love and for marriage based on love. Love, she argues, is Allah's will. It is something of the hereafter, the eternal, something of paradise. The union of two people is first and foremost the will of Allah.]

> No one should shame their sharer of secrets
> Do not say your inner words to a gossip.
> No slave knows Allah.

['Slave' (*jon*) is here understood as 'slave of God,' a human being. No one can claim to know the ways of God.]

> Giving your word is misery.
> Ah! Giving your word is hard.
> Giving your word is hard.
> Nobles must hold to their word.
> Ah! Giving your word is hard.
> Nobles must hold to their word.
> If you are not a bastard,
> Then giving your word is your misery, Allah!

[Sira Mori here is using *horon* to refer to a kind of noble behavior which is not limited to social structural categories. Anyone may be called *horon* if they behave in a certain way. As Yamuru said, a person becomes a slave by his or her behavior. *Horon* are those who can trace their patrilineal descent and be proud of it. This is opposed to *nyamogoden*, literally 'before-person child,' 'the child of someone who came before' (the wedding, we assume), hence, a bastard. Bastards cannot trace their ancestors through their fathers and are thus cursed by a biological lack of dignity and are therefore untrustworthy.]

> The wedding people came,
> Sara's wedding people came.
> Sara's husband-to-be did not please her,
> BUT SHE SAID, "I will not shame my fathers.
> "I will not shame my grandfathers.
> "I will not shame my uncles.
> "If Allah is not in the matter
> "It does not happen,
> "Because my word has been spoken to another."
> Sara's bride-price had been taken.
> The wedding cows had been taken.
> Sara's wedding date had been set.
> Oh Sara, Allah!
> > (This part calls to Sira Mori Nana. They did not break their promise.)
> The wedding escort rose up.
> Sara's promise-sharer spoke.
> HE SAID: "Ayi! Giving your word is hard. Oh, la, la!
> "Oh, oh! Giving your word is hard.
> "Your bride-price has been taken.
> "Your wedding cows have been taken today.
> "Your wedding escort has risen up.
> "Long-necked Sara, giving your word is hard.

"Do not think about those cows, my twin-alike.
"Do not think about this marriage, my pair-alike."

[We have translated *filanin-nyogon* as 'twin-alike,' which is a literal translation of the Maninka. It is a term of endearment used for someone who is like a twin to you, someone with whom you giggle, laugh, and cry. The meaning of *ma-nyogon* is 'person-alike' roughly 'each other's person.' We wanted to preserve Sira Mori's Maninka parallelism in our translation which explains the idiosyncratic English.]

I will not shame my grandfathers.
Giving your word is hard.
Do you not take me at my word?
Do not hurry so.
Giving your word is hard.
    (Amazing! If you spit out your saliva, it can
    not be gathered up again. That's the truth!)

[The following section describes the wedding party leaving Sara's village for the village of her husband-to-be, where she will reside. The wedding party will be met outside the new village by a party consisting mostly of her new female in-laws.]

The wedding arrangers rose up, Sara.
They all went off passing the boundary.
The birds in the trees were crying.
The *ko-n-kan-ko* birds all were crying, Sara.

[*Ko-n-kan-ko* is held to be the cry of the messenger bird. It is a way of gaining the floor when you have something to say: "Say, my voice says. . . ."]

The wedding arrangers said: "This is amazing!"
This is what the *ko-n-kan-ko* birds sang:
"No slave knows Allah.
"Giving your word is hard."
    (Your father makes you noble.
    You mother makes you that. You
      make yourself a slave. This calls
    to Sira Mori Nana's child. Bati Hayidara,
      this must call to him. He is noble.)
Sara arrived outside the village.
Those meeting the wedding party came.
The *jembe*-drummers began.
The balafon-players began.
The gong-playing bard women began.
The bride who was being met . . .
When those meeting the wedding party saw Sara,
She said her belly was in pain,
Ah! Those meeting the wedding came up.
SHE SAID: "Laila! Laila!
    Mahamadarasurudilahi!"

[The above expressions are Arabic and mean, "There is no God but Allah, and Mohammad is His Prophet." In Maninka, it is used in situations similar to those in which an English speaker might say in swearing, "Jesus Christ Almighty God. "We have not broken the expression up into its Arabic words, because we do not believe that the majority of Maninka who use it do so.]

SHE SAID: "Ah! Allah! My belly pains me."
The wedding arrangers said: "It's amazing!"
Those meeting the wedding party having come,
THEY SAID: "Sara says her belly pains her."
"Get away from me!
"My belly pains me, lalala layi!
"My belly won't cool down.
"Ah! My belly pains me!"
One old brave spoke up:
"Calm down!
"Let the *jembe*-drummers return,
"Let the bard women return."
He took the end of Sara's staff to lead her.

[The image here is of Sara debilitated by her illness, leaning on a staff like a blind person who is often led around by a young boy or girl holding the end of the staff. There is a very material sense of language in this story. Sara's promise is embodied; it is in her belly. Words are things that enter into people and cause them to behave in particular ways. Some phrases, like the Arabic expressions above, are known only by their use, by their potential effects on one's life. They have no analyzable meanings independent of that.]

They went to her groom's compound, Allah!
They went there with Sara,
Ah! World!
The belly-pain men came up to her.
The medicine-powder men came up to her.
The string-knotters came up to her.
The belly-spitters came up to her.

[There are hundreds, if not thousands, of practitioners of traditional medicine in the Mande world. They are brought into the story named for the devices they use. Some medicines, like ours, involve the use of powders: ground roots, bark, or leaves. Some medical interventions involve the knotting of string which may then be wrapped around the problem. The knots draw the badness out. They say that some of these knotted strings wrapped around a fetish can kill your enemies.]

SHE SAID: "My belly pains me.
"If you don't get away from me,
"My belly will not cool down, lalala layi!
"My belly pains me."
    (Amazing! Her stomach does not
      pain her. It is the sound of her
      promise that pains her.)
SARA'S MAN SAID: "Laila, eee! Laila!
Mahamadarasurudilahi!"

HE SAID: "Ah! World! My bride who has come thus,
"Three days, her belly does not cool.
"Four days, her belly does not cool.
"Five days, a headache is added to it.
"Ah, Sara! What will cool your belly?
"Long-necked Sara!
"The medicine powder men have failed on you.
"The string-knotters have failed on you.
"The belly-spitters have failed on you.
"Ah! Long-necked Sara!
"What will cool your belly then?"
SHE SAID: "My belly pains me.
"If you don't leave me alone,
"My belly will not cool. Laila!
"Ayi! My belly hurts me. Allah!
"My belly will not cool."
SARA'S MAN-TO-BE SAID: "Laila,
"No slave knows Allah.
"The wedding arrangers are troubled.
"Sara's bride-price should go back.
"I am shamed before my ill-wishing *faden*.
"I am shamed before my ill-wishing *faden*."

[*Faden* is literally 'father-child.' *Baden* is literally 'mother-child.' These terms, as you might expect, are polyphonous. Perhaps early meanings referred, in the case of *faden*, to the children of the same father but not the same mother in polygamous households. *Baden* refers from this point of view to children of the same mother. Perhaps by extension, *faden* came to refer to those people with whom you compete, against whom you measure yourself. *Baden* refers to those people with whom you cooperate, with whom you subordinate your self-interest and suppress matters of ego. Your b*aden* pushes you away. Your *faden* pulls you close. We have translated the Maninka word jugu as 'ill-wishing.' As a noun, it can mean 'enemy.' Modifying a noun, it can translate 'mean, cruel, dangerous, bad,' and 'ill-wishing.']

"My bride having come
"Three days, her belly does not cool.
"Four days her belly does not cool.
"Five days, a headache is added to it.
"Let the wedding arrangers go back."
Two young boys had run up *biribiribiri*.
And climbed out on a branch of a *dubalen* tree
To look out on the world.
"Well, the world is thus!"
The two boys ran *biribiribiri*.
They came to stop before the promise-sharer's door.
ONE SAID: "Cool off my mouth!
"Sara's wedding is dead!
"Those ten kola nuts in the container there,
"That is the mouth-cooler, my father.
"Thus a promise is not paid just once."

[The expression *n da lafige*, literally, 'fan/blow on my mouth,' is used by the bringer of news, which, it is said, makes his or her mouth hot. The heat dispels with a gift. Thus, *n da lafige* means, in Wittgenstein the Elder's sense of the word, 'give me a tip.']

Sara stood before her father.
SHE SAID: "It's Allah's work."
"Mama, this child of yours,
"Long-necked Sara! . . . and her belly will not cool."
SARA'S MOTHER SAID: "Laila, no slave knows Allah.
"Will your belly not cool?"
SHE SAID: "Mothers do not cry!
"Ayi! Mother, do not cry, ay!
"King White Guts did this to me."

['King White Guts' translates word for word the expression *Mansa nagalagwe*. This is a metaphor for God, whose white, gutlike clouds pass across his great belly, the sky.]

SARA SAID TO HER FATHER:
"Baba won't you gather the men for me today?
"Gather the riverbank village men for me today.
"Gather the men in the village for me.
"Whoever will cool my belly today,
"Father, that will be my husband
"And get you out of this talk.
"Won't you gather the men?"
          (Amazing! Her belly does not hurt her.
              It's the spoken words that hurt her.
              Her spoken words are hurting her.)
Iyo! He gathered the men,
Gathered the men in the village.
The medicine-powder men came.
The men of importance came.

[We have translated *cebakoro* as 'men of importance.' In some contexts, one might think of a *cebakoro* as a seasoned brave, a mature warrior.]

The big money men came.
The Koran men came.
The *nasi*-writing men all came.

[Islamic holy men are heavily involved in traditional medical practices. Some specialize in writing verses of the Koran on a chalkboard, which is then washed and the water collected. This *nasi* water can be used for washing or drinking, and its uses extend to all manners of illness and social problems.]

Three days, Sara's belly was hurting.
They all had failed. Sara remained in it.
SARA'S MOTHER SAID: "How is it going to go today, Sara?"
"Mother, hush up, my mother.
"King White Guts did this to me.
"Do not hurry Allah, my mother."

With the night half gone,
With the night half gone,
She stopped before her promise-sharer's door.
"Is there no one in the house, my twin-together?"
"There is someone in the house, my mother.
"Whose voice is that in the deep, dark night?
"Whose voice is that in the dawn?"
"It's the voice of your embrace-together.
"It's the voice of your sharer of inner words."
"Well, won't you sit, Long-necked Sara?"
"I am sitting down, my father.
"The powder medicine men have failed on me.
"The string-knotters have failed on me.
"The belly-spitters have failed on me.
"What will cool this belly,
"If there is no meaning to it?
"You should find ironstone tomorrow,
"And put it in the fire and embers.
"I say, when the ironstone gets hot,
"You should put it in drinking water, my
     promise-sharer.
"Wiii! My belly will cool tomorrow,
"Because of my spoken words, Allah!"
          (Yes! That is just the answer she
was looking for. Her belly was not hurting her.
     The promise that she gave him, that
     was what was hurting her. That is the
     reason for this part, to detail it and show
     to the people. The children of Adam
          must stick to their word.)

[There is certainly an interpretation of this story in
which Sara is construed to be duplicitous, faking her
illness to avoid her marriage; but both Sira Mori
and Yamuru go to considerable pains to show that
her pain was real, coming from the promise she had
given to another man. The ruse that she constructs
to allow her "promise-sharer "to cure her and win
her hand may, in the view of some readers, detract
from her moral standing somewhat, but her
*horonoya*, her nobility, comes from her keeping her
promise; and it must be pointed out that the ruse is
in fact a way for her father to save face. Sara does
not defy authority in this story. Rather, like Brer
Rabbit, she finds ways to use it to her advantage.]

From the time the cock cried,
When the first cock cried,
He went to find the ironstone.
Allah came to lay the stone before him. Iyo!

Mid-morning prayer time arrived,
He took the ironstone *co*!
And put it in the fire and embers.
When the ironstone boiled,
He put some in drinking water.
He was off with the water an hour later.
The men of importance said:
"No one should even speak with you.
"The thing that caused the medicine powder to
     fail,
"The thing that caused the *nasi*-waters to fail,
"And you think it's just dead water that will
     cool it for you!"
"I beg your pardon, big money men.
"I beg your pardon, medicine men.
"Let her try the water for me.
"Sara should try my fresh water for me."
Ah Sara! Sara drank the water, unnnh!
She drank the water at midmorning.
As the early afternoon prayer was called,
She went before her birth father.

[In the Mande social world, there are many people
that you call *n fa*, 'my father.' To refer to the
biological father, the Maninka use the expression,
*wolo-fa*' birth father.']

"Ah! Baba! "SHE SAID: "My belly has cooled,
"Baba, ah, my belly has cooled, lalala! Woyi!
"My belly has cooled today.
"I passed the night my belly did not rise up.
"Baba, my belly has cooled.
"Make this my true wedded husband."
SARA'S MOTHER SAID: "Won't you calm down?
"The late afternoon prayer has not been called.
"And you say your belly has cooled?"
"Mama, won't you prepare the baggage today?
"Prepare my wedding baggage today
"Let my wedding arrangers come forward.
"This one will be my true wedded husband."

SIRA MORI: Ah! Sara! Sara is sung for those of
     one voice.
     Ah! Long-necked Sara!
     CHORUS: Ah! Sara is sung for those of one
          voice.
     Don't you see it?
SIRA MORI: Ah! Sara! Sara is sung for those of
     one voice.
     No slave knows God.

CHORUS: Ah! Sara is sung for those of one
        voice.
        Don't you see it?


**Study Question**

1.  What are Sara's three main concerns in this
    epic? How does she resolve them? In what way
    is this epic different from others?

# THE NATURAL

# AND THE UNNATURAL

# THE MISMEASURE OF MAN

*Stephen Jay Gould (1941- )*

*Stephen J. Gould is an evolutionary biologist who is a Professor of Earth and Planatary Sciences at Harvard University. He has also been the Curator of the Museum of Comparative Zoology at Harvard University. He has written numerous books on the history of science, which analyze the social and political implications of scientific theories and movements. This essay, from* The Mismeasure of Man *(1981), analyzes the ways in which "scientific" measurements of intelligence work to perpetuate racial hierarchies in the U.S. This book was awarded a National Book Critics Circle award, among others.*

Citizens of the Republic, Socrates advised, should be educated and assigned by merit to three classes: rulers, auxiliaries, and craftsmen. A stable society demands that these ranks be honored and that citizens accept the status conferred upon them. But how can this acquiescence be secured? Socrates, unable to devise a logical argument, fabricates a myth. With some embarrassment, he tells Glaucon:

I will speak, although I really know not how to look you in the face, or in what words to utter the audacious fiction . . . They [the citizens] are to be told that their youth was a dream, and the education and training which they received from us, an appearance only; in reality during all that time they were being formed and fed in the womb of the earth. . . .

Glaucon, overwhelmed, exclaims: "You had good reason to be ashamed of the lie which you were going to tell." "True," replied Socrates, "but there is more coming; I have only told you half."

Citizens, we shall say to them in our tale, you are brothers, yet God has framed you differently.

Some of you have the power of command, and in the composition of these he has mingled gold, wherefore also they have the greatest honor; others he has made of Silver. To be auxiliaries; others again who are to be husbandmen and craftsmen he has composed of brass and iron; and the species will generally be preserved in the children. . . . An oracle says that when a man of brass or iron guards the State, it will be destroyed. Such is the tale; is there any possibility of making our citizens believe in it?

Glaucon replies: "Not in the present generation; there is no way of accomplishing this; but their sons may be made to believe in the tale, and their son's sons, and posterity after them."

Glaucon had uttered a prophesy. The same tale, in different versions, has been promulgated and believed ever since. The justification for ranking groups by inborn worth has varied with the tides of Western history. Plato relied upon dialectic, the Church upon dogma. For the past two centuries, scientific claims have become the primary agent for validating Plato's myth.

This book is about the scientific version of Plato's tale. The general argument may be called *biological determinism*. It holds that shared behavioral norms, and the social and economic differences between human groups—primarily races, classes, and sexes—arise from inherited, inborn distinctions and that society, in this sense, is an accurate reflection of biology. This book discusses, in historical perspective, a principal theme within biological determinism: the claim that worth can be assigned to individuals and groups by *measuring intelligence as a single quantity*. Two major sources of data have supported this theme: craniometry (or measurement of the skull) and certain styles of psychological testing.

Metals have ceded to genes (though we retain an etymological vestige of Plato's tale in speaking of people's worthiness as their "mettle"). But the basic argument has not changed: that social and economic roles accurately reflect the innate construction of people. One aspect of the intellectual strategy has altered, however. Socrates knew that he was telling a lie.

Determinists have often invoked the traditional prestige of science as objective knowledge, free from social and political taint. They portray themselves as purveyors of harsh truth and their opponents as sentimentalists, ideologues, and wishful thinkers. Louis Agassiz (1850, p. 111), defending his assignment of blacks to a separate species, wrote: "Naturalists have a right to consider the questions growing out of men's physical relations as merely scientific questions, and to investigate them without reference to either politics or religion." Carl C. Brigham (1923), arguing for the exclusion of southern and eastern European immigrants who had scored poorly on supposed tests of innate intelligence stated: "The steps that should be taken to preserve or increase our present intellectual capacity must of course be dictated by science and not by political expediency." And Cyril Burt, invoking faked data compiled by the nonexistent Ms. Conway, complained that doubts about the genetic foundation of IQ "appear to be based rather on the social ideals or the subjective preferences of the critics than on any first-hand examination of the evidence supporting the opposite view" (in Conway, 1959, p. 15).

Since biological determinism possesses such evident utility for groups in power, one might be excused for suspecting that it also arises in a political context, despite the denials quoted above. After all, if the status quo is an extension of nature, then any major change, if possible at all, must inflict an enormous cost—psychological for individuals, or economic for society—in forcing people into unnatural arrangements. In his epochal book, *An American Dilemma* (1944), Swedish sociologist Gunnar Myrdal discussed the thrust of biological and medical arguments about human nature: "They have been associated in America, as in the rest of the world, with conservative and even reactionary ideologies. Under their long hegemony, there has been a tendency to assume biological causation without question, and to accept social explanations only under the duress of a siege of irresistible evidence. In political questions, this tendency favored a do—nothing policy." Or, as Condorcet said more succinctly a long time ago: they "make nature herself an accomplice in the crime of political inequality."

This book seeks to demonstrate both the scientific weaknesses and political contexts of determinist arguments. Even so, I do not intend to contrast evil determinists who stray from the path of scientific objectivity with enlightened antideterminists who approach data with an open mind and therefore see truth. Rather, I criticize the myth that science itself is an objective enterprise, done properly only when scientists can shuck the constraints of their culture and view the world as it really is.

Among scientists, few conscious ideologues have entered these debates on either side. Scientists needn't become explicit apologists for their class or culture in order to reflect these pervasive aspects of life. My message is not that biological determinists were bad scientists or even that they were always wrong. Rather, I believe that science must be understood as a social phenomenon, a gutsy, human enterprise, not the work of robots programed to collect pure information. I also present this view as an upbeat for science, not as a gloomy epitaph for a noble hope sacrificed on the altar of human limitations.

Science, since people must do it, is a socially embedded activity. It progresses by hunch, vision, and intuition. Much of its change through time does not record a closer approach to absolute truth, but the alteration of cultural contexts that influence it so strongly. Facts are not pure and unsullied bits of information; culture also influences what we see and how we see it. Theories, moreover, are not inexorable inductions from facts. The most creative theories are often imaginative visions imposed upon facts; the source of imagination is also strongly cultural.

This argument, although still anathema to many practicing scientists, would, I think, be accepted by nearly every historian of science. In advancing it, however, I do not ally myself with an overextension now popular in some historical circles: the purely relativistic claim that scientific change only reflects the modification of social contexts, that truth is a meaningless notion outside cultural assumptions, and that science can therefore provide no enduring answers. As a practicing scientist, I share the credo of my colleagues: I believe that a factual reality exists and that science, though often in an obtuse and erratic manner, can learn about it. Galileo was not shown the instruments of torture in an abstract debate about lunar motion. He had threatened the Church's conventional argument for social and doctrinal stability: the static world order with planets circling about a central earth, priests subordinate to the Pope and serfs to their lord. But the Church soon made its peace with Galileo's cosmology. They had no choice; the earth really does revolve about the sun.

Yet the history of many scientific subjects is virtually free from such constraints of fact for two major reasons. First, some topics are invested with enormous social importance but blessed with very little reliable information. When the ratio of data to social impact is so low, a history of scientific attitudes may be little more than an oblique record of social change. The history of scientific views on race, for example, serves as a mirror of social movements (Provine, 1973). This mirror reflects in good times and bad, in periods of belief in equality and in eras of rampant racism. The death knell of the old eugenics in America was sounded more by Hitler's particular use of once-favored arguments for sterilization and racial purification than by advances in genetic knowledge.

Second, many questions are formulated by scientists in such a restricted way that any legitimate answer can only validate a social preference. Much of the debate on racial differences in mental worth, for example, proceeded upon the assumption that intelligence is a thing in the head. Until this notion was swept aside, no amount of data could dislodge a strong Western tradition for ordering related items into a progressive chain of being.

Science cannot escape its curious dialectic. Embedded in surrounding culture, it can, nonetheless, be a powerful agent for questioning and even overturning the assumptions that nurture it. Science can provide information to reduce the ratio of data to social importance. Scientists can struggle to identify the cultural assumptions of their trade and to ask how answers might be formulated under different assertions. Scientists can propose creative theories that force startled colleagues to confront unquestioned procedures. But science's potential as an instrument for identifying the cultural constraints upon it cannot be fully realized until scientists give up the twin myths of objectivity and inexorable march toward truth. One must, indeed, locate the beam in one's own eye before interpreting correctly the pervasive motes in everybody else's. The beams can then become facilitators, rather than impediments.

Gunnar Myrdal (1944) captured both sides of this dialectic when he wrote:

*A handful of social and biological scientists over the last 50 years have gradually forced informed people to give up some of the more blatant of our biological errors. But there must be still other countless errors of the same sort that no living man can yet detect, because of the fog within which our type of Western culture envelops us. Cultural influences have set up the assumptions about the mind, the body, and the universe with which we begin; pose the questions we ask; influence the facts we seek; determine the interpretation we give these facts;*

*and direct our reaction to these interpretations and conclusions.*

Biological determinism is too large a subject for one man and one book—for it touches virtually every aspect of the interaction between biology and society since the dawn of modern science. I have therefore confined myself to one central and manageable argument in the edifice of biological determinism—an argument in two historical chapters, based on two deep fallacies, and carried forth in one common style.

The argument begins with one of the fallacies—*reification*, or our tendency to convert abstract concepts into entities (from the Latin *res*, or thing). We recognize the importance of mentality in our lives and wish to characterize it, in part so that we can make the divisions and distinctions among people that our cultural and political systems dictate. We therefore give the word "intelligence" to this wondrously complex and multifaceted set of human capabilities. This shorthand symbol is then reified and intelligence achieves its dubious status as a unitary thing.

Once intelligence becomes an entity, standard procedures of science virtually dictate that a location and physical substrate be sought for it. Since the brain is the seat of mentality, intelligence must reside there.

We now encounter the second fallacy—*ranking*, or our propensity for ordering complex variation as a gradual ascending scale. Metaphors of progress and gradualism have been among the most pervasive in Western thought—see Lovejoy's classic essay (1936) on the great chain of being or Bury's famous treatment (1920) of the idea of progress. Their social utility should be evident in the following advice from Booker T. Washington (1904, p. 245) to black America:

*For my race, one of its dangers is that it may grow impatient and feel that it can get upon its feet by artificial and superficial efforts rather than by the slower but surer process which means one step at a time through all the constructive grades of industrial, mental, moral and social development which all races have had to follow that have become independent and strong.*

But ranking requires a criterion for assigning all individuals to their proper status in the single series. And what better criterion than an objective number? Thus, the common style embodying both fallacies of thought has been quantification, or the measurement of intelligence as a single number for each person.[1] This book, then, is about the abstraction of intelligence as a single entity, its location within the brain, its quantification as one number for each individual, and the use of these numbers to rank people in a single series of worthiness, invariably to find that oppressed and disadvantaged groups—races, classes, or sexes— are innately inferior and deserve their status. In short, this book is about the Mismeasure of Man.[2]

Different arguments for ranking have characterized the last two centuries. Craniometry was the leading numerical science of biological determinism during the nineteenth century. I discuss (Chapter 2) the most extensive data compiled before Darwin to rank races by the sizes of their brains—the skull collection of Philadelphia physician Samuel George Morton. Chapter 3 treats the flowering of craniometry as a rigorous and respectable science in the school of Paul Broca in late nineteenth-century Europe. Chapter 4 then underscores the impact of quantified approaches to human anatomy in nineteenth-century biological determinism. It presents two case studies: the theory of recapitulation as evolution's primary criterion for unilinear ranking of human groups, and the attempt to explain criminal behavior as a biological atavism reflected in the apish morphology of murderers and other miscreants.

What craniometry was for the nineteenth century, intelligence testing has become for the twentieth, when it assumes that intelligence (or at least a dominant part of it) is a single, innate, heritable, and measurable thing. I discuss the two components of this invalid approach to mental testing in Chapter 5 (the hereditarian version of the IQ scale as an American product) and Chapter 6 (the argument for reifying intelligence as a single entity by the mathematical technique of factor analysis). Factor analysis is a difficult mathematical subject almost invariably omitted from documents written for nonprofessionals. Yet I believe that it can be made accessible and explained in a pictorial and nonnumerical way. The material of Chapter 6 is still not "easy reading," but I could not leave it out for the history of intelligence testing cannot be understood without grasping the factor—analytic argument and understanding its deep conceptual fallacy. The great IQ debate makes no sense without this conventionally missing subject.

I have tried to treat these subjects in an unconventional way by using a method that falls outside the traditional purview of either a scientist or historian operating alone. Historians rarely treat the quantitative details in sets of primary data. They write, as I cannot adequately, about social context, biography, or general intellectual history. Scientists are used to analyzing the data of their peers, but few are sufficiently interested in history to apply the method to their predecessors. Thus, many scholars have written about Broca's impact, but no one has recalculated his sums.

I have focused upon the reanalysis of classical data sets in craniometry and intelligence testing for two reasons beyond my incompetence to proceed in any other fruitful way and my desire to do something a bit different. I believe, first of all, that Satan also dwells with God in the details. If the cultural influences upon science can be detected in the humdrum minutiae of a supposedly objective, almost automatic quantification, then the status of biological determinism as a social prejudice reflected by scientists in their own particular medium seems secure.

The second reason for analyzing quantitative data arises from the special status that numbers enjoy. The mystique of science proclaims that numbers are the ultimate test of objectivity. Surely we can weigh a brain or score an intelligence test without recording our social preferences. If ranks are displayed in hard numbers obtained by rigorous and standardized procedures, then they must reflect reality, even if they confirm what we wanted to believe from the start. Antideterminists have understood the particular prestige of numbers and the special difficulty that their refutation entails. Leonce Manouvrier (1903, p. 406), the nondeterminist black sheep of Broca's fold, and a fine statistician himself, wrote of Broca's data on the small brains of women:

> Women displayed their talents and their diplomas. They also invoked philosophical authorities. But they were opposed by numbers unknown to Condorcet or to John Stuart Mill. These numbers fell upon poor women like a sledge hammer, and they were accompanied by commentaries and sarcasms more ferocious than the most misogynist imprecations of certain church fathers. The theologians had asked if women had a soul. Several centuries later, some scientists were ready to refuse them a human intelligence.

If—as I believe I have shown—quantitative data are as subject to cultural constraint as any other aspect of science, then they have no special claim upon final truth.

In reanalyzing these classical data sets, I have continually located a priori prejudice, leading scientists to invalid conclusions from adequate data, or distorting the gathering of data itself. In a few cases—Cyril Burt's documented fabrication of data—on IQ of identical twins, and my discovery that Goddard altered photographs to suggest mental retardation in the Kallikaks—we can specify conscious fraud as the cause of inserted social prejudice. But fraud is not historically interesting except as gossip because the perpetrators know what they are doing and the unconscious biases that record subtle and inescapable constraints of culture are not illustrated. In most cases discussed in this book, we can be fairly certain that biases—though often expressed as egregiously as in cases of conscious fraud—were unknowingly influential and that scientists believed they were pursuing unsullied truth.

Since many of the cases presented here are so patent, even risible, by today's standards, I wish to emphasize that I have not taken cheap shots at marginal figures (with the possible exceptions of Mr. Bean in Chapter 3, whom I use as a curtain-raiser to illustrate a general point, and Mr. Cartwright in Chapter 2. whose statements are too precious to exclude). Cheap shots come in thick catalogues— from a eugenicist named W. D. McKim, Ph.D. (1900), who thought that all nocturnal housebreakers should be dispatched with carbonic acid gas, to a certain English professor who toured the United States during the late nineteenth century, offering the unsolicited advice that we might solve our racial problems if every Irishman killed a Negro and got hanged for it.[3] Cheap shots are also gossip, not history; they are ephemeral and uninfluential, however amusing. I have focused upon the leading and most influential scientists of their times and have analyzed their major works.

I have enjoyed playing detective in most of the case studies that make up this book: finding passages expurgated without comment in published letters, recalculating sums to locate errors that support expectations, discovering how adequate data can be filtered through prejudices to predetermined results, even giving the Army Mental Test for illiterates to my own students with interesting results. But I trust that whatever zeal any investigator must invest in details has not obscured the general message: that determinist arguments for ranking people according to a single scale of intelligence, no matter now numerically sophisticated, have recorded little more than social prejudice—and that we learn something hopeful about the nature of science in pursuing such an analysis.

If this subject were merely a scholar's abstract concern, I could approach it in more measured tone. But few biological subjects have had a more direct influence upon millions of lives. Biological determinism is, in its essence, a *theory of limits*. It takes the current status of groups as a measure of where they should and must be (even while it allows some rare individuals to rise as a consequence of their fortunate biology).

I have said little about the current resurgence of biological determinism because its individual claims are usually so ephemeral that their refutation belongs in a magazine article or newspaper story. Who even remembers the hot topics of ten years ago: Shockley's proposals for reimbursing voluntarily sterilized individuals according to their number of IQ points below 100, the great XYY debate, or the attempt to explain urban riots by diseased neurology of rioters? I thought that it would be more valuable and interesting to examine the original sources of the arguments that still surround us. These, at least, display great and enlightening errors. But I was inspired to write this book because biological determinism is rising in popularity again, as it always does in times of political retrenchment. The cocktail party circuit has been buzzing with its usual profundity about innate aggression, sex roles, and the naked ape. Millions of people are now suspecting that their social prejudices are scientific facts after all. Yet these latent prejudices themselves, not fresh data, are the primary source of renewed attention.

We pass through this world but once. Few tragedies can be more extensive than the stunting of life, few injustices deeper than the denial of an opportunity to strive or even to hope, by a limit imposed from without, but falsely identified as lying within. Cicero tells the story of Zopyrus, who claimed that Socrates had inborn vices evident in his physiognomy. His disciples rejected the claim, but Socrates defended Zopyrus and stated that he did indeed possess the vices, but had cancelled their effects through the exercise of reason. We inhabit a world of human differences and predilections, but the extrapolation of these facts to theories of rigid limits is ideology.

George Eliot well appreciated the special tragedy that biological labeling imposed upon members of disadvantaged groups. She expressed it for people like herself—women of extraordinary talent. I would apply it more widely—not only to those whose dreams are flouted but also to those who never realize that they may dream. But I cannot match her prose (from the prelude to *Middlemarch*):

> *Some have felt that these blundering lives are due to the inconvenient indefiniteness with which Supreme Power has fashioned the natures of women: if there were one level of feminine incompetence as strict as the ability to count three and no more, the social lot of women might be treated with scientific certitude. The limits of variation are really much wider than anyone would imagine from the sameness of women's coiffure and the favorite love stories in prose and verse. Here*

*and there a cygnet is reared uneasily among the ducklings in the brown pond, and never finds the living stream in Fellowship with its own oary-footed kind. Here and there is born a Saint Theresa, foundress of nothing, whose loving heartbeats and sobs after an unattained goodness tremble off and are dispersed among hindrances instead of centering in some long-recognizable deed.*

## ENDNOTES

1. Peter Medawar (1977, p. 13) has presented other interesting examples of "the illusion embodied in the ambition to attach a single number valuation to complex quantities"—for example, the attempts made by demographers to seek causes for trends in population in a single measure of "reproductive prowess," or the desire of soil scientist to abstract the "quality" of a soil as a single number.

2. Following strictures of the argument outlined above, I do not treat all theories of craniometrics (I omit phrenology, for example, because it did not reify intelligence as a single entity but sought multiple organs within the brain). Likewise, I exclude many important and often quantified styles of determinism that did not seek to measure intelligence as a property of the brain—for example, most of eugenics.

3. Also too precious to exclude is my favorite modern invocation of biological determinism as an excuse for dubious behavior. Bill Lee, baseball's self-style philosopher, justifying the beanball (*New York Times*, 24 July 1976): "I read a book in college called 'Territorial Imperative.' A fellow always has to protect his master's home much stronger than anything down the street; My territory is down and away from the hitters. If they're going out there and getting the ball, I'll have to come in close."

## Study Questions

1. What is the main point of this essay?

2. What is biological determinism? What two fallacies give rise to biological determinism, according to Gould?

3. How does he criticize the notion of objective knowledge? Why does he focus on science particularly?

4. Why are measurements of intelligence so significant in our culture? We see here how they apply to uphold racial hierarchies; could we make a similar argument about gender?

5. What are the ramifications of his argument for education?

# RACIAL FORMATION

## Michael Omi And Howard Winant

*Howard Winant states that he is a child of the new left and the black freedom movement. His work focuses on the continued centrality of racial identity and racial inequality in the United States. He is currently a professor of Sociology at Temple University.*

*Michael Omi is associate professor of Asian American Studies and Ethnic Studies at Berkeley. He is the author of "Shifting the Blame: Ideology and Politics in the Post-Civil Rights Era" (1972).*

*This essay is an excerpt from Winant and Omi's book Racial Formation in the United States (2nd edition, 1994). They argue for understanding race as a social and political construction.*

In 1982–83, Susie Guillory Phipps unsuccessfully sued the Louisiana Bureau of Vital Records to change her racial classification from black to white. The descendant of an 18th–century white planter and a black slave, Phipps was designated "black" in her birth certificate in accordance with a 1970 state law which declared anyone with at least 1/32nd "Negro blood" to be black.

The Phipps case raised intriguing questions about the concept of race, its meaning in contemporary society, and its use (and abuse) in public policy. Assistant Attorney General Ron Davis defended the law by pointing out that some type of racial classification was necessary to comply with federal record-keeping requirements and to facilitate programs for the prevention of genetic diseases. Phipps's attorney, Brian Begue, argued that the assignment of racial categories on birth certificates was unconstitutional and that the 1/32nd desig-

nation was inaccurate. He called on a retired Tulane University professor who cited research indicating that most Louisiana whites have a least 1/20th "Negro" ancestry.

In the end, Phipps lost. The court upheld the state's right to classify and quantify racial identity.

Phipps's problematic racial identity, and her effort to resolve it through state action, is in many ways a parable of America's unsolved racial dilemma. It illustrates the difficulties of defining race and assigning individuals or groups to racial categories. It shows how the racial legacies of the past —slavery and bigotry—continue to shape the present. It reveals both the deep involvement of the state in the organization and interpretation of race, and the inadequacy of state institutions to carry out these functions. It demonstrates how deeply Americans both as individuals and as a civilization are shaped, and indeed haunted, by race.

Having lived her whole life thinking that she was white, Phipps suddenly discovers that by legal definition she is not. In U.S. society, such an event is indeed catastrophic. But if she is not white, of what race is she? The *state* claims that she is black, based on its rules of classification, and another state agency, the court, upholds this judgment. But despite these classificatory standards which have imposed an either-or logic on racial identity, Phipps will not in fact "change color." Unlike what would have happened during slavery times if one's claim to whiteness was successfully challenged, we can assume that despite the outcome of her legal challenge, Phipps will remain in most of the social relationships she had occupied before the trial. Her socialization, her familial and friendship networks, her cultural orientation, will not change. She will simply have to wrestle with her newly acquired "hybridized" condition. She will have to confront the "Other" within.

The designation of racial categories and the determination of racial identity is no simple task. For centuries, this question has precipitated intense debates and conflicts, particularly in the U.S.— disputes over natural and legal rights, over the distribution of resources, and indeed, over who shall live and who shall die.

A crucial dimension of the Phipps case is that it illustrates the inadequacy of claims that race is a mere matter of variations in human physiognomy, that it is simply a matter of skin color. But if race cannot be understood in this manner, how can it be understood? We cannot fully hope to address this topic—no less than the meaning of race, its role in society, and the forces which shape it—in one chapter, nor indeed in one book. Our goal in this chapter, however, is far from modest: we wish to offer at least the outlines of a theory of race and racism.

## WHAT IS RACE?

There is a continuous temptation to think of race as an *essence*, as something fixed, concrete, and objective. And there is also an opposite temptation: to imagine race as a mere *illusion*, a purely ideological construct which some ideal non-racist social order would eliminate. It is necessary to challenge both these positions, to disrupt and reframe the rigid and bipolar manner in which they are posed and debated, and to transcend the presumably irreconcilable relationship between them.

The effort must be made to understand race as an unstable and "decentered" complex of social meanings constantly being transformed by political struggle. With this in mind, let us propose a definition: *race is a concept which signifies and symbolizes social conflicts and interests by referring to different types of human bodies.* Although the concept of race invokes biologically based human characteristics (so-called "phenotypes"), selection of these particular human features for purposes of racial signification is always and necessarily a social and historical process. In contrast to the other major distinction of this type, that of gender, there is no biological basis for distinguishing among human groups along the lines of race. Indeed, the categories employed to differentiate among human groups along racial lines reveal themselves, upon serious examination, to be at best imprecise, and at worst completely arbitrary.

If the concept of race is so nebulous, can we not dispense with it? Can we not "do without" race, at least in the "enlightened" present? This question has been posed often, and with greater frequency in recent years. An affirmative answer would of course present obvious practical difficulties: it is rather difficult to jettison widely held beliefs, beliefs which moreover are central to everyone's identity and understanding of the social world. So the attempt to banish the concept as an archaism is at best counter-intuitive. But a deeper difficulty, we believe, is inherent in the very formulation of this schema, in its way of posing race as a *problem,* a misconception left over front the past, and suitable now only for the dustbin of history.

A more effective starting point is the recognition that despite its uncertainties and contradictions, the concept of race continues to play a fundamental role in structuring and representing the social world. The task for theory is to explain this situation. It is to avoid both the utopian framework which sees race as an illusion we can somehow "get beyond," and also the essentialist formulation which sees race as something objective and fixed, a biological datum. Thus we should think of race as an element of social structure rather than as an irregularity within it; we should see race as a dimension of human representation rather than an illusion. These perspectives inform the theoretical approach we call racial formation.

## RACIAL FORMATION

We define *racial formation* as the sociohistorical process by which racial categories are created, inhabited, transformed, and destroyed. Our attempt to elaborate a theory of racial formation will proceed in two steps. First, we argue that racial formation is a process of historically situated *projects* in which human bodies and social structures are represented and organized. Next we link racial formation to the evolution of hegemony, the way in which society is organized and ruled. Such an approach, we believe, can facilitate understanding of a whole range of contemporary controversies and dilemmas involving race, including the nature of racism, the relationship of race to other forms of differences, inequalities, and oppression such as sexism and nationalism, and the dilemmas of racial identity today.

From a racial formation perspective, race is a matter of both social structure and cultural representation. Too often, the attempt is made to understand race simply or primarily in terms of only one of these two analytical dimensions. For example, efforts to explain racial inequality as a purely social structural phenomenon are unable to account for the origins, patterning, and transformation of racial difference.

Conversely, many examinations of racial difference—understood as a matter of cultural attributes *á la* ethnicity theory, or as a society-wide signification system, *á la* some poststructuralist accounts—cannot comprehend such structural phenomena as racial stratification in the labor market or patterns of residential segregation.

An alternative approach is to think of racial formation processes as occurring through a linkage between structure and representation. Racial *projects* do the ideological "work" of making these links. *A racial project is simultaneously an interpretation, representation, or explanation of racial dynamics, and an effort to reorganize and redistribute resources along particular racial lines.* Racial projects connect what race *means* in a particular discursive practice and the ways in which both social structures and everyday experiences are racially *organized*, based upon that meaning. Let us consider this proposition, first in terms of large-scale or macro-level social processes, and then in terms of other dimensions of the racial formation process.

## RACIAL FORMATION AS A MACRO-LEVEL SOCIAL PROCESS

To *interpret the meaning of race is to frame it social structurally.* Consider for example, this statement by Charles Murray on welfare reform:

> *My proposal for dealing with the racial issue in social welfare is to repeal every bit of legislation and reverse every court decision that in any way requires, recommends, or awards differential treatment according to race, and thereby put us back onto the track that we left in 1965. We may argue about the appropriate limits of government intervention in trying to enforce the ideal, but it least it should be possible to identify the ideal: Race is not a morally admissible reason for treating one person differently from another. Period.*

Here there is a partial but significant analysis of the meaning of race: it is not a morally valid basis upon which to treat people "differently from one another." We may notice someone's race, but we cannot act upon that awareness. We must act in a "color-blind" fashion. This analysis of the meaning of race is immediately linked to a specific conception of the role of race in the social structure: it can play no part in government action, save in "the enforcement of the ideal." No state policy can legitimately require, recommend, or award different status according to race. This example can be classified is a particular type of racial project in the present-day U.S.—a "neoconservative" one.

Conversely, *to recognize the racial dimension in social structure is to interpret the meaning of race.* Consider the following statement by the late Supreme Court Justice Thurgood Marshall on minority "set-aside" programs:

> *A profound difference separates governmental actions that themselves are racist, and governmental actions that seek to remedy the effects of prior racism or to prevent neutral government activity from perpetuating the effects of such racism.*

Here the focus is on the racial dimensions of *social structure*—in this case of state activity and policy. The argument is that state actions in the past and present have treated people in very different ways according to their race, and thus the government cannot retreat from its policy responsibilities in this area. It cannot suddenly declare itself "color-blind" without in fact perpetuating the same type of differential, racist treatment. Thus, race continues to signify difference and structure inequality. Here, racialized social structure is immediately linked to an interpretation of the meaning of race. This example too can be classified as a particular type of racial project in the present-day U.S.—a "liberal" one.

To be sure, such political labels as "neoconservative or "liberal" can not fully capture the complexity of racial projects, for these are always multiply determined, politically contested, and deeply shaped by their historical context. Thus, encapsulated within the neoconservative example cited here are certain egalitarian commitments which derive from a previous historical context in which they played a very different role, and which are rearticulated in neoconservative racial discourse precisely to oppose a more open-ended, more capacious conception of the meaning of equality. Similarly, in the liberal example, Justice Marshall recognizes that the contemporary state, which was formerly the architect of segregation and the chief enforcer of racial difference, has a tendency to reproduce those patterns of inequality in a new guise. Thus he admonishes it (in dissent, significantly) to fulfill its responsibilities to uphold a robust conception of equality. These particular instances, then, demonstrate how racial projects are always concretely framed, and thus are always contested and unstable. The social structures they uphold or attack, and the representations of race they articulate, are never invented out of the air, but exist in a definite historical context, having descended from previous conflicts. This contestation appears to be permanent in respect to race.

These two examples of contemporary racial projects are drawn from mainstream political debate; they may be characterized as center-right and center-left expressions of contemporary racial politics. We can, however, expand the discussion of racial formation processes far beyond these familiar examples. In fact, we can identify racial projects in at least three other analytical dimensions: first, the political spectrum can be broadened to include radical projects, on both the left and right, as well is along other political axes. Second, analysis of racial projects can take place not only at the macro-level of racial policy-making, state activity, and collective action, but also at the micro-level of everyday experience. Third, the concept of racial projects can be applied across historical time, to identify racial formation dynamics in the past. We shall now offer examples of each of these types of racial projects.

## THE POLITICAL SPECTRUM OF RACIAL FORMATION

We have encountered examples of a neoconservative racial project, in which the significance of race is denied, leading to a "color-blind" racial politics and "hands off" policy orientation; and of a "liberal" racial project, in which the significance of race is affirmed, leading to an egalitarian and "activist" state policy. But these by no means exhaust the political possibilities. Other racial projects can be readily identified on the contemporary U.S. scene. For example, "far right" projects, which uphold biologistic and racist views of difference, explicitly argue for white supremacist policies. "New right" projects overtly claim to hold "color-blind" views, but covertly manipulate racial fears in order to achieve political gains. On the left, "radical democratic" projects invoke notions of racial "difference" in combination with egalitarian politics and policy.

Further variations can also be noted. For example, "nationalist" projects, both conservative and radical, stress the incompatibility of racially defined group identity with the legacy of white supremacy, and therefore advocate a social structural solution of separation, either complete or partial. Nationalist currents represent a profound legacy of the centuries of racial absolutism, that initially defined the meaning of race in the U.S. Nationalist concerns continue to influence racial debate in the form of Afrocentrism and other expressions of identity politics.

Taking the range of politically organized racial projects as a whole, we can "map" the current pattern of racial formation at the level of the public sphere, the "macro-level" in which public debate and mobilization takes place. But important as this is, the terrain on which racial formation occurs is broader yet.

## RACIAL FORMATION AS EVERYDAY EXPERIENCE

At the micro-social level, racial projects also link signification and structure, not so much as efforts to shape policy or define large-scale meaning, but as the applications of "common sense." To see racial projects operating it the level of everyday life, we have only to examine the many ways in which, often unconsciously, we "notice" race.

One of the first things we notice about people when we meet them (along with their sex) is their race. We utilize race to provide clues about *who* a person is. This fact is made painfully obvious when we encounter someone whom we cannot conveniently racially categorize—someone who is, for example, racially "mixed" or of an ethnic/racial group we are not familiar with. Such in encounter becomes a source of discomfort and momentarily a crisis of racial meaning.

Our ability to interpret racial meanings depends on preconceived notions of a racialized social structure. Comments such as, "Funny, you don't look black," betray in underlying image of what black should be. We expect people to act out their apparent racial identities; indeed we become disoriented when they do not. The black banker harassed by police while walking in casual clothes through his own well-off neighborhood, the Latino or white kid rapping in perfect Afro patois, the unending *faux pas* committed by whites who assume that the non-whites they encounter are servants or tradespeople, the belief that non-white colleagues are less qualified persons hired to fulfill affirmative action guidelines, indeed the whole gamut of racial stereotypes—that "white men can't jump," that Asians can't dance, etc., etc.—all testify to the way a racialized social structure shapes racial experience and conditions meaning. Analysis of such stereotypes reveals the always present, already active link between our view of the social structure—its demography, its laws, its customs, its threats—and our conception of what race means.

Conversely, our ongoing interpretation of our experience in racial terms shapes our relations to the institutions and organizations through which we are imbedded in social structure. Thus we expect differences in skin color, or other racially coded characteristics, to explain social differences. Temperament, sexuality, intelligence, athletic ability, aesthetic preferences, and so on are presumed to be fixed and discernible from the palpable mark of race. Such diverse questions as our confidence and trust in others (for example, clerks or salespeople, media figures, neighbors), our sexual preferences and romantic images, our tastes in music, films, dance, or sports, and our very ways of talking, walking, eating, and dreaming become racially coded simply because we live in a society where racial awareness is so pervasive. Thus in ways too comprehensive even to monitor consciously, and despite periodic calls—neoconservative and otherwise—for us to ignore race and adopt "color-blind" racial attitudes, skin color "differences" continue to rationalize distinct treatment of racially identified individuals and groups.

To summarize the argument so far: the theory of racial formation suggests that society is suffused with racial projects, large and small, to which all are subjected. This racial "subjection" is quintessentially ideological. Everybody learns some combination, some version, of the rules of racial classification, and of her own racial identity, often without obvious teaching or conscious inculcation. Thus are we inserted in a comprehensively racialized social structure. Race becomes "common sense"— a way of comprehending, explaining, and acting in the world. A vast web of racial projects mediates between the discursive or representational means in which race is identified and signified on the one hand, and the institutional and organizational forms in which it is routinized and standardized on the other. These projects are the heart of the racial formation process.

Under such circumstances, it is not possible to represent race discursively without simultaneously locating it, explicitly or implicitly, in a social structural (and historical) context. Nor is it possible to organize, maintain, or transform social structures without simultaneously engaging, once more either explicitly or implicitly, in racial signification. Racial formation, therefore, is a kind of synthesis, an outcome, of the interaction of racial projects on a society-wide level. These projects are, of course, vastly different in scope and effect. They include large-scale public action, state activities, and interpretations of racial conditions in artistic, journalistic, or academic fora, as well as the seemingly infinite number of racial judgments and practices we carry out at the level of individual experience.

Since racial formation is always historically situated, our understanding of the significance of race, and of the way race structures society, has changed enormously over time. The processes of racial formation we encounter today, the racial projects large and small which structure U.S. society in so many ways, are merely the present-day outcomes of a complex historical evolution. The contemporary racial order remains transient. By knowing something of how it evolved, we can perhaps better discern where it is heading. We therefore turn next to a historical survey of the racial formation process, and the conflicts and debates it has engendered.

## THE EVOLUTION OF MODERN RACIAL AWARENESS

The identification of distinctive human groups, and their association with differences in physical appearance, goes back to prehistory, and can be found in the earliest documents—in the Bible, for example, or in Herodotus. But the emergence of a modern conception of race does not occur until the rise of Europe and the arrival of Europeans in the Americas. Even the hostility and suspicion with which Christian Europe viewed its two significant non-Christian "Others"—the Muslims and the Jews—cannot be viewed as more than a rehearsal for racial formation, since these antagonisms, for all their bloodletting and chauvinism, were always and everywhere religiously interpreted.

It was only when European explorers reached the Western Hemisphere, when the oceanic seal separating the "old" and the "new" worlds was breached, that the distinctions and categorizations fundamental to a racialized social structure, and to a discourse of race, began to appear. The European explorers were the advance guard of merchant capitalism, which sought new openings for trade. What they found exceeded their wildest dreams, for never before and never again in human history has an opportunity for the appropriation of wealth remotely approached that presented by the "discovery."

But the Europeans also "discovered" people, people who looked and acted differently. These "natives" challenged their "discoverers'" pre-existing conceptions of the origins and possibilities of the human species. The representation and interpretation of the meaning of the indigenous peoples' existence became a crucial matter, one which would affect the outcome of the enterprise of conquest. For the "discovery" raised disturbing questions as to whether *all* could be considered part of the same "family of man," and more practically, the extent to which native peoples could be exploited and enslaved. Thus religious debates flared over the attempt to reconcile the various Christian metaphysics with the existence of peoples who were more "different" than any whom Europe had previously known.

In practice, of course, the seizure of territories and goods, the introduction of slavery through the *encomienda* and other forms of coerced native labor, and then through the organization of the African slave trade—not to mention the practice of outright extermination—all presupposed a worldview which distinguished Europeans, as children of God, full-fledged human beings, etc., from "Others." Given the dimensions and the ineluctability of the European onslaught, given the conquerors determination to appropriate both labor and goods, and given the presence of an axiomatic and unquestioned Christianity among them, the ferocious division of society into Europeans and "Others" soon coalesced. This was true despite the famous 16th-century theological and philosophical debates about the identity of indigenous peoples.

Indeed debates about the nature of the "Others" reached their practical limits with a certain dispatch. Plainly they would never touch the essential: nothing, after all, would induce the Europeans to pack up and go home. We cannot examine here the early controversies over the status of American souls. We simply wish to emphasize that the "discovery" signalled a break from the previous proto-racial awareness by which Europe contemplated its "Others" in a relatively disorganized fashion. In other words, the "conquest of America" was not simply an epochal historical event—however unparalleled in its importance. It was also the advent of a consolidated social structure of exploitation, appropriation, domination. Its representation, first in religious terms, but soon enough in scientific and political ones, initiated modern racial awareness.

The conquest, therefore, was the first—and given the dramatic nature of the case, perhaps the greatest—racial formation project. Its significance was by no means limited to the Western Hemisphere, for it begin the work of constituting Europe as the metropole, the center, of a group of empires which could take, as Marx would later write, "the globe for a theater." It represented this new imperial structure as a struggle between civilization and barbarism, and implicated in this representation all the great European philosophies, literary traditions, and social theories of the modern age. In short, just as the noise of the "big bang" still resonates through the universe, so the, over-determined construction of world "civilization." as a product of the rise of Europe and the subjugation of the rest of us, still defines the race concept.

## FROM RELIGION TO SCIENCE

After the initial depredations of conquest, religious justifications for racial difference gradually gave way to scientific ones. By the time of the Enlightenment, a general awareness of race was pervasive, and most of the great philosophers of Europe, such as Hegel, Kant, Hume, and Locke, had issued virulently racist opinions.

The problem posed by race during the late 18th century was markedly different than it had been in the age of "discovery," expropriation, and slaughter. The social structures in which race operated were no longer primarily those of military conquest and plunder, nor of the establishment of thin beachheads of colonization on the edge of what had once seemed a limitless wilderness. Now the issues were much more complicated: nationbuilding, establishment of national economies in the world trading system, resistance to the arbitrary authority of monarchs, and the assertion of the "natural rights" of "man," including the right of revolution. In such a situation, racially organized exploitation, in the form of slavery, the expansion of colonies, and the continuing expulsion of native peoples, was both necessary and newly difficult to justify.

The invocation of scientific criteria to demonstrate the "natural" basis of racial hierarchy was both a logical consequence of the rise of this form of knowledge, and in attempt to provide a more subtle and nuanced account of human complexity in the new, "enlightened" age. Spurred on by the classificatory scheme of living organisms devised by Linnaeus in *Systema Naturae* (1735), many scholars in the 18th and 19th centuries dedicated themselves to the identification and ranking of variations in humankind. Race was conceived as a *biological* concept, a matter of species. Voltaire wrote that "the negro race is a species of men (sic) as different from ours is the breed of spaniels is from that of greyhounds," and in a formulation echoing down from his century to our own, declared that

> If their understanding is not of a different nature from ours... it is at least greatly inferior. They are not capable of any great application or association of ideas, and seem formed neither for the advantages nor the abuses of philosophy.

Jefferson, the preeminent exponent of the Enlightenment doctrine of "the rights of man" on North American shores, echoed these sentiments:

> In general their existence appears to participate more of sensation than reflection.... In memory they are equal to whites, in reason much inferior . . . [and] in imagination they are dull, tasteless, and anomalous.... I advance it therefore . . . that the blacks, whether originally a different race, or made distinct by time and circumstances are inferior to the whites.... Will not a lover of natural history, then, one who views the gradations in all the animals with the eye of philosophy, excuse an effort to keep those in the department of Man (sic) as distinct as nature has formed them?

Such claims of species distinctiveness among humans justified the inequitable allocation of political and social rights, while still upholding the doctrine of "the rights of man." The quest to obtain a precise scientific definition of race sustained debates which continue to rage today. Yet despite efforts ranging from Dr. Samuel Morton's studies of cranial capacity to contemporary attempts to base racial classification on shared gene pools, the concept of race has defied biological definition.

In the 19th century, Count Joseph Arthur de Gobineau drew upon the most respected scientific studies of his day to compose his four-volume *Essay on the Inequality of Races* (1853–1855). He not only greatly influenced the racial thinking of the period, but his themes would be echoed in the racist ideologies of the next one hundred years: beliefs that superior races produced superior cultures and that racial intermixtures resulted in the degradation of the superior racial stock. These ideas found expression, for instance, in the eugenics movement launched by Darwin's cousin, Francis Galton, which had an immense impact on scientific and sociopolitical thought in Europe and the U.S. In the wake of civil war and emancipation and with immigration from southern and Eastern Europe as well as East Asia running high, the U.S. was particularly fertile ground for notions such as social darwinism and eugenics.

Attempts to discern the *scientific meaning* of race continue to the present day. For instance, an essay by Arthur Jensen which argued that hereditary factors shape intelligence not only revived the "nature or nurture" controversy, but also raised highly volatile questions about racial equality itself. All such attempts seek to remove the concept of race from the historical context in which it arose and developed. They employ an *essentialist* approach which suggests instead that the truth of race is a matter of innate characteristics, skin color and other physical attributes provide only the most obvious, and in some respects most superficial, indicators.

## FROM SCIENCE TO POLITICS

It has taken scholars more than a century to reject biologistic notions of race in favor of an approach which regards race as a *social* concept. This trend has been slow, and uneven, and even today remains somewhat embattled, but its overall direction seems clear. At the turn of the century Max Weber discounted biological explanations for racial conflict and instead highlighted the social and political factors which engendered such conflict. W. E. B. Du Bois argued for a sociopolitical definition of race by identifying "the color line" as "the problem of the 20th century." Pioneering anthropologist Franz Boas rejected attempts to link racial identifications and cultural traits, labelling as pseudoscientific any assumption of a continuum of "higher" and

"lower" cultural groups. Other early exponents of social, as opposed to biological, views of race included Robert E. Park, founder of the "Chicago school" of sociology, and Alain Leroy Locke, philosopher and theorist of the Harlem Renaissance.

Perhaps more important than these and subsequent intellectual efforts, however, were the political struggles of racially defined groups themselves. Waged all around the globe under a variety of banners such as anticolonialism and civil rights, these battles to challenge various structural and cultural racisms have been a major feature of 20th-century politics. The racial horrors of the 20th century—colonial slaughter and apartheid, the genocide of the holocaust, and the massive bloodlettings required to end these evils—have also indelibly marked the theme of race as a political issue *par excellence*.

As a result of prior efforts and struggles, we have now reached the point of fairly general agreement that race is not a biologically given but rather a socially constructed way of differentiating human beings. While a tremendous achievement, the transcendence of biologistic conceptions of race does not provide any reprieve from the dilemmas of racial injustice and conflict, nor from controversies over the significance of race in the present. Views of race as socially constructed simply recognize the fact that these conflicts and controversies are now more properly framed on the terrain of politics. By privileging politics in the analysis which follows we do not mean to suggest that race has been displaced as a concern of scientific inquiry, that struggles over cultural representation are no longer important. We do argue, however, that race is now a preeminently political phenomenon.

## WHAT IS RACISM?

Since the ambiguous triumph of the civil rights movement in the mid-1960s, clarity about what racism means has been eroding. The concept entered the lexicon of "common sense" only in the 1960s. Before that, although the term had surfaced occasionally, the problem of racial injustice and inequality was generally understood in a more limited fashion, as a matter of prejudiced attitudes or bigotry on the one hand, and discriminatory practices on the other. Solutions, it was believed, would therefore involve the overcoming of such attitudes, the achievement of tolerance, the acceptance of "brotherhood," etc., and the passage of laws which prohibited discrimination with respect to access to public accommodations, jobs, education, etc. The early civil rights movement explicitly reflected such views. In its espousal of integration and its quest for a "beloved community" it sought to overcome racial prejudice. In its litigation activities and agitation for civil rights legislation it sought to challenge discriminatory practices.

The later 1960s, however, signalled a sharp break with this vision. The emergence of the slogan "black power" (and soon after, of "brown power," "red power," and "yellow power"), the wave of riots that swept the urban ghettos from 1964 to 1968, and the founding of radical movement organizations of nationalist and Marxist orientation, coincided with the recognition that racial inequality and injustice had much deeper roots. They were not simply the product of prejudice, nor was discrimination only a matter of intentionally informed action. Rather, prejudice was an almost unavoidable outcome of patterns of socialization which were "bred in the bone," affecting not only whites but even minorities themselves. Discrimination, far from manifesting itself only (or even principally) through individual actions or conscious policies, was a structural feature of U.S. society, the product of centuries of systematic exclusion, exploitation, and of racially defined minorities. It was this combination of relationships—prejudice, discrimination, and institutional inequality—which defined the concept of racism it the end of the 1960s.

Such a synthesis was better able to confront the political realities of the period. Its emphasis on the structural dimensions of racism allowed it to address the intransigence which racial injustice and inequality continued to exhibit, even after discrimination had supposedly been outlawed and bigoted expression stigmatized. But such an approach also had clear limitations. As Robert Miles has argued, it tended to "inflate" the concept of racism to a point at which it lost precision." If the "institutional" component of racism were so pervasive and deeply rooted, it became difficult to see how the democratization of U.S. society could be achieved, and difficult to explain what progress had been made. The result was a levelling critique which denied any distinction between the Jim Crow era (or even the whole *longue durée* of racial dictatorship since the conquest) and the present. Similarly, if the prejudice component of racism were so deeply inbred, it became difficult to account for the evident hybridity and interpenetration that characterizes civil society in the U.S., as evidenced by the shaping of popular culture, language, and style, for example. The result of the "inflation" of the concept of racism was thus a deep pessimism about any efforts to overcome racial barriers, in the workplace, the community, or any other sphere of lived experience. An overly comprehensive view of racism, then, potentially served as a self-fulfilling prophecy.

Yet the alternative view—which surfaced with a vengeance in the 1970s—urging a return to the conception of racism held before the movement's "radical turn," was equally inadequate. This was the neoconservative perspective, which deliberately restricted its attention to injury done to the individual as opposed to the group, and to advocacy of a color-blind racial policy. Such an approach reduced race to ethnicity, and almost entirely neglected the continuing organization of social inequality and oppression along racial lines. Worse yet, it tended to rationalize racial injustice as a supposedly natural outcome of group attributes in competition.

The distinct, and contested, meanings of racism which have been advanced over the past three decades have contributed to an overall crisis of meaning for the concept today. Today, the absence of a clear "common sense" understanding of what racism means has become a significant obstacle to efforts aimed at challenging it. Bob Blauner has noted that in classroom discussions of racism, white and non-white students tend to talk past one another. Whites tend to locate racism in color consciousness and to locate find in its absence color-blindness. In so doing, they see the affirmation of difference and racial identity among racially defined minority students as racist. Non-white students, by contrast, see racism as a system of power, and correspondingly argue that blacks, for example, cannot be racist because they lack power. Blauner concludes that there are two "languages" of race, one in which members of racial minorities, especially blacks, see the centrality of race in history and everyday experience, and another in which whites see race as "a peripheral, nonessential reality."

Given this crisis of meaning, and in the absence of any "common sense" understanding, does the concept of racism retain any validity? If so, what view of racism should we adopt? Is a more coherent theoretical approach possible? We believe it is.

We employ racial formation theory to reformulate the concept of racism. Our approach recognizes that racism, like race, has changed over time. It is obvious that the attitudes, practices, and institutions of the epochs of slavery, say, or of Jim Crow, no longer exist today. Employing a similar logic, it is reasonable to question whether concepts of racism which developed in the early days of the post-civil rights era, when the limitations of both moderate reform and militant racial radicalism of various types had not yet been encountered, remain adequate to explain circumstances and conflicts a quarter-century later.

Racial formation theory allows us to differentiate between race and racism. The two concepts should not be used interchangeably. We have argued that race has no fixed meaning, but is constructed and transformed sociohistorically through competing political projects, through the necessary and ineluctable link between the structural and cultural dimensions of race in the U.S. This emphasis on projects allows us to refocus our understanding of racism as well for racism can now be seen as characterizing some, but not all, racial projects.

A racial project can be defined as *racist* if and only if it *creates or reproduces structures of domination based on essentialist categories of race.* Such a definition recognizes the importance of locating racism within a fluid and contested history of racially based social structures and discourses. Thus there call be no timeless and absolute standard for what constitutes racism, for social structures change and discourses are subject to rearticulation. Our definition therefore focuses instead on the "work" essentialism does for domination, and the "need" domination displays to essentialize the subordinated.

Further, it is important to distinguish racial awareness from racial essentialism. To attribute merits, allocate values or resources to, and/or represent individuals or groups on the basis of racial identity should not be considered racist in and of itself. Such projects may in fact be quite benign.

Consider the following examples: first, the statement, "Many Asian Americans are highly entrepreneurial": second, the organization of an association of, say, black accountants.

The first racial project, in our view, signifies or represents a racial category ("Asian Americans") and locates that representation within the social structure of the contemporary U.S. (in regard to business, class issues, socialization, etc.). The second racial project is organizational or social structural, and therefore must engage in racial signification. Black accountants, the organizers might maintain, have certain common experiences, can offer each other certain support, etc. Neither of these racial projects is essentialist, and neither can fairly be labelled racist. Of course, racial representations may be biased or misinterpret their subjects, just as racially based organizational efforts may be unfair or unjustifiably exclusive. If such were the case, if for instance in our first example the statement in question were "Asian Americans are naturally entrepreneurial," this would by our criterion be racist. Similarly, if the effort to organize black accountants had as its rationale the raiding of clients from white accountants, it would by our criterion be racist as well.

Similarly, to allocate values or resources—let us say, academic scholarships—on the basis of racial categories is not racist. Scholarships are awarded on a preferential basis to Rotarians, children of insurance company employees, and residents of the Pittsburgh metropolitan area. Why then should they not also be offered, in particular cases, to Chicanos or Native Americans?

In order to identify a social project as racist, one must in our view demonstrate a link between essentialist representations of race and social structures of domination. Such a link might be revealed in efforts to protect dominant interests, framed in racial terms, from democratizing racial initiatives. But it might also consist of efforts simply to reverse the roles of racially dominant and racially subordinate. There is nothing inherently white about racism.

Obviously a key problem with essentialism is its denial, or flattening, of differences within a particular racially defined group. Members of subordinate racial groups, when faced with racist practices such as exclusion or discrimination, are frequently forced to band together in order to defend their interests (if not, in some instances, their very lives). Such "strategic essentialism" should not, however, be simply equated with the essentialism practiced by dominant groups, nor should it prevent the interrogation of internal group differences.

Without question, any abstract concept of racism is severely put to the test by the untidy world of reality. To illustrate our discussion, we analyze the following examples, chosen from current racial issues because of their complexity and the rancorous debates they have engendered:

- Is the allocation of employment opportunities through programs restricted to racially defined minorities, so-called "preferential treatment" or affirmative action policies, racist? Do such policies practice "racism in reverse"? We think not, with certain qualifications. Although such programs necessarily employ racial criteria in assessing eligibility, they do not generally essentialize race, because they seek to overcome specific socially and historically constructed inequalities. Criteria of effectiveness and feasibility, therefore, must be considered in evaluating such programs. They must balance egalitarian and context—specific objectives, such as academic potential or job—related qualifications. It should be acknowledged that such programs often do have deleterious consequences for whites who are not personally the source of the discriminatory practices the programs seek to overcome. In this case, compensatory measures should be enacted to vitiate the charge of "reverse discrimination."

- Is all racism the same, or is there a distinction between white and non-white versions of racism? We have little patience with the argument that racism is solely a white problem, or even a "white disease. The idea that non-whites cannot act in a racist manner, since they do not possess "power," is another variant of this formulation.

For many years now, racism has operated in a more complex fashion than this, sometimes taking such forms as self-hatred or self-aggrandizement at the expense of more vulnerable members of racially subordinate groups. Whites can at times be the victims of racism—by other white—or non-whites—as is the case with anti-Jewish and anti-Arab prejudice. Furthermore, unless one is prepared to argue that there his been no transformation of the U.S. racial order over the years, and that racism consequently has remained unchanged—an essentialist position *par excellence*—it is difficult to contend that racially defined minorities have attained no power or influence, especially in recent years.

Having said this, we still do not consider that all racism is the same. This is because of the crucial importance we place in situating various "racisms" within the dominant hegemonic discourse about race. We have little doubt that the rantings of a Louis Farrakhan or Leonard Jeffries—to pick two currently demonized black ideologues—meet the criteria we have set out for judging a discourse to be racist. But if we compare Jeffries, for example, with a white racist such as Toni Metzger of the White Aryan Resistance, we find the latter's racial project to be far more menacing than the former's. Metzger's views are far more easily associated with in essentializing (and once very powerful) legacy: that of white supremacy and racial dictatorship in the U. S., and fascism in the world at large. Jeffries's project has far fewer examples with which to associate: no more than some ancient African empires and the (usually far less bigoted) radical phase of the black power movement. Thus black supremacy may be an instance of racism, just as its advocacy may be offensive, but it can hardly constitute the threat that white supremacy has represented in the U.S., nor can it be so easily absorbed and rearticulated in the dominant hegemonic discourse on race as white supremacy can. All racisms, all racist political projects, are not the same.

• Is the redrawing—or gerrymandering—of adjacent electoral districts to incorporate large numbers of racially defined minority voters in one, and largely white voters in the other, racist? Do such policies amount to "segregation" of the electorate? Certainly this alternative is preferable to the pre-Voting Rights Act practice of simply denying racial minorities the franchise. But does it achieve the Act's purpose of fostering electoral equality across and within racial lines? In our view such practices, in which the post-1990 redistricting process engaged rather widely—are vulnerable to charges of essentialism. They often operate through "racial lumping," tend to freeze rather than overcome

racial inequalities, and frequently subvert or defuse political processes through which racially defined groups could otherwise negotiate their differences and interests. They worsen rather than ameliorate the denial of effective representation to those whom they could not effectively redistrict— since no redrawing of electoral boundaries is perfect, those who get stuck on the "wrong side" of the line are particularly disempowered. Thus we think such policies merit the designation of "tokenism"—a relatively mild form of racism—which they have received.

Parallel to the debates on the concept of race, recent academic and political controversies about the nature of racism have centered on whether it is primarily an ideological act or structural phenomenon. Proponents of the former position argue that racism is first and foremost a matter of beliefs and attitudes, doctrines and discourse, which only then give rise to unequal and unjust practices and structures. Advocates of the latter view see racism as primarily a matter of economic stratification, residential segregation, and other institutionalized forms of inequality which then give rise to ideologies of privileges.

From the standpoint of racial formation, these debates are fundamentally misguided. They frame the problem of racism in a rigid "either—or" manner. We believe it is crucial to disrupt the fixity of these positions by simultaneously arguing that ideological beliefs have structural consequences, and that social structures give rise to beliefs. Racial ideology and social structure, therefore, mutually shape the nature of racism in a complex, dialectical, and overdetermined manner.

Even those racist projects which at first glance appear chiefly ideological turn out upon closer examination to have significant institutional and social structural dimensions. For example, what we have called "far right" projects appear at first glance to be centrally ideological. They are rooted in biologistic doctrine, after all. The same seems to hold for certain conservative black nationalist projects which have deep commitments to biologism. But the unending stream of racist assaults initiated by the far right, the apparently increasing presence of skinheads in high schools, the proliferation of neo-Nazi computer bulletin boards, and the appearance of racist talk shows on cable access channels, all suggest that the organizational manifestations of the far right racial projects exist and will endure. Perhaps less threatening but still quite worrisome is the diffusion of doctrines of black superiority through some (though by no means all) university-based African American Studies departments and student organizations, surely a serious institutional or structural development.

By contrast, even those racisms which at first glance appear to be chiefly structural upon closer examination reveal a deeply ideological component. For example, since the racial right abandoned its explicit advocacy of segregation, it has not seemed to uphold—in the main—an ideologically racist project, but more primarily a structurally racist one. Yet this, very transformation required tremendous efforts of ideological production. It demanded the rearticulation of civil rights doctrines of equality in suitably conservative form and indeed the defense of continuing large-scale racial inequality as an outcome preferable to (what its advocates have seen as) the threat to democracy that affirmative action, busing, and large-scale "race-specific" social spending would entail. Even more tellingly, this project took shape through a deeply manipulative coding of subtextual appeals to white racism, notably in a series of political campaigns for high office which have occurred over recent decades. The retreat of social policy from any practical commitment to racial justice, and the relentless reproduction and divulgation of this theme at the level of everyday life—where whites are now "fed up" with all the "special treatment" received by non-whites, etc.—constitutes the hegemonic racial project at this time. It therefore exhibits an unabashed structural racism all the more brazen because on the ideological or signification level, it adheres to a principle of "treating everyone alike."

In summary, the racism of today is no longer a virtual monolith, as was the racism of yore. Today, racial hegemony is "messy." The complexity of the present situation is the product of a vast historical legacy of structural inequality and invidious racial representation, which his been confronted during the post-World War II period with an opposition more serious and effective than any it had faced before. The result is a deeply ambiguous and contradictory spectrum of racial projects, unremittingly conflictual racial politics, and confused and ambivalent racial identities of all sorts.

## Study Questions

1. How do Omi and Winant define the terms race, racial formation, and racial project?

2. What do they mean by saying that race is both a social structure and a cultural representation?

3. According to the authors what are the main ways that racial differences have been explained throughout history?

4. How do they define racism? Do you agree with their definition? Why or why not?

5. Why is it important to examine race theoretically? Why do the authors feel their theory is important? What are the practical applications of their theory of racial formation?

# WHITE PRIVILEGE AND MALE PRIVILEGE

### Peggy McIntosh

*Peggy McIntosh is the associate director of the Wellesley College Center for Research on Women. She is also the co-director of the National SEED Project on Inclusive Curriculum: Seeking Educational Equity and Diversity. Her work has been foundational in analyzing not only the way that oppression negatively impacts those who are oppressed, but also confers privilege on those who benefit from domination.*

Through work to bring materials and perspectives from Women's Studies into the rest of the curriculum, I have often noticed men's unwillingness to grant that they are over privileged in the curriculum, even though they may grant that women are disadvantaged. Denials that amount to taboos surround the subject of advantages that men gain from women's disadvantages. These denials protect male privilege from being fully recognized, acknowledge, lessened, or ended.

Thinking through unacknowledged male privilege as a phenomenon with a life of its own, I realized that since hierarchies in our society are interlocking, there was most likely a phenomenon of white privilege that was similarly denied and protected, but alive and real in its effects. As a white person, I realized I had been taught about racism as something that puts others at a disadvantage, but had been taught not to see one of its corollary aspects, white privilege, which puts me at an advantage.

I think whites are carefully taught not to recognize white privilege, as males are taught not to recognize male privilege. So I have begun in an untutored way to ask what it is like to have white privilege. This paper is a partial record of my personal observations and not a scholarly analysis. It is based on my daily experiences within my particular circumstances.

I have come to see white privilege as an invisible package of unearned assets that I can count on cashing in each day, but about which I was "meant" to remain oblivious. White privilege is like an invisible weightless knapsack of special provisions, assurances, tools, maps, guides, codebooks, passports, visas, clothes, compass, emergency gear, and blank checks.

Since I have had trouble facing white privilege, and describing its results in my life, I saw parallels here with men's reluctance to acknowledge male privilege. Only rarely will a man go beyond acknowledging that women are disadvantaged to acknowledging that men have unearned advantage, or that unearned privilege has not been good for men's development as human beings, or for society's development, or that privilege systems might ever be challenged and changed.

I will review here several types or layers of denial that I see as work protecting, and preventing awareness about, entrenched male privilege. Then I will draw parallels, from my own experience, with the denials that veil the facts of white privilege. Finally, I will list forty-six ordinary and daily ways in which I experience having white privilege, by contrast with my African American colleagues in the same building. This list is not intended to be generalize able. Others can make their own lists from within their own life circumstances.

Writing this paper has been difficult, despite warm receptions for the talks on which it is based.* For describing white privilege makes one newly accountable. As we in Women's Studies work reveal male privilege and ask men to give up some of their power, so one who writes about having white privilege must ask, "Having described it, what will I do to lessen or end it?"

The denial of men's over privileged state takes many forms in discussions of curriculum change work. Some claim that men must be central in the curriculum because they have done most of what is important or distinctive in life or in civilization. Some recognize sexism in the curriculum but deny that it makes male students seem unduly important in life. Others agree that certain individual thinkers are male oriented but deny that there is any systemic tendency in disciplinary frameworks or epistemology to over empower men as a group. Those men who do grant that male privilege takes institutionalized and embedded forms are still likely to deny that male hegemony has opened doors for them personally. Virtually all men deny that male over reward alone can explain men's centrality in all the inner sanctums of our most powerful institutions. Moreover, those few who will acknowledge that male privilege systems have over empowered them usually end up doubting that we could dismantle these privilege systems. They may say they will work to improve women's status, in the society or in the university, but they can't or won't support the idea of lessening men's. In curricular terms, this is the point at which they say that they regret they cannot use any of the interesting new scholarship on women because the syllabus is full. When the talk turns to giving men less cultural room, even the most thoughtful and fair-minded of the men I know will tend to reflect, or fall back on, conservative assumptions about the inevitability of present gender relations and distributions of power, calling on precedent or sociobiology and psychobiology to demonstrate that male domination is natural and follows inevitably from evolutionary pressures. Others resort to arguments from "experience" or religion or social responsibility or wishing and dreaming.

After I realized, through faculty development work in Women's Studies, the extent to which men work from a base of unacknowledged privilege, I understood that much of their oppressiveness was unconscious. Then I remembered the frequent charges from women of color that white women whom they encounter are oppressive. I began to understand why we are justly seen as oppressive, even when we

don't see ourselves that way. At the very least, obliviousness of one's privileged state can make a person or group irritating to be with. I began to count the ways in which I enjoy unearned skin privilege and have been conditioned into oblivion about its existence, unable to see that it put me "ahead" in any way, or put my people ahead, over rewarding us and yet also paradoxically damaging us, or that it could or should be changed.

My schooling gave me no training in seeing myself as an oppressor, as an unfairly advantaged person, or as a participant in a damaged culture. I was taught to see myself as an individual whose moral state depended on her individual moral will. At school, we were not taught about slavery in any depth; we were not taught to see slaveholders as damaged people. Slaves were seen as the only group at risk of being dehumanized. My schooling followed the pattern which Elizabeth Minnich has pointed out: whites are taught to think of their lives as morally neutral, normative, and average, and also ideal, so that when we work to benefit others, this is seen as work that will allow "them" to be more like "us." I think many of us know how obnoxious this attitude can be in men.

After frustration with men who would not recognize male privilege, I decided to try to work on myself at least by identifying some of the daily effects of white privilege in my life. It is crude work, at this stage, but I will give here a list of special circumstances and conditions I experience that I did not earn but that I have been made to feel are mine by birth, by citizenship, and by virtue of being a conscientious law-abiding "normal" person of goodwill. I have chosen those conditions that I think in my case attach somewhat more to skin-color privilege than to class, religion, ethnic status, or geographical location, though these other privileging factors are intricately intertwined. As far as I can see, my Afro-American co-workers, friends, and acquaintances with whom I come into daily or frequent contact in this particular time, place, and line of work cannot count on most of these condition.

1. I can, if I wish, arrange to be in the company of people of my race most of the time.

2. I can avoid spending time with people whom I was trained to mistrust and who have learned to mistrust my kind or me.

3. If I should need to move, I can be pretty sure of renting or purchasing housing in an area which I can afford in which I would want to live.

*.   This paper was presented at the Virginia Women's Studies Association conference in Richmond in April, 1986, and the American Education Research Association conference in Boston in October, 1986, and discussed with two groups of participants in the Dodge seminars for Secondary School Teachers in New York and Boston in the spring of 1987.

4. I can be reasonably sure that my neighbors in such a location will be neutral or pleasant to me.

5. I can go shopping alone most of the time, fairly well assured that I will not be followed or harassed by store detectives.

6. I can turn on the television or open the front page of the paper and see people of my race widely and positively represented.

7. When I am told about our national heritage or about "civilization," I am shown that people of my color made it what it is.

8. I can be sure that my children will be given curricular materials that testify to the existence of their race.

9. If I want to, I can be pretty sure of finding a publisher for this piece on white privilege.

10. I can be fairly sure of having my voice heard in a group in which I am the only member of my race.

11. I can be casual about whether or not to listen to another woman's voice in a group in which she is the only member of her race.

12. I can go into a book shop and count on finding the writing of my race represented, into a supermarket and find the staple foods that fit with my cultural traditions, into a hairdresser's shop and find someone who can deal with my hair.

13. Whether I use checks, credit cards, or cash, I can count on my skin color not to work against the appearance that I am financially reliable.

14. I could arrange to protect our young children most of the time from people who might not like them.

15. I did not have to educate our children to be aware of systemic racism for their own daily physical protection.

16. I can be pretty sure that my children's teachers and employers will tolerate them if they fit school and workplace norms; my chief worries about them do not concern other's attitudes toward their race.

17. I can talk with my mouth full and not have people put this down to my color.

18. I can swear, or dress in secondhand clothes, or not answer letters, without having people attribute these choices to the bad morals, the poverty, or the illiteracy of my race.

19. I can speak in public to a powerful male group without putting my race on trial.

20. I can do well in a challenging situation without being called a credit to my race.

21. I am never asked to speak for all the people of my racial group.

22. I can remain oblivious to the language and customs of persons of color who constitute the world's majority without feeling in my culture any penalty for such oblivion.

23. I can criticize our government and talk about how much I fear its policies and behavior without being seen as a cultural outsider.

24. I can be reasonably sure that if I ask to talk to "the person in charge," I will be facing a person of my race.

25. If a traffic cop pulls me over or if the IRS audits my tax return, I can be sure I haven't been singled out because of my race.

26. I can easily buy posters, postcards, picture books, greeting cards, dolls, toys, and children's magazines featuring people of my race.

27. I can go home from most meetings of organizations I belong to feeling somewhat tied in, rather than isolate, out of place, outnumbered, unheard, held at a distance, or feared.

28. I can be pretty sure that if I argue for the promotion of a person of another race, or a program centering on race, this is not likely to cost me heavily within my present setting, even if my colleagues disagree with me.

29. I can be fairly sure that if I argue for the promotion of a person of another race, or a program centering on race, this is not likely to cost me heavily within my present setting, even if my colleagues disagree with me.

30. If I declare there is a racial issue at hand, or there isn't a racial issue at hand, my race will lend me more credibility for either position than a person of color will have.

31. I can choose to ignore developments in minority writing and minority activist programs, or disparage them, or learn from them, but in any case, I can find ways to be more or less protected from negative consequences of any of these choices.

32. My culture gives me little fear about ignoring the perspectives and powers of people of other races.

33. I am not made acutely are that my shape, bearing, or body odor will be taken as a reflection on my race.

34. I can worry about racism without being seen as self-interested or self-seeking.

35. I can take a job with an affirmative action employer without having my co-workers on the job suspect that I got it because of my race.

36. If my day, week, or year is going badly, I need not ask of each negative episode or situation whether it has racial overtones.

37. I can be pretty sure of finding people who would be willing to talk with me and advise me about my next steps, professionally.

38. I can think over my options, social, political, imaginative, or professional, without asking whether a person of my race would be accepted or allowed to do what I want to do.

39. I can be late to a meeting without having the lateness reflect on my race.

40. I can choose public accommodation without fearing that people of my race cannot get in or will be mistreated in places I have chosen.

41. I can be sure that if I need legal or medical help, my race will not work against me.

42. I can arrange my activities so that I will never have to experience feelings of rejection owing to my race.

43. If I have low credibility as a leader, I can be sure that my race is not the problem.

44. I can easily find academic courses and institutions that give attention only to people of my race.

45. I can expect figurative language and imagery in all of the arts to testify to experiences of my race.

46. I can choose blemish cover or bandages in "flesh" color that have them more or less match my skin.

I repeatedly forgot each of the realizations on this list until I wrote it down. For me, white privilege has turned out to be an elusive and fugitive subject. The pressure to avoid it is great, for in facing it I must give up the myth of meritocracy. If these things are true, this is not such a free country; one's life is not what one makes it; many doors open for certain people through no virtues of their own. These perceptions mean also that my moral condition is not what I had been led to believe. The appearance of being a good citizen rather than a troublemaker comes in large part from having all sorts of doors open automatically because of my color.

A further paralysis of nerve comes from literary silence protecting privilege. My clearest memories of finding such analysis are in Lillian Smith's unparalleled Killers of the Dream and Margaret Andersen's review of Karen and Mamie Fields' Lemon Swamp. Smith, for example, wrote about walking toward black children on the street and knowing they would step into the gutter; Andersen contrasted the pleasure that she, as a white child, took on summer driving trips to the south with Karen Fields' memories of driving in a closed car stocked with all necessities lest, in stopping, her black family should suffer "insult, or worse." Adrienne Rich also recognizes and writes about daily experiences of privilege, but in my observation, white women's writing in this area is far more often on systemic racism than on our daily lives as light-skinned women.*

In unpacking this invisible knapsack of white privilege, I have listed conditions of daily experience that I once took for granted, as neutral, normal, and universally available to everybody, just as I once thought of a male-focused curriculum as the neutral or accurate account that can speak for all. Nor did I think of any of these perquisites as bad for the holder. I now think that we need a more finely differentiated taxonomy of privilege, for some of these varieties are only what one would want for everyone in a just society, and others give license to be ignorant, oblivious, arrogant, and destructive. Before proposing some more finely tuned categorization, I will make some observations about the general effects of these conditions on my life and expectations.

In this potpourri of examples, some privileges make me feel at home in the world. Others allow me to escape penalties and dangers that others suffer. Through some, I escape fear, anxiety, insult, injury, or a sense of not being welcome, not being real. Some keep me from having to hide, to be in disguise, to feel sick or crazy, to negotiate each transaction from the position of being an outsider or, within my group, a person who is suspected of having too close links with a dominant culture. Most keep me from having to be angry.

---

*· Andersen, Margaret, "Race and the Social Science Curriculum: A Teaching and Learning Discussion." Radical Teacher, November, 1984, pp. 17-20. Smith, Lillian, Killers of the Dream, New York: W.W. Norton, 1949.

I see a pattern running through the matrix of white privilege, a pattern of assumptions that were passed on to me as a white person. There was one main piece of cultural turf; it was my own turf, and I was among those who could control the turf. I could measure up to the cultural standards and take advantage of the many options I saw around me to make what the culture would call a success of my life. My skin color was an asset for any move I was educated to want to make. I could think of myself as "belonging" in major ways and of making social systems work for me. I could freely disparage, fear, neglect, or be oblivious to anything outside of the dominant cultural forms. Being of the main culture, I could also criticize it fairly freely. My life was reflected back to me frequently enough so that I felt, with regard to my own race, if not to my sex, like one of the real people.

Whether through the curriculum or in the newspaper, the television, the economic system, or the general look of people in the streets, I received daily signals and indications that my people counted and that others either didn't exist or must be trying, not very successfully, to be like people of my race. I was given cultural permission not to hear voices of people of other races or a tepid cultural tolerance for hearing or acting on such voices. I was also raised not to suffer seriously from anything that darker-skinned people might say about my group, "protected," though perhaps I should more accurately say prohibited, through the habits of my economic class and social group, from living in racially mixed groups or being reflective about inter-actions between people of differing races.

In proportion as my racial group was being made confident, comfortable, and oblivious, other groups were likely being made unconfident, uncomfortable, and alienated. Whiteness protected me from many kinds of hostility, distress, and violence, which I was being subtly trained to visit in turn upon people of color.

For this reason, the word "privilege" now seems to me misleading. Its connotations are too positive to fit the conditions and behaviors which "privilege systems" produce. We usually think of privilege as being a favored state, whether earned, or conferred by birth or luck. School graduates are reminded they are privileged and urged to use their (enviable) assets well. The word "privilege" carries the conno-tation of being something everyone must want. Yet some of the conditions I have described here work to systemically over-empower certain groups. Such privilege simply confers dominance, gives permission to control, because of one's race or sex. The kind of privilege that gives license to some people to be, at best, thoughtless and, at worst,

murderous should not continue to bee referred to as a desirable attribute. Such "privilege" may be widely desired without being in any way beneficial t the whole society.

Moreover, through "privilege" may confer power, it does not confer moral strength. Those who do not depend on conferred dominance have traits and qualities that may never develop in those who do. Just as Women's Studies courses indicate that women survive their political circumstances to lead lives that hold the human race together, so "under-privileged" people of color who are the world's majority have survived their oppression and lived survivors' lives from which the white global minority can and must learn. In some groups, those dominated have actually become strong through not having all of these unearned advantages, and this give them a great deal to teach others. Members of so-called privileged groups can seem foolish, ridic-ulous, infantile, or dangerous by contrast.

I want, then, to distinguish between earned strength and unearned power conferred systemically. Power from unearned privilege can look like strength when it is, in fact, permission to escape or to dominate. But not all of the privileges on my list are inevitably damaging. Some, like the expectation that neighbors will be decent to you, or that your race will not count against you in court, should be the norm in a just society and should be considered as the enti-tlement of everyone. Others, like the privilege not to listen to less powerful people, distort the humanity of the holders as well as the ignored groups. Still others, like finding one's staple foods everywhere, may be a function of being a member of a numerical majority in the population. Others have to do with not having to labor under pervasive negative stereo-typing and mythology.

We might at least start by distinguishing between positive advantages that we can work to spread, to the point where they are not advantages at all but simply part of the normal civic and social fabric, and negative types of advantage that unless rejected will always reinforce and present hierarchies. For example, the positive "privilege" of belonging, the feeling that one belongs within the human circle, as Native Americans say, fosters development and should not be seen as privilege for a few. It is, let us say, an entitlement that none of us should have to earn; ideally it is an unearned entitlement. At present, since only a few have it, it is an unearned advantage for them. The negative "privilege" that gave me cultural permission not to take darker-skinned others seriously can be seen as arbitrarily conferred dominance and should not be desired for anyone. This paper results from a process of coming to see that some of the power that I organically saw as attendant on being a human being in the United States consisted in unearned advantage and conferred dominance, as well as other kinds of special circumstance not universally taken for granted.

In writing this paper I have also realized that white identity and status (as well as class identity and status) give me considerable power to choose whether to broach this subject and its trouble. I can pretty well decide whether to disappear and avoid and not listen and escape the dislike I may engender in other people though this essay, or interrupt, answer, interpret, preach, correct, criticize, and control to some extent what goes on in reaction to it. Being white, I am given considerable power to escape many kinds of danger or penalty as well as to choose which risks I want to take.

There is an analogy here, once again, with Women's Studies. Our male colleagues do not have a great deal to lose in supporting Women's Studies, they do not have a great deal to lose if they oppose it either. They simply have the power to decide whether to commit themselves to more equitable distributions of power. They will probably feel few penalties whatever choice they make; they do not seem, in any obvious short-term sense, the ones at risk, though they and we are all at risk because of the behaviors that have been rewarded in them.

Through Women's Studies work I have met very few men who are truly distressed about systemic, unearned male advantage and conferred dominance. And so one question for me and others like me is whether we will be like them, or whatever we will get truly distressed, even outraged, about unearned race advantage and conferred dominance and if so, what we will do to lessen them. In any case, we need to do more work in identifying how they actually affect our daily lives. We need more down-to-earth writing by people about these taboo subjects. We need more understanding of the ways in which white "privilege" damages white people, for these are not the same ways in which it damages the victimized. Skewed white psyches are an inseparable part of the picture, though I do not want to confuse the kinds of damage done to the holders of special assets and to those who suffer the deficits. Many, perhaps most, of our white students in the United States think that racism doesn't affect them because they are not people of color; they do not see "whiteness" as a racial identity. Many men likewise think that Women's Studies does not bear on their own existences because they are not female; they do not see themselves as having gendered identities. Insisting on the universal "effects" of "privilege" systems, then, becomes one of our chief tasks, and being more explicit about the particular effects in

particular contexts in another. Men need to join us in this work.

In addition, since race and sex are not the only advantaging systems at work, we need to similarly examine the daily experience of having age advantage, or ethnic advantage, or physical ability, or advantage related to nationality, religion, or sexual orientation. Professor Marnie Evans suggested to me that in many ways the list I made also applies directly to heterosexual privilege. This is a still more taboo subject than race privilege: the daily ways in which heterosexual privilege makes some persons comfortable or powerful, providing supports, assets, approvals, and rewards to those who live or expect to live in heterosexual pairs. Unpacking that content is still more difficult, owing to the deeper imbeddedness of heterosexual advantage and dominance and stricter taboos surrounding these.

But to start such an analysis I would put this observation from my own experience: the fact that I live under the same roof with a man triggers all kinds of societal assumptions about my worth, politics, life, and values and triggers a host of unearned advantages and powers. After recasting many elements from the original list I would add further observations like these:

1. My children do not have to answer questions about why I live with my partner (my husband).

2. I have no difficulty finding neighborhoods where people approve of our household.

3. Our children are given texts and classes that implicitly support our kind of family unit and do not turn them against my choice of domestic partnership.

4. I can travel alone or with my husband without expecting embarrassment or hostility in those who deal with us.

5. Most people I meet will see my marital arrangements as an asset to my life or as a favorable comment on my likability, my competence, or my mental health.

6. I can talk about the social events of a weekend without fearing most listeners' reactions.

7. I will feel welcomed and "normal" in the usual walks of public life, institutional and social.

8. In many contexts, I am seen as "all right" in daily work on women because I do not live chiefly with women.

Difficulties and dangers surrounding the task of finding parallels are many. Since racism, sexism, and heterosexism are not the same, the advantages associated with them should not be seen as the same. In addition, it is hard to isolate aspects of unearned advantage that derive chiefly from social class, economic class, race, religion, sex, or ethnic identity. The oppressions are both distinct and interlocking, as the Combahee River Collective statement of 1977 continues to remind us eloquently.[*]

One factor seems clear about all of the interlocking oppressions. They take both active forms that we can see and embedded forms that members of the dominant group are taught not to see. In my class and place, I did not see myself as racist because I was taught to recognize racism only in individual acts of meanness by members of my group, never in invisible systems conferring racial dominance on my group from birth. Likewise, we are taught to think that sexism or heterosexism is carried on only through intentional, individual acts of discrimination, meanness, or cruelty, rather than in invisible systems conferring unsought dominance on certain groups. Disapproving of the systems won't be enough to change them. I was taught to think that racism could end if white individuals changed their attitudes; many men think sexism can be ended by individual changes in daily behavior toward women. But a man's sex provides advantage for him whether or not he approves of the way in which dominance has been conferred on his group. A "white" skin in the United States opens many doors for whites whether or not we approve the way dominance has been conferred on us. Individual acts can palliate, but cannot end, these problems. To redesign social systems, we need first to acknowledge their colossal unseen dimensions. The silences and denials surrounding privilege are the

key political tools here. They keep the thinking about equality or equity incomplete, protecting unearned advantage and conferred dominance by making these taboo subjects. Most talk by whites about equal opportunity seems to me now to be about equal opportunity to try to get into a position of dominance while denying that systems of dominance exist.

Obliviousness about white advantage, like obliviousness about male advantage, is kept strongly acculturated in the United States so as to maintain the myth of meritocracy, the myth that democratic choice is equally available to all. Keeping most people unaware that freedom of confident action is there for just a small number of people props up those in power and serves to keep power in the hands of the same groups that have most of it already. Though systemic change takes many decades, there are pressing questions for me and I imagine for some others like me if we raise our daily consciousness on the perquisites of being light-skinned. What will we do with such knowledge? As we know from watching men, it is an open question whether we will choose to use unearned advantage to weaken invisible privilege systems and whether we will use any of our arbitrarily awarded power to try to reconstruct power systems on a broader base.

## Study Questions

1. According to McIntosh, why do we focus on oppression and not privilege? How does that limit us in our struggle for social justice?

2. What American mythology does an understanding of privilege subvert? What do privileges do for us?

3. Which of the specific items on the list do you find most persuasive and why?

4. What does she want to do with these privileges?

---

[*]. "A Black Feminist Statement," The Combahee River Collective, pp. 13-22 in G.Hull, P.Scott, B. Smith, Eds., <u>All the Women Are White, All the Blacks are Men, But Some of Us Are Brave</u>: Black Women's Studies, Old Westbury, NY: The Feminist Press, 1982.

# BLOODCHILD

## Octavia Butler (1947- )

*Butler lives in Los Angeles and is the only African-American woman science fiction writer whose work is self-supporting. She describes herself as a feminist, a former Baptist, and a combination of ambition, laziness, insecurity, certainty, and drive. Her more than ten novels include* Kindred *(1979),* Wild Seed *(1980),* Imago *(1989), and* The Parable of the Sower *(1993). In 1995, she was awarded a MacArthur Foundation 'Genius' Grant. Her work examines issues of power, race, survival, and stretches the limits of our understanding of the meaning and place of humans in the universe. The following example won both the Hugo (1985) and Nebula (1984) awards for best science fiction novelette.*

My last night of childhood began with a visit home. T'Gatoi's sister had given us two sterile eggs. T'Gatoi gave one to my mother, brother, and sisters. She insisted that I eat the other one alone. It didn't matter. There was still enough to leave everyone feeling good. Almost everyone. My mother wouldn't take any. She sat, watching everyone drifting and dreaming without her. Most of the time she watched me.

I lay against T'Gatoi's long, velvet underside, sipping from my egg now and then, wondering why my mother denied herself such a harmless pleasure. Less of her hair would be gray if she indulged now and then. The eggs prolonged life, prolonged vigor. My father, who had never refused one in his life, had lived more than twice as long as he should have. And toward the end of his life, when he should have been slowing down, he had married my mother and fathered four children.

But my mother seemed content to age before she had to. I saw her turn away as several of T'Gatoi's limbs secured me closer. T'Gatoi liked our body heat and took advantage of it whenever she could. When I was little and at home more, my mother used to try to tell me how to behave with T'Gatoi—how to be respectful and always obedient because T'Gatoi was the government official in charge of the Preserve, and thus the most important of her kind to deal directly with Terrans. It was an honor, my mother said, that such a person had chosen to come into the family. My mother was at her most formal and severe when she was lying.

I had no idea why she was lying, or even what she was lying about. It *was* an honor to have T'Gatoi in the family, but it was hardly a novelty. T'Gatoi and my mother had been friends all my mother's life, and T'Gatoi was not interested in being honored in the house she considered her second home. She simply came in, climbed onto one of her special couches, and called me over to keep her warm. It was impossible to be formal with her while lying against her and hearing her complain as usual that I was too skinny.

"You're better," she said this time, probing me with six or seven of her limbs. "You're gaining weight finally. Thinness is dangerous." The probing changed subtly, became a series of caresses.

"He's still too thin," my mother said sharply.

T'Gatoi lifted her head and perhaps a meter of her body off the couch as though she were sitting up. She looked at my mother, and my mother, her face lined and old looking, turned away.

"Lien, I would like you to have what's left of Gan's egg."

"The eggs are for the children," my mother said.

"They are for the family. Please take it."

Unwillingly obedient, my mother took it from me and put it to her mouth. There were only a few drops left in the now—shrunken, elastic shell, but she squeezed them out, swallowed them, and after a few moments some of the lines of tension began to smooth from her face.

"It's good," she whispered. "Sometimes I forget how good it is."

"You should take more," T'Gatoi said. "Why are you in such a hurry to be old?"

My mother said nothing.

"I like being able to come here," T'Gatoi said. "This place is a refuge because of you, yet you won't take care of yourself."

T'Gatoi was hounded on the outside. Her people wanted more of us made available. Only she and her political faction stood between us and the hordes who did not understand why there was a Preserve — why any Terran could not be courted, paid, drafted, in some way made available to them. Or they did understand, but in their desperation, they did not care. She parceled us out to the desperate and sold us to the rich and powerful for their political support. Thus, we were necessities, status symbols, and an independent people. She oversaw the joining of families, putting an end to the final remnants of the earlier system of breaking up Terran families to suit impatient Tlic. I had lived outside with her. I had seen the desperate eagerness in the way some people looked at me. It was a little frightening to know that only she stood between us and that desperation that could so easily swallow us. My mother would look at her sometimes and say to me, "Take care of her." And I would remember that she too had been outside, had seen.

Now T'Gatoi used four of her limbs to push me away from her onto the floor. "Go on, Gan," she said. "Sit down there with your sisters and enjoy not being sober. You had most of the egg. Lien, come warm me."

My mother hesitated for no reason that I could see. One of my earliest memories is of my mother stretched alongside T'Gatoi, talking about things I could not understand, picking me up from the floor and laughing as she sat me on one of T'Gatoi's segments. She ate her share of eggs then. I wondered when she had stopped, and why.

She lay down now against T'Gatoi, and the whole left row of T'Gatoi's limbs closed around her, holding her loosely, but securely. I had always found it comfortable to lie that way, but except for my older sister, no one else in the family liked it. They said it made them feel caged.

T'Gatoi meant to cage my mother. Once she had, she moved her tail slightly, then spoke. "Not

enough egg, Lien. You should have taken it when it was passed to you. You need it badly now."

T'Gatoi's tail moved once more, its whip motion so swift I wouldn't have seen it if I hadn't been watching for it. Her sting drew only a single drop of blood from my mother's bare leg.

My mother cried out—probably in surprise. Being stung doesn't hurt. Then she sighed and I could see her body relax. She moved languidly into a more comfortable position within the cage of T'Gatoi's limbs. "Why did you do that?" she asked, sounding half asleep.

"I could not watch you sitting and suffering any longer."

My mother managed to move her shoulders in a small shrug. "Tomorrow," she said.

"Yes. Tomorrow you will resume your suffering—if you must. But just now, just for now, lie here and warm me and let me ease your way a little."

"He's still mine, you know," my mother said suddenly.

"Nothing can buy him from me." Sober, she would not have permitted herself to refer to such things.

"Nothing," T'Gatoi agreed, humoring her.

"Did you think I would sell him for eggs? For long life? My son?"

"Not for anything," T'Gatoi said, stroking my mother's shoulders, toying with her long, graying hair.

I would like to have touched my mother, shared that moment with her. She would take my hand if I touched her now. Freed by the egg and the sting, she would smile and perhaps say things long held in. But tomorrow, she would remember all this as a humiliation. I did not want to be part of a remembered humiliation. Best just be still and know she loved me under all the duty and pride and pain.

"Xuan Hoa, take off her shoes," T'Gatoi said. "In a little while I'll sting her again and she can sleep."

My older sister obeyed, swaying drunkenly as she stood up. When she had finished, she sat down beside me and took my hand. We had always been a unit, she and I.

My mother put the back of her head against T'Gatoi's underside and tried from that impossible angle to look up into the broad, round face. "You're going to sting me again?"

"Yes, Lien."

"I'll sleep until tomorrow noon."

"Good. You need it. When did you sleep last?"

My mother made a wordless sound of annoyance. "I should have stepped on you when you were small enough," she muttered.

It was an old joke between them. They had grown up together, sort of, though T'Gatoi had not, in my mother's life time, been small enough for any Terran to step on. She was nearly three times my mother's present age, yet would still be young when my mother died of age. But T'Gatoi and my mother had met as T'Gatoi was coming into a period of rapid development—a kind of Tlic adolescence. My mother was only a child, but for a while they developed at the same rate and had no better friends than each other.

T'Gatoi had even introduced my mother to the man who became my father. My parents, pleased with each other in spite of their different ages, married as T'Gatoi was going into her family's business—politics. She and my mother saw each other less. But sometime before my older sister was born, my mother promised T'Gatoi one of her children. She would have to give one of us to someone, and she preferred T'Gatoi to some stranger.

Years passed. T'Gatoi traveled and increased her influence. The Preserve was hers by the time she came back to my mother to collect what she probably saw as her just reward for her hard work. My older sister took an instant liking to her and wanted to be chosen, but my mother was just coming to term with me and T'Gatoi liked the idea of choosing an infant and watching and taking part in all the phases of development. I'm told I was first caged within T'Gatoi's many limbs only three minutes after my birth. A few days later, I was given my first taste of egg. I tell Terrans that when they ask whether I was ever afraid of her. And I tell it to Tlic when T'Gatoi suggests a young Terran child for them and they, anxious and ignorant, demand an adolescent. Even my brother who had somehow grown up to fear and distrust the Tlic could probably have gone smoothly into one of their families if he had been adopted early enough. Sometimes, I think for his sake he should have been. I looked at him, stretched out on the floor across the room, his eyes open, but glazed as he dreamed his egg dream. No matter what he felt toward the Tlic, he always demanded his share of egg.

"Lien, can you stand up?" T'Gatoi asked suddenly.

"Stand?" my mother said. "I thought I was going to sleep."

"Later. Something sounds wrong outside." The cage was abruptly gone.

"What?"

"Up, Lien!"

My mother recognized her tone and got up just in time to avoid being dumped on the floor. T'Gatoi whipped her three meters of body off her couch, toward the door, and out at full speed. She had bones—ribs, a long spine, a skull, four sets of limb bones per segment. But when she moved that way, twisting, hurling herself into controlled falls, landing, running, she seemed not only boneless, but aquatic—something swimming through the air as though it were water. I loved watching her move.

I left my sister and started to follow her out the door, though I wasn't very steady on my own feet. It would have been better to sit and dream, better yet to find a girl and share a waking dream with her. Back when the Tlic saw us as not much more than convenient, big, warm-blooded animals, they would pen several of us together, male and female, and feed us only eggs. That way they could be sure of getting another generation of us no matter how we tried to hold out. We were lucky that didn't go on long. A few generations of it and we would have been little more than convenient, big animals.

"Hold the door open, Gan," T'Gatoi said. "And tell the family to stay back."

"What is it?" I asked.

"N'Tlic."

I shrank back against the door. "Here? Alone?"

"He was trying to reach a call box, I suppose." She carried the man past me, unconscious, folded like a coat over some of her limbs. He looked young —my brother's age perhaps—and he was thinner than he should have been. What T'Gatoi would have called dangerously thin.

"Gan, go to the call box," she said. She put the man on the floor and began stripping off his clothing.

I did not move.

After a moment, she looked up at me, her sudden stillness a sign of deep impatience.

"Send Qui," I told her. "I'll stay here. Maybe I can help."

She let her limbs begin to move again, lifting the man and pulling his shirt over his head. "You don't want to see this," she said. "It will be hard. I can't help this man the way his Tlic could."

"I know. But send Qui. He won't want to be of any help here. I'm at least willing to try."

She looked at my brother—older, bigger, stronger, certainly more able to help her here. He was sitting up now, braced against the wall, staring at the man on the floor with undisguised fear and revulsion. Even she could see that he would be useless.

"Qui, go!" she said.

He didn't argue. He stood up, swayed briefly, then steadied, frightened sober.

"This man's name is Bram Lomas," she told him, reading from the man's armband. I fingered my own armband in sympathy. "He needs T'Khotgif Teh. Do you hear?"

"Bram Lomas, T'Khotgif Teh," my brother said. "I'm going." He edged around Lomas and ran out the door.

Lomas began to regain consciousness. He only moaned at first and clutched spasmodically at a pair of T'Gatoi's limbs. My younger sister, finally awake from her egg dream, came close to look at him, until my mother pulled her back.

T'Gatoi removed the man's shoes, then his pants, all the while leaving him two of her limbs to grip. Except for the final few, all her limbs were equally dexterous. "I want no argument from you this time, Gan," she said.

I straightened. "What shall I do?"

"Go out and slaughter an animal that is at least half your size.

"Slaughter? But I've never—"

She knocked me across the room. Her tail was an efficient weapon whether she exposed the sting or not.

I got up, feeling stupid for having ignored her warning, and went into the kitchen. Maybe I could kill something with a knife or an ax. My mother raised a few Terran animals for the table and several thousand local ones for their fur. T'Gatoi would probably prefer something local. An achti, perhaps. Some of those were the right size, though they had about three times as many teeth as I did and a real love of using them. My mother, Hoa, and Qui could kill them with knives. I had never killed one at all, had never slaughtered any animal. I had spent most of my time with T'Gatoi while my brother and sisters were learning the family business. T'Gatoi

had been right. I should have been the one to go to the call box. At least I could do that.

I went to the corner cabinet where my mother kept her large house and garden tools. At the back of the cabinet there was a pipe that carried off waste water from the kitchen—except that it didn't anymore. My father had rerouted the waste water below before I was born. Now the pipe could be turned so that one half slid around the other and a rifle could be stored inside. This wasn't our only gun, but it was our most easily accessible one. I would have to use it to shoot one of the biggest of the achti. Then T'Gatoi would probably confiscate it. Firearms were illegal in the Preserve. There had been incidents right after the Preserve was established—Terrans shooting Tlic, shooting N'Tlic. This was before the joining of families began, before everyone had a personal stake in keeping the peace. No one had shot a Tlic in my lifetime or my mother's, but the law still stood—for our protection, we were told. There were stories of whole Terran families wiped out in reprisal back during the assassinations.

I went out to the cages and shot the biggest achti I could find. It was a handsome breeding male, and my mother would not be pleased to see me bring it in. But it was the right size, and I was in a hurry.

I put the achti's long, warm body over my shoulder—glad that some of the weight I'd gained was muscle—and took it to the kitchen. There, I put the gun back in its hiding place. If T'Gatoi noticed the achti's wounds and demanded the gun, I would give it to her. Otherwise, let it stay where my father wanted it.

I turned to take the achti to her, then hesitated. For several seconds, I stood in front of the closed door wondering why I was suddenly afraid. I knew what was going to happen. I hadn't seen it before but T'Gatoi had shown me diagrams and drawings. She had made sure I knew the truth as soon as I was old enough to understand it.

Yet I did not want to go into that room. I wasted a little time choosing a knife from the carved, wooden box in which my mother kept them. T'Gatoi might want one, I told myself, for the tough, heavily furred hide of the achti.

"Gan!" T'Gatoi called, her voice harsh with urgency.

I swallowed. I had not imagined a single moving of the feet could be so difficult. I realized I was trembling and that shamed me. Shame impelled me through the door.

I put the achti down near T'Gatoi and saw that Lomas was unconscious again. She, Lomas, and I were alone in the room—my mother and sisters probably sent out so they would not have to watch. I envied them.

But my mother came back into the room as T'Gatoi seized the achti. Ignoring the knife I offered her, she extended claws from several of her limbs and slit the achti from throat to anus. She looked at me, her yellow eyes intent. "Hold this man's shoulders, Gan."

I stared at Lomas in panic, realizing that I did not want to touch him, let alone hold him. This would not be like shooting an animal. Not as quick, not as merciful, and, I hoped, not as final, but there was nothing I wanted less than to be part of it.

My mother came forward. "Gan, you hold his right side," she said. "I'll hold his left." And if he came to, he would throw her off without realizing he had done it. She was a tiny woman. She often wondered aloud how she had produced, as she said, such "huge" children.

"Never mind," I told her, taking the man's shoulders. "I'll do it." She hovered nearby.

"Don't worry," I said. "I won't shame you. You don't have to stay and watch."

She looked at me uncertainly, then touched my face in a rare caress. Finally, she went back to her bedroom.

T'Gatoi lowered her head in relief "Thank you, Gan," she said with courtesy more Terran than Tlic. "That one . . . she is always finding new ways for me to make her suffer."

Lomas began to groan and make choked sounds. I had hoped he would stay unconscious. T'Gatoi put her face near his so that he focused on her.

"I've stung you as much as I dare for now," she told him. "When this is over, I'll sting you to sleep and you won't hurt anymore."

"Please," the man begged. "Wait . . . "

"There's no more time, Bram. I'll sting you as soon as it's over. When T'Khotgif arrives she'll give you eggs to help you heal. It will be over soon."

"T'Khotgif!' the man shouted, straining against my hands.

"Soon, Bram." T'Gatoi glanced at me, then placed a claw against his abdomen slightly to the right of the middle, just below the left rib. There was movement on the right side—tiny, seemingly random pulsations moving his brown flesh, creating a concavity here, a convexity there, over and over

until I could see the rhythm of it and knew where the next pulse would be.

Lomas's entire body stiffened under T'Gatoi's claw, though she merely rested it against him as she wound the rear section of her body around his legs. He might break my grip, but he would not break hers. He wept helplessly as she used his pants to tie his hands, then pushed his hands above his head so that I could kneel on the cloth between them and pin them in place. She rolled up his shirt and gave it to him to bite down on.

And she opened him.

His body convulsed with the first cut. He almost tore himself away from me. The sound he made . . . I had never heard such sounds come from anything human. T'Gatoi seemed to pay no attention as she lengthened and deepened the cut, now and then pausing to lick away blood. His blood vessels contracted, reacting to the chemistry of her saliva, and the bleeding slowed.

I felt as though I were helping her torture him, helping her consume him. I knew I would vomit soon, didn't know why I hadn't already. I couldn't possibly last until she was finished.

She found the first grub. It was fat and deep red with his blood—both inside and out. It had already eaten its own egg case but apparently had not yet begun to eat its host. At this stage, it would eat any flesh except its mother's. Let alone, it would have gone on excreting the poisons that had both sickened and alerted Lomas. Eventually it would have begun to eat. By the time it ate its way out of Lomas's flesh, Lomas would be dead or dying—and unable to take revenge on the thing that was killing him. There was always a grace period between the time the host sickened and the time the grubs began to eat him.

T'Gatoi picked up the writhing grub carefully and looked at it, somehow ignoring the terrible groans of the man.

Abruptly, the man lost consciousness.

"Good," T'Gatoi looked down at him. "I wish you Terrans could do that at will." She felt nothing. And the thing she held . . .

It was limbless and boneless at this stage, perhaps fifteen centimeters long and two thick, blind and slimy with blood. It was like a large worm. T'Gatoi put it into the belly of the achti, and it began at once to burrow. It would stay there and eat as long as there was anything to eat.

Probing through Lomas's flesh, she found two more, one of them smaller and more vigorous. "A male!" she said happily. He would be dead before I would. He would be through his metamorphosis and screwing everything that would hold still before his sisters even had limbs. He was the only one to make a serious effort to bite T'Gatoi as she placed him in the achti.

Paler worms oozed to visibility in Lomas's flesh. I closed my eyes. It was worse than finding something dead, rotting, and filled with tiny animal grubs. And it was far worse than any drawing or diagram.

"Ah, there are more," T'Gatoi said, plucking out two long, thick grubs. You may have to kill another animal, Gan. Everything lives inside you Terrans."

I had been told all my life that this was a good and necessary thing Tlic and Terran did together—a kind of birth. I had believed it until now. I knew birth was painful and bloody, no matter what. But this was something else, something worse. And I wasn't ready to see it. Maybe I never would be. Yet I couldn't not see it. Closing my eyes didn't help.

T'Gatoi found a grub still eating its egg case. The remains of the case were still wired into a blood vessel by their own little tube or hook or whatever. That was the way the grubs were anchored and the way they fed. They took only blood until they were ready to emerge. Then they ate their stretched, elastic egg cases. Then they ate their hosts.

T'Gatoi bit away the egg case, licked away the blood. Did she like the taste? Did childhood habits die hard—or not die at all?

The whole procedure was wrong, alien. I wouldn't have thought anything about her could seem alien to me.

"One more, I think," she said. "Perhaps two. A good family. In a host animal these days, we would be happy to find one or two alive." She glanced at me. "Go outside, Gan, and empty your stomach. Go now while the man is unconscious."

I staggered out, barely made it. Beneath the tree just beyond the front door, I vomited until there was nothing left to bring up. Finally, I stood shaking, tears streaming down my face. I did not know why I was crying, but I could not stop. I went further from the house to avoid being seen. Every time I closed my eyes I saw red worms crawling over redder human flesh.

There was a car coming toward the house. Since Terrans were forbidden motorized vehicles except for certain farm equipment, I knew this must be Lomas's Tlic with Qui and perhaps a Terran doctor. I wiped my face on my shirt, struggled for control.

"Gan," Qui called as the car stopped. "What happened?" He crawled out of the low, round, Tlic-convenient car door. Another Terran crawled out the other side and went into the house without speaking to me. The doctor. With his help and a few eggs, Lomas might make it.

"T'Khotgif Teh?" I said.

The Tlic driver surged out of her car, reared up half her length before me. She was paler and smaller than T'Gatoi—probably born from the body of an animal. Tlic from Terran bodies were always larger as well as more numerous.

"Six young "I told her. "Maybe seven, all alive. At least one male."

"Lomas?" she said harshly. I liked her for the question and the concern in her voice when she asked it. The last coherent thing he had said was her name.

"He's alive," I said.

She surged away to the house without another word.

"She's been sick," my brother said, watching her go. "When I called, I could hear people telling her she wasn't well enough to go out even for this."

I said nothing. I had extended courtesy to the Tlic. Now I didn't want to talk to anyone. I hoped he would go in—out of curiosity if nothing else.

"Finally found out more than you wanted to know, eh?"

I looked at him.

"Don't give me one of *her* looks," he said. "You're not her. You're just her property."

One of her looks. Had I picked up even an ability to imitate her expressions?

"What'd you do, puke?" He sniffed the air. "So now you know what you're in for."

I walked away from him. He and I had been close when we were kids. He would let me follow him around when I was home, and sometimes T'Gatoi would let me bring him along when she took me into the city. But something had happened when he reached adolescence. I never knew what. He began keeping out of T'Gatoi's way. Then he began running away—until he realized there was no "away." Not in the Preserve. Certainly not outside. After that he concentrated on getting his share of every egg that came into the house and on looking out for me in a way that made me all but hate him—a way that clearly said, as long as I was all right, he was safe from the Tlic.

"How was it, really?" he demanded, following me.

"I killed an achti. The young ate it."

"You didn't run out of the house and puke because they ate an achti."

"I had . . . never seen a person cut open before." That was true, and enough for him to know. I couldn't talk about the other. Not with him.

"Oh," he said. He glanced at me as though he wanted to say more, but he kept quiet.

We walked, not really headed anywhere. Toward the back, toward the cages, toward the fields.

"Did he say anything?" Qui asked. "Lomas, I mean."

Who else would he mean? "He said 'T'Khotgif.'"

Qui shuddered. "If she had done that to me, she'd be the last person I'd call for."

"You'd call for her. Her sting would ease your pain without killing the grubs in you."

"You think I'd care if they died?"

No. Of course he wouldn't. Would I?

"Shit!" He drew a deep breath. "I've seen what they do. You think this thing with Lomas was bad? It was nothing."

I didn't argue. He didn't know what he was talking about.

"I saw them eat a man," he said.

I turned to face him. "You're lying!"

"*I saw them eat a man.*" He paused. "It was when I was little. I had been to the Hartmund house and I was on my way home. Halfway here, I saw a man and a Tlic and the man was N'Tlic. The ground was hilly. I was able to hide from them and watch. The Tlic wouldn't open the man because she had nothing to feed the grubs. The man couldn't go any further and there were no houses around. He was in so much pain, he told her to kill him. He begged her to kill him. Finally, she did. She cut his throat. One swipe of one claw. I saw the grubs eat their way out, then burrow in again, still eating."

His words made me see Lomas's flesh again, parasitized, crawling. "Why didn't you tell me that?" I whispered.

He looked startled as though he'd forgotten I was listening. "I don't know."

"You started to run away not long after that, didn't you?"

"Yeah. Stupid. Running inside the Preserve. Running in a cage."

I shook my head, said what I should have said to him long ago. "She wouldn't take you, Qui. You don't have to worry."

"She would if anything happened to you."

"No. She'd take Xuan Hoa. Hoa... wants it." She wouldn't if she had stayed to watch Lomas.

"They don't take women," he said with contempt.

"They do sometimes." I glanced at him. "Actually, they prefer women. You should be around them when they talk among themselves. They say women have more body fat to protect the grubs. But they usually take men to leave the women free to bear their own young."

"To provide the next generation of host animals," he said, switching from contempt to bitterness.

"It's more than that!" I countered. Was it?

"If it were going to happen to me, I'd want to believe it was more, too."

"It *is* more!" I felt like a kid. Stupid argument.

"Did you think so while T'Gatoi was picking worms out of that guy's guts?"

"It's not supposed to happen that way."

"Sure it is. You weren't supposed to see it, that's all. And his Tlic was supposed to do it. She could sting him unconscious and the operation wouldn't have been as painful. But she'd still open him, pick out the grubs, and if she missed even one, it would poison him and eat him from the inside out."

There was actually a time when my mother told me to show respect for Qui because he was my older brother. I walked away, hating him. In his way, he was gloating. He was safe and I wasn't. I could have hit him, but I didn't think I would be able to stand it when he refused to hit back, when he looked at me with contempt and pity.

He wouldn't let me get away. Longer legged, he swung ahead of me and made me feel as though I were following him.

"I'm sorry," he said.

I strode on, sick and furious.

"Look, it probably won't be that bad with you. T'Gatoi likes you. She'll be careful."

I turned back toward the house, almost running from him.

"Has she done it to you yet?" he asked, keeping up easily. "I mean, you're about the right age for implantation. Has she—"

I hit him. I didn't know I was going to do it, but I think I meant to kill him. If he hadn't been bigger and stronger, I think I would have.

He tried to hold me off, but in the end, had to defend himself He only hit me a couple of times. That was plenty. I don't remember going down, but when I came to, he was gone. It was worth the pain to be rid of him.

I got up and walked slowly toward the house. The back was dark. No one was in the kitchen. My mother and sisters were sleeping in their bedrooms—or pretending to.

Once I was in the kitchen, I could hear voices—Tlic and Terran from the next room. I couldn't make out what they were saying—didn't want to make it out.

I sat down at my mother's table, waiting for quiet. The table was smooth and worn, heavy and well crafted. My father had made it for her just before he died. I remembered hanging around underfoot when he built it. He didn't mind. Now I sat leaning on it, missing him. I could have talked to him. He had done it three times in his long life. Three clutches of eggs, three times being opened up and sewed up. How had he done it? How did anyone do it?

I got up, took the rifle from its hiding place, and sat down again with it. It needed cleaning, oiling,

All I did was load it.

"Gan?"

She made a lot of little clicking sounds when she walked on bare floor, each limb clicking in succession as it touched down. Waves of little clicks.

She came to the table, raised the front half of her body above it, and surged onto it. Sometimes she moved so smoothly she seemed to flow like water itself. She coiled herself into a small hill in the middle of the table and looked at me.

"That was bad," she said softly. "You should not have seen it. It need not be that way."

"I know."

"T'Khotgif—Ch'Khotgif now—she will die of her disease. She will not live to raise her children. But her sister will provide for them, and for Bram Lomas." Sterile sister. One fertile female in every,

lot. One to keep the family going. That sister owed Lomas more than she ever repay.

"He'll live then?"

"Yes."

"I wonder if he would do it again."

"No one would ask him to do that again."

I looked into the yellow eyes, wondering how much I saw and understood there, and how much I only imagined.

"No one ever asks us," I said. "You never asked me."

She moved her head slightly. "What's the matter with your face?"

"Nothing. Nothing important." Human eyes probably wouldn't have noticed the swelling in the darkness. The only light was from one of the moons, shining through a window across the room.

"Did you use the rifle to shoot the achti?"

"Yes."

"And do you mean to use it to shoot me?"

I stared at her, outlined in the moonlight—coiled, graceful body. "What does Terran blood taste like to you?"

She said nothing.

"What are you?" I whispered. "What are we to you?"

She lay still, rested her head on her topmost coil. "You know me as no other does," she said softly. "You must decide."

"That's what happened to my face," I told her.

"What?"

"Qui goaded me into deciding to do something. It didn't turn out very well." I moved the gun slightly, brought the barrel up diagonally under my own chin. "At least it was a decision I made."

"As this will be."

"Ask me, Gatoi."

"For my children's lives?"

She would say something like that. She knew how to manipulate people, Terran and Tlic. But not this time.

"I don't want to be a host animal," I said. "Not even yours."

It took her a long time to answer. "We use almost no host animals these days," she said. "You know that."

"You use us."

"We do. We wait long years for you and teach you and join our families to yours." She moved restlessly. "You know you aren't animals to us."

I stared at her, saying nothing.

"The animals we once used began killing most of our eggs after implantation long before your ancestors arrived," she said softly. "You know these things, Gan. Because your people arrived, we are relearning what it means to be a healthy, thriving people. And your ancestors, fleeing from their homeworld, from their own kind who would have killed or enslaved them—they survived because of us. We saw them as people and gave them the Preserve when they still tried to kill us as worms."

At the word "worms," I jumped. I couldn't help it, and she couldn't help noticing it.

"I see," she said quietly. "Would you really rather die than bear my young, Gan?"

I didn't answer.

"Shall I go to Xuan Hoa?"

"Yes!" Hoa wanted it. Let her have it. She hadn't had to watch Lomas. She'd be proud. Not terrified.

T'Gatoi flowed off the table onto the floor, startling me almost too much.

"I'll sleep in Hoa's room tonight," she said. "And sometime tonight or in the morning, I'll tell her."

This was going too fast. My sister Hoa had had almost as much to do with raising me as my mother. I was still close to her—not like Qui. She could want T'Gatoi and still love me.

"Wait! Gatoi!"

She looked back, then raised nearly half her length off the floor and turned to face me. "These are adult things, Gan. This is my life, my family!"

"But she's my sister."

"I have done what you demanded. I have asked you!"

"But—"

"It will be easier for Hoa. She has always expected to carry other lives inside her."

Human lives. Human young who should someday drink at her breasts, not at her veins.

I shook my head. "Don't do it to her, Gatoi." I was not Qui. It seemed I could become him, though, with no effort at all. I could make Xuan Hoa my shield. Would it be easier to know that red worms were growing in her flesh instead of mine?

"Don't do it to Hoa," I repeated.

She stared at me, utterly still.

I looked away, then back at her. "Do it to me."

I lowered the gun from my throat and she leaned forward to take it.

"No," I told her.

"It's the law," she said.

"Leave it for the family. One of them might use it to save my life someday."

She grasped the rifle barrel, but I wouldn't let go. I was pulled into a standing position over her.

"Leave it here!" I repeated. "If we're not your animals, if these are adult things, accept the risk. There is risk, Gatoi, in dealing with a partner."

It was clearly hard for her to let go of the rifle. A shudder went through her and she made a hissing sound of distress. It occurred to me that she was afraid. She was old enough to have seen what guns could do to people. Now her young and this gun would be together in the same house. She did not know about the other guns. In this dispute, they did not matter.

"I will implant the first egg tonight," she said as I put the gun away. "Do you hear, Gan?"

Why else had I been given a whole egg to eat while the rest of the family was left to share one? Why else had my mother kept looking at me as though I were going away from her, going where she could not follow? Did T'Gatoi imagine I hadn't known?

"I hear."

"Now!" I let her push me out of the kitchen, then walked ahead of her toward my bedroom. The sudden urgency in her voice sounded real. "You would have done it to Hoa tonight!" I accused.

"I must do it to someone tonight."

I stopped in spite of her urgency and stood in her way. "Don't you care who?"

She flowed around me and into my bedroom. I found her waiting on the couch we shared. There was nothing in Hoa's room that she could have used. She would have done it to Hoa on the floor. The thought of her doing it to Hoa at all disturbed me in a different way now, and I was suddenly angry.

Yet I undressed and lay down beside her. I knew what to do, what to expect. I had been told all my life. I felt the familiar sting, narcotic, mildly pleasant. Then the blind probing of her ovipositor. The puncture was painless, easy. So easy going in. She undulated slowly against me, her muscles forcing the egg from her body into mine. I held on to a pair of her limbs until I remembered Lomas holding her that way. Then I let go, moved inadvertently, and hurt her. She gave a low cry of pain and I expected to be caged at once within her limbs. When I wasn't, I held on to her again, feeling oddly ashamed.

"I'm sorry," I whispered.

She rubbed my shoulders with four of her limbs.

"Do you care?" I asked. "Do you care that it's me?"

She did not answer for some time. Finally, "You were the one making the choices tonight, Gan. I made mine long ago."

"Would you have gone to Hoa?"

"Yes. How could I put my children into the care of one who hates them?"

"It wasn't . . . hate."

"I know what it was."

"I was afraid."

Silence.

"I still am." I could admit it to her here, now.

"But you came to me . . . to save Hoa."

"Yes." I leaned my forehead against her. She was cool velvet, deceptively soft. "And to keep you for myself," I said. It was so. I didn't understand it, but it was so.

She made a soft hum of contentment. "I couldn't believe I had made such a mistake with you," she said. "I chose you. I believed you had grown to choose me."

"I had, but . . ."

"Lomas."

"Yes."

"I had never known a Terran to see a birth and take it well. Qui has seen one, hasn't he?"

"Yes."

"Terrans should be protected from seeing."

I didn't like the sound of that—and I doubted that it was possible. "Not protected," I said. "Shown. Shown when we're young kids, and shown more than once. Gatoi, no Terran ever sees a birth that goes right. All we see is N'Tlic—pain and terror and maybe death."

She looked down at me. "It is a private thing. It has always been a private thing."

Her tone kept me from insisting—that and the knowledge that if she changed her mind, I might be the first public example. But I had planted the thought in her mind. Chances were it would grow, and eventually she would experiment.

"You won't see it again," she said. "I don't want you thinking any more about shooting me."

The small amount of fluid that came into me with her egg relaxed me as completely as a sterile egg would have, so that I could remember the rifle in my hands and my feelings of fear and revulsion, anger and despair. I could remember the feelings without reviving them. I could talk about them.

"I wouldn't have shot you," I said. "Not you." She had been taken from my father's flesh when he was my age.

"You could have," she insisted.

"Not you." She stood between us and her own people, protecting, interweaving.

"Would you have destroyed yourself?"

I moved carefully, uncomfortable. "I could have done that. I nearly did. That's Qui's 'away.' I wonder if he knows."

"What?"

I did not answer.

"You will live now."

"Yes." *Take care of her*, my mother used to say. Yes.

"I'm healthy and young," she said. "I won't leave you as Lomas was left—alone, N'Tlic. I'll take care of you."

## AFTERWORD

It amazes me that some people have seen "Bloodchild" as a story of slavery. It isn't. It's a number of other things, though. On one level, it's a love story between two very different beings. On another, it's a coming-of-age story in which a boy must absorb disturbing information and use it to make a decision that will affect the rest of his life.

On a third level, "Bloodchild" is my pregnant man story. I've always wanted to explore what it might be like for a man to be put into that most unlikely of all positions. Could I write a story in which a man chose to become pregnant not through some sort of misplaced competitiveness to prove that a man could do anything a woman could do, not because he was forced to, not even out of curiosity? I wanted to see whether I could write a dramatic story of a man becoming pregnant as an act of love—choosing pregnancy in spite of as well as because of surrounding difficulties.

Also, "Bloodchild" was my effort to ease an old fear of mine. I was going to travel to the Peruvian Amazon to do research for my Xenogenesis books (*Dawn, Adulthood Rites,* and *Imago*), and I worried about my possible reactions to some of the insect life of the area. In particular, I worried about the botfly—an insect with, what seemed to me then, horror movie habits. There was no shortage of botflies in the part of Peru that I intended to visit.

The botfly lays its eggs in wounds left by the bites of other insects. I found the idea of a maggot living and growing under my skin, eating my flesh as it grew, to be so intolerable, so terrifying that I didn't know how I could stand it if it happened to me. To make matters worse, all that I heard and read advised botfly victims not to try to get rid of their maggot passengers until they got back home to the United States and were able to go to a doctor—or until the fly finished the larval part of its growth cycle, crawled our of its host, and flew away.

The problem was to do what would seem to be the normal thing, to squeeze out the maggot and throw it away, was to invite infection. The maggot becomes literally attached to its host and leaves part of itself behind, broken off, if it's squeezed or cut out. Of course, the part left behind dies and rots, causing infection. Lovely.

When I have to deal with something that disturbs me as much as the botfly did, I write about it. I sort out my problems by writing about them. In a high school classroom on November 22, 1963, I remember grabbing a notebook and beginning to write my response to news of John Kennedy's assassination. Whether I write journal pages, an essay, a short story, or weave my problems into a novel, I find the writing helps me get through the trouble and get on with my life. Writing "Bloodchild" didn't —make me like botflies, but for a while, it made them seem more interesting than horrifying.

There's one more thing I tried to do in "Bloodchild." I tried to write a story about paying the rent —a story about an isolated colony of human beings on an inhabited, extrasolar world. At best, they would be a lifetime away from reinforcements. It wouldn't be the British Empire in space, and it wouldn't be *Star Trek*. Sooner or later, the humans would have to make some kind of accommodation with their um . . .their hosts. Chances are this would be an unusual accommodation. Who knows what we humans have that others might be willing to take in trade for a livable space on a world not our own?

## Study Questions

1. What are the characteristics of science fiction? Is there such a thing as "black" science fiction? Why or why not? What does he genre of science fiction allow Butler to do that might be more difficult in other genres?

2. Why do you think Butler explores the idea of male pregnancy? What does this story suggest about male pregnancy?

3. What is the relationship between the two species? Is it equitable? What compromises have both species made? Would you like to live in such a world? Explain.

4. What is the relationship between Gan and T'Gatoi? Is it "natural" or "moral"? Explain.

5. Why do you think readers often think that this is a story about slavery? Do you agree with the author that it is not?

# GENDER AND SCIENCE

## Ruth Bleier

*Science, it would seem, is not sexless; she is a man, a father, and infected, too. Virginia Wolfe,*

*1938, p. 139*

*Ruth Bleier was a professor of Neurophysiology and a member of the Women's Studies Program at the University of Wisconsin, Madison. She was also politically active in feminist and lesbian groups in Madison. This essay comes from her book,* Gender and Science *(1984), which critically analyzes biological theories of male and female "nature," to show the logical errors and scientific weaknesses of these claims.*

Because Wilsonian sociobiology is a particularly dramatic contemporary version of biological determinist theories of human behavior, because it is powerful and persuasive, because it is a particularly good example of bad science, because it provides "scientific" support for a dominant political ideology that directly opposes every goal and issue raised by the women's movement, and because it has been aggressively marketed and perceptibly incorporated into our culture, it seems a fitting area with which to begin the examination of science and scientific theories of biological determinism.

While the general field of sociobiology has a long and solid tradition of studying the social behavior of animals, in 1975 E. O. Wilson, whose area of expertise is insect behaviors, sought to establish sociobiology "as the systematic study of the biological basis of all social behavior." He stated his conviction that "It may not be too much to say that sociology and the other social sciences, as well as the humanities, are the last branches of biology waiting to be included in the Modern Syntheses" (Wilson, 1975b, p. 4). Thus, Wilson and those in his school of human sociobiology believe that all human behaviors, social relationships, and

organization are genetically evolved adaptations, as I will describe below. Before proceeding, however, to a critique of the work of Wilsonian sociobiology's, it is important to distinguish it from the general field of sociobiology. There are many other scientists who study the social behaviors and characteristics of animals and are therefore sociobiology's but do not make reckless extrapolations to human social relationships and behaviors. Their observations and interpretations form an important part of the evidence I use to support my arguments concerning the inadequacies and distortions inherent in the "science" that Wilson and his followers popularize.

By reducing human behavior and complex social phenomena to genes and to inherited and programmed mechanisms of neuronal functioning, the message of the new Wilsonia Sociobiology becomes rapidly clear: we had best resign ourselves to the fact that the more unsavory aspects of human behavior, like wars, racism, and class struggle, are inevitable results of evolutionary adaptations based in our genes. And of key importance is the fact that the particular roles performed by women and men in society are also biologically, genetically determined; in fact, civilization as we know it, or perhaps any at all, could not have evolved in any other way. Thus the Sociobiologist and popular writer David Barash says, "There is good reason to believe that we are (genetically) primed to be much less sexually egalitarian than we appear to be" (Barash, 1979, p. 47)

But it is not only that the direct political and social statements and theories of Sociobiologists are dangerous to the interests and well being of women and minorities. If Sociobiology were a valid science, by even traditional standards, we should have to find ways to cope with the consequences of incontrovertible "truths." But this Sociobiology is deeply flawed conceptually, methodologically, and logically as a science. It is only because it concerns itself with the most complex aspects of human behaviors and social relationships, about which we suffer enormous depths of both ignorance and emotion, that Sociobiology achieves acceptance as a science: The same kinds of logical and methodological flaws in the sciences, say, of ant or camel behavior would be immediately obvious and unacceptable.

In this chapter I first review some basic postulates and assumptions of Sociobiological theory and outline the methodologies used for theory building. I then offer a detailed critique of Sociobiologists' theories and methods and indicate some alternative observations and interpretations that contradict their assumptions and conclusions. Finally, since the fundamental scientific issue is the validity of a theory based on the genetic determination of human behavior, I explore the relationship between genes and the fetal environment and between biology and learning..

## SOME PREMISES AND APPROACHES OF SOCIOBIOLOGY

### Natural Selection of Behaviors Through Gene Transmission

The basic premise of Sociobiology is that human behaviors and certain aspects of social organization have evolved, like our bodies, through adaptations based on Darwinian natural selection. It is important to understand Darwin's theory of evolution of the physical forms of animals by adaptation in order to understand its application by Sociobiologists to behavior. In its modern version, the theory assumes that by some genetic recombination or mutation, a particular anatomical characteristic appears anew in a species, let us say gray body color in a family of orange moths. If the gray color in the moths' particular ecological setting permits more gray than orange moths to survive predation and other causes of an early demise and therefore to reach sexual maturity so that more gray moths are reproduced than their relatives of the original orange color, then an increasing proportion of moths will be gray in successive generations. Over time, the genes for gray will be present in increasing numbers of moths and become a predominant feature of moths in that ecological setting. The new genetic feature for gray is then considered, in the language of Darwinian evolution, to be adaptive through natural selection since it contributes to the maximum fitness of the moths, with maximum fitness being defined as the ability to leave many healthy descendants that are themselves

able to reproduce and thus spread the genes for gray body color.

Sociobiologists suggest and assume that behaviors also evolve in similar ways so that "adaptive" and "successful" behaviors become based in our genes, and that certain genetic configurations became selected because they result in behaviors that are adaptive for survival. Our "innate" predisposing to display these behaviors constitute our human nature. It is important to note at this point that to be valid the theory requires that human behaviors be represented by a particular genetic configuration, because evolution through natural selection requires genetic variations (that is, mutant forms) from which to select. But Sociobiologists themselves, as well as geneticists, agree that it is not possible to link any specific human behavior with any specific gene or genetic configuration. The only evidence for such a link is that which is provided by Sociobiologists' circular logic. This logic makes a premise of the genetic basis of behaviors, then cites a certain animal or human behavior, constructs a speculative story to explain how the behavior (if it were genetically based) could have served or could serve to maximize the reproductive success of the individual, and this conjecture then becomes evidence for the premise that the behavior was genetically determined.

This is the central principle of sociobiology: insofar as a behavior reflects at least some component of gene action, individuals will tend to behave so as to maximize their fitness…The result is a very strange sort of purposefulness, in which a goal - maximization of fitness - appears to be sought, but without any of the participants necessarily having awareness of what they are doing, or why. (Barash, 1979, pp. 29 and 25)

Notice the insofar clause is key and serves to confuse the issue. All behavior of course reflects at least some component of gene action. Individuals of any species of animal behave within the limits of the broad range of biological capabilities defined by their genes. Humans walk rather than fly. Birds peck at their food. When we are frightened, our hearts beat faster. But what is really at issue in Sociobiological theory is not the physical capacity for behavior that biology provides but rather the genetic encoding of the entire range of complex human behaviors and characteristics that are expressed in a nearly infinite variety of ways by different individuals and cultures and often not expressed at all; such an altruism, loyalty, dominance, competitiveness, aggressively. In addition, Sociobiology claims genetic encoding for such arbitrarily chosen and questionably sexually differentiated "traits" as coyness, fickleness, promiscuity, rapaciousness, or maternalism.

Sociobiologists make a passing attempt to acknowledge that learning, culture, or environment plays a role in human behavior, but it is clear that their hearts (and minds) are not engaged by this idea. David Barash clearly states his position on the contribution of learning to behavior.

Core elements are the essential person, an entity bequeathed by evolution to each of us; they are the us upon which experience acts. The great strength of sociobiology is that its conception of the "core" is grounded in evolution...(1079, p. 10)

Biology and culture undoubtedly work together, but it is tempting to speculate that our biology is somehow more real, lying unnoticed within each of us, quietly but forcefully manipulating much of our behavior. Culture, which is overwhelmingly important in shaping the myriad details of our lives, is more likely seen as a think veneer, compared to the underlying ground substance of our biology. (1979, p. 14)

Richard Dawkins, the Sociobiologist who coined the catchy anthropomorphic phrase, selfish genes, explains that genes and their expression are unaffected by environment:

Now they swarm in huge colonies, safe inside gigantic lumbering robots, sealed off from the outside world, communicating with it by tortuous indirect routes, manipulating it by remote control. They are in you and in me; they created us, body and mind and their preservation is the ultimate rationale for our existence. They have come a long way, those replicators. Now they go by the name of genes, and we are their survival machines. (1976, p. 21)

Mary Midgley, the British philosopher, suggests that "Dawkin's crude, cheap blurred genetics is not just an expository device. It is the kingpin of his ??? Cheap, blurred psychology" (1980a, p. 120). She further notes how the message of such "science" was transmitted to the general public by the cover of Time magazine's sociobiology number, which showed two puppets making love "while invisible genes twitch the strings above them..." (1980b, p. 26).

SEX DIFFERENCES IN REPRODUCTIVE
STRATEGIES

Since a key concept for Sociobiological theory is that behaviors are programmed to maximize the ability of the body's genes to reproduce themselves,

an important area for Sociobiological speculation is that of reproduction itself. The second key postulate, then, is that the two sexes have a different strategy for maximizing their fitness through the reproduction of the largest possible number of offspring, and it is to this difference that Sociobiologists are able to attribute what they consider to be differences in female and male natures, behaviors, and social behaviors for assuring the reproduction and survival of their genes because they have an "unequal" biological investment in each offspring. Their reasoning is that since human males produce millions of sperm a day and can theoretically "sire offspring with different women at hourly or at most daily intervals" (Van Den Berghe and Barash, 1977, p. 814), their investment in the future in terms of the maximum reproduction of their genes in offspring lies in inseminating as many women as possible. Also, their relative investment in any one offspring is small. The human female, however, has a much greater investment in each of her offspring because her egg is 85,000 times larger than a sperm (hence more "expensive" to produce), because she ordinarily produces but one egg at a time and only about 400 in her lifetime, and because she usually produces no more than one offspring a year. Furthermore, since she is the one who gestates the fetus in her body, her expenditure of energy for those months for the subsequent year or two of lactation and infant care is considerably greater than the father's. Therefore, while the genetic contribution from each parent is equivalent (23 chromosomes), the mother contributes a larger portion of her total reproductive potential and a larger investment of time and energy. These facts, according to Sociobiologists, result in different reproductive strategies in the two sexes: women are selective and choosy - they go for quality: men go for quantity. Thus, E. O. Wilson writes:

It pays males to be aggressive, hasty, fickle, and undiscriminating. In theory it is more profitable for females to be coy, to hold back until they can identify males with the best genes...Human beings obey this biological principle faithfully. (1978, p. 125)

And Barash explains further:

The evolutionary mechanism should be clear. Genes that allow females to accept the sorts of mates who make lesser contributions to their reproductive successes will leave fewer copies of themselves than will genes that influence the females to be more selective...For males, a very different strategy applies. The maximum advantages goes to individuals with fewer inhibitions. A genetically influenced tendency to "play fast and loose" - "love 'em and leave 'em" - may well reflect more

*biological reality than most of us care to admit.*
(1979, p. 48)

### The Leap to Sex Differences in Human Social Roles and Characteristics

Thus, we can see that Sociobiologists leap from some obvious facts such as the relative sizes and available numbers of eggs and sperm to sweeping and unwarranted generalizations about the explanations for presumed female and male innate characteristics: women are coy, choosy, and fussy: males are fickle to such social phenomena and arrangements as marital fidelity for women and adultery, polygyny (harems), and rape by men. Sociobiologists explain that a woman stands to lose much less by her husband's sexual infidelity and by his fathering of children outside the marriage than a husband stands to lose by his wife's infidelity, since he would, in the latter case, be helping to rear children who do not bear his genes. It is for this reason, they claim, that there is a sexual double standard: a differential valuation of virginity and a differential condemnation of marital infidelity (Van Den Berghe and Barash, 1977).

Sociobiologists derive two other important postulates from the observation that the eggs and sperms that women and men contribute to the process of conception are different. The first is predictable: since a woman has a greater investment in terms of egg size and the time and energy spent in gestation, she also invests the major portion of total parental care in her offspring. She does this in order to protect her biological investment and her genes, since each of her offspring represents a greater proportion of her total reproductive capacity than it does for the father. An added factor is that women know with certainty that their genes have been passed on in their children; men have to take it on faith.

Throughout their evolutionary history, males have generally been ill advised to devote themselves too strongly to the care of children, since the undertaking might turn out to be a wasted effort. (Barash, 1979, pp. 108-9).

There is a second important Sociobiological postulate derived from the fact that the total number of eggs available for fertilization is far fewer than the number of sperm available to fertilize them: competition among males for females is inevitable; since females, with their limited reproductive potential, are a scarce resource. Because of this competition on the time scale of evolution, the most reproductively successful males came to be those who were larger and more aggressive. It is this

inherited male aggressively that provides the biological basis for male dominance over females, male dominance hierarchies, competitiveness, territoriality, and war.

This, then, is how Sociobiology sees itself as replacing psychology and sociology. It is a social theory in the guise of biology; Sociobiologists provide the biological basis for all social phenomena and, in particular, for the social roles and the cultural representations of women and men. Thus Dawkins blandly declares:

The female sex is exploited, and the fundamental evolutionary basis for the exploitation is the fact that eggs are larger than sperms. (1976, p. 158)

And Wilson explains:

*In hunter-gatherer societies, men hunt and women stay home. This strong bias persists in most agricultural and industrial societies and, on that ground alone, appears to have a genetic origin (1975, p. 47)*

This quotation is particularly perplexing in view of Wilson's obvious and known familiarity with the renowned work of his Harvard colleagues, Richard Lee and Irven DeVore and their coworkers, on hunter-gatherer societies extensively documenting the exact opposite of this claim; that, in fact, women gatherers are away from "home" as much as the men. His knowledge of what women do in agricultural and industrial societies appears similarly based in mythic imagery rather than in modern anthropological scholarship let alone in the real world of agricultural and industrial economies where 50 to 100 percent of women may work outside the home. The most generous interpretation may be that extrapolations to human societies from insects is a hazardous (though not unrewarding) intellectual undertaking even for eminent entomologists. And, finally, to complete the unanimity of the Sociobiological voice, Barash speaks:

*...women have almost universally found themselves relegated to the nursery while men derive their greatest satisfaction from their jobs...such differences in male-female attachment to family versus vocation could derive in part from hormonal differences between sexes...(1977, p. 301)*

I should like to call attention to the last quotation as an example of Sociobiologists;' tendency to play loose with both language and logic. Barash speaks of women being relegated (assigned, banished) to the nursery, while men derive satisfaction from their jobs, hardly equivalent states, conditions, or situations; he then proceeds to base them both in biology as though they were equivalent. It is like claiming that repeatedly jailed offenders have an innate attachment to their cells.

### Sociobiological Methodology in Theory Building

Having stated the basic postulates of their theory. Sociobiologists then go on to catalogue the behaviors they consider to be universal and characteristic of humans and thus to be either explainable by or supportive of their theory. These behaviors and characteristics are never defined so that we all can know that we are talking about the same thing, nor are they selected according to any agreed upon criteria from psychology, anthropology, or sociology. The behaviors and characteristics they choose to discuss and explain as universals of human societies are what upper/middle class white male North American and English scientists consider to be characteristic: male aggressivity, territoriality, and tribalism; in doctrinability and conformity; male competitiveness and entrepreneurship; altruism and selfishness. The existence of these supposedly genetically determined human characteristic ("traits") then obviously and logically explains such social phenomena as national chauvinism, xenophobia and war; slavery and capitalism; ethnocentrism and racism; dominance hierarchies and sexism. In order to establish that these presumed universal human characteristics and social phenomena have evolved genetically, the next step in Sociobiological theory building is to demonstrate their existence throughout the animal world. The methodology consists essentially of flipping through the encyclopedic catalogue of animal behaviors and selecting particular behaviors of fishes, birds, insects or mammals that can be readily made to exemplify the various categories of human "traits" and social arrangements that Sociobiologists claim to be universal and genetically based. It is this step that introduces a number of methodological flaws into a theory already suffering from the conceptual ailments I have described.

But before discussing these flaws, I should like to place this critical next step within the context of the basic postulates and methodology of Sociobiology that I have described thus far. First, a picture is presented of human social organizations and relationships. These are said to have universal elements that are based upon the existence of universal human behavioral traits that have evolved through natural selection because they were optimally adaptive; that is, the best alternative for survival from among several genetic variations. This assumes a specific genetic coding for specific behavioral "traits" and characteristics. It is not possible to adduce scientific proof for the presence or absence of specific behavioral traits in evolving

hominids since traits leave no fossil record. Therefore, there is no way to identify the possible genetic variations from which current behavioral solutions have been selected. This forces Sociobiologists to demonstrate biological and evolutionary continuity by establishing similarities with other living nonhuman species that are viewed as representing an evolutionary continuum culminating in the human species. This is done by then describing carefully selected behaviors of particular species that represent and demonstrate some presumed human universal, such as female "coyness." But since we also do not know what the environmental, ecological, or reproductive problems were that such behaviors or characteristics were solving over the past several hundred million years, Sociobiologists attempt to reconstruct evolutionary history by inventing plausible stories that attempt to show how a particular behavior or social interaction in humans or other species could have or would have been adaptive and therefore favored by natural selection and genetically carried through subsequent generations. Basically, the aim is to establish the biological "innateness" and inevitability of present-day human behaviors and forms of social organization.

### Flaws in Sociobiological Theory and Methodology

In the methodology, and arguments used by Sociobiologists and other biological determinists, one can detect a number of recurring and interrelated flaws. The problems begin with the categories and definition of behaviors that they consider characteristic of all people. When they proceed to draw analogies to animal behaviors, the problems are compounded by their selective use of particular animal models and by the language and concepts they apply to their descriptions of animal behaviors. We will find that these problems are intimately interrelated, but I shall try to analyze each, giving examples from important Sociobiological concepts, and then discuss two other kinds of methodological problems: the scientific tests one uses to validate hypotheses, and the classical and recurring issue of gene-environment, biology-culture interactions.

### Ethnocentricity of Behavioral Description

The first problem lies in the Sociobiological descriptions of presumably universal human behaviors and social relationships, which are curiously similar to social organizations in the white Western industrial capitalist world. In this sense, Sociobiology is in fact an anachronism. It incorporates into its methodology the naïve ethnocentric, andocentric, and anthropocentric fallacies discarded at least a decade or two ago by most competent and aware anthropologists and primatologists. Throughout Sociobiological writings there is a pervasive sense of the investigator's perception of his own self as a universal reference point, as equivalent to humanity, viewing all others - the other sex, other classes, races, cultures and civilizations, species, and epochs - in the light and language of his own experiences, values, and beliefs. He and his fraternity become the norm against which all others are measured and interpreted. (I use the male pronoun since Sociobiologists with few exceptions are male.) Thus, Sociobiologists make unwarranted generalizations about characteristic human behaviors , such as that "men would rather believe than know" (Wilson, 1975b, p. 561) or that women are coy and marry for upward social mobility. This means that much of the argument of Sociobiologists is devised to explain what they define as universal behavioral traits, the existence of which is, however, highly problematic to many students of human behavior. As the anthropologist Nancy Howell has said, "...they seem to be innocently ignorant of much of the complexity of human social life and cultures that sociobiology sets out to explain" (1979, p. 1295), though one wonders, when they see rape in the reproductive mechanism of flowers and war as a collective expression of individual male's innate aggressivity, just how "innocently ignorant" they can be. At the same time they seem also to be unconscious of any of the methodological problems that pervade attempts to describe human behavior, problems with which social scientists continue to struggle. As Richard Lewontin has pointed out, "anthropologists have long been acutely conscious of the difficulties of describing human behavior in such a way as not to dictate the analysis by the categories of description:" (1976, p. 24). Sociobiologists simply declare what they consider to be categories of behavioral description, for example, entrepreneurship, territoriality, aggression dominance, without relationship to any cultural or historical context, and then proceed to arbitrarily assign examples of human and animal behavior to that category to demonstrate its universality in the animal world.

The concept of dominance hierarchies is an example of both ethnocentrism of descriptions of human "traits" and the trap of dictating analysis by the use of arbitrary categorization of behavior. Barash asserts that we are "a species organized along distinct lines of dominance" (1979, p. 186). But as Ruth Hubbard points out:

We in the industrialized countries have grown up in hierarchically structured societies, so that, to us, dominance hierarchies appear natural and inevitable. But it is a mistake to apply the same categories to societies that function quite differently and to pretend that differences between our society and

theirs can be expressed merely as matters of degree...To take widely and complexly different social manifestations and scale them along one dimension does violence to the sources and significances of human social behavior. Western technological societies have developed in their ways for their own historical reasons. Other societies have their histories that have led to their social forms. (1978, p. 134)

As I discuss in detail in Chapter 6, many anthropological studies suggest that dominance hierarchies have not uniformly characterized the organization of human societies either in the past or today. In order to prove both the universality and the evolutionary inevitability of male dominance and dominance hierarchies, Sociobiologists and other biological determinists cite the example of the prototypical primate troop with its chest-pounding leader that has become familiar to us all. I shall discuss the fallacies of this approach in a section to follow on anthropomorphism.

Another example of the ethnocentric and androcentric application of concepts of human behavior to animals can be found in Sociobiological explanations of polygyny (marriage of one man to many wives) and hypergamy (marriage for upward mobility). I have already alluded to the Sociobiological postulate that men, being producers of millions of sperm a day, maximize their fitness by impregnating as many women as possible and, therefore, have traditionally established systems of polygyny, and that women have evolved to be more selective. Van Den Berghe and Barash (1977) describe the fact that in some bird species the females "prefer" polygynous males (here used to mean males that mate with many females) over bachelors. Wondering why, biologists have concluded that it is because the polygynous males command better territory than bachelors, more land providing more food and more protection for the young. This leads Van Den Berghe and Barash (1977) then to another Sociobiological universal of female behavior, hypergamy, marrying males of higher socioeconomic status for upward social mobility:

Extrapolating to humans, we suggest that men are selected for engaging in male-male competition over resources appropriate to reproductive success, and that women are selected for preferring men who are successful in that endeavor. Any genetically influenced tendencies in these directions will necessarily be favored by natural selection.

It is true, of course, that social advantages of wealth, power, or rank need not, indeed often do not, coincide with physical superiority. Women in all societies have found a way of resolving this dilemma by marrying wealthy and powerful men while taking young and attractive ones as lovers" the object of the game is to have the husband assume parental obligations for the lover's children. Understandably, men in most societies do not take kindly to such female strategies on the part of their wives, though they are not averse to philandering with other men's wives. The solution to this moral dilemma is the double standard, independently invented in countless societies. In any case, ethnographic evidence points to different reproductive strategies on the part of men and women, and to a remarkable consistency in the institutionalized means of accommodating these biological predispositions. (pp. 814, 815)

In this way the authors postulate a genetic tendency and a "biological predisposition" for women to marry men of wealth, power, and rank. Yet it is perfectly obvious that this "predisposition" can govern the behavior of only a small percentage of the world's women, since only a tiny minority of men in all countries of the world have any wealth, power, or rank. Thus, the vast majority of women everywhere, who are in lower socioeconomic classes and marry within their class, are excluded from biological universality. Their "universal" hypergamy is what happens only in romantic fiction. Sociobiologists attempt to establish human species universals of behavior by using an extraordinary ethnocentric and class-biased model based on the behavior of a relatively small group of people in their own countries and others where the sexual and marital exploits of the rich and powerful are familiar topics in the international press. Furthermore, they also imply that there exists a related biological predisposition that expresses itself in the sexual double standard "independently invented in countless societies" because of men's unwillingness to assume obligation for the offspring (genes) of their wives' lovers. There is no suggestion that the double standard could have social origins independent of genes, that it may be but one more reflection of the economic and political domination of men over women in "countless" patriarchal societies.

Since even biological determinists recognize that many so-called human characteristics or behaviors are not universal, they postulate "predispositions," that is, traits that are genetically determined but not always expressed. It is very difficult, however, to take seriously the existence of a "predisposition" if it is not manifested in the a majority of human beings. Just as Sociobiologists claim territoriality to be an evolutionary predisposition even though it is not manifested in a large number, perhaps the majority , of species, one could use their reasoning to argue that the sharing of territory is based on a biological predisposition, since the majority of species do just that.

It is a remarkable feature of Sociobiologists' descriptions of human "traits" that there appears to be no recognition of the possibility that there may be something arbitrary, selective, or subjective in their characterizations of females and males; that if some other group, for example, women or black males or American Indian males, were to list what they consider to be characteristic of women and men, the lists would be quite different. There is no acknowledgement, for example, that there are many women who are not coy and would use other adjectives to describe women. Also my guess is that it would come as a surprise to Sociobiologists to know that many American women because of their experiences, would include in their list of male characteristics helplessness, impracticality, and dependence. One is then left to wonder hwy this kind of list is any less "scientific" than the list of "human" characteristic Sociobiologists have chosen to describe.

### Lack of Definition of Behavioral Units

A further difficulty that one encounters in Sociobiological accounts of human behavioral categories is the absence of any precise description or definition of the behaviors Sociobiologists are seeking to explain. It is a requirement for any science to define the units or the phenomena that are the subjects of its investigations so as to ensure that different scientists, writers, and their readers are using the same terms to mean the same thing. Certainly a theory of social behavior needs to describe the behaviors it explains. But Sociobiologists do not describe or define what they mean, for example, by entrepreneurship or aggressivity. Is aggressively fighting in bars, getting ahead in business, being creative, being a football star, a Don Juan, a war hero, a professor? Or is it being a mother who pursues City Hall and all of its politicians until a stoplight is installed where her children have to cross the street on their way to school?

Sociobiologists do not provide the answers to these questions. Every person who reads their literature has her/his own impression of what is being discussed, and perhaps that is precisely where Sociobiology's wide appeal and acceptance lies. Its statements can be interpreted in accordance with any person's subjective experiences, expectations, frame of reference, or prejudices rather than needing to be measured or judged against generally accepted standards of meaning or definition. This omission of a definition of the behavioral units that are being "explained" makes for further difficulty when we try to understand how Sociobiologists relate behaviors to genes. For example, if aggressivity is genetic and biological, what is it that is being inherited? Is it a physiological state of high energy;

is it overactive adrenal glands with high levels of adrenalin in the blood; is it high intelligence and creativity; is it good body coordination; is it being "too" short and "therefore" insecure; is it "maternalism?" Or, as another example, what exactly do genes "encode" when they encode for hypergamy in females or entrepreneurship in males? Would biological determinists simply have to agree that what is biologically based is the perception of hunger and the drive for survival, and that both hypergamy and the different forms that entrepreneurship takes are simply those among an infinite variety of behavioral strategies that human beings learn and select as solutions to the problems of hunger and survival in their particular ecological and cultural niche? Or do they really mean that all females inherit a gene or a cluster of genes that drive them to look for and, of course, scheme to marry a rich man? Would they concede the possibility that, rather than genes for "entrepreneurship," the more successful gatherer-hunters may have been distinguished from the rest by their greater inventiveness (of tools), better memory (for plants and fertile sites), quicker intelligence, more energy or speed, or by superior ecological circumstances? Surely to understand the evolution of complex behaviors, a multiplicity of such characteristics can be considered and perhaps profitably analyzed, but invoking a murky concept like entrepreneurship seems useless, in contrast, except perhaps as a means of justifying the inevitability of our economic system.

Anthropomorphizing: The Choice
of Animal Models and Use of
Language

Following close on the heels of the first, large problems of Sociobiological methodology that I have just discussed - its subjective and fuzzy conceptualizations and categorizations of human behavioral "traits" and social relationships - is the next great problem: anthropomorphizing, the substitution of human "equivalents" for real or postulated animal behaviors. In efforts to uncover the biological origins of human behavior, some investigators select an animal model that reflects their image of relationships presumed to exist in human society and then impose the language and concepts ordinarily used to describe human behavior upon their observations and interpretations of animal behaviors. The conclusions are inevitable, for the entire structure is a self-fulfilling prophecy. It involves a method, long in disrepute, or reading human motivation and intent into animal behavior. This make for poor science because it cannot lead to an understanding of an animal species' behaviors or how the behaviors have come to solve th animal's problems of survival in its particular environment; it

is also a circular and ineffectual way to approach human behavior even if one could understand human behavior by extrapolating from animals. (For reasons I discuss later, I do not believe one can.) If you initially interpret an animal's behavior in terms of what you believe about human behavior, you cannot then use your interpretation of that animal's behavior to explain something about human behavior.

Anthropomorphizing makes for a poor science of animal behavior for several reasons. The one I have discussed is that applying to animals assumptions that one has about human behavior or relationships structures and distorts the actual observations that investigators make as well as those they fail to make, and, in so doing, biases the course and outcome of the research. A second related reason is that the technique makes the assumption that simply because an animal and a human behavior look alike, they are the same. But the two behaviors could have a superficial similarity and at the same time have a totally different significance for the body economy and represent different solutions to two completely different sets of problems of survival in their respective ecological circumstances. To apply human terminology to animals not only totally ignores these distinctions, but in the process circumvents or cancels out all the relevant questions and investigations that could lead one to understand either the animal or the human behavior. Examples of some of these biasing concepts are the concepts of dominance hierarchies, rape, and harem to be discussed in the following pages.

The technique of describing animal behaviors in human terms was characteristic of primate studies in this country until the last decade or two and was especially incisively criticized and parodied by Ruth Herschberger in *Adam's Rib*, which was first published in 1948, but today is still fresh and apt in its wit and viewpoint. Herschberger describes the work of Robert Yerkes, a pioneer investigator in the field of primatology, and quotes a passage from his book, Chimpanzees:

*In the picture of behavior which is characteristic of which is characteristic of femininity in the chimpanzee, the biological basis of prostitution of sexual function stands revealed. The mature and sexually experienced female trades upon her ability to satisfy the sexual urge of the male.* (1943, p. 86)

By imagining how Josie (a female member of the world-renowned chimpanzee colony collected and studied by Yerkes in the 1920s and later) might view the situation, Herschberger criticizes Yerkes' concept of prostitution:

*Jack (the largest male chimp in the colony) and I can go through almost the same motions, but by the time it gets down on paper, it has one name when Jack does it, and another if it was me. For instance, when Jack was at the (food) chute, and I gestured in sexual invitation to him, and after his acquiescence obtained the chute, this was put down...as downright prostitution. Please note that on March 21, as well as on other occasions, Jack came up to me repeatedly at the chute and similarly gestured in sexual invitation. Doesn't this suggest that he was trying to get me away from the chute by carnal lure? Or was Jack just being (as everyone wants to think) an impulsive male? The experimenter took it as the latter. (1918, p. 11).*

But that didn't end Josie's complaints:

*When Jack takes over the food chute, the report calls it his "natural dominance." When I do, it's "privilege" - conferred by him. If you humans could get enough perspective on your language, you'd find it as much fun as a zoo. While I'm up there lording it over the food chute, the investigator writes down "the male temporarily defers to her and allows her to act as if dominant over him." Can't I get any satisfaction out of life that isn't allowed by me some male chimp? Damn it! (p. 10)*

Apes and Dominance Hierarchies

The behavioral category of dominance hierarchies was for decades a major organizing principle for investigators of primate social behavior. Assuming presumably from their own perceptions of their world, and possibly from observations of caged primate, that primate species were naturally organized within male dominance hierarchies, they indeed saw male dominance hierarchies among the primate troops they observed whether they existed or not. An important function of the concept of dominance hierarchies, of particular relevance to Sociobiological theory, is that it was and is used to explain the evolution of male aggressivity and dominance, and therefore the inevitability of patriarchy. The theory is that the dominant (therefore presumably more aggressive and larger) males have more frequent access to the estrous females (those in heat) and thus pass on their "genes for aggressively" and dominance. Now that the questions of dominance hierarchies and the relationships between an individual male's status within the group and his access to females have begun to be investigated by primatologists, anthropologists, and sociobiology's who are not motivated to justify the sexual status quo, important observations clearly contradict the stereotyped descriptions and the evolutionary formula that was derived from it (Lancaster, 1975; Leavitt, 1975; Liebowitz, 1975, 1978; Rowell,

1972, 1974). It has now been shown that dominance hierarchies are neither universal nor always male. In many primate species dominance hierarchies cannot be discerned and in our closest relatives, the chimpanzees, interactions involving dominance appear to form a small fraction of total behaviors. In some species dominance is matrilineal and males derive their status from their mothers. For example, rank order among Japanese macaques, rhesus macaques, and vervets runs from the mother through the older daughter to the younger one, and the rank of male depends on that of his mother so long as he remains in her troop. Secondly, across primate species there is no correlation between dominance status in the group and sex, size, aggressiveness, leadership, territoriality, or mating behavior. In some carefully studied baboon and Japanese macaque troops, no evidence was found that dominant males have more frequent access to females than less dominant males (Eaton, 1974). The large silver-backed male gorilla may set troop movement, but he is mild-mannered and has no sexual prerogatives (Schaller, 1963). It has been suggested that some studies correlating mating frequency with dominance are weighed in favor of the dominant males who, being prominent, receive disproportionate observer attention, while the less dominant males wisely receive disproportionate observer attention, while the less dominant males wisely mate only when out of sight of the dominant males and human observers. Furthermore, estrous females usually are the ones who select mating partners, they are not passive recipients and they do not select only dominant males. Finally, when dominance interactions exist, they are usually situation dependent and change frequently. In some species and troops, rank among females appears to remain stable for long periods while rank among males may change with age and seniority in the troop. But in some species, whether males remain in a troop long enough to achieve seniority is determined by the females (Kolata, 1976; Pilbeam, 1973).

Models were chosen that fit stereotypic views of human relationships and social organization into male dominance hierarchies, while disregarding or ignoring animals whose behaviors failed to lend support to the stereotype. A favorite and highly popularized primate has been the savanna baboon, since early descriptions presented a familiar vignette: the large aggressive male who defends the troop and its territory, dominates the hierarchy of other males and all females, decides troop movements, and has first choice in food, sex and grooming. But this was a description of baboon life that had been observed in game parks and is a form of social organization that develops when predators are common and food availability is outside of the control of the baboons (Pilbeam, 1973). As the primatologist Thelma Rowell has shown, a wide range of life-styles exists among baboons in their natural habitats, and ecological factors are important in determining the social organization that any troop assumes. Among the population of forest baboons that Rowell observed for a period of five years (1972), the females and their young formed the stable core of the troop while the males moved periodically from troop to troop. It was the older females who decided when and in what direction the troop would move. Males did not establish rank ordering or hierarchies; they engaged in few aggressive encounters with other males and appeared largely to enjoy cooperative relations in their main task as lookouts for the troop. She concluded that "there is no evidence for any 'quality of dominance' either inherent or acquired by the animals which could influence the way in which rank relationships become structured" (1974, p. 151). Males did not defend the troop, since each member of the troop fled in response to danger, each being on its own, including the mothers with babies clinging to their fur. Rowell rarely saw encounters of any kind between troops, and they did not appear to be territorial. But when such generally peaceable primate troops are captured and/or fed by humans, aggressive encounters and hierarchies appear, clearly learned responses to environmental change.

In short, a reading of the recent literature on primate behavior reveals much richness and diversity of social arrangements and behaviors not only between primate species but also between troops within any particular species and within individual troops under differing ecological circumstances. As the primatologist Jane Lancaster has pointed out, "dominance is only one principle of social organization and even for the most dominance-oriented species, it is only one aspect of social life" (1975, p. 19). The elevation of the ideology of dominance hierarchies to a scientific principle underlying the social organization of primate did in fact structure and distort the observations that were made of primate behaviors and, consequently, also the course of primate research for many decades.

In a recent book, Sarah Blaffer Hrdy (1981) has written an extensive description of the innumerable varieties of sex differences and relationships between the sexes among primate species and an analysis of their possible significance. She emphasizes that while it is possible to support any proposition about primate or human characteristics by citing isolated examples, the meaningful approach is to look for patterns and find under what circumstances certain phenomena exist. For example, why or under what circumstances do males in polyg-

ynous species defer to females, who may "take priority at feeding sites and control social access to other group members" (p. 60), or what are the circumstances that explain females competing with each other, as well as with males, or, on the other hand, bonding together? Whatever the relationships may be of females to males in their troop - and indeed in some species they are subordinate under some circumstances - they do not conform, with a few exceptions, to the stereotype of them as one-dimensional male-protected mothers. Hrdy's important point is that those who seek to explain women's subordinate status as an inevitable evolutionary consequence of genetic patters laid down in and inherited from our primate ancestors, have to ignore a mass of contradictory evidence offered by modern female apes and monkeys who are, by and large, "highly competitive, socially involved and sexually assertive individuals" (p. 189). They protect territory, fight for their own or other mothers' young, take food from males, and bond with other females to fight aggressive males.

It is fortunate that some primatologists are replacing stereotypical notions careful observations of monkeys and apes and the cultures that they evolve within their particular ecological niches. But just as primatologists obviously would not study chimpanzees if they wanted to understand orangutan behavior, it should be equally obvious that we shall never understand human behavior by studying baboons or by trying to hunt down some prototypical primate. Observations of other primates can provide valuable clues about the range of biological and social possibilities that existed for evolving hominids, just as do observations of modern gathering and hunting societies. More complete understanding of the evolution of modern human societies, of dominance hierarchies, and of relationships based on gender depend upon the careful accumulation of cross-cultural data and upon the reconstruction of the archeological/anthropological record of our own evolving species, as well as the continuing study and re-analysis of our recorded social history.

Flowers, Ducks, and Rape

We can find a particularly extravagant use of human behavioral concepts and language in the descriptions of animals in Barash's second book, *The Whisperings Within*. He claims he does not want to be a "racy modern Aesop," but says he will, nonetheless, be telling many animal stories about "rape in ducks, adultery in bluebirds, prostitution in hummingbirds, divorce and lesbian pairing in gulls, even homosexual rape in parasitic worms" (p. 2). Noteworthy for its relevance to a key contemporary issue for women is Barash's view of the origins of rape. Among Sociobiologists, Barash in particular sees rape rampant in nature. First he cites the work of Daniel Janzen, "one of our most creative ecologists," who has pointed out that even plants "perform courtship displays, rape, promiscuity, and fickleness just as do animals." Barash goes on to describe what he evidently considers to be rape in flowers:

For example, plants with male flowers will "attempt" to achieve as many fertilizations as possible. How is this done? Among other things, they bombard female flowers with incredible amounts of pollen, and some even seem to have specially evolved capacities to rape female flowers, by growing a pollen tube which forces its way to the ovary within each female. (1979, p. 30).

So by defining the insertion of a pollen tube into a female flower as a rape, Barash begins to set the scene for the naturalness and - yes - the innocence of rape:

Plants that commit rape...are following evolutionary strategies that maximize their fitness. And, clearly, in neither case do the actors know what they are doing, or why. We human beings like to think we are different. We introspect, we are confident that we know what we are doing, and why. But we may have to open our minds and admit the possibility that our need to maximize our fitness may be whispering somewhere deep within us and that, now it or not, most of the time we are heeding these whisperings. (p. 31)

Barash here strongly suggests that rapists are simply unwitting tools of a blind genetic drive; that rape is an unconscious urge for reproductive success and hence, biologically speaking, both advantageous and inevitable. But he seems unaware that there may be a different definition of rape; that most women see it as an act of violence expressing hatred, contempt, and fear of women and also as a weapon of social control that keeps women from asserting autonomy and freedom of movement, and forces them to depend on male "protectors." If that is the definition of rape, and I would say women have the right and the knowledge to decide that, then it is not relevant to flowers. And to name what flowers do as "rape" is specifically to deny that rape is a sexual act of physical violence committed by men against women, an act embodying and enforcing the political power wielded by men over women.

Later in the book, Barash turns to rape among the birds and bees, especially mallard ducks. He explains that mallard ducks pair up for breeding, leaving some males unmated since there are usually more males than females. He then describes how one male or a group of unmated males may copulate

with a mated female without the normal preliminary courtship rituals that mated couples engage in and "despite her obvious and vigorous protest. If that's not rape, it is certainly very much like it" (p. 54). But first of all, he gives no indication whether this is a frequent or a rare occurrence nor does he describe the circumstances of the observation. Secondly, there is again the problem of language, in the use of the word protest. Courtship rituals are complex behaviors set in motion as a result of complex interactions between the hormonal and nervous systems of the animal, usually the female, and certain environmental conditions, for example, season of year. The female's state stimulates the male and, in turn, sets in motion the courtship rituals between partners, which further sequentially prime the reproductive systems for biological readiness to mate, ovulate, and fertilize - an intricate, balanced interplay between sight, smell, the brain, hormones, and gonads.

Thus, we could accommodate Barash's description of resisted copulation within the concept of the female's being biologically not primed for mating at the time of the bachelor's intrusion, but to impute rape and protest - intent and motivation - to ducks is again to use words for some purpose other than the clarity and accuracy required of scientific description and analysis. And the next page provides us with a lead to his purpose:

Rape in humans is by no means as simple, influenced as it is by an extremely complex overlay of cultural attitudes. Nevertheless mallard rape and bluebird adultery may have a degree of relevance to human behavior. Perhaps human rapists, in their own criminally misguided way are doing the best they can to maximize their fitness. If so, they are not that different from the sexually excluded bachelor mallards. (p. 55)

So Barash completes his portrait of the pitiful rapist: a lonesome fellow, left out of the mainstream of socially acceptable ways to copulate and so spread his genes about, he must force himself upon an unwilling female for the purpose of ensuring their reproduction.

In these examples, then, Barash used the word rape, which has a specific connotation in human terms, to describe behavior of a plant and a bird. This serves two purposes for Sociobiology: to establish that rape is biological and hence natural to defuse rape as an urgent political issue, which has at is heart a cultural tradition of misogyny and male violence directed against women.

Harems

Thus far in the discussion of methodology, the basic problem has been the projection of investigators' personal and cultural values and biases about human behavior in their society onto their observations and interpretations of animals and other cultures' behaviors. Since what is involved in these anthropomorphic and ethnocentric descriptions is language, we see that words become burdened with heavy implications. Language can be used to mold reality to a particular "truth," to impose a particular perception of the world as reality. Sociobiologists use language to mold the truth when they say that courted females are coy or the insects have evolved "rampant machismo" (Wilson, 1975b, p. 320), or that aggressivity is a universal trait of males. When Barash and other Sociobiologists use the word rape to describe a male flower's act of pollinating a female flower, they appropriate the word in order to remove rape from its sociopolitical context of male violence against women, to make it an act of sexual desire and of reproductive need, and finally, to claim for rape a biological basis and inevitability because of its universality in the animal world.

The traditional use of the word harem in primatology to describe a single-male troop of females is another example of biased language and andocentric fantasy that served to structure observations and conceptualizations concerning the social organization of such troops. In our culture, harem has a generally accepted connotation of a group of women who are dependent economically, socially, and presumably sexually on a powerful male whose bodily needs are their central concern and occupation.1 When that word was then used to signify single-male troops of female primates and their offspring, it automatically carried with it the entire complex of meanings and assumptions stereotypically associated with humans. It was assumed that the male was of central importance, defending the troop, making decisions, having his choice of sex partners, and in return was groomed, fed, and sexed by his harem of dependent females. Language substituted for actual observations, but it served ideology and circular logic by "demonstrating" that human male dominance and polygyny are innate since they are rooted in our primate ancestors. While hierarchical organization around a central male exists for some primate species under some circumstances, for many species, the solitary male is peripheral, functions mainly as a stud, and remains only so long as the females want him (Lancaster, 1975).

The Omission of Unwelcome
Animal Data

Another problem in Sociobiological writings is the omission of unwelcome data that confound the stereotype. For example, rather than being engaged by red winged blackbirds that exhibit polygyny and hypergamy, Sociobiologists, in the true scientific spirit of inquiry, could find it challenging to try to understand the South American male rhea bird that incubates and tends the 50 or so eggs that are laid by several females in the nest he builds. Or they could find it fascinating to explore shared parenting by examining the phenomenon of "double clutching," a situation in which female shore birds produce two clutches of eggs in quick succession, one of which becomes her responsibility and the other the male's. Or there is the female South American jacana bird who has a territory where she keeps a "harem" of males. She fills with eggs the nest that each male builds in his own sub territory and leaves him to incubate them and tend the brood (Bonner, 1980). Many bonded sea bird pairs take turns sitting on the nest while the partner goes out to sea to bring back fish. Some penguins have an even more elaborate system whereby both partners fish together leaving the young in a huge crèche tended by a few adults. The emperor penguin father remains nearly immobile during the two months he incubates his offspring's egg in a fold of skin about his feet, while the mother hunts for food. Bonner notes that monogamy is the main mating system among animals in which both sexes share in parental care (p. 156), and I wonder why Sociobiologists do not use this phenomenon as a "natural" model for human social organization as much as they do examples of male promiscuity and female domesticity.

ENDNOTES
1 For a different and multidimensional view of harems and the Muslim women who inhabit them, see Ahmed (1982).

**Study Questions**

1. What does she say about biological determination? Compare her ideas to those of Gould.

2. What purpose does a simple concept of male and female nature serve? Why would dominant culture put forth these ideas?

3. What do you think she would say about the nature versus nurture argument?

4. What is sociobiology? Why is she particularly critical of it?

5. What logical flaws does she see with sociobiology? What examples does she use?

6. Do you think there are sex-based characteristics that are "natural"? What are they? How would Bleier respond?

.

# "THE CLAN OF ONE-BREASTED WOMEN"

## Terry Tempest Williams

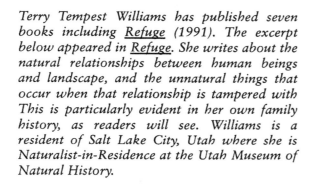

*Terry Tempest Williams has published seven books including Refuge (1991). The excerpt below appeared in Refuge. She writes about the natural relationships between human beings and landscape, and the unnatural things that occur when that relationship is tampered with This is particularly evident in her own family history, as readers will see. Williams is a resident of Salt Lake City, Utah where she is Naturalist-in-Residence at the Utah Museum of Natural History.*

I belong to a Clan of One-breasted Women. My mother, my grandmothers, and six aunts have all had mastectomies. Seven are dead. The two who survive have just completed rounds of chemotherapy and radiation.

I've had my own problems: two biopsies for breast cancer and a small tumor between my ribs diagnosed as "a border-line malignancy."

This is my family history.

Most statistics tell us breast cancer is genetic, hereditary, with rising percentages attached to fatty diets, childlessness, or becoming pregnant after thirty. What they don't say is living in Utah may be the greatest hazard of all.

We are a Mormon family with roots in Utah since 1847. The word-of-wisdom, a religious doctrine of health, kept the women in my family aligned with good foods: no coffee, no tea, tobacco, or alcohol. For the most part, these women were finished having their babies by the time they were thirty. And only one faced breast cancer prior to 1960. Traditionally, as a group of people, Mormons have a low rate of cancer.

Is our family a cultural anomaly? The truth is we didn't think about it. Those who did, usually the men, simply said, "bad genes." The women's attitude was stoic. Cancer was part of life. On February 16, 1971, the eve before my mother's surgery, I accidently picked up the telephone and overheard her ask my grandmother what she could expect.

"Diane, it is one of the most spiritual experiences you will ever encounter."

I quietly put down the receiver.

Two days later, my father took my three brothers and me to the hospital to visit her. She met us in the lobby in a wheelchair. No bandages were visible. I'll never forget her radiance, the way she held herself in a purple velour robe and how she gathered us around her.

"Children, I am fine. I want you to know I felt the arms of God around me."

We believed her. My father cried. Our mother, his wife, was thirty-eight years old.

Two years ago, after my mother's death from cancer, my father and I were having dinner together. He had just returned from St. George where his construction company was putting in natural gas lines for towns in southern Utah. He spoke of his love for the country: the sandstoned landscape, bare-boned and beautiful. He had just finished hiking the Kolob trail in Zion National Park. We got caught up in reminiscing, recalling with fondness our walk up Angle's Landing on his fiftieth birthday and the years our family had vacationed there. This was a remembered landscape where we had been raised.

Over dessert, I shared a recurring dream of mine. I told my father that for years, as long as I could remember, I saw this flash of light in the night in the desert. That this image had so permeated my being, I could not venture south without seeing it again, on the horizon, illuminating buttes and mesas.

"You did see it," he said.

"Saw what?" I asked, a bit tentative.

"The bomb. The cloud. We were driving home from Riverside, California. You were sitting on your mother's lap. She was pregnant. In fact, I remember the date, September 7, 1957. We had just gotten out of the Service. We were driving north, past Las Vegas. It was an hour or so before dawn, when this explosion went off. We not only heard it, but felt it. I thought the oil tanker in front of us had blown up. We pulled over and suddenly, rising from the desert floor, we saw it, clearly, this golden-stemmed cloud, the mushroom. The sky seemed to vibrate with an eerie pink glow. Within a few minutes, a light ash was raining on the car."

I stared at my father. This was new information to me.

"I thought you knew that," my father said. "It was a common occurrence in the fifties."

It was at this moment I realized the deceit I had been living under. Children growing up in the American Southwest, drinking contaminated milk from contaminated cows, even from the contaminated breasts of their mother, my mother—members, years later, of the Clan of One-breasted Women.

It is a well-known story in the Desert West, "The Day We Bombed Utah," or perhaps, "The Years We Bombed Utah."[1] Above ground atomic testing in Nevada took place from January 27, 1951, through July 11, 1962. Not only were the winds blowing north, covering "low use segments of the population" with fallout and leaving sheep dead in their tracks, but the climate was right.[2] The United States of the 1950s was red, white, and blue. The Korean War was raging. McCarthyism was rampant. Ike was it and the Cold War was hot. If you were against nuclear testing, you were for a Communist regime.

Much has been written about this "American nuclear tragedy." Public health was secondary to national security. The Atomic Energy Commissioner, Thomas Murray, said, "Gentlemen, we must not let anything interfere with this series of tests, nothing."[3]

Again and again, the American public was told by its government, in spite of burns, blisters, and nausea, "It has been found that the tests may be conducted with adequate assurance of safety under conditions prevailing at the bombing reserva-

tions."[4] Assuaging public fears was simply a matter of public relations. "Your best action," an Atomic Energy Commission booklet read, "is not to be worried about fallout." A news release typical of the times stated, "We find no basis for concluding that harm to any individual has resulted from radioactive fallout."[5]

On August 30, 1979, during Jimmy Carter's presidency, a suit was filed entitled "Irene Allen vs. the United States of America." Mrs. Allen was the first to be alphabetically listed with twenty-four test cases, representative of nearly 1200 plaintiffs seeking compensation from the United States government for cancers caused from nuclear testing in Nevada.

Irene Allen lived in Hurricane, Utah. She was the mother of five children and had been widowed twice. Her first husband with their two oldest boys had watched the tests from the roof of the local high school. He died of leukemia in 1956. Her second husband died of pancreatic cancer in 1978.

In a town meeting conducted by Utah Senator Orrin Hatch, shortly before the suit was filed, Mrs. Allen said, "I am not blaming the government, I want you to know that, Senator Hatch. But I thought if my testimony could help in any way so this wouldn't happen again to any of the generations coming up after us . . . I am really happy to be here this day to bear testimony of this."[6]

God-fearing people. This is just one story in an anthology of thousands.

On May 10, 1984, Judge Bruce S. Jenkins handed down his opinion. Ten of the plaintiffs were awarded damages. It was the first time a federal court had determined that nuclear tests had been the cause of cancers. For the remaining fourteen test cases, the proof of causation was not sufficient. In spite of the split decision, it was considered a landmark ruling.[7] It was not to remain so for long.

In April, 1987, the 10th Circuit Court of Appeals overturned Judge Jenkins' ruling on the basis that the United States was protected from suit by the legal doctrine of sovereign immunity, the centuries-old idea from England in the days of absolute monarchs.[8]

In January, 1988, the Supreme Court refused to review the Appeals Court decision. To our court system, it does not matter whether the United States Government was irresponsible, whether it lied to its citizens or even that citizens died from the fallout of nuclear testing. What matters is that our government is immune. "The King can do no wrong."

In Mormon culture, authority is respected, obedience is revered, and independent thinking is not. I was taught as a young girl not to "make waves" or "rock the boat."

"Just let it go—" my mother would say. "You know how you feel, that's what counts."

For many years, I did just that—listened, observed, and quietly formed my own opinions within a culture that rarely asked questions because they had all the answers. But one by one, I watched the women in my family die common, heroic deaths. We sat in waiting rooms hoping for good news, always receiving the bad. I cared for them, bathed their scarred bodies and kept their secrets. I watched beautiful women become bald as cytoxan, cisplatin and adriamycin were injected into their veins. I held their foreheads as they vomited green-black bile and I shot them with morphine when the pain became inhuman. In the end, I witnessed their last peaceful breaths, becoming a midwife to the rebirth of their souls. But the price of obedience became too high.

The fear and inability to question authority that ultimately killed rural communities in Utah during atmospheric testing of atomic weapons was the same fear I saw being held in my mother's body. Sheep. Dead sheep. The evidence is buried.

I cannot prove that my mother, Diane Dixon Tempest, or my grandmothers, Lettie Romney Dixon and Kathryn Blackett Tempest, along with my aunts contracted cancer from nuclear fallout in Utah. But I can't prove they didn't.

My father's memory was correct, the September blast we drove through in 1957 was part of Operation Plumbbob, one of the most intensive series of bomb tests to be initiated. The flash of light in the night in the desert I had always thought was a dream developed into a family nightmare. It took fourteen years, from 1957 to 1971, for cancer to show up in my mother-the same time, Howard L. Andrews, an authority on radioactive fallout at the National Institutes of Health, says radiation cancer requires to become evident. The more I learn about what it means to be a "downwinder," the more questions I drown in.

What I do know, however, is that as a Mormon woman of the fifth generation of "Latter-Day-Saints," I must question everything, even if it means losing my faith, even if it means becoming a member of a border tribe among my own people. Tolerating blind obedience in the name of patriotism or religion ultimately takes our lives.

When the Atomic Energy Commission described the country north of the Nevada Test Site as "virtually uninhabited desert terrain," my family members were some of the "virtual uninhabitants."

One night, I dreamed women from all over the world circling a blazing fire in the desert. They spoke of change, of how they hold the moon in their bellies and wax and wane with its phases. They mocked at the presumption of even-tempered beings and made promises that they would never fear the witch inside themselves. The women danced wildly as sparks broke away from the flames and entered the night sky as stars.

And they sang a song given to them by Shoshoni grandmothers:

Ah ne nah, nah
nin nah nah—
Ah ne nah, nah
nin nah nah—
Nyaga mutzi
oh ne nay—
Nyaga mutzi
oh ne nay—[10]

The women danced and drummed and sang for weeks, preparing themselves for what was to come. They would reclaim the desert for the sake of their children, for the sake of the land.

A few miles downwind from the fire circle, bombs were being, tested. Rabbits felt the tremors. Their soft leather pads on paws and get recognized the shaking sands while the roots of mesquite and sage were smoldering. Rocks were hot from the inside out and dust devils hummed unnaturally. And each time there was another nuclear test, ravens watched the desert heave. Stretch marks appeared. The land was losing its muscle.

The women couldn't bear it any longer. They were mothers. They had suffered labor pains but always under the promise of birth. The red hot pains beneath the desert promised death only as each bomb became a stillborn. A contract had been broken between human beings and the land. A new contract was being drawn by the women who understood the fate of the earth as their own.

Under the cover of darkness, ten women slipped under the barbed wire fence and entered the contaminated country. They were trespassing. They walked toward the town of Mercury in moonlight, taking their cues from coyote, kit fox, antelope squirrel, and quail. They moved quietly and deliberately through the maze of Joshua trees. When a hint of daylight appeared they rested, drinking tea and sharing their rations of food. The women closed their eyes. The time had come to protest with the heart, that to deny one's genealogy with the earth was to commit treason against one's soul.

At dawn, the women draped themselves in mylar, wrapping long streamers of silver plastic around their arms to blow in the breeze. They wore clear masks that became the faces of humanity. And when they arrived on the edge of Mercury, they carried all the butterflies of a summer day in their wombs. They paused to allow their courage to settle.

The town which forbids pregnant women and children to enter because of radiation risks to their health was asleep. The women moved through the streets as winged messengers, twirling around each other in slow motion, peeking inside homes and watching the easy sleep of men and women. They were astonished by such stillness and periodically would utter a shrill note or low cry just to verify life.

The residents finally awoke to what appeared as strange apparitions. Some simply stared. Others called authorities, and in time, the women were apprehended by wary soldiers dressed in desert fatigues. They were taken to a white, square building on the other edge of Mercury. When asked who they were and why they were there, the women replied, "We are mothers and we have come to reclaim the desert for our children."

The soldiers arrested them. As the ten women were blindfolded and handcuffed, they began singing:

You can't forbid us everything
You can't forbid us to think—
You can't forbid our tears to flow
And you can't stop the songs that we sing.

The women continued to sing louder and louder, until they heard the voices of their sisters moving across the mesa.

Ah ne nah, nah
nin nah nah—
Ah ne nah, nah
nin nah nah—
Nyaga mutzi
oh ne nay—
Nyaga mutzi
oh ne nay—

"Call for re-enforcement," one soldier said.

"We have," interrupted one woman. "We have —and you have no idea of our numbers."

On March 18, 1988, I crossed the line at the Nevada Test Site and was arrested with nine other Utahns for trespassing on military lands. They are still conducting nuclear tests in the desert. Ours was an act of civil disobedience. But as I walked toward the town of Mercury, it was more than a gesture of peace. It was a gesture on behalf of the Clan of One-breasted Women.

As one officer cinched the handcuffs around my wrists, another frisked my body. She found a pen and a pad of paper tucked inside my left boot.

"And these?" she asked sternly.

"Weapons," I replied.

Our eyes met. I smiled. She pulled the leg of my trousers back over my boot.

"Step forward, please," she said as she took my arm.

We were booked under an afternoon sun and bussed to Tonapah, Nevada. It was a two-hour ride. This was familiar country to me. The Joshua trees standing their ground had been named by my ancestors who believed they looked like prophets pointing west to the promised land. These were the same trees that bloomed each spring, flowers appearing like white flames in the Mojave. And I recalled a full moon in May when my mother and I had walked among them, flushing out mourning doves and owls.

The bus stopped short of town. We were released. The officials thought it was a cruel joke to leave us stranded in the desert with no way to get home. What they didn't realize is that we were home, soul-centered and strong, women who recognized the sweet smell of sage as fuel for our spirits.

## ENDNOTES

1. Fuller, John G., *The Day We Bombed Utah* (New York: New American Library, 1984).

2. Discussion on March 14, 1988, with Carole Gallagher, photographer and author, *Nuclear Towns: The Secret War in the American Southwest,* to be published by Doubleday, Spring, 1990.

3. Szasz, Ferenc M., "Downwind From the Bomb," *Nevada Historical Society Quarterly,* Fall 1987 Vol. XXX, No. 3, p. 185.

4. Fradkin, Philip L., *Fallout* (Tucson: University of Arizona Press, 1989), 98.

5. Ibid., 109.

6. Town meeting held be Senator Orrin Hatch in St. George, Utah, April 17, 1979, transcript, 26–28.

7. Fradkin, Op. cit., 228.

8. U. S. vs Allen, 816 Federal Reporter, 2nd/1417 (10th Circuit Court 1987), cert. denied, 108 S. CT. 694 (1988).

9. Fradkin, Op.cit., 116.

10. This song was sung by the Western Shoshone women as they crossed the line at the Nevada Test Site on March 18, 1988, as part of their "Reclaim the Land" action. The translation they gave was: "Consider the rabbit how gently they walk on the earth. Consider the rabbits how gently they walk on the earth. We remember them. We can walk gently also. We remember them. We can walk gently also."

**Study Questions**

1. Explain the significance of the title.

2. How can cancer be "spiritual"?

# IDENTITY

# WHO'S PASSING FOR WHO?

*Langston Hughes (1902-1967)*

*Langston Hughes was born in Joplin, Missouri, in 1902. After graduating from high school in Cleveland, Ohio, Hughes lived and traveled in Mexico, Europe, and Africa for about five years. He moved to Harlem in 1924 and his first collection of poems,* The Weary Blues, *was published in 1926. While Hughes acknowledged the influence of Paul Lawrence Dunbar and Carl Sandburg upon his writing, he creatively used the black folk expressions of spirituals, blues, and jazz as the basis of his poetic expression. He became one of the most influenial writers of the Harlem Renaissance of the 1920s through his powerful depiction of urban black life. He was a prolific writer who published poetry, fiction, drama, essay, and history. Hughes is one of the dominant voices in American literature of this century.*

*This short story is an example of his use of humor to expose both the pretensions of American bourgeois life and the hypocritical nature of American racism.*

One of the great difficulties about being a member of a minority race is that so many kindhearted, well-meaning bores gather around to help you. Usually, to tell the truth, they have nothing to help with, except their company—which is often appallingly dull.

Some members of the Negro race seem very well able to put up with it, though, in these uplifting years. Such was Caleb Johnson, colored social worker, who was always dragging around with him some nondescript white person or two, inviting them to dinner, showing them Harlem, ending up at the Savoy—much to the displeasure of whatever friends of his might be out that evening for fun, not sociology.

Friends are friends and, unfortunately, over-earnest uplifters are uplifters—no matter what color they may be. If it were the white race that was ground down instead of Negroes, Caleb Johnson would be one of the first to offer Nordics the sympathy of his utterly inane society, under the impression that somehow he would be doing them a great deal of good.

You see, Caleb, and his white friends, too, were all bores. Or so we, who lived in Harlem's literary bohemia during the "Negro Renaissance," thought. We literary ones in those days considered ourselves too broad-minded to be bothered with questions of color. We liked people of any race who smoked incessantly, drank liberally, wore complexion and morality as loose garments, and made fun of anyone who didn't do likewise. We snubbed and high-hatted any Negro or white luckless enough not to understand Gertrude Stein, Ulysses, Man Ray, the theremin, Jean Toomer or George Antheil. By the end of the 1920's Caleb was just catching up to Dos Passos. He thought H. G. Wells good.

We met Caleb one night in Small's. He had three assorted white folks in tow. We would have passed him by with but a nod had he not hailed us enthusiastically, risen, and introduced us with great acclaim to his friends, who turned out to be schoolteachers from Iowa, a woman and two men. They appeared amazed and delighted to meet all at once two Negro writers and a black painter in the flesh. They invited us to have a drink with them. Money being scarce with us, we deigned to sit down at their table.

The white lady said, "I've never met a Negro writer before."

The two men added, "Neither have we."

"Why, we know any number of *white* writers," we three dark bohemians declared with bored nonchalance.

"But Negro writers are much more rare," said the lady.

"There are plenty in Harlem," we said.

"But not in Iowa," said one of the men, shaking his mop of red hair.

"There are no good *white* writers in Iowa either, are there?" we asked superciliously.

"Oh yes, Ruth Suckow came from there."

Whereupon we proceeded to light in upon Ruth Suckow as old hat and to annihilate her in favor of Kay Boyle. The way we flung names around seemed to impress both Caleb and his white guests. This, of course, delighted us, though we were too young and too proud to admit it.

The drinks came and everything was going well, all of us drinking, and we three showing off in a high-brow manner, when suddenly at the table just behind us a man got up and knocked down a woman. He was a brownskin man. The woman was blonde. As she rose, he knocked her down again. Then the red-haired man from Iowa got up and knocked the colored man down.

He said, "Keep your hands off that white woman."

The man got up and said, "She's not a white woman. She's my wife."

One of the waiters added, "She's not white, sir, she's colored."

Whereupon the man from Iowa looked puzzled, dropped his fists, and said, "I'm sorry."

The colored man said, "What are you doing up here in Harlem anyway, interfering with my family affairs?"

The white man said, "I thought she was a white woman."

The woman who had been on the floor rose and said, "Well, I'm not a white woman, I'm colored, and you leave my husband alone."

Then they both lit in on the gentleman from Iowa. It took all of us and several waiters, too, to separate them. When it was over, the manager requested us to kindly pay our bill and get out. He said we were disturbing the peace. So we all left. We went to a fish restaurant down the street. Caleb was terribly apologetic to his white friends. We artists were both mad and amused.

"Why did you say you were sorry," Said the colored painter to the visitor from Iowa, "after you'd hit that man—and then found out it wasn't a white woman you were defending, but merely a light colored woman who looked white?"

"Well," answered the red-haired Iowan, "I didn't mean to be butting in if they were all the same race."

"Don't you think a woman needs defending from a brute, no matter what race she may be?" asked the painter.

"Yes, but I think it's up to you to defend your own women."

"Oh, so you'd divide up a brawl according to races, no matter who was right?"

"Well, I wouldn't say that."

"You mean you wouldn't defend a colored woman whose husband was knocking her down?" asked the poet.

Before the visitor had time to answer, the painter said, "No! You just got mad because you thought a black man was hitting a *white* woman."

"But she *looked* like a white woman," countered the man.

"Maybe she was just passing for colored," I said.

"Like some Negroes pass for white," Caleb interposed.

"Anyhow, I don't like it," said the colored painter, "the way you stopped defending her when you found out she wasn't white."

"No, we don't like it," we all agreed except Caleb.

Caleb said in extenuation, "But Mr. Stubblefield is new to Harlem."

The red-haired white man said, "Yes, it's my first time here."

"Maybe Mr. Stubblefield ought to stay out of Harlem," we observed.

"I agree," Mr. Stubblefield said. "Good night."

He got up then and there and left the café. He stalked as he walked. His red head disappeared into the night.

"Oh, that's too bad," said the white couple who remained. "Stubby's temper just got the best of him. But explain to us, are many, colored folks really as fair as that woman?"

"Sure, lots of them have more white blood than colored, and pass for white."

"Do they?" said the lady and gentleman from Iowa.

"You never read Nella Larsen?" we asked.

"She writes novels," Caleb explained. "She's part white herself."

"Read her," we advised. "Also read the *Autobiography of an Ex-Coloured Man*." Not that we had read it ourselves—because we paid but little attention to the older colored writers—but we knew it was about passing for white.

We all ordered fish and settled down comfortably to shocking our white friends with tales about how many Negroes there were passing for white all over America. We were determined to *épater le burgeois* real good via this white couple we had cornered, when the woman leaned over the table in the midst of our dissertations and said, "Listen, gentlemen, you needn't spread the word, but me and my husband aren't white either. We've just been *passing* for white for the last fifteen years."

"What?"

"We're colored, too, just like you," said the husband. "But it's better passing for white because we make more money."

Well, that took the wind out of us. It took the wind out of Caleb, too. He thought all the time he was showing some fine white folks Harlem—and they were as colored as he was!

Caleb almost never cursed. But this time he said, "I'll be damned!"

Then everybody laughed. And laughed! We almost had hysterics. All at once we dropped our professionally self-conscious "Negro" manners, became natural, ate fish, and talked and kidded freely like colored folks do when there are no white folks around. We really had fun then, joking about that red-haired guy who mistook a fair colored woman for white. After the fish we went to two or three more night spots and drank, until five o'clock in the morning.

Finally we put the light-colored people in a taxi heading downtown. They turned to shout a last

good-by. The cab was just about to move off when the woman called to the driver to stop.

She leaned out the window and said with a grin, "Listen, boys! I hate to confuse you again. But, to tell the truth my husband and I aren't really colored at all. We're white. We just thought we'd kid you by passing for colored a little while—just as you said Negroes sometimes pass for white."

She laughed as they sped off toward Central Park, waving, "Good-by!"

We didn't say a thing. We just stood there on the corner in Harlem dumbfounded—not knowing now *which* way we'd been fooled. Were they really white—passing for colored? Or colored—passing for white?

Whatever race they were, they had had too much fun at our expense—even if they did pay for the drinks.

**Study Questions**

1. Describe the narrator of this story. What are his values, beliefs, and attitudes?

2. How is racial or ethnic identity formed in America? How do we know what race someone is?

3. What does "passing" mean? Are there different ways to define it? Who do people pass? Is it wrong? Explain.

4. Does this story hasve anything to say about domestic violence? Male-Female relationships?

5. Has the racial climate changed in America since this story was published in the 1930s? Could the events in this story happen today? Why or why not?

6. Who is passing in this story? Explain.

# "RECITATIF"

## Toni Morrison

*Toni Morrison was born in 1931. She has written numerous novels, beginning with* The Bluest Eye *in 1970,* Sula *in 1973, and she is perhaps best known for her Pultizer Award winning* Beloved *in 1987. She also received the Nobel Prize for Literature in 1993. Currently, she is the Robert F. Goheen Professsor of the Humanities at Princeton University. This short story was published in 1991. It analyzes the intersections of race and class in terms of the relationship of two young girls from their meeting in an orphanage until they become adults.*

My mother danced all night and Roberta was sick. That's why we were taken to St. Bonny's. People want to put their arms around you when you tell them you were in a shelter, but it really wasn't bad. No big long room with one hundred beds like Bellevue. There were four to a room, and when Roberta and me came, there was a shortage of state kids, so we were the only ones assigned to 406 and could go from bed to bed if we wanted to. And we wanted to, too. We changed beds every night and for the whole four months we were there we never picked one out as our own permanent bed.

It didn't start out that way. The minute I walked in and the Big Bozo introduced us, I got sick to my stomach. It was one thing to be taken out of your own bed early in the morning—it was something else to be stuck in a strange place with a girl from a whole other race. And Mary, that's my mother, she was right. Every now and then she would stop dancing long enough to tell me something important and one of the things she said was that they never washed their hair and they smelled funny. Roberta sure did. Smell funny, I mean. So when the Big Bozo

(nobody ever called her Mrs. Itkin, just like nobody every said St. Bonaventure)—when she said, "Twyla, this is Roberta. Roberta, this Twyla. Make each other welcome." I said, "My mother won't like you putting me in here."

"Good," said Bozo. "Maybe then she'll come and take you home."

How's that for mean? If Roberta had laughed I would have killed her, but she didn't. She just walked over to the window and stood with her back to us.

"Turn around," said the Bozo. "Don't be rude. Now Twyla. Roberta. When you hear a loud buzzer, that's the call for dinner. Come down to the first floor. Any fights and no movie." And then, just to make sure we knew what we would be missing, *The Wizard of Oz.*

Roberta must have thought I meant that my mother would be mad about my being put in the shelter. Not about rooming with her, because as soon as Bozo left she came over to me and said, "Is your mother sick too?"

"No," I said. "She just likes to dance all night."

"Oh," she nodded her head and I liked the way she understood things so fast. So for the moment it didn't matter that we looked like salt and pepper standing there and that's what the other kids called us sometimes. We were eight years old and got F's all the time. Me because I couldn't remember what I read or what the teacher said. And Roberta because she couldn't read at all and didn't even listen to the teacher. She wasn't good at anything except jacks, at which she was a killer: pow scoop pow scoop pow scoop.

We didn't like each other all that much at first, but nobody else wanted to play with us because we weren't real orphans with beautiful dead parents in the sky. We were dumped. Even the New York City

Puerto Ricans and the upstate Indians ignored us. All kinds of kids were in there, black ones, white ones, even two Koreans. The food was good, though. At least I thought so. Roberta hated it and left whole pieces of things on her plate: Spam, Salisbury steak—even jello with fruit cocktail in it, and she didn't care if I ate what she wouldn't. Mary's idea of supper was popcorn and a can of Yoo-Hoo. Hot mashed potatoes and two weenies was like Thanksgiving for me.

It really wasn't bad, St. Bonny's. The big girls on the second floor pushed us around now and then. But that was all. They wore lipstick and eyebrow pencil and wobbled their knees while they watched TV. Fifteen, sixteen, even, some of them were. They were put-out girls, scared runaways most of them. Poor little girls who fought their uncles off but looked tough to us, and mean. God did they look mean. The staff tried to keep them separate from the younger children, but sometimes they caught us watching them in the orchard where they played radios and danced with each other. They'd light out after us and pull our hair or twist our arms. We were scared of them, Roberta and me, but neither of us wanted the other one to know it. So we got a good list of dirty names we could shout back when we ran from them through the orchard. I used to dream a lot and almost always the orchard was there. Two acres, four maybe, of these little apple trees. Hundreds of them. Empty and crooked like beggar women when I first came to St. Bonny's but fat with flowers when I left. I don't know why I dreamt about that orchard so much. Nothing really happened there. Nothing all that important, I mean. Just the big girls dancing and playing the radio. Roberta and me watching. Maggie fell down there once. The kitchen woman with legs like parentheses. And the big girls laughed at her. We should have helped her up, I know, but we were scared of those girls with lipstick and eyebrow pencil. Maggie couldn't talk. The kids said she had her tongue cut out, but I think she was just born that way: mute. She was old and sandy-colored and she worked in the kitchen. I don't know if she was nice or not. I just remember her legs like parentheses and how she rocked when she walked. She worked from early in the morning till two o'clock, and if she was late, if she had too much cleaning and didn't get out till two-fifteen or so, she'd cut through the orchard so she wouldn't miss her bus and have to wait another hour. She wore this really stupid little hat—a kid's hat with ear flaps—and she wasn't much taller than we were. A really awful little hat. Even for a mute, it was dumb—dressing like a kid and never saying anything at all.

"But what about if somebody tries to kill her?" I used to wonder about that. "Or what if she wants to cry? Can she cry?"

"Sure," Roberta said. "But just tears. No sounds come out."

"She can't scream?"

"Nope. Nothing."

"Can she hear?"

"I guess."

"Let's call her," I said. And we did.

"Dummy! Dummy!" She never turned her head.

"Bow legs! Bow legs!" Nothing. She just rocked on, the chin straps of her baby-boy hat swaying from side to side. I think we were wrong. I think she could hear and didn't let on. And it shames me even now to think there was somebody in there after all who heard us call her those names and couldn't tell on us.

We got along all right, Roberta and me. Changed beds every night, got F's in civics and communication skills and gym. The Bozo was disappointed in us, she said. Out of 130 of us state cases, 90 were under twelve. Almost all were real orphans with beautiful dead parents in the sky. We were the only ones dumped and the only ones with F's in three classes including gym. So we got along—what with her leaving whole pieces of things on her plate and being nice about not asking questions.

I think it was the day before Maggie fell down that we found out our mothers were coming to visit us on the same Sunday. We had been at the shelter twenty-eight days (Roberta twenty-eight and a half) and this was their first visit with us. Our mothers would come at ten o'clock in time for chapel, then lunch with us in the teachers' lounge. I thought if my dancing mother met her sick mother it might be good for her. And Roberta thought her sick mother would get a big bang out of a dancing one. We got excited about it and curled each other's hair. After breakfast we sat on the bed watching the road from the window. Roberta's socks were still wet. She washed them the night before and put them on the radiator to dry. They hadn't, but she put them on anyway because their tops were so pretty—scalloped in pink. Each of us had a purple construction-paper basket that we had made in craft class. Mine had a yellow crayon rabbit on it. Roberta's had eggs with wiggly lines of color. Inside were cellophane grass and just the jelly beans because I'd eaten the two marshmallow eggs they gave us. The Big Bozo came herself to get us. Smiling she told us we looked very nice and to come downstairs. We were so surprised by the smile we'd never seen before, neither of us moved.

"Don't you want to see your mommies?"

I stood up first and spilled the jelly beans all over the floor. Bozo's smile disappeared while we scrambled to get the candy up off the floor and put it back in the grass.

She escorted us downstairs to the first floor, where the other girls were lining up to file into the chapel. A bunch of grown-ups stood to one side. Viewers mostly. The old biddies who wanted servants and the fags who wanted company looking for children they might want to adopt. Once in a while a grandmother. Almost never anybody young or anybody whose face wouldn't scare you in the night. Because if any of the real orphans had young relatives they wouldn't be real orphans. I saw Mary right away. She had on those green slacks I hated and hated even more now because didn't she know we were going to chapel? And that fur jacket with the pocket linings so ripped she had to pull to get her hands out of them. But her face was pretty—like always, and she smiled and waved like she was the little girl looking for her mother—not me.

I walked slowly, trying not to drop the jelly beans and hoping the paper handle would hold. I had to use my last Chiclet because by the time I finished cutting everything out, all the Elmer's was gone. I am left-handed and the scissors never worked for me. It didn't matter, though; I might just as well have chewed the gum. Mary dropped to her knees and grabbed me, mashing the basket, the jelly beans, and the grass into her ratty fur jacket.

"Twyla, baby. Twyla, baby,"

I could have killed her. Already I heard the big girls in the orchard the next time saying, "Twyyyyyla, baby!" But I couldn't stay mad at Mary while she was smiling and hugging me and smelling of Lady Esther dusting powder. I wanted to stay buried in her fur all day.

To tell the truth I forgot about Roberta. Mary and I got in line for the traipse into chapel and I was feeling proud because she looked so beautiful even in those ugly green slacks that made her behind stick out. A pretty mother on earth is better than a beautiful dead one in the sky even if she did leave you all alone to go dancing.

I felt a tap on my shoulder, turned, and saw Roberta smiling. I smiled back, but not too much lest somebody think this visit was the biggest thing that ever happened in my life. Then Roberta said, "Mother, I want you to meet my roommate, Twyla. And that's Twyla's mother."

I looked up it seemed for miles. She was big. Bigger than any man and on her chest was the biggest cross I'd ever seen. I swear it was six inches long each way. And in the crook of her arm was the biggest Bible ever made.

Mary, simple-minded as ever, grinned and tried to yank her hand out of the pocket with the raggedy lining—to shake hands, I guess. Roberta's mother looked down at me and then looked down at Mary too. She didn't say anything, just grabbed Roberta with her Bible-free hand and stepped out of line, walking quickly to the rear of it. Mary was still grinning because she's not too swift when it comes to what's really going on. Then this light bulb goes off in her head and she says "That bitch!" really loud and us almost in the chapel now. Organ music whining; the Bonny Angels singing sweetly. Everybody in the world turned around to look. And Mary would have kept it up—kept calling names if I hadn't squeezed her hand as hard as I could. That helped a little, but she still twitched and crossed and uncrossed her legs all through service. Even groaned a couple of times. Why did I think she would come there and act right? Slacks. No hat like the grandmothers and viewers, and groaning all the while. When we stood for hymns she kept her mouth shut. Wouldn't even look at the words on the page. She actually reached in her purse for a mirror to check her lipstick. All I could think of was that she really needed to be killed. The sermon lasted a year, and I knew the real orphans were looking smug again.

We were supposed to have lunch in the teacher's lounge, but Mary didn't bring anything, so we picked fur and cellophane grass off the mashed jelly beans and ate them. I could have killed her. I sneaked a look at Roberta. Her mother had brought chicken legs and ham sandwiches and oranges and a whole box of chocolate-covered grahams. Roberta drank milk from a thermos while her mother read the Bible to her.

Things are not right. The wrong food is always with the wrong people. Maybe that's why I got into waitress work later—to match up the right people with the right food. Roberta just let those chicken legs sit there, but she did bring a stack of grahams up to me later when the visit was over. I think she was sorry that her mother would not shake my mother's hand. And I liked that and I liked the fact that she didn't say a word about Mary groaning all the way through the service and not bringing any lunch.

Roberta left in May when the apple trees were heavy and white. On her last day we went to the orchard to watch the big girls smoke and dance by the radio. It didn't matter that they said, "Twyyyyyla, baby." We sat on the ground and breathed. Lady Esther. Apple blossoms. I still go soft when I smell one or the other. Roberta was going home. The big cross and the big Bible was coming to get her and she seemed sort of glad and sort of not. I thought I would die in that room of four beds without her and I knew Bozo had plans to move some other dumped kid in there with me. Roberta promised to write every day, which was really sweet of her because she couldn't read a lick so how could she write anybody. I would have drawn pictures and sent them to her but she never gave me her address. Little by little she faded. Her wet socks with the pink scalloped tops and her big serious-looking eyes—that's all I could catch when I tried to bring her to mind.

I was working behind the counter at the Howard Johnson's on the Thruway just before the Kingston exit. Not a bad job. Kind of a long ride from Newburgh, but okay once I got there. Mine was the second night shift—eleven to seven. Very light until a Greyhound checked in for breakfast around six-thirty. At that hour the sun was all the way clear of the hills behind the restaurant. The place looked better at night—more like shelter—but I loved it when the sun broke in, even if it did show all the cracks in the vinyl and the speckled floor looked dirty no matter what the mop boy did.

It was August and a bus crowd was just unloading. They would stand around a long while: going to the john, and looking at gifts and junk-for-sale machines, reluctant to sit down so soon. Even to eat. I was trying to fill the coffee pots and get them all situated on the electric burners when I saw her. She was sitting in a booth smoking a cigarette with two guys smothered in head and facial hair. Her own hair was so big and wild I could hardly see her face. But the eyes. I would know them anywhere. She had on a powder-blue halter and shorts outfit and earrings the size of bracelets. Talk about lipstick and eyebrow pencil. She made the big girls look like nuns. I couldn't get off the counter until seven o'clock, but I kept watching the booth in case they got up to leave before that. My replacement was on time for a change, so I counted and stacked my receipts as fast as I could and signed off. I walked over to the booth, smiling and wondering if she would remember me. Or even if she wanted to remember me. Maybe she didn't want to be reminded of St. Bonny's or to have anybody know she was ever there. I know I never talked about it to anybody.

I put my hands in my apron pockets and leaned against the back of the booth facing them.

"Roberta? Roberta Fisk?"

She looked up. "Yeah?"

"Twyla."

She squinted for a second and then said, "Wow."

"Remember me?"

"Sure. Hey. Wow."

"It's been a while," I said, and gave a smile to the two hairy guys.

"Yeah. Wow. You work here?"

"Yeah," I said. "I live in Newburgh."

"Newburgh? No kidding?" She laughed then a private laugh that included the guys but only the guys, and they laughed with her. What could I do but laugh too and wonder why I was standing there with my knees showing out from under that uniform. Without looking I could see the blue and white triangle on my head, my hair shapeless in a net, my ankles thick in white oxfords. Nothing could have been less sheer than my stockings. There was this silence that came down right after I laughed. A silence it was her turn to fill up. With introductions, maybe, to her boyfriends on an invitation to sit down and have a Coke. Instead she lit a cigarette off the one she'd just finished and said, "We're on our way to the Coast. He's got an appointment with Hendrix." She gestured casually toward the boy next to her.

"Hendrix? Fantastic," I said. "Really fantastic. What's she doing now?"

Roberta coughed on her cigarette and the two guys rolled their eyes up at the ceiling.

"Hendrix. Jimi Hendrix, asshole. He's only the biggest—Oh, wow. Forget it."

I was dismissed without anyone saying goodbye, so I thought I would do it for her.

"How's your mother?" I asked. Her grin cracked her whole face. She swallowed. "Fine," she said. "How's yours?"

"Pretty as a picture," I said and turned away. The backs of my knees were damp. Howard Johnson's really was a dump in the sunlight.

James is as comfortable as a house slipper. He liked my cooking and I liked his big loud family. They have lived in Newburgh all of their lives and talk about it the way people do who have always known a home. His grandmother is a porch swing older than his father and when they talk about streets and avenues and buildings they call them names they no longer have. They still call the A & P Rico's because it stands on property once a mom and pop store owned by Mr. Rico. And they call the new community college Town Hall because it once was. My mother-in-law puts up jelly and cucumbers and buys butter wrapped in cloth from a dairy. James and his father talk about fishing and baseball and I can see them all together on the Hudson in a raggedy skiff. Half the population of Newburgh is on welfare now, but to my husband's family it was still some upstate paradise of a time long past. A time of ice houses and vegetable wagons, coal furnaces and children weeding gardens. When our son was born my mother-in-law gave me the crib blanket that had been hers.

But the town they remembered had changed. Something quick was in the air. Magnificent old houses, so mined they had become shelter for squatters and rent risks, were bought and renovated. Smart IBM people moved out of their suburbs back into the city and put shutters up and herb gardens in their backyards. A brochure came in the mail announcing the opening of a Food Emporium Gourmet food it said—and listed items the rich IBM crowd would want. It was located in a new mall at the edge of town and I drove out to shop there one day—just to see. It was late in June. After the tulips were gone and the Queen Elizabeth roses were open everywhere. I trailed my cart along the aisle tossing in smoked oysters and Robert's sauce and things I knew would sit in my cupboard for years. Only when I found some Klondike ice cream bars did I feel less guilty about spending James's fireman's salary so foolishly. My father-in-law ate them with the same gusto little Joseph did.

Waiting in the check-out line I heard a voice say, "Twyla!"

The classical music piped over the aisles had affected me and the woman leaning toward me was dressed to kill. Diamonds on her hand, a smart white summer dress. "I'm Mrs. Benson," I said.

"Ho. Ho. The Big Bozo" she sang.

For a split second I didn't know what she was talking about. She had a bunch of asparagus and two cartons of fancy water.

"Roberta!"

"Right."

"For heaven's sake. Roberta."

"You look great," she said.

"So do you. Where are you? Here? In Newburgh?"

"Yes. Over in Annandale."

I was opening my mouth to say more when the cashier called my attention to her empty counter.

"Meet you outside." Roberta pointed her finger and went into the express line.

I placed the groceries and kept myself from glancing around to check Roberta's progress. I remembered Howard Johnson's and looking for a chance to speak only to be greeted with a stingy "wow." But she was waiting for me and her huge hair was sleek now, smooth around a small, nicely shaped head. Shoes, dress, everything lovely and summery and rich. I was dying to know what happened to her, how she got from Jimi Hendrix to Annandale, a neighborhood full of doctors and IBM executives. Easy, I thought. Everything is so easy for them. They think they own the world.

"How long," I asked her. "How long have you been here?"

"A year. I got married to a man who lives here. And you, you're married too, right? Benson, you said."

"Yeah. James Benson."

"And is he nice?"

"On, is he nice?"

"Well, is he?" Roberta's eyes were steady as though she really meant the question and wanted an answer.

"He's wonderful, Roberta. Wonderful."

"So you're happy."

"Very."

"That's good," she said and nodded her head. "I always hoped you'd be happy. Any kids? I know you have kids."

"One. A boy. How about you?"

"Four."

"Four?"

She laughed. "Step kids. He's a widower."

"Oh."

"Got a minute? Let's have a coffee."

I thought about the Klondikes melting and the inconvenience of going all the way to my car and putting the bags in the trunk. Served me right for buying all that stuff I didn't need. Roberta was ahead of me.

"Put them in my car. It's right here."

And then I saw the dark blue limousine.

"You married a Chinaman?"

"No," she laughed. "He's the driver."

"Oh, my. If the Big Bozo could see you now."

We both giggled. Really giggled. Suddenly, in just a pulse beat, twenty years disappeared and all of it came rushing back. The big girls (whom we called gar girls—Roberta's misheard word for the evil stone faces described in a civics class) there dancing in the orchard, the ploppy mashed potatoes, the double weenies, the Spam with pineapple. We went into the coffee shop holding on to one another and I tried to think why we were glad to see each other this time and not before. Once, twelve years ago, we passed like strangers. A black girl and a white girl meeting in a Howard Johnson's on the road and having nothing to say. One in a blue and white triangle waitress hat—the other on her way to see Hendrix. Now we were behaving like sisters separated for much too long. These four short months were nothing in time. Maybe it was the thing itself. Just being there, together. Two little girls who knew what nobody else in the world knew—how not to ask questions. How to believe what had to be believed. There was politeness in that reluctance and generosity as well. Is your mother sick too? No, she dances all night. Oh—and an understanding nod.

We sat in a booth by the window and fell into recollection like veterans.

"Did you ever learn to read?"

"Watch." She picked up the menu. "Special of the day. Cream of corn soup. Entrées. Two dots and a wriggly line. Quiche. Chef salad, scallops . . . "

I was laughing and applauding when the waitress came up.

"Remember the Easter baskets?"

"And how we tried to *introduce* them?"

"Your mother with that cross like two telephone poles."

"And yours with those tight slacks."

We laughed so loudly heads turned and made the laughter hard to suppress.

"What happened to the Jimi Hendrix date?"

Roberta made a blow-out sound with her lips.

"When he died I thought about you."

"Oh, you heard about him finally?"

"Finally. Come on, I was a small-town country waitress."

"And I was a small-town country dropout. God, were we wild. I still don't know how I got out of there alive."

"But you did."

"I did. I really did. Now I'm Mrs. Kenneth Norton."

"Sounds like a mouthful."

"It is."

"Servants and all?"

Roberta held up two fingers.

"Ow! What does he do?"

"Computers and stuff. What do I know?"

"I don't remember a hell of a lot from those days, but Lord, St. Bonny's is as clear as daylight. Remember Maggie? The day she fell down and those gar girls laughed at her?"

Roberta looked up from her salad and stared at me. "Maggie didn't fall," she said.

"Yes, she did. You remember."

"No, Twyla. They knocked her down. Those girls pushed her down and tore her clothes. In the orchard."

"I don't—that's not what happened."

"Sure it is. In the orchard. Remember how scared we were?"

"Wait a minute. I don't remember any of that."

"And Bozo was fired."

"You're crazy. She was there when I left. You left before me."

"I went back. You weren't there when they fired Bozo."

"What?"

"Twice. Once for a year when I was about ten, another for two months when I was fourteen. That's when I ran away."

"You ran away from St. Bonny's?"

"I had to. What do you want? Me dancing in that orchard?"

"Are you sure about Maggie?"

"Of course I'm sure. You've blocked it, Twyla. It happened. Those girls had behavior problems, you know."

"Didn't they, though. But why can't I remember the Maggie thing?"

"Believe me. It happened. And we were there."

"Who did you room with when you went back?" I asked her as if I would know her. The Maggie thing was troubling me.

"Creeps. They tickled themselves in the night."

My ears were itching and I wanted to go home suddenly. This was all very well but she couldn't just comb her hair, wash her face and pretend everything was hunky-dory. After the Howard Johnson's snub. And no apology. Nothing.

"Were you on dope or what that time at Howard Johnson's?" I tried to make my voice sound friendlier than I felt.

"Maybe, a little. I never did drugs much. Why?"

"I don't know, you acted sort of like you didn't want to know me then."

"Oh, Twyla, you know how it was in those days: black—white. You know how everything was."

But I didn't know. I thought it was just the opposite. Busloads of blacks and whites came into Howard Johnson's together. They roamed together then: students, musicians, lovers, protesters. You got to see everything at Howard Johnson's and blacks were very friendly with whites in those days. But sitting there with nothing on my plate but two hard tomato wedges wondering about the melting klondikes it seemed childish remembering the slight. We went to her car, and with the help of the driver, got my stuff into my station wagon.

"We'll keep in touch this time," she said.

"Sure," I said. "Sure. Give me a call."

"I will," she said, and then just as I was sliding behind the wheel, she leaned into the window. "By the way. Your mother. Did she ever stop dancing?"

I shook my head. "No. Never."

Roberta nodded.

"And yours? Did she ever get well?"

She smiled a tiny sad smile. "No. She never did. Look, call me, okay?"

"Okay," I said, but I knew I wouldn't. Roberta had messed up my past somehow with that business about Maggie. I wouldn't forget a thing like that. Would I?

Strife came to us that fall. At least that's what the paper called it. Strife. Racial strife. The word made me think of a bird—a big shrieking bird out of 1,000,000,000 B. C. Flapping its wings and cawing. Its eye with no lid always bearing down on you. All day it screeched and at night it slept on the rooftops.

It woke you in the morning and from the *Today* show to the eleven o'clock news it kept you an awful company. I couldn't figure it out from one day to the next. I knew I was supposed to feel something strong, but I didn't know what, and James wasn't any help. Joseph was on the list of kids to be transferred from the junior high school to another one at some far-out-of-the-way place and I thought it was a good thing until I heard it was a bad thing. I mean I didn't know. All the schools seemed dumps to me, and the fact that one was nicer looking didn't hold much weight. But the papers were full of it and then the kids began to get jumpy. In August, mind you. Schools weren't even open yet. I thought Joseph might be frightened to go over there, but he didn't seem scared so I forgot about it, until I found myself driving along Hudson Street out there by the school they were trying to integrate and saw a line of women marching. And who do you suppose was in line, big as life, holding a sign in front of her bigger than her mother's cross? MOTHERS HAVE RIGHTS TOO! it said.

I drove on, and then changed my mind. I circled the block, slowed down, and honked my horn.

Roberta looked over and when she saw me she waved. I didn't wave back, but I didn't move either. She handed her sign to another woman and came over to where I was parked.

"Hi."

"What are you doing?"

"Picketing. What's it look like?"

"What for?"

"What do you mean 'What for?' They want to take my kids and send them out of the neighborhood. They don't want to go."

"So what if they go to another school? My boy's being bussed too, and I don't mind. Why should you?

"It's not about us. Twyla, Me and you. It's about our kids."

"What's more *us* than that?"

"Well, it is a free country."

"Not yet, but it will be."

"What the hell does that mean? I'm not doing anything to you."

"You really think that?"

"I know it."

"I wonder what made me think you were different."

"I wonder what made me think you were different."

"Look at them," I said. "Just look. Who do they think they are? Swarming all over the place like they own it. And now they think they can decide where my child goes to school. Look at them, Roberta. They're Bozos."

Roberta turned around and looked at the women. Almost all of them were standing still now, waiting. Some were even edging toward us. Roberta looked at me out of some refrigerator behind her eyes. "No, they're not. They're just mothers."

"And what am I? Swiss cheese?"

"I used to curl your hair."

"I hated your hands in my hair."

The women were moving. Our faces looked mean to them of course and they looked as though they could not wait to throw themselves in front of a police car, or better yet, into my car and drag me away by my ankles. Now they surrounded my car and gently, gently began to rock it. I swayed back and forth like a sideways yo yo. Automatically I reached for Roberta, like the old days in the orchard when they saw us watching them and we had to get out of there, and if one of us fell the other pulled her and if one of us was caught the other stayed to kick and scratch, and neither would leave the other behind. My arm shot out of the car window but no receiving hand was there. Roberta was looking at me sway from side to side in the car and her face was still. My purse slid from the car seat down under the dashboard. The four policemen who had been drinking Tab in their car finally got the message and strolled over, forcing their way through the women. Quietly, firmly they spoke. "Okay, ladies. Back in line or off the streets."

Some of them went away willingly; others had to be urged away front the car doors and the hood. Roberta didn't move. She was looking steadily at me. I was fumbling to turn on the ignition, which wouldn't catch because the gear shift was still in drive. The seats of the car were a mess because the swaying had thrown my grocery coupons all over it and my purse was sprawled on the floor.

"Maybe I am different now, Twyla. But you're not. You're the same little state kid who kicked a poor old black lady when she was down on the ground. You kicked a black lady and you have the nerve to call me a bigot."

The coupons were everywhere and the guts of my purse were bunched under the dashboard. What was she saying? Black? Maggie wasn't black.

"She wasn't black," I said.

"Like hell she wasn't, and you kicked her. We both did. You kicked a black lady who couldn't even scream."

"Liar!"

"You're the liar! Why don't you just go on home and leave us alone, huh?"

She turned away and I skidded away from the curb.

The next morning I went into the garage and cut the side out of the carton our portable TV had come in. It wasn't nearly big enough, but after a while I had a decent sign: red spray-painted letters on a white background—AND SO DO CHILDREN. I meant just to go down to the school and tack it up somewhere so those cows on the picket line across the street could see it, but when I got there, some ten or so others had already assembled—protesting the cows across the street. Police permits and everything. I got in line and we strutted in time on our side while Roberta's group strutted on theirs. That first day we were all dignified, pretending the other side didn't exist. The second day there was name calling and finger gestures. But that was about all. People changed signs from time to time, but Roberta never did and neither did I. Actually my sign didn't make sense without Roberta's. "And so do children what?" one of the women on my side asked me. Have rights, I said, as though it was obvious.

Roberta didn't acknowledge my presence in any way and I got to thinking maybe she didn't know I was there. I began to pace myself in the line, jostling people one minute and lagging behind the next, so Roberta and I could reach the end of our respective lines at the same time and there would be a moment in our turn when we would face each other. Still, I couldn't tell whether she saw me and knew my sign was for her. The next day I went early before we were scheduled to assemble. I waited until she got there before I exposed my new creation. As soon as she hoisted her MOTHERS HAVE RIGHTS TOO I began to wave my new one, which said, HOW WOULD YOU KNOW? I know she saw that one, but I had gotten addicted now. My signs got crazier each day, and the women on my side decided that I was a kook. They couldn't make heads or tails out of my brilliant screaming posters.

I brought a painted sign in queenly red with huge black letters that said, IS YOUR MOTHER WELL? Roberta took her lunch break and didn't come back for the rest of the day or any day after. Two days later I stopped going too and couldn't have been missed because nobody understood my signs anyway.

It was a nasty six weeks. Classes were suspended and Joseph didn't go to anybody's school until October. The children—everybody's children—soon got bored with that extended vacation they thought was going to be so great. They looked at TV until their eyes flattened. I spent a couple of mornings tutoring my son, as the other mothers said we should. Twice I opened a text from last year that he had never turned in. Twice he yawned in my face. Other mothers organized living room sessions so the kids would keep up. None of the kids could concentrate so they drifted back to *The Price Is Right* and *The Brady Bunch*. When the school finally opened there were fights once or twice and some sirens roared through the streets every once in a while. There were a lot of photographers from Albany. And just when ABC was about to send up a news crew, the kids settled down like nothing in the world had happened. Joseph hung my HOW WOULD YOU KNOW? sign in his bedroom. I don't know what became of AND SO DO CHILDREN****. I think my father-in-law cleaned some fish on it. He was always puttering around in our garage. Each of his five children lived in Newburgh and he acted as though he had five extra homes.

I couldn't help looking for Roberta when Joseph graduated from high school, but I didn't see her. It didn't trouble me much what she had said to me in the car. I mean the kicking part. I know I didn't do that, I couldn't do that. But I was puzzled by her telling me Maggie was black. When I thought about it I actually couldn't be certain. She wasn't pitch-black, I knew, or I would have remembered that. What I remember was the kiddie hat, and the semicircle legs. I tried to reassure myself about the race thing for a long time until it dawned on me that the truth was already there and Roberta knew it. I didn't kick her; I didn't join in with the gar girls and kick that lady, but I sure did want to. We watched and never tried to help her and never called for help. Maggie was my dancing mother. Deaf, I thought, and dumb. Nobody inside. Nobody who would hear you if you cried in the night. Nobody who could tell you anything important that you could use. Rocking, dancing, swaying as she walked. And when the gar girls pushed her down, and started roughhousing, I knew she wouldn't scream, couldn't—just like me—and I was glad about that.

We decided not to have a tree, because Christmas would be at my mother-in-law's house, so why have a tree at both places? Joseph was at SUNY New Paltz and we had to economize, we said. But at the last minute, I changed my mind. Nothing could be that bad. So I rushed around town looking for a tree, something small but wide. By the time I found a place, it was snowing and very late. I dawdled like it was the most important purchase in the world and the tree man was fed up with me. Finally I chose one and had it tied onto the trunk of the car. I drove away slowly because the sand trucks were not out yet and the streets could be murder at the beginning of a snowfall. Downtown the streets were wide and rather empty except for a cluster of people coming out of the Newburgh Hotel. The one hotel in town that wasn't built out of cardboard and Plexiglas. A party, probably. The men huddled in the snow were dressed in tails and the women had on furs. Shiny things glittered from underneath their coats. It made me tired to look at them. Tired, tired, tired. On the next corner was a small diner with loops and loops of paper bells in the window. I stopped the car, and went in. Just for a cup of coffee and twenty minutes of peace before I went home and tried to finish everything before Christmas Eve.

"Twyla?"

There she was. In a silvery evening gown and dark fur coat. A man and another woman were with her, the man fumbling for change to put in the cigarette machine. The woman was humming and tapping on the counter with her fingernails. They all looked a little bit drunk.

"Well. It's you."

"How are you?"

I shrugged. "Pretty good. Frazzled. Christmas and all."

"Regular?" called the woman from the counter.

"Fine," Roberta called back and then, "Wait for me in the car"

She slipped into the booth beside me. "I have to tell you something. Twyla. I made up my mind if I ever saw you again, I'd tell you."

"I'd just as soon not hear anything, Roberta. It doesn't matter now, anyway."

"No," she said. "Not about that."

"Don't be long," said the woman. She carried two regulars to go and the man peeled his cigarette pack as they left.

"It's about St. Bonny's and Maggie."

"Oh, please."

"Listen to me. I really did think she was black. I didn't make that up. I really thought so. But now I can't be sure. I just remember her as old, so old. And because she couldn't talk—well, you know, I thought she was crazy. She'd been brought up in an institution like my mother was and like I thought I would be too. And you were right. We didn't kick her. It was the gar girls. Only them. But, well, I wanted to. I really wanted them to hurt her. I said we did it, too. You and me, but that's not true. And I don't want you to carry that around. It was just that I wanted to do it so bad that day—wanting to is doing it."

Her eyes were watery from the drinks she'd had, I guess. I know it's that way with me. One glass of wine and I start bawling over the littlest thing.

"We were kids, Roberta."

"Yeah. Yeah. I know, just kids."

"Eight."

"Eight."

"And lonely."

"Scared, too."

She wiped her checks with the heel of her hand and smiled. "Well, that's all I wanted to say."

I nodded and couldn't think of any way to fill the silence that went from the diner past the paper bells on out into the snow. It was heavy now. I thought I'd better wait for the sand trucks before starting home.

"Thanks, Roberta."

"Sure."

"Did I tell you? My mother, she never did stop dancing."

"Yes. You told me. And mine, she never got well." Roberta lifted her hands from the tabletop and covered her face with her palms. When she took them away she really was crying. "On shit, Twyla. Shit, shit, shit. What the hell happened to Maggie?"

## Study Questions

1. This story is about two girls / women (Twyla and Roberta), one black and one white. Which one is which? Find at least four things fron the story that support your answer. Find at least two other things that might support the other choice.

2. Does it matter which one is black and which one is white? Why does Morrison not clearly identify which one is which? How does she describe the girls / women and their behaviors without clearly identifying their race?

3. Describe the class backgrounds and experiences of Twyla and Roberta. How do these backgrounds impact their values and politics? (For example, their positions on school bussing.)

4. Why do Twyla and Roberta hate Maggie so much? At the end of the story, how do they understand their feelings towards Maggie? What does Maggie represent to them?

5. What does the story say about the relationship of race, class and gender? About interracial friendships? Will Twyla and Roberta stay in touch in the future? Why or why not?

3

# "AIN'T I A WOMAN?"

*Sojourner Truth (1795-1853)*

*Sojourner Truth, an ex-slave, was a writer and supporter of progressive causes. She is best known for her advocacy of anti-slavery and women's rights, and wa a gifted and powerful orator. The text below is a speech she made at the 1851 Women's Rights Convention in Akron, Ohio. Note how she artfully blends themes racial equality and women's rights in her plainly spoken commentary.*

*A very religious woman, Truth began hearning "voices" in 1843 that instructed her to change her name and become a wandering preacher. Her mission was to "sojourn" America and speak God's "truth."*

Well, children, where there is so much racket there must be something out of kilter. I think that 'twixt the negroes of the South and the women at the North, all talking about rights, the white men will be in a fix pretty soon. But what's all this here talking about?

That man over there says that women need to be helped into carriages, and lifted over ditches, and to have the best place everywhere. Nobody ever helps me into carriages, or over mud-puddles, or gives me any best place! And ain't I a woman? Look at me! Look at my arm! I have ploughed and planted, and gathered into barns, and no man could head me! And ain't I a woman? I could work as much and eat as much as a man—when I could get it—and bear the lash as well! And ain't I a woman? I have borne thirteen children, and seen them most all sold off to slavery, and when I cried out with my mother's grief, none but Jesus heard me! And ain't I a woman?

Then they talk about this thing in the head; what's this they call it? (Intellect, someone whispers.) That's it, honey. What's that got to do with women's rights or negro's rights? If my cup won't hold but a pint, and yours holds a quart, wouldn't you be mean not to let me have my little half-measure full?

Then that little man in black there, he says women can't have as much rights as men, 'cause Christ wasn't a woman! Where did your Christ come from? Where did your Christ come from? From God and a woman! Man had nothing to do with Him.

If the first woman God ever made was strong enough to turn the world upside down all alone, these women together ought to be able to turn it back, and get it right side up again! And now they is asking to do it, the men better let them.

Obliged to you for hearing me, and now old Sojourner ain't got nothing more to say.

## Study Questions

1. How does Sojourner Truth expose the contradiction between the ideal of "Womanhood" and the lived realities of African-American women?

2. How does she confront popular arguments against women's rights?

3. How does she argue against the social and racial assumptions of her day?

# LA GÜERA

## Cherríe Moraga (1952- )

*It requires something more than personal experience to gain a philosophy or point of view from any specific event. It is the quality of our response to the event and our capacity to enter into the lives of others that help us to make their lives and experiences our own.*

*Emma Goldman*[*]

*Cherri Moraga teaches in the Drama Department a the University of California at Berkeley. She has written numerous plays, as well as* Loving in the War Years: Lo que nunca paso por sus labios, *a mixture of prose, poetry, and memoir, in 1983. She is perhaps best known for co-editing the ground-breaking anthology* This Bridge Called My Back: Writings by Radical Women of Color *with Gloria Anzaldua in 1981. "La Guera" is taken from this collection.*

I am the very well-educated daughter of a woman who, by the standards in this country, would be considered largely illiterate. My mother was born in Santa Paula, Southern California, at a time when much of the central valley there was still farm land. Nearly thirty-five years later, in 1948, she was the only daughter of six to marry an anglo, my father.

I remember all of my mother's stories, probably much better than she realizes. She is a fine story-teller, recalling every event of her life with the vividness of the present, noting each detail right down to the cut and color of her dress. I remember stories of her being pulled out of school at the ages of five, seven, nine, and eleven to work in the fields, along with her brothers and sisters; stories of her father drinking away whatever small profit she was able to make for

the family; of her going the long way home to avoid meeting him on the street, staggering toward the same destination. I remember stories of my mother lying about her age in order to get a job as a hat-check girl at Agua Caliente Racetrack in Tijuana. At fourteen, she was the main support of the family. I call still see her walking home alone at 3 A.M., only to turn all of her salary and tips over to her mother, who was pregnant again.

The stories continue through the war years and on: walnut-cracking factories, the Voit Rubber factory, and then the computer boom. I remember my mother doing piecework for the electronics plant in our neighborhood. In the late evening, she would sit in front of the T. V. set, wrapping copper wires into the backs of circuit boards, talking about "keeping up with the younger girls." By that time, she was already in her mid-fifties.

Meanwhile, I was college-prep in school. After classes, I would go with my mother to fill out job applications for her, or write checks for her at the supermarket. We would have the scenario all worked out ahead of time. My mother would sign the check before we'd get to the store. Then, as we'd approach the checkstand, she would say— within earshot of the cashier –"oh honey, you go ahead and make out the check," as if she couldn't be bothered with such an insignificant detail. No one asked any questions.

I was educated, and wore it with a keen sense of pride and satisfaction, my head propped up with the knowledge, from my mother, that my life would be easier than hers. I was educated; but more than this,

[*] Alix Kates Shulman, "Was My Life Worth Living?" *Red Emma Speaks.* (New York: Random House, 1972). p. 388

I was "la güera": fair-skinned. Born with the features of my Chicana mother, but the skin of my Anglo father, I had it made.

No one ever quite told me this (that light was right), but I knew that being light was something valued in my family (who were all chicano, with the exception of my father). In fact, everything about my upbringing (at least what occurred on a conscious level) attempted to bleach me of what color I did have. Although my mother was fluent in it, I was never taught much Spanish at home. I picked up what I did learn from school and from over-heard snatches of conversation among my relatives and mother. She often called other lower-income Mexicans "braceros," or "wet-backs," referring to herself and her family as "a different class of people." And yet, the real story was that my family, too, had been poor (some still are) and farmworkers. My mother can remember this in her blood as if it were yesterday. But this is something she would like to forget (and rightfully), for to her, on a basic economic level, being Chicana meant being "less." It was through my mother's desire to protect her children from poverty and illiteracy that we became "anglocized"; the more effectively we could pass in the white world, the better guaranteed our future.

From all of this, I experience, daily, a huge disparity between what I was born into and what I was to grow up to become. Because (as Goldman suggests) these stories my mother told me crept under my "güera" skin. I had no choice but to enter into the life of my mother. *I had no choice.* I took her life into my heart, but managed to keep a lid on it as long as I feigned being the happy, upwardly mobile heterosexual.

When I finally lifted the lid to my lesbianism, a profound connection with my mother reawakened in me. It wasn't until I acknowledged and confronted my own lesbianism in the flesh, that my heartfelt identification with and empathy for my mother's oppression—due to being poor, uneducated, and Chicana—was realized. My lesbianism is the avenue through which I have learned the most about silence and oppression, and it continues to be the most tactile reminder to me that we are not free human beings.

You see, one follows the other. I had known for years that I was a lesbian, had felt it in my bones, had ached with the knowledge, gone crazed with the knowledge, wallowed in the silence of it. Silence *is* like starvation. Don't be fooled. It's nothing short of that, and felt most sharply when one has had a full belly most of her life. When we are not physically starving, we have the luxury to realize psychic and emotional starvation. It is from

this starvation that other starvations can be recognized—if one is willing to take the risk of making the connection—if one is willing to be responsible to the result of the connection. For me, the connection is an inevitable one.

What I am saying is that the joys of looking like a white girl ain't so great since I realized I could be beaten on the street for being a dyke. If my sister's being beaten because she's Black, it's pretty much the same principle. We're both getting beaten any way you look at it. The connection is blatant; and in the case of my own family, the difference in the privileges attached to looking white instead of brown are merely a generation apart.

In this country, lesbianism is a poverty—as is being brown, as is being a woman, as is being just plain poor. *The danger lies in ranking the oppressions.* The danger lies in failing to acknowledge the specificity of the oppression. The danger lies in attempting to deal with oppression purely from a theoretical base. Without an emotional, heartfelt grappling with the source of our own oppression, without naming the enemy within ourselves and outside of us, no authentic, non-hierarchical connection among oppressed groups can take place.

When the going gets rough, will we abandon our so-called comrades in a flurry of racist/heterosexist/what-have-you panic? To whose camp, then, should the lesbian of color retreat? Her very presence violates the ranking and abstraction of oppression. Do we merely live hand to mouth? Do we merely struggle with the "ism" that's sitting on top of our own heads?

The answer is: yes, I think first we do; and we must do so thoroughly and deeply. But to fail to move out from there will only isolate us in our own oppression—will only insulate, rather than radicalize us.

To illustrate: a gay male friend of mine once confided to me that he continued to feel that, on some level, I didn't trust him because he was male; that he felt, really, if it ever came down to a "battle of the sexes," I might kill him. I admitted that I might very well. He wanted to understand the source of my distrust. I responded, "You're not a woman. Be a woman for a day. Imagine being a woman." He confessed that the thought terrified him because to him, being a woman meant being raped by men. He *had* felt raped by men; he wanted to forget what that meant. What grew from that discussion was the realization that in order for him to create an authentic alliance with me, he must deal with the primary source of his own sense of oppression. He must, first, emotionally come to terms with what it feels like to be a victim. If he—or anyone—were to truly do this, it would be impossible to discount the oppression of other, except by again forgetting how we have been hurt.

And yet, oppressed groups are forgetting all the time. There are instances of this in the rising Black middle class, and certainly an obvious trend of such "unconsciousness" among white gay men. Because to remember may mean giving up whatever privileges we have managed to squeeze out of this society by virtue of our gender, race, class, or sexuality.

Within the women's movement, the connections among women of different backgrounds and sexual orientations have been fragile, at best. I think this phenomenon is indicative of our failure to seriously address ourselves to some very frightening questions: How have I internalized my own oppression? How have I oppressed? Instead we have let rhetoric do the job of poetry. Even the word "oppression" has lost its power. We need a new language, better words that can more closely describe women's fear of and resistance to one another; words that will not always come out sounding like dogma.

What prompted me in the first place to work on an anthology by radical women of color was a deep sense that I had a valuable insight to contribute, by virtue of my birthright and background. And yet, I don't really understand first-hand what it feels like being shitted on for being brown. I understand much more about the joys of it—being Chicana and having family are synonymous for me. What I know about loving, singing, crying, telling stories, speaking with my heart and hands, even having a sense of my own soul comes from the love of my mother, aunts, cousins . . .

But at the age of twenty-seven, it is frightening to acknowledge that I have internalized a racism and classism, where the object of oppression is not only someone outside of my skin, but the someone inside my skin. In fact, to a large degree, the real battle with such oppression, for all of us, begins under the skin. I have had to confront the fact that much of what I value about being Chicana, about my family, has been subverted by anglo culture and my own cooperation with it. This realization did not occur to me overnight. For example, it wasn't until long after my graduation, from the private college I'd attended in Los Angeles, that I realized the major reason for my total alienation from and fear of my classmates was rooted in class and culture. CLICK.

Three years after graduation, in an apple-orchard in Sonoma, a friend of mine (who comes from an Italian Irish working-class family) says to me, "Cherríe, no wonder you felt like such a nut in school. Most of the people there were white and rich." It was true. All along I had felt the difference, but not until I had put the words "class" and "color" to the experience, did my feelings make any sense. For years, I had berated myself for not being as "free" as my classmates. I completely bought that they simply had more guts than I did—to rebel against their parents and run around the country hitch-hiking, reading books and studying "art." They had enough privilege to be atheists, for chrissake. There was no one around filling in the disparity for me between their parents, who were Hollywood filmmakers, and my parents, who wouldn't know the name of a filmmaker if their lives depended on it (and precisely because their lives didn't depend on it, they couldn't be bothered). But I knew nothing about "privilege" then. White was right. Period. I could pass. If I got educated enough, there would never be any telling.

Three years after that, another CLICK. In a letter to Barbara Smith, I wrote:

> I went to a concert where Ntosake Shange was reading. There, everything exploded for me. She was speaking a language that I knew—in the deepest parts of me—existed, and that I had ignored in my own feminist studies and even in my own writing. What Ntosake caught in me is the realization that in my development as a poet, I have, in many ways, denied the voice of my brown mother—the brown in me. I have acclimated to the sound of a white, language which, as my father represents, it does not speak to the emotions in my poems—emotions which stem from the love of my mother.
>
> The reading was agitating. Made me uncomfortable. Threw me into a week-long terror of how deeply I was affected. I felt that I had to start all over again. That I turned only to the perceptions of white middle—class women to speak for me and all women. I am shocked by my own ignorance.

Sitting in that auditorium chair was the first time I had realized to the core of me that for years I had disowned the language I knew best—ignored the words and rhythms that were the closest to me. The sounds of my mother and aunts gossiping—half in English, half in Spanish—while drinking cerveza in the kitchen. And the hands—I had cut off the hands in my poems. But not in conversation; still the hands could not be kept down. Still they insisted on moving.

The reading had forced me to remember that I knew things from my roots. But to remember puts me up against what I don't know. Shange's reading agitated me because she spoke with power about a world that is both alien and common to me: "the capacity to enter into the lives of others." But you can't just take the goods and run. I knew that then, sitting in the Oakland auditorium (as I know in my poetry), that the only thing worth writing about is what seems to be unknown and, therefore, fearful.

The "unknown" is often depicted in racist literature as the "darkness" within a person. Similarly, sexist writers will refer to fear in the form of the vagina, calling it "the orifice of death." In contrast, it is a pleasure to read works such as Maxine Hong Kingston's *Woman Warrior*, where fear and alienation are described as "the white ghosts." And yet, the bulk of literature in this country reinforces the myth that what is dark and female is evil. Consequently, each of us—whether dark, female, or both—has in some way *internalized* this oppressive imagery. What the oppressor often succeeds in doing is simply *externalizing* his fears, projecting them into the bodies of women, Asians, gays, disabled folks, whoever seems most "other."

> *call me*
> *roach and presumptuous*
> *nightmare on your white pillow*
> *your itch to destroy*
> *the indestructible*
> *part of yourself*

Audre Lorde[*]

But it is not really difference the oppressor fears so much as similarity. He fears he will discover in himself the same aches, the same longings as those of the people he has shitted on. He fears the immobilization threatened by his own incipient guilt. He fears he will have to change his life once he has seen himself in the bodies of the people he has called different. He fears the hatred, anger, and vengeance of those he has hurt.

This is the oppressor's nightmare, but it is not exclusive to him. We women have a similar nightmare, for each of us in some way has been both oppressed and the oppressor. We are afraid to look at how we have failed each other. We are afraid to see how we have taken the values of our oppressor into our hearts and turned them against ourselves and one another. We are afraid to admit how deeply "the man's" words have been ingrained in us.

To assess the damage is a dangerous act. I think of how, even as a feminist lesbian, I have so wanted to ignore my own homophobia, my own hatred of myself for being queer. I have not wanted to admit that my deepest personal sense of myself has not

quite "caught up" with my 'woman-identified" politics. I have been afraid to criticize lesbian writers who choose to "skip over" these issues in the name of feminism. In 1979, we talk of "old gay" and "butch and femme" roles as if they were ancient history. We toss them aside as merely patriarchal notions. And yet, the truth of the matter is that I have sometimes taken society's fear and hatred of lesbians to bed with me. I have sometimes hated my lover for loving me. I have sometimes felt "not woman enough" for her. I have sometimes felt "not man enough." For a lesbian trying to survive in a heterosexist society, there is no easy way around these emotions. Similarly, in a white-dominated world, there is little getting around racism and our own internalization of it. It's always there, embodied in some one we least expect to rub up against.

When we do rub up against this person, *there* then is the challenge. *There* then is the opportunity to look at the nightmare within us. But we usually shrink from such a challenge.

Time and time again, I have observed that the usual response among white women's groups when the "racism issue" comes up is to deny the difference. I have heard comments like, "Well, we're open to *all* women; why don't they (women of color) come? You can only do so much . . . " But there is seldom any analysis of how the very nature and structure of the group itself may be founded on racist or classist assumptions. More importantly, so often the women seem to feel no loss, no lack, no absence when women of color are not involved; therefore, there is little desire to change the situation. This has hurt me deeply. I have come to believe that the only reason women of a privileged class will dare to look at *how* it is that *they* oppress, is when they've come to know the meaning of their own oppression. And understand that the oppression of others hurts them personally.

The other side of the story is that women of color and working-class women often shrink from challenging white middle-class women. It is much easier to rank oppressions and set up a hierarchy, rather than take responsibility for changing our own lives. We have failed to demand that white women, particularly those who claim to be speaking for all women, be accountable for their racism.

The dialogue has simply not gone deep enough.

I have many times questioned my right to even work on an anthology which is to be written "exclusively by Third World women." I have had to look critically at my claim to color, at a time when, among white feminist ranks, it is a "politically correct" (and sometimes peripherally advantageous) assertion to make. I must acknowledge the fact that,

---

[*] From "The Brown Menace or Poem to the Survival of Roaches", *The New York Head Shop and Museum* (Detroit: Broadside, 1974), p. 48

physically, I have had a *choice* about making that claim, in contrast to women who have not had such a choice, and have been abused for their color. I must reckon with the fact that for most of my life, by virtue of the very fact that I am white-looking, I identified with and aspired toward white values, and that I rode the wave of that Southern Californian privilege as far as conscience would let me.

Well, now I feel both bleached and beached. I feel angry about this—the years when I refused to recognize privilege, both when it worked against me, and when I worked it, ignorantly, at the expense of others. These are not settled issues. That is why this work feels so risky to me. It continues to be discovery. It has brought me into contact with women who invariably know a hell of a lot more than I do about racism, as experienced in the flesh, as revealed in the flesh of their writing.

I think: what is my responsibility to my roots—both white and brown, Spanish-speaking and English? I am a woman with a foot in both worlds; and I refuse the split. I feel the necessity for dialogue. Sometimes I feel it urgently.

But one voice is not enough, nor two, although this is where dialogue begins. It is essential that radical feminists confront their fear of and resistance to each other, because without this, there *will* be no bread on the table. Simply, we will not survive. If we could make this connection in our heart of hearts, that if we are serious about a revolution—better—if we seriously believe there should be joy in our lives (real joy, not just "good times"), then we need one another. We women need each other. Because my/your solitary, self -asserting "go-for-the-throat-of-fear" power is not enough. The real power, as you and I well know, is collective. I can't afford to be afraid of you, nor you of me. If it

takes head-on collisions, let's do it: this polite timidity is killing us.

As Lorde suggests in the passage I cited earlier, it is in looking to the nightmare that the dream is found. There, the survivor emerges to insist on a future, a vision, yes, born out of what is dark and female. The feminist movement must be a movement of such survivors, a movement with a future.

## Study Questions

1. Why does Moraga's mother want her to become "anglocized"? How is her identity connected tot he identity of her mother? What conflict does this cause in her life?

2. What is she saying about skin color? What about sexual identity? How do they interact?

3. What problems does Moraga have witht he way people talk about oppression? Why is it so hard to come to terms with oneself as an oppressor? Why is it so important?

4. Does Moraga emphasize differences or similarities between oppressed groups in America? Explain.

5. How does her analysis of passing relate to Langston Hughes'?

6. What point is she making about silence and denial? How are they connected to oppression?

# 5

# THE COMBAHEE RIVER COLLECTIVE STATEMENT

*The Combahee River Collective was a Black feminist group in Boston whose name came from the guerrilla action conceptualized and led by Harriet Tubman on June 2, 1863, in the Port Royal region of South Carolina. This action freed more than 750 slaves and is the only military campaign in American history planned and led by a woman.*

We are a collective of Black feminists who have been meeting together since 1974.[1] During that time we have been involved in the process of defining and clarifying our politics, while at the same time doing political work within our own group and in coalition with other progressive organizations and movements. The most general statement of our politics at the present time would be that we are actively committed to struggling against racial, sexual, heterosexual, and class oppression, and see as our particular task the development of integrated analysis and practice based upon the fact that the major systems of oppression are interlocking. The synthesis of these oppressions creates the conditions of our lives. As Black women we see Black feminism as the logical political movement to combat the manifold and simultaneous oppressions that all women of color face.

We will discuss four major topics in the paper that follows: the genesis of contemporary Black feminism; what we believe, i.e., the specific province of our politics; the problems in organizing Black feminists, including a brief herstory of our collective; and Black feminist issues and practice.

## THE GENESIS OF CONTEMPORARY BLACK FEMINISM

Before looking at the recent development of Black feminism we would like to affirm that we find our origins in the historical reality of Afro-American women's continuous life-and-death struggle for survival and liberation. Black women's extremely negative relationship to the American political system (a system of white male rule) has always been determined by our membership in two oppressed racial and sexual castes. As Angela Davis points out in "Reflections on the Black Woman's Role in the Community of Slaves," Black women have always embodied, if only in their physical manifestation, an adversary stance to white male rule and have actively resisted its inroads upon them and their communities in both dramatic and subtle ways. There have always been Black women activists—some known, like Sojourner Truth, Harriet Tubman, Frances E. W. Harper, Ida B. Wells Barnett, and Mary Church Terrell, and thousands upon thousands unknown—who have had a shared awareness of how their sexual identity combined with their racial identity to make their whole life situation and the focus of their political struggles unique. Contemporary Black feminism is the outgrowth of countless generations of personal sacrifice, militancy, and work by our mothers and sisters.

A Black feminist presence has evolved most obviously in connection with the second wave of the American women's movement beginning in the late 1960s. Black, other Third World, and working women have been involved in the feminist movement from its start but both outside reactionary forces and racism and elitism within the movement itself have served to obscure our participation. In 1973, Black feminists, primarily located in New York, felt the necessity of forming a separate Black feminist group. This became the National Black Feminist Organization (NBFO).

Black feminist politics also have an obvious connection to movements for Black liberation, particulary those of the 1960s and 1970s. Many of us were active in those movements (Civil Rights, Black nationalism, the Black Panthers), and all of our lives were greatly affected and changed by their ideologies, their goals, and the tactics used to achieve their goals. It was our experience and disillusionment within these liberation movements, as well as experience on the periphery of the white male left, that led to the need to develop a politics that was anti-racist, unlike those of white women, and anti-sexist, unlike those of Black and white men.

There is also undeniably a personal genesis for Black feminism, that is, the political realization that comes from the seemingly personal experiences of individual Black women's lives. Black feminists and many more Black women who do not define themselves as feminists have all experienced sexual oppression as a constant factor in our day-to-day existence. As children we realized that we were different from boys and that we were treated differently. For example, we were told in the same breath to be quiet both for the sake of being "ladylike" and to make us less objectionable in the eyes of white people. As we grew older we became aware of the threat of physical and sexual abuse by men. However, we had no way of conceptualizing what was so apparent to us, what we *knew* was really happening.

Black feminists often talk about their feelings of craziness before becoming conscious of the concepts of sexual politics, patriarchal rule, and most importantly, feminism, the political analysis and practice that we women use to struggle against our oppression. The fact that racial politics and indeed racism are pervasive factors in our lives did not allow us, and still does not allow most Black women, to look more deeply into our own experiences and, from that sharing and growing consciousness, to build a politics that will change our lives and inevitably end our oppression. Our development must also be tied to the contemporary economic and political position of Black people. The post World War II generation of Black youth was the first to be able to minimally partake of certain educational and employment options, previously closed completely to Black people. Although our economic position is still at the very bottom of the American capitalistic economy, a handful of us have been able to gain certain tools as a result of tokenism in education and employment which potentially enable us to more effectively fight our oppression.

A combined anti-racist and anti-sexist position drew us together initially, and as we developed politically we addressed ourselves to heterosexism and economic oppression under capitalism.

## WHAT WE BELIEVE

Above all else, our politics initially sprang from the shared belief that Black women are inherently valuable, that our liberation is a necessity not as an adjunct to somebody else's but because of our need as human persons for autonomy. This may seem so obvious as to sound simplistic, but it is apparent that no other ostensibly progressive movement has ever considered our specific oppression as a priority or worked seriously for the ending of that oppression. Merely naming the pejorative stereotypes attributed to Black women (e.g. mammy, matriarch, Sapphire, whore, bulldagger), let alone cataloguing the cruel, often murderous, treatment we receive, indicates how little value has been placed upon our lives during four centuries of bondage in the Western hemisphere. We realize that the only people who care enough about its to work consistently for our liberation are us. Our politics evolve from a healthy love for ourselves, our sisters and our community which allows us to continue our struggle and work.

This focusing upon our own oppression is embodied in the concept of identity politics. We believe that the most profound and potentially most radical politics come directly out of our own identity, as opposed to working to end somebody else's oppression. In the case of Black women this is a particularly repugnant, dangerous, threatening, and therefore revolutionary concept because it is obvious from looking at all the political movements that have preceded us that anyone is more worthy of liberation than ourselves. We reject pedestals, queenhood, and walking ten paces behind. To be recognized as human, levelly human, is enough.

We believe that sexual politics under patriarchy is as pervasive in Black women's lives as are the politics of class and race. We also often find it difficult to separate race from class from sex oppression because in our lives they are most often experienced simultaneously. We know that there is such a thing as racial-sexual oppression which is neither solely racial nor solely sexual, e.g., the history of rape of Black women by white men as a weapon of political repression.

Although we are feminists and Lesbians, we feel solidarity with progressive Black men and do not advocate the fractionalization that white women who are separatists demand. Our situation as Black people necessitates that we have solidarity around the fact of race, which white women of course do not need to have with white men, unless it is their negative solidarity as racial oppressors. We struggle together with Black men against racism; while we also struggle with Black men about sexism.

We realize that the liberation of all oppressed peoples necessitates the destruction of the political-economic systems of capitalism and imperialism as well as patriarchy. We are socialists because we believe that work must be organized for the collective benefit of those who do the work and create the products, and not for the profit of the bosses. Material resources must be equally distributed among those who create these resources. We are not convinced, however, that a socialist revolution that is not also a feminist and anti-racist revolution will guarantee our liberation. We have arrived at the necessity for developing an understanding of class relationships that takes into account the specific class position of Black women who are generally marginal in the labor force, while at this particular time some of us are temporarily viewed as doubly desirable tokens at white-collar and professional levels. We need to articulate the real class situation of persons who are not merely raceless, sexless workers, but for whom racial and sexual oppression are significant determinants in their working/economic lives. Although we are in essential agreement with Marx's theory as it applied to the very specific economic relationships he analyzed, we know that his anaylsis must be extended further in order for us to understand our specific economic situation as Black women.

A political contribution which we feel we have already made is the expansion of the feminist principle that the personal is political. In our consciousness-raising sessions, for example, we have in many ways gone beyond white women's revelations because we are dealing with the implications of race and class as well as sex. Even our Black women's style of talking/testifying in Black language about what we have experienced has a resonance that is both cultural and political. We have spent a great deal of energy delving into the cultural and experiential nature of our oppression out of necessity because none of these matters has ever been looked at before. No one before has ever examined the multilayered texture of Black women's lives. An example of this kind of revelation/conceptualization occurred at a meeting as we discussed the ways in which our early intellectual interests had been attacked by our peers, particularly Black males. We discovered that all of us, because we were "smart" had also been considered "ugly," i.e., "smart-ugly." "Smart-ugly" crystallized the way in which most of us had been forced to develop our intellects at great cost to our "social" lives. The sanctions in the Black and white communities against Black women thinkers is comparatively much higher than for white women, particularly ones from the educated middle and upper classes.

As we have already stated, we reject the stance of Lesbian separatism because it is not a viable political analysis or strategy for us. It leaves out far too much and far too many people, particularly Black men, women, and children. We have a great deal of criticism and loathing for what men have been socialized to be in this society: what they support, how they act, and how they oppress. But we do not have the misguided notion that it is their maleness, *per se*—i.e., their biological maleness—that makes them what they are. As Black women we find any type of biological determinism a particularly dangerous and reactionary basis upon which to build a politic. We must also question whether Lesbian separatism is an adequate and progressive political analysis and strategy, even for those who practice it, since it so completely denies any but the sexual sources of women's oppression, negating the facts of class and race.

## PROBLEMS IN ORGANIZING BLACK FEMINISTS

During our years together as a Black feminist collective we have experienced success and defeat, joy and pain, victory and failure. We have found that it is very difficult to organize around Black feminist issues, difficult even to announce in certain contexts that we *are* Black feminists. We have tried to think about the reasons for our difficulties, particularly since the white women's movement continues to be strong and to grow in many directions. In this section we will discuss some of the general reasons for the organizing problems we face and also talk specifically about the stages in organizing our own collective.

The major source of difficulty in our political work is that we are not just trying to fight oppression on one front or even two, but instead to address a whole range of oppressions. We do not have racial, sexual, heterosexual, or class privilege to rely upon, nor do we have even the minimal access to resources and power that groups who possess any one of these types of privilege have.

The psychological toll of being a Black woman and the difficulties this presents in reaching political consciousness and doing political work can never be underestimated. There is a very low value placed upon Black women's psyches in this society, which is both racist and sexist. As an early group member once said, "We are all damaged people merely by virture of being Black women." We are dispossessed psychologically and on every other level, and yet we feel the necessity to struggle to change the condition of all Black women. In "A Black Feminist's Search for Sisterhood," Michele Wallace arrives at this conclusion:

*We exist as women who are Black who are feminists, each stranded for the moment, working independently because there is not yet an environment in this society remotely congenial to our struggle—because, being on the bottom, we would have to do what no one else has done: we would have to fight the world.*[2]

Wallace is pessimistic but realistic in her assessment of Black feminists' position, particularly in her allusion to the nearly classic isolation most of us face. We might use our position at the bottom, however, to make a clear leap into revolutionary action. If Black women were free, it would mean that everyone else would have to be free since our freedom would necessitate the destruction of all the systems of oppression.

Feminism is, nevertheless, very threatening to the majority of Black people because it calls into question some of the most basic assumptions about our existence, i.e., that sex should be a determinant of power relationships. Here is the way male and female roles were defined in a Black nationalist pamphlet from the early 1970s:

> *We understand that it is and has been traditional that the man is the head of the house. He is the leader of the house/nation because his knowledge of the world is broader, his awareness is greater, his understanding is fuller and his application of this information is wiser . . . After all, it is only reasonable that the man be the head of the house because he is able to defend and protect the development of his home . . . Women cannot do the same things as men—they are made by nature to function differently. Equality of men and women is something that cannot happen even in the abstract world. Men are not equal to other men, i.e. ability, experience or even understanding. The value of men and women can be seen as in the value of gold and silver—they are not equal but both have great value. We must realize that men and women are a complement to each other because there is no house/ family without a man and his wife. Both are essential to the development of any life.*[3]

The material conditions of most Black women would hardly lead them to upset both economic and sexual arrangements that seem to represent some stability in their lives. Many Black women have a good understanding of both sexism and racism, but because of the everyday constrictions of their lives, cannot risk struggling against them both.

The reaction of Black men to feminism has been notoriously negative. They are, of course, even more threatened than Black women by the possibility that Black feminists might organize around our own needs. They realize that they might not only lose valuable and hardworking allies in their struggles

but that they might also be forced to change their habitually sexist ways of interacting with and oppressing Black women. Accusations that Black feminism divides the Black struggle are powerful deterrents to the growth of an autonomous Black women's movement.

Still, hundreds of women have been active at different times during the three-year existence of our group. And every Black woman who came, came out of a strongly-felt need for some level of possibility that did not previously exist in her life.

When we first started meeting early in 1974 after the NBFO first eastern regional conference, we did not have a strategy for organizing, or even a focus. We just wanted to see what we had. After a period of months of not meeting, we began to meet again late in the year and started doing an intense variety of consciousness—raising. The overwhelming feeling that we had is that after years and years we had finally found each other. Although we were not doing political work as a group, individuals continued their involvement in Lesbian politics, sterilization abuse and abortion rights work, Third World Women's International Women's Day activities, and support activity for the trials of Dr. Kenneth Edelin, Joan Little, and Inéz García. During our first summer, when membership had dropped off considerably, those of us remaining devoted serious discussion to the possibility of opening a refuge for battered women in a Black community. (There was no refuge in Boston at that time.) We also decided around that time to become an independent collective since we had serious disagreements with NBFO's bourgeois-feminist stance and their lack of a clear political focus.

We also were contacted at that time by socialist feminists, with whom we had worked on abortion rights activities, who wanted to encourage us to attend the National Socialist Feminist Conference in Yellow Springs. One of our members did attend and despite the narrowness of the ideology that was promoted at that particular conference, we became more aware of the need for us to understand our own economic situation and to make our own economic analysis.

In the fall, when some members returned, we experienced several months of comparative inactivity and internal disagreements which were first conceptualized as a Lesbian-straight split but which were also the result of class and political differences. During the summer those of us who were still meeting had determined the need to do political work and to move beyond consciousness-raising and serving exclusively as an emotional support group. At the beginning of 1976, when some of the women who had not wanted to do political work and who also had voiced disagreements stopped attending of their own accord, we again looked for a focus. We decided at that time, with the addition of new members, to become a study group. We had always shared our reading with each other and some of us had written papers on Black feminism for group discussion a few months before this decision was made. We began functioning as a study group and also began discussing the possibility of starting a Black feminist publication. We had a retreat in the late spring which provided a time for both political discussion and working out interpersonal issues. Currently we are planning to gather together a collection of Black feminist writing. We feel that it is absolutely essential to demonstrate the reality of our politics to other Black women and believe that we can do this through writing and distributing our work. The fact that individual Black feminists are living in isolation all over the country, that our own numbers are small, and that we have some skills in writing, printing, and publishing makes us want to carry out these kinds of projects as a means of organizing Black feminists as we continue to do political work in coalition with other groups.

## BLACK FEMINIST ISSUES AND PROJECTS

During our time together we have identified and worked on many issues of particular relevance to Black women. The inclusiveness of our politics makes us concerned with any situation that impinges upon the lives of women, Third World and working people. We are of course particularly committed to working on those struggles in which race, sex and class are simultaneous factors in oppression. We might, for example, become involved in workplace organizing at a factory that employs Third World women or picket a hospital that is cutting back on already inadequate health care to a Third World community, or set up a rape crisis center in a Black neighborhood. Organizing around welfare and daycare concerns might also be a focus. The work to be done and the countless issues that this work represents merely reflect the pervasiveness of our oppression.

Issues and projects that collective members have actually worked on are sterilization abuse, abortion rights, battered women, rape and health care. We have also done many workshops and educationals on Black feminism on college campuses, at women's conferences, and most recently for high school women.

One issue that is of major concern to us and that we have begun to publicly address is racism in the white women's movement. As Black feminists we are made constantly and painfully aware of how little effort white women have made to understand and combat their racism, which requires among other things that they have a more than superficial comprehension of race, color, and Black history and culture. Eliminating racism in the white women's movement is by definition work for white women to do, but we will continue to speak to and demand accountability on this issue.

In the practice of our politics we do not believe that the end always justifies the means. Many reactionary and destructive acts have been done in the name of achieving "correct" political goals. As feminists we do not want to mess over people in the name of politics. We believe in collective process and a nonhierarchical distribution of power within our own group and in our vision of a revolutionary society. We are committed to a continual examination of our politics as they develop through criticism and self-criticism as an essential aspect of our practice. In her introduction to *Sisterhood is Powerful* Robin Morgan writes:

> *I haven't the faintest notion what possible revolutionary role white heterosexual men could fulfill, since they are the very embodiment of reactionary-vested-interest-power.*

As Black feminists and Lesbians we know that we have a very definite revolutionary task to perform and we are ready for the lifetime of work and struggle before us.

## ENDNOTES

1. This statement is dated April 1977.
2. Wallace, Michele. "A Black Feminist's Search for Sisterhood," The Village Voice, 28 July 1975, pp. 6-7.
3. Mumininas of Committee for Unified Newark, Mwanamke Mwananchi (The Nationalist Woman), Newark, N.J., ©1971, pp. 4-5.

### Study Questions

1. How do the authors understand oppression? How does this impact their politics?

2. What do they argue is the relationship between th personal and the political? What do they mean by identity politics? How do their personal lives affect their analysis?

3. What analysis of privilege do they have? Why are they critical of other progressive movements? What are their specific critisms?

4. Are the authors "anti-male"? Explain.

5. What strategies to fight oppression do they suggest are most effective? Do you agree? Why or why not?

# 6

# NO NAME WOMAN

*Maxine Hong Kingston (1940- )*

*Maxine Hong Kingston has successfully placed the Chinese-American experience into American literature. She is committed to showing that Chinese people have the right to claim themselves as Americans as a result of investing their physical labor into building the nation and exhibiting the ability to be self-sustaining. In her writing,she also strives to dispel the fear and distrust that Americans have had toward the Chinese since the first wave of immigrants landed here during the late nineteenth century. She combats exploitation, racism and ignorance by addressing them directly in her writings. She is best known as the author of* The Woman Warrior: Memoirs of a Girlhood Among Ghosts *(1976), from which the excerpt below is taken, and* China Men *(1980) which describes the patriarchial aspects of Chinese society.*

*Blending morality, Chinese rhythms and American slang, Kingston relates the cautionary tale of an aunt who has been deliberately erased from the family history and whose personal misfortune haunts Kingston's memory. This tale is one of many derived from those her mother told her when she was growing up. What you will find is that this is Kingston's rebellion against the low opinion Chinese culture has of women and the oppression that they experience.*

"You must not tell anyone," my mother said, "what I am about to tell you. In China your father had a sister who killed herself. She jumped into the family well. We say that your father has all brothers because it is as if she had never been born.

"In 1924 just a few days after our village celebrated seventeen hurry-up weddings—to make sure that every young man who went 'out on the road' would responsibly come home—your father and his brothers and your grandfather and his brothers and your aunt's new husband sailed for America, the Gold Mountain. It was your grandfather's last trip. Those lucky enough to get contracts waved goodbye from the decks. They fed and guarded the stowaways and helped them off in Cuba, New York, Bali, Hawaii. 'We'll meet in California next year,' they said. All of them sent money home.

"I remember looking at your aunt one day when she and I were dressing; I had not noticed before that she had such a protruding melon of a stomach. But I did not think, 'She's pregnant' until she began to look like other pregnant women, her shirt pulling and the white tops of her black pants showing. She could not have been pregnant, you see, because her husband had been gone for years. No one said anything. We did not discuss it. In early summer she was ready to have the child, long after the time when it could have been possible.

"The village had also been counting. On the night the baby was to be born the villagers raided our house. Some were crying. Like a great saw, teeth strung with lights, files of people walked zigzag across our land, tearing the rice. Their lanterns doubled in the disturbed black water, which drained away through the broken bunds. As the villagers closed in, we could see that some of them, probably men and women we knew well, wore white masks. The people with long hair hung it over their faces. Women with short hair made it stand up on end. Some had tied white bands around their foreheads, arms, and legs.

"At first they threw mud and rocks at the house. Then they threw eggs and began slaughtering our stock. We could hear the animals scream their deaths—the roosters, the pigs, a last great roar from the ox. Familiar wild heads flared in our night windows; the villagers encircled us. Some of the faces stopped to peer at us, their eyes rushing like search-lights. The hands flattened against the panes, framed heads, and left red prints.

"The villagers broke in the front and the back doors at the same time, even though we had not locked the doors against them. Their knives dripped with the blood of our animals. They smeared blood on the doors and walls. One woman swung a chicken, whose throat she had slit, splattering blood in red areas about her. We stood together in the middle of our house, in the family hall with the pictures and tables of the ancestors around us, and looked straight ahead.

"At that time the house had only two wings. When the men came back, we would build two more to enclose our courtyard and a third one to begin a second courtyard. The villagers pushed through both wings, even your grandparents' rooms, to find your aunt's, which was also mine until the men returned. From this room a new wing for one of the younger families would grow. They ripped up her clothes and shoes and broke her combs, grinding them underfoot. They tore her work from the loom. They scattered the cooking fire and rolled the new weaving in it. We could hear them in the kitchen breaking our bowls and banging the pots. They overturned the great waist-high earthenware jugs; duck eggs, pickled fruits, vegetables burst out and mixed in acrid torrents. The old woman from the next field swept a broom through the air and loosed the spirits-of-the-broom over our heads. 'Pig.' 'Ghost.' 'Pig,' they sobbed and scolded while they ruined our house.

"When they left, they took sugar and oranges to bless themselves. They cut pieces from the dead animals. Some of them took bowls that were not broken and clothes that were not torn. Afterward we swept up the rice and sewed it back up into sacks. But the smells from the spilled preserves lasted. Your aunt gave birth in the pigsty that night. The next morning when I went for the water, I found her and the baby plugging up the family well.

"Don't let your father know that I told you. He denies her. Now that you have started to menstruate, what happened to her could happen to you. Don't humiliate us. You wouldn't like to be forgotten as if you had never been born. The villagers are watchful."

Whenever she had to warn us about life, my mother told stories that ran like this one, a story to grow up on. She tested our strength to establish realities. Those in the emigrant generations who could not reassert brute survival died young and far from home. Those of us in the first American generations have had to figure out how the invisible world the emigrants built around our childhoods fits in solid America.

The emigrants confused the gods by diverting their curses, misleading them with crooked streets and false names. They must try to confuse their offspring as well, who, I suppose, threaten them in similar ways—always trying to get things straight, always trying to name the unspeakable. The Chinese I know hide their names; sojourners take new names when their lives change and guard their real names with silence.

Chinese-Americans, when you try to understand what things in you are Chinese, how do you separate what is peculiar to childhood, to poverty, insanities, one family, your mother who marked your growing with stories, from what is Chinese? What is Chinese tradition and what is the movies?

If I want to learn what clothes my aunt wore, whether flashy or ordinary, I would have to begin, "Remember Father's drowned-in-the-well sister?" I cannot ask that. My mother has told me once and for all the useful parts. She will add nothing unless powered by Necessity, a riverbank that guides her life. She plants vegetable gardens rather than lawns; she carries the odd-shaped tomatoes home from the fields and eats food left for the gods.

Whenever we did frivolous things, we used up energy; we flew high kites. We children came up off the ground over the melting cones our parents brought home from work and the American movie on New Year's Day—Oh, *You Beautiful Doll* with Betty Grable one year, and *She Wore a Yellow Ribbon* with John Wayne another year. After the one carnival ride each, we paid in guilt; our tired father counted his change on the dark walk home.

Adultery is extravagance. Could people who hatch their own chicks and eat the embryos and the heads for delicacies and boil the feet in vinegar for party food, leaving only the gravel, eating even the gizzard lining—could such people engender a prodigal aunt? To be a woman, to have a daughter in starvation time was a waste enough. My aunt could not have been the lone romantic who gave up everything for sex. Women in the old China did not choose. Some man had commanded her to lie with him and be his secret evil. I wonder whether he masked himself when he joined the raid on her family.

Perhaps she had encountered him in the fields or on the mountain where the daughters-in-law collected fuel. Or perhaps he first noticed her in the marketplace. He was not a stranger because the village housed no strangers. She had to have dealings with him other than sex. Perhaps he worked an adjoining field, or he sold her the cloth for the dress she sewed and wore. His demand must have surprised, then terrified her. She obeyed him; she always did as she was told.

When the family found a young man in the next village to be her husband, she had stood tractably beside the best rooster, his proxy, and promised before they met that she would be his forever. She was lucky that he was her age and she would be the first wife, an advantage secure now. The night she first saw him, he had sex with her. Then he left for America. She had almost forgotten what he looked like. When she tried to envision him, she only saw the black and white face in the group photograph the men had had taken before leaving.

The other man was not, after all, much different from her husband. They both gave orders: she followed. "If you tell your family, I'll beat you. I'll kill you. Be here again next week." No one talked sex, ever. And she might have separated the rapes from the rest of living if only she did not have to buy her oil from him or gather wood in the same forest. I want her fear to have lasted just as long as rape lasted so that the fear could have been contained. No drawn-out fear. But women at sex hazarded birth and hence lifetimes. The fear did not stop but permeated everywhere. She told the man, "I think I'm pregnant." He organized the raid against her.

On nights when my mother and father talked about their life back home, sometimes they mentioned an "outcast table" whose business they still seemed to be settling, their voices tight. In a commensal tradition, where food is precious, the powerful older people made wrongdoers eat alone. Instead of letting them start separate new lives like the Japanese, who could become samurais and geishas, the Chinese family, faces averted but eyes glowering sideways, hung on to the offenders and fed them leftovers. My aunt must have lived in the same house as my parents and eaten at an outcast table. My mother spoke about the raid as if she had seen it, when she and my aunt, a daughter-in-law to a different household, should not have been living together at all. Daughters-in-law lived with their husbands' parents, not their own; a synonym for marriage in Chinese is "taking a daughter-in-law." Her husband's parents could have sold her, mortgaged her, stoned her. But they had sent her back to her own mother and father, a mysterious act hinting at disgraces not told me. Perhaps they had thrown her out to deflect the avengers.

She was the only daughter; her four brothers went with her father, husband, and uncles "out on the road" and for some years became western men. When the goods were divided among the family, three of the brothers took land, and the youngest, my father, chose an education. After my grandparents gave their daughter away to her husband's family, they had dispensed all the adventure and all the property. They expected her alone to keep the traditional ways, which her brothers, now among the barbarians, could fumble without detection. The heavy, deeprooted women were to maintain the past against the flood, safe for returning. But the rare urge west had fixed upon our family, and so my aunt crossed boundaries not delineated in space.

The work of preservation demands that the feelings playing about in one's guts not be turned into action. Just watch their passing like cherry blossoms. But perhaps my aunt, my forerunner, caught in a slow life, let dreams grow and fade and after some months or years went toward what persisted. Fear at the enormities of the forbidden kept her desires delicate, wire and bone. She looked at a man because she liked the way the hair was tucked behind his ears, or she liked the question-mark line of a long torso curving at the shoulder and straight at the hip. For warm eyes or a soft voice or a slow walk—that's all—a few hairs, a line, a brightness, a sound, a pace, she gave up family. She offered us up for a charm that vanished with tiredness, a pigtail that didn't toss when the wind died. Why, the wrong lighting could erase the dearest thing about him.

It could very well have been, however, that my aunt did not take subtle enjoyment of her friend, but, a wild woman, kept rollicking company. Imagining her free with sex doesn't fit, though. I don't know any women like that, or men either. Unless I see her life branching into mine, she gives me no ancestral help.

To sustain her being in love, she often worked at herself in the mirror, guessing at the colors and shapes that would interest him, changing them frequently in order to hit on the right combination. She wanted him to look back.

On a farm near the sea, a woman who tended her appearance reaped a reputation for eccentricity. All the married women blunt-cut their hair in flaps about their ears or pulled it back in tight buns. No nonsense. Neither style blew easily into heart-catching tangles. And at their weddings they displayed themselves in their long hair for the last time. "It brushed the backs of my knees," my mother tells me. "It was braided, and even so, it brushed the backs of my knees."

At the mirror my aunt combed individuality into her bob. A bun could have been contrived to escape into black streamers blowing in the wind or in quiet wisps about her face, but only the older women in our picture album wear buns. She brushed her hair back from her forehead, tucking the flaps behind her ears. She looped a piece of thread, knotted into a circle between her index fingers and thumbs, and ran the double strand across her forehead. When she closed her fingers as if she were making a pair of shadow geese bite, the string twisted together catching the little hairs. Then she pulled the thread away from her skin, ripping the hairs out neatly, her eyes watering from the needles of pain. Opening her fingers, she cleaned the thread, then rolled it along her hairline and the tops of her eyebrows. My mother did the same to me and my sisters and herself. I used to believe that the expression "caught by the short hairs" meant a captive held with a depilatory string. It especially hurt at the temples, but my mother said we were lucky we didn't have to have our feet bound when we were seven. Sisters used to sit on their beds and cry together, she said, as their mothers or their slaves removed the bandages for a few minutes each night and let the blood gush back into their veins. I hope that the man my aunt loved appreciated a smooth brow, that he wasn't just a tits-and-ass man.

Once my aunt found a freckle on her chin, at a spot that the almanac said predestined her for unhappiness. She dug it out with a hot needle and washed the wound with peroxide.

More attention to her looks than these pullings of hairs and pickings at spots would have caused gossip among the villagers. They owned work clothes and good clothes, and they wore good clothes for feasting the new seasons. But since a woman combing her hair hexes beginnings, my aunt rarely found an occasion to look her best. Women looked like great sea snails—the corded wood, babies, and laundry they carried were the whorls on their backs. The Chinese did not admire a bent back; goddesses and warriors stood straight. Still there must have been a marvelous freeing of beauty when a worker laid down her burden and stretched and arched.

Such commonplace loveliness, however, was not enough for my aunt. She dreamed of a lover for the fifteen days of New Year's, the time for families to exchange visits, money, and food. She plied her secret comb. And sure enough she cursed the year, the family, the village, and herself.

Even as her hair lured her imminent lover, many other men looked at her. Uncles, cousins, nephews, brothers would have looked, too, had they been home between journeys. Perhaps they had already been restraining their curiosity, and they left, fearful that their glances, like a field of

nesting birds, might be startled and caught. Poverty hurt, and that was their first reason for leaving. But another, final reason for leaving the crowded house was the never-said.

She may have been unusually beloved, the precious only daughter, spoiled and mirror gazing because of the affection the family lavished on her. When her husband left, they welcomed the chance to take her back from the in-laws; she could live like the little daughter for just a while longer. There are stories that my grandfather was different from other people, "crazy ever since the little Jap bayoneted him in the head." He used to put his naked penis on the dinner table, laughing. And one day he brought home a baby girl, wrapped up inside his brown western-style greatcoat. He had traded one of his sons, probably my father, the youngest, for her. My grandmother made him trade back. When he finally got a daughter of his own, he doted on her. They must have all loved her, except perhaps my father, the only brother who never went back to China, having once been traded for a girl.

Brothers and sisters, newly men and women, had to efface their sexual color and present plain miens. Disturbing hair and eyes, a smile like no other, threatened the ideal of five generations living under one roof. To focus blurs, people shouted face to face and yelled from room to room. The immigrants I know have loud voices, unmodulated to American tones even after years away from the village where they called their friendships out across the fields. I have not been able to stop my mother's screams in public libraries or over telephones. Walking erect (knees straight, toes pointed forward, not pigeon-toed, which is Chinese-feminine) and speaking in an inaudible voice, I have tried to turn myself American-feminine. Chinese communication was loud, public. Only sick people had to whisper. But at the dinner table, where the family members came nearest one another, no one could talk, not the outcasts nor any eaters. Every word that falls from the mouth is a coin lost. Silently they gave and accepted food with both hands. A preoccupied child who took his bowl with one hand got a sideways glare. A complete moment of total attention is due everyone alike. Children and lovers have no singularity here, but my aunt used a secret voice, a separate attentiveness.

She kept the man's name to herself throughout her labor and dying; she did not accuse him that he be punished with her. To save her inseminator's name she gave silent birth.

He may have been somebody in her own household, but intercourse with a man outside the family would have been no less abhorrent. All the village were kinsmen, and the titles shouted in loud country voices never let kinship be forgotten. Any man within visiting distance would have been neutralized as a lover—"brother," "younger brother," "older brother"—one hundred and fifteen relationship titles. Parents researched birth charts probably not so much to assure good fortune as to circumvent incest in a population that has but one hundred surnames. Everybody has eight million relatives. How useless then sexual mannerisms, how dangerous.

As if it came from an atavism deeper than fear, I used to add "brother" silently to boys' names. It hexed the boys, who would or would not ask me to dance, and made them less scary and as familiar and deserving of benevolence as girls.

But, of course, I hexed myself also—no dates. I should have stood up, both arms waving, and shouted out across libraries, "Hey, you! Love me back." I had no idea, though, how to make attraction selective, how to control its direction and magnitude. If I made myself American—pretty so that the five or six Chinese boys in the class fell in love with me, everyone else—the Caucasian, Negro, and Japanese boys—would too. Sisterliness, dignified and honorable, made much more sense.

Attraction eludes control so stubbornly that whole societies designed to organize relationships among people cannot keep order, not even when they bind people to one another from childhood and raise them together. Among the very poor and the wealthy, brothers married their adopted sisters, like doves. Our family allowed some romance, paying adult brides' prices and providing dowries so that their sons and daughters could marry strangers. Marriage promises to turn strangers into friendly relatives—a nation of siblings.

In the village structure, spirits shimmered among the live creatures, balanced and held in equilibrium by time and land. But one human being flaring up into violence could open up a black hole, a maelstrom that pulled in the sky. The frightened villagers, who depended on one another to maintain the real, went to my aunt to show her a personal, physical representation of the break she had made in the "roundness." Misallying couples snapped off the future, which was to be embodied in true offspring. The villagers punished her for acting as if she could have a private life, secret and apart from them.

If my aunt had betrayed the family at a time of large grain yields and peace, when many boys were born, and wings were being built on many houses, perhaps she might have escaped such severe punishment. But the men—hungry, greedy, tired of planting in dry soil—had been forced to leave the village in order to send food money home. There were ghost plagues, bandit plagues, wars with the Japanese, floods. My Chinese brother and sister had died of an unknown sickness. Adultery, perhaps only a mistake during good times, became a crime when the village needed food.

The round moon cakes and round doorways, the round tables of graduated sizes that fit one roundness inside another, round windows and rice bowls—these talismans had lost their power to warn this family of the law: a family must be whole, faithfully keeping the descent line by having sons to feed the old and the dead, who in turn look after the family. The villagers came to show my aunt and her lover-in-hiding a broken house. The villagers were speeding up the circling of events because she was too shortsighted to see that her infidelity had already harmed the village, that waves of consequences would return unpredictably, sometimes in disguise, as now, to hurt her. This roundness had to be made coin-sized so that she would see its circumference: punish her at the birth of her baby. Awaken her to the inexorable. People who refused fatalism because they could invent small resources insisted on culpability. Deny accidents and wrest fault from the stars.

After the villagers left, their lanterns now scattering in various directions toward home, the family broke their silence and cursed her. "Aiaa, we're going to die. Death is coming. Death is coming. Look what you've done. You've killed us. Ghost! Dead ghost! Ghost! You've never been born." She ran out into the fields, far enough from the house so that she could no longer hear their voices, and pressed herself against the earth, her own land no more. When she felt the birth coming, she thought that she had been hurt. Her body seized together. "They've hurt me too much," she thought. "This is gall, and it will kill me." With forehead and knees against the earth, her body convulsed and then relaxed. She turned on her back, lay on the ground. The black well of sky and stars went out and out and out forever; her body and her complexity seemed to disappear. She was one of the stars, a bright dot in blackness, without home, without a companion, in eternal cold and silence. An agoraphobia rose in her, speeding higher and higher, bigger and bigger; she would not be able to contain it; there would be no end to fear.

Flayed, unprotected against space, she felt pain return, focusing her body. This pain chilled her—a cold, steady kind of surface pain. Inside, spasmodically, the other pain, the pain of the child, heated her. For hours she lay on the ground, alternately body and space. Sometimes a vision of normal comfort obliterated reality: she saw the family in the evening gambling at the dinner table, the young people massaging their elders' backs. She saw them congratulating one another, high joy on the mornings the rice shoots came up. When these pictures burst, the stars drew yet further apart. Black space opened.

She got to her feet to fight better and remembered that old-fashioned women gave birth in their pigsties to fool the jealous, pain-dealing gods, who do not snatch piglets. Before the next spasms could stop her, she ran to the pigsty, each step a rushing out into emptiness. She climbed over the fence and knelt in the dirt. It was good to have a fence enclosing her, a tribal person alone.

Laboring, this woman who had carried her child as a foreign growth that sickened her every day, expelled it at last. She reached down to touch the hot, wet, moving mass, surely smaller than anything human, and could feel that it was human after all-fingers, toes, nails, nose. She pulled it up on to her belly, and it lay curled there, butt in the air, feet precisely tucked one under the other. She opened her loose shirt and buttoned the child inside. After resting, it squirmed and thrashed and she pushed it up to her breast. It turned its head this way and that until it found her nipple. There, it made little snuffling noises. She clenched her teeth at its preciousness, lovely as a young calf, a piglet, a little dog.

She may have gone to the pigsty as a last act of responsibility: she would protect this child as she had protected its father. It would look after her soul, leaving supplies on her grave. But how would this tiny child without family find her grave when there would be no marker for her anywhere, neither in the earth nor the family hall? No one would give her a family hall name. She had taken the child with her into the wastes. At its birth the two of them had felt the same raw pain of separation, a wound that only the family pressing tight could close. A child with no descent line would not soften her life but only trail after her, ghostlike, begging her to give it purpose. At dawn the villagers on their way to the fields would stand around the fence and look.

Full of milk, the little ghost slept. When it awoke, she hardened her breasts against the milk that crying loosens. Toward morning she picked up the baby and walked to the well.

Carrying the baby to the well shows loving. Otherwise abandon it. Turn its face into the mud. Mothers who love their children take them along. It was probably a girl; there is some hope of forgiveness for boys.

"Don't tell anyone you had an aunt. Your father does not want to hear her name. She has never been born." I have believed that sex was unspeakable and words so strong and fathers so frail that "aunt" would do my father mysterious harm. I have thought that my family, having settled among immigrants who had also been their neighbors in the ancestral land, needed to clean their name, and a wrong word would incite the kinspeople even here. But there is more to this silence: they want me to participate in her punishment. And I have.

In the twenty years since I heard this story I have not asked for details nor said my aunt's name; I do not know it. People who can comfort the dead can also chase after them to hurt them further—a reverse ancestor worship. The real punishment was not the raid swiftly inflicted by the villagers, but the family's deliberately forgetting her. Her betrayal so maddened them, they saw to it that she would suffer forever, even after death. Always hungry, always needing, she would have to beg food from other ghosts, snatch and steal it from those whose living descendants give them gifts. She would have to fight the ghosts massed at crossroads for the buns a few thoughtful citizens leave to decoy her away from village and home so that the ancestral spirits could feast unharassed. At peace, they could act like gods, not ghosts, their descent lines providing them with paper suits and dresses, spirit money, paper houses, paper automobiles, chicken, meat, and rice into eternity—essences delivered up in smoke and flames, steam and incense rising from each rice bowl. In an attempt to make the Chinese care for people outside the family, Chairman Mao encourages us now to give our paper replicas to the spirits of outstanding soldiers and workers, no matter whose ancestors they may be. My aunt remains forever hungry. Goods are not distributed evenly among the dead.

My aunt haunts me—her ghost drawn to me because now, after fifty years of neglect, I alone devote pages of paper to her, though not origamied into houses and clothes. I do not think she always means me well. I am telling on her, and she was a spite suicide, drowning herself in the drinking water. The Chinese are always very frightened of the drowned one, whose weeping ghost, wet hair hanging and skin bloated, waits silently by the water to pull down a substitute.

**Study Questions**

1. Why would Hong Kingston begin her entire autobiography with this piece? What does this story have have to do with the life of the author in America?

2. What point is she making about silence here? Can you compare it to Moraga's?

3. Is this piece fiction, biography, or autobiography? Why does she go through various scenarios about her aunt? What does this say about objectivity?

4. Which account of the "No Name Woman's" pregnancy do you think is "true"? Why" What difference does it make?

5. According to Kingston, how do standards of femininity differ between China and the U.S.? What does that suggest about these standards?

6. Why did the village react so harshly against the "No Name Woman"? What does this piece reveal about family relationships and the influence of the community?

7. How does family folklore influence the manner in which an individual views the wider society?

# EXCERPT FROM *FAREWELL TO MANZANAR*

*Jeanne Wakatsuki Houston and James Houston*

*Jeanne Wakatsuki Houston was born and raised in Southern California. In 1942 at the age of seven she and her family were evacuated from their home and taken to Manzanar, a Japanese internment camp. She and her family spent the next three years there. Years later she studied sociology and journalism at San Jose State College.*

*James D. Houston, Jeanne's husband, was born in San Francisco, California in 1933. He has published several novels, a collection of short stories, and a few non-fiction works.*

*This excerpt is taken from their book by the same name which tells the story of Jeanne Houston and her family during World War II.*

## Tragic Transition: The Internment of Japanese Americans (1942 - 1945)

In the aftermath of the Japanese bombing of Pearl Harbor on December 7, 1941, wartime hysteria and decades of prejudice against people of Asian descent created one of the great horrors of American history - the mass relocation and imprisonment of Japanese Americans in internment camps. From 1942 through 1945, more than 120,000 Japanese Americans, American citizens and Japanese nationals alike, were uprooted from their lives on the West Coast and Hawaii and incarcerated in detention camps.

Despite reports by the FBI, the War Department, and the President's own investigative team that Japanese Americans posed no military threat, xenophobic military and political leaders pushed for the internment of first-, second-, and third-generation Japanese Americans, declaring that they constituted an internal threat to national security as possible spies and saboteurs. Racist anti-Japanese sentiment was fueled by mainstream press editorials and articles in publications such as Time, The Los Angeles Times, and The Washington Post, and bolstered the position of relocation movement leaders such as Lieutenant General John L. DeWitt, head of the Western Defense Command.

On February 19, 1942, President Franklin Delano Roosevelt signed Executive Order 9066. Order 9066 directed the Secretary of War to prescribe military areas from which persons could be excluded at the discretion of the U.S. military. Although the order directly violated the constitutional rights of Japanese -American citizens, who comprised two-thirds of the interned population, it gave full authority to remove them from their homes and place them first in assembly centers and then in internment camps.

Most internees (119,000) were taken from the states of California, Washington, and Oregon. Due to their vital importance to Hawaii's labor pool (as over one third of the population) and because of Hawaii's multiethnic history, a much smaller number of Japanese Americans were interned from the Hawaiian Islands (1,444).

Instructed to bring only what they could carry, internees were given little notice - a week or less - to get ready for evacuation, and many lost their homes and livelihoods in the process. Families were forced to register by number and were taken to assembly centers, which were often stockyards, fairgrounds, and racetracks ordinarily used to house animals. Later, they were taken by train to one of ten camp locations: Topaz in Utah, Poston and Gila River in Arizona, Amache in Colorado, Jerome and Rohwer in Arkansas, Minidoka in Idaho, Manzanar and Tule Lake in California, and Heart Mountain in Wyoming. Most of these sites were in desolate desert areas.

As Jeanne Wakatsuki Houston recounts in Farewell to Manzanar, conditions in the guarded, barbed wire-enclosed camps were bleak. Only the bare necessities were provided for and there was little or no privacy.

Some families were split up among different camps. Prior to the internment, Japanese Americans were subjected to raids on their homes by government officials looking for evidence of treason. Many men, especially community leaders, were taken in for questioning only because they were of Japanese descent. Following the interrogations, some men were deported to all-male relocation camps and interned separately from their families.

In September of 1942, the Selective Service had classified all men of Japanese descent as IV-C, or enemy aliens. However, on February 1, 1943, President Roosevelt wrote a letter to Secretary of War Henry L. Stimson stating that all U.S. citizens regardless of their ancestry would be allowed to fight in the armed forces. In spite of his earlier evacuation order, President Roosevelt thereby made many male Nisei (second-generation Japanese Americans) eligible for the draft. These orders often forced young men to choose between fighting for a country that was imprisoning their families or being sentenced and jailed separately for draft resistance.

Some Nisei defied the relocation orders because they believed they were unconstitutional. Acting independently, Minoru Yasui of Portland, Fred Korematsu in California, and Gordon Hirabayashi in Washington were among those who refused to obey the evacuation orders and the curfew orders that preceded the internment. All three men were arrested, convicted, and sent to prison. At the time, their cases were heard in the Supreme Court, which upheld their criminal convictions, stating that the government's policies were based on "military necessity." It wasn't until the 1980s that their cases were appealed and overturned by courts that found that the U.S. government had suppressed evidence indicating that Japanese Americans posed no security threat and therefore no "military necessity" for their removal existed.

During the 1970s and 1980s, many Asian American and civil-rights groups campaigned for redress for interned Japanese Americans. These efforts resulted in the signing into law of the Civil Liberties Act of 1988 on August 10, 1988. The act provided for an official apology for the government's internment survivors, as well as a fund for a public educational program to prevent the recurrence of such injustice. The act is significant in its recognition that the U.S. government had committed an egregious violation of rights against its own people.

Even after the internment had ended, Japanese Americans felt the devastating effects of this injustice for many years. After being released from the concentration camps, some returned to their hometowns only to find their homes and businesses destroyed and struggled to rebuild their lives. The sense of being singled out as untrusted members of American society also haunted younger Nisei, who passed this on to later generations.

In addition to the following passages, which illustrate life during this period, many Sansei and Yonsei (third- and fourth-generation Japanese Americans) have written about how their parents' and grandparents' internment memories affected their lives.

## From *Farewell to Manzanar*

### SHIKATA GA NAI

In December of 1941 Papa's disappearance didn't' bother me nearly so much as the world I soon found myself in.

He had been a jack-of-all-trades. When I was born he was farming near Inglewood. Later, when he started fishing, we moved to Ocean Park, near Santa Monica, and until they picked him up, that's where we lived, in a big frame house with a brick fireplace, a block back from the beach. We were the only Japanese family in the neighborhood. Papa liked it that way. He didn't want to be labeled or grouped by anyone. But with him gone and no way of knowing what to expect, my mother moved all of us down to Terminal Island. Woody already lived there, and one of my older sisters had married a Terminal Island boy. Mama's first concern now was to keep the family together; and once the war began, she felt safer there than isolated racially in Ocean Park. But for me, at age seven, the island was a country as foreign as India or Arabia would have been. It was the first time I had lived among other Japanese, or gone to school with them, and I was terrified all the time.

This was partly Papa's fault. One of his threats to keep us younger kids in line was "I'm going to sell you to the Chinaman." When I had entered kindergarten two years earlier, I was the only Oriental in the class. They sat me next to a Caucasian girl who happened to have very slanted eyes. I looked at her and began to scream, certain Papa had sold me out at last. My fear of her ran so deep I could not speak of it, even to Mama, couldn't explain why I was screaming. For two weeks I had nightmares about this girl, until the teachers finally moved me to the other side of the room. And it was still with me, this fear of Oriental faces, when we moved to Terminal Island.

In those days it was a company town, a ghetto owned and controlled by the canneries. The men went after fish, and whenever the boats came back - day or night - the women would be called to process the catch while it was fresh. One in the afternoon or four in the morning, it made no difference. My mother had to go to work right after we moved there. I can still hear the whistle - two toots for French's three for Van Camp's - and she and Chizu would be out of bed in the middle of the night, heading for the cannery.

The house we lived in was nothing more than a shack, a barracks with single-plank walls and rough wooden floors, like the cheapest kind of migrant workers' housing. The people around us were hard-working, boisterous, a little proud of their nickname, yo-go-re, which meant literally uncouth one, or roughneck, or dead-end kid. They not only spoke Japanese exclusively, they spoke a dialect peculiar to Kyushu, where their families had come from in Japan, a rough, fisherman's language, full of oaths and insults. Instead of saying ba-ka-at-re, a common insult meaning stupid, Terminal Islanders would say ba-ka-ya-ro, a coarser and exclusively masculine use of the word, which implies gross stupidity. They would swagger and pick on outsiders and persecute anyone who didn't speak as they did. That was what made my own time there so hateful. I had never spoken anything but English, and the other kids in the second grade despised me for it. They were tough and mean, like ghetto kids anywhere. Each day after school I dreaded their ambush. My brother Kiyo, three years older, would wait for me at the door, where we would decide whether to run straight home together, or split up, or try a new and unexpected route.

None of these kids ever actually attacked. It was the threat that frightened us, their fearful looks, and the noises they would make, like miniature Samurai, in a language we couldn't understand.

At the time it seemed we had been living under this reign of fear for years. In fact, we lived there

about two months. Late in February the navy decided to clear Terminal Island completely. Even though most of us were American-born, it was dangerous having that many Orientals so close to the Long Beach Naval Station, on the opposite end of the island. We had known something like this was coming. But, like Papa's arrest, not much could be done ahead of time. There were four of us kids still young enough to be living with Mama, plus Granny, her mother, sixty-five then, speaking no English, and nearly blind. Mama didn't know where else she could get work, and we had nowhere else to move to. On February 25 the choice was made for us. We were given forty-eight hours to clear out.

The secondhand dealers had been prowling for weeks, like wolves, offering humiliating prices for good and furniture they knew many of us would have to sell sooner or later. Mama had left all but her most valuable possessions in Ocean Park, simply because she had nowhere to put them. She had brought along her pottery, her silver, heirlooms like the kimonos Granny had brought from Japan, tea sets, lacquered tables, and one fine old set of china, blue and white porcelain, almost translucent. On the day we were leaving, Woody's car was so crammed with boxes and luggage and kids we had just run out of room. Mama had to sell this china.

One of the dealers offered her fifteen dollars for it. She said it was a full setting for twelve and worth at least two hundred. He said fifteen was his top price. Mama started to quiver. Her eyes blazed up at him. She had been packing all night and trying to calm down Granny, who didn't understand why we were moving again and what all the rush was about. Mama's nerves were shot, and now navy jeeps were patrolling the streets. She didn't say another word. She just glared at this man, all the rage and frustration channeled at him through her eyes.

He watched her for a moment and said he was sure he couldn't pay more than seventeen fifty for that china. She reached into the red velvet case, took out a dinner plate and hurled it at the floor right in front of his feet.

The man leaped back shouting, "Hey! Hey, don't do that! Those are valuable dishes!"

Mama took out another dinner plate and hurled it at the floor, then another and another, never moving, never opening her mouth, just quivering and glaring at the retreating dealer, with tears streaming down her cheeks. He finally turned and scuttled out the door, heading for the next house. When he was gone she stood there smashing cups and bowls and platters until the whole set lay in scattered blue and white fragments across the wooden floor.

The American Friends Service helped us find a small house in Boyle Heights, another minority ghetto, in downtown Los Angeles, now inhabited briefly by a few hundred Terminal Island refugees. Executive Order 9066 had been signed by President Roosevelt, giving the War Department authority to define military areas in the western states and to exclude from them anyone who might threaten the war effort. There was a lot of talk about internment, or moving inland, or something like that in store for all Japanese Americans. I remember my brothers sitting around the table talking very intently about what we were going to do, how we would keep the family together. They had seen how quickly Papa was removed, and they knew now that he would not be back for quite a while. Just before leaving Terminal Island Mama had received her first letter, from Bismarck, North Dakota. He had been imprisoned at Fort Lincoln, in an all-male camp for enemy aliens.

Papa had been the patriarch. He had always decided everything in the family. With him gone, my brothers, like councilors in the absence of a chief, worried about what should be done. The ironic thing is, there wasn't much left to decide. These were mainly days of quiet, desperate waiting for what seemed at the time to be inevitable. There is a phrase the Japanese use in such situation, when something difficult must be endured. You would hear the older heads, the Issue, telling others very quietly, "Shikata ga nai" (it cannot be helped). "Shikata ga nai" (It must be done).

Mama and Woody went to work packing celery for a Japanese produce dealer. Kiyo and my sister May and I enrolled in the local school, and what sticks in my memory from those few weeks is the teacher - not her looks, her remoteness. In Ocean Park my teacher had been a kind, grandmotherly woman who used to sail with us in Papa's boat from time to time and who wept the day we had to leave. In Boyle Heights the teacher felt cold and distant. I was confused by all the moving and was having trouble with the class work, but she would never help me out. She would have nothing to do with me.

This was the first time I had felt outright hostility from a Caucasian. Looking back, it is easy enough to explain. Public attitudes toward the Japanese in California were shifting rapidly. In the first few months of the Pacific war, America was on the run. Tolerance had turned to distrust the irrational fear. The hundred-year-old tradition of anti-Orientalism on the West Coast soon resurfaced, more vicious than ever. Its result became clear about a month later, when we were told to make our third and final move.

The name Manzanar meant nothing to us when we left Boyle Heights. We didn't know where it was or what it was. We went because the government ordered us to. And, in the case of my older brothers and sisters, we went with a certain amount of relief. They had all heard stories of Japanese homes being attacked, of beatings in the streets of California towns. They were as frightened of the Caucasians as Caucasians were of us. Moving, under what appeared to be government protection, to an area less directly threatened by the war seemed not such a bad idea at all. For some it actually sounded like a fine adventure.

Our pickup point was a Buddhist church in Los Angeles. It was very early, and misty, when we got there with our luggage. Mama had bought heavy coats for all of us. She grew up in eastern Washington and knew that anywhere inland in early April would be cold. I was proud of my new coat, and I remember sitting on a duffel bag trying to be friendly with the Greyhound driver. I smiled at him. He didn't smile back. He was befriending no one. Someone tied a number tag to my collar and to the duffel bag (each family was given a number, and that became our official designation until the camps were closed), someone else passed out box lunches for the trip, and we climbed aboard.

I had never been outside Los Angeles County, never traveled more than ten miles from the coast, but never even ridden on a bus. I was full of excitement, the way any kid would be, and wanted to look out the window. But for the first few hours the shades were drawn. Around me other people played cards, read magazines, dozed, waiting. I settled back, waiting too, and finally fell asleep. The bus felt very secure to me. Almost half its passengers were immediate relatives. Mama and my older brothers had succeeded in keeping most of us together, on the same bus, headed for the same camp. I didn't realize until much later what a job that was. The strategy had been, first, to have everyone living in the same district when the evacuation began, and then to get all of us included under the same family number, even though names had been changed by marriage. Many families weren't as lucky as ours and suffered months of anguish while trying to arrange transfers from one camp to another.

We rode all day. By the time we reached our destination, the shades were up. It was late afternoon. The first thing I saw was a yellow swirl across a blurred, reddish setting sun. The bus was being pelted by what sounded like splattering rain. It wasn't rain. This was my first look at something I would soon know very well, a billowing flurry of dust and sand churned up by the wind through Owens Valley.

We drove past a barbed-wire fence, through a gate, and into an open space where trunks and sacks and packages had been dumped from the baggage trucks that drove out ahead of us. I could see a few tents set up, the first rows of black barracks, and beyond them, blurred by sand, rows of barracks that seemed to spread for miles across this plain. People were sitting on cartons or milling around, with their backs to the wind, waiting to see which friends or relatives might be on this bus. As we approached, they turned or stood up, and some moved toward us unrepentantly. But inside the bus no one stirred. No one waved or spoke. They just stared out the windows, ominously silent. I didn't understand this. Hadn't we finally arrived, our whole family intact? I opened a window, leaned out, and yelled happily. "Hey! This whole bus is full of Wakatsukis!"

Outside, the greeters smiled. Inside there was an explosion of laughter, hysterical, tension-breaking laughter that left my brothers choking and whacking each other across the shoulders.

We had pulled up just in time for dinner. The mess halls weren't completed yet. An outdoor chow line snaked around a half-finished building that broke a good part of the wind. They issued us army mess kits, the round metal kind that fold over, and plopped in scoops of canned Vienna sausage, canned string beans, steamed rice that had been cooked too long, and on top of the rice a serving of canned apricots. The Caucasian servers were thinking that the fruit poured over the rice would make a good desert. Among the Japanese of course, rice is never eaten with sweet foods, only with salty or savory foots. Few of us could eat such a mixture. But at this point no one dared protest. It would have been impolite. I was horrified when I saw the apricot syrup seeping through my little mound of rice. I opened my mouth to complain. My mother jabbed me in the back to keep quiet. We moved on through the line and joined the others squatting in the lee of half-raised walls, dabbing courteously at what was, for almost everyone there, an inedible concoction.

After dinner we were taken to Block 16, a cluster of fifteen barracks that had just been finished a day or so earlier - although finished was hardly the word for it. The shacks were built of one thickness of pine planking covered with tarpaper. They sat on concrete footings, with about two feet of open space between the floorboards and the ground. Gaps showed between the planks, and as the weeks passed and the green wood dried out, the gaps widened. Knotholes gaped in the uncovered floor.

Each barracks was divided into six units, sixteen by twenty feet, about the size of a living room, with one bare bulb hanging from the ceiling and an oil stove for heat. We were assigned two of these for the twelve people in our family group; and our official family "number" was enlarged by three digits - 16 plus the number of this barracks. We were issued steel army cots, two brown army blankets each, and some mattress covers, which my brothers stuffed with straw.

The first task was to divide up what space we had for sleeping. Bill and Woody contributed a blanket each and portioned off the first room: one side for Bill and Tomi, one side for Woody and Chizu and their baby girl. Woody also got the stove, for heating formulas.

The people who had it hardest during the first few months were young couples like these, many of whom had married just before evacuation began, in order not to be separated and sent to different camps. Our two rooms were crowded, but at least it was all in the family. My oldest sister and her husband were shoved into one of those sixteen-by-twenty-foot compartments with six people they had never seen before - two other couples, one recently married like themselves, the other with two teenage boys. Partitioning off a room like that wasn't easy. It was bitter cold when we arrived, and the wind did not abate. All they had to use for room dividers were those army blankets, two of which were barely enough to keep one person warm. They argued over whose blanket should be sacrificed and later argued about noise at night - the parents wanted their boys asleep by 9:00 p.m. - and they continued arguing over matters like that for six months, until my sister and her husband left to harvest sugar beets in Idaho. It was grueling work up there, and wages were pitiful, but when the call came through camp for workers to alleviate the wartime labor shortage, it sounded better than their life at Manzanar. They knew they'd have, if nothing else, a room, perhaps a cabin of their own.

That first night in Block 16, the rest of us squeezed into the second room - Granny, Lillian, age fourteen, Ray, thirteen, May, eleven, Kiyo, ten, Mama, and me. I didn't mind this at all at the time. Being youngest meant I got to sleep with Mama. And before we went to bed I had a great time jumping up and down on the mattress. The boys had stuffed so much straw into her, we had to flatten it some so we wouldn't slide off. I slept with her every night after that until Papa came back.

## A DIFFERENT KIND OF SAND

We woke early, shivering and coated with dust that had blown up through the knotholes and in through the slits around the doorway. During the night Mama had unpacked all our clothes and heaped them on our beds for warmth. Now our cubicle look as if a great laundry bag had exploded and then been sprayed with fine dust. A skin of sand covered the floor. I looked over Mama's shoulder at Kiyo, on top of his fat mattress, buried under jeans and overcoats and sweaters. His eyebrows were gray, and he was starting to giggle. He was looking at me, at my gray eyebrows and coated hair, and pretty soon we were both giggling. I looked at Mama's face to see if she thought Kiyo was funny. She lay very still next to me on our mattress, her eyes scanning everything - bare rafters, walls, dusty kids - scanning slowly, and I think the mask of her face would have cracked had not Woody's voice just then come at us through the wall. He was rapping on the planks as if testing to see if they were hollow.

Hey!" he yelled. "you guys fall into the same flour barrel as us?"

No," Kiyo yelled back. "Ours is full of Japs."

All of us laughed at this.

Well, tell 'em it's time to get up," Woody said "If we're gonna live in this place, we better get to work."

He gave us ten minutes to dress, then he came in carrying a broom, a hammer, and a sack full of tin canlids he had scrounged somewhere. Woody would be our leader for a while now, short, stocky, grinning behind his mustache. He had just turned twenty-four. In later years he would tour the country with Mr. Moto, the Japanese tag-team wrestler, as his sinister assistant Suki - karate chops through the ropes from outside the ring, a chunky leg reaching from under his kimono to trip up Mr. Moto's foe. In the ring Woody's smile looked sly and crafty; he hammed it up. Offstage it was whimsical, as if some joke were busting to be told.

Hey, brother Ray, Kiyo," he said. "You see these tin can lids?"

Yeah, yeah," the boys said drowsily, as if going back to sleep.

They were both young versions of Woody.

You see all them knotholes in the floor and in the walls?"

They looked around. You could see about a dozen.

Woody said, "You get those covered up before breakfast time. Any more sand comes in here through one of them knotholes, you have to eat it off the floor with ketchup."

"What about sand that comes in through the cracks?" Kiyo said.

Woody stood up very straight, which in itself was funny, since he was only about five-foot-six.

"Don't worry about the cracks," he said. Different kind of sand comes in through the cracks."

He put his hands on his hips and gave Kiyo a sternly comic look, squinting at him through one eye the way Papa would when he was asserting his authority. Woody mimicked Papa's voice: "And I can tell the difference. So be careful."

The boys laughed and went to work nailing down lids. May started sweeping out the sand. I was helping Mama fold the clothes we'd used for cover, when Woody came over and put his arm around her shoulder. He was short; she was even shorter, under five feet.

He said softly, "You okay, Mama?"

She didn't look at him she just kept folding clothes and said, "Can we get the cracks covered too, Woody?"

Outside the sky was clear, but icy gusts of wind were buffeting our barracks every few minutes, sending fresh dust puffs up through the floorboards. May's broom could barely keep up with it, and our oil heater could scarcely hold its own against the drafts.

We'll get this whole place as tight as a barrel, Mama. I already met a guy who told me where they pile all the scrap lumber."

"Scrap?"

"That's all they got. I mean they're still building the camp, you know. Sixteen blocks left to go. After that, they say maybe we'll get some stuff to fix the insides a little bit."

Her eyes blazed then, her voice quietly furious. "Woody, we can't live like this. Animals live like this."

It was hard to get Woody down. He'd keep smiling when everybody else was ready to explode. Grief flickered in his eyes. He blinked it away and hugged her tighter. "We'll make it better, Mama. You watch."

We could hear voices in other cubicles now. Beyond the wall Woody's baby girl started to cry.

"I have to go over to the kitchen," he said, "see if those guys got a pot for heating bottles. That oil stove takes too long - something wrong with the fuel line. I'll find out what they're giving us for breakfast."

Probably hotcakes with soy sauce," Kiyo said, on his hands and knees between the bunks.

"No." Woody grinned, heading out the door. "Rice. With Log Cabin Syrup and melted butter."

## A COMMON MASTER PLAN

I don't remember what we ate that first morning. I know we stood for half an hour in cutting wind waiting to get our food. Then we took it back to the cubicle and ate huddled around the stove. Inside, it was warmer than when we left, because Woody was already making good his promise to Mama, tacking up some ends of lath he'd found, stuffing rolled paper around the door frame.

Trouble was, he had almost nothing to work with. Beyond this temporary weather stripping, there was little else he could do. Months went by, in fact, before our "home" changed much at all from what it was the day we moved in - bare floors, blanket partitions, one bulb in each compartment dangling from a roof beam, and open ceilings overhead so that mischievous boys like Ray and Kiyo could climb up into the rafters and peek into anyone's life.

The simple truth is the camp was no more ready for us when we got there than we were ready for it. We had only the dimmest ideas of what to expect. Most of the families, like us, had moved out from southern California with as much luggage as each person could carry. Some old men left Los Angeles wearing Hawaiian shirts and Panama hats and stepped off the bus at an altitude of 400 feet, with nothing available but sagebrush and tarpaper to stop the April winds pouring down off the back side of the Sierras.

The War Department was in charge of all the camps at this point. They began to issue military

surplus from the First World War - olive-drab knit caps, earmuffs, pea coats, canvas leggings. Later on, sewing machines were shipped in, and our barracks was turned into a clothing factory. An old seamstress took a peacoat of mine, tore the lining out, opened and flattened the sleeves, added a collar, put arm holes in and handed me back a beautiful cape. By fall dozens of seamstresses were working full-time transforming thousands of these old army clothes into capes, slacks and stylish coats. But until that factory got going and packages from friends outside began to fill out our wardrobes, warmth was more important than style. I couldn't help laughing at Mama walking around in army earmuffs and a pair of wide-cuffed, khaki-colored wool trousers several sizes too big for her. Japanese are generally smaller than Caucasians, and almost all these clothes were oversize. They flopped, they dangled, they hung.

It seems comical, looking back; we were a band of Charlie Chaplins marooned in the California desert. But at the time, it was pure chaos. That's the only way to describe it. The evacuation had been so hurriedly planned, the camps so hastily thrown together, nothing was completed when we got there, and almost nothing worked.

I was sick continually, with stomach cramps and diarrhea. At first it was from the shots they gave us for typhoid, in very heavy doses and in assembly-line fashion: swab, jab, swab, Move along now, swab, jab, swab, Keep it moving. That knocked all of us younger kids down at once, with fevers and vomiting. Later it was the food that made us sick, young and old alike. The kitchens were too small and badly ventilated. Food would spoil from being left out too long. That summer, when the heat got fierce, it would spoil faster. The refrigeration kept breaking down. The cooks, in many cases, had never cooked before. Each block had to provide its own volunteers. Some were lucky and had a professional or two in their midst. But the first chef in our block had been a gardener all his life and suddenly found himself preparing three meals a day for 250 people.

"The Manzanar runs" became a condition of life, and you only hoped that when you rushed to the latrine, one would be in working order.

That first morning, on our way to the chow line, Mama and I tried to use the women's latrine in our block. The smell of it spoiled what little appetite we had. Outside, men were working in an open trench, up to their knees in muck - a common sight in the months to come. Inside, the floor was covered with excrement, and all twelve bowls were erupting like a row of tiny volcanoes.

Mama stopped a kimono-wrapped woman stepping past us with her sleeve pushed up against her nose and asked, "What do you do?"

"Try Block Twelve," the woman said, grimacing. "They have just finished repairing the pipes."

It was about two city blocks away. We followed her over there and found a line of women waiting in the wind outside the latrine. We had no choice but to join the line and wait with them.

Inside it was like all the other latrines. Each block was built to the same design, just as each of the ten camps, from California to Arkansas, was built to a common master plan. It was an open room, over a concrete slab. The sink was a long metal trough against one wall, with a row of spigots for hot and cold water. Down the center of the room twelve toilet bowls were arranged in six pairs, back to back, with no partitions. My mother was sitting down in public, among strangers.

One old woman had already solved the problem for herself by dragging in a large cardboard carton. She set it up around one of the bowls, like a three-sided screen. She set it up around one of the bowls, like a three-sided screen. Oxydol was printed in large black letters down the front. I remember this well, because that was the soap we were issued for laundry; later on, the smell of it would permeate these rooms. The upended carton was about four feet high. The old woman behind it wasn't much taller. When she stood, only her head showed over the top.

She was about Granny's age. With great effort she was trying to fold the sides of the screen together. Mama happened to be at the head of the line now. As she approached the vacant bowl, she and the old woman bowed to each other from the waist. Mama then moved to help her with the carton, and the old woman said very graciously, in Japanese, "Would you like to use it?"

Happily, gratefully, Mama bowed again and said, "Arigato" (Thank you). "Arigato gozaimas" (Thank you very much). "I will return it to you barracks."

"Oh, no. It is not necessary. I will be glad to wait."

The old woman unfolded one side of the cardboard, while Mama opened the other; then she bowed again and scurried out the door.

Those big cartons were a common sight in the spring of 1942. Eventually sturdier partitions appeared, one or two at a time. The first were built of scrap lumber. Word would get around that Block such and such had partitions now, and Mama and my older sisters would walk halfway across the camp to use them. Even after every latrine in camp was screened, this quest for privacy continued. Many would wait until late at night. Ironically, because of this, midnight was often the most crowded time of all.

Like so many of the women there, Mama never did get used to the latrines. It was humiliation she just learned to endure: shikata ga nai, this cannot be helped. She would quickly subordinate her own desires to those of the family or the community, because she knew cooperation was the only way to survive. At the same time she placed a high premium on personal privacy, respected it in others and insisted upon it for herself. Almost everyone at Manzanar had inherited this pair of traits from the generations before them who had learned to live in a small, crowded country like Japan. Because of the first they were able to take a desolate stretch of wasteland and gradually make it livable. But the entire situation there, especially in the beginning - the packed sleeping quarters, the communal mess halls, the open toilets - all this was an open insult to that other, private self, a slap in the face you were powerless to challenge.

## Study Questions

1. What was the Civil Liberties Act of 1988 and what do you think about it? Was it fair? Helpful? Was its impact materially substantial or more symbolic?

2. What would you think about a similar act by the U.S. government acknowledging the violations of the rights of African-Americans under the system of slavery? Under the system of Jim Crow and/or legal segregation? Assuming that there was enough political support for such an act, what provisions should it have? What do you think about recent proposals that the President and/or Congress ought to officially apologize for slavery?

3. What were conditions like in the internment camps? What was the worst thing about living in them? Explain how cultural influences might affect ones answer to this question.

4. Could such a thing happen again? If so, under what conditions?

5. What is the emotional tone of the account? How do the authors use humor in this piece?

# 8

# INVISIBILITY IS AN UNNATURAL DISASTER: REFLECTIONS OF AN ASIAN AMERICAN WOMAN

## Mitsuye Yamada

*Mitsuye Yamada is the founder of Multicultural Women Writers, in addition to her work as a poet and teacher. She is also a published poet; her books include* Camp Notes and Other Poems *(1976) and* Desert Run: Poems and Stories *(1980). Her first collection consists of poems that were written during and after World War II; however, they were not published until later due to the anti-Japanese sentiment of the time. This essay was published in* This Bridge Called My Back: Writings by Radical Women of Color *(1981).*

Last year for the Asian segment of the Ethnic American Literature course I was teaching, I selected a new anthology entitled *Aiiieeeee!* compiled by a group of outspoken Asian American writers. During the discussion of the long but thought-provoking introduction to this anthology, one of my students blurted out that she was offended by its militant tone and that as a white person she was tired of always being blamed for the oppression of all the minorities. I noticed several of her classmates' eyes nodding in tacit agreement. A discussion of the "militant" voices in some of the other writings we had read in the course ensued. Surely, I pointed out, some of these other writings have been just as, if not more, militant as the words in this introduction? Had they been offended by those also but failed to express their feelings about them? To my surprise they said they were not offended by any of the Black American, Chicano or

American Indian writings, but were hard-pressed to explain why when I asked for an explanation. A little further discussion revealed that they "understood" the anger expressed by the Black and Chicanos and they "empathized" with the frustrations and sorrow expressed by the American Indian. But the Asian Americans?

Then finally, one student said it for all of them: "it made me angry. *Their* anger made *me* angry, because I didn't even know the Asian Americans felt oppressed. I didn't expect their anger."

At this time I was involved in an academic due process procedure begun as a result of a grievance I had filed the previous semester against the administrators at my college. I had filed a grievance for violation of my rights as a teacher who had worked in the district for almost eleven years. My student's remark "Their anger made me angry . . . I didn't expect their anger," explained for me the reactions of some of my own colleagues as well as the reactions of the administrators during those previous months. The grievance procedure was a time-consuming and emotionally draining process, but the basic principle was too important for me to ignore. That basic principle was that I, an individual teacher, do have certain rights which are given and my superiors cannot, should not, violate them with impunity. When this was pointed out to them, however, they responded with shocked surprise that I, of all people, would take them to task for violation of what was clearly written policy in our college district. They all seemed to exclaim, "We don't understand this; this is so uncharacteristic of her; she seemed such a nice person, so polite, so obedient, so non-troublemaking." What was even more surprising was once they were forced to acknowledge that I was determined to start the due process action, they assumed I was not doing it on my own. One of the administrators suggested someone must have pushed me into this, undoubtedly some of "those feminists" on our campus, he said wryly.

In this age when women are clearly making themselves visible on all fronts, I, an Asian American woman, am still functioning as a "front for those feminists" and therefore invisible. The realization of this sinks in slowly. Asian Americans as a whole are finally coming to claim their own, demanding that they be included in the multicultural history of our country. I like to think in spite of my administrator's myopia, that the most stereotyped minority of them all, the Asian American woman, is just now emerging to become part of that group. It took forever. Perhaps it is important to ask ourselves why it took so long. We should ask ourselves this question just when we think we are emerging as a viable minority in the fabric of our society. I should add to my student's words, "because I didn't even know they felt oppressed," that it took this long because we Asian American women have not admitted to ourselves that we were oppressed. We, the visible minority that is invisible.

I say this because until a few years ago I have been an Asian American woman working among non-Asians in an educational institution where most of the decision-makers were men; an Asian American woman thriving under the smug illusion that I was *not* the stereotypic image of the Asian woman because I had a career teaching English in a community college. I did not think anything assertive was necessary to make my point. People who know me, I reasoned, the ones who count, know who I am and what I think. Thus, even when what I considered a veiled racist remark was made in a casual social setting, I would "let it go" because it was pointless to argue with people who didn't even know their remark was racist. I had supposed that I was practicing passive resistance while being stereotyped, but it was so passive no one noticed I was resisting; it was so much my expected role that it ultimately rendered me invisible.

My experience leads me to believe that contrary to what I thought; I had actually been contributing to my own stereotyping. Like the hero in Ralph Ellison's novel *The Invisible Man,* I had become invisible to white Americans, and it clung to me like a bad habit. Like most bad habits, this one crept up on me because I took it in minute doses like Mithra-

dates' poison and my mind and body adapted so well to it I hardly noticed it was there.

For the past eleven years I have busied myself with the usual chores of an English teacher, a wife of a research chemist, and a mother of four rapidly growing children. I hadn't even done much to shatter this particular stereotype: the middle class woman happy to be bringing home the extra income and quietly fitting into the man's world of work. When the Asian American woman is lulled into believing that people perceive her as being different from other Asian women (the submissive, subservient, ready-to-please, easy-to-get-along-with Asian woman), she is kept comfortably content with the state of things. She becomes ineffectual in the milieu in which she moves. The seemingly apolitical middle class woman and the apolitical Asian woman constituted a double invisibility.

I had created an underground culture of survival for myself and had become in the eyes of others the person I was trying not to be. Because I was permitted to go to college, permitted to take a stab at a career or two along the way, given "free choice" to marry and have a family, given a "choice" to eventually do both, I had assumed I was more or less free, not realizing that those who are free make and take choices; they do not choose from options proffered by "those out there."

I, personally, had not "emerged" until I was almost fifty years old. Apparently through a long conditioning process, I had learned how *not* to be seen for what I am. A long history of ineffectual activities had been, I realize now, initiation rites toward my eventual invisibility. The training begins, in childhood; and for women and minorities, whatever is started in childhood is continued throughout their adult lives. I first recognized just how invisible I was in my first real confrontation with my parents a few years after the outbreak of World War II.

During the early years of the war, my older brother, Mike, and I left the concentration camp in Idaho to work and study at the University of Cincinnati. My parents came to Cincinnati soon after my father's release from Internment Camp (these were POW camps to which many of the Issei* men, leaders in their communities, were sent by the FBI), and worked as domestics in the suburbs. I did not see them too often because by this time I had met and was much influenced by a pacifist who was out on a furlough from a conscientious objectors camp in Trenton, North Dakota. When my parents learned about my "boy friend" they were appalled

---

* Issei — Immigrant Japanese living in the U.S.

and frightened. After all, this was the period when everyone in the country was expected to be one-hundred percent behind the war effort, and the Nisei boys who had volunteered for the Armed Forces were out there fighting and dying to prove how American we really were. However, during interminable arguments with my father and over-heard arguments between my parents, I was devastated to learn they were not so much concerned about my having become a pacifist, but they were more concerned about the possibility of my marrying one. They were understandably frightened (my father's prison years of course were still fresh on his mind) about repercussions on the rest of the family. In an attempt to make my father understand me, I argued that even if I didn't marry him, I'd still be a pacifist; but my father reassured me that it was "all right" for me to be a pacifist because as a Japanese national and a "girl" *it didn't make any difference to anyone.* In frustration I remember shouting, "But can't you see, *I'm* philosophically committed to the pacifist cause," but he dismissed this with "In my college days we used to call philosophy, foolosophy," and that was the end of that. When they were finally convinced I was not going to marry "my pacifist," the subject was dropped and we never discussed it again.

As if to confirm my father's assessment of the harmlessness of my opinions, my brother Mike, an American citizen, was suddenly expelled from the University of Cincinnati while I, "an enemy alien," was permitted to stay. We assumed that his stand as a pacifist, although he was classified a 4-F because of his health, contributed to his expulsion. We were told the Air Force was conducting sensitive wartime research on campus and requested his removal, but they apparently felt my presence on campus was not as threatening.

I left Cincinnati in 1945, hoping to leave behind this and other unpleasant memories gathered there during the war years, and plunged right into the politically active atmosphere at New York University where students, many of them returning veterans, were continuously promoting one cause or other by making speeches in Washington Square, passing out petitions, or staging demonstrations. On one occasion, I tagged along with a group of students who took a train to Albany to demonstrate on the steps of the State Capitol. I think I was the only Asian in this group of predominantly Jewish students from NYU. People who passed us were amused and shouted "Go home and grow up." I suppose Governor Dewey, who refused to see us, assumed we were a group of adolescents without a cause as most college students were considered to be during those days. It appears they weren't expecting any results from our demonstration. There were no

newspersons, no security persons, no police. No one tried to stop us from doing what we were doing. We simply did "our thing" and went back to our studies until next time, and my father's words were again confirmed: it made no difference to anyone, being a young student demonstrator in peacetime, 1947.

Not only the young, but those who feel powerless over their own lives, know what it is like not to make a difference on anyone or anything. The poor know it only too well, and we women have known it since we were little girls. The most insidious part of this conditioning process, I realize now, was that we have been trained not to expect a response in ways that mattered. We may be listened to and responded to with placating words and gestures, but our psychological mind set has already told us time and again that we were born into a readymade world into which we must fit ourselves, and that many of us do it very well.

This mind set is the result of not believing that the political and social forces affecting our lives are determined by some person, or a group of persons, probably sitting behind a desk or around a conference table.

Just recently I read an article about "the remarkable track record of success" of the Nisei in the United States. One Nisei was quoted as saying he attributed our stamina and endurance to our ancestors whose characters had been shaped, he said, by their living in a country which has been contantly besieged by all manner of natural disasters, such as earthquakes and hurricanes. He said the Nisei has inherited a steely will, a will to endure and hence, to survive.

This evolutionary explanation disturbs me, because it equates the "act of God" (i.e. natural disasters) to the "act of man" (i.e., the war, the evacuation). The former is not within our power to alter, but the latter, I should think, is. By putting the "acts of God" on par with the acts of man, we shrug off personal responsibilities.

I have, for too long a period of time accepted the opinion of others (even though they were directly affecting my life) as if they were objective events totally out of my control. Because I separated such opinions from the persons who were making them, I accepted them the way I accepted natural disasters; and I endured them as inevitable. I have tried to cope with people whose points of view alarmed me in the same way that I had adjusted to natural phenomena, such as hurricanes, which plowed into my life from time to time. I would readjust my dismantled feelings in the same way that we repaired the broken shutters after the storm. The Japanese have an all-purpose expression in their language for this attitude of resigned acceptance: "Shikataganai." "It can't be helped." "There's nothing I can do about it." It is said with the shrug of the shoulders and tone of finality, perhaps not unlike the "those-were-my-orders" tone that was used at the Nuremberg trials. With all the sociological studies that have been made about the causes of the evacuations of the Japanese Americans during World War II, we should know by now that "they" knew that the West Coast Japanese Americans would go without too much protest, and of course "they" were right, for most of us (with the exception of those notable few), resigned to our fate, albeit bewildered and not willingly. We were not perceived by our government as responsive Americans; we were objects that happened to be standing in the path of the storm.

Perhaps this kind of acceptance is a way of coping with the "real" world. One stands against the wind for a time, and then succumbs eventually because there is no point to being stubborn against all odds. The wind will not respond to entreaties anyway, one reasons; one should have sense enough to know that. I'm not ready to accept this evolutionary reasoning. It is too rigid for me; I would like to think that my new awareness is going to make me more visible than ever, and to allow me to make some changes in the "man made disaster" I live in at the present time. Part of being visible is refusing to separate the actors from their actions, and demanding that they be responsible for them.

By now, riding along with the minorities and women's movements, I think we are making a wedge into the main body of American life, but people are still looking right through and around us, assuming we are simply tagging along. Asian American women still remain in the background and we are heard but not really listened to. Like Musak, they think we are piped into the airwaves by someone else. We must remember that one of the most insidious ways of keeping women and minorities powerless is to let them only talk about harmless and inconsequential subjects, or let them

speak freely and not listen to them with serious intent.

We need to raise our voices a little more, even as they say to us "This is so uncharacteristic of you." To finally recognize our own invisibility is to finally be on the path toward visibility. Invisibility is not a natural state for anyone.

**Study Questions**

1. Why were Yamada's students upset about the Asian-American anthology they were reading?

2. What stereotypes of Asian-American women does she raise? What stereotypes do you think of when you think of Asian-American women?

3. Explain why Yamada believes that in certain cases she was contributing to her own stereotyping? Do you think this ever happens with other racial or ethnic groups? How do people "learn" to be oppressed? Explain.

4. What disturbed Yamada's parents when they discovered she was considering marrying a pacifist? What were the political implications of a Japanese-American being a pacifist during World War II.

5. What is she saying about the relationship between silence and invisibility? How would you compare that to Maxine Hong Kingston?

6. What are the internment camps? What do they have to do with invisibility?

7. According to Yamada, what are the relationships among freedom, responsibility, and accountability?

# 9

# WE, THE DANGEROUS

## Janice Mirikitani

*Janice Mirikatani was born in 1942 as a third-generation Japanese-American, during World War II when many Japanese-American citizens were placed in internment camps. Her poetry often describes the injustices and oppression that Japanese and other Asian-Americans have suffered in the U.S. This poem is taken from her collection,* Awake in the River *(1978), and she also published* Shedding Silence *in 1987. Currently, she is a teacher and community activitst in San Francisco.*

I swore
it would not devour me
I swore
it would not humble me
I swore
it would not break me.

     And they commanded we dwell in the desert
     Our children be spawn of barbed wire and barracks

We, closer to the earth,
squat, short thighed,
knowing the dust better.

     And they would have us make the garden
     Rake the grass to soothe their feet

We, akin to the jungle,
plotting with the snake,
tails shedding in civilized America.

     And they would have us skin their fish
     deft hands like blades/ sliding back flesh/bloodless

We, who awake in the river
Ocean's child
Whale eater.

And they would have us strange scented women,
Round shouldered/strong and yellow/like the moon
to pull the thread to the cloth
to loosen their backs massaged in myth

We, who fill the secret bed,
the sweat shops
the laundries.

And they would dress us in napalm,
Skin shred to clothe the earth,
Bodies filling pock marked fields.
Dead fish bloating our harbors.

We, the dangerous,
Dwelling in the ocean.
Akin to the jungle.
Close to the earth.

Hiroshima
Vietnam
Tule Lake[1]

And yet we were not devoured.
And yet we were not humbled
And yet we are not broken

**Study Questions**

1. Who are "the dangerous"?

2. What associations with Asian people does she mention? What stereotypes does she allude to?

3. Pay attention to the pronouns here. Who are "they"? Why does she switch from "I" to "we"?

---

[1.] Tule Lake: The largest of the camps where Japanese immigrants and their children were imprisoned in the United States during WWII.

# THREE THOUSAND DOLLAR DEATH SONG

*Wendy Rose*

*Wendy Rose is a mixed blood Hopi/Miwok. She is a visual artist and professor of American Indian Studies at Fresno City College. Her collections of poetry include* Going to War with All My Relations: New and Selected Poems *(1983) and* Now Poof She is Gone *(1994). This poem comes from her 1980 collection,* Lost Copper. *It analyzes the ways in which contemporary Americans treat Native American cultures as dead and gone.*

> 19 American Indian Skeletons from Nevada...
> valued at $3000.00
> Museum Invoice, 1975

Is it in cold hard cash? the kind
that dusts the insides of men's pockets
lying silver-polished surface along the cloth.
Or in bills? papering the wallets of they
who thread the night with dark words. Or
checks? paper promises weighing the same
as words spoken once on the other side
of the grown grass and damned rivers
of history. However it goes, it goes
Through my body it goes assessing each nerve, running its edges
along my arteries, planning ahead
for whose hands will rip me
into pieces of dusty red paper,
whose hands will smooth or smatter me
into traces of rubble. Invoiced now,
it's official how our bones are valued
that stretch out pointing to sunrise
or are flexed into one last foetal bend,[1]
that are removed and tossed about,
catalogued, numbered with black ink
on newly-white foreheads.
As we were formed to the white soldier's voice,
so we explode under white students' hands.
Death is a long trail of days
in our fleshless prison.

From this distant point we watch our bones
auctioned with our careful beadwork,
our quilled medicine bundles, even the bridles
of our shot-down horses. You: who have

147

priced us, you who have removed us: at what cost?
What price the pits where our bones share
a single bit of memory, how one century
turns our dead into specimens, our history
into dust, our survivors into clowns.
Our memory might be catching, you know;
picture the mortars,[2] the arrowheads, the labrets[3]
shaking off their labels like bears
suddenly awake to find the seasons have ended
while they slept. Watch them touch each other,
measure reality, march out the museum door!
Watch as they lift their faces
and smell about for us; watch our bones rise
to meet them and mount the horses once again!
The cost, then, will be paid
for our sweetgrass-smelling having-been
in clam shell beads and steatite.[4]
dentalia[5] and woodpecker scalp, turquoise
and copper, blood and oil, coal
and uranium, children, a universe
of stolen things.

## ENDNOTES

1. Foetal bend: Throughout history, many cultures have buried their dead in a curled position resembling that of a fetus.
2. Mortars: Bowl-shaped vessels.
3. Labrets: Ornaments of wood or bone worn in holes pierced through the lip.
4. Steatite: A soft, easily carved stone; soapstone.
5. Dentalia: A type of mollusk shell resembling a tooth.

## Study Questions

1. What does Rose mean by calling this poem a "death song"?

2. Who is this poem addressed to? Explain.

3. What is Rose saying about museum displays of Native Americans and their culture? What is she saying about heritage?

4. What do skeletons represent? Why does she compare students to soldiers?

5. What vision does Rose conjure up in the last few lines?

6. In the list of stolen things, do any seem out of place? Why?

7. Does this poem have anything to say about sports teams named "Indians," Redskins," "Braves," etc.? Explain.

# 11

# The Only Traffic Signal on the Reservation Doesn't Flash Red Anymore

## Sherman Alexie

*Sherman Alexie, Jr. is a Spokane/Coeur d'Alene Indian who was born and raised on the Spokane Indian Reservation in Washington. Alexie prefers to be called an Indian, believing that 'Native American' is a term reflecting the guilt of liberal white Americans. His works have won numerous awards and include the novels* Reservation Blues_(1996) and Indian Killer *(1998). This story comes from his collection of short stories titled* The Lone Ranger and Tonto Fistfight in Heaven *(1993). This story contans some of the same characters found in his movie* Smoke Signals *(1998).*

"Go ahead," Adrian said. "Pull the trigger."

I held a pistol to my temple. I was sober but wished I was drunk enough to pull the trigger.

"Go for it," Adrian said. "You chickenshit."

While I still held that pistol to my temple, I used my other hand to flip Adrian off. Then I made a fist with my third hand to gather a little bit of courage or stupidity, and wiped sweat from my forehead with my fourth hand.

"Here," Adrian said. "Give me the damn thing."

Adrian took the pistol, put the barrel in his mouth, smiled around the metal, and pulled the trigger. Then he cussed wildly, laughed, and spit out the BB.

"Are you dead yet!" I asked.

"Nope," he said. "Not yet. Give me, another beer."

"Hey, we don't drink no more, remember? How about a Diet Pepsi?"

"That's right, enit? I forgot. Give me a Pepsi."

Adrian and I sat on the porch and watched the reservation. Nothing happened. From our chairs made rockers by unsteady legs, we could see that the only traffic signal on the reservation had stopped working.

"Hey, Victor," Adrian asked. "Now when did that thing quit flashing?"

"Don't know," I said.

It was summer. Hot. But we kept our shirts on to hide our beer bellies and chicken-pox scars. At least, I wanted to hide my beer belly. I was a former basketball star fallen out of shape. It's always kind of sad when that happens. There's nothing more unattractive than a vain man, and that goes double for an Indian man.

"So," Adrian asked. "What you want to do today?"

"Don't know."

We watched a group of Indian boys, walk by. I'd like to think there were ten of them. But there were actually only four or five. They were skinny, darkened by sun, their hair long and wild. None of them looked like they had showered for a week.

Their smell made me jealous.

They were off to cause trouble somewhere, I'm sure. Little warriors looking for honor in some twentieth-century vandalism. Throw a few rocks through windows, kick a dog, slash a tire. Run like hell when the tribal cops drove slowly by the scene of the crime.

"Hey," Adrian asked. "Isn't that the Windmaker boy?"

"Yeah," I said and watched Adrian lean forward to study Julius Windmaker, the best basketball player on the reservation, even though he was only fifteen years old.

"He looks good," Adrian said.

"Yeah, he must not be drinking."

"Yet."

"Yeah, yet."

Julius Windmaker was the latest in a long line of reservation basketball heroes, going all the way back to Aristotle Polatkin, who was shooting jump-shots exactly one year before James Naismith supposedly invented basketball.

I'd only seen Julius play a few times, but he had that gift, that grace, those fingers like a goddamn medicine man. One time, when the tribal school traveled to Spokane to play this white high school team, Julius scored sixty-seven points and the Indians won by forty.

"I didn't know they'd be riding horses," I heard the coach of the white team say when I was leaving.

I mean, Julius was an artist, moody. A couple times he walked right off the court during the middle of a game because there wasn't enough competition. That's how he was. Julius could throw a crazy pass, surprise us all, and send it out of bounds. But nobody called it a turnover because we all knew that one of his teammates should've been there to catch the pass. We loved him.

"Hey, Julius," Adrian yelled from the porch. "You ain't shit."

Julius and his friends laughed, flipped us off, and shook their tail feathers a little as they kept walking down the road. They all knew Julius was the best ballplayer on the reservation these days, maybe the best ever, and they knew Adrian was just confirming that fact.

It was easier for Adrian to tease Julius because he never really played basketball. He was more detached about the whole thing. But I used to be quite a ballplayer. Maybe not as good as some, certainly not as good as Julius, but I still felt that ache in my bones, that need to be better than everyone else. It's that need to be the best, that feeling of immortality, that drives a ballplayer. And when it disappears, for whatever reason, that ballplayer is never the same person, on or off the court.

I know when I lost it, that edge. During my senior year in high school we made it to the state finals. I'd been playing like crazy, hitting everything. It was like throwing rocks into the ocean from a little rowboat. I couldn't miss. Then, right before the championship game, we had our pregame meeting in the first-aid room of the college where the tournament was held every year.

It took a while for our coach to show up so we spent the time looking at these first-aid manuals. These books had all kinds of horrible injuries. Hands and feet smashed flat in printing presses, torn apart by lawnmowers, burned and dismembered. Faces that had gone through windshields, dragged over gravel, split open by garden tools. The stuff was disgusting, but we kept looking, flipping through photograph after photograph, trading books, until we all wanted to throw up.

While I looked at those close-ups of death and destruction, I lost it. I think everybody in that room, everybody on the team, lost that feeling of immortality. We went out and lost the championship game by twenty points. I missed every shot I took. I missed everything.

"So," I asked Adrian. "You think Julius will make it all the way?"

"Maybe, maybe."

There's a definite history of reservation heroes who never finish high school, who never finish basketball seasons. Hell, there's been one or two guys who played just a few minutes of one game, just enough to show what they could have been. And there's the famous case of Silas Sirius, who made one move and scored one basket in his entire basketball career. People still talk about it.

"Hey," I asked Adrian. "Remember Silas Sirius?"

"Hell," Adrian said. "Do I remember? I was there when he grabbed that defensive rebound, took a step, and flew the length of the court, did a full spin in midair, and then dunked that fucking ball. And I don't mean it looked like he flew, or it was so beautiful it was almost like he flew. I mean, he flew, period."

I laughed, slapped my legs, and knew that I believed Adrian's story more as it sounded less true.

"Shit" he continued. "And he didn't grow no wings. He just kicked his legs a little. Held that ball like a baby in his hand. And he was smiling. Really. Smiling when he flew. Smiling when he dunked it, smiling when he walked off the court and never came back. Hell he was still smiling ten years after that."

I laughed some more, quit for a second, then laughed a little longer because it was the right thing to do.

"Yeah," I said. "Silas was a ballplayer."

"Real ballplayer," Adrian agreed.

In the outside world, a person can be a hero one second and a nobody the next. Think about it. Do white people remember the names of those guys who dove into that icy river to rescue passengers front that plane wreck a few years back? Hell, white people don't even remember the names of the dogs who save entire families from burning up in house fires by barking. And, to be honest, I don't remember none of those names either, but a reservation hero is remembered. A reservation hero is a hero forever. In fact, their status grows over the years as the stories are told and retold.

"Yeah," Adrian said. "It's too bad that damn diabetes got him. Silas was always talking about a comeback."

"Too bad, too bad."

We both leaned further back into our chairs. Silence. We watched the grass grow, the rivers flow, the winds blow.

"Damn," Adrian asked. "When did that fucking traffic signal quit working?"

"Don't know."

"Shit, they better fix it. Might cause an accident."

We both looked at each other, looked at the traffic signal, knew that about only one car an hour passed by, and laughed our asses off. Laughed so hard that when we tried to rearrange ourselves, Adrian ended up with my ass and I ended up with his. That looked so funny that we laughed them off again and it took us most of an hour to get them back right again.

Then we heard glass breaking in the distance.

"Sounds like beer bottles," Adrian said

"Yeah, Coors Light, I think."

"Bottled 1988."

We started to laugh, but a tribal cop drove by and cruised down the road where Julius and his friends had walked earlier.

Think they'll catch them?" I asked Adrian.

"Always do."

After a few minutes, the tribal cop drove by again, with Julius in the backseat and his friends running behind.

"Hey," Adrian asked. "What did he do?"

"Threw a brick through a BIA pickup's windshield," one of the Indian boys yelled back.

"Told you it sounded like a pickup window," I said.

"Yeah, yeah, a 1982 Chevy."

"With red paint."

"No, blue."

We laughed for just a second. Then Adrian sighed long and deep. He rubbed his head, ran his fingers through his hair, scratched his scalp hard.

"I think Julius is going to go bad," he said.

"No way," I said. "He's just horsing around."

"Maybe, maybe."

It's hard to be optimistic on the reservation. When a glass sits on a table here, people don't wonder if it's half filled or half empty. They just hope it's good beer. Still, Indians have a way of surviving. But it's almost like Indians can easily survive the big stuff. Mass murder, loss of language and land rights. It's the small things that hurt the most. The white waitress who wouldn't take an order, Tonto, the Washington Redskins.

And, just like everybody else, Indians need heroes to help them learn how to survive. But what happens when our heroes don't even know how to pay their bills?

"Shit, Adrian," I said. "He's just a kid."

"Ain't no children on a reservation."

"Yeah, yeah, I've heard that before. Well," I said. "I guess that Julius is pretty good in school, too."

"And?"

"And he wants to maybe go to college."

"Really?"

"Really," I said and laughed. And I laughed because half of me was happy and half of me wasn't sure what else to do.

A year later, Adrian and I sat on the same porch in the same chairs. We'd done things in between, like ate and slept and read the newspaper. It was another hot summer. Then again, summer is supposed to be hot.

"I'm thirsty," Adrian said. "Give me a beer."

"How many times do I have to tell you? We don't drink anymore."

"Shit," Adrian said. "I keep forgetting. Give me a goddamn Pepsi."

"That's a whole case for you today already."

"Yeah, yeah, fuck these substitute addictions."

We sat there for a few minutes, hours and then Julius Windmaker staggered down the road.

"Oh, look at that," Adrian said. "Not even two in the afternoon and he's drunk as a skunk."

"Don't he have a game tonight?"

"Yeah, he does."

"Well, I hope he sobers up in time."

"Me, too."

I'd only played one game drunk and it was in an all-Indian basketball tournament after I got out of high school. I'd been drinking the night before and woke up feeling kind of sick, so I got drunk again. Then I went out and played a game. I felt disconnected the whole time. Nothing seemed to fit right. Even my shoes, which had fit perfectly before, felt too big for my feet. I couldn't even see the basketball or basket clearly. They were more like ideas. I mean, I knew where they were generally supposed to be, so I guessed at where I should be. Somehow or another, I scored ten points.

"He's been drinking quite a bit, enit?" Adrian asked.

"Yeah, I hear he's even been drinking Sterno."

"Shit, that'll kill his brain quicker than shit."

Adrian and I left the porch that night and went to the tribal school to watch Julius play. He still looked good in his uniform, although he was a little puffy around the edges. But he just wasn't the ballplayer we all remembered or expected. He missed shots, traveled, threw dumb passes that we all knew were dumb passes. By the fourth quarter, Julius sat at the end of the bench, hanging his head, and the crowd filed out, all talking about which of the younger players looked good. We talked about some kid named Lucy in the third grade who already had a nice move or two.

Everybody told their favorite Julius Windmaker stories, too. Times like that, on a reservation, a basketball game felt like a funeral and wake all rolled up together.

Back at home, on the porch, Adrian and I sat wrapped in shawls because the evening was kind of cold.

"It's too bad, too bad," I said. "I thought Julius might be the one to make it all the way."

"I told you he wouldn't. I told you so."

"Yeah, yeah. Don't rub it in."

We sat there in silence and remembered all of our heroes, ballplayers from seven generations, all the way back. It hurts to lose any of them because Indians kind of see ballplayers as saviors. I mean, if basketball would have been around, I'm sure Jesus Christ would've been the best point guard in Nazareth. Probably the best player in the entire world. And in the beyond. I just can't explain how much losing Julius Windmaker hurt us all.

"Well," Adrian asked. "What do you want to do tomorrow?"

"Don't know."

"Shit, that damn traffic signal is still broken. Look."

Adrian pointed down the road and he was right. But what's the point of fixing it in a place where the stop signs are just suggestions?

"What time is it?" Adrian asked.

"I don't know. Ten, I think."

"Let's go somewhere."

"Where?"

"I don't know, Spokane, anywhere. Let's just go."

"Okay," I said, and we both walked inside the house, shut the door, and locked it tight. No. We left it open just a little bit in case some crazy Indian needed a place to sleep. And in the morning we found crazy Julius passed out on the living room carpet.

"Hey, you bum," Adrian yelled. "Get off my floor."

"This is my house, Adrian," I said.

"That's right. I forgot. Hey, you bum, get your ass off Victor's floor."

Julius groaned and farted but he didn't wake up. It really didn't bother Adrian that Julius was on the floor, so he threw an old blanket on top of him. Adrian and I grabbed our morning coffee and went back out to sit on the porch. We had both just about finished our cups when a group of Indian kids walked by, all holding basketballs of various shapes and conditions.

"Hey, look," Adrian said. "Ain't that the Lucy girl?"

I saw that it was, a little brown girl with scarred knees, wearing her daddy's shirt.

"Yeah, that's her," I said.

"I heard she's so good that she plays for the sixth grade boys team."

"Really? She's only in third grade herself, isn't she?"

"Yeah, yeah, she's a little warrior."

Adrian and I watched those Indian children walk down the road, walking toward another basketball game.

"God, I hope she makes it all the way," I said.

"Yeah, yeah," Adrian said, stared into the bottom of his cup, and then threw it across the yard. And we both watched it with all of our eyes, while the sun rose straight up above us and settled down behind the house, watched that cup revolve, revolve, until it came down whole to the ground.

## Study Questions

1. What is the significance of the story's title?

2. How does Alexie deal with the issue /stereotype of alcoholism on the reservation?

3. How does he deal with the Indian stereotypes in general? Which ones does he mention? Does this story maintain or question these images? How? What is the difference between stereotypes and cultural "norms"?

4. What is the relationship of Indian cultural traditions to contemporary Indian life on a reservation? How does Alexie characterize life on the reservation?

5. Why are heroes so important to the characters? What kinds of heroes are there on the reservation?

6. What does basketball mean to the characters? In what sense are basketball players "warriors"?

# 12

# EXCERPT FROM OEDIPUS REX

*Sophocles (496-406 BCE)*

*Translation by Dudley Fitts and Robert Fitzgerald*

*Sophocles has dramatized human tragedy in a series of plays well known to modern audiences. This tale of the proud Oedipus Rex (king) comes to a head in this scene IV where the dawning realization of the horror of his life creates a dramatic tension that encapsulates the moral dilemma of the person who has sinned and desperately seeks redemption, knowing there is none. It also illustrates the proverb "Pride goeth before destruction and a haughtly spirit before a fall" since Oedipus' pride of place and power has brought him to the terrifying reality of what he has done. Sophocles also wrote about Oedipus' daughters, Ismene and Antigone in the play* Antigone.

## CHARACTERS

OEDIPUS, *King of Thebes, supposed son of Polybos and Meropê, King and Queen of Corinth*

IOKASTÊ, *wife of Oedipus and widow of the late King Laïos*

KREON, *brother of Iokastê, a prince of Thebes*

TEIRESIAS, *a blind seer who serves Apollo*

PRIEST

MESSENGER, *from Corinth*

SHEPHERD, *former servant of Laïos*

SECOND MESSENGER, *from the palace*

CHORUS OF THEBAN ELDERS

CHORAGOS, *leader of the Chorus*

ANTIGONE *and* ISMENE, *young daughters of Oedipus and Iokastê. They appear in the Éxodos but do not speak.*

SUPPLIANTS, GUARDS, SERVANTS

## SCENE IV

OEDIPUS     SIRS: though I do not know the man, I think I see him coming, this shepherd we want: He is old, like our friend here, and the men Bringing him seem to be servants of my house. But you can tell, if you have ever seen him.

(*Enter* SHEPHERD *escorted by* SERVANTS)

CHORAGOS     I know him, he was Laïos' man. You can trust him.

OEDIPUS     Tell me first, you from Corinth: is this the Shepherd
We were discussing?

MESSENGER     This is the very man.

OEDIPUS (*to* SHEPHERD)     Come here. No, look at me. You must answer
Everything I ask.—You belonged to Laïos?

SHEPHERD     Yes: born his slave, brought us in his house.

OEDIPUS     Tell me: what kind of work did you do for him?

SHEPHERD     I was a shepherd of his, most of my life.

OEDIPUS     Where mainly did you go for pasturage?

SHEPHERD     Sometimes Kithairon, sometimes the hills near-by.

OEDIPUS     Do you remember ever seeing this man out there?

SHEPHERD     What would he be doing there? This man?

OEDIPUS     This man standing here. Have you ever seen him before?

SHEPHERD     No. At least, not to my recollection.

MESSENGER     And that is not strange, my lord. But I'll refresh

His memory: he must remember when we two
Spend three whole seasons together. March to
September,
On Kithairon or thereabouts. He had two
flocks;
I had one. Each autumn I'd drive mine home
And he would go back with his to Laïos'
sheepfold.—
Is this not true, just as I have described it?
SHEPHERD     True, yes; but it was all so long
ago.
MESSENGER     Well, then: do you remember,
back in those days,
That you gave me a baby boy to bring up as
my own?
SHEPHERD     What if I did? What are you
trying to say?
MESSENGER     King Oedipus was once that little
child.
SHEPHERD     Damn you, hold your tongue!
OEDIPUS                        No more of that!
It is your tongue needs watching, not this
man's.
SHEPHERD     My king, my master, what is it I
have done wrong?
OEDIPUS     You have not answered his
question about the boy.
SHEPHERD     He does not know . . . He is only
making trouble . . .
OEDIPUS     Come, speak plainly, or it will go
hard with you.
SHEPHERD     In God's name, do not torture an
old man!
OEDIPUS     Come here, one of you; bind his
arms behind him.
SHEPHERD     Unhappy king! What more do you
wish to learn?
OEDIPUS     Did you give this man the child he
speaks of?
SHEPHERD                              I did.
And I would to God I had died that very day.
OEDIPUS     You will die now unless you speak
the truth.
SHEPHERD     Yet if I speak the truth, I am worse
than dead.
OEDIPUS (to ATTENDANT)     He intends to
draw it out, apparently—
SHEPHERD     No! I have told you already that I
gave him the boy.
OEDIPUS     Where did you get him? From your
house?
From somewhere else?
SHEPHERD     Not from mine, no. A man gave
him to me.
OEDIPUS     Is that man here? Whose house did
he belong to?
SHEPHERD     For God's love, my king, do not ask
me any more!

OEDIPUS     You are a dead man if I have to ask
you again.
SHEPHERD     Then . . . Then the child was from
the palace of Laïos.
OEDIPUS     A slave child? Or a child of his own
line?
SHEPHERD     Ah, I am on the brink of a dreadful
speech!
OEDIPUS     And I of dreadful hearing. Yet I
must hear.
SHEPHERD     If you must be told, then . . .
                    They said it was Laïos' child;
But it is your wife who can tell you about that.
OEDIPUS     My wife!—Did she give it to you?
SHEPHERD                        My lord, she did.
OEDIPUS     Do you know why?
SHEPHERD                    I was told to get rid of it.
OEDIPUS     Oh heartless mother!
SHEPHERD          But in dread of prophecies . . .
OEDIPUS     Tell me.
SHEPHERD     It was said that the boy would kill
his own father.
OEDIPUS     Then why did you give him over to
this old man?
SHEPHERD     I pitied the baby, my king,
And I thought that this man would take him
far away
To his own country.
                    He saved him—but for what a fate!
For if you are what this man says you are,
No man living is more wretched than
Oedipus.
OEDIPUS     Ah God!
It was true!
                    All the prophecies!
                              —Now,
O Light, may I look on you for the last time!
I, Oedipus,
Oedipus, damned in his birth, in his marriage
damned,
Damned in the blood he shed with his own
hand!

(*He rushes into the palace*)


## ODE IV

STROPHE 1

CHORUS     Alas for the seed of men.
What measure shall I give these generations
That breathe on the void and are void
And exist and do not exist?
Who bears more weight of joy
Than mass of sunlight shifting in images,
Or who shall make his thought stay on
That down time drifts away?
Your splendor is all fallen.

O naked brow of wrath and tears,
O change of Oedipus!
I who saw your days call no man blest—
Your great days like ghosts gone.

ANTISTROPHE 1

That mind was a strong bow.
Deep, how deep you drew it then, hard archer,
At a dim fearful range,
And brought dear glory down!
You overcame the stranger[1]—
The virgin with her hooking lion claws—
And though death sang, stood like a tower
To make pale Thebes take heart.
Fortress against our sorrow!
True king, giver of laws,
Majestic Oedipus!
No prince in Thebes had ever such renown,
No prince won such grace of power.

STROPHE 2

And now of all men ever known
Most pitiful is this man's story:
His fortunes are most changed, his state
Fallen to a low slave's
Ground under bitter fate.
O Oedipus, most royal one!
The great door[2] that expelled you to the light
Gave at night—ah, gave night to your glory:
As to the father, to the fathering son.
All understood too late.
How could that queen whom Laïos won,
The garden that he harrowed at his height,
Be silent when that act was done?

ANTISTROPHE 2

But all eyes fail before time's eye,
All actions come to justice there.
Though never willed, though far down the
    deep past,
Your bed, your dread sirings,
Are brought to book at last.
Child by Laïos doomed to die,
Then doomed to lose that fortunate little
    death,
Would God you never took breath in this air
That with my wailing lips I take to cry:
For I weep the world's outcast.
I was blind, and now I can tell why:
Asleep, for you had given ease of breath
To Thebes, while the false years went by.

EXODOS[3]

(Enter, from the palace, SECOND MESSENGER)

SECOND MESSENGER    Elders of Thebes, most
    honored in this land,
What horrors are yours to see and hear, what
    weight
Of sorrow to be endured, if, true to your
    birth,
You venerate the line of Labdakos!
I think neither Istros nor Phasis, those great
    rivers,
Could purify this place of all the evil
It shelters now, or soon must bring to light—
Evil not done unconsciously, but willed.

The greatest griefs are those we cause
    ourselves.
CHORAGOS    Surely, friend, we have grief
    enough already;
What new sorrow do you mean?
SECOND MESSENGER        The queen is dead.
CHORAGOS    O miserable queen! But at
    whose hand?
SECOND MESSENGER            Her own.
The full horror of what happened you can not
    know,
For you did not see it; but I, who did, will tell
    you
As clearly as I can how she met her death.

When she had left us,
In passionate silence, passing through the
    court,
She ran to her apartment in the house,
Her hair clutched by the fingers of both hands.
She closed the doors behind her; then, by that
    bed
Where long ago the fatal son was conceived—
That son who should bring about his father's
    death—
We heard her call upon Laïos, dead so many
    years,
And heard her wail for the double fruit of her
    marriage,
A husband by her husband, children by her
    child.
Exactly how she died I do not know:
For Oedipus burst in moaning and would not
    let us
Keep vigil to the end: it was by him
As he stormed about the room that our eyes
    were caught.
From one to another of us he went, begging a
    sword,
Hunting the wife who was not his wife, the
    mother
Whose womb had carried his own children
    and himself.
I do not know: it was none of us aided him,
But surely one of the gods was in control!
For with a dreadful cry

He hurled his weight, as though wrenched out
    of himself,
At the twin doors: the bolts gave, and he
    rushed in.
And there we saw her hanging, her body
    swaying
From the cruel cord she had noosed about her
    neck.
A great sob broke from him, heartbreaking to
    hear,
As he loosed the rope and lowered her to the
    ground.

I would blot out from my mind what
    happened next!
For the king ripped from her gown the golden
    brooches
That were her ornament, and raised them, and
    plunged them down
Straight into his own eyeballs, crying, "No
    more,
No more shall you look on the misery about
    me,
The horrors of my own doing! Too long you
    have known
The faces of those whom I should never have
    seen,
Too long been blind to those for whom I was
    searching!
From this hour, go in darkness!" And as he
    spoke,
He struck at his eyes-not once, but many
    times;
And the blood spattered his beard,
Bursting from his ruined sockets like red hail.

So from the unhappiness of two this evil has
    sprung,
A curse on the man and woman alike. The old
Happiness of the house of Labdakos
Was happiness enough: where is it today?
It is all wailing and ruin, disgrace, death—all
The misery of mankind that has a name—
And it is wholly and for ever theirs.
CHORAGOS        Is he in agony still? Is there no
    rest for him?
SECOND MESSENGER              He is calling for
    someone to open the doors wide
So that all the children of Kadmos may look
    upon
His father's murderer, his mother's—no,
I can not say it!
                    then he will leave Thebes,
Self-exiled, in order that the curse
Which he himself pronounced may depart
    from the house.
He is weak, and there is none to lead him,
So terrible is his suffering.
                            But you will see:

Look, the doors are opening; in a moment
You will see a thing that would crush a heart
    of stone.

(*The central door is opened,* OEDIPUS, *blinded,
    is led in*)

CHORAGOS        Dreadful indeed for men to see.
  Never have my own eyes
  Looked on a sight so full of fear.

  Oedipus!
  What madness came upon you, what daemon
  Leaped on your life with heavier
  Punishment than a mortal man can bear?
  No: I can not even
  Look at you, poor ruined one.
  And I would speak, question, ponder,
  If I were able. No.
  You make me shudder.
OEDIPUS        God. God.
  Is there a sorrow greater?
  Where shall I find harbor in this world?
  My voice is hurled far on a dark wind.
  What has God done to me?
CHORAGOS        Too terrible to think of, or to see.

STROPHE 1

OEDIPUS        O cloud of night,
  Never to be turned away: night coming on,
  I can not tell how: night like a shroud!
  My fair winds brought me here.
                              O God. Again
  The pain of the spikes where I had sight,
  The flooding pain
  Of memory, never to be gouged out.
CHORAGOS        This is not strange.
  You suffer it all twice over, remorse in pain,
  Pain in remorse.

ANTISTROPHE 1

OEDIPUS        Ah dear friend
  Are you faithful even yet, you alone?
  Are you still standing near me, will you stay
    here,
  Patient, to care for the blind?
                                  The blind man!
  Yet even blind I know who it is attends me,
  By the voice's tone—
  Though my new darkness hide the comforter.
CHORAGOS        Oh fearful act!
  What god was it drove you to rake black
  Night across your eyes?

STROPHE 2

OEDIPUS        Apollo. Apollo. Dear
  Children, the god was Apollo.
  He brought my sick, sick fate upon me.
  But the blinding hand was my own!

How could I bear to see
When all my sight was horror everywhere?
CHORAGOS     Everywhere; that is true.
OEDIPUS          And now what is left?
Images? Love? A greeting even,
Sweet to the senses? Is there anything?
Ah, no, friends: lead me away.
Lead me away from Thebes.
Lead the great wreck
And hell of Oedipus, whom the gods hate.
CHORAGOS     Your misery, you are not blind to
     that.
Would God you had never found it out!

ANTISTROPHE 2

OEDIPUS          Death take the man who unbound
My feet on that hillside
And delivered me from death to life!
What life? If only I had died,
This weight of monstrous doom
Could not have dragged me and my darlings
     down.
CHORAGOS  I would have wished the same.
OEDIPUS          Oh never to have come here
With my father's blood upon me! Never
To have been the man they call his mother's
     husband!
Oh accurst! Oh child of evil,
To have entered that wretched bed-
                              the selfsame one!
More primal than sin itself, this fell to me.
CHORAGOS  I do not know what words to offer
     you.
You were better dead than alive and blind.
OEDIPUS          Do not counsel me any more. This
     punishment
That I have laid upon myself is just.
If I had eyes,
I do not know how I could bear the sight
Of my father, when I came to the house of
     Death,
Or my mother: for I have sinned against them
     both
So vilely that I could not make my peace
By strangling my own life.
                    Or do you think my children,
Born as they were born, would be sweet to my
     eyes?
Ah never, never! Nor this town with its high
     walls,
Nor the holy images of the gods.
                                        For I,
Thrice miserable!—Oedipus, noblest of all the
     line
Of Kadmos, have condemned myself to enjoy
These things no more, by my own malediction
Expelling that man whom the gods declared
To be a defilement in the house of Laïos.

After exposing the rankness of my own guilt,
How could I look men frankly in the eyes?
No, I swear it,
If I could have stifled my hearing at its source,
I would have done it and made all this body
A tight cell of misery, blank to light and
     sound:
So I should have been safe in my dark mind
Beyond external evil.
                              Ah Kithairon!
Why did you shelter me? When I was cast
     upon you,
Why did I not die? Then I should never
Have shown the world my execrable birth.

Ah Polybos! Corinth, city that I believed
The ancient seat of my ancestors: how fair
I seemed, your child! And all the while this
     evil
Was cancerous within me!
                                        For I am sick
In my own being, sick in my origin.

O three roads, dark ravine, woodland and
     way
Where three roads met: you, drinking my
     father's blood,
My own blood, spilled by my own hand: can
     you remember
The unspeakable things I did there, and the
     things
I went on from there to do?
                                   O marriage, marriage!
That act that engendered me, and again the
     act
Performed by the son in the same bed—
                                        Ah, the net
Of incest, mingling fathers, brothers, sons,
With brides, wives, mothers: the last evil
That can be known by men: no tongue can say
How evil!
          No. For the love of God, conceal me
Somewhere far from Thebes; or kill me; or
     hurl me
Into the sea, away from men's eyes for ever.

Come, lead me. You need not fear to touch
     me.
Of all men, I alone can bear this guilt.

(Enter KREON)

CHORAGOS     Kreon is here now. As to what
     you ask,
He may decide the course to take. He only
Is left to protect the city in your place.
OEDIPUS          Alas, how can I speak to him?
     What right have I
To beg his courtesy whom I have deeply
     wronged?

KREON     I have not come to mock you, Oedipus,
Or to reproach you, either. (*To* ATTENDANTS)
                    —You, standing there:
If you have lost all respect for man's dignity,
At least respect the flame of Lord Helios:
Do not allow this pollution to show itself
Openly here, an affront to the earth
And Heaven's rain and the light of day. No, take him
Into the house as quickly as you can.
For it is proper
That only the close kindred see his grief.
OEDIPUS     I pray you in God's name, since your courtesy
Ignores my dark expectation, visiting
With mercy this man of all men most execrable:
Give me what I ask—for your good, not for mine.
KREON     And what is it that you turn to me begging for?
OEDIPUS     Drive me out of this country as quickly as may be
To a place where no human voice can ever greet me.
KREON     I should have done that before now—only,
God's will had not been wholly revealed to me.
OEDIPUS     But his command is plain: the parricide
Must be destroyed. I am that evil man.
KREON     That is the sense of it, yes; but as things are,
We had best discover clearly what is to be done.
OEDIPUS     You would learn more about a man like me?
KREON     You are ready now to listen to the god.
OEDIPUS     I will listen. But it is to you
That I must turn for help. I beg you, hear me.

The woman in there—
Give her whatever funeral you think proper:
She is your sister.
                    —But let me go, Kreon!
Let me purge my father's Thebes of the pollution
Of my living here, and go out to the wild hills,
To Kithairon, that has won such fame with me,
The tomb my mother and father appointed for me,
And let me die there, as they willed I should.

And yet I know
Death will not ever come to me through sickness
Or in any natural way: I have been preserved

For some unthinkable fate. But let that be.

As for my sons, you need not care for them.
They are men, they will find some way to live.
But my poor daughters, who have shared my table,
Who never before have been parted from their father—
Take care of them, Kreon; do this for me.

And will you let me touch them with my hands
A last time, and let us weep together?
Be kind, my lord,
Great prince, be kind!
                    Could I but touch them,
They would be mine again, as when I had my eyes.

(*Enter* ANTIGONE *and* ISMENE, *attended*)

Ah God!
Is it my dearest children I hear weeping?
Has Kreon pitied me and sent my daughters?
KREON     Yes, Oedipus: I knew that they were dear to you
In the old days, and know you must love them still.
OEDIPUS     May God bless you for this—and be a friendlier
Guardian to you than he has been to me!
Children, where are you?
Come quickly to my hands: they are your brother's—
Hands that have brought your father's once clear eyes
To this way of seeing—
                    Ah dearest ones,
I had neither sight nor knowledge then, your father
By the woman who was the source of his own life!
And I weep for you—having no strength to see you—,
I weep for you when I think of the bitterness
That men will visit upon you all your lives.
What homes, what festivals can you attend
Without being forced to depart again in tears?
And when you come to marriageable age,
Where is the man, my daughters, who would dare
Risk the bane that lies on all my children?
Is there any evil wanting? Your father killed
His father; sowed the womb of her who bore him;
Engendered you at the fount of his own existence!
That is what they will say of you.
                    Then, whom

Can you ever marry? There are no bride-
  grooms for you,
And your lives must wither away in sterile
  dreaming.

O Kreon, son of Menoikeus!
You are the only father my daughters have,
Since we, their parents, are both of us gone for
  ever.
They are your own blood: you will not let
  them
Fall into beggary and loneliness;
You will keep them from the miseries that are
  mine!
Take pity on them; see, they are only children,
Friendless except for you. Promise me this,
Great prince, and give me your hand in token
  of it.

(KREON *clasps his right hand*)

Children:
I could say much, if you could understand me,
But as it is, I have only this prayer for you:
Live where you can, be as happy as you can—
Happier, please God, than God has made your
  father.

KREON      Enough. You have wept enough.
  Now go within.
OEDIPUS    I must; but it is hard.
KREON            Time eases all things.
OEDIPUS    You know my mind, then?
KREON            Say what you desire.
OEDIPUS    Send me from Thebes!
KREON           God grant that I may!

OEDIPUS    But since God hates me . . .
KREON       No, he will grant your wish.
OEDIPUS    You promise?
KREON      I can not speak beyond my
  knowledge.
OEDIPUS    Then lead me in.
KREON      Come now, and leave your
  children.
OEDIPUS    No! Do not take them from me!
KREON            Think no longer
  That you are in command here, but rather
    think
  How, when you were, you served your own
    destruction.

(*Exeunt into the house all but the* CHORUS; *the*
  CHORAGOS *chants directly to the audience*)

CHORAGOS    Men of Thebes: look upon
  Oedipus.

This is the king who solved the famous riddle
And towered up, most powerful of men.
No mortal eyes but looked on him with envy,
Yet in the end ruin swept over him.
Let every man in mankind's frailty
Consider his last day; and let none
Presume on his good fortune until he find
Life, at his death, a memory without pain.

## ENDNOTES

1. The Sphinx.
2. Iokastê's womb.
3. Final scene.

# INDIVIDUAL AND COMMUNITY

# "STRANGER IN THE VILLAGE"

### James Baldwin (1926-1987)

James Baldwin was born in Harlem during the period in African-American cultural history known as the Harlem Renaissance. During his long literary career, Baldwin authored essays, short stories, novels, and two plays. His first collection of essays, Notes of a Native Son (1955), brought him critical acclaim and earned him preeminence as a voice for the urban African-American experience. He subsequently became an incisive, articulate spokesman during the early Civil Rights Movement, and his activism eventually consumed him to the degree that his literary craft suffered. Baldwin not only fought the injustice of racism, but the rampant homophobia and anti-intellectualism he confronted as a young man. Alienated by the racial climate in America, he moved to Paris in 1948, and except for returning to America for brief periods to visit his family, remained there until the end of his life.

While living in Paris proved to be liberating, Baldwin nevertheless grappled with the scars of racism, poverty, self-identity and depression. He was also struggling to complete his first novel, Go Tell It On The Mountain (1953). Baldwin accepted an invitation to spend a winter in a Swiss village finishing the novel while staying at the family chalet of a close friend. As a literal stranger to the village, he deals with his feelings of alienation, ponders his past and his future, and juxtaposes European racial attitudes with American race relations.

From all available evidence no black man had ever set foot in this tiny Swiss village before I came. I was told before arriving that I would probably be a "sight" for the village; I took this to mean that people of my complexion were rarely seen in Switzerland, and also that city people are always something of a "sight" outside of the city. It did not occur to me—possibly because I am an American—that there could be people anywhere who had never seen a Negro.

It is a fact that cannot be explained on the basis of the inaccessibility of the village. The village is very high, but it is only four hours from Milan and three hours from Lausanne. It is true that it is virtually unknown. Few people making plans for a holiday would elect to come here. On the other hand, the villagers are able, presumably, to come and go as they please—which they do: to another town at the foot of the mountain, with a population of approximately five thousand, the nearest place to see a movie or go to the bank. In the village there is no movie house, no bank, no library, no theater; very few radios, one jeep, one station wagon; and, at the moment, one typewriter, mine, an invention which the woman next door to me here had never seen. There are about six hundred people living here, all Catholic—I conclude this from the fact that the Catholic church is open all year round, whereas the Protestant chapel, set off on a hill a little removed from the village, is open only in the summertime when the tourists arrive. There are four or five hotels, all closed now, and four or five bistros, of which, however, only two do any business during the winter. These two do not do a great deal, for life in the village seems to end around nine or ten o'clock. There are a few stores, butcher, baker, épicerie, a hardware store, and a money-changer—who cannot change travelers' checks, but must send them down to the bank, an operation which takes two or three days. There is something called the Ballet Haus, closed in the winter and used for God knows what, certainly not ballet, during the summer. There seems to be only one schoolhouse in the village, and this for the quite young children; I suppose this to mean that their older brothers and sisters at some point descend from these mountains in order to complete their education—possibly, again, to the town just below. The landscape is absolutely forbidding, mountains towering on all four sides, ice and snow as far as the eye can reach. In this white wilderness, men and women and children move all day, carrying washing, wood, buckets of milk or water, sometimes skiing on Sunday afternoons. All week long boys and young men are to be seen shoveling snow off the rooftops, or dragging wood down from the forest in sleds.

The village's only real attraction, which explains the tourist season, is the hot spring water. A disquietingly high proportion of these tourists are cripples, or semi-cripples, who come year after year—from other parts of Switzerland, usually—to take the waters. This lends the village, at the height of the season, a rather terrifying air of sanctity, as though it were a lesser Lourdes. There is often something beautiful, there is always something awful, in the spectacle of a person who has lost one of his faculties, a faculty he never questioned until it was gone, and who struggles to recover it. Yet people remain people, on crutches or indeed on deathbeds; and wherever I passed, the first summer I was here, among the native villagers or among the lame, a wind passed with me—of astonishment, curiosity, amusement, and outrage. That first summer I stayed two weeks and never intended to return. But I did return in the winter, to work; the village offers, obviously, no distractions whatever and has the further advantage of being extremely cheap. Now it is winter again, a year later, and I am here again. Everyone in the village knows my name, though they scarcely ever use it, knows that I come from America—though, this, apparently, they will never really believe: black men come from Africa—and everyone knows that I am the friend of the son of a woman who was born here, and that I am staying in their chalet. But I remain as much a stranger today as I was the first day I arrived, and the children shout *Neger! Neger!* as I walk along the streets.

It must be admitted that in the beginning I was far too shocked to have any real reaction. In so far as I reacted at all, I reacted by trying to be pleasant —it being a great part of the American Negro's education (long before he goes to school) that he must make people "like" him. This smile-and-the-world-smiles-with-you routine worked about as well in this situation as it had in the situation for which it was designed, which is to say that it did not work at all. No one, after all, can be liked whose human weight and complexity cannot be, or

has not been, admitted. My smile was simply another unheard-of phenomenon which allowed them to see my teeth—they did not, really, see my smile and I began to think that, should I take to snarling, no one would notice any difference. All of the physical characteristics of the Negro which had caused me, in America, a very different and almost forgotten pain were nothing less than miraculous— or infernal—in the eyes of the village people. Some thought my hair was the color of tar, that it had the texture of wire, or the texture of cotton. It was jocularly suggested that I might let it all grow long and make myself a winter coat. If I sat in the sun for more than five minutes some daring creature was certain to come along and gingerly put his fingers on my hair, as though he were afraid of an electric shock, or put out his hand on my hand, astonished that the color did not rub off. In all of this, in which it must be conceded there was the charm of genuine wonder and in which there was certainly no element of intentional unkindness, there was yet no suggestion that I was human: I was simply a living wonder.

I knew that they did not mean to be unkind, and I know it now; it is necessary, nevertheless, for me to repeat this to myself each time that I walk out of the chalet. The children who shout *Neger!* have no way of knowing the echoes this sound raises in me. They are brimming with good humor and the more daring swell with pride when I stop to speak with them. Just the same, there are days when I cannot pause and smile, when I have no heart to play with then; when, indeed, I mutter sourly to myself, exactly as I muttered on the streets of a city these children have never seen, when I was no bigger than these children are now: *Your mother was a nigger.* Joyce is right about history being a nightmare—but it may be the nightmare from which no one can awaken. People are trapped in history and history is trapped in them.

There is a custom in the village—I am told it is repeated in many villages—of "buying" African natives for the purpose of converting them to Christianity. There stands in the church all year round a small box with a slot for money, decorated with a black figurine, and into this box the villagers drop their francs. During the *carnaval* which precedes Lent, two village children have their faces blackened —out of which bloodless darkness their blue eyes shine like ice—and fantastic horsehair wigs are placed on their blond heads; thus disguised, they solicit among the villagers for money for the missionaries in Africa. Between the box in the church and the blackened children, the village "bought" last year six or eight African natives. This was reported to me with pride by the wife of one of the bistro owners and I was careful to express astonishment and pleasure at the solicitude shown by the village for the souls of black folk. The *bistro* owner's wife beamed with pleasure far more genuine than my own and seemed to feel that I might now breathe more easily concerning the souls of at least six of my kinsmen.

I tried not to think of these so lately baptized kinsmen, of the price paid for them, or the peculiar price they themselves would pay, and said nothing about my father, who having taken his own conversion too literally never, at bottom, forgave the white world (which he described as heathen) for having saddled him with a Christ in whom, to judge at least from their treatment of him, they themselves no longer believed. I thought of white men arriving for the first time in an African village, strangers there, as I am a stranger here, and tried to imagine the astounded populace touching their hair and marveling at the color of their skin. But there is a great difference between being the first white man to be seen by Africans and being the first black man to be seen by whites. The white man takes the astonishment as tribute, for he arrives to conquer and to convert the natives, whose inferiority in relation to himself is not even to be questioned; whereas I, without a thought of conquest, find myself among a people whose culture controls me, has even, in a sense, created me, people who have cost me more in anguish and rage than they will ever know, who yet do not even know of my existence. The astonishment with which I might have greeted them, should they have stumbled into my African village a few hundred years ago, might have rejoiced their hearts. But the astonishment with which they greet me today can only poison mine.

And this is so despite everything I may do to feel differently, despite my friendly conversations with the bistro owner's wife, despite their three-year-old son who has at last become my friend, despite the *saluts* and *bonsoirs* which I exchange with people as I walk, despite the fact that I know that no individual can be taken to task for what history is doing, or has done. I say that the culture of these people controls me—but they can scarcely be held responsible for European culture. America comes out of Europe, but these people have never seen America, nor have most of them seen more of Europe than the hamlet at the foot of their mountain. Yet they move with an authority which I shall never have; and they regard me, quite rightly, not as a stranger in their village but as a suspect latecomer, bearing no credentials, to everything they have—however unconsciously—inherited.

For this village, even were it incomparably more remote and incredibly more primitive, is the West, the West onto which I have been so strangely grafted. These people cannot be, from the point of view of power, strangers anywhere in the world; they have made the modern world, in effect, even if they do not know it. The most illiterate among them is related, in a way that I am not, to Dante, Shakespeare, Michelangelo, Aeschylus, Da Vinci, Rembrandt, and Racine; the cathedral at Chartres says something to them which it cannot say to me, as indeed would New York's Empire State Building, should anyone here ever see it; out of their hymns and dances come Beethoven and Bach. Go back a few centuries and they are in their full glory—but I am in Africa, watching the conquerors arrive.

The rage of the disesteemed is personally fruitless, but it is also absolutely inevitable; this rage, so generally discounted, so little understood even among the people whose daily bread it is, is one of the things that makes history. Rage can only with difficulty, and never entirely, be brought under the domination of the intelligence and is therefore not susceptible to any arguments whatever. This is a fact which ordinary representatives of the Herrenvolk, having never felt this rage and being unable to imagine it, quite fail to understand. Also, rage cannot be hidden, it can only be dissembled. This dissembling deludes the thoughtless, and strengthens rage and adds, to rage, contempt. There are, no doubt, as many ways of coping with the resulting complex of tensions as there are black men in the world, but no black man can hope ever to be entirely liberated from this internal warfare—rage, dissembling, and contempt having inevitably accompanied his first realization of the power of white men. What is crucial here is that, since white men represent in the black man's world so heavy a weight, white men have for black men a reality which is far from being reciprocal; and hence all black men have toward all white men an attitude which is designed, really, either to rob the white man of the jewel of his naivete, or else to make it cost him dear.

The black man insists, by whatever means he finds at his disposal, that the white man cease to regard him as an exotic rarity and recognize him as a human being. This is a very charged and difficult moment, for there is a great deal of will power involved in the white man's naivete. Most people are not naturally reflective any more than they are naturally malicious, and the white man prefers to keep the black man at a certain human remove because it is easier for him thus to preserve his simplicity and avoid being called to account for crimes committed by his forefathers, or his neighbors. He is inescapably aware, nevertheless, that he is in a better position in the world than black men are, nor can he quite put to death the suspicion that he is hated by black men therefore. He does not wish to be hated, neither does he wish to change places, and at this point in his uneasiness he can scarcely avoid having recourse to those legends which white men have created about black men, the most usual effect of which is that the white man finds himself enmeshed, so to speak, in his own language which describes hell, as well as the attributes which lead one to hell, as being as black as night.

Every legend, moreover, contains its residuum of truth, and the root function of language is to control the universe by describing it. It is of quite considerable significance that black men remain, in the imagination, and in overwhelming numbers in fact, beyond the disciplines of salvation; and this despite the fact that the West has been "buying" African natives for centuries. There is, I should hazard, an instantaneous necessity to be divorced from this so visibly unsaved stranger, in whose heart, moreover, one cannot guess what dreams of vengeance are being nourished; and, at the same time, there are few things on earth more attractive than the idea of the unspeakable liberty which is allowed the unredeemed. When, beneath the black mask, a human being begins to make himself felt one cannot escape a certain awful wonder as to what kind of human being it is. What one's imagination makes of other people is dictated, of course, by the laws of one's own personality and it is one of the ironies of black-white relations that, by means of what the white man imagines the black man to be, the black man is enabled to know who the white man is.

I have said, for example, that I am as much a stranger in this village today as I was the first summer I arrived, but this is not quite true. The villagers wonder less about the texture of my hair than they did then, and wonder rather more about me. And the fact that their wonder now exists on another level is reflected in their attitudes and in their eyes. There are the children who make those delightful, hilarious, sometimes astonishingly grave overtures of friendship in the unpredictable fashion of children; other children, having been taught that the devil is a black man, scream in genuine anguish as I approach. Some of the older women never pass without a friendly greeting, never pass, indeed, if it seems that they will be able to engage me in conversation; other women look down or look away or rather contemptuously smirk. Some of the men drink with me and suggest that I learn how to ski—partly, I gather, because they cannot imagine what I would look like on skis and want to know if I am married, and ask questions about my *metier*. But some of the men have accused *le sale negre*— behind my back—of stealing wood and there is already in the eyes of some of them that peculiar, intent, paranoiac malevolence which one sometimes surprises in

the eyes of American white men when, out walking with their Sunday girl, they see a Negro male approach.

There is a dreadful abyss between the streets of this village and the streets of the city in which I was born, between the children who shout *Neger* today and those who shouted *Nigger* yesterday—the abyss is experience, the American experience. The syllable hurled behind me today expresses, above all, wonder: I am a stranger here. But I am not a stranger in America and the same syllable riding on the American air expresses the war my presence has occasioned in the American soul.

For this village brings home to me this fact: that there was a day, and not really a very distant day, when Americans were scarcely Americans at all but discontented Europeans, facing a great unconquered continent and strolling, say, into a marketplace and seeing black men for the first time. The shock this spectacle afforded is suggested, surely, by the promptness with which they decided that these black men were not really men but cattle. It is true that the necessity on the part of the settlers of the New World of reconciling their moral assumptions with the fact—and the necessity—of slavery enhanced immensely the charm of this idea, and it is also true that the idea expresses, with a truly American bluntness, the attitude which to varying extents all masters have had toward all slaves.

But between all former slaves and slave-owners and the drama which begins for Americans over three hundred years ago at Jamestown, there are at least two differences to be observed. The American Negro slave could not suppose, for one thing, as slaves in past epochs had supposed and often done, that he would ever be able to wrest the power from his master's hands. This was a supposition which the modern era, which was to bring about such vast changes in the aims and dimensions of power, put to death; it only begins, in unprecedented fashion, and with dreadful implications, to be resurrected today. But even had this supposition persisted with undiminished force, the American Negro slave could not have used it to lend his condition dignity, for the reason that this supposition rests on another: that the slave in exile yet remains related to his past, has some means—if only in memory—of revering and sustaining the forms of his former life, is able, in short, to maintain his identity.

This was not the case with the American Negro slave. He is unique among the black men of the world in that his past was taken from him, almost literally, at one blow. One wonders what on earth the first slave found to say to the first dark child he bore. I am told that there are Haitians able to trace their ancestry back to African kings, but any

American Negro wishing to go back so far will find his journey through time abruptly arrested by the signature on the bill of sale which served as the entrance paper for his ancestor. At the time—to say nothing of the circumstances—of the enslavement of the captive black man who was to become the American Negro, there was not the remotest possibility that he would ever take power from his master's hands. There was no reason to suppose that his situation would ever change, nor was there, shortly, anything to indicate that his situation had ever been different. It was his necessity, in the words of E. Franklin Frazier, to find a "motive for living under American culture or die." The identity of the American Negro comes out of this extreme situation, and the evolution of this identity was a source of the most intolerable anxiety in the minds and lives of his masters.

For the history of the American Negro is unique also in this: that the question of his humanity, and of his rights therefore as a human being, became a burning one for several generations of Americans, so burning a question that it ultimately became one of those used to divide the nation. It is out of this argument that the venom of the epithet *Nigger!* is derived. It is an argument which Europe has never had, and hence Europe quite sincerely fails to understand how or why the argument arose in the first place, why its effects are so frequently disastrous and always so unpredictable, why it refuses until today to be entirely settled. Europe's black possessions remained—and do remain—in Europe's colonies, at which remove they represented no threat whatever to European identity. If they posed any problem at all for the European conscience, it was a problem which remained comfortingly abstract: in effect, the black man, *as a man*, did not exist for Europe. But in America, even as a slave, he was an inescapable part of the general social fabric and no American could escape having an attitude toward him. Americans attempt until today to make an abstraction of the Negro, but the very nature of these abstractions reveals the tremendous effects the presence of the Negro has had on the American character.

When one considers the history of the Negro in America it is of the greatest importance to recognize that the moral beliefs of a person, or a people, are never really as tenuous as life—which is not moral —very often causes them to appear; these create for them a frame of reference and a necessary hope, the hope being that when life has done its worst they will be enabled to rise above themselves and to triumph over life. Life would scarcely be bearable if this hope did not exist. Again, even when the worst has been said, to betray a belief is not by any means to have put oneself beyond its power; the betrayal of

a belief is not the same thing as ceasing to believe. If this were not so there would be no moral standards in the world at all. Yet one must also recognize that morality is based on ideas and that all ideas are dangerous—dangerous because ideas can only lead to action and where the action leads no man can say. And dangerous in this respect: that confronted with the impossibility of remaining faithful to one's beliefs, and the equal impossibility of becoming free of them, one can be driven to the most inhuman excesses. The ideas on which American beliefs are based are not, though Americans often seem to think so, ideas which originated in America. They came out of Europe. And the establishment of democracy on the American continent was scarcely as radical a break with the past as was the necessity, which Americans faced, of broadening this concept to include black men.

This was, literally, a hard necessity. It was impossible, for one thing, for Americans to abandon their beliefs, not only because these beliefs alone seemed able to justify the sacrifices they had endured and the blood that they had spilled, but also because these beliefs afforded them their only bulwark against a moral chaos as absolute as the physical chaos of the continent it was their destiny to conquer. But in the situation in which Americans found themselves, these beliefs threatened an idea which, whether or not one likes to think so, is the very warp and woof of the heritage of the West, the idea of white supremacy.

Americans have made themselves notorious by the shrillness and the brutality with which they have insisted on this idea, but they did not invent it; and it has escaped the world's notice that those very excesses of which Americans have been guilty imply a certain, unprecedented uneasiness over the idea's life and power, if not, indeed, the idea's validity. The idea of white supremacy rests simply on the fact that white men are the creators of civilization (the present civilization, which is the only one that matters; all previous civilizations are simply "contributions" to our own) and are therefore civilization's guardians and defenders. Thus it was impossible for Americans to accept the black man as one of themselves, for to do so was to jeopardize their status as white men. But not to accept him was to deny his human reality; his human weight and complexity, and the strain of denying the overwhelmingly undeniable forced Americans into rationalizations so fantastic that they approached the pathological.

At the root of the American Negro problem is the necessity of the American white man to find a way of living with the Negro in order to be able to live with himself. And the history of this problem can be reduced to the means used by Americans—

lynch law and law, segregation and legal acceptance, terrorization and concession-either to come to terms with this necessity, or to find a way around it, or (most usually) to find a way of doing both these things at once. The resulting spectacle, at once foolish and dreadful, led someone to make the quite accurate observation that "the Negro-in-America is a form of insanity which overtakes the white man."

In this long battle, a battle by no means finished, the unforeseeable effects of which will be felt by many future generations, the white man's motive was the protection of his identity; the black man was motivated by the need to establish an identity. And despite the terrorization which the Negro in America endured and endures sporadically until today, despite the cruel and totally inescapable ambivalence of his status in his country, the battle for his identity has long ago been won. He is not a visitor to the West, but a citizen there, an American; as American as the Americans who despise him, the Americans who fear him, the Americans who love him—the Americans who became less than themselves, or rose to be greater than themselves by virtue of the fact that the challenge he represented was inescapable. He is perhaps the only black man in the world whose relationship to white men is more terrible, more subtle, and more meaningful than the relationship of bitter possessed to uncertain possessor. His survival depended, and his development depends, on his ability to turn his peculiar status in the Western world to his own advantage and, it may be, to the very great advantage of that world. It remains for him to fashion out of his experience that which will give him sustenance, and a voice.

The cathedral at Chartres, I have said, says something to the people of this village which it cannot say to me; but it is important to understand that this cathedral says something to me which it cannot say to them. Perhaps they are struck by the power of the spires, the glory of the windows; but they have known God, after all, longer than I have known him, and in a different way, and I am terrified by the slippery bottomless well to be found in the crypt, down which heretics were hurled to death, and by the obscene, inescapable gargoyles jutting out of the stone and seeming to say that God and the devil can never be divorced. I doubt that the villagers think of the devil when they face a cathedral because they have never been identified with the devil. But I must accept the status which myth, if nothing else, gives me in the West before I can hope to change the myth.

Yet, if the American Negro has arrived at his identity by virtue of the absoluteness of his estrangement from his past, American white men

still nourish the illusion that there is some means of recovering the European innocence, of returning to a state in which black men do not exist. This is one of the greatest errors Americans can make. The identity they fought so hard to protect has, by virtue of that battle, undergone a change: Americans are as unlike any other white people in the world as it is possible to be. I do not think, for example, that it is too much to suggest that the American vision of the world—which allows so little reality, generally speaking, for any of the darker forces in human life, which tends until today to paint moral issues in glaring black and white—owes a great deal to the battle waged by Americans to maintain between themselves and black men a human separation which could not be bridged. It is only now beginning to be borne in on us—very faintly, it must be admitted, very slowly, and very much against our will—that this vision of the world is dangerously inaccurate, and perfectly useless. For it protects our moral high-mindedness at the terrible expense of weakening our grasp of reality. People who shut their eyes to reality simply invite their own destruction, and anyone who insists on remaining in a state of innocence long after that innocence is dead turns himself into a monster.

The time has come to realize that the interracial drama acted out on the American continent has not only created a new black man, it has created a new white man, too. No road whatever will lead Americans back to the simplicity of this European village where white men still have the luxury of looking on me as a stranger. I am not, really, a stranger any longer for any American alive. One of the things that distinguishes Americans from other people is that no other people has ever been so deeply involved in the lives of black men, and vice versa. This fact faced, with all its implications, it can be seen that the history of the American Negro problem is not merely shameful, it is also something of an achievement. For even when the worst has been said, it must also be added that the perpetual challenge posed by this problem was always, somehow, perpetually met. It is precisely this black-white experience which may prove of indispensable value to us in the world we face today. This world is white no longer, and it will never be white again.

## Study Questions

1. In what way does Baldwin distinguish Europe's vision of racial differences from that of American race relations?

2. Why does Baldwin say that Americans are unlike any other white people in the world?

3. What does this essay say about black identity in America? About American identity in general?

# 2

# CLARENCE THOMAS AND THE CRISIS OF BLACK POLITICAL CULTURE

## Manning Marable

*Manning Marable is a professor of History and Political Science, as well as the Director of the Institute for Research in African-American Studies at Columbia University. He has published numerous books, including* Beyond Black and White: Race in America's Past, Present, and Future. *This essay comes from an anthology, edited by Toni Morrison, entitled* Race-ing Justice, En-gendering Power: Essays on Anita Hill, Clarence Thomas, and the Construction of Social Reality *(1992).*

The controversy surrounding Clarence Thomas's nomination and confirmation as an associate justice of the Supreme Court represents the first decisive national debate in the post-civil-rights era. The Second Reconstruction, the great historical epoch characterized by the democratic upsurgence of African Americans against the structures of racial discrimination and social inequality, effectively ended with the Reagan administration. Although much of the commentary on Thomas focused largely on the sexual harassment charges against him by former aide Anita Hill, the case must be seen against even larger political currents that symbolize the contemporary crisis within the African American political culture. This crisis is represented by the overlapping contradictions of gender, race, and the flawed ideology of liberalism. Each of these elements simultaneously illuminates and obscures the actual character of American politics and the status of African Americans within the apparatus of state power. Beyond the dimensions of personality, they alone explain how and why Clarence Thomas succeeded in being appointed to the Supreme Court

and why the majority of African Americans were persuaded to support his nomination.

Clarence Thomas's climb to power is directly related to his abandonment of the principles of the black-freedom struggle. A quarter century ago, as a college student in the late 1960s, Thomas proclaimed himself a devoted disciple of Malcolm X. Thomas wore the black beret of the Black Panther Party and signed his letters "Power to the People." He secured a position at Yale Law School because of its aggressive affirmative-action program, which had set aside roughly 10 percent of all places in each class to racial minorities. Yet less than a decade later Thomas would condemn affirmative action as being destructive to blacks' interests. When initially appointed head of the Equal Employment Opportunity Commission, Thomas embraced for a time the use of numerical hiring goals and timetables as a means to increase the employment of blacks. Yet following Reagan's landslide electoral victory in 1984, he reversed himself and strongly attacked affirmative-action goals and timetables. Two years later, when seeking reappointment to the EEOC from a Democratic-controlled Congress, Thomas solemnly promised that he would reinstate affirmative-action measures inside his office.

In dozens of published articles and in more than one hundred public speeches, Thomas repeatedly attacked the entire civil rights agenda as hopelessly anachronistic and irrelevant to the more conservative political environment of the 1980s. Thomas denounced welfare and other liberal reforms of the Great Society as a form of government-sponsored paternalism that reinforced dependency and undermined self-help and practical initiative within the black community. Thomas even went so far as to criticize the famous 1954 Supreme Court decision *Brown v. Board of Education* of Topeka, Kansas, which abolished racially segregated schools, as being based on "dubious social science" evidence. Thomas's subsequent appointment to a federal judgeship in Washington, D.C., was due less to his reputation as a legal scholar and for his judicial temperament, which was nonexistent, but for his noteworthy service as a partisan ideologue for conservative Republicanism.

Moreover, Thomas was one of the few people of color elevated by both former President Reagan and President Bush to federal judgeships. During Bush's first two years as president, he appointed seventy federal judges, nearly all of whom were white, affluent males. Less than 12 percent of Bush's federal judges were women; only 6.5 percent were from racial minority groups. Virtually all of his selections were deeply hostile to civil rights, affirmative-action enforcement, civil liberties for those charged with criminal offenses, environmental-protection laws, and the freedom of choice for women on the issue of abortion. Thus, the reality of Thomas's racial identity, and any personal or political connections he might have had with the African-American community, were secondary to his role as legal apologist for reactionary politics. Indeed, during these years Thomas attempted to "transcend" his blackness and condemned those who argued that his race necessarily imposed an obligation to conform to certain progressive political attitudes or policies.

From the moment of Bush's nomination of Thomas to replace liberal Associate Justice Thurgood Marshall on the Supreme Court, the president's justification and defense of the black conservative was essentially a series of unambiguous lies. No one in Congress or the legal profession seriously believed Bush's assertion that Thomas was nominated because he was "the best-qualified" jurist in the nation. No one was convinced by Bush's initial claims that Thomas's race had "nothing" to do with the decision to advance his candidacy. At best, Thomas's published writings revealed the working of a mediocre mind. If Bush had genuinely desired to nominate a black Republican judge with outstanding legal credentials, he would have ignored Thomas entirely and selected Amalya Kearse, an African American currently serving on the federal appeals court in New York. But Kearse's legal reputation as a moderate, despite her Republican Party affiliation, made her unacceptable to the extreme right wing. Bush's objective in selecting Thomas was, in part, to gain political capital at the expense of the core constituencies within the Demo-cratic Party, astutely pitting feminists against civil rights activists.

By contrast, other Republican presidents when considering Supreme Court appointments frequently have chosen quality over narrow partisanship. Dwight Eisenhower appointed two of the most liberal Supreme Court justices in American history—Chief Justice Earl Warren and Associate Justice William Brennan. Gerald Ford appointed Justice John Paul Stevens to the court, who is viewed today as a moderate. Even Reagan nominated Sandra Day O'Connor, who is essentially a moderate conservative. Bush's goal clearly was not judicial excellence. He wanted a nominee who was opposed to a woman's freedom of choice on abortion, an ideologue with slim intellectual qualifications who would attack the liberal political agenda from the protected confines of the court for the next thirty years.

Even before Professor Anita Hill's charges of sexual misconduct began to circulate, thoughtful observers noted in Thomas's record a disturbing characteristic of contempt for African-American women. This perception was not directly linked to his divorce from his first wife, an African American, and his remarriage in 1987 to Virginia Bess Lamp, a white Republican attorney. Thomas had first come to the attention of white conservatives nationally at a San Francisco conference sponsored by black Reaganites in the late 1980s. In his remarks before the conference, Thomas attacked welfare programs for perpetuating dependent behavior among blacks by focusing his negative remarks on his own sister, Emma Mae Martin. "She gets mad when the mailman is late with her welfare check," Thomas announced, as other black conservatives laughed aloud. "That's how dependent she is," Thomas affirmed.

Years later, journalists investigated Thomas's statements and discovered that they were false, because his sister was not on welfare at the time of his speech. Thomas didn't mention that his sister had received none of the educational advantages and affirmative-action benefits that he had taken for granted. It was also Thomas's sister who had assumed the responsibility of caring for their mother, and had taken two part-time jobs to get off welfare. As economist Julianne Malveaux critically observed: "For providing that kind of support in her family, Emma Mae Martin earned her brother's public scorn. What can the rest of us women expect from Supreme Court Justice Clarence Thomas as issues of pay equity and family policy come before this court?"

As Hill's charges of sexual harassment by Thomas reached the headlines, other disturbing evidence surfaced. Classmates of Thomas during his years at Yale Law School had already informed members of the Senate Judiciary Committee that he had displayed a strong "interest in pornographical films" at that time. Most damaging was Hill's testimony before the committee, which was detailed, credible, and persuasive. Witnesses also corroborated her testimony. Hill's charges of sexual misconduct echoed sharply across the country and transcended the specific case of Thomas, largely because the experience of sexual harassment was so common to millions of working women, regardless of their race, ethnicity, education, or class background. According to an October 1991 New York Times/ CBS News poll, about four out of ten women across the country have been the "object of sexual advances, propositions, or unwanted sexual discussions from men" in supervisory positions at their places of employment. Only one out of eight women who had been sexually harassed actually reported the incident. Like Hill, they knew that without hard evidence their assertions were unlikely to be believed. Their professional careers would suffer. Interestingly, even one-half of all men polled admitted that they have "said or done something which could have been construed by a female colleague as harassment."

The Senate and the Bush administration were first inclined to ignore the gravity of Hill's charges, which had originally been made in private, and to rush a confirmation vote on Thomas. But the public outcry, particularly from women's groups, was so profound that the leaders of both parties were forced to retreat. Part of the dilemma for the White House was the collapse of its basic strategy, which had avoided any analysis of Thomas's meager record as a legal scholar or federal judge, and had concentrated totally on his Horatio Alger, "Up from Slavery" saga. Now it was exactly Thomas's personality, character, and private morals that were seriously open to question.

But as the Senate committee was forced to reopen the hearings to evaluate Hill's testimony, the scales were tipped decisively in Thomas's favor. First, both the White House and the Senate were determined to keep the hearings from becoming, as Bush lieutenants put it, a "referendum on sexual harassment." Thomas should not be the "victim of two thousand years of male dominance." None of the senators had any familiarity with the legal requirements for sexual harassment, and had no knowledge of the massive body of scholarship and legal decisions on the issue. Second, a strategic error was committed by Senate Judiciary Committee Chairman Joseph Biden. Biden perceived Hill's accusations in the context of a criminal trial, with the presumption of innocence resting with Thomas. But

this was completely erroneous; no one had filed criminal charges against Thomas. The process should not have been seen as a trial, with the issue of establishing witness credibility, but as a political hearing to determine the qualifications and fitness of Thomas to serve on the Supreme Court. The point should have been made repeatedly that even if Hill did not exist, or even if grave doubts could be established concerning her testimony, there was already more than sufficient evidence to reject Thomas's nomination to the court.

Thomas helped his own case by taking the offensive. "If someone wanted to block me from the Supreme Court of the United States because of my views on the Constitution, that's fine," he declared before the committee. "But to destroy me? . . . I would have preferred an assassin's bullet to this kind of living hell that they have put me and my family through." Thomas proclaimed himself a martyr of an elaborate smear campaign inspired by racism. Without even listening to Hill's testimony or specific charges, Thomas declared that he was the victim of a "high-tech lynching." This was, of course, the most supreme irony: the black conservative who had done so much to destroy affirmative-action and civil rights programs designed to attack racial discrimination now sought refuge on the grounds of racism. As Janelle Byrd, a lawyer with the NAACP Legal Defense Fund, observed: "Thomas has run from his blackness, and now that he is backed into a corner, all of a sudden, Judge Thomas is black. He has used race in the most manipulative way." Nevertheless, Thomas's strategy was effective. The white liberal Democratic senators did not wish to be accused of racism, and they deliberately permitted Thomas to dictate the terms of the discourse. They were so effectively cowed that they neglected even to ask Thomas about the evidence of his long-time interest in pornographic films.

As the Democrats equivocated, the Reaganite Republicans smelled blood and circled for the political kill. The Senate's leading demagogue, Alan Simpson of Wyoming, vowed that Hill would be "destroyed, belittled, hounded, and harassed." With sinister innuendoes, he claimed to have faxes and letters attacking Hill's credibility "hanging out of my pockets," which warned him to "watch out for this woman." Senator Strom Thurmond of South Carolina declared Hill's allegations to be "totally without merit," even *before* listening to her testimony!

In a racist, sexist society, it is relatively easy for white men with power to discredit and to dismiss a black woman. The media contributed to the political assassination of Hill by projecting the controversy as part soap opera, part public trial, and by accepting the interpretation that Thomas merited the presumption of innocence. In this context it was not terribly surprising that the majority of Americans witnessing the spectacle concluded that Thomas was telling the truth and that Hill was lying. But in response those who smeared Anita Hill for possessing the courage and dignity to step forward, one should ask: Why would she lie? What did she actually gain from her actions? Politically a conservative and identified with her tenure in the Reagan administration, she clearly was not a liberal. Conservative politicians, ideologues, and sexists may attack her personal integrity and professionalism for decades to come. Her probable goal of one day becoming a federal judge is lost forever. As University of Maryland law professor Tanya Banks observed, Hill certainly "would not have taken this step without full consideration of consequences."

But at the moment of truth the liberals lacked the courage of their convictions. They sacrificed their principles before the volatile politics of gender and race. They physically recoiled when Thomas, in a moment of desperation, cynically charged "racism." They refused to acknowledge the reality that Anita Hill, not Thomas, was the real victim of "lynching"—not once but twice: the first time a decade ago, when she was sexually humiliated and harassed in private, and the second time on Capital Hill before the eyes of the world.

From the vantage point of African-American politics, the most crucial factor that contributed to Thomas's narrow confirmation by the Senate was the obvious support he had received from the majority of blacks. In several polls about 60 percent of all African Americans expressed support for Thomas's confirmation, even after Hill's charges were widely circulated. The Southern Christian Leadership Conference, established in 1957 by Martin Luther King, Jr., announced its endorsement of Thomas. The National Urban League took no official position against Thomas's nomination. The reality of black support for Thomas was a major reason that several southern Democrats who faced reelection in 1992 gave their votes to the black nominee. These senators included Wyche Fowler, Jr., of Georgia, Richard Shelby of Alabama, and John B. Breaux of Louisiana. Several other southern Democrats who had voted against Robert Bork's nomination to the Supreme Court four years before, Senators J. Bennett Johnston of Louisiana and Sam Nunn of Georgia, also cast their votes for Thomas. Black southern votes were absolutely essential for these white Democrats to survive politically.

When Bush first selected Thomas to replace Marshall, most African-American leaders and national organizations expressed strong opposition. The Congressional Black Caucus, with few exceptions, condemned Thomas as unfit to serve in Marshall's place. After some initial hesitancy, the NAACP came out against the black Reaganite on the grounds of his bitter hostility to civil rights and affirmative action. Many powerful black religious and trade-union leaders also issued similar condemnations of Thomas's nomination.

But the initial opinion polls of African Americans clearly indicated a willingness to support Thomas's appointment. There were at least three reasons for this curious response. The first factor was due to the growth of black "neoaccommodation." Since the rise of Reaganism within national politics more than a decade ago, white conservatives have made an effort to establish a base of political support within the African-American community. One primary reason for this can be attributed to racial patterns in national presidential and congressional politics. Since 1948 the majority of white voters have given a Democratic presidential candidate their support only once—Lyndon Johnson in 1964. Neither John F. Kennedy nor Jimmy Carter received a majority of whites' votes in their successful presidential elections. White middle-class voters, especially males, consistently support Republican candidates. Conversely, since 1964 an average of 88 percent of all African Americans have supported Democratic presidential candidates. Black support for Democratic senatorial candidates usually exceeds 90 percent. Republicans recognized that they would only need to increase their electoral support among blacks to roughly 20 to 25 percent—a realistic figure, given that Dwight Eisenhower had received over 40 percent of blacks' votes in 1956. With this increased black support, the Republicans would regain control over Congress, and would be virtually unbeatable in presidential contests, regardless of the Democratic candidate.

Thus, despite Reagan's vicious posturing and rhetoric against the civil rights community and most black officials, the Republicans began to fashion a "black-middle-class agenda": federal governmental support for black-owned banks and entrepreneurship, criticism of social welfare programs, endorsement of all-black male public schools, embracing the discourse of "self-reliance" historically associated with Booker T. Washington and Elijah Muhammad. A series of neoaccommodationist-conservative black spokespersons were promoted in the national media: economists Thomas Sowell and Walter Williams; journalist Tony Brown; Glenn C. Loury, professor at Harvard University's Kennedy School of Government; Robert Woodson, president of the National Center for Neighborhood Enterprises; J. A. Y. Parker, president of the Lincoln Institute for Research and Education; and of course Thomas.

The collaboration between black Democrats and conservative Republicans began to grow in statewide and congressional elections throughout the 1980s. In a half-million-dollar project, Benjamin L. Ginsberg, the chief counsel of the Republican National Committee, assisted civil rights organizations in their legal challenges to redraft congressional district boundaries, which might increase the number of African-American and Latino representatives. Republicans frequently observed that about eighty white Democrats represented congressional districts that were at least 30 percent black; for blacks to gain greater political power, they would have to do so at the expense of the Democratic Party's white establishment. Republicans began to provide Chicano and African-American groups free computer time, legal assistance, and political support. In several statewide races blacks began to support "moderate" Republicans. In 1986, 60 percent of all blacks voted for Republican incumbent Thomas Kean in New Jersey's gubernatorial race. In 1990, in Illinois, Republican gubernatorial candidate James Edgar received more than one-fifth of the black vote, and with this slender percentage was elected. Many black Chicagoans who had supported progressive mayor Harold Washington announced their support for Edgar.

Bush was well aware of these trends, and he sought to advance some public policy positions that would appeal to the black middle class. One central example is provided by the Bush administration's inconsistent position on the desegregation of historically black state colleges. In July 1991, U.S. Solicitor General Kenneth Starr was ordered to file an initial brief with the Supreme Court on a major school desegregation case, taking the position that states did not have to increase funds to black public colleges. The initial brief stated that there was no "independent obligation" for states "to correct disparities" between white and black public institutions. In protest, Bush's board of advisors on historically black colleges, chaired by former Howard University President James Cheek, demanded a meeting with the president. On September 9, 1991, Bush was told by his black advisors that Starr's brief had created a "crisis" among African-American educators. Partially due to the pressures of the Thomas nomination, Bush totally repudiated his earlier position, ordering Starr to issue a new brief stating that it was "incumbent" for states to "eradicate discrimination" by implementing "equitable and fair funding to historically black institutions." Just in case the Supreme Court overlooked the significance of Bush's new position, the revised brief added: "Suggestions to the contrary in our opening brief no longer reflect the position of the United States."

The second factor contributing to black support for Thomas was the ideology of "liberal integrationism" that permeated the strategic and tactical vision of the entire black middle class. For nearly a century, since the founding of the NAACP, most middle-class blacks have espoused a political ideology of integrationism, a commitment to the eradication of racial barriers within government, business, and society. In its simplest terms, "liberal integrationism" argues that if individual African Americans are advanced to positions of political, cultural, or corporate prominence, then the entire black community will benefit. This concept is essentially "symbolic representation": the conviction that the individual accomplishments of a Bill Cosby, Michael Jordan, Douglas Wilder, or Oprah Winfrey trickle down to empower millions of less fortunate African Americans. In municipal politics liberal integrationism's "symbolic representation" means that if the number of African Americans appointed to the police department increases, or if a black professional becomes police commissioner, working-class black neighborhoods will eventually become safer, or police brutality gradually will be reduced. The 1989 mayoral victory of David Dinkins in New York, for example, is broadly interpreted in the black media as yet another "gain" for the entire race.

The fundamental contradiction inherent in the notion of integrationist "symbolic representation" is that it presumes a degree of structural accountability and racial solidarity that binds the black public figure with the larger masses of African Americans. During the period of Jim Crow, the oppressive external constraints of legal discrimination imposed norms of racial conformity and solidarity. Despite an individual's educational attainments, capital formation, or excellence on the athletic field, for example, a person could never entirely escape the oppressive reality of segregation. The very definition of "race" was a social category defined by the presumed and very real hierarchies within the socioeconomic and political system, preserving and perpetuating black subordination. Black conservatives in an earlier era, such as George Schuyler, felt an obligation to their "race" that was imposed by the burden of exploitation, commonly experienced by all. But in the post-civil-rights period, in the absence of the legal structures of formal discrimination, the bonds of cultural kinship, social familiarity, and human responsibility that had once linked the most affluent and upwardly mobile African Americans with their economically marginalized sisters and brothers were severely weakened. It is now possible for a member of the present-day

Negro elite to live in the white suburbs, work in a white professional office, attend religious services in an all-white church or synagogue, belong to a white country club, and never come into intimate contact with the most oppressed segments of the black community. Moreover, for those privileged blacks within the expanding elite, the benefits of betraying the commonly-held perceptions of the liberal politics and social democratic assumptions deeply entrenched within the black working class are greater than ever. So the argument that, regardless of individual personal histories, class affinities, and cultural identities, the professional successes of individuals within the African-American elite benefit the entire black community is no longer valid.

But old beliefs die hard. A number of black liberal intellectuals, whose worldviews and political perceptions were hardened by the turmoil of the sixties and the heroic struggles against legal segregation, implicitly accept the notion of symbolic representation, and the totality of the ideological baggage of liberal integration. Noted author Maya Angelou expressed her support for Thomas in a *New York Times* editorial. Stephen Carter of Yale University, author of the controversial book *Reflections of an Affirmative Action Baby*, termed many of the charges leveled against Thomas by blacks irrelevant and "ridiculous." Carter declared that he "admire[d] much of what [Thomas] stands for," and that the black conservative who had done so much to undermine the black struggle for equality nevertheless represented "an important voice in the black community and in national affairs. His ostracism as a traitor, an enemy, an Uncle Tom, reflects no credit on those who have sought to cast him out." Carter's effort to salvage a degree of credibility from Thomas's shabby and shameful record was based on a faulty set of political assumptions. Carter never questioned the belief that a Thomas victory in the Senate would translate into a type of political advancement for other African Americans.

However, the most articulate defense of Thomas from liberal black quarters was offered by Harvard sociologist Orlando Patterson. Thomas was probably guilty of violating the cultural norms of "his white, upper-middle-class work world," Patterson suggested. But he had only offered sexual advances "to an aloof woman who is esthetically and socially very similar to himself, who had made no secret of her own deep admiration for him." In short, Thomas was guilty of bad judgment and poor office manners. If anyone was to blame, it was Hill. Patterson argues: "Raising the issue ten years later was unfair and disingenuous: unfair because, while she may well have been offended by his coarseness, there is no evidence that she suffered any emotional or career damage, and the punishment she belatedly

sought was in no way commensurate with the offense; and disingenuous because she has lifted a verbal style that carries only minor sanction in one subcultural context and thrown it in the overheated cultural arena of mainstream, neo-Puritan America, where it incurs professional extinction." The approach to redeem Thomas taken by Patterson is familiar to many African Americans schooled in cultural norms of their own people. How can any man be blamed for expressing his sexual interest in an available, attractive black woman? Doesn't the punishment for these sweet words uttered in the executive suite so many years ago far exceed the crime? Patterson goes so far as to defend Thomas's falsehoods given under oath because the black conservative's behavior did not merit censure. "Judge Thomas was justified in denying making the remarks, even if he had in fact made them," Patterson concluded, "not only because the deliberate displacement of his remarks made them something else but on the utilitarian moral grounds that any admission would have immediately incurred a self-destructive and grossly unfair punishment."

Patterson's thesis is grounded in several contradictory falsehoods. There is certainly a deep tradition of sexism within the black community, a pattern of denying human rights and leadership for women within our own institutions. In both black nationalist and integrationist formations, practices and policies of gender discrimination are apparent. But to dismiss the brutal language and offensive actions of Thomas by recalling similar behavior by other black men makes absolutely no sense. Shouldn't it matter that when this incident occurred, Thomas was the head of the Equal Employment Opportunity Commission, the agency responsible for outlawing sexual harassment in the workplace? Patterson's query concerning the number of years that had transpired between the alleged act of harassment and its public revelation blatantly ignores the legal evolution that has occurred in the past decade in such cases. The EEOC did not issue guidelines concerning sexual harassment, which was defined as any behavior that has the "purpose of unreasonably interfering with an individual's work performance or creating an intimidating or hostile or offensive environment," until 1980. It was not until 1986, in *Meritor Savings Bank v. Vinson*, that the Supreme Court actually ruled that sexual harassment in the workplace was a form of sex discrimination covered under Title VII of the 1964 Civil Rights Act. At the time of her harassment in the early 1980s, Hill would have had few legal avenues for redress. If she had filed a grievance, she would not have had a federal case, because judges viewed sexist intimidation as merely "bad manners." Even as late as 1991, Hill would not

CLARENCE THOMAS AND THE CRISIS OF BLACK POLITICAL CULTURE

have been able to recover damages from such a suit. Most professional women in this situation would have done what Hill did: stay with the position, hoping that her supervisor would change, or seek employment elsewhere without alienating her boss. But to claim as Patterson does that Thomas's obnoxious behavior was just a "down-home style of courting" is dishonest and disturbing.

A third factor that explains African-American support for Thomas can be attributed to the quasi-black-nationalist sentiment among millions of African-American working-class people and elements of the black middle class that were radicalized during the 1960s. A distinguishing feature of black nationalism is the belief that "race" is more important than other factors, such as gender or class, in determining social and political outcomes. Given the reality of Thomas's racial background, some black nationalists could support him on the grounds that Bush would simply appoint a white reactionary to the court if he was rejected by the Senate. Some even argued that any black person, regardless of his or her public record as a reactionary, nevertheless had experienced daily life as a black person. The factor of race was inescapable, and certainly this meant that Thomas ought to be given the benefit of the doubt. With the security of a permanent judicial appointment, he might eventually come to embrace the progressive perspectives of other African Americans.

The most articulate neoaccommodationist of Thomas from a "black-nationalist" perspective was Dr. Niara Sudarkasa, noted anthropologist and president of Lincoln University in Pennsylvania. Sudarkasa has previously identified herself as a black nationalist, and has claimed that one of the most influential African Americans in her own political development was Malcolm X. She has informed Lincoln University students and alumni that the *n* in the university's name stands for "nation-building," a phrase taken directly from the black-nationalist cultural upsurgence of two decades ago. Nevertheless, Sudarkasa went before the Senate Judiciary Committee to praise Thomas's conservative credentials. She insisted that Thomas was "an openminded and independent thinker" who should not be attacked for holding views in opposition to liberal integrationists in the civil rights establishment. African Americans "have been fortunate in having a long line of leaders who, in retrospect, seem right for their times," she argued. "These leaders did not always have the same ideology or agree on strategies, but they all agreed that the goal was to secure freedom and justice for our people. . . . Who can say that we are not better off for having the benefit of their separate and distinct voices?" Invoking black history, Sudarkasa

perceived Thomas in the "nation-building" tradition of Frederick Douglass, Marcus Garvey, and Martin Luther King, Jr.

Sudarkasa's thesis is only partially true. Throughout African-American history the political ideology of black people has been characterized by a struggle for both human equality and political democracy. Different leaders have approached these goals with different strategies. Black nationalists such as Malcolm X and Marcus Garvey have sought to build strong, black-controlled economic, political, and social institutions that could empower the black community from within. They have linked our struggles for freedom with the larger currents of political protest in Africa and the Caribbean. Other black leaders, such as Frederick Douglass and Martin Luther King, Jr., have emphasized the necessity of achieving full integration and the eradication of all barriers to equality within this country.

Sudarkasa's analysis presumes that Thomas and other upper-middle-class blacks who favor the repressive policies of the Reagan-Bush agenda are consciously working on behalf of other African Americans as an oppressed national minority. Actually, they are working fundamentally to promote their own careers, manipulating the mantle of blackness to cloak political perfidy. No doubt Thomas feels some ambiguous connections with the historical achievements of previous African-American leaders, who sacrificed to advance the boundaries of freedom for their people. The critical difference that separates him from this earlier leadership is a rupture between "race" and "ethnicity." Racially, Thomas remains "black": both by governmental definition and societal recognition, he belongs to a specific racial group characterized in part by physical appearance and political condition. Racial identity is essentially passive, a reality of being within a social formation stratified by the oppressive concept of race. Yet ethnically Thomas has ceased to be an African American, in the context of political culture, social values and ideals, and commitment to collective interests. Thomas feels absolutely no active ideological or cultural obligations to the dispossessed, the hungry and homeless who share the ethnic rituals, customs, and traditions of blackness. Thomas's accomplishment is a logical product not simply of personal cynicism but of the flawed perspective of liberal integrationism, which all too frequently made no distinction between race and ethnicity in black life. This is the reason that Louisiana racist politician and former neo-Nazi David Duke had little difficulty endorsing Thomas for appointment to the Supreme Court. Thomas was racially black, but in most other respects stood in bitter opposition to the resistance traditions in the culture of African-American people.

The great danger of Thomas's appointment will be measured in the political outlook and ideological attitudes of a new generation of African Americans, who were born after the period of Jim Crow and have no personal memories or involvement in civil rights demonstrations, protest marches, and Black Power activism. Like Thomas, they stand outside a period of history that binds them to a political culture of resistance and social transformation. Many seek not to challenge the established structures of power but to prepare themselves to assimilate within these systems. This tremendous sense of impending crisis for the future of young African Americans was reinforced for me during a visit to Lincoln University, in the midst of the national debate over Thomas-Hill. One of Lincoln's most articulate young male students argued passionately after I presented several critical comments on the Thomas nomination. The student did not deny that the evidence in the case weighed heavily against Thomas. Nevertheless, he insisted that African Americans had no choice except to applaud this appointment to the Supreme Court. After all, Thomas claimed to be opposed to welfare and the white liberal policies of dependency; didn't this place Thomas in harmony with black activists such as Malcolm X and black nationalists like Elijah Muhammad, who advocated "self-help"? In brief, he forcefully presented Sudarkasa's thesis of neo-accomodationism. I was deeply impressed with the student's seriousness, and tried to raise every counterargument conceivable. I argued just as passionately that Thomas's opposition to a woman's freedom of choice on abortion would mean that thousands of pregnant black women annually would be subjected to back-alley butchers. Thomas's hatred of affirmative action meant a monolithically conservative Supreme Court that would reduce blacks' opportunities in education and the job market.

The Lincoln University student replied: "That's the problem with black people today. We aren't willing to settle for half a loaf. Sometimes less than half a loaf is all we can expect, and we should be happy to get even that." This is not the political perspective of resistance, the enthusiastic defiance of youth that characterized the Student Nonviolent Coordinating Committee and the cadre of the Black Panther Party. This is not the aggressive posture of young people who oppose oppression and who are unwilling to accept anything less than freedom. The central tragedy of Thomas for black America is his powerful image as a negative role model for millions of young people who have never walked a picket line or occupied a public building in protest. Thomas's victory reinforces the tendencies toward compromise, accommodation, and pessimism. His

elevation to the court illustrates to our next generation that any instincts toward the political culture of resistance must be forgotten, that the way forward is by accepting the "less than half a loaf" offered to us by our oppressors.

The price of Thomas's personal advancement into the corridors of national power thus has been achieved at an unprecedented price. Our young people have witnessed an unprincipled individual who possesses a deep hostility toward African-American women, possibly committing acts of sexual harassment, who is nevertheless rewarded and praised at the highest levels of government. Seldom has the black intelligentsia and political leadership been in such disarray, debating the merits of supporting an obvious opportunist. Seldom has the black middle class so confused its actual material interests with the symbolic satisfaction of seeing one of its own being appointed to high judicial office. The Thomas case is one of the rare instances in which the majority of the African-American community has supported the wrong person for the wrong position for the wrong reasons. Unfortunately, given the profound level of confusion in both the strategic and ideological perspectives of the African-American middle class, its present inability to transcend the bankrupt politics of liberal integrationism, it is probable that we will witness more Clarence Thomases in the near future.

## Study Questions

1. What is Manning's primary criticism of Clarence Thomas, in terms of his relationship to affirmative action? What about Thomas's behavior toward women?

2. What does he say went wrong in the Senate hearings?

3. He argues that there are three main reasons for black communities' support of Thomas. What are these reasons? Do they reflect black cultural reality as a whole? What do you think?

4. Do you think Thomas has the good of black communities at heart? Why or why not?

5. What does he see as the single most important danger of this appointment? Evaluate his analysis of "your" generation.

# THE SECOND SEX

## *Simone de Beauvoir (1908-1986)*

*Society, being codified by man, decrees that woman is inferior: she can do away with this inferiority only by destroying the male's superiority. She sets about mutilating, dominating man, she contradicts him, she denies his truth and his values. But in doing this she is only defending herself; it was neither a changeless essence nor a mistaken choice that doomed her to immanence, to inferiority. They were imposed upon her. All oppression creates a state of war. And this is no exception. The existent who is regarded as inessential cannot fail to demand the reestablishment of her sovereignty*

*Today the combat takes a different shape; instead of wishing to put man in a prison, woman endeavors to escape from one; she no longer seeks to drag him into the realms of immanence but to emerge, herself, into the light of transcendence. Now the attitude of the males creates a new conflict: it is with a bad grace that the man lets her go. He is very well pleased to remain the sovereign subject, the absolute superior, the essential being; he refuses to accept his companion as an equal in any concrete way. She replies to his lack of confidence in her by assuming an aggressive attitude. It is no longer a question of a war between individuals each shut up in his or her sphere: a caste claiming its rights goes over the top and it is resisted by the privileged caste. Here two transcendences are face to face; instead of displaying mutual recognition, each free being wishes to dominate the other.*

*This difference of attitude is manifest on the sexual plane as on the spiritual plane. The "feminine" woman in making herself prey tries to reduce man, also, to her carnal passivity; she occupies herself in catching him in her trap, in enchaining him by means of the desire she arouses in him in submissively making herself a thing. The emancipated woman, on the contrary, wants to be active, a taker, and refuses the passivity man means to impose on her.*

*Simone de Beauvoir was a member of the French intellectual and literary elite during much of the twentieth century. Much of her writings (novels, essays, memoirs) are drawn from the philosophy of existentialism, which was mainly the work of Jean-Paul Sartre, with whom she was intimately involved. The excerpt below is the final chapter of her classical feminist work,* The Second Sex *(1952). Herein she caustically describes the adversarial relationship between the sexes and concludes by outlining how a new society can be forged where men and women can live together in freedom and equality.*

The quarrel will go on as long as men and women fail to recognize each other as peers; that is to say, as long as femininity is perpetuated as such. Which sex is the more eager to maintain it? Woman, who is being emancipated from it, wishes none the less to retain its privileges; and man, in that case, wants her to assume its limitations. "It is easier to accuse one sex than to excuse the other," says Montaigne.[1] It is vain to apportion praise and blame. The truth is that if the vicious circle is so hard to break, it is because the two sexes are each the victim at once of the other and of itself. Between two adversaries confronting each other in their pure liberty, an agreement could be easily reached: the more so as the war profits neither. But the complexity of the whole affair derives from the fact that each camp is giving aid and comfort to the enemy; woman is pursuing a dream of submission, man a dream of identification. Want of authenticity does not pay: each blames the other for the unhappiness he or she has incurred in yielding to the temptations of the easy way; what man and woman loathe in each other is the shattering frustration of each one's own bad faith and baseness.

We have seen why men enslaved women in the first place; the devaluation of femininity has been a necessary step in human evolution, but it might have led to collaboration between the two sexes; oppression is to be explained by the tendency of the existent to flee from himself by means of identification with the other, whom he oppresses to that end. In each individual man that tendency exists today; and the vast majority yield to it. The husband wants to find himself in his wife, the lover in his mistress, in the form of a stone image; he is seeking in her the myth of his virility, of his sovereignty, of his immediate reality. "My husband never goes to the movies," says his wife, and the dubious masculine opinion is graved in the marble of eternity. But he is himself the slave of his double: what an effort to build up an image in which he is always in danger! In spite of everything his success in this depends upon the capricious freedom of women: he must constantly try to keep this propitious to him. Man is concerned with the effort to appear male, important, superior; he pretends so as to get pretense in return; he, too, is aggressive, uneasy; he feels hostility for women because he is afraid of them, he is afraid of them because he is afraid of the personage, the image, with which he identifies himself. What time and strength he squanders in liquidating, sublimating, transferring complexes, in talking about women, in seducing them, in fearing them! He would be liberated himself in their liberation. But this is precisely what he dreads, and so he obstinately persists in the mystifications intended to keep woman in her chains.

That she is being tricked, many men have realized. 'What a misfortune to be a woman! And yet the misfortune, when one is a woman, is at bottom not to comprehend that it is one," says Kierkegaard.[2] For a long time there have been efforts to disguise this misfortune. For example, guardianship has been done away with: women have been given "protectors," and if they are invested with the rights of the old-time guardians, it is in woman's own interest. To forbid her working, to keep her at home, is to defend her against herself and to assure her happiness. We have seen what poetic veils are thrown over her monotonous burdens of housekeeping and maternity: in exchange for her liberty she has received the false treasures of her "femininity." Balzac[3] illustrates this maneuver very well in counseling man to treat her as a slave while persuading her that she is a queen. Less cynical, many men try to convince themselves that she is really privileged. There are American sociologists who seriously teach today the theory of "low-class gain." In France, also, it has often been proclaimed—although in a less scientific manner— that the workers are very fortunate in not being obliged to "keep up appearances" and still more so the bums who can dress in rags and sleep on the sidewalks, pleasures forbidden to the Count de Beaumont and the Wendels. Like the carefree wretches gaily scratching at their vermin, like the merry Negroes laughing under the lash and those joyous Tunisian Arabs burying their starved children with a smile, woman enjoys that incomparable privilege: irresponsibility. Free from troublesome burdens and cares, she obviously has "the better part." But it is disturbing that with an obstinate perversity-connected no doubt with original sin—down through the centuries and in all countries, the people who have the better part are always crying to their benefactors: "It is too much! I will be satisfied with yours!" But the munificent capitalists, the generous colonists, the superb males, stick to their guns: "Keep the better part, hold on to it!"

It must be admitted that the males find in woman more complicity than the oppressor usually finds in the oppressed. And in bad faith they take authorization from this to declare that she has *desired* the destiny they have imposed on her. We have seen that all the main features of her training combine to bar her from the roads of revolt and adventure. Society in general—beginning with her respected parents—lies to her by praising the lofty values of love, devotion, the gift of herself, and then concealing from her the fact that neither lover nor husband nor yet her children will be inclined to accept the burdensome charge of all that. She cheerfully believes these lies because they invite her to follow the easy slope: in this others commit their worst crime against her; throughout her life from childhood on, they damage and corrupt her by designating as her true vocation this submission, which is the temptation of every existent in the anxiety of liberty. If a child is taught idleness by being amused all day long and never being led to study, or shown its usefulness, it will hardly be said, when he grows up, that he chose to be incapable and ignorant; yet this is how woman is brought up, without ever being impressed with the necessity of taking charge of her own existence. So she readily lets herself come to count on the protection, love, assistance, and supervision of others, she lets herself be fascinated with the hope of self-realization without *doing* anything. She does wrong in yielding to the temptation; but man is in no position to blame her, since he has led her into the temptation. When conflict arises between them, each will hold the other responsible for the situation; she will reproach him with having made her what she is: "No one taught me to reason or to earn my own living"; he will reproach her with having accepted the consequences. "You don't know anything, you are an incompetent," and so on. Each sex thinks it can justify itself by taking the offensive;

but the wrongs done by one do not make the other innocent.

The innumerable conflicts that set men and women against one another come from the fact that neither is prepared to assume all the consequences of this situation which the one has offered and the other accepted. The doubtful concept of "equality in inequality," which the one uses to mask his despotism and the other to mask her cowardice, does not stand the test of experience: in their exchanges, woman appeals to the theoretical equality she has been guaranteed, and man the concrete inequality that exists. The result is that in every association an endless debate goes on concerning the ambiguous meaning of the words *give* and *take*. She complains of giving her all, he protests that she takes his all. Woman has to learn that exchanges—it is a fundamental law of political economy—are based on the value the merchandise offered has for the buyer, and not for the seller: she has been deceived in being persuaded that her worth is priceless. The truth is that for man she is an amusement, a pleasure, company, an inessential boon; he is for her the meaning, the justification of her existence. The exchange, therefore, is not of two items of equal value.

This inequality will be especially brought out in the fact that the time they spend together—which fallaciously seems to be the same time does not have the same value for both partners. During the evening the lover spends with his mistress he could be doing something of advantage to his career, seeing friends, cultivating business relationships, seeking recreation; for a man normally integrated in society, time is a positive value: money, reputation, pleasure. For the idle, bored woman, on the contrary, it is a burden she wishes to get rid of; when she succeeds in killing time, it is a benefit to her: the man's presence is pure profit. In a liaison what most clearly interests the man, in many cases, is the sexual benefit he gets from it: if need be, he can be content to spend no more time with his mistress than is required for the sexual act; but—with exceptions—what she, on her part, wants is to kill all the excess time she has on her hands; and—like the storekeeper who will not sell potatoes unless the customer will take turnips also—she will not yield her body unless her lover will take hours of conversation and "going out" into the bargain. A balance is reached if, on the whole, the cost does not seem too high to the man, and this depends, of course, on the strength of his desire and the importance he gives to what is to be sacrificed. But if the woman demands—offers—too much time, she becomes wholly intrusive, like the river overflowing its banks, and the man will prefer to have nothing rather than too much. Then she reduces her

demands; but very often the balance is reached at the cost of a double tension: she feels that the man has "had" her at a bargain, and he thinks her price is too high. This analysis, of course, is put in somewhat humorous terms; but—except for those affairs of jealous and exclusive passion in which the man wants total possession of the woman—this conflict constantly appears in cases of affection, desire, and even love. He always has "other things to do" with his time; whereas she has time to burn; and he considers much of the time she gives him not as a gift but as a burden.

As a rule he consents to assume the burden because he knows very well that he is on the privileged side, he has a bad conscience; and if he is of reasonable good will he tries to compensate for the inequality by being generous. He prides himself on his compassion, however, and at the first clash he treats the woman as ungrateful and thinks, with some irritation: "I'm too good to her." She feels she is behaving like a beggar when she is convinced of the high value of her gifts, and that humiliates her.

Here we find the explanation of the cruelty that woman often shows she is capable of practicing; she has a good conscience because she is on the unprivileged side; she feels she is under no obligation to deal gently with the favored caste, and her only thought is to defend herself. She will even be very happy if she has occasion to show her resentment to a lover who has not been able to satisfy all her demands: since he does not give her enough, she takes savage delight in taking back everything from him. At this point the wounded lover suddenly discovers the value *in toto* of a liaison each moment of which he held more or less in contempt: he is ready to promise her everything, even though he will feel exploited again when he has to make good. He accuses his mistress of blackmailing him: she calls him stingy; both feel wronged.

Once again it is useless to apportion blame and excuses: justice can never be done in the midst of injustice. A colonial administrator has no possibility of acting rightly toward the natives, nor a general toward his soldiers; the only solution is to be neither colonist nor military chief; but a man could not prevent himself from being a man. So there he is, culpable in spite of himself and laboring under the effects of a fault he did not himself commit; and here she is, victim and shrew in spite of herself. Sometimes he rebels and becomes cruel, but then he makes himself an accomplice of the injustice, and the fault becomes really his. Sometimes he lets himself be annihilated, devoured, by his demanding victim; but in that case he feels duped. Often he stops at a compromise that at once belittles him and leaves him ill at ease. A well-disposed man will be more tortured by the situation than the woman herself. In a sense it is always better to be on the side of the vanquished; but if she is well-disposed also, incapable of self-sufficiency, reluctant to crush the man with the weight of her destiny, she struggles in hopeless confusion.

In daily life we meet with an abundance of these cases which are incapable of satisfactory solution because they are determined by unsatisfactory conditions. A man who is compelled to go on materially and morally supporting a woman whom he no longer loves feels he is victimized; but if he abandons without resources the woman who has pledged her whole life to him, she will be quite as unjustly victimized. The evil originates not in the perversity of individuals—and bad faith first appears when each blames the other—it originates rather in a situation against which all individual action is powerless. Women are "clinging," they are a dead weight, and they suffer for it; the point is that their situation is like that of a parasite sucking out the living strength of another organism. Let them be provided with living strength of their own, let them have the means to attack the world and wrest from it their own subsistence, and their dependence will be abolished— that of man also. There is no doubt that both men and women will profit greatly from the new situation.

A world where men and women would be equal is easy to visualize, for that precisely is what the Soviet Revolution *promised*: women raised and trained exactly like men were to work under the same conditions[4] and for the same wages. Erotic liberty was to be recognized by custom, but the sexual act was not to be considered a "service" to be paid for; woman was to be *obliged* to provide herself with other ways of earning a living; marriage was to be based on a free agreement that the spouses could break at will; maternity was to be voluntary, which meant that contraception and abortion were to be authorized and that, on the other hand, all mothers and their children were to have exactly the same rights, in or out of marriage; pregnancy leaves were to be paid for by the State, which would assume charge of the children, signifying not that they would be *taken away* from their parents, but that they would not be *abandoned* to them.

But is it enough to change laws, institutions, customs, public opinion, and the whole social context, for men and women to become truly equal? "Women will always be women," say the skeptics. Other seers prophesy that in casting off their femininity they will not succeed in changing themselves into men and they will become monsters. This would be to admit that the woman of today is a creation of nature; it must be repeated once more

that in human society nothing is natural and that woman, like much else, is a product elaborated by civilization. The intervention of others in her destiny is fundamental: if this action took a different direction, it would produce a quite different result. Woman is determined not by her hormones or by mysterious instincts, but by the manner in which her body and her relation to the world are modified through the action of others than herself. The abyss that separates the adolescent boy and girl has been deliberately opened out between them since earliest childhood; later on, woman could not be other than what she *was made,* and that past was bound to shadow her for life. If we appreciate its influence, we see clearly that her destiny is not predetermined for all eternity.

We must not believe, certainly, that a change in woman's economic condition alone is enough to transform her, though this factor has been and remains the basic factor in her evolution; but until it has brought about the moral, social, cultural, and other consequences that it promises and requires, the new woman cannot appear. At this moment they have been realized nowhere, in Russia no more than in France or the United States; and this explains why the woman of today is torn between the past and the future. She appears most often as a "true woman" disguised as a man, and she feels herself as ill at ease in her flesh as in her masculine garb. She must shed her old skin and cut her own new clothes. This she could do only through a social evolution. No single educator could fashion a *female human being* today who would be the exact homologue of the *male human being*, if she is raised like a boy, the young girl feels she is an oddity and thereby she is given a new kind of sex specification. Stendhal[5] understood this when he said: "The forest must be planted all at once." But if we imagine, on the contrary, a society in which the equality of the sexes would be concretely realized, this equality would find new expression in each individual.

If the little girl were brought up from the first with the same demands and rewards, the same severity and the same freedom, as her brothers, taking part in the same studies, the same games, promised the same future, surrounded with women and men who seemed to her undoubted equals, the meanings of the castration complex and of the Œdipus complex would be profoundly modified. Assuming on the same basis as the father the material and moral responsibility of the couple, the mother would enjoy the same lasting prestige; the child would perceive around her an androgynous world and not a masculine world. Were she emotionally more attracted to her father—which is not even sure—her love for him would be tinged with a will to emulation and not a feeling of powerlessness; she would not be oriented toward passivity. Authorized to test her powers in work and sports, competing actively with the boys, she would not find the absence of the penis—compensated by the promise of a child—enough to give rise to an inferiority complex; correlatively, the boy would not have a superiority complex if it were not instilled into him and if he looked up to women with as much respect as to men.[6] The little girl would not seek sterile compensation in narcissism and dreaming, she would not take her fate for granted; she would be interested in what she was *doing*, she would throw herself without reserve into undertakings.

I have already pointed out how much easier the transformation of puberty would be if she looked beyond it, like the boys, toward a free adult future: menstruation horrifies her only because it is an abrupt descent into femininity. She would also take her young eroticism in much more tranquil fashion if she did not feel a frightened disgust for her destiny as a whole; coherent sexual information would do much to help her over this crisis. And thanks to coeducational schooling, the august mystery of Man would have no occasion to enter her mind: it would be eliminated by everyday familiarity and open rivalry.

Objections raised against this system always imply respect for sexual taboos; but the effort to inhibit all sex curiosity and pleasure in the child is quite useless; one succeeds only in creating repressions, obsessions, neuroses. The excessive sentimentality, homosexual fervors, and platonic crushes of adolescent girls, with all their train of silliness and frivolity, are much more injurious than a little childish sex play and a few definite sex experiences. It would be beneficial above all for the young girl not to be influenced against taking charge herself of her own existence, for then she would not seek a demigod in the male—merely a comrade, a friend, a partner. Eroticism and love would take on the nature of free transcendence and not that of resignation; she could experience them as a relation between equals. There is no intention, of course, to remove by a stroke of the pen all the difficulties that the child has to overcome in changing into an adult; the most intelligent, the most tolerant education could not relieve the child of experiencing things for herself; what could be asked is that obstacles should not be piled gratuitously in her path. Progress is already shown by the fact that "vicious" little girls are no longer cauterized with a red-hot iron. Psychoanalysis has given parents some instruction, but the conditions under which, at the present time, the sexual training and initiation of woman are accomplished are so deplorable that none of the objections advanced against the idea of a radical change could be considered valid. It is not a question of abolishing in woman the contingencies and miseries of the human condition, but of giving her the means for transcending them.

Woman is the victim of no mysterious fatality; the peculiarities that identify her as specifically a woman get their importance from the significance placed upon them. They can be surmounted, in the future, when they are regarded in new perspectives. Thus, as we have seen, through her erotic experience woman feels—and often detests—the domination of the male; but this is no reason to conclude that her ovaries condemn her to live forever on her knees. Virile aggressiveness seems like a lordly privilege only within a system that in its entirety conspires to affirm masculine sovereignty; and woman *feels* herself profoundly passive in the sexual act only because she already *thinks* of herself as such. Many modern women who lay claim to their dignity as human beings still envisage their erotic life from the standpoint of a tradition of slavery: since it seems to them humiliating to be beneath the man, to be penetrated by him, they grow tense in frigidity. But if the reality were different, the meaning expressed symbolically in amorous gestures and postures would be different, too: a woman who pays and dominates her lover can, for example, take pride in her superb idleness and consider that she is enslaving the male who is actively exerting himself. And here and now there are many sexually well-balanced couples whose notions of victory and defeat are giving place to the idea of an exchange.

As a matter of fact, man, like woman, is flesh, therefore passive, the plaything of his hormones and of the species, the restless prey of his desires. And she, like him, in the midst of the carnal fever, is a consenting, a voluntary gift, an activity; they live out in their several fashions the strange ambiguity of existence made body. In those combats where they think they confront one another, it is really against the self that each one struggles, projecting into the partner that part of the self which is repudiated; instead of living out the ambiguities of their situation, each tries to make the other bear the abjection and tries to reserve the honor for the self. If, however, both should assume the ambiguity with a clear-sighted modesty, correlative of an authentic pride, they would see each other as equals and would live out their erotic drama in amity. The fact that we are human beings is infinitely more important than all the peculiarities that distinguish human beings from one another; it is never the given that confers superiorities: "virtue," as the ancients called it, is defined at the level of "that which depends on us." In both sexes is played out the same drama of the flesh and the spirit, of finitude and transcendence; both are gnawed away by time and laid in wait for by death, they have the same essential need for one another; and they can gain from their liberty the same glory. If they were to taste it, they would no longer be tempted to dispute fallacious privileges, and fraternity between them could then come into existence.

I shall be told that all this is utopian fancy, because woman cannot be "made over" unless society has first made her really the equal of man. Conservatives have never failed in such circumstances to refer to that vicious circle; history, however, does not revolve. If a caste is kept in a state of inferiority, no doubt it remains inferior; but liberty can break the circle. Let the Negroes vote and they become worthy of having the vote; let woman be given responsibilities and she is able to assume them. The fact is that oppressors cannot be expected to make a move of gratuitous generosity; but at one time the revolt of the oppressed, at another time even the very evolution of the privileged caste itself, creates new situations; thus men have been led, in their own interest, to give partial emancipation to women: it remains only for women to continue their ascent, and the successes they are obtaining are an encouragement for them to do so. It seems almost certain that sooner or later they will arrive at complete economic and social equality, which will bring about an inner metamorphosis.

However this may be, there will be some to object that if such a world is possible it is not desirable. When woman is "the same" as her male, life will lose its salt and spice. This argument, also, has lost its novelty: those interested in perpetuating present conditions are always in tears about the marvelous past that is about to disappear, without having so much as a smile for the young future. It is quite true that doing away with the slave trade meant death to the great plantations, magnificent with azaleas and camellias, it meant ruin to the whole refined Southern civilization. The attics of time have received its rare old laces along with the clear pure voices of the Sistine *castrati*,[7] and there is a certain "feminine charm" that is also on the way to the same dusty repository. I agree that he would be a barbarian indeed who failed to appreciate exquisite flowers, rare lace, the crystal-clear voice of the eunuch, and feminine charm.

And it is true that the evolution now in progress threatens more than feminine charm alone: in beginning to exist for herself, woman will relinquish the function as double and mediator to which she owes her privileged place in the masculine universe; to man, caught between the silence of nature and the demanding presence of other free beings, a creature who is at once his like and a passive thing seems a great treasure. The guise in which he conceives his companion may be mythical, but the experiences for which she is the source or the pretext are none the less real: there are hardly any more precious, more intimate, more ardent. There is no denying that feminine dependence, inferiority, woe, give women their special character; assuredly woman's autonomy, if it spares men many troubles, will also deny them many conveniences; assuredly there are certain forms of the sexual adventure which will be lost in the world of tomorrow. But this does not mean that love, happiness, poetry, dream, will be banished from it.

Let us not forget that our lack of imagination always depopulates the future; for us it is only an abstraction; each one of us secretly deplores the absence there of the one who was himself. But the humanity of tomorrow will be living in its flesh and in its conscious liberty; that time will be its present and it will in turn prefer it. New relations of flesh and sentiment of which we have no conception will arise between the sexes; already, indeed, there have appeared between men and women friendships, rivalries, complicities, comradeships—chaste or sensual—which past centuries could not have conceived. To mention one point, nothing could seem to me more debatable than the opinion that dooms the new world to uniformity and hence to boredom. I fail to see that this present world is free from boredom or that liberty ever creates uniformity.

To begin with, there will always be certain differences between man and woman; her eroticism, and therefore her sexual world, have a special form of their own and therefore cannot fail to engender a sensuality, a sensitivity, of a special nature. This means that her relations to her own body, to that of the male, to the child, will never be identical with those the male bears to his own body, to that of the female, and to the child; those who make much of "equality in difference" could not with good grace refuse to grant me the possible existence of differences in equality. Then again, it is institutions that create uniformity. Young and pretty, the slaves of the harem are always the same in the sultan's embrace; Christianity gave erotism its savor of sin and legend when it endowed the human female with a soul; if society restores her sovereign individuality to woman, it will not therefore destroy the power of love's embrace to move the heart.

It is nonsense to assert that revelry, vice, ecstasy, passion, would become impossible if man and woman were equal in concrete matters; the contradictions that put the flesh in opposition to the spirit, the instant to time, the swoon of immanence to the challenge of transcendence, the absolute of pleasure to the nothingness of forgetting, will never be resolved; in sexuality will always be materialized the tension, the anguish, the joy, the frustration, and the triumph of existence. To emancipate woman is to refuse to confine her to the relations she bears to man, not to deny them to her; let her have her independent existence and she will continue none the less to exist for him also: mutually recognizing each other as subject, each will yet remain for the other an *other*. The reciprocity of their relations will not do away with the miracles—-desire, possession, love, dream, adventure—worked by the division of human beings into two separate categories; and the words that move us—giving, conquering, uniting—will not lose their meaning. On the contrary, when we abolish the slavery of half of humanity, together with the whole system of hypocrisy that it implies, then the "division" of humanity will reveal its genuine significance and the human couple will find its true form.

# ENDNOTES

1. [French essayist (1533–1592)—Ed.]

2. *In Vino Veritas*. He says further: "Politeness is pleasing—essentially—to woman, and the fact that she accepts it without hesitation is explained by nature's care for the weaker, for the unfavored being, and for one whom an illusion means more than a material compensation. But this illusion, precisely, is fatal to her. . . . To feel oneself freed from distress thanks to something imaginary, is that not a still deeper mockery? . . . Woman is very far from being *verwahrlost* (neglected), but in another sense she is, since she can never free herself from the illusion that nature has used to console her."

3. [French novelist (1799–1850)—Ed.]

4. That certain too laborious occupations were to be closed to women is not in contradiction to this project. Even among men there is an increasing effort to obtain adaption to profession; their varying physical and mental capacities limit their possibilities of choice; what is asked is that, in any case, no line of sex or caste be drawn.

5. [Pen name of Marie Henri Beyle, French Novelist (1783–1842)—Ed].

6. I knew a little boy of eight who lived with his mother, aunt, and grandmother, all independent and active women, and his weak old half-crippled grandfather. He had a crushing inferiority complex in regard to the feminine sex, although he made efforts to combat it. At school he scorned comrades and teachers because they were miserable males.

7. Eunuchs were long used in the male choirs of the Sistine Chapel in Rome, until the practice was forbidden by Pope Leo XIII in 1880. The operation of castration caused the boy's soprano voice to be retained into adulthood, and it was performed for this purpose.—Tr.

**Study Questions**

1. How does de Beauvoir define sexism?

2. Why does she bring up the issue of complicity? How does that complicate notions of oppression?

3. What values are women taught that make resistance difficult?

4. What does she think about femininity? Does she believe it is "natural"?

5. Why does she argue that freedom would benefit both men and women? Do you agree?

6. How does she envision male/female relationships for the future?

# TO BE A RADICAL JEW IN THE LATE TWENTIETH CENTURY

## Melanie Kaye/Kantrowitz (1952- )

*Melanie Kaye/Kantrowitz has worked as a professor and editor of* Sinister Wisdom, *a journal which focuses on lesbian politics and literature. Currently, she is a member of the New York-based non-profit Jews for Racial and Economic Justice. She has published both fiction and non-fiction, including* My Jewish Face and Other Stories *in 1990 and* The Issue is Power: Essays on Women, Jews, Violence and Resistance *in 1992. This essay was published in* <u>Out the Other Side</u>, *edited by Christian McEwen and Sue O Sullivan in 1989.*

*For Irena Klepfisz who pushed me*

To be a Jew in the twentieth century
Is to be offered a gift. . .

Muriel Rukeyser, 'Letter to the Front, VIII,' 1944

*So, Melanie, what's with all the Jewish?* This was my father speaking sometime in 1982, the year he died. I answered him clearly, carefully, the way I did that year because he often got confused, but the answer was not hard to find. I had been away from NY since I was 20 - I was then 37 - and I had noticed two things: my own hunger for Jewish culture, music, food, language, humor, perspective, Jewish *people*; and, the anti-Semitism palpable - and growing - around me.

Twenty years earlier I had marched on my first demonstration, against nuclear testing. My parents had not pushed me into activism, yet clearly they raised me to do these things. Their parents had come to this country from Eastern Europe, Poland Russia. None had been political. Yet, as a teenager in the

Depression, my father had belonged to the Young Communist League; and, even as an adult, his major hero remained his dead friend Aaron, a Communist who had spoken on street corners and fought in Spain. My mother had circulated petitions against the Korean War, walking up to people on the streets of Flatbush during peak McCarthy period, and she had been spat on. Later she became president of the PTA at Walt Whitman Jr. High, and fought to bring blacklisted performers to sing at the annual PTA meeting.

My mother often says, "When Melanie was 3 years old, I knew it would be Melanie against the world, and I was betting on Melanie.' One of her favorite stories of me dates from 1950, when my class and my older sister's had been given dog tags - issued to NYC schoolchildren, as to soldiers - so that in the event of a bomb, our bodies could be identified. My sister, 7 years old, asked what the dog tag was for, and my mother told her. I listened. And had bombs ever been dropped? Roni asked. Imagine the discussion, my mother explaining to a 7-year-old about war, about Hiroshima and Nagasaki...And the next time the 5-bell signal rang for a shelter drill and my kindergarten teacher said, "now, children, it's only a game, remember, under your desk, head down,' I, 5 years old, stood up and said it was not a game, it was about dropping bombs on children and they our own government had dropped bombs on children and their eyes had melted and people were burned and killed. The other 5-year-olds began crying and screaming, and the principal summoned my mother to school. 'What are you, crazy, telling a kid things like that,' the principle is reputed to have said, and my mother to have answered: 'I will not lie to my children.'

My mother's version of this story emphasizes my role: as class conscience and rebel. But what delights me in the story is *her* courage: though a good student, she had dropped out of high school at 15 and was always convinced that educated people were smarter. Yet she had the political and intellectual backbone to defend me and defy authority.

This was my Jewish upbringing, as much as the candles we lit for Hanukkah, or the seders where bread and matzoh shared the table. My father had been raised observant, my mother, not. But to us breaking religious observance was progressive, the opposite of superstitious; when we ate on Yom Kippur, it never occurred to me that this was un-Jewish. I knew I was a Jew. I knew Hitler had been evil. I knew Negroes - we said then - had been slaves and that was evil too. I knew prejudice was wrong, stupid. I knew Jews believed in freedom and justice. When Eisenhower-Nixon ran in 1952, I noticed Nixon's dark wavy hair, like my father's, and said: 'He looks like Daddy.' My mother was furious: 'Nothing like him!' and went on and on explaining how Nixon had gotten elected to Congress only by smearing Helen Gahagan Douglas (the liberal Congresswoman). I was 7 years old.

Soon we would get our first TV, so my mother (and I) could watch the McCarthy hearings. I knew the whole fate of humanity hinged on these hearings, as surely as I knew the Rosenbergs had been good people, like my parents, with children the same age as my sister and me. I knew government people, like McCarthy, had killed the Rosenbergs, and I was terrified, but it literally did not occur to me that real people, people I might meet, people who had children and went to work, hated the Rosenbergs, thought they should die. Nor did it occur to me that there were people who thought unions were bad, people who did not know you never cross a picket line, did not know prejudice was wrong and stupid.

This is not to say I never heard alternate views, but my parents - though not formally educated or trained in political analysis - had very definite opinions about right and wrong which they passed on to me like the 10 Commandments, ideas I have yet to find wanting.

That this set of principles was Jewish never occurred to me. Around me was Flatbush, a swirling Jewish ghetto/community of first and second generation immigrants, including Holocaust survivors (though they were noted in my mind simply as the parents who brought umbrellas to school when it rained, spoke with my grandparents' accents); there were clerks, trade unionists, salespeople, plumbers; small business people, radio and TV repairmen, people like my parents and their friends; there were teachers and there were even doctors who lived in what we called 'private houses' in the outreaches of the neighborhood at the point where not everyone was Jewish.

But where I lived, everyone was, or almost. Jewish was the air I breathed, nothing I articulated, everything I took for granted.

1963. I was 17, working in the Harlem Education Project.[1] HEP had organized a tutoring project, several rent strikes, an anti-rat campaign;[2] had pressured schools for decent facilities and a Black history curriculum, and helped to create freedom schools for children to attend in protest. A block organization was gradually turning a lot filled with garbage (and once or twice dead bodies) into a park. It was my first experience with a mobilizing proud community and with the possibilities of collective action. I was hooked, though it took me years to recognize how my upbringing had brought me to 133rd St. and Lenox, and primed me for this commitment.

It was also my first experience in a non-Jewish environment. Harlem was the center of Northern Black culture; there were community people, students - some from other cities and communities - some from middle-class homes, some traveling back and forth from the South with stories of Fannie Lou Hamer, James Farmer or of the past: a grandfather lynched in Florida, a great-great-aunt who learned to read in slavery in Mississippi (and Mississippi is still the most frightening word I know). And there were white people, these almost all young, almost all students, some who were my first contact with WASPs; some Jews, though I barely registered that fact since they were not like the Jews I knew. All these students went to colleges like Columbia and Sarah Lawrence, while I went to no-tuition City College, riding the subway 3 hours a day to classes and to Harlem, and would the next year - at 18 - move into my own apartment and become financially self-supporting.

At the end of my first summer in Harlem, on the bus returning from the historic March on Washington, a Black man my age flirted with me and I flirted back, and he sang me this song:

*Jew girls from Brooklyn they go wild over me*
*And they hold my hand where everyone can see*
*O they paint their face like whores*
*Have me leave them at their doors*
*They go wild, simply wild over me*

Intensely focused on white racism, utterly unaware of racism against Jews, or of the possibility of Jewish danger (the Holocaust was eons ago, irrelevant), I felt only shame at the label - Jew girl from Brooklyn - and at the stereotype - hypocrite, liberal in public but won't bring him home to meet the family. I determined not to be like the others; not to be like myself...

1966. I was 20, preparing to leave NY for graduate school at Berkeley. I wanted to get away from NY, from my family, my people to be part of the radical politics developing on the West Coast. At a summer demonstration against the war in Viet Nam, I marched with a slim pale woman from California. She had long straight blond hair, wore some easy cotton shift and sandals; she seemed not to sweat and her voice lilted when she spoke. I had the same body I still have: sturdy, strong legs, heavy black eyebrows, dark hair which in NY's August frizzed and bushed; my skin glistened with oil. I could not imagine how I would fit into the West Coast.

I discovered in Berkeley that the Brooklyn Jewish accent which in NY had always marked me as lower class now marked me as one of those smart Jews from NY. Apart from this observation, passed on by an admiring gentile friend, I have few memories of being a Jew in Berkeley, little consciousness that people's reactions to or assumptions about me had something to do with my particular style of Jewish culture. Jewish political issues moved me not at all, including the 1967 war in the Middle East - I did not identify with Israel - and, when in 1968 I had a minor operation, like Tillie Olsen's Anna I wrote 'none' next to *religion* on the hospital registration form because 'I didn't want anyone mumbling religion at me if I died.'

1972. I had just moved to Portland, Oregon and was attending a feminist conference, talking with a woman while we waited for the elevator. I have forgotten the context for what she said: that she did not like Jews. They were loud and pushy and aggressive. This was the first time I had heard someone say this outright. I was stunned, didn't know what to say - 'no they're not'? - and I couldn't believe she didn't know I was Jewish. I said, loud, flat, 'I'm Jewish.' I can't remember what happened next or even her face, only the moment by the elevator.

1975. Yellow Springs, Ohio, at the Feminist Socialist Conference, on the lunch line, the woman in back of me was talking about a Jewish caucus. I didn't ask her anything, didn't even seriously eavesdrop. I couldn't relate to it. I went to a workshop on economics instead. Years later I wonder what they talked about.

1978. I was working at Rape Relief Hotline in downtown Portland doing counseling, advocacy, community education and organizing. I was talking with my best friend and sister organizer - a middle-class WASP woman - about my sense of awkwardness and ineffectiveness with 'straight' women - meaning some combination of middle-aged heterosexual non-movement women; that I seemed to have no social skills, everything I said had the wrong beat. A couple of days later a woman called the hotline to talk about her experience some years back of being battered. She wanted to get involved in

hotline activities, and I invited her to stop by. She did. The woman was some 30 years older than I, had raised 2 kids, worked in an office, had never considered herself political. I might have been the first lesbian she'd ever knowingly met. She was everything I was supposed to by my own analysis feel awkward around. We went out for coffee, talked for hours, easy. She was a Jew, an east coast Jew. I realized in some ways I was in the wrong city, the wrong part of the world; I was an alien.

By the time I left Oregon in 1979, I had developed an interest in Jewish immigrant history and an obsession with the Holocaust. I read avidly, vaguely aware that I needed Jews but feeling as out of place as ever with those who'd received religious education, as with those women in Portland who had started getting together on Friday nights to eat and *shmooz*, to 'socialize.' I was political. My rejection of these Jewish women's gatherings paralleled closely my pre-feminist contempt for women's consciousness-raising groups. My failure to register this similarity is a tribute to the mind's ability to resist information which threatens.

And then a time of moving, from one *goyish* environment to another. A summer in Maine, Down East, the easternmost point in the US, and if I thought I had seen a Jewish vacuum before, I hadn't. The house we moved into had a swastika smeared on the bedroom door in what looked like blood. A car parked down the road had swastikas and crosses painted on the doors (we spay-painted over them one night). I was becoming very very conscious. Driving out west, passing signs for Greensboro, Atlanta, Birmingham, Montgomery, Jackson, names I knew as sites of struggle and danger, listening to the radio's furious anti-Arab anti-Iranian aggressively fundamentalist Christian tirades unleashed by the taking of hostages in the Tehran embassy complex; hearing Christian hymn after Christian hymn, seeing more crosses, more churches than I had ever imagined: I was afraid.

By the time I got to northern New Mexico - where I lived for the next two year - I knew I needed Jews, nothing vague about it. I sought out a Jewish women's group which met on and off. I was reading and writing about Jewishness. My political work was still not Jewish-related - I helped to organize a women's coffeehouse, and a demonstration against militarism at Los Alamos Science Museum, and at these and other women's events I read work with strong Jewish content. Some women hugged and thanked me, especially Jews and others strongly grounded in their own culture; responses which warmed, emboldened and confirmed me. And some looked blank, perhaps wondering why I was bothering, or why I was being divisive, identifying with a patriarchal religion, or...responses which alienated me, pushed me deeper into my Jewishness, sharpened my awareness of difference so that I began to notice and respond to cultural stimuli or casual remarks or jokes or, even, political analysis differently.

1980. I recognized in Reagan's election that the liberalism I had for years seen as the real danger was being superceded, that the right was gaining power, with all its Jew-hating, racist, sexist, homophobic capitalist thrust. At the same time the anti-Semitism I was encountering in the women's movement and on the left hurt me more, not because it was more threatening but because the feminist left was where I needed to be: this added to my sense of isolation as a Jew.

I was also reading analyses of racism and discussions of identity, mostly by Black women, and my proximity to Chicana and Native American cultures allowed me tangible lessons in diversity and in non-mainstream survival. Cultures, people were being defined as Third World or white; where I lived it was Chicana, Indian or Anglo. But none of these categories, none of the descriptive analyses fit me or my culture. I was an English-speaker, my people came from Europe, but we were not Anglo and neither was our culture.

There are many more details, scenes, some I remember and some which still elude me. What is clear to me is this: the more outside of a Jewish ambiance I was, the more conscious I became of Jewishness. For me, it was like Marshall McLuhan's perhaps apocryphal remark: I don't know who discovered water, but I'm sure it wasn't a fish. Inside a Jewish environment, where I could take for granted a somewhat shared culture, an expectation about Jewish survival, where my body type and appearance were familiar, my voice ordinary, my laughter not too loud but hearty and normal, above all, normal ...in this environment, I did not know what it meant to be a Jew, only what it meant to be a *mentsh*. I did not know that *mentsh* was a Jewish word in a Jewish language.

As I lived longer outside Jewish culture, as I became more fully aware of anti-Semitism, internal as well as external, as I understood my own hunger for home, kin, for *my people*, I was walking further and further along a mostly unconscious, gradual, zig-zag and retrospectively inevitable path.

## I. IF I AM NOT FOR MYSELF...

There were many of us on distinct but similarly inevitable paths. What happened as Jewish women began raising Jewish issues inside the women's movement?

Even at the beginning, some of the issues we were raising seemed almost mundane, obvious: issues of direct insult, stereotypes, omission, exclusion, indifference, discrimination, assumptions of sameness, passing, invisibility, cultural difference, concern for cultural survival...I - and I think many of us - expected that the groundwork on these issues had been laid, that the heroic and tedious labor undertaken by women of color, with some white and Jewish support, to raise everyone's consciousness about racism would carry over somewhat to inform response to Jewish women.

Not that I thought white - or Jewish - women had always been adequate in their commitment to fight racism. Not that I assumed experience and issues for Jewish women and for gentile women of color were the same; nor did I expect identical experience and issues for all women of color, including Jewish women of color. But I did expect some analogy to be apprehended. I expected that the movement would continue building on general principles, as well as differentiate what was unique.

And this did not happen. I saw resistance, overt rejection, ridicule, a willful ignorance. Not from everyone. From some I saw respect, support and desire to extend themselves. From many I saw hypocritical silence masquerading as respect. From some, hostility. And - most often - I saw bewilderment, and inability to grasp what was being said about anti-Semitism or Jewish identity, an incapacity to recognize why it mattered. And, of course, the too-polite silence, the bewilderment, the hostility intensified my self-consciousness as a Jew.

Examples are not hard to find. The policy statement that doesn't mention opposition to anti-Semitism.[3] many courses that include readings by women from a variety of cultures but, somehow, no Jews. The decision that to have a Jew as keynote speaker is too particular, too specialized.[4] The 1984 Women & the Law conference, with its theme *Bread and Roses*, which offered, out of nearly 200 workshops, none on Jews or Jewish issues. (Let me honor those Jewish women who ensured that the 1985 conference would have several Jewish workshops and events.[5]) The flyer for an anti-militarist protest which voiced opposition to misogyny, racism, homophobia, ableism, a number of other -isms, but not anti-Semitism; named a string of identities including 'Black, Latina, Asian, Palestinian ...' but not Jewish.[6] A flyer soliciting material for a feminist journal on issues such as:

Imperialist Intervention

Racism, Sexism, Heterosexism, Ageism...

Hunger Education Reproductive Rights

Disarmament    Health    Self-Determination
Housing [7]

I guess the '...' after 'Ageism' is supposed to leave room for the inclusion of anti-Semitism, but the general effect is to make Jews feel invisible, unwelcome, or worse.

Why? Why have the basic points been so hard to get? Why have so many radicals been impermeable to a pro-Jewish analysis and activity? Why are we getting the message that many of our erstwhile political comrades and sister - including some Jews - think it contradictory to be a radical Jew?

The explanation, as I have tried to track it down, is as tangled as the nature of anti-Semitism; as unconscious, as willfully ignorant as an ordinary American's relationship to the rest of the world; as inadequately grasped and developed as the women's movement understanding of race and class and why the movement should oppose racism and class hierarchy.

### Anti-Semitism, Race, and Class

I am not one who believes anti-Semitism is inevitable, yet I confess my heart sinks when I consider how resilient this hatred is: Jew as an anti-Christ, embodying materialism, money, Shylock's pound of flesh; Marx's analysis of the Jew as irrelevant parasite; shameful victims, who went like sheep to the slaughter; the UN General Assembly's proclamations on Zionism; killer Israelis.

Nor does Jewish oppression fit into previously established analysis. If capitalism is your primary contradiction, the Jewish people is not a class category. If racism, many Jews have light skin, pass as gentile if they wish. If sexism, why should Jewish women identify with Jewish men? If Jewish is an ethnicity, a peoplehood, why don't you live in Israel, or call yourself Israeli? If it's a religion, how are you Jewish if you don't observe?

But not only does Jewish oppression elude conventional categories, Jewish stereotypes prove that anti-Semitism does not exist. Jews are rich, powerful, privileged, control the media, the schools, the business world, international banking: the Zionist conspiracy rides again. How could such powerhouses ever be in trouble. These stereotypes, I've realized, prevent recognition of how we are threatened or demeaned as Jews.

For example: in 1982 when WBAI, NYC progressive radio station, broadcast the disarmament march and interviewed - as the lone voice against demonstration - an Orthodox Jew, I was one of several who phoned to complain. 'Why pick on an Orthodox as the single representative of conservative politics?' I asked. 'Why not?' a man answered. 'I've always wanted to pick on an Orthodox Jew.' When I expressed shock/tried to explain (obviously I was in shock if I tried to explain), he immediately said, 'I'm so sick of hearing about the fucking Holocaust' (which I hadn't mentioned). So I called the station manager, who apologized and proceeded to explain how when someone was making $7000 a year and someone next door was making $15,000 a year (clearly this man knew a lot about neighborhoods) I could understand the resentment.

Sure I could understand. But I had been talking about Jewhatred, not class antagonism. The station manager of NYC's progressive station had leaped from one to the other instantly, automatically. As if all Jews were wealthy. As if all wealth were Jewish. As if anti-Semitism were indulged in only by the poor.

By speaking about anti-Semitism, Jewish women unsettle an unspoken equation in the radical women's movement: in a society like ours, deeply racist and absurdly pretending to classlessness, class comes to be seen as identical to race. People of color are considered the same as working and poor people. Other aspects of racism - cultural erasure, assimilation, self-hate, just to name a few - are simply not heeded, nor are - god forbid - strengths of ethnic or racial minorities acknowledged unless - in a wash of white self-hate - people of color are romanticized as stronger, more authentic, somehow better than whites; but better because they are seen as such victims that mere survival is a miracle.

Meanwhile, these same analyses which ignore class as an independent category, related to but separate from race, ignore the variety of class experience and location of Jews: Jews, you remember, are all rich or at least middle class. Why, then, are we complaining?

Such a non-analysis not only belies the experience of middle-class people of color - the upper middle-class Black families, for example, whose LA neighborhood was firebombed in June, 1985; the middle-class Japanese home-land-and-business-owners on the West Coast who had everything confiscated and were imprisoned in camps during the second World War. This perspective also erases the existence of Jews of color and working-class Jews, and the entire white poor and working class; a very substantial group of women.

Related to this unspoken equation: analyses of racism - both on the left and in the feminist movement - have been spearheaded by Black people, and to some extent the experience of Black people in the US provides the model by which we understand racism. And despite the existence and even growth of a Black middle class, the continued grinding poverty of most Black people in this country also suggests an equation of race and class.

And it's true: most immigrant groups have moved up the class ladder, at least to lower middle class or trade union status (which - for men - means pretty good pay), usually pushed up in what has been called "the queuing effect" by a newer group of immigrants against whom prejudice is fresher and stronger.[8] But American Blacks, in their forced passage to this country, in the destruction of many elements of African culture by slavery, in their confrontation with classic American racism against the darkest skin, and in the exploitation of this racism by capitalists to 'explain' inequality, have been painfully excluded from the process of queuing. This is evident from the progress of Puerto Ricans and Koreans in NYC, for example, or Cubans in Miami; though more recently arrived than Blacks, these groups have, in effect, cut in ahead of Blacks economically.

But there's another kind of distortion. I have lived outside of NYC for half my 40 years now, and have come to think that the usual explanations of racism and anti-Semitism focus unduly on New York, a focus which has everything to do with location of media and ambitious intellectuals, not to mention a huge Jewish and a huge Black community, each deeply rooted in the city, each a cultural center for their people. And these two communities have often, in the past 20 years, been at odds, not utterly, but noticeably: on community control of schools, in the struggle for the city's limited resources, on affirmative action and quotas...And the contrast - between a visible relatively secure Jewish community, mostly (except for the old) employed, and a continuing impoverished Black community with an unequal share of the city's resources, unequally protected and unequally harassed by the police, with an astronomical rate of unemployment among Black teenage males and not much prospect of improvement - the contrast has got to seem stark.

It is this sense of contrast that is drawn upon again and again in people's discussion of anti-Semitism as opposed to racism. But when I look more closely at places other than New York - at Boston, where working class Italians and Blacks have been at odds over school busing; at Detroit, where Iraqi small merchants and Blacks have had racial tension reminiscent of the "Jewish shopkeeper in Harlem'; at northern New Mexico where Chicana/o and Native American communities may have differences, and where Anglos moving to the area are wresting political control from the Chicanas/so; at Miami, where non-Spanish speakers may resent the bilingualism requirement for civil service jobs dealing with the public - my grasp of the complexities of race, Jewishness, ethnicity, class, and culture is greatly enhanced. Instead of being characterized by polarization, in which anti-Semitism is treated as a phenomenon different *in nature* from racism, anti-Semitism can be clearly seen as a *form of racism.*

## The World According to America

There are other factors blocking recognition of the weight of anti-Semitism on Jews. Jewish experience in the US, isolated from the experience of Jews around the world, seems fairly rosy. But Jews are an international people, and the nature of Jewish identity, oppression, fear and danger derive from and connect to experiences outside this country.

Wars between the US and other countries have always been fought *in* other countries; most people in the US live in an extraordinarily protected context. Not only is our country vast and populous and proud of an isolationist spirit (often masking an imperialist reality); but, in addition, the strictly limited immigration during the middle portion of this century has restricted most Americans' knowledge about war, persecution, torture, the experience of refugees. Most Americans seem to believe ourselves peculiarly unaffected by what goes on in the rest of the world. If it didn't happen here, if it isn't happening now, why worry? Nor does a nation busy constructing a California or Texas future over Native American and Chicana/o culture care much about history.

From this vantage point, Jews seem ridiculous when we talk about Jewish danger. We are up against a failure of Americans to take seriously the pitch Jewhating attained so quickly in Europe in the thirties, for example, because Americans think Europe and the thirties so far away. They know about evil Germans, sheeplike Jews, and heroic Americans, but are not taught to see the war against the Jews as a culmination to centuries of Jewhating. Americans are told lies about the base of Nazism, so that we imagine Jewhating goes with a lack of education: working-class people are - as with white racism in this country - blamed. We are not told of the doctors and doctorates trained in Europe's finest universities. For most Americans the Holocaust blurs safely, almost pleasantly, with other terrible events of the past, like Bubonic Plague in the Middle Ages.

Nor have most Americans paid much attention to the persecution of Jews in the Soviet Union, or Argentina, or Ethiopia, unless an ideological point is to be scored against these nations. As for the fact that Jews are not in danger in some communities around the world because Jews have been exiled or violently excised from those communities - this is not recognized as a legitimate source of grief and suspicion for Jews to reckon with, a loss - of our people, our culture. Women in the feminist movement, not necessarily educated on these issues, respond pretty much like other Americans.

## The Scarcity Assumption

Then, too, an assumption deeply integral to capitalism has been absorbed by all of us, since it is reflected in so much of what we see. I have called this the Scarcity Theory,[9] not enough to go around: not enough love, not enough time, not enough appointments at the foodstamps office, not enough food stamps, not enough money, not enough seats on the subway. It's pervasive. We learn mistrust of each other, bone deep: everything is skin off somebody's nose.

And in the short run, certain things *are* scarce. To what causes do I apply my limited 'free' time? Where do I donate 'extra' money? What books do I read, what issues do I follow and become knowledgeable about? Where will my passion be deep and informed, able to make connections and inspire others, and where will it be superficial, giving lip service only? The women's movement has only in the last few years and under considerable pressure begun to face its own racism; class is still addressed in the most minimal ways. Meanwhile, international crises - apartheid in South Africa, intervention in Nicaragua, torture and repression in Salvador and Guatemala - compel attention.

Few of us have learned to trust our own rhetoric, that people will fight harder as they also fight for themselves. So when Jews begin talking about anti-Semitism, it's only 'natural' that even the left, which should welcome a people's coming to consciousness, responds as if we're asking for handouts-and whose pocket will they come out of? Ignoring how much political energy can be generated as groups develop a cohesive identity and analysis, the left accuses Jews of draining the movement, of competing for status as victims, of ignoring advantages and options open to us.

Identity politics of all kinds do contain an inherent potential not only for victim-competition but for splintering movements into 1000 groups whose members at last feel sufficiently the same: comfy but not a powerful resource.[10] But while the focus of some Jewish women on identity as a source of personal discovery and support is hardly unique, criticism of identity politics has been aimed disproportionately at Jews, sometimes by Jews. I'll put this another way: anti-Semitism has sometimes masqueraded as a disdain for identity politics.[11]

## Hurry Hurry

Some - including some Jews who identify, as I do, with the left - if not disdainful of our attention to Jewish identity, seem to be rushing us, implying that we are lingering over what Rosa Luxemburg - a Jewish leftist - called 'petty Jewish concerns'; that we

are evading important struggles, being selfish or self-indulgent. Aren't we done already?

A Jewish lesbian/feminist who has written about racism publishes, as part of a long essay on anti-Semitism and racism, 5 pages of consciousness-raising questions directed at Jewish women, prefaced by:

*Since many women have engaged in consciousness-raising about Jewish identity and anti-Semitism...I have skipped over a basic avenue of inquiry...*[12]

New Jewish Agenda, a progressive Jewish organization founded six years ago - and to which I belong - holds its second national convention, Summer'85, inspired by Hillel's second question: *If we are only for ourselves, what are we?* The question has two possible takes: an ethical one (the answer is, 'less than human'); and a practical one (the answer is, 'a failure,' because we are tiny minority who needs allies.) This is the question which prompts joining with others, the question of coalition.[13]

But before Hillel asked, 'If I am only for myself...' he asked, 'If I am not for myself, who will be?' This is the question of separatism, the question that prompts a gathering of one's people. Literally, who will stick up for me if I don't respect myself enough to stand up for myself, if I can't articulate my own concerns so that others understand and care about them? Here is our beginning. Have we been for ourselves sufficiently already? Do we even know who ourselves are?

## II. Jewish Diversity, Assimilation and Identity

Who, what is the Jewish people? This question dazed me when I first voiced it. I had always known the Jewish people: we lived in Brooklyn, and those whose fathers made money moved to Long Island. It was simple.

And suddenly it was not simple at all. I began to discover the different experiences, cultures, languages of Jews. I was 34 when I learned about Ladino, a couple of years older when I learned of Arab Jews, Kurds, the Beta Israel of Ethiopia, the Colchins of India. The diversity of the Jewish people shocked me.

Even in this country, I realized, there are vast differences: place of origin, part of the country, class background, religious or secular upbringing practice, knowledge of and attachment to Jewish culture (which one?!), degree of assimilation.

For some Jews, 'passing' seems a choice; for others, passing means total denial and pain; for still others, passing is something they do without even thinking, and for still others, passing - as white/American/normal is impossible. Some Jews have never felt a moment of Jewish fear; others smell it daily. Some were raised in comfortable suburbs, sheltered from knowledge of anti-Semitism; others came from Europe or the Middle East and relive their own nightmares or those of their families; others grew up in mixed neighborhoods where they were beat up every day after school for being the Jew, and especially on Easter.

To observant Jews, a persistent reluctance by others to take Jewish holidays, *shabes*, dietary customs into account means that they - observant Jews - are not welcome;[14] to others, ignoring these traditions embodies anti-patriarchal struggle. Some Jews are passionately attached to yiddish culture and want to preserve this; other feel alienated by a Yiddish emphasis: they grew up with Ladino or Arabic, and resent the assumption that Jewish means Ashkenazi roots; some share the rejection of much of the New Left for European anything, and, seeing the future in the Third World and only a moribund or embarrassing past in the remnants of Europeans Jewry, feel no desire to preserve Ashkenazi culture. (Though one might question this last position as self-hating, the people who feel this way do not perceive what they hate as their *selves*.)

Some Jews identify deeply with other Jews; others identify only with white middle-class privilege; some consider themselves people of color. Some invalidate, trivialize or otherwise deny Jewish experience, oppression, and values, say 'I'm a Jew' only as a label or a credential, not a perspective. With the diversity of our experience unarticulated in a way that supports all of it, even Jews tend to perceive the needs, complaints, experience of other Jews as extreme, atypical, threatening, not really or not necessarily *Jewish*.[15] Given this lack of agreement about even such basics as the nature of Jewish experience and identity, the parameters of anti-Semitism, how are Jews supposed to work politically *as Jews*?

America is famous for gobbling up cultures, immigrant and native. But in addition, the nature of the Jewish people on the face of this earth has been totally transformed in the past 45 years by three facts:

> The Holocaust: the partial extermination of European Jewry and the virtual destruction of Ashkenazi culture.

> The expulsion of Jews from the Arab countries and destruction of these centers of Judeo-Arab culture.

The founding of the state of Israel and the ingathering of many Jews.

We have not yet absorbed these transformations. We don't yet know what it means to be a Jew in the late 20th century.

For many North American Jews (in the US and Canada, half the world's Jews) a key issue is assimilation, a seepage of Jewishness out of Diaspora Jewry, except for those who retain or return to religious practice. Assimilation is often treated, by those who would belittle Jewish issues, as privilege, the *ability* to pass, a ticket out of Jewish oppression.

Anyone who has heard - as I have - Jew-hating remarks said to her face because to the speaker she didn't look Jewish knows both the survival value and the knife twist of passing. (And consider how some Jews came to look non-Jewish: Jewish women raped by gentile men during pogroms; Jewish women with lighter skin, hair, more gentile features, considered prettier, more desirable than their darker, more Semitic-looking sisters.)

But assimilation is a much larger issue than who you do or don't look like. Assimilation *is the blurring* or erasure of identity and culture. As I have come to recognize Jewish identity and culture not as givens, there for the taking, but as profoundly valuable *and vulnerable*, assimilation has become a source of pain: loss, some of which I can retrieve, some not: gone.

The point is that Jewish identity is not just about oppression, about anti-Semitism and survival, though clearly this is part of our history and we need our history. We also need our culture, need to know *where we grew*. We need *not* to disappear into the vague flesh of America, even if this disappearance were possible.

Those who call resistance to assimilation a luxury might do well to think about calling 'sexual preference' a luxury, or reproductive rights, or access to education or creative expression. None of these is *bread*, but 'Bread *and* Roses' was a demand voiced by Rose Schneiderman, a union organizer and a Jew.

What are the roses? As Jews we need our people hood, our culture, history, languages, music, calendar, tradition, literature…We need these things because they are beautiful and ours, and because the point of struggle is not bare survival but lives full of possibility.

But Rose Schneiderman's metaphor flounders. Our culture is not a rose, it is our backbone. To say it matters that we're Jews; to bond with our people; for a tiny minority, these acts trigger intense fear - fear of being boxed into a perspective that is assumed to be narrow and selfish, fear of being isolated, as we have often historically been isolated.

And the only thing that counters this fear is love for our people, pride in our culture.

*If I am not for myself, who will be?* Hillel could not have predicted the need American Jews in the late 20th century would bring to his first question: the need to know the self, the people, the culture. For several years I have given workshops across the country on anti-Semitism, racism, and more recently, Jewish identity. I have heard Jews talk about gathering as a group, loving the comfort, the opportunity to discuss anti-Semitism, offer support, eat wonderful food, laugh…but then uncertain what to do next, as Jews. I have watched Jews sob as they grappled for the first time with the meaning of Jewish resistance, of violence and non-violence in the context of the Holocaust. Jewish radicals are just beginning to tangle with Jewish identity and its relationship to Jewish culture, tradition and politics.

So it's not surprising that we are still, many of us, uncertain in our responses. What *is* a good radical Jewish response? How do we take positions that won't be used against us or where we won't be invisible as Jews? How, for example, do we support the struggle against apartheid, confront the anti-Semitic emphasis on Israel as well as the assumption that as Jews we support the Israeli government's position, do all of this without getting crazed or isolated? What is our position on arms sales to Israel? What's our position on Israel generally? Why do we, as Jews, need a position on Israel - on another country's foreign and domestic policy? What is our relationship to the mainstream Jewish community? How do we look clearly at the strength we have, as a people, without worrying that they'll see us as running the world again?

These questions need to be answered by Jews talking with one another, developing political and emotional clarity and cohesion. And this requires Jewish space in which to piece together a deeply felt Jewish identity and perspective inch by inch from the various threads of tradition, literature, ritual, religion, culture, values, politics, language. Some of us will spend our lives building Jewish identity; others will draw on this work as a strong foundation from which to live our politics. Particularly for those of us who are not religiously observant, much confusion attends our grasping - through anti-Semitism and often prodded by anti-Semitism - for something beyond common danger. We need to figure out how to undo assimilation without being nostalgic or xenophobic: how to reach in and out at the same time.

## III. Guilt vs. Solidarity

Most feminist theory on identity was developed by women of color and focused on fighting racism.[16] I have come to think that had white women fully grasped the nature of this fight and *their own reasons for joining it*, they would now be grasping what Jewish women are trying to do. For the suspicion which greets a developing Jewish identity - from some Jews as well as gentiles - is only partly explained by anti-Semitism (the sense that Jewish identity *in particular* has no value) and by scarcity (the fear that focus on Jews will detract from other pressing issues). The way Jews have been met with 'not you too,' the way anti-Semitism becomes the one issue too many, suggest that many white women are angry and resistant to dealing with racism but are too frightened to express that anger openly;[17] suggest further how little our movement has taught us to see struggles against racism as life-giving, nourishing; as our own.

Most white women have learned, instead; guilt: to oppose racism because it's their - I am tempted to say Christian - duty, for they seem to offer two models: the missionary and the crusader.

### Guilt: How Not to Build a Movement

If you join a struggle because you know your life depends on it - even if remotely: because you identify with the people, because people you love are involved - you have one attitude toward the people and their struggle.

But if you join because lucky you, you should help out those less fortunate - you have a different attitude: you consider those you deign to help pathetic victims. (It's no wonder Jews remain outside the paradigm, because Jews are pegged as over privileged powerhouses: gentiles don't feel guilty about Jews.) The missionary in some way sees herself stooping to pick up the white woman's burden, a dangerous attitude, reeking of condescension, of failure to believe in the value or capacity of other people. Besides, 'the white man's burden' was a polite name for imperialism. I don't imagine that white women in the women's movement are the British Empire but people who take this attitude are - at best - focused on themselves. They want that rosy do-gooder glow.

They can be harmless. And sometimes they *do* good. Guilt has prompted some white women to act against racism: white teachers who make sure to include books by Third World writers; white women with access to funds, grants, etc., who make sure that women of color get heard, solicited, funded. These acts are not negligible, whatever their motives. And though people acting from guilt may not be reliable allies, they will do in the short run. Sometimes they're all the allies there are.

The crusader, another sort of frail ally, plays on white guilt. She attacks white women whose racism has showed, isolating and shaming them. I have seen her in women's communities all over the US: in crisis centers, in print, in women's studies programs…Sometimes, I confess, I have been her. And just as crusaders were supposed to gather souls but really killed, so the white knight, I have come to call her, destroys more than she saves.[18]

By doing so, she gains power in her own community - white women are afraid of her, and, besides, she is on to something. The white knight often does useful work: were this not true she would have no credibility - people aren't fools. But instead of enlarging the circle of women doing anti-racist work, fostering an atmosphere in which people believe they can change - by struggling compassionately with other white women (by communicating a vision of why one struggles) the white knight banishes most potential allies, leaving herself and a few others as the only decent white women in town.

Her power thus depends on racism, making her, in the end, no more reliable as an ally than the guilt-responsive missionary, since she has, objectively speaking, a stake in maintaining racism. She can, of course, function overtly as a Christian knight and attack other Christians who exhibit anti-Semitic behavior, etc.; but since the guilt quotient on Jewish issues is low, she's less likely to get response.

Sometimes acts inspired by gilt or fear of acting wrong have a positive impact. And, for the most cockamamie reasons, people land in situations from which they change and wisen. I did not take the D-train to Harlem when I was 17 with my present consciousness, yet I would not have developed my present consciousness without those formative experiences.

But guilt itself, as a motivating factor, is rooted in a way of thinking which does not promote change. Guilt asks: am I bad or am I good? Guilty or innocent? Racist or not? Very different from asking 'is this a racist act?' which allows me not to commit it, or to do the work that ensures I never commit it again. For in order to change you have to be willing to expose yourself - and observe and examine and understand. This takes time, patience, and a respect for process. Guilt prompts a longing to purge all impure impulses quickly, get it over and done with once and for all. Impulses which seem impure are not examined or transformed; they are stifled while you keep busy trying to act as though you have the right impulses.

We've all seen white women act like corpses around women of color, so afraid of doing the wrong thing: meaning, anything natural, treating a person like a person. For guilt is a freeze emotion: you can't think, you can't feel, you can only knee jerk. This is the infantilizing function of guilt: you lose faith in your own responses because the risk of their being wrong is more than you can handle.

In addition to militating against real change, guilt exercises an uneasy influence over the real difference in resources and options which women may enjoy, leading to downward mobility, pretending to have less, gleefully selecting the most oppressed possible identity: *office worker,* not *daughter of a lawyer and dropout from a prestigious college most office workers never get near (as students).*

And why does someone embrace an identity of oppression? Because it's groovy? The insult of this must be apparent. Because she feels guilty about what she's got? Are money, power, privilege worthless resources to ignore, bury, pretend away? The insult of this ought to be apparent too.

And besides: behind the guilt, the desire to belong, be one with the people, etc., the resources remain, quietly drawn on or untouched by anyone, but ready to be picked up and used at some future date. So guilt helps people hoard what they've got, because they never come to terms with how to use resources productively.

The thing is: anyone who really wants to hoard her money, power and privilege sooner or later will. She can be targeted for guilt trips - to let go of some of what she wishes no on knew she had - but beneath the guilt had better be fear: fear of exposure, fear of conflict, so she'll stay in line and act right. And how does any sane person react after a while to fear, guilt? Is this a way to build a movement?

Nor can guilt mobilize those who don't feel guilty. Try telling a white working-class woman, for example, to fight racism because of how privileged she is. She may think racism is wrong and may be committed to fight it; she may also think that movement analyses of racism are ridiculous because she is not living the easy life her white skin is supposed to guarantee her. Whatever privilege she may have, she clings to - things are tough - but she hardly feels guilty. Only recognition of a common goal, the possibilities and - I want to say - the joys of solidarity will inspire women who don't feel guilty to join another struggle as their own.

## Solidarity: How To Build a Movement

Solidarity requires the bonding together of a people engaged in common struggle. But solidarity also means standing alongside another struggle, not because you feel guilty but because you recognize it as your own; it means using what you have on behalf of struggle.

Angela Davis notes, for example, Prudence Crandall, a white woman who risked her life in defense of education for Black girls.[19] Or the strategy suggested by Maria Chapman Weston, a white leader of the Boston Female Anti-Slavery Society; when a white pro-slavery mob burst into a meeting chaired by Weston, she realized that the mob sought to isolate and perhaps violently attack the Black women in attendance, and thus insisted that each white woman leave the building with a Black woman at her side.[20] Or, at the world anti-slavery convention in London, at which the notorious decision was made to bar women from the floor, there were a few men who refused to join the floor but stood with the women in the gallery, silent. Among them was the Black abolitionist Charles Remond, and the white abolitionists William Lloyd Garrison and Nathaniel Rogers.[21] Black leader Frederick A Douglas, too, at least initially supported the then-radical demand of women's suffrage and used his male privilege on behalf of the emerging women's right movement.[22] Or, the women workers in the stockyards (mostly Irish and Poles) and in the garment industry (mostly Jews and Italians) who deliberately - and contrary to the practice of the AFL and most of their peers - sought to include and organize with Black women.[23] Or the Women's Trade Union League, upper middle-class college-educated white suffragists who worked in support of immigrant women's unions.[24] Or the Black and white college students - including many Jews - who went south to challenge segregation.

All these actions are examples of informed coalition work. None is a passive giving something up; they are all an aggressive wrapping of two peoples in a cloak only one has. These are acts which build trust between peoples.

But those who performed these acts which build and justify trust - I can't believe that they did not understand that these acts were also in defense of *their own freedom*, a freedom without which they, the actors, could not breathe.

*If I am only for myself, what am I?* Lonely. Hungry for sister, comrades. Listen to the words of the fiery Grimke sisters, white abolitionists who recognized 'the special bond, linking them with Black women who suffered the pain of slavery..."They are our countrywomen - they are our sister."'[25] Or the slogan displayed at the April '85 march in Paris to protest increasing violence against Jews and Arabs (many of whom are also Jews) and to protest increasing racist propaganda about purifying France for the French:

*Ne touche pas a mon pote.* 'Keep your hands off my buddy.'

None of the passionless rhetoric which has come to dominate our movement's discussions of race, class. Obviously, if your friends, if your sisters are suffering you put everything you have into the struggle to free them *because you need their freedom as your own.*

Your privilege, insofar as it divides you from others, is in your way, unless you resolve how to use it for others, as well as for yourself. This is a non-guilt approach: drawing on what is best in people, not suppressing what is worst.

And let me say something which in this (Christian) culture may come as a surprise: what is best in people is not self-abnegation. What is best in people is a sturdy connection between respect for the self and respect for the other: reaching in and out at the same time:

*If I am not for myself, who will be?*

*If I am only for myself, what am I?*

## IV. Some Strategies for Action

As we come into our Jewish identity, we feel somehow that to be justified in asserting it, in opposing anti-Semitism, we must be innocent victims, trying to make our oppression palpable to those who don't understand it. My beginning search for Jewish identity focused on the Holocaust and on the immigrant experience only partly because such a search must.

We need our history/herstory, and these are our handles, what we know. These are also all images of greater persecution than most American Jews are subject to today. As Jews, afraid of the myth of Jewish power; as (white?) feminists, guilty about our skin privilege, we are so hungry for innocence that images of oppression come almost as a relief. Innocence, even suffering, seems the only alternative to guilt.

But innocence has its price: while it relieves us of responsibility, it also denies us our strength. The assumption is: since we have been victims, we cannot ever be anything else. Witness Begin, involving the Holocaust to justify the invasion of Lebanon. *How could Jews be oppressive after all we've suffered?* From this perspective, class hostility, for example, has no basis in class distinctions but is only a front for Jewhating. We have to recognize that Jews are relatively well-off economically compared with most people of color in this country, as with the rural white poor; and that Jews endure about the same level of poverty as other ethnic groups who immigrated around the same time. Our job is to untangle class hostility from anti-Semitism, not to pretend the Jewish people still work in the sweatshop.

Non-Jews rely on this innocence too, including people of color. Witness how some excused Farrakhan's description of Hitler as a great German. Was it because support for Jackson's presidential candidacy transcended Jewish danger (which, given Jewish wealth and power, could not possibly be *real* danger)? Or was it because Farrakhan is Black, and a cry of hatred against Jews carries no threat when the speaker is, by definition, powerless? (Need it be said that this is racist as well as anti-Semitic?) From this perspective, the fears of elderly Jews in racially mixed neighborhoods that they will be mugged and robbed are merely a front for racism, instead of reflecting the reality of urban violence: old people are marks, especially when living in communities no longer theirs. Our job here is to untangle concern for safety from racism, not to come up with justifications for mugging.

How this need for innocence translates politically is a disaster. The attitude that claims we - of any group - are essentially victims and so can't be charged with our behavior is destructive to all of us. If we can't do *anything* wrong, the fact is we can't do anything at all - and how in that state of powerlessness are we to build a vast movement sufficient to transform the exceedingly powerful state we live in? Defensive, protective of that dubious privilege of having our suffering acknowledged, we are at something of a standstill. Can't we look at each other and begin to see what we might build? Can't we extend towards each other so that we can draw on each other's strengths, learn to trust that we can use our power in positive ways?

## Working Alone/Working Together

True coalition is not a smattering of tokens. True coalition forms between groups; the premise is that each group has a strong base in a larger community. Thus Jews who want to work in coalition need not only to know who we are but to be bonded with other Jews.

For feminists, for lesbians, this presents its own complications. Some of us won't work with men. This is not a flawed choice. Some of us will have to be separatist - as Jews, as women, as lesbians, as whoever we are. Separatism gives strength, a base from which coalition is possible. Some of us - because of desire or need - will choose to be with our own. There are different forms of struggle, and separatists often are in the vanguard, creating a strong identity and consciousness for the whole community, including those who are not themselves separatist.

Those of us who choose to work in coalitions can assert that identity and consciousness to others. I know many Jewish women, myself among them, have participated in anti-racist, anti-apartheid, anti-intervention work, but not visibly as Jews. It is time we became visible as Jews, as some are doing.

Yet we need at the same time strategies for combating anti-Semitism, for Jewish visibility fans the coals of indifference and passive contempt. An individual visible as a Jew simply attracts, like a magnet, all available anti-Jewish prejudice, or gets written off as an exception. And sometimes we even need strategies to ensure visibility. A Jew who traveled to Nicaragua recently tells of her attempts to be visible as Jew to the Nicaraguan Press, attempts frustrated by her travel group's leader, whose job it was to inform the press about the group members who kept 'forgetting' to mention the Jewish member. Just as women, as lesbians, need our own groups - for support and as bases for coalitions, a Jewish group traveling to Nicaragua might have had the desired impact, built Jewish pride *and* Jewish-Nicaraguan solidarity. To reach in and out at the same time.

The particular example of Nicaragua offers another possibility for solidarity and coalition. Progressive Jews have something in common with progressive Native Americans who oppose US intervention in Nicaragua, yet are concerned about the status of the Miskito Indians. We might learn from each other ways to express concern about our people without having this concern either used by the right or discredited by the left.

Again, focusing on Nicaragua, there is work to do in the Jewish community, to make sure the justified fear of anti-Semitism is not exploited by the US government, that Jews have access to the facts. There's a need for community education by strongly identified Jews; there is also a need for honest discussion of liberation theology, of its potential for anti-Semitism (if the revolutionary impulse is Christian, where does that leave us?), and of ways we can support the revolution without supporting an unexamined Christianity.

## Fears

But there are fears. Mine are that non-Jews won't care about working with us. Who are *we* that they should bother? Our numbers so small, we are so disposable, a liability almost; dislike of us a point of unity among everyone else. And as women, as lesbians, as underemployed professionals or workers at traditional women's jobs, most of us don't even have money to contribute. Sometimes I am simply afraid that radical Jews are on the wrong side of history, trapped between self-respect, love for our people and culture and what we, politically, ideologically would support were it not tangled with Jewhating. I know I am not the only radical Jew whose stomach ties in knots reading the radical press or attending a rally.

Non-Jews, especially people of color, may fear that Jews will deny differences in experience, will aim for the great white American marshmallow of 'you're oppressed/I'm oppressed'.

No doubt on every side there is prejudice, ignorance and mistrust. I think of the Jew who uses the names Palestinian and Lebanese interchangeably, has not bothered to distinguish between the two peoples; the Arab who blames Leon Klinghoffer's death on 'the fact that the whole country of Palestine has been hijacked by the ...Zionist Jews of Europe, America and elsewhere,' not only condoning the brutal death of an old man in a wheelchair, but also hiding - with the words 'and elsewhere' - the thousands of Jews forced to leave *their* homes in Arab countries.[26] The Jew who says 'We made it, why can't they?' or 'Who cares, they're all *goyim*!' The Black who says '*They* made it on my back.' The Chicana/o who says '*They're* all landlords.' There is work to do on all sides.

James Baldwin, in 1967, wrote: 'A genuinely candid confrontation between Negroes and American Jews would certainly prove of inestimable value. But the aspirations of the country are wretchedly middle-class and the middle class can never afford candor.' [27] A genuinely candid confrontation amongst all of us - a genuinely *specific* and candid confrontation - is much needed; and Baldwin is precise, as ever, in indicating that we must be prepared to go further than liberal acceptance, further than maneuvering for our own (larger) slice of the pie. The theme re-emerges: we must *want* equality, and we must grasp that equality does not coexist with class structure.

As a feminist and a Jew, I am asking women of color not to abandon us as we assert our Jewishness, not to hear this assertion as a lowered vigilance against racism.

And I am asking Jews not to withdraw into self-righteousness, not to insist that gentiles understand everything immediately, yesterday. We are not without dignity if we explain our issues. I am also asking Jews not to be so afraid of being trapped with other Jews - including, perhaps, some whose politics or attitudes offend us - that we forget that people can change, including our own people; including ourselves.

## Commonality

I am saying there have got to be many points of unity among us. Even in my fear that non-Jews won't care because we are a small - useless - minority I find

a connection - with Native Americans who express the same fear, of irrelevance; and another similar fear, genocide - historical and cultural. And I see difference: the grinding poverty in which most Native American people live.

And in my recognition that Jews are better off economically than most people of color, I find connection with some Asian Americans, not the recent immigrants, from Southeast Asian, who tend to be very poor, but with many Japanese Americans. Looking specifically at the situation of Japanese Americans I see a people also traumatized by events of the past 40 years - internment in camps; the atomic bombs dropped on civilian cities of Hiroshima and Nagasaki; a fear of cultural loss and assimilation; and continued economic discrimination, despite their apparent integration into professional and business life. And I see differences: Japanese -and other Asian-Americans - pressed into the sciences, engineering, computers, pushed away from the humanities, the arts, where much Jewish talent has been channeled.[28]

I could go on. And if I am doing my work, I *will* go on, understanding the ways in which Jewish history and experience are like and unlike the experience of other groups, the ways in which the light skin of some Jews has and has not protected them, the issues *as defined by Jews* and the *issues as defined by other groups*.

We might then, as Jews, offer support to Japanese Americans seeking restitution from the US government for their internment and confiscation of property during World War II, and to those still fighting their convictions for refusing to report for 'relocation.'

We might express - in unison with Japanese American women - our disgust at the stereotype and acronym JAP - a racist name for Japanese people as well as a sexist scapegoat of Jewish middle-class women for crimes of capitalism.

We might, as Jews, press our religious and community institutions to offer sanctuary to refugees, from El Salvador and other countries, as some are doing, recognizing our own history as refugees. We might, as Jews, support attempts of women garment workers - jobs once held by Jewish and Italian women - to organize for better conditions and pay. We might support bilingual efforts of Chicana, Latina and Francophone communities, grasping through our own linguistic losses the importance of retaining one's language.

We might decide that even in the midst of vitriolic disagreement about peace in the Middle East, we must never accept or leave unchallenged instances of

INDIVIDUAL AND COMMUNITY

racism against Arabs, remembering our own history of prejudice and stereotypes.

We might even, as Jews, offer support to people whose struggles and issues are different form ours now and in the past simply because we care about justice; because we know that while nothing guarantees allies, callousness guarantees callousness.

Of late, there are positive instances of coalition. An event in NYC of Jews and Latinas/os (including some who are both) reading and performing their work, much of which is bilingual (Spring, 1984). Prior to several of Farrakhan's most recent appearances, coalitions of Black and Jewish leaders joined to denounce him. (In Baltimore, th esame group joined to condem Kahane prior to his appearance there).[29] In the feminist movement, a Jewish-Arab-Black coalition which prepared for the International Women's Conference at Nairobi has been speaking about this gathering, including information on Jewish-Palestinian dialogue.[30] A workshop for Black-Jewish dialogue was offered at the 1986 Women and the Law conference for the second year. It seems that many of us may have learned something form drawing close to the precipice of total withdrawal and isolation.

If we could start working together *before* we trust, understand, or like each other, we might learn to. Black activist and performer Bernice Reagon says we are stumbling because we have to take the next step.[31] We have gotten entirely too theoretical about these issues, expecting that with words, with ideas, we can work it all out in advance. Perhaps we need to engage, even in uncertainty, and work out issues as they arise. Maulana Karenga, a theorist for the Black movement, has pointed out that a coalition on a specific issue does not create reliable allies: he is critical of what he calls the reliance of middle-class Black movement leaders on alliance with Jews.[32]

But the positive side to Karenga's depressing analysis is that you don't need to be reliable allies to form a coalition. Having formed one, it may be possible to overcome mistrust and establish a larger common ground. It is impossible to do this without some concrete basis of unity, and focusing on the task at hand can help reveal commonality.

The problem is not a lack of common issues, not a lack of desperate need. The problem for us, as Jews, is that we are often afraid, afraid to gather with other Jews, afraid to be visibly Jewish, afraid - too often with reason - to know the extent of anti-Semitism in our comrades, neighbors, co-workers, friends. We are afraid of being or of seeming racist; afraid of our own ignorance of Jewish culture and tradition.

And because, as radicals, we have been taught to see dignity in resistance, in the struggle against oppression, we must remember not to idealize oppression, but to respect the struggles Jews have waged on behalf of their children, who are, sometimes, us. We must remember: What is beautiful is the resistance, and that people can - and must - resist from their own authentic place in the world.

This means we must reach out to Israelis fighting for peace, civil rights, and feminism without secretly feeling the Palestinians are more beautiful, because apparently more besieged. One of the hardest acts of self-love for American radical Jews is to identify in this way with Israelis, and I have come to believe it is a crucial stretch, for the alternative is denial of the Jewish connection. It is from this solid, self-knowing place that we can work towards peace and justice in the Middle East.

It is also from this place of valuing resistance that we are able to reach out to those in the Jewish community who have themselves been fighters for justice, or supporters of this fight, to ask them to continue this tradition; to ask them for what is best in themselves too.

Last Rosh Hashonah I stood with my friend Mitzi Lichtman at the edge of the Atlantic performing (in our own way) the ancient ritual of *tashlekh* - casting our sins into the water, in the form of stones. And among all the sins we hurled into the ocean, the sin of self-hate and the sin of failing to feel compassion for others mingled, as indeed they should, for they are the same sin.

And Hillel had a third question: *If not now, when?*

*Portions of this essay were first developed as talks given in Mankato and Minneapolis, MN, on Anti-Semitism, Racism, and Coalitions' (1984); a workshop given at the 1985 Women & Law Conference on 'Dealing with Racism as Jewish Women'; and as a review of Yours in Struggle which appeared in off our backs (October 1985). I thank the women who attended these events and talked with me about these issues. Much of the essay was also developed in conversation with Irena Klepfisz. I thank Linda Vance for her critical acumen, generous editorial attention, humor and patience. Responsibility for the opinions and analysis is mine alone.*

Endnotes
1. The Harlem Education Project (HEP) was a branch of the Northern Student Movement (NSM), founded in New Haven as the northern arm of the Student Non-Violent Coordinating Committee (SNCC), the most militant of the southern civil rights activist organizations.
2. The anti-rat campaign consisted of a number of young Black people armed with rifles very visibly hinting rats in

Harlem apartment buildings. The sluggish city health department responded immediately to combat the rats.

3. The National Women's Studies Association, pressed by angry Jewish women, agreed to mention opposition 'to anti-Semitism against Arabs and Jews.' Since hatred and discrimination against Arabs are regularly included by the term 'racism' - and since, oddly enough, these same phenomena directed against Jews are often excluded - I wonder why Jews are not allowed to use 'anti-Semitism' to mean anti-Jewish racism, its historic meaning.

4. I have heard this a number of times from women who attended conference planning sessions.

5. Cynthia Kern deserves particular credit for her work. Let me mention that these Jewish events were mostly open to gentiles but were attended almost exclusively by Jews.

6. Flyer for Not in Our Name/Women Resistance Action, Boston Office. See exchange of letters - a critical letter by me and Mitzi Lichtman, and a self-critical response by several Not in Our Name women - in Gay Community News (17 November 1984).

7. Heresies.

8. For a discussion of the queuing effect, see Stanley Lieberson, A Piece of the Pie: Blacks and White Immigrants Since 1880 (Berkeley, Univ. of Calif., 1980), pp. 296-326; 377-81.

9. See my earlier discussion, 'Anti-Semitism, Homophobia, and the Good White Knight,' Off Our Backs (May 1982).

10. Cf. Black activist Bernice Johnson Reagon, on the discomfort of working in coalitions: '[Coalition is] a monster. It never gets enough. It always want more. So you better be sure you got your home someplace for you to go to so that you will not become a martyr to the coalition.' See Reagon's fine discussion, 'Coalition Politics: Turning the Century,' Home Girls, ed. Barbara Smith (NY: Kitchen Table/Women of Color Press, 1983), p. 361.

11. The felicitous wording is Linda Vance's.

12. Elly Bulkin, Appendix to 'Hard Ground: Jewish Identity, Racism, and Anti-Semitism,' Yours in Struggle (Brooklyn: Long Haul Press, 1984), pp. 194-98. See Bernice Mennis' review, below; also, my review in off our backs (October 1985).

13. Adrienne Rich, speaking at the NJA Convention, added another question - 'If not with others, how?' - showing a peculiar failure to note that Hillel's second question already confronts the need for coalition. Her question also places the burden on Jews, as if we have refused to work in alliance with Gentiles, whereas in fact the opposite has often been true. The history of Jews engaged in political activity hardly suggests a people unwilling to work with others; what this history reveals, rather, is erasure of Jewish participation, Jews drummed out of movements by anti-Semitism, as well as substantial Jewish contributions to revolutionary activity. See, for example, Elinor Learner, 'Jewish Involvement in the New York City Woman Suffrage Movement,' American Jewish History, LXX (1981), 442-61.

14. See below for Sushi Gaynes' moving statement about recognizing how some Jewish women were made to feel unwelcome by just such a reluctance.

15. In this discussion, I am drawing heavily on Irena Klepfisz, 'When Jewish Women Disagree, unpublished (1983).

16. For an early clear statement of identity politics, see the Combahee River Collective, 'A Black Feminist Statement,' reprinted in Capitalist Patriarchy and the Case for Socialist Feminism, ed. Zillah R. Eisenstein (NY: Monthly Review Press, 1979).

17. See Susanna Sturgis' analysis of feminist resistance to dealing with fat oppression, 'Is this the new thing I'm going to have to be p c about?' Sinister Wisdom 28 (1985).

18. See Kaye/Kantrowitz, '...the Good White Knight.'

19. Angela Davis, Women, Race, & Class (NY: Random House, 1981), pp. 34 ff.

20. Davis, p. 38.

21. Davis, p. 48.

22. Davis, pp. 50 ff.

23. See Eleanor Flexner, Century of Struggle: a History of the Women's Rights Movement in the US (Cambridge, MA: Belknap/Harvard Univ., 1978). But also see Rosalyn Terborg-Penn, 'Survival strategies among African-American women workers: A continuing process,' Women, Work & Protest: A Century of US Women's Labor History, ed. Ruth Milkman (Boston: Routledge & Kegan Paul, 1985). Terborg-Penn cites the occasional interest of mostly white CIO Unions in organizing with Black women, but the more common lack of interest.

24. Nancy Schrom Dye, As Equals As Sisters: Feminism, The Labor Movement and The Women's Trade Union League of New York (Columbia: Univ. of Missouri Press, 1980), p. 93.

25. Quoted in Davis, p. 44

26. M.T. Mehdi, letter, NY Times (17 October 1985).

27. James Baldwin, 'Negroes Are Anti-Semitic Because They're Anti-White,' 1st pub. NY Times Magazine (1967); reprinted in Black Anti-Semitism and Jewish Racism (NY: Schocken, 1972), p. 11.

28. See Prof. Ronald Takaki's remarks, quoted in the NY Times (4 September 1985).

29. See Earl Raab, 'Poisoned Good: Understanding the Farrakhan Factor,' Moment, vol. 11, no. 2 (Jan. - Feb. 1986), pp. 13-17.

30. The dialogue was organized by New Jewish Agenda.

31. Reagon, p. 368.

32. Maulana Karenga, 'The Crisis of Black Middle-Class Leadership: A Critical Analysis,' The Black Scholar (Fall '82), pp. 16-32.

## Study Questions

1. Why is it so important to analyze anti-Semitism?

2. What kinds of pressures exist to prevent this analysis?

3. What does she say about the relationship between
   racism and anti-Semitism? What do you think?

4. What is the "scarcity theory"? Do you agree?

5. What is she calling for?

# HOW TO TAME A WILD TONGUE

## Gloria Anzaldúa

*Gloria Anzaldúa lives in Santa Cruz, California. She is a poet and essayist whose work includes her autobiographical* Borderlands/La Frontera: The New Mestiza *(1987), from which this selection is excepted. Along with Cherríe Moraga, she edited* This Bridge Called My Back: Writings by Radical Women of Color *(1981), and she also edited the anthology* Making Face/Making Soul: Haciendo Caras *(1990).*

"We're going to have to control your tongue," the dentist says, pulling out all the metal from my mouth. Silver bits plop and tinkle into the basin. My mouth is a motherlode.

The dentist is cleaning out my roots. I get a whiff of the stench when I gasp. "I can't cap that tooth yet, you're still draining," he says.

"We're going to have to do something about your tongue," I hear the anger rising in his voice. My tongue keeps pushing out the wads of cotton, pushing back the drills, the long thin needles. "I've never seen anything as strong or as stubborn," he says. And I think, how do you tame a wild tongue, train it to be quiet, how do you bridle and saddle it? How do you make it lie down?

"Who is to say that robbing a people of its language is less violent than war?"
—Ray Gwyn Smith

I remember being caught speaking Spanish at recess—that was good for three licks on the knuckles with a sharp ruler. I remember being sent to the corner of the classroom for "talking back" to the Anglo teacher when all I was trying to do was tell her how to pronounce my name. "If you want to be American, speak 'American.' If you don't like it, go back to Mexico where you belong."

"I want you to speak English. *Pa'hallar buen trabajo tienes que saber hablar el inglés bien. Qué vale toda tu educación si todavia hablas inglés con un* 'accent,'" my mother would say, mortified that I spoke English like a Mexican. At Pan American University, I and all Chicano students were required to take two speech classes. Their purpose: to get rid of our accents.

Attacks on one's form of expression with the intent to censor are a violation of the First Amendment. *El Anglo con cara de inocente nos arrancó la lengua.* Wild tongues can't be tamed, they can only be cut out.

## OVERCOMING THE TRADITION OF SILENCE

Abogadas, escupimos el oscuro
Peleando con nuestra propia sombra
el silencio nos sepulta

*En boca cerrada no entran moscas.* "Flies don't enter a closed mouth" is a saying I kept hearing when I was a child. *Ser habladora* was to be a gossip and a liar, to talk too much. *Muchachitas bien criadas,* well bred girls don't answer back. *Es una falta de respeto* to talk back to one's mother or father. I remember one of the sins I'd recite to the priest in the confession box the few times I went to confession: talking back to my mother, *hablar pa' tras, repelar. Hocicona, repelona, chismosa* having a big mouth, questioning, carrying tales are all signs of being *mal criada.* In my culture they are all words that are derogatory if applied to women—I've never heard them applied to men.

The first time I heard two women, a Puerto Rican and a Cuban, say the word *"nosotras,"* I was shocked. I had not known the word existed. Chicanas use nosotros whether we're male or female. We are robbed of our female being by the masculine plural. Language is a male discourse.

> And our tongues have become
> dry the wilderness has
> dried out our tongues and
> we have forgotten speech.
>
> —Irena Klepfisz

Even our own people, other Spanish speakers *nos quieren poner candados en la boca.* They would hold us back with their bag of *reglas de academia.*

## OYÉ COMO LADRA: EL LENGUAJE DE LA FRONTERA

*Quien tiene boca se equivoca.*
—Mexican saying,

"*Pocho,* cultural traitor, you're speaking the oppressor's language by speaking English, you're ruining the Spanish language," I have been accused by various Latinos and Latinas. Chicano Spanish is considered by the purist and by most Latinos deficient, a mutilation of Spanish.

But Chicano Spanish is a border tongue which developed naturally. Change, *evolución, enriquecimiento de palabras nuevas por invención o adopción* have created variants of Chicano Spanish, *un nuevo lenguaje enguaje. Un lenguaje que corresponde a un modo de vivir.* Chicano Spanish is not incorrect, it is a living language.

For a people who are neither Spanish nor live in a country in which Spanish is the first language; for a people who live in a country in which English is the reigning tongue but who are not Anglo; for a people who cannot entirely identify with either standard (formal, Castillian) Spanish nor standard English, what recourse is left to them but to create their own language? A language which they can connect their identity to, one capable of communicating the realities and values true to themselves—a language with terms that are neither *español ni inglés,* but both. We speak a patois, a forked tongue, a variation of two languages.

Chicano Spanish sprang out of the Chicanos' need to identify ourselves as a distinct people. We needed a language with which we could communicate with ourselves, a secret language. For some of us, language is a homeland closer than the southwest—for many Chicanos today live in the Midwest and the East. And because we are a complex, heterogeneous people, we speak many languages. Some of the languages we speak are:

1. Standard English
2. Working class and slang English
3. Standard Spanish
4. Standard Mexican Spanish
5. North Mexican Spanish dialect
6. Chicano Spanish (Texas, New Mexico, Arizona and California have regional variations)
7. Tex-Mex
8. *Pachuco* (called *caló*)

My "home" tongues are the languages I speak with my sister and brothers, with my friends. They are the last five listed with 6 and 7 being closest to my heart. From school, the media and job situations, I've picked up standard and working class English. From Mamagrande Locha and from reading Spanish and Mexican literature, I've picked up standard Spanish and standard Mexican Spanish. From *los recién llegados,* Mexican immigrants, and *braceros,* I learned the North Mexican dialect. With Mexicans I'll try to speak either Standard Mexican Spanish or the North Mexican dialect. From my parents and Chicanos living in the Valley, I picked up Chicano Texas Spanish, and I speak it with my mom, younger brother (who married a Mexican and who rarely mixes Spanish with English), aunts and older relatives.

With Chicanas from *Nuevo México or Arizona* I will speak Chicano Spanish a little, but often they don't understand what I'm saying. With most California Chicanas I speak entirely in English (unless I forget). When I first moved to San Francisco, I'd rattle off something in Spanish, unintentionally embarrassing them. Often it is only with another Chicana *tejana* that I can talk freely.

Words distorted by English are known as anglicisms or *pochismos.* The *pocho* is an anglicized Mexican or American of Mexican origin who speaks Spanish with an accent characteristic of North Americans and who distorts and reconstructs the language according to the influence of English. Tex-Mex, or Spanglish, comes most naturally to me. I may switch back and forth from English to Spanish in the same sentence or in the same word. With my sister and my brother Nune and with Chicano *tejano* contemporaries I speak in Tex-Mex.

From kids and people my own age I picked up *Pachuco. Pachuco* (the language of the zoot suiters) is a language of rebellion, both against standard Spanish and Standard English. It is a secret language. Adults of the culture and outsiders cannot understand it. It is made up of slang words from both English and Spanish. *Ruca* means girl or woman, *vato* means guy or dude, *chale* means no, *simón* means yes, *churro* is sure, talk is *periquiar*, *pigionear* means petting, *que gacho* means how nerdy, *ponte águila* means watch out, death is called *la pelona*. Through lack of practice and not having others who can speak it, I've lost most of the *pachuco* tongue.

## Chicano Spanish

Chicanos, after 250 years of Spanish/Anglo colonization have developed significant differences in the Spanish we speak. We collapse two adjacent vowels into a single syllable and sometimes shift the stress in certain words such as *maíz/maiz, cohetel/ cuete*. We leave out certain consonants when they appear between vowels: *lado/lao, mojado/mojao*. Chicanos from South Texas pronounce *f* as *j* as in *jue (fue)*. Chicanos use "archaisms," words that are no longer in the Spanish language, words that have been evolved out. We say *semos, truje, haiga, ansina* and *naiden*. We retain the "archaic" *j*, as in *jalar*, that derives from an earlier *h*, (the French *halar* or the Germanic *halon* which was lost to standard Spanish in the 16th century), but which is still found in several regional dialects such as the one spoken in South Texas. (Due to geography, Chicanos from the Valley of South Texas were cut off linguistically from other Spanish speakers. We tend to use words that the Spaniards brought over from Medieval Spain. The majority of the Spanish colonizers in Mexico and the Southwest came from Extremadura—Hernán Cortés was one of them—and Andalucia. Andalucians pronounce *ll* like a *y*, and their *d*'s tend to be absorbed by adjacent vowels: *tirado* becomes *tirao*. They brought *el lenguaje popular, dialectos y regionalismos*.)

Chicanos and other Spanish speakers also shift *ll* to *y* and *z* to *s*. We leave out initial syllables, saying *tar* for *estar, toy* for *estoy, hora* for *ahora* (*cubanos* and *puertorriqueños* also leave out initial letters of some words.) We also leave out the final syllable such as *pa* for *para*. The intervocalic *y*, the *ll* as in *tortilla, ella, botella*, gets replaced by *tortia* or *tortiya, ea, botea*. We add an additional syllable at the beginning of certain words: *atocar* for *tocar, agastar* for *gastar*. Sometimes we'll say *lavaste las vacijas*, other times *lavates* (substituting the *ates* verb endings for the *aste*).

We use anglicisms, words borrowed from English: *bola* from ball, *carpeta* from carpet, *máchina de lavar* (instead of *lavadora*) from washing machine. Tex-Mex argot, created by adding a Spanish sound at the beginning or end of an English word such as *cookiar* for cook, *watchar* for watch, *parkiar* for park, and *rapiar* for rape, is the result of the pressures on Spanish speakers to adapt to English.

We don't use the word *vosotros/as* or its accompanying verb form. We don't say *claro* (to mean yes), *imagínate*, or *me emociona*, unless we picked up Spanish from Latinas, out of a book, or in a classroom. Other Spanish-speaking groups are going through the same, or similar, development in their Spanish.

## Linguistic Terrorism

*Deslenguadas. Somos los del español deficiente.* We are your linguistic nightmare, your linguistic aberration, your linguistic *mestisaje* the subject of your *burla*. Because we speak with tongues of fire we are culturally crucified. Racially, culturally and linguistically *somos huérfanos*— we speak an orphan tongue.

Chicanas who grew up speaking Chicano Spanish have internalized the belief that we speak poor Spanish. It is illegitimate, a bastard language. And because we internalize how our language has been used against us by the dominant culture, we use our language differences against each other.

Chicana feminists often skirt around each other with suspicion and hesitation. For the longest time I couldn't figure it out. Then it dawned on me. To be close to another Chicana is like looking into the mirror. We are afraid of what we'll see there. *Pena*. Shame. Low estimation of self. In childhood we are told that our language is wrong. Repeated attacks on our native tongue diminish our sense of self. The attacks continue through out our lives.

Chicanas feel uncomfortable talking in Spanish to Latinas, afraid of their censure. Their language was not out outlawed in their countries. They had a whole lifetime of being immersed in their native tongue; generations, centuries in which Spanish was a first language, taught in school, heard on radio and TV, and read in the newspaper.

If a person, Chicana or Latina, has a low estimation of my native tongue, she also has a low estimation of me. Often with *mexicanas y latinas* we'll speak English as a neutral language. Even among Chicanas we tend to speak English at parties or conferences. Yet, at the same time, we're afraid the other will think we're *agringadas* because we don't speak Chicano Spanish. We oppress each other trying to out-Chicano each other, vying to be the "real" Chicanas, to speak like Chicanos. There is no one Chicano language just as there is no one Chicano experience. A monolingual Chicana whose first language is English or Spanish is just as much a

Chicana as one who speaks several variants of Spanish. A Chicana from Michigan or Chicago or Detroit is just as much a Chicana as one from the Southwest. Chicano Spanish is as diverse linguistically as it is regionally.

By the end of this century, Spanish speakers will comprise the biggest minority group in the U.S., a country where students in high schools and colleges are encouraged to take French classes because French is considered more "cultured." But for a language to remain alive it must be used. By the end of this century English, and not Spanish, will be the mother tongue of most Chicanos and Latinos.

So, if you want to really hurt me, talk badly about my language. Ethnic identity is twin skin to linguistic identity—I am my language. Until I can take pride in my language, I cannot take pride in myself. Until I can accept as legitimate Chicano Texas Spanish, Tex-Mex and all the other languages I speak, I cannot accept the legitimacy of myself. Until I am free to write bilingually and to switch codes without having always to translate, while I still have to speak English or Spanish when I would rather speak Spanglish, and as long as I have to accommodate the English speakers rather than having them accommodate me, my tongue will be illegitimate.

I will no longer be made to feel ashamed of existing. I will have my voice: Indian, Spanish, white. I will have my serpent's tongue—my woman's voice, my sexual voice, my poet's voice. I will overcome the tradition of silence.

My fingers
move sly against your palm
Like women everywhere, we speak in code. . . .
—Melanie Kaye/Kantrowitz

## "VISTAS," CORRIDOS, Y COMIDA: MY NATIVE TONGUE

In the 1960s, I read my first Chicano novel. It was *City of Night* by John Rechy, a gay Texan, son of a Scottish father and a Mexican mother. For days I walked around in stunned amazement that a Chicano could write and could get published. When I read *I Am Joaquín* I was surprised to see a bilingual book by a Chicano in print. When I saw poetry written in Tex-Mex for the first time, a feeling of pure joy flashed through me. I felt like we really existed as a people. In 1971, when I started teaching High School English to Chicano students, I tried to supplement the required texts with works by Chicanos, only to be reprimanded and forbidden to do so by the principal. He claimed that I was supposed to teach "American" and English liter-

ature. At the risk of being fired, I swore my students to secrecy and slipped in Chicano short stories, poems, a play. In graduate school, while working toward a Ph.D., I had to "argue" with one advisor after the other, semester after semester, before I was allowed to make Chicano literature an area of focus.

Even before I read books by Chicanos or Mexicans, it was the Mexican movies I saw at the drive-in—the Thursday night special of $1.00 a carload—that gave me a sense of belonging. "*Vámonos a las vistas*," my mother would call out and we'd all—grandmother, brothers, sister and cousins-squeeze into the car. We'd wolf down cheese and bologna white bread sandwiches while watching Pedro Infante in melodramatic tear jerkers like *Nosotros los pobres*, the first "real" Mexican movie (that was not an imitation of European movies). I remember seeing *Cuando los hijos se van* and surmising that all Mexican movies played up the love a mother has for her children and what ungrateful sons and daughters suffer when they are not devoted to their mothers. I remember the singing-type "westerns" of Jorge Negrete and Miquel Aceves Mejia. When watching Mexican movies, I felt a sense of homecoming as well as alienation. People who were to amount to something didn't go to Mexican movies, or *bailes* or tune their radios to *bolero, rancherita,* and *corrido* music.

The whole time I was growing up, there was *norteño* music sometimes called North Mexican border music, or Tex-Mex music, or Chicano music, or *cantina* (bar) music. I grew up listening to *conjuntos*, three- or four-piece bands made up of folk musicians playing guitar, *bajo sexto*, drums and button accordion, which Chicanos had borrowed from the German immigrants who had come to Central Texas and Mexico to farm and build breweries. In the Rio Grande Valley, Steve Jordan and Little Joe Hernandez were popular, and Flaco Jiménez was the accordian king. The rhythms of Tex-Mex music are those of the polka, also adapted from the Germans, who in turn had borrowed the polka from the Czechs and Bohemians.

I remember the hot, sultry evenings when *corridos*—songs of love and death on the Texas-Mexican borderlands—reverberated out of cheap amplifiers from the local *cantinas* and wafted in through my bedroom window.

*Corridos* first became widely used along the South Texas/Mexican border during the early conflict between Chicanos and Anglos. The corridos are usually about Mexican heroes who do valiant deeds against the Anglo oppressors. Pancho Villa's song, "*La cucaracha*," is the most famous one. Corridos of John F. Kennedy and his death are still very popular in the Valley. Older Chicanos remember Lydia Mendoza, one of the great border corrido singers who was called *la Gloria de Tejas.* Her *"El tango negro,"* sung during the Great Depression, made her a singer of the people. The ever-present *corridos* narrated one hundred years of border history, bringing news of events as well as entertaining. These folk musicians and folk songs are our chief cultural mythmakers, and they made our hard lives seem bearable.

I grew up feeling ambivalent about our music. Country-western and rock-and-roll had more status. In the 50s and 60s, for the slightly educated and *agringado* Chicanos, there existed a sense of shame at being caught listening to our music. Yet I couldn't stop my feet from thumping to the music, could not stop humming the words, nor hide from myself the exhilaration I felt when I heard it.

There are more subtle ways that we internalize identification, especially in the forms of images and emotions. For me food and certain smells are tied to my identity, to my homeland. Woodsmoke curling up to an immense blue sky; woodsmoke perfuming my grandmother's clothes, her skin. The stench of cow manure and the yellow patches on the ground; the crack of a .22 rifle and the reek of cordite. Homemade white cheese sizzling in a pan, melting inside a folded *tortilla.* My sister Hilda's hot, spicy *menudo, chile colorado* making it deep red, pieces of *panza* and hominy floating on top. My brother Carito barbequing *fajitas* in the backyard. Even now and 3,000 miles away, I can see my mother spicing the ground beef, pork and venison with *chile.* My mouth salivates at the thought of the hot steaming *tamales* I would be eating if I were home.

## SI LE PREGUNTAS A MI MAMÁ, *"¿QUÉ ERES?"*

"Identity is the essential core of who we are as individuals, the conscious experience of the self inside."
-Kaufman[9]

*Nosotros los* Chicanos straddle the borderlands. On one side of us, we are constantly exposed to the Spanish of the Mexicans, on the other side we hear the Anglos' incessant clamoring so that we forget our language. Among ourselves we don't say *nosotros los americanos, o nosotros los españoles, o nosotros los hispanos.* We say *nosotros los mexicanos* (by *mexicanos* we do not mean citizens of Mexico; we do not mean a national identity, but a racial one). We distinguish between *mexicanos del otro lado* and *mexicanos de este lado.* Deep in our hearts we believe that being Mexican has nothing to do with which country one lives in. Being Mexican is a state of soul-not one of mind, not one of citizenship. Neither eagle nor serpent, but both. And like the ocean, neither animal respects borders.

*Dime con quien andas y te diré quien eres.*
(Tell me who your friends are and I'll tell you who you are.)
—Mexican saying

*Si le preguntas a mi mamá, "¿Qué eres?" te dirá, "Soy mexicana."* My brothers and sister say the same. I sometimes will answer *"soy mexicana"* and at others will say *"soy Chicana"* o *"soy tejana."* But I identified as *"Raza"* before I ever identified as *"mexicana"* or *"Chicana."*

As a culture, we call ourselves Spanish when referring to ourselves as a linguistic group and when copping out. It is then that we forget our predominant Indian genes. We are 70-80% Indian.[10] We call ourselves Hispanic.[11] or Spanish-American or Latin American or Latin when linking ourselves to other Spanish-speaking peoples of the Western hemisphere and when copping out. We call ourselves Mexican-American to signify we are neither Mexican nor American, but more the noun "American" than the adjective "Mexican" (and when copping out).

Chicanos and other people of color suffer economically for not acculturating. This voluntary (yet forced) alienation makes for psychological conflict, a kind of dual identity—we don't identify with the Anglo-American cultural values and we don't totally identify with the Mexican cultural values. We are a synergy of two cultures with various degrees of Mexicanness or Angloness. I have so internalized the borderland conflict that sometimes I feel like one cancels out the other and we are zero, nothing, no one. *A veces no soy nada ni nadie. Pero hasta cuando no lo soy, lo soy.*

When not copping out, when we know we are more than nothing, we call ourselves Mexican, referring to race and ancestry; *mestizo* when affirming both our Indian and Spanish (but we hardly ever own our Black ancestry); Chicano when referring to a politically aware people born and/or raised in the U.S.; *Raza* when referring to Chicanos; *tejanos* when we are Chicanos from Texas.

Chicanos did not know we were a people until 1965 when Ceasar Chavez and the farmworkers united and *I Am Joaquín* was published and *la Raza Unida* party was formed in Texas. With that recognition, we became a distinct people. Something momentous happened to the Chicano soul—we became aware of our reality and acquired a name and a language (Chicano Spanish) that reflected that reality. Now that we had a name, some of the fragmented pieces began to fall together—who we were, what we were, how we had evolved. We began to get glimpses of what we might eventually become.

Yet the struggle of identities continues, the struggle of borders is our reality still. One day the inner struggle will cease and a true integration take place. In the meantime, *tenémos que hacer la lucha. ¿Quién está protegiendo los ranchos de mi gente? ¿Quién está tratando de cerrar la fisura entre la india y el blanco en nuestra sangre? El Chicano, si, el Chicano que anda como un ladrón en su propia casa.*

*Los Chicanos,* how patient we seem, how very patient. There is the quiet of the Indian about us. We know how to survive. When other races have given up their tongue, we've kept ours. We know what it is to live under the hammer blow of the dominant *norteamericano* culture. But more than we count the blows, we count the days the weeks the years the centuries the eons until the white laws and commerce and customs will rot in the deserts they've created, lie bleached. *Humildes* yet proud, *quietos* yet wild, *nosotros los mexicanos-Chicanos* will walk by the crumbling ashes as we go about our business. Stubborn, persevering, impenetrable as stone, yet possessing a malleability that renders us unbreakable, we, the *mestizas* and *mestizos*, will remain.

**Study Questions**

1. According to Anzaldúa, why is language so significant? What is its relationship to identity?

2. Why is it important for her to list so many languages? How is that connected to a mestiza heritage?

3. Why is she so angry at those who criticize those who do not speak "proper" English or Spanish?

4. What does this issue have to do with other forms of cultural production, such as music and film?

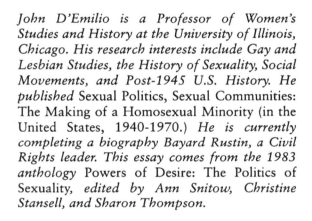

# CAPITALISM AND GAY IDENTITY

## John D'Emilio

*John D'Emilio is a Professor of Women's Studies and History at the University of Illinois, Chicago. His research interests include Gay and Lesbian Studies, the History of Sexuality, Social Movements, and Post-1945 U.S. History. He* published Sexual Politics, Sexual Communities: The Making of a Homosexual Minority (in the United States, 1940-1970.) *He is currently completing a biography Bayard Rustin, a Civil Rights leader. This essay comes from the 1983 anthology* Powers of Desire: The Politics of Sexuality, *edited by Ann Snitow, Christine Stansell, and Sharon Thompson.*

For gay men and lesbians, the 1970s were years of significant achievement. Gay liberation and women's liberation changed the sexual landscape of the nation. Hundreds of thousands of gay women and men came out and openly affirmed same-sex eroticism. We won repeal of sodomy laws in half the states, a partial lifting of the exclusion of lesbians and gay men from federal employment, civil rights protection in a few dozen cities, the inclusion of gay rights in the platform of the Democratic Party, and the elimination of homosexuality from the psychiatric profession's list of mental illnesses. The gay male subculture expanded and became increasingly visible in large cities, and lesbian feminists pioneered in building alternative institutions and an alternative culture that attempted to embody a liberatory vision of the future.

In the 1980s, however, with the resurgence of an active right wing, gay men and lesbians face the future warily. Our victories appear tenuous and fragile: the relative freedom of the past few years seems too recent to be permanent. In some parts of the lesbian and gay male community, a feeling of

doom is growing: analogies with McCarthy's America, when "sexual perverts" were a special target of the Right, and with Nazi Germany, where gays were shipped to concentration camps, surface with increasing frequency. Everywhere there is the sense that new strategies are in order if we want to preserve our gains and move ahead.

I believe that a new, more accurate theory of gay history must be part of this political enterprise. When the gay liberation movement began at the end of the 1960s, gay men and lesbians had no history that we could use to fashion our goals and strategy. In the ensuing years, in building a movement without a knowledge of our history, we instead invented a mythology. This mythical history drew on personal experience, which we read backward in time. For instance, most lesbians and gay men in the 1960s first discovered their homosexual desires in isolation, unaware of others, and without resources for naming and understanding what they felt. From this experience, we constructed a myth of silence, invisibility, and isolation as the essential characteristics of gay life in the past as well as the present. Moreover, because we faced so many oppressive laws, public policies, and cultural beliefs, we projected this into an image of the abysmal past: until gay liberation, lesbians and gay men were always the victims of systematic, undifferentiated, terrible oppression.

These myths have limited our political perspective. The have contributed, for instance, to an overreliance on a strategy of coming out—if every gay man and lesbian in America came out, gay oppression would end—and have allowed us to ignore the institutionalized ways in which homophobia and heterosexism are reproduced. They have encouraged, at times, an incapacitating despair, especially at moments like the present: How can we unravel a gay oppression so pervasive and unchanging?

There is another historical myth that enjoys nearly universal acceptance in the gay movement, the myth of the "eternal homosexual." The argument runs something like this: gay men and lesbians always were and always will be. We are everywhere; not just now, but throughout history, in all societies and all periods. This myth served a positive political function in the first years of gay liberation. In the early 1970s, when we battled an ideology that either denied our existence or defined us as psychopathic individuals or freaks of nature, it was empowering to assert that "we are everywhere." But in recent years it has confined us as surely as the most homophobic medical theories, and locked our movement in place.

Here I wish to challenge this myth. I want to argue that gay men and lesbians have *not* always existed. Instead, they are a product of history, and have come into existence in a specific historical era. Their emergence is associated with the relations of capitalism; it has been the historical development of capitalism—more specifically, its free labor system—that has allowed large numbers of men and women in the late twentieth century to call themselves gay, to see themselves as part of a community of similar men and women, and to organize politically on the basis of that identity.[1] Finally, I want to suggest some political lessons we can draw from this view of history.

What, then, are the relationships between the free labor system of capitalism and homosexuality? First, let me review some features of capitalism. Under capitalism, workers are "free" laborers in two ways. We have the freedom to look for a job. We own our ability to work and have the freedom to sell our labor power for wages to anyone willing to buy it. We are also freed from the ownership of anything except our labor power. Most of us do not own the land or the tools that produce what we need, but rather have to work for a living in order to survive. So, if we are free to sell our labor power in the positive sense, we are also freed, in the negative sense, from any other alternative. This dialectic— the constant interplay between exploitation and some measure of autonomy—informs all of the history of those who have lived under capitalism.

As capital—money used to make more money— expands, so does this system of free labor. Capital expands in several ways. Usually it expands in the same place, transforming small firms into larger ones, but it also expands by taking over new areas of production: the weaving of cloth, for instance, or the baking of bread. Finally, capital expands geographically. In the United States, capitalism initially took root in the Northeast, at a time when slavery was the dominant system in the South and when noncapitalist Native American societies occupied the western half of the continent. During the nineteenth century, capital spread from the Atlantic to the Pacific, and in the twentieth, U.S. capital has penetrated almost every part of the world.

The expansion of capital and the spread of wage labor have effected a profound transformation in the structure and functions of the nuclear family, the ideology of family life, and the meaning of heterosexual relations. It is these changes in the family that are most directly linked to the appearance of a collective gay life.

The white colonist in seventeenth-century New England established villages structured around a household economy, composed of family units that were basically self-sufficient, independent, and patriarchal. Men, women, and children farmed land owned by the male head of household. Although there was a division of labor between men and women, the family was truly an interdependent unit of production: the survival of each member depended on the cooperation of all. The home was a workplace where women processed raw farm products into food for daily consumption, where they made clothing, soap, and candles, and where husbands, wives, and children worked together to produce the goods they consumed.

By the nineteenth century, this system of household production was in decline. In the Northeast, as merchant capitalists invested the money accumulated through trade in the production of goods, wage labor became more common. Men and women were drawn out of the largely self-sufficient household economy of the colonial era into the capitalist system of free labor. For women in the nineteenth century, working for wages rarely lasted beyond marriage; for men, it became a permanent condition.

The family was thus no longer an independent unit of production. But although no longer independent, the family was still interdependent. Because capitalism had not expanded very far, because it had not yet taken over—or socialized— the production of consumer goods, women still performed necessary productive labor in the home. Many families no longer produced grain, but wives still baked into bread the flour they bought with their husbands' wages; or, when they purchased yarn or cloth, they still made clothing for their families. By the mid-1860s, capitalism had destroyed the economic self-sufficiency of many families, but not the mutual dependence of the members.

This transition away from the household family-based economy to a fully developed capitalist free labor economy occurred very slowly, over almost two centuries. As late as 1920, 50 percent of the U.S. population lived in communities of fewer than 2,500 people. The vast majority of blacks in the early twentieth century lived outside the free labor economy, in a system of sharecropping and tenancy that rested on the family. Not only did independent farming as a way of life still exist for millions of Americans, but even in towns and small cities women continued to grow and process food, make clothing, and engage in other kinds of domestic production.

But for those people who felt the brunt of these changes, the family took on new significance as an affective unit, an institution that produced not goods but emotional satisfaction and happiness. By the 1920s among the white middle class, the ideology surrounding the family described it as the means through which men and women formed satisfying, mutually enhancing relationships and created an environment that nurtured children. The family became the setting for a "personal life," sharply distinguished and disconnected from the public world of work and production.[2]

The meaning of heterosexual relations also changed. In colonial New England, the birthrate averaged over seven children per woman of child-bearing age. Men and women needed the labor of children. Producing offspring was as necessary for survival as producing grain. Sex was harnessed to procreation. The Puritans did not celebrate *hetero-sexuality* but rather marriage; they condemned *all* sexual expression outside the marriage bond and did not differentiate sharply between sodomy and heterosexual fornication.

By the 1970s, however, the birthrate had dropped to under two. With the exception of the post-World War II baby boom, the decline has been continuous for two centuries, paralleling the spread of capitalist relations of production. It occurred even when access to contraceptive devices and abortion was systematically curtailed. The decline has included every segment of the population—urban and rural families, blacks and whites, ethnics and WASPs, the middle class and the working class.

As wage labor spread and production became socialized, then, it became possible to release sexuality from the "imperative" to procreate. Ideologically, heterosexual expression came to be a means of establishing intimacy, promoting happiness, and experiencing pleasure. In divesting the household of its economic independence and fostering the separation of sexuality from procreation, capitalism has created conditions that allow some men and women to organize a personal life around their erotic/emotional attraction to their own sex. It has made possible the formation of urban communities of lesbians and gay men and, more recently, of a politics based on a sexual identity.

Evidence from colonial New England court records and church sermons indicates that male and female homosexual behavior existed in the seventeenth century. Homosexual *behavior*, however, is different from homosexual *identity*. There was, quite simply, no "social space" in the colonial system of production that allowed men and women to be gay. Survival was structured around participation in a nuclear family. There were certain homosexual acts—sodomy among men, "lewdness" among women—in which individuals engaged, but family was so pervasive that colonial society lacked even the category of homosexual or lesbian to describe a person. It is quite possible that some men and women experienced a stronger attraction to their own sex than to the opposite sex—in fact, some colonial court cases refer to men who persisted in their "unnatural" attractions—but one could not fashion out of that preference a way of life. Colonial Massachusetts even had laws prohibiting unmarried adults from living outside family units.[3]

By the second half of the nineteenth century, this situation was noticeably changing as the capitalist system of free labor took hold. Only when *individuals* began to make their living through wage labor, instead of as parts of an interdependent family unit, was it possible for homosexual desire to coalesce into a personal identity—an identity based on the ability to remain outside the heterosexual nuclear family and to construct a personal life based on attraction to one's own sex. By the end of the century, a class of men and women existed who recognized their erotic interest in their own sex, saw it as a trait that set them apart from the majority, and sought others like themselves. These early gay lives came from a wide social spectrum: civil servants and business executives, department store clerks and college professors, factory operatives, ministers, lawyers, cooks, domestics, hoboes, and the idle rich: men and women, black and white, immigrant and native born.

In this period, gay men and lesbians began to invent ways of meeting each other and sustaining a group life. Already, in the early twentieth century, large cities contained male homosexual bars. Gay men staked out cruising areas, such as Riverside Drive in New York City and Lafayette Park in Washington. In St. Louis and the nation's capital, annual drag balls brought together large numbers of black gay men. Public bathhouses and YMCAs became gathering spots for male homosexuals.

Lesbians formed literary societies and private social clubs. Some working-class women "passed" as men to obtain better paying jobs and lived with other women—lesbian couples who appeared to the world as husband and wife. Among the faculties of women's colleges, in the settlement houses, and in the professional associations and clubs that women formed one could find lifelong intimate relationships supported by a web of lesbian friends. By the 1920s and 1930s, large cities such as New York and Chicago contained lesbian bars. These patterns of living could evolve because capitalism allowed individuals to survive beyond the confines of the family.[4]

Simultaneously, ideological definitions of homosexual behavior changed. Doctors developed theories about homosexuality, describing it as a condition, something that was inherent in a person, a part of his or her "nature." These theories did not represent scientific breakthroughs, elucidations of previously undiscovered areas of knowledge; rather, they were an ideological response to a new way of organizing one's personal life. The popularization of the medical model, in turn, affected the consciousness of women and men who experienced homosexual desire, so that they came to define themselves through their erotic life.[5]

These new forms of gay identity and patterns of group life also reflected the differentiation of people according to gender, race, and class that is so pervasive in capitalist societies. Among whites, for instance, gay men have traditionally been more visible than lesbians. This partly stems from the division between the public male sphere and the private female sphere. Streets, parks, and bars, especially at night, were "male space." Yet the greater visibility of white gay men also reflected their larger numbers. The Kinsey studies of the 1940s and 1950s found significantly more men than women with predominantly homosexual histories, a situation caused, I would argue, by the fact that capitalism had drawn far more men than women into the labor force, and at higher wages. Men could more easily construct a personal life independent of attachments to the opposite sex, whereas women were more likely to remain economically dependent on men. Kinsey also found a strong positive correlation between years of schooling and lesbian activity. College-educated white women are far more able than their working-class sisters to support themselves, could survive more easily without intimate relationships with men.[6]

Among working-class immigrants in the early twentieth century, closely knit kin networks and an ethic of family solidarity placed constraints on individual autonomy that made gayness a difficult option to pursue. In contrast, for reasons not altogether clear, urban black communities appeared relatively tolerant of homosexuality. The popularity in the 1920s and 1930s of songs with lesbian and gay male themes—"B.D. Woman," "Prove It on Me," "Sissy Man," "Fairey Blues"—suggests an openness about homosexual expression at odds with the mores of whites. Among men in the rural West in the 1940s, Kinsey found extensive incidence of homosexual behavior, but, in contrast with the men in large cities, little consciousness of gay identity. Thus even as capitalism exerted a homogenizing influence by gradually transforming more individuals into wage laborers and separating them from traditional communities, different groups of people were also affected in different ways.[7]

The decisions of particular men and women to act on their erotic/emotional preference for the same sex, along with the new consciousness that this preference made them different, led to the formation of an urban subculture of gay men and lesbians. Yet at least through the 1930s this subculture remained rudimentary, unstable, and difficult to find. How, then, did the complex, well-developed gay community emerge that existed by the time the gay liberation movement exploded? The answer is to be found during World War II, a time when the cumulative changes of several decades coalesced into a qualitatively new shape.

The war severely disrupted traditional patterns of gender relations and sexuality, and temporarily created a new erotic situation conducive to homosexual expression. It plucked millions of young men and women, whose sexual identities were just forming, out of their homes, out of towns and small cities and into a heterosexual environment of the family, and dropped them into sex-segregated situations—as GIs, as WACs and as WAVEs, in same-sex rooming houses for women workers who relocated to seek employment. The war freed millions of men and women from the settings where heterosexuality was normally imposed. For men and women already gay, it provided an opportunity to meet people like themselves. Others could become gay because of the temporary freedom to explore sexuality that the war provided.[8]

Lisa Ben, for instance, came out during the war. She left the small California town where she was raised, came to Los Angeles to find work, and lived in a women's boarding house. There she met for the first time lesbians who took her to gay bars and introduced her to other gay women. Donald Vining was a young man with lots of homosexual desire and few gay experiences. He moved to New York City during the war and worked at a large YMCA. His diary reveals numerous erotic adventures with soldiers, sailors, marines, and civilians at the Y where he worked, as well as at the men's residence club where he lived, and in parks, bars, and movie theaters. Many GIs stayed in port cities like New York, at YMCAs like the one where Vining worked. In his oral histories of gay men in San Francisco, focusing on the 1940s, Allan Bérubé has found that the war years were critical in the formation of a gay male *community* in the city. Places as different as San Jose, Denver, and Kansas City had their first gay bars in the 1940s. Even severe repression could have positive side effects. Pat Bond, a lesbian from Davenport, Iowa, joined the WACs during the 1940s. Caught in a purge of hundreds of lesbians from the WACs in the Pacific, she did not return to Iowa. She stayed in San Francisco and became part of a community of lesbians. How many other women and men had comparable experiences? How many other cities saw a rapid growth of lesbian and gay male communities?[9]

The gay men and women of the 1940s were pioneers. Their decisions to act on their desires formed the underpinnings of an urban subculture of gay men and lesbians. Throughout the 1950s and 1960s, the gay subculture grew and stabilized so that people coming out then could more easily find other gay women and men than in the past. Newspapers and magazines published articles describing gay male life. Literally hundreds of novels with lesbian themes were published.[10] Psychoanalysts complained about the new ease with which their gay male patients found sexual partners. And the gay subculture was not just to be found in the largest cities. Lesbian and gay male bars existed in places like Worcester, Massachusetts, and Buffalo, New York; in Columbia, South Carolina, and Des Moines, Iowa. Gay life in the 1950s and 1960s became a nationwide phenomenon. By the time of the Stonewall Riots in New York City in 1969—the event that ignited the gay liberation movement—our situation was hardly one of silence, invisibility, and isolation. A massive, grass-roots liberation movement could form almost overnight precisely because communities of lesbians and gay men existed.

Although gay community was a precondition for a mass movement, the oppression of lesbians and gay men was the force that propelled the movement into existence. As the subculture expanded and grew more visible in the post-World War II era, oppression by the state intensified, becoming more systematic and inclusive. The Right-wing scapegoated "sexual perverts" during the McCarthy era. Eisenhower imposed a total ban on the employment of gay women and men by the federal government and government contractors. Purges of lesbians and homosexuals from the military rose sharply. The FBI instituted widespread surveillance of gay meeting places and of lesbian and gay organizations, such as the Daughters of Bilitis and the Mattachine Society. The Post Office placed tracers on the correspondence of gay men and passed evidence of homosexual activity on to employers. Urban vice squads invaded private homes, made sweeps of lesbian and gay male bars, entrapped gay men in public places, and fomented local witch hunts. The danger involved in being gay rose even as the possibilities of being gay were enhanced. Gay liberation was a response to this contradiction.

Although lesbians and gay men won significant victories in the 1970s and opened up some safe social space in which to exist, we can hardly claim to have dealt a fatal blow to heterosexism and homophobia. One could even argue that the enforcement of gay oppression has merely changed locales, shifting somewhat from the state to the arena of extralegal violence in the form of increasingly open physical attacks on lesbians and gay men. And, as our movements have grown, they have generated a backlash that threatens to wipe out our gains. Significantly, this New Right opposition has taken shape as a "pro-family" movement. How is it that capitalism, whose structure made possible the emergence of a gay identity and the creation of urban gay communities, appears unable to accept gay men and lesbians in its midst? Why do heterosexism and homophobia appear so resistant to assault?

The answers, I think, can be found in the contradictory relationship of capitalism to the family. On the one hand, as I argued earlier, capitalism has gradually undermined the material basis of the nuclear family by taking away the economic functions that cemented the ties between family members. As more adults have been drawn into the free labor system, and as capital has expanded its sphere until it produces as commodities most goods and services we need for our survival, the forces that propelled men and women into families and kept them there have weakened. On the other hand the ideology of capitalist society has enshrined the family as the source of love, affection, and emotional security, the place where our need for stable, intimate human relationships is satisfied.

This elevation of the nuclear family to preeminence in the sphere of personal life is not accidental. Every society needs structures for reproduction and childbearing, but the possibilities are not limited to the nuclear family. Yet the privatized family fits well with capitalist relations of production. Capitalism has socialized production while maintaining that the products of socialized labor belong to the owners of private property. In many ways, childrearing has also been progressively socialized over the last two centuries, with schools, the media, peer groups, and employers taking over functions that once belonged to parents. Nevertheless, capitalist society maintains that reproduction and childrearing are private tasks, that children "belong" to parents, who exercise the rights of ownership. Ideologically, capitalism drives people into heterosexual families: each generation comes of age having internalized a heterosexist model of intimacy and personal relationships. Materially, capitalism weakens the bonds that once kept families together so that their members experience a growing instability in the place they have come to expect happiness and emotional security. Thus, while capitalism has knocked the material foundation away from family life, lesbians, gay men, and heterosexual feminists have become the scapegoats for the social instability of the system.

This analysis, if persuasive, has implications for us today. It can affect our perception of our identity, our formulation of political goals, and our decisions about strategy.

I have argued that lesbian and gay identity and communities are historically created, the result of a process of capitalist development that has spanned many generations. A corollary of this argument is that we are *not* a fixed social minority composed for all time of a certain percentage of the population. *There are more of us* than one hundred years ago, more of us than forty years ago. And there may very well be more gay men and lesbians in the future. Claims made by gays and nongays that sexual orientation is fixed at an early age, that large numbers of visible gay men and lesbians in society, the media, and the schools will have no influence on the sexual identities of the young, are wrong. Capitalism has created the material conditions for homosexual desire to express itself as a central component of some individuals' lives; now, our political movements are changing consciousness, creating the ideological conditions that make it easier for people to make that choice.

To be sure, this argument confirms the worst fears and most rabid rhetoric of our political opponents. But our response must be to challenge the underlying belief that homosexual relations are bad, a poor second choice. We must not slip into the opportunistic defense that society need not worry about tolerating us, since only homosexuals become homosexuals. At best, a minority group analysis and a civil rights strategy pertain to those of us who already are gay. It leaves today's youth—tomorrow's lesbians and gay men—to internalize heterosexist models that it can take a lifetime to expunge.

I have also argued that capitalism has led to the separation of sexuality from procreation. Human sexual desire need no longer be harnessed to repro-

ductive imperatives, to procreation; its expression has increasingly entered the realm of choice. Lesbians and homosexuals most clearly embody the potential of this split, since our gay relationships stand entirely outside a procreative framework. The acceptance of our erotic choices ultimately depends on the degree to which society is willing to affirm sexual expression as a form of play, positive and life-enhancing. Our movement may have begun as the struggle of a "minority," but what we should now be trying to "liberate" is an aspect of the personal lives of all people—sexual expression.[11]

Finally, I have suggested that the relationship between capitalism and the family is fundamentally contradictory. On the one hand, capitalism continually weakens the material foundation of family life, making it possible for individuals to live outside the family, and for a lesbian and gay male identity to develop. On the other, it needs to push men and women into families, at least long enough to reproduce the next generation of workers. The elevation of the family to ideological preeminence guarantees that capitalist society will reproduce not just children but heterosexism and homophobia. In the most profound sense, capitalism is the problem.[12]

How do we avoid remaining the scapegoats, the political victims of the social instability that capitalism generates? How can we take this contradictory relationship and use it to move toward liberation?

Gay men and lesbians exist on social terrain beyond the boundaries of the heterosexual nuclear family. Our communities have formed in that social space. Our survival and liberation depend on our ability to defend and expand that terrain, not just for ourselves but for everyone. That means, in part, support for issues that broaden the opportunities for living outside traditional heterosexual family units: issues like the availability of abortion and the ratification of the Equal Rights Amendment, affirmative action for people of color and for women, publicly funded daycare and other essential social services, decent welfare payments, full employment, the rights of young people -- in other words, programs and issues that provide a material basis for personal autonomy.

The rights of young people are especially critical. The acceptance of children as dependents, as belonging to parents, is so deeply ingrained that we can scarcely imagine what it would mean to treat them as autonomous human beings, particularly in the realm of sexual expression and choice. Yet until that happens, gay liberation will remain out of our reach.

But personal autonomy is only half the story. The instability of families and the sense of impermanence and insecurity that people are now experiencing in their personal relationships are real social problems that need to be addressed. We need political solutions for these difficulties of personal life. These solutions should not come in the form of a radical version of the pro-family position, of some left-wing proposals to strengthen the family. Socialists do not generally respond to the exploitation and economic inequality of industrial capitalism by calling for a return to the family farm and handicraft production. We recognize that the vastly increased productivity that capitalism has made possible by socializing production is one of its progressive features. Similarly, we should not be trying to turn back the clock to some mythic age of the happy family.

We do need, however, structures and programs that will help to dissolve the boundaries that isolate the family, particularly those that privatize childrearing. We need community- or worker-controlled daycare, housing where privacy and community coexist, neighborhood institutions—from medical clinics to performance centers—that enlarge the social unit where each of us has a secure place. As we create structures beyond the nuclear family that provide a sense of belonging, the family will wane in significance. Less and less will it seem to make or break our emotional security.

In this respect gay men and lesbians are well situated to play a special role. Already excluded from families as most of us are, we have had to create, for our survival, networks of support that do not depend on the bonds of blood or the license of the state, but that are freely chosen and nurtured. The building of an "affectional community" must be as much a part of our political movement as are campaigns for civil rights. In this way we may change the shape of personal relationships in a society grounded in equality and justice rather than exploration and oppression, a society where autonomy and security do not preclude each other but coexist.

## ENDNOTES

This essay is a revised version of a lecture given before several audiences in 1979 and 1980. I am grateful to the following groups for giving me a forum in which to talk and get feedback: the Baltimore Gay Alliance, the San Francisco Lesbian and Gay History Project, the organizers of Gay Awareness Week 1980 at San Jose State University and the University of California at Irvine, and the coordinators of the Student Affairs Lectures at the University of California at Irvine.

Lisa Duggan, Estelle Freedman, Jonathan Katz, Carole Vance, Paula Webster, Bert Hansen, Ann Snitow, Christine Stansell, and Sharon Thompson provided helpful criticisms of an earlier draft. I especially want to thank Allan Berube and Jonathan Katz for generously sharing with me their own research, and Amber Hollibaugh for many exciting hours of nonstop conversation about Marxism and sexuality.

1. I do not mean to suggest that no one has ever proposed that gay identity is a product of historical change. See, for instance: Mary McIntosh, "The Homosexual Role" Social Problems 16 (1968): 182–92: Jeffrey Weeks, Coming Out: Homosexual Politics in Britain (New York: Quartet Books, 1977). It is also implied in Michel Foucault, The History of Sexuality, vol. 1: An Introduction, tr. Robert Hurley (New York: Pantheon, 1978). However, this does represent a minority viewpoint and the works cited above have not specified how it is that capitalism as a system of production has allowed for the emergence of a gay male and lesbian identity. As an example of the "eternal homosexual" thesis, see John Boswell, Christianity, Social Tolerance, and Homosexuality (Chicago: University of Chicago Press, 1980), where "gay people" remains an unchanging social category through fifteen centuries of Mediterranean and Western European history.

2. See Eli Zaretsky, Capitalism, the Family, and Personal Life (New York: Harper and Row, 1976); and Paula Fass, The Damned and the Beautiful: American Youth in the 1920s (New York: Oxford University Press, 1977).

3. Robert F. Oaks, "'Things Fearful to Name': Sodomy and Buggery in Seventeenth Century New England," Journal of Social History 12 (1978): 268–81; J.R. Roberts, "The Case of Sarah Norman and Mary Hammond," Sinister Wisdom 24 (1980): 57–62; and Jonathan Katz, Gay American History (New York: Crowell, 1976), pp. 16–24, 568–71.

4. For the period from 1870 to 1940 see the documents in Katz; Gay American History, and in, Gay/Lesbian Almanac (New York: Crowell, 1983). Other sources include Allan Berube, "Lesbians and Gay Men in Early San Francisco: Notes Toward a Social History of Lesbians and Gay Men in America," unpublished paper, 1979; Vern Bullough and Bonnie Bullough, "Lesbianism in the 1920s and 1930s: A Newfound Study," Signs 2 (Summer 1977): 895–904.

5. On the medical model see Weeks, Coming Out, pp. 23–32. The impact of the medical model on the consciousness of men and women can be seen in Louis Hyde, ed., Rat and the Devil: The Journal Letters of F.O. Matthiessen and Russell Cheney (Hamden, Conn.: Archon, 1978), p. 47, and in the story of Lucille Hart in Katz, Gay American History, pp. 258–79. Radclyffe Hall's classic novel about lesbianism, The Well of Loneliness, published in 1928, was perhaps one of the most important vehicles for the popularization of the medical model.

6. See Alfred Kinsey et al., Sexual Behavior in the Human Male (Philadelphia: W.B. Saunders, 1948) and Sexual Behavior in the Human Female (Philadelphia: W.B. Saunders, 1953).

7. On black music, see "AC/DC Blues: Gay Jazz Reissues," Stash Records, ST–106 (1977) and Chris

Albertson, *Bessie* (New York: Stein and Day, 1974); on the persistence of kin networks in white ethnic communities see Judith Smith, "'Our Own Kind: Family and Community Networks in Providence," in *A Heritage of Her Own*, ed. Nancy F. Cott and Elizabeth H. Pleck (New York: Simon and Schuster, 1979), pp. 393–411; on differences between rural and urban male homoeroticism see Kinsey et al., *Sexual Behavior in the Human Male*, pp. 455–57, 630–31.

8. The argument and the information in this and the following paragraphs come from my book *Sexual Politics, Sexual Communities: The Making of a Homosexual Minority in the United States, 1940–1970* (Chicago: University of Chicago Press, 1983). I have also developed it with reference to San Francisco in "Gay Politics, Gay Community: San Francisco's Experience," *Socialist Review* 55 (January-February 1981): 77–104.

9. Donald Vining, *A Gay Diary*, 1933–1946 (New York: Pepys Press, 1979); "Pat Bond," in Nancy Adair and Casey Adair, Word Is Out (New, York: New Glide Publications, 1978), pp. 55–65; and Allan Berube, "Marching to a Different Drummer: Coming Out During World War II" a slide/talk presented at the annual meeting of the American Historical Association, December 1981, Los Angeles. A shorter version of Berube's presentation can be found in *The Advocate*, October 15, 1981, pp. 20–24.

10. On lesbian novels see *The Ladder*, March 1958, p. 18; February 1960, pp. 14–15; April 1961, pp. 12–13; February 1962, pp. 6–11; January 1963, pp. 6–13; February 1964, pp. 12–19; February 1965, pp. 19–23; March 1966, pp. 22–26; and April 1967, pp. 8–13. *The Ladder* was the magazine published by the Daughters of Bilitis.

11. This especially needs to be emphasized today. The 1980 annual conference of the National Organization for Women, for instance, passed a lesbian rights resolution that defined the issue as one of "discrimination based on affectional/sexual preference/orientation," and explicitly disassociated the issue from other questions of sexuality such as pornography, sadomasochism, public sex, and pederasty.

12. I do not mean to suggest that homophobia is "caused" by capitalism, or is to be found only in capitalist societies. Severe sanctions against homoeroticism can be found in European feudal society and in contemporary socialist countries. But my focus in this essay has been the emergence of a gay identity under capitalism, and the mechanisms specific to capitalism that made this possible and that reproduce homophobia as well.

## Study Questions

1. D'Emilio begins by identifying two myths about gay history. What are these myths and how does he argue against them?

2. D'Emilio discusses the institutionalization of heterosexism. Do you agree or disagree? Can you think of any examples of this institutionalization?

3. What is the relationship between capitalism and ideologies about the family?

4. How does capitalism allow for a distinction between private and public?

5. In this article, D'Emilio specifically separates sexual behavior from sexual identity. Why is this distinction important to him?

6. What kinds of directions does he want gay politics to go in? What do you think?

# RELIGION AND
# BELIEF SYSTEMS

# THE PROBLEM OF CREATION

## Vine Deloria, Jr.

*Vine Deloria, Jr. is a member of the Lakota (western or plains Sioux) nation from South Dakota. He has earned both a Master of Theology degree from the Lutheran School of Theology in Rock Island, Illinois and a Doctor of Laws from the University of Colorado. He has been executive director of the National Congress of American Indians and is currently a professor at the Center for Native American Studies at the University of Colorado.*

*This excerpt is a chapter from his book* God is Red: A Native View of Religion (1994). *In his work Deloria examines the impact of the Christian religion on Native Americans and on American society as a whole. He argues that certain Christian doctrines have contributed to the environmental crises facing us today.*

Indian tribal religions and Christianity differ considerably on numerous theological points, but a very major distinction that can be made between the two types of thinking concerns the idea of creation. Christianity has traditionally appeared to place its major emphasis on creation as a specific event while the Indian tribal religions could be said to consider creation as an ecosystem present in a definable place. In this distinction we have again the fundamental problem of whether we consider the reality of our experience as capable of being described in terms of space or time—as "what happened here" or "what happened then."

Both religions can be said to agree on the role and activity of a creator. Outside of that specific thing, there would appear to be little that the two views share. Tribal religions appear to be thereafter confronted with the question of the interrelationship of all things. Christians see creation as the beginning event of a linear time sequence in which a divine plan is worked out, the conclusion of the sequence being an act of destruction bringing the world to an end. The beginning and end of time are of no apparent concern for many tribal religions.

The act of creation is a singularly important event for the Christian. It describes the sequence in which the tangible features of human existence are brought into being, and although some sermons have made much of the element of light that appears in the creation account of Genesis and the prologue of St. John's Gospel, the similarity of the two books and their use of light do not appear to be of crucial importance in the doctrine of creation. For the Christian it would appear that the importance of the creation event is that it sets the scene for an understanding of the entrance of sin into the world.

Intimately tied with the actual creation event in the Christian theological scheme is the appearance of the first people, Adam and Eve. They are made after the image of God. It is important that this point be recognized, as it has affected popular conceptions held by Christians and seems to have some relevance to central theological doctrines. As the Genesis story relates that the first people were made after God's image, Christians, although not necessarily their Hebrew predecessors and Jewish contemporaries, have popularly conceived God as having a human form. That is to say, God looks like a man. Paintings represent Him generally as an old man, deriving perhaps from the old Hebrew conception of the "Ancient of Days."

The first distinction between Indian tribal religions and Christianity would appear to be in the manner in which deity is popularly conceived. The overwhelming majority of American Indian tribal religions refused to represent deity anthropomorphically.[1] To be sure many tribes used the term *grand-*

*father* when praying to God, but there was no effort to use that concept as the basis for a theological doctrine by which a series of complex relationships and related doctrines could be developed. While there was an acknowledgment that the Great Spirit has some resemblance to the role of a grandfather in the tribal society, there was no great demand to have a "personal relationship" with the Great Spirit in the same manner as popular Christianity has emphasized personal relationships with God.[2]

The difference between conceiving God as an anthropomorphic being and as an undefinable presence carries over into the distinction in the views of creation. Closely following the creation of the world in Christian theology comes the disobedience of man, Adam, in eating the forbidden fruit growing on a tree in the Garden of Eden.

In this act as recorded in Genesis, humankind "fell" from God's grace and was driven out of the garden by the angry God. The major thesis of the Christian religion is thus contained in its creation story, because it is for the redemption of man that the atonement of Jesus of Nazareth is considered to make sense.

With the fall of Adam the rest of nature also falls out of grace with God, Adam being a surrogate for the whole of creation. This particular point has been a very difficult problem for Christian theologians. While it adequately explains the entrance of evil into the world, just how it could occur in a universe conceived as perfect has been difficult for theologians to answer. St. Augustine preferred to think that God Himself had taken the form of the snake that, in the story, talked Eve into eating the forbidden fruit.[3] St. Augustine's solution has not generally been accepted, even though it appears to explain the logical sequence.

Perhaps of more importance are two aspects of the Christian doctrine of creation bearing directly on us today. One aspect is that the natural world is thereafter considered as corrupted, and it becomes theoretically beyond redemption. Many Christian theologians have attempted to avoid this conclusion, but it appears to have been a central, doctrine of the Christian religion during most of the Christian era. No less a thinker than Paul Tillich attempted to reconstruct the doctrine into more satisfying terms that would be acceptable to the modern world. In a rather complex analysis in his *Systematic Theology,* Tillich wrestled with the problem.

*Christianity must reject the idealistic separation of an innocent nature from guilty man. Such a rejection has become comparatively easy in our period because of the insights gained about the growth of man and his relation to nature within and outside himself. First, it can be shown that in the development of man there is no absolute discontinuity between animal bondage and human freedom. There are leaps between different stages, but there is also a slow and continuous transformation. It is impossible to say at which point in the process of natural evolution animal nature is replaced by the nature which, in our present experience we know as human, a nature which is qualitatively different from animal nature.[4]*

*And, as there are analogies to human freedom in nature, so there are also analogies to human good and evil in all parts of the universe. It is worthy of note that Isaiah prophesied peace in nature for the new eon, thereby showing that he would not call nature "innocent." Nor would the writer who, in Genesis, chapter 3, tells about the curse over the land declare nature innocent. Nor would Paul do so in Romans, chapter 8, when he speaks about the bondage to futility which is the fate of nature. Certainly, all these expressions are poetic-mythical. They could not be otherwise, since only poetic empathy opens the inner life of nature. Nevertheless, they are realistic in substance and certainly more realistic than the moral utopianism which confronts immoral man with innocent nature. Just as, within man, nature participates in the good and evil he does, so nature, outside man, shows analogies to man's good and evil doing. Man reaches into nature, as nature reaches into man. They participate in each other and cannot be separated from each other. This makes it possible and necessary to use the term "fallen world" and to apply the concept of existence (in contrast to essence) to the universe as well as man.[5]*

Like many other Christian thinkers, Tillich cannot break the relationship between humans and the natural world in which both share a corrupt nature. Even his dependence on evolution appears to be but a temporary nod to the reflections of science, because he stands ready to label the nature of people corrupt at whatever point in the evolutionary process a human being comparable in psychological processes to ourselves emerges.

Indian tribal religions also held a fundamental relationship between human beings and the rest of nature, but the conception was radically different. For many Indian tribal religions the whole of creation was good, and because the creation event did not include a "fall," the meaning of creation was that all parts of it functioned together to sustain it. Young Chief, a Cayuse, refused to sign the Treaty of Walla Walla because he felt the rest of the creation was not represented in the transaction.

*I wonder if the ground has anything to say? I wonder if the ground is listening to what is said? I wonder if the ground would come alive and what is on it? Though I hear what the ground says. The ground says, It is the Great Spirit that placed me here. The Great Spirit tells me to take care of the Indians, to feed them aright. The Great Spirit appointed the roots to feed the Indians on. The water says the same thing. The Great Spirit directs me, Feed the Indians well. The grass says the same thing, Feed the Indians well. The ground, water and grass say, the Great Spirit has given us our names. We have these names and hold these names. The ground says, The Great Spirit placed me here to produce all that grows on me, trees and fruit. The same way the ground says, It was from me man was made. The Great Spirit, in placing men on earth, desired them to take good care of the ground and to do each other no harm.* [6]

The similarity between Young Chief's conception of creation and the Genesis story is striking, but when one understands that the Genesis story is merely the starting place for theological doctrines of a rather abstract nature while Young Chief's beliefs are the practical articulations of his understanding of the relationship between the various entities of the creation, the difference becomes apparent. In the Indian tribal religions, man and the rest of creation are cooperative and respectful of the task set for them by the Great Spirit. In the Christian religion both are doomed from shortly after the creation event until the end of the world.

The second aspect of the Christian doctrine of creation that concerns us today is the idea that man receives domination over the rest of creation. Harvey Cox, a popular Protestant theologian, articulates rather precisely the attitude derived from this idea of Genesis: "Just after his creation man is given the crucial responsibility of naming the animals. He is their master and commander. It is his task to subdue the earth." [7] It is this attitude that has been adopted wholeheartedly by Western peoples in their economic exploitation of the earth. The creation becomes a mere object when this view is carried to its logical conclusion—a directly opposite result from that of the Indian religions.

Whether or not Christians wanted to carry their doctrine of human dominance as far as it has been carried, the fact remains that the modern world is just now beginning to identify the Christian religion's failure to show adequate concern for the planet as a major factor in our present ecological crisis. Among the earliest scholars to recognize the Christian responsibility for our present situation of ecological chaos was Lynn White, Jr., who gave a presentation titled "The Historical Roots of Our Ecological Crisis" in 1967 before the American Association for the Advancement of Science. White presented the same previously discussed criticism of Christian theology, emphasizing the tendency of the Christian religion to downgrade the natural world and its life forms in favor of the supernatural world of the Christian post judgment world of eternal life. [8] But he was extremely kind for a man who had his intellectual arguments honed so fine that he could have gone for the jugular vein had he wanted. White proposed that St. Francis be made the ecological saint, elevating Francis to a pedestal he did not deserve.

A number of Christians appear to be taking up White's thesis, and one frequently hears arguments that St. Francis represents the true Christian tradition. The Franciscan tradition is not a major theme of either Christian or Western thought however, and it would appear as if advocating St. Francis as a patron of the Christian attitude toward creation is not only historically late but uncertain. White's thesis proved unbearable to Dr. René Dubos, of New York City Rockefeller University, who gave a presentation in 1969 at the Smithsonian Institution in Washington, D.C., on "A Theology of the Earth." In it Dubos disclaimed White's charge against Christianity. Dubos contended that other societies had also created ecological disasters. He felt that Christianity was therefore not to be held accountable for the shortcomings of Westerners. He buttressed his thesis by references to St. Francis and, more particularly, to St. Benedict, founder of the Benedictine Order. Dubos found that the Benedictine work rules, which at that time included draining swamps and filling in lowlands, were more suitable for modern man than St. Francis' ideas of nature worship. [9]

Dubos' valiant defense of Christian thought lacks a number of substantial considerations. While other societies did create ecological disasters Dubos would be hard put to find in the theologies of other religions either a command to subdue the earth or the doctrine that the creation had "fallen" and shared responsibility for a man's direct violation of divine commands. There is also little evidence that destroying wetlands is ecologically sound, a fact the Bush administration ignores as it proposes to weaken federal law against tampering with the wetlands.

Further indications of Dubos's miscalculation of Christian sincerity—and evidence, perhaps, that Christians have not yet understood the complexity of the ecological crisis—were evidenced by the liturgy of the earth created by the National Cathedral in Washington, D.C. The confession used in this liturgy exemplifies the extent to which even concerned Christians have misunderstood the seriousness of the ecological problem.

> *Lord God, we say here in your presence and before each other that we, both individually and collectively, have not been good stewards of your earth. We have fouled the air, spoiled the water, poisoned the land, and by these acts have gravely hurt each other. We know now that this has and will cost us, and for these and all other sins we are truly sorry. Give us, we pray, the strength and guidance to undo what we have done and grant us inspiration for a new style of living.*[10]

Even in this attempt to bring religious sensitivity to the problem of ecological destruction, one can see the shallow understanding of the basis of the religious attitude that has been largely responsible for the crisis. No effort is made to begin a new theory of the meaning of creation. Indeed, the popular attitude of *stewardship* is invoked, as if it had no relationship to the cause of the ecological crisis whatsoever. Perhaps the best summary of the attitude inherent in the liturgy is, "Please, God, help us cut the cost, and we'll try to find a new life-style that won't be quite as destructive." The response is inadequate because it has not reached any fundamental problem; it is only a patch job over a serious theological problem. But at least in this liturgy we humans are bad and nature is good—a marked advance over earlier conceptions.

It would be difficult to find an Indian counterpart to this proposed liturgy. In the first place, traditional religions do not have the point-counterpoint recitation of beliefs that we find in the Near Eastern traditions. Singers and individual medicine people sing specific songs that compose the ceremony. While there is the expression of humility as humans stand before the higher spiritual powers, the Indian tradition lacks the admission of individual and corporate guilt which Near Eastern religions make the central part of their doctrines. The phrase "all my relatives" is frequently invoked by Indians performing ceremonies and this phrase is used to invite all other forms of life to participate as well as to inform them that the ceremony is being done on their behalf.

There is another, more serious problem involved in the Christian doctrine of creation. For most of the history of the Christian religion, people have been taught that the description of the event of creation as recorded in Genesis is historical fact. Although many Christian theologians have recognized that at best the Genesis account is mythological, it would be fair to conclude on the basis of what is known of the Christian religion that many Christian theologians and a substantial portion of the populace take the Genesis account as historical fact.

This issue has been a particularly difficult problem in the last century in America. The 1925 Scopes trial in Tennessee is perhaps the most publicized of the incidents marking the conflict between literal believers of Genesis and those who regard it symbolically, either as an analogy or as a mythological representation of a greater spiritual reality. Because people in a number of states, most prominently California, have petitioned their state legislatures to require the Genesis account of creation in the school curriculum indicates that the desire of many Christians is to believe in spite of the evidence, not because of it.[11]

Indian tribal religions have not had this problem. The tribes confront and interact with a particular land along with its life forms. The task or role of the tribal religions is to relate the community of people to each and every facet of creation as they have experienced it. Dr. Charles Eastman, the famous Sioux physician, relates a story in which the Indian viewpoint of the historicity of creation legends is illustrated.

> *A missionary once undertook to instruct a group of Indians in the truths of his holy religion. He told them of the creation of the earth in six days, and of the fall of our first parents by eating an apple.*

The courteous savages listened attentively, and, after thanking him one related in his turn a very ancient tradition concerning the origin of maize. But the missionary plainly showed his disgust and disbelief, indignantly saying:

> *"What I delivered to you were sacred truths, but this that you tell me is mere fable and falsehood!"*
> *"My Brother," gravely replied the offended Indian, "it seems that you have not been well grounded in the rules of civility. You saw that we, who practice these rules, believed your stories; why, then, do you refuse to credit ours?"*[12]

The difference in approach goes back to the basic consideration discussed earlier. If a religion is tied to a sense of time then everything forming a part of it must have some validity because it occurs within the temporal scheme. Christians are thus stuck with the assertion that the account of Genesis is an actual historical recording of the proceedings whether or not some of the theologians consent to such an interpretation.

Most important, perhaps, is that the major Christian theologian, the apostle Paul, made the historicity of the Genesis account cut the most important aspect of his theory of redemption. Paul's theory has formed a major part of the Christian teachings, and while some of the Christian sects would not agree with everything Paul wrote, he is not an insignificant figure in Christian history. Paul writes in Romans:

> *Sin, you see, was in the world long before the Law, though I suppose, technically speaking, it was not sin where there was no law to define it. Nevertheless death, the complement of sin, held sway over mankind from Adam to Moses, even over those whose sin was quite unlike Adam's.*
>
> *Adam, the first man, corresponds in some degree to the Man who was to come. But the gift of God through Christ is a very different matter from the 'account rendered' through the sin of Adam. For while as a result of one man's sin death by natural consequence became the common lot of men, it was by the generosity of God, the free giving of the grace of the One Man Jesus Christ, that the love of God overflowed for the benefit of all men.*
>
> *We see, then, that as one act of sin exposed the whole race of men to God's judgment and condemnation, so one Act of Perfect Righteousness presents all men freely acquitted in the sight of God. One man's disobedience placed all men under the threat of condemnation, but one Man's obedience has the power to present all men righteous before God.*[13]

It would appear that if the Genesis account of Adam's disobedience is not a historical event (that is, an event that can be located at some specific time and place on the planet), subsequent explanations of the meaning of the death of Jesus of Nazareth are without validity. We have no need to question the historical existence of Jesus of Nazareth, although that particular conflict has also consumed considerable energy in the past. But we cannot project from the historical reality of Jesus as a man existing in Palestine during the time of Augustus and his successors to affirm the historical existence of a man called Adam in a garden someplace in Asia Minor. Without the historical existence of Adam, we are powerless to explain the death of Jesus as a religious event of cosmic or historic significance.

At best we can conclude that the Christian doctrine of creation has serious shortcomings. It is too often considered not only as a historical event but also as the event that determined all other facts of our existence. It is bad enough to consider Genesis as a historical account in view of what we know today of the nature of our world. But when we consider that the Genesis account places nature and non-human life systems in a polarity with us, tinged with evil and without hope of redemption except at the last judgment, the whole idea appears intolerable.

There are, to be sure, numerous accounts from the various tribal religious traditions relating how an animal, bird, or reptile participated in a creation event. We have already seen how some Indian people regarded such stories and the lack of belief in the historical nature of the event. Within the tribal accounts is contained, perhaps, an even greater problem, the problem of origins of peoples and religions, which we shall take up in chapter 8. At no point, however, does any tribal religion insist that its particular version of the creation is an absolute historical recording of the creation event or that the story necessarily leads to conclusions about humankind's good or evil nature. At best the tribal stories recount how the people experience the creative process which continues today.

The relationships that serve to form the unity of nature are of vastly more importance to most tribal religions. The Indian is confronted with a bountiful earth in which all things and experiences have a role to play. The task of the tribal religion, if such a religion can be said to have a task, is to determine the proper relationship that the people of the tribe must have with other living things and to develop the self-discipline within the tribal community so that man acts harmoniously with other creatures. The world that he experiences is dominated by the presence of power, the manifestation of life energies, the whole life-flow of a creation. Recognition that the human being holds an important place in such a creation is tempered by the thought that they are dependent on everything in creation for their existence. There is not, therefore, that determined cause that Harvey Cox projects to subdue Earth and its living things. Instead the awareness of the meaning of life comes from observing how the various living things appear to mesh to provide a whole tapestry.

Each form of life has its own purposes, and there is no form of life that does not have a unique quality to its existence. Shooter, a Sioux Indian, explained the view held by many tribal religions in terms of individuality as follows:

*Animals and plants are taught by Wakan Tanka what they are to do. Wakan Tanka teaches the birds to make nests, yet the nests of all birds are not alike. Wakan Tanka gives them merely the outline. Some make better nests than others.*

*In the same way some animals are satisfied with very rough dwellings, while others make attractive places in which to live. Some animals also take better care of their young than others. The forest is the home of many birds and other animals, and the water is the home of fish and reptiles. All birds, even those of the same species, are not alike, and it is the same with animals, or human beings. The reason Wakan Tanka does not make two birds, or animals, or human beings exactly alike is because each is placed here by Wakan Tanka to be an independent individuality and to rely upon itself.*[14]

To recognize or admit differences, even among the species of life, does not require then that human beings create forces to forge to gain a sense of unity or homogeneity. To exist in a creation means that living is more than tolerance for other life forms—it is recognition that in differences there is the strength of creation and that this strength is a deliberate desire of the creator.

Tribal religions find a great affinity among species of living creatures, and it is at this point that the fellowship of life is a strong part of the Indian way. The Hopi, for example, revere not only the lands on which they live but also the animals with which they have a particular relationship. The dance for rain, which involves the use of reptiles in its ceremonies, holds a great fascination for whites, primarily because they have traditionally considered reptiles, particularly snakes, as their mortal enemy. In this attitude and its ensuing fascination, we may illustrate, perhaps, the alienation between the various life forms that Christian peoples read into the story in Genesis. This alienation is not present in tribal religions.

Behind the apparent kinship between animals, reptiles, birds, and human beings in the Indian way stands a great conception shared by a great majority of the tribes. Other living things are not regarded as insensitive species. Rather they are "people" in the same manner as the various tribes of human beings are people. The reason why the Hopi use live reptiles in their ceremony goes back to one of their folk heroes who lived with the snake people for a while and learned from them the secret of making rain for the crops.[15] It was a ceremony freely given by the snake people to the Hopi. In the same manner the Plains Indians considered the buffalo as a distinct people, the Northwest Coast Indians regarded the salmon as a people. Equality is thus

not simply a human attribute but recognition of the creatureness of all creation.

Very important in some of the tribal religions is the idea that humans can change into animals and birds and that other species can change into human beings. In this way species can communicate and learn from each other. Some of these tribal ideas have been classified as witchcraft by anthropologists, primarily because such phenomena occurring within the Western tradition would naturally be interpreted as evil and satanic. What Westerners miss is the rather logical implication of the unity of life. If all living things share a creator and a creation, is it not logical to suppose that all have the ability to relate to every part of the creation? How Westerners can believe in evolution and not see the logical consequences of this doctrine in the religious life of people is incomprehensible for many Indians. Recent studies with the dolphin and other animals may indicate that Westerners are beginning to shed superstitions and consider the possibility of having communication with other life forms.

But many tribal religions go even farther. The manifestation of power is simply not limited to mobile life forms. For some tribes the idea extends to plants, rocks, and natural features that Westerners consider inanimate. Walking Buffalo, a Stoney Indian from Canada, explained the nature of the unity of creation and the possibility of communicating with any aspect of creation when he remarked:

*Did you know that trees talk? Well they do. They talk to each other, and they'll talk to you if you listen. Trouble is, white people don't listen. They never learned to listen to the Indians, so I don't suppose they'll listen to other voices in nature. But I have learned a lot from trees; sometimes about the weather, sometimes about animals, sometimes about the Great Spirit.*[16]

Again we must return to the Christian idea of the complete alienation of nature and the world from human beings as a result of Adam's immediate postcreation act in determining the Western and Christian attitude toward nature. Some theologians have felt that man's alienation from nature is a natural result of his coming to a sense of self-consciousness, and people dealing with psychological problems seem to have a tendency to emphasize the sense in which humans are alienated from nature by promulgating theories of childhood fear based on the unfolding of natural growth processes. Even Western poets have been articulating the Western fears of "I, a stranger and afraid, in a world I never made."[17]

By and large there was no fear of nature in the Indian view of the world. Chief Luther Standing Bear remarked on the wildness of nature in his autobiography as follows:

*We did not think of the great open plains, the beautiful rolling hills, and winding streams with tangled growth as "wild." Only to the white men was nature a "wilderness" and only to him was the land "infested" with "wild" animals and "savage" people. To us it was tame. Earth was bountiful and we were surrounded with the blessings of the Great Mystery. Not until the hairy man from the east came and with brutal frenzy heaped injustices upon us and the families that we loved was it "wild" for us. When the very animals of the forest began fleeing from his approach, then it was that for us the "Wild West" began.[18]*

In some sense, part of the alienation of human beings from nature is caused by the action of humans against nature and not as the result of some obscure and corrupted relationship that came into being as a result of the human's inability to relate to the creator. It is doubtful if Western Christians can change their understanding of creation at this point in their existence. Their religion is firmly grounded in their escape from a fallen nature, and it is highly unlikely to suppose at this late date that they can find a reconciliation with nature while maintaining the remainder of their theological understanding of salvation.

We have one final aspect to cover with respect to the creation. Whether it be considered as a specific event or as a tenet of faith that need not be explained, certain empirical data exists today that was unavailable to humankind when tribal religions and Christianity originated. Modern science has in large part pierced the veil of nature. We are becoming increasingly aware of some of the basic processes of the universe to a much greater degree than was ever possible. With the explosion of the atomic bomb, humankind moved far beyond the speculations of earlier science and philosophy. It may be yet too soon to conclude that our science can determine everything about the universe. Yet the possibility of almost instantaneous destruction through misuse of science should indicate that we are close to describing in an approximate manner how the universe works.

Our further question, therefore, should concern how religious statements are to be made which are either broad enough or specific enough to parallel what we are discovering in nature through scientific experiments. Christian theology has traditionally fluctuated between the philosophical views of Plato and Aristotle. Occasionally some theologian will go to the ideas of Kant or Descartes to find a usable system to explain religious ideas in a scientific manner. Some theologians have gone so far as Alfred North Whitehead's view of the universe to find a way to describe religious ideas by the same basic form of articulation as followed in scientific circles and created *process theology.*

Which religious atmosphere, Christian or Indian, would appear to be more compatible with contemporary scientific ideas? The question may appear absurd, but it has the highest relevance for a number of reasons. First, we must determine on what basis religious ideas are considered to be mere superstitions and on what basis religious ideas are said to be either valid or possible in the world in which we live. Indian dances for rain, for example, were said to be mere superstitions; songs to make corn grow were said to be even more absurd. Today people can make plants grow with music, and the information on the power of sound vibrations is coming into its own. The principles used by Indian tribal religions have tremendous parallels with contemporary scientific experiments. This can be either coincidental, which is very difficult to prove, or it can all mean that the Indian tribal religions have been dealing at least partially with a fairly accurate conception of reality, which is difficult to argue convincingly to the scientific mind.

The second reason for determining compatibility of religion and science is to lay the groundwork for bringing our view of the world back to a unified whole, if at all possible. The competition between ministers and psychoanalysts, for example, to determine the sense of spiritual or psychological infirmity in effect promotes two distinct views of reality. Karl Heim relates in his incisive book, *Christian Faith and Natural Science,* as follows:

*In cases of physiologically conditioned depression, in which the religious responses are often involved, modern medicine applies with great success the electric shock treatment, passing an electric current through leads placed in contact with the patient's temples. These are often people who in their state of depression also despaired of their spiritual salvation, who were a prey in other words to what has been called in theological literature "certainty of damnation." And lo and behold! What the minister of religion had tried in vain to achieve with comforting exhortations and encouraging from the Bible and the Catechism has now been accomplished by the electric current! The depression has gone and the patient not only faces his life with new courage but is filled with a joyful belief in God's forgiveness and in his own eternal salvation.*[19]

It would thus appear that unless some new effort in the field of religion is made to provide a more realistic understanding of the universe there may be no solution to people's problems except manipulation by artificial means—the *1984* solution, that we all dread.

The Indian tribal religions would probably suggest that the unity of life is manifested in the existence of the tribal community for, it is only in the tribal community that any Indian religions— have relevance. James Jeans, in his book *Physics and Philosophy*, suggests that a profound view of nature lies in the concept of community:

> *Space and time are inhabited by distinct individuals, but when we pass beyond space and time, from the world of phenomena towards reality, individuality is replaced by community.*
> *When we pass beyond space and time, they (separate individuals) may perhaps form ingredients of a single continuous stream of life.*[20]

The parallel with conceptions of the basic unity of existence held by American Indian tribal religions is striking. If the nature of the world is a "single continuous stream of life," there is no reason to reject the idea that one can learn to hear the trees talk. It would be strange if they did not have the power to communicate.

R. G. Collingwood in the *Idea of Nature*, attempts to sketch out Alexander's cosmology as it applies to a whole continuant of life:

> *In the physical world before the emergence of life, there are already various orders of being, each consisting of a pattern composed of elements belonging to the order next below it: point-instants form a pattern which is the electron having physical qualities, electrons form an atom having higher chemical qualities of a new and higher order, molecules like those of air form wave-patterns having sonority and so on.*
> *Living organisms in their turn are patterns whose elements are bits of matter. In themselves these bits of matter are inorganic; it is only the whole pattern which they compose that is alive, and its life is the time-aspect or rhythmic process of its material parts.*[21]

We apparently have order and orders. We have time, but a time that is not a universal value, only a time internal to the complex relationships themselves. Above all, we have no disruption of the unity of the creation, only a variation on a general

theme. If there is anything to the similarity of things, it is that a sense of alienation does not exist at a significant level.

We even have the startling statement of Whitehead about the nature of God: "Not only does God [primordial nature] arrange the eternal objects; he also makes them available for use by other actual entities. This is God's function as the principle of concretion."[22] Again we are dealing with a complexity of relationships in which no particular object is given primacy over any other object or entity. Energy or spirit and the manifestation of purposeful order seem to characterize both modern scientific speculations and Indian beliefs.

What is important is not an attempt to show that either Indian tribal religions or Christianity prefigured contemporary science, modern concern for ecological sanity, or a startlingly new idea of what the universe might eventually be. Rather we should find what religious ideas can credibly encompass the broadest field of both our thoughts and actions. We must show that religious ideas are at least not tied to any particular view of man, nature, or the relationship of man and nature that is clearly in conflict with what we know. In this sense, American Indian tribal religions certainly appear to be more at home in the modern world than Christian ideas and Westerners' traditional religious concepts.

## ENDNOTES

1. Frederick Webb Hodge, *Handbook of American Indians North of Mexico*, vol. 11 (Lanham, Md.: Rowman & Littlefield, 1965), 366.

Something more needs to be said about anthropomorphic images. Medicine men report the existence of spiritual beings that have or take on human forms. Thus Black Elk and other Sioux mystics report that they have sat with the Six Grandfathers and counseled with them. Much more thought needs to be given to the question of whether the Indians had "gods" in the same sense as Near Eastern peoples. Was the mysterious power—*wakan tanka* in the Dakota language—the same as the spiritual power that provided life and was superior to any specific personifications of itself? If so, the ultimate representation of this sacred universe—and other sacred Indian universes—was without a deity in the Near Eastern sense.

2. For example, see Joseph Epes Brown, *The Sacred Pipe* (Norman: University of Oklahoma Press, 1953, 3–6) for Black Elk's discussion of this relationship.

3. In *The Confessions* by St. Augustine (London: Burns & Oates, 1954), the solution to the problem of evil seems to be completing the circle and suggesting that the deity himself is the tempter. Carl Jung also folds back the problem of good and evil to make a complete circle or circuit. The Plains Indian concept is considerably more complex and seems to involve the related question of the

structure of conscious life—the difference between probable future events and the realization of existing possibilities. It is too complicated to deal with here except to note that there is a considerable difference between the two traditions.

4. Paul Tillich, *Systematic Theology*, vol. 11 (Chicago: University of Chicago Press, 1957), 41–42.

5. *Ibid.*

In all of North American Indian traditions there is, of course no sense of "animal bondage" but rather relationships with the specific peoples of creation; hence, creation is ultimately good and humans are a part of it.

6. T. C. McLuhan, *Touch the Earth* (New York: Outerbridge & Dienstfrey, 1971), 8.

7. Harvey Cox, *The Secular City* (New York: Macmillan, 1965), 20.

8. Lynne White, Jr., "The Historical Roots of Our Ecological Crisis," paper. American Association for the Advancement of Science, 1967.

9. Rene Dubois' address is published as a small booklet by the Smithsonian Institution, Washington, D.C. It is singularly instructive, however, to note that filling in marshes and wetlands destroys habitat for a significant number of species and moves the planet toward ecological unbalance. Thus, White's thesis holds even when applied to what Christians believe is their most benign behavior.

10. Quoted in an article by Louis Cassels in the Religion Section, *The Denver Post* (March 7, 1970).

11. The Creation Science Research Center in San Diego has been extremely active in submitting textbooks to the State Board of Education which allege to give equal treatment to both Darwin and Genesis. There has apparently been some talk by people who support the center of forcing acceptance of their textbooks through court action. (Reported in *The Denver Post* Religion Section, August 12, 1972.)

12. Charles Eastman, *The Soul of the Indian* (Boston: Houghton Mifflin, 1911), 119–20.

13. Romans 5: 13–19

14. *Touch the Earth*, 18.

15. The ceremony is briefly described in *Book of the Hopi* by Frank Waters and Oswald White Bear Fredericks (Viking Press, 1963).

16. *Touch the Earth*, 23.

17. A. E. Houseman, *A Shropshire Lad* (New York: Grosset & Dunlap, 1932).

18. Luther Standing Bear, *Land of the Spotted Eagle* (Boston: Houghton Mifflin, 1933).

19. Karl Heim, *Christian Faith and Natural Science* (New York: Harper Torchbooks, 1957), 15.

20. James Jeans, *Physics and Philosophy*, Ann Arbor Papers (Ann Arbor: University of Michigan Press, 1958), 204.

21. R. G. Collingwood, *The Idea of Nature* (London: Oxford University Press, 1945), 160.

22. A. H. Johnson, *Whitehead's Theory of Reality* (New York: Dover Publications, 1962), 60–61.

**Study Questions**

1. According to Deloria, how do Christians characterize creation? How do Indians characterize creation?

2. What differences are there between the Indian and Christian conceptions of God?

3. What two aspects of the Christian doctrine of creation does Deloria highlight?

4. Why does Deloria claim that the nature of the Christian religion forces it to interpret the Genesis account as a historical fact?

5. How have many Christian theologians tied the creation account with other key Christian doctrines?

6. What is the "task" of tribal religion?

7. How do Christians and Indian religions understand human alienation from nature?

8. Deloria argues that tribal religions are more compatible with contemporary scientific ideas. Do you agree or disagree?

# 2

# CREATION LEGENDS OF THE HOPI

*Margot Edmonds and Ella E. Clark*

*Margot Edmonds (b. 1910) and the late Ella E. Clark (1896--1989) were collaborators on several books and anthologies of Native American legends. Margot Edmonds still lives and works in California. Ella E. Clark was a Washington State University professor of English. She visited many Indian reservations and wrote a number of books recounting American Indian legends. In 1979, Edmonds and Clark wrote* Sacagawea of the Lewis and Clark Expedition, *the story of the famous Shoshoni Indian woman who served as guide and interpreter for the previously mentioned explorers. Their last collaboration was* Voices in the Winds: Native American Legends, *a comprehensive anthology of the myths, stories and religious practices of Native tribes in North America.*

*The Hopi Indians reside mainly in northwestern Arizona, and their Native American culture is regarded as one of the best preserved. The Hopi creation legends are an integral part of their religious beliefs.*

## HOW THE HOPI INDIANS REACHED THEIR WORLD

When the world was new, the ancient people and the ancient creatures did not live on the top of the earth. They lived under it. All was darkness, all was blackness, above the earth as well as below it.

There were four worlds: this one on top of the earth, and below it three cave worlds, one below the other. None of the cave worlds was large enough for all the people and the creatures.

They increased so fast in the lowest cave world that they crowded it. They were poor and did not know where to turn in the blackness. When they moved, they jostled one another. The cave was filled with the filth of the people who lived in it. No one could turn to spit without spitting on another. No one could cast slime from his nose without its falling on someone else. The people filled the place with their complaints and with their expressions of disgust.

Some people said, "It is not good for us to live in this way."

"How can it be made better?" one man asked.

"Let it be tried and seen!" answered another.

Two Brothers, one older and one younger, spoke to the priest-chiefs of the people in the cave world, "Yes, let it be tried and seen. Then it shall be well. By our wills it shall be well."

The Two Brothers pierced the roofs of the caves and descended to the lowest world, where people lived. The Two Brothers sowed one plant after another, hoping that one of them would grow up to the opening through which they themselves had descended and yet would have the strength to bear the weight of men and creatures. These, the Two Brothers hoped, might climb up the plant into the second cave world. One of these plants was a cane.

At last, after many trials, the cane became so tall that it grew through the opening in the roof, and it was so strong that men could climb to its top. It was jointed so that it was like a ladder, easily ascended. Ever since then, the cane has grown in joints as we see it today along the Colorado River.

Up this cane many people and beings climbed to the second cave world. When a part of them had climbed out, they feared that that cave also would be too small. It was so dark that they could not see how large it was. So they shook the ladder and caused those who were coming up it to fall back. Then they pulled the ladder out. It is said that those who were left came out of the lowest cave later. They are our brothers west of us.

After a long time the second cave became filled with men and beings, as the first had been. Complaining and wrangling were heard as in the beginning. Again the cane was placed under the roof vent, and once more men and beings entered the upper cave world. Again, those who were slow to climb out were shaken back or left behind. Though larger, the third cave was as dark as the first and second. The Two Brothers found fire. Torches were set ablaze, and by their light men built their huts and kivas, or traveled from place to place.

While people and the beings lived in this third cave world, times of evil came to them. Women became so crazed that they neglected all things for the dance. They even forgot their babies. Wives became mixed with wives, so that husbands did not know their own from others. At that time there was no day, only night, black night. Throughout this night, women danced in the kivas (men's "club-houses"), ceasing only to sleep. So the fathers had to be the mothers of the little ones. When these little ones cried from hunger, the fathers carried them to the kivas, where the women were dancing. Hearing their cries, the mothers came and nursed them, and then went back to their dancing. Again the fathers took care of the children.

These troubles caused people to long for the light and to seek again an escape from darkness. They climbed to the fourth world, which was this world. But it too was in darkness, for the earth was closed in by the sky, just as the cave worlds had been closed in by their roofs. Men went from their lodges and worked by the light of torches and fires. They found the tracks of only one being, the single ruler of the unpeopled world, the tracks of Corpse Demon or Death. The people tried to follow these tracks, which led eastward. But the world was damp and dark, and people did not know what to do in the darkness. The waters seemed to surround them, and the tracks seemed to lead out into the waters.

With the people were five beings that had come forth with them from the cave worlds: Spider, Vulture, Swallow, Coyote, and Locust. The people and these beings consulted together, trying to think of some way of making light. Many, many attempts were made, but without success. Spider was asked to try first. She spun a mantle of pure white cotton. It gave some light but not enough. Spider therefore became our grandmother.

Then the people obtained and prepared a very white deerskin that had not been pierced in any spot. From this they made a shield case, which they painted with turquoise paint. It shed forth such brilliant light that it lighted the whole world. It made the light from the cotton mantle look faded. So the people sent the shield-light to the east, where it became the moon.

Down in the cave world Coyote had stolen a jar that was very heavy, so very heavy that he grew weary of carrying it. He decided to leave it behind, but he was curious to see what it contained. Now that light had taken the place of darkness, he opened the jar. From it many shining fragments and sparks flew out and upward, singeing his face as they passed him. That is why the coyote has a black face to this day. The shining fragments and sparks flew up to the sky and became stars.

By these lights the people found that the world was indeed very small and surrounded by waters, which made it damp. The people appealed to Vulture for help. He spread his wings and fanned the waters, which flowed away to the east and to the west until mountains began to appear.

Across the mountains the Two Brothers cut channels. Water rushed through the channels, and wore their courses deeper and deeper. Thus the great canyons and valleys of the world were formed. The waters have kept on flowing and flowing for ages. The world has grown drier, and continues to grow drier and drier.

Now that there was light, the people easily followed the tracks of Death eastward over the new land that was appearing. Hence Death is our greatest father and master. We followed his tracks when we left the cave worlds, and he was the only being that awaited us on the great world of waters where this world is now.

Although all the water had flowed away, the people found the earth soft and damp. That is why we can see today the tracks of men and of many strange creatures between the place toward the west and the place where we came from the cave world.

Since the days of the first people, the earth has been changed to stone, and all the tracks have been preserved as they were when they were first made.

When people had followed in the tracks of Corpse Demon but a short distance, they overtook him. Among them were two little girls. One was the beautiful daughter of a great priest. The other was the child of somebody-or-other. She was not beautiful, and she was jealous of the little beauty. With the aid of Corpse Demon the jealous girl caused the death of the other child. This was the first death.

When people saw that the girl slept and could not be awakened, that she grew cold and that her heart had stopped beating, her father, the great priest, grew angry.

"Who has caused my daughter to die?" he cried loudly.

But the people only looked at each other.

"I will make a ball of sacred meal," said the priest. "I will throw it into the air, and when it falls it will strike someone on the head. The one it will strike I shall know as the one whose magic and evil art have brought my tragedy upon me."

The priest made a ball of sacred flour and pollen and threw it into the air. When it fell, it struck the head of the jealous little girl, the daughter of somebody-or-other. Then the priest exclaimed, "So you have caused this thing! You have caused the death of my daughter."

He called a council of the people, and they tried the girl. They would have killed her if she had not cried for mercy and a little time. Then she begged the priest and his people to return to the hole they had all come out of and look down it.

"If you still wish to destroy me, after you have looked into the hole," she said, "I will die willingly."

So the people were persuaded to return to the hole leading from the cave world. When they looked down, they saw plains of beautiful flowers in a land of everlasting summer and fruitfulness. And they saw the beautiful little girl, the priest's daughter, wandering among the flowers. She was so happy that she paid no attention to the people. She seemed to have no desire to return to this world.

"Look!" said the girl who had caused her death. "Thus it shall be with all the children of men."

"When we die," the people said to each other, "we will return to the world we have come from. There we shall be happy. Why should we fear to die? Why should we resent death?"

So they did not kill the little girl. Her children became the powerful wizards and witches of the world, who increased in numbers as people increased. Her children still live and still have wonderful and dreadful powers.

Then the people journeyed still farther eastward. As they went, they discovered Locust in their midst.

"Where did you come from?" they asked.

"I came out with you and the other beings," he replied. "Why did you come with us on our journey?" they asked.

"So that I might be useful," replied Locust.

But the people, thinking that he could not be useful, said to him, "You must return to the place you came from."

But Locust would not obey them. Then the people became so angry at him that they ran arrows through him, even through his heart. All the blood oozed out of his body and he died. After a long time he came to life again and ran about, looking as he had looked before, except that he was black.

The people said to one another, "Locust lives again, although we have pierced him through and through. Now he shall indeed be useful and shall journey with us. Who besides Locust has this wonderful power of renewing his life? He must possess the medicine for the renewal of the lives of others. He shall become the medicine of mortal wounds and of war."

So today the locust is at first white, as was the first locust that came forth with the ancients. Like him, the locust dies, and after he has been dead a long time, he comes to life again — black. He is our father, too. Having his medicine, we are the greatest of men. The locust medicine still heals mortal wounds.

After the ancient people had journeyed a long distance, they became very hungry. In their hurry to get away from the lower cave world, they had forgotten to bring seed. After they had done much lamenting, the Spirit of Dew sent the Swallow back to bring the seed of corn and of other foods. When Swallow returned, the Spirit of Dew planted the seed in the ground and chanted prayers to it. Through the power of these prayers, the corn grew and ripened in a single day.

So for a long time, as the people continued their journey, they carried only enough seed for a day's planting. They depended upon the Spirit of Dew to raise for them in a single day an abundance of corn and other foods. To the Corn Clan, he gave this seed, and for a long time they were able to raise enough corn for their needs in a very short time.

But the powers of the witches and wizards made the time for raising foods grow longer and longer. Now, sometimes, our corn does not have time to grow old and ripen in the ear, and our other foods do not ripen. If it had not been for the children of the little girl whom the ancient people let live, even now we would not need to watch our cornfields whole summers through, and we would not have to carry heavy packs of food on our journeys.

As the ancient people traveled on, the children of the little girl tried their powers and caused other troubles. These mischief-makers stirred up people who had come out of the cave worlds before our ancients had come. They made war upon our ancients. The wars made it necessary for the people to build houses whenever they stopped traveling. They built their houses on high mountains reached by only one trail, or in caves with but one path leading to them, or in the sides of deep canyons. Only in such places could they sleep in peace.

Only a small number of people were able to climb up from their secret hiding places and emerge into the Fourth World. Legends reveal the Grand Canyon is where these people emerged. From there they began their search for the homes the Two Brothers intended for them.

These few were the Hopi Indians that now live on the Three Mesas of northeastern Arizona.

## HOW THE GREAT CHIEFS MADE THE MOON AND THE SUN

("Haliksai" was the usual beginning when a Hopi told a story in his own language. "Once upon a time" was his beginning when he told it in English.)

Once upon a time, when our people first came up from the villages of the underworld, there was no sun. There was no moon. They saw only dreary darkness and felt the coldness. They looked hard for firewood, but in the darkness they found little.

One day as they stumbled around, they saw a light in the distance. The Chief sent a messenger to see what caused the light. As the messenger approached it, he saw a small field containing corn, beans, squash, watermelons, and other foods. All around the field a great fire was burning. Nearby stood a straight, handsome man wearing around his neck a turquoise necklace of four strands. Turquoise pendants hung from his ears.

"Who are you?" the owner of the field asked the messenger.

"My people and I have come from the cave world below," the messenger replied. "And we suffer from the lack of light and the lack of food."

"My name is Skeleton," said the owner of the field. He showed the stranger the terrible mask he often wore and then gave him some food. "Now return to your people and guide them to my field."

When all the people had arrived, Skeleton began to give them food from his field. They marveled that, although the crops seemed so small, there was enough food for everyone. He gave them ears of corn for roasting; he gave them beans, squashes, and

watermelons. The people built fires for themselves and were happy.

Later, Skeleton helped them prepare fields of their own and to make fires around them. There they planted corn and soon harvested a good crop.

"Now we should move on," the people said. "We want to find the place where we will live always."

Away from the fires it was still dark. The Great Chiefs, at a council with Skeleton, decided to make a moon like the one they had enjoyed in the underworld.

They took a piece of well-prepared buffalo hide and cut from it a great circle. They stretched the circle tightly over a wooden hoop and then painted it carefully with white paint. When it was entirely dry, they mixed some black paint and painted, all around its edge, completing the picture of the moon. When all of this was done, they attached a stick to the disk and placed it on a large square of white cloth. Thus they made a symbol of the moon.

Then the Great Chiefs selected one of the young men and bade him stand on top of the moon symbol. They took up the cloth by its corners and began to swing it back and forth, higher and higher. As they were swinging it, they sang a magic song. Finally, with a mighty heave, they threw the moon disk upward. It continued to fly swiftly, upward and eastward.

As the people watched, they suddenly saw light in the eastern sky. The light became brighter and brighter. Surely something was burning there, they thought. Then something bright with light rose in the east. That was the moon!

Although the moon made it possible for the people to move around with less stumbling, its light was so dim that frequently the workers in the fields would cut up their food plants instead of the weeds. It was so cold that fires had to be kept burning around the fields all the time.

Again the Great Chiefs held a council with Skeleton, and again they decided that something better must be done.

This time, instead of taking a piece of buffalo hide, they took a piece of warm cloth that they themselves had woven while they were still in the underworld. They fashioned this as they had fashioned the disk of buffalo hide, except that this time they painted the face of the circle with a copper colored paint.

They painted eyes and a mouth on the disk and decorated the forehead with colors that the Great Chiefs decided upon according to their desires.

Around the circle, they then wove a ring of corn husks, arranged in a zig zag design. Around the circle of corn husks, they threaded a string of red hair from some animal. To the back of the disk, they fastened a small ring of corn husks. Through that ring they poked a circle of eagle feathers.

To the top of each eagle feather, the old Chief tied a few little red feathers taken from the top of the head of a small bird. On the forehead of the circle, he attached an abalone shell. Then the sun disk was completed.

Again the Great Chiefs chose a young man to stand on top of the disk, which they had placed on a large sheet. As they had done with the moon disk, they raised the cloth by holding its corners. Then they swung the sun disk back and forth, back and forth, again and again. With a mighty thrust, they threw the man and the disk far into the air. It traveled fast into the eastern sky and disappeared.

All the people watched it carefully. In a short time, they saw light in the east as if a great fire were burning. Soon the new sun rose and warmed the earth with its kindly rays.

Now with the moon to light the earth at night and the sun to light and warm it by day, all the people decided to pick up their provisions and go on. As they started, the White people took a trail that led them far to the south. The Hopis took one to the north, and the Pueblos took one midway between the two. Thus they wandered on to the places where they were to live.

The Hopis wandered a long time, building houses and planting crops until they reached the mesas where they now live. The ruins of the ancient villages are scattered to the very beginnings of the great river of the canyon—the Colorado.

**Study Questions**

1. In what ways do the Hopi stories differ from the biblical creation stories?

2. What aspects of Hopi society are revealed by these stories?

3. What do the two young girls represent?

4. Draw a diagram of the Hopi cosmology as described in these stories.

# 3

# THE SERMON ON THE FOUR NOBLE TRUTHS

## *Gautama Buddha*

*Siddhartha Gautauma (563 BCE - 483 BCE) was born in what is known today as Nepal, India to royal parents. As a prince, he lived a privileged existence while growing up. His father wanted him to be a successful politician, despite fotunetellers' predictions of great religious leadership. To safeguard his dissuasion from politics, efforts were made to shield him from the harsh realities of life: disease, old age and death. Nevertheless, while outside of the palace Siddhartha encountered a sick man, an old man, a corpse, and a monk - these encounters became known as the Passing Sights. Because he realized there were mysteries of life he knew nothing about, Siddhartha left home to seek answers for his questions.*

*Over the course of six years, Siddhartha renounced his life of luxury and traveled with five monks. Suffering from extreme hunger and deprivation, he decided that since he could find no answers in luxury or poverty there must be a middle path. He began to practice a less severe form of meditation and vowed that he would sit under a bodhi tree and not rise until he discovered the truth. He became the Buddha or "the enlightened one" after much temptation to give up. Following three days of intense meditations on his insights, he went to Deer Park on the outskirts of Benares and preached his first sermon to the five monks who had traveled with him before. Below is an excerpt from this sermon.*

Reverence to the Blessed One, the Holy One, the Fully Enlightened One!

Thus have I heard. The Blessed one was once staying at Benares, at the hermitage called Migadaya. The Blessed One addressed the company of the five monks, and said, "There are two extremes, O monks, which the man who has given up the world ought not to follow. The first is the habitual practice of those things whose attraction depends upon the passions. This is especially true of sensuality. It is a low and pagan way, unworthy, unprofitable, and fit only for the worldly minded. Second is the habitual practice of asceticism, which is painful, unworthy, and unprofitable.

"There is a middle path, O monks, avoiding these two extremes, discovered by the Tathagata. This path opens the eyes, bestows understanding, leads to peace of mind, to the higher wisdom, to full enlightenment, and to Nirvana! What is that middle path, O monks, avoiding these two extremes, discovered by the Tathagata, the path that opens the eyes, and bestows understanding, which leads to peace of mind, to the higher wisdom, to full enlightenment, to Nirvana? Truly, it is this Noble Eightfold Path, that is to say: Right views; Right aspirations; Right speech; Right conduct; Right livelihood; Right effort; Right mindfulness; and Right contemplation. . . .

"Now this, O monks, is the noble truth concerning suffering. Birth brings pain, decay is painful, disease is painful, death is painful. Union with the unpleasant is painful, painful is separation from the pleasant. Any craving that is unsatisfied, that too is painful. In brief, the five aggregates that spring from attachment, the conditions of individuality and their cause, are painful. This, O monks, is the noble truth concerning suffering.

"Now this, O monks, is the noble truth concerning the origin of suffering. Truly, it is the thirst or craving, causing the renewal of existence, accompanied by sensual delight, seeking satisfaction now here, now there. That is to say, it is the craving for the gratification of the passions, or the craving for a future life, or the craving for success in this present life. This, O monks, is the noble truth concerning the origin of suffering.

"Now this, O monks, is the noble truth concerning the destruction of suffering. Truly, it is the destruction, in which no passion remains, of this very thirst. It is the laying aside of, the getting rid of, the being free from, the harboring no longer of this thirst. This, O monks, is the noble truth concerning the destruction of suffering.

"Now this, O monks, is the noble truth concerning the way which leads to the destruction of sorrow. Truly, it is this Noble Eightfold Path. . . .

"As long, O monks, as my knowledge and insight were not quite clear regarding each of these Four Noble Truths in this triple order, in this twelve fold manner, I was uncertain whether I had attained to the full insight of that wisdom that is unsurpassed in the heavens or on earth, among the whole race of Samanas and Brahmins, or of gods or men. But as soon as my knowledge and insight were quite clear regarding each of these four noble truths, in this triple order, in this twelvefold manner, then I became certain that I had attained to the full insight of that wisdom that is unsurpassed in the heavens or on earth, among the whole race of Samanas and Brahmins, or of gods or men. Now this knowledge and this insight has arisen within me. The emancipation of my heart is immovable. This is my last existence. Now there will be no rebirth for me!"

Thus spoke the Blessed One. The five monks praised the words of the Blessed One and were glad. When the discourse had been uttered, there arose within the venerable Kondanna the eye of truth, spotless, and without a stain. He saw that whatever has an origin also inherently must end.

And when the royal chariot wheel of the truth had been set rolling by the Blessed One, the gods of the earth . . . the attendant gods of the four great kings . . . and the gods in the highest heaven gave forth a shout. They said, "In Benares, at the hermitage of the Migadaya, the supreme wheel of the empire of Truth has been set rolling by the Blessed One. That wheel can never be turned back by any Samana or Brahmin, nor by any god, nor by any Brahma or Mara, not by anyone in the universe!" In an instant, a second, a moment, this sound went up to the world of Brahma. This great ten-thousand-world-system quaked and trembled and was shaken violently. An immeasurably bright light appeared in the universe, beyond even the power of the gods!

## Study Questions

1. What do the four noble truths teach?

2. Who is the Blessed One?

3. How does the theology of the Blessed One avoid both sensuality and asceticism?

4. How does he characterize sensuality? Asceticism?

5. Does this philosophy compare to Socrates' "Everything in moderation"?

# THE KORAN

## As Revealed To Muhammad

*Muhammed (570-632) was born in the city of Mecca. By the time he reached the age of six, both of his parents died. He lived with his grandfather and his uncle until he married and began his own household. In 610 Muhammed received a revelation through the angel Gabriel while he was meditating. His revelation instructed him to call people to Islam, that is, to surrender to the will of God. Islam has grown into a major religious tradition throughout the world despite its humble origins.*

*The Koran, the sacred writings of Islam, are known as the standing miracle; although associated with Muhammed, they are not his work, as he was illiterate. These are the words of Allah (the name of God) that were recited to Muhammed ("Koran" literally means recitation). As is the case with most oral traditions, those who heard the recitation memorized them. Eventually the words were recorded on leaves and stones in fragments. Twenty years after Muhammed's death, the fragments were compiled into a final collection. The original Arabic text remains one of the great religious documents of the world and retains its beauty and value as a literary text. This section is taken from the Suras, or chapters 47,55, and 56.*

God will bring to nothing the deeds of those who disbelieve and debar others from His path. As for the faithful who do good works and believe in what is revealed to Muhammad—which is the Truth from their Lord—He will forgive them their sins and ennoble their state.

This, because the unbelievers follow falsehood, while the faithful follow the truth from their Lord.

Thus God lays down for mankind their rules of conduct.

When you meet the unbelievers in the battlefield strike off their heads and, when you have laid them low, bind your captives firmly. Then grant them their freedom or take ransom from them, until War shall lay down her burdens.

Thus shall you do. Had God willed, He could Himself have punished them; but He has ordained it thus that He might test you, the one by the other.

As for those who are slain in the cause of God, He will not allow their works to perish. He will vouchsafe them guidance and ennoble their state; He will admit them to the Paradise He has made known to them.

Believers, if you help God, God will help you and make you strong. But the unbelievers shall be consigned to perdition. He will bring their deeds to nothing. Because they have abhorred His revelations, He will frustrate their works.

Have they never journeyed through the land and seen what was the end of those who have gone before them? God destroyed them utterly. A similar fate awaits the unbelievers, because God is the protector of the faithful: because the unbelievers have no protector.

God will admit those who embrace the true Faith and do good works to gardens watered by running streams. The unbelievers take their fill of pleasure and eat as cattle eat: but the Fire shall be their home.

How many cities were mightier than your own city, which has cast you out![1] We destroyed them all, and there was none to help them.

Can he who follows the guidance of his Lord be compared to him who is led by his desires and whose foul deeds seem fair to him?

This is the Paradise which the righteous have been promised. Therein shall flow rivers of water undefiled, and rivers of milk for ever fresh; rivers of wine delectable to those that drink it, and rivers of clarified honey. They shall eat therein of every fruit and receive forgiveness from their Lord. Is this like the lot of those who shall abide in Hell for ever, and drink scalding water which will tear their bowels?

Some of them indeed listen to you, but no sooner do they leave your presence than they ask those endowed with knowledge: 'What did he say just now?' Such are the men whose hearts are sealed by God, and who follow their base desires.

As for those who follow the right path, He will increase their guidance and show them the way to righteousness.

Are they waiting for the Hour of Doom to overtake them unawares? Its portents have already come. How else will they be warned when it does overtake them?

Know that there is no deity but God. Implore Him to forgive your sins and to forgive the true believers, men and women. God knows your busy haunts and resting places.

## THE MERCIFUL[2]

*In the Name of God, the Compassionate, the Merciful*

It is the Merciful who has taught the Koran.

He created man and taught him articulate speech. The sun and the moon pursue their ordered course. The plants and the trees bow down in adoration.

He raised the heaven on high and set the balance of all things, that you might not transgress that balance. Give just weight and full measure.

He laid the earth for His creatures, with all its fruits and blossom—bearing palm, chaff—covered grain and scented herbs. Which of your Lord's blessings would you[3] deny?

He created man from potter's clay, and the jinn from smokeless fire. Which of your Lord's blessings would you deny?

The Lord of the two easts[4] is He, and the Lord, of the two wests. Which of your Lord's blessings would you deny?

He has let loose the two oceans:[5] they meet one another. Yet between them stands a barrier which they cannot overrun. Which of your Lord's blessings would you deny?

Pearls and corals come from both. Which of your Lord's blessings would you deny?

His are the ships that sail like mountains upon the ocean. Which of your Lord's blessings would you deny?

All that lives on earth is doomed to die. But the face of your Lord will abide for ever, in all its majesty and glory. Which of your Lord's blessings would you deny?

All who dwell in heaven and earth entreat Him. Each day some mighty task engages Him. Which of your Lord's blessings would you deny?

Mankind and jinn, We shall surely find the time to judge you! Which of your Lord's blessings would you deny?

Mankind and jinn, if you have power to penetrate the confines of heaven and earth, then penetrate them! But this you shall not do except with Our own authority. Which of your Lord's blessings would you deny?

Flames of fire shall be lashed at you, and molten brass. There shall be none to help you. Which of your Lord's blessings would you deny?

When the sky splits asunder, and reddens like a rose or stained leather, which of your Lord's blessings would you deny?, on that day neither man nor jinn will be asked about his sins. Which of your Lord's blessings would you deny?

The wrongdoers will be known by their looks; they shall be seized by their forelocks and their feet. Which of your Lord's blessings would you deny?

That is the Hell which the sinners deny. They shall wander between fire and water fiercely seething. Which of your Lord's blessings would you deny?

But for those that fear the majesty of their Lord there are two gardens (which of your Lord's blessings would you deny?) planted with shady trees. Which of your Lord's blessings would you deny?

Each is watered by a flowing spring. Which of your Lord's blessings would you deny?

Each bears every kind of fruit in pairs. Which of your Lord's blessings would you deny?

They shall recline on couches lined with thick brocade, and within reach will hang the fruits of both gardens. Which of your Lord's blessings would you deny?

Therein are bashful virgins whom neither man nor jinn will have touched before. Which of your Lord's blessings would you deny?

Virgins as fair as corals and rubies. Which of your Lord's blessings would you deny?

Shall the reward of goodness be anything but good? Which of your Lord's blessings would you deny?

And beside these there shall be two other gardens (which of your Lord's blessings would you deny?) of darkest green. Which of your Lord's blessings would you deny?

A gushing fountain shall flow in each. Which of your Lord's blessings would you deny?

Each planted with fruit-trees, the palm and the pomegranate. Which of your Lord's blessings would you deny?

In each there shall be virgins chaste and fair. Which of your Lord's blessings would you deny?

Dark-eyed virgins sheltered in their tents (which of your Lord's blessings would you deny?) whom neither man nor jinn will have touched before. Which of your Lord's blessings would you deny?

They shall recline on green cushions and fine carpets. Which of your Lord's blessings would you deny?

Blessed be the name of your Lord, the Lord of majesty and glory!

## THAT WHICH IS COMING

*In the Name of God, the Compassionate, the Merciful*

When that which is coming comes—and no soul shall then deny its coming—some shall be abased and others exalted.

When the earth shakes and quivers, and the mountains crumble away and scatter abroad into fine dust, you shall be divided into three multitudes: those on the right (blessed shall be those on the right); those on the left (damned shall be those on the left); and those to the fore (foremost shall be those). Such are they that shall be brought near to their Lord in the gardens of delight: a whole multitude from the men of old, but only a few from the latter generations.

They shall recline on jewelled couches face to face, and there shall wait on them immortal youths with bowls and ewers and a cup of purest wine (that will neither pain their heads nor take away their reason); with fruits of their own choice and flesh of fowls that they relish. And theirs shall be the dark-eyed hours, chaste as hidden pearls: a guerdon for their deeds.

There they shall hear no idle talk, no sinful speech, but only the greeting, 'Peace! Peace!'

Those on the right hand—happy shall be those on the right hand! They shall recline on couches raised on high in the shade of thornless sidrs and clusters of talh[6] amidst gushing waters and abundant fruits, unforbidden, neverending.

We created the houris and made them virgins, loving companions for those on the right hand: a multitude from the men of old, and a multitude from the latter generations.

As for those on the left hand (wretched shall be those on the left hand!) they shall dwell amidst scorching winds and seething water: in the shade of pitch-black smoke, neither cool nor refreshing. For they have lived in comfort and persisted in the heinous sin,[7] saying: 'When we are once dead and turned to dust and bones, shall we be raised to life? And our forefathers, too?'

Say: 'Those of old, and those of the present age, shall be brought together on an appointed day. As for you sinners who deny the truth, you shall eat the fruit of the Zaqqum tree and fill your bellies with it. You shall drink scalding water: yet you shall drink it as the thirsty camel drinks.'

Such shall be their fare on the Day of Reckoning.

*We* created you: will you not believe then in Our power?

Behold the semen you discharge: did you create it, or We?

It was We that ordained death among you. Nothing can hinder Us from replacing you by others like yourselves or transforming you into beings you know nothing of.

You surely know of the First Creation. Why, then, do you not reflect? Consider the seeds you grow. Is it you that give them growth, or We? If We pleased, We could turn your harvest into chaff, so that, filled with wonderment, you would exclaim: 'We are laden with debts! Surely we have been robbed?'

Consider the water which you drink. Was it you that poured it from the cloud, or We? If We pleased, We could turn it bitter. Why, then, do you not give thanks?

Observe the fire which you light. Is it you that create its wood, or We? We have made it a reminder for man, and for the traveller a comfort.

Praise, then, the name of your Lord, the Supreme One. I swear by the shelter of the stars (a mighty oath, if you but knew it) that this is a glorious Koran, safeguarded in a book which none may touch except the purified; a revelation from the Lord of the Universe.

Would you scorn a scripture such as this, and earn your daily bread by denying it?

When under your very eyes a man's soul is about to leave him (We are nearer to him than you, although you cannot see Us), why do you not restore it, if you will not be judged hereafter? Answer this, if what you say be true!

Thus, if he is favoured, his lot will be repose and plenty, and a garden of delight. If he is one of those on the right hand, he will be greeted with, 'Peace be to you!' by those on the right hand.

But if he is an erring disbeliever, his welcome will be scalding water, and he will burn in Hell.

This is the indubitable truth. Praise, then, the name of your Lord, the Supreme One.

## ENDNOTES

1. Muhammad
2. Compare this chapter with Psalm 126 of the Old Testament.
3. The promoun is in the dual number, the words being addressed to mankind and the jinn. This refrain is repeated no fewer than 31 times.
4. The points at which the sun rises in summer and in winter.
5. Salt water and fresh water.
6. Probably the banana fruit.
7. Idolatry

**Study Question**

1. Consider what the Koran reveals about the Islamic conception of God. Do you see similarities between the Islamic understanding of God and your own?

# THE TEACHINGS OF PTAHHOTEP

## The Oldest Book In The World (2575 BCE-2551 BCE)

Then the majesty of the Diety said to Ptahhotep, go ahead and instruct him in the Ancient Wisdom. May he become a model for the children of the great. May obedience enter into him, and may he be devoted to the one who speaks to him. No one is born wise.

And so begins the formulation of Mdw Ntr, *good speech*, to be spoken by the Prince, the Count, God's beloved, the eldest son of the Pharoah, the son of his body, Mayor of the City and Vizier, Ptahhotep, instructs the ignorant in the knowledge and in the standards of *good speech*. It will profit those who hear. It will be a loss to those who transgress. Ptahhotep began to speak to "Pharoah's son" (to posterity).

1. Do not be proud and arrogant with your knowledge. Consult and converse with the ignorant and the wise, for the limits of art are not reached. No artist ever possesses that perfection to which he should aspire. *Good speech* is more hidden than greenstone (emeralds), yet it may be found among maids at the grindstones.

2. If you meet a disputant in the heat of action, one who is more powerful than you, simply fold your arms and bend your back. To confront him will not make him agree with you. Pay no attention to his *evil speech*. If you do not confront him while he is raging, people will call him an ignoramus. Your self-control will be the match for his evil utterances.

3. If you meet a disputant in action, one who is your equal, one who is on your level, you will overcome him by being silent while he is speaking evilly. There will be much talk among those who hear and your name will be held in high regard among the great.

4. If you meet a disputant in action who is a poor man and who is not your equal do not attack him because he is weak. Leave him alone. He will confound himself. Do not answer him just so that you can relieve your own heart. Do not vent yourself against your opponent. Wretched is he who injures a poor man. If you ignore him listeners will wish to do what you want. You will beat him through their reproof.

5. If you are a man who leads, a man who controls the affairs of many, then seek the most perfect way of performing your responsibility so that your conduct will be blameless. Great is Maat (truth, justice and righteousness). It is everlasting. Maat has been unchanged since the time of Osiris. To create obstacles to the following of laws, is to open a way to a condition of violence. The transgressor of laws is punished, although the greedy person over-looks this. Baseness may obtain riches, yet crime never lands its wares on the shore. In the end only Maat lasts. Man says, "Maat is my father's ground."

6. Do not scheme against people. God will punish accordingly. If a man says, "I shall live by scheming," he will lack bread for his mouth. If a man says, "I will be rich," he will have to say, "My cleverness has trapped me." If he says, "I will trap for myself" he will not be able to say, "I trapped for my profit." If a man says, "I will rob someone," he will end by being given to a stranger. People's schemes do not prevail. God's command is what prevails. Therefore, live in the midst of peace. What God gives comes by itself.

7. If you are one among guests at the table of a person who is more powerful than you, take

what that person gives just as it is set before you. Look at what is before you. Don't stare at your host. Don't speak to him until he asks. One does not know what may displease him. Speak when he has spoken to you. Then your words will please the heart. The man who has plenty of the means of existence acts as his Ka commands. He will give food to those who he favors. It is the Ka that makes his hand stretch out. The great man gives to the chosen man, thus eating is under the direction of God. It is a fool who complains about it.

8.   If you are a person of trust sent by one great person to another great person, be careful to stick to the essence of the message that you were asked to transmit. Give the message exactly as he gave it to you. Guard against provocative speech which makes one great person angry with another. Just keep to the truth. Do not exceed it. However, even though there may have been an out-burst in the message you should not repeat it. Do not malign anyone, great or small, the Ka abhors it.

9.   If you plow and if there is growth in your field and God lets it prosper in your hand, don't boast to your neighbor. One has great respect for the silent person. A person of character is a person of wealth. If that person robs, he or she is like a crocodile in the middle of the waters. If God gives you children, don't impose on one who has no children. Neither should you decry or brag about having your own children, for there is many a father who has grief and many a mother with children who is less content than another. It is the lonely whom God nurtures while the family man prays for a follower.

10. If you are poor, then serve a person of worth so that your conduct may be well with God. Do not bring up the fact that he was once poor. Do not be arrogant towards him just because you know about his former state. Respect him now for his position of authority. As for fortune, it obeys its own law and that is her will. It is God's gift. It is God who makes him worthy and who protects him while he sleeps, or who can turn away from him.

11. Follow your heart as long as you live. Do more than is required of you. Do not shorten the time of "follow the heart," since that offends the Ka. Don't waste time on daily cares over and beyond providing for your household. When wealth finally comes, then follow your heart. Wealth does no good if you are glum.

12. If you are a wise man, train up a son who will be pleasing to God. If he is, straight and takes after you, take good care of him. Do everything that is good for him. He is your son, your Ka begot him. Don't withdraw your heart from him. But an offspring can make trouble. If your son strays and neglects your council and disobeys all that is said, with his mouth spouting evil speech, then punish him for all his talk. God will hate him who crosses you. His guilt was determined in the womb. He who God makes boatless cannot cross the water.

13. If you are a guard in the storehouse, stand or sit rather than leave your post and trespass into someone else's place. Follow this rule from the first. Never leave your post, even when fatigued. Keen is the face to him who enters announced, and spacious is the seat of him who has been asked to come in. The storehouse has fixed rules. All behavior is strictly by the rule. Only a God can penetrate the secure warehouse where the rules are followed, even by privileged persons.

14. If you are among the people then gain your supporters by building trust. The trusted man is one who does not speak the first thing that comes to mind; and he will become a leader. A man of means has a good name, and his face is benign. People will praise him even without his knowledge. On the other hand, he whose heart obeys his belly asks for contempt of himself in the place of love. His heart is naked. His body is unanointed. The great hearted is a gift of God. He who is ruled by his appetite belongs to the enemy.

15. Report the thing that you were commissioned to report without error. Give your advice in the high council. If you are fluent in your speech, it will not be hard for you to report. Nor will anyone say of you, "who is he to know this?" As to the authorities, their affairs will fail if they punish you for speaking truth. They should be silent upon hearing the report that you have rendered as you have been told.

16. If you are a man who leads, a man whose authority reaches widely, then you should do perfect things, those which posterity will remember. Don't listen to the words of flatterers or to words that puff you up with pride and vanity.

17. If you are a person who judges, listen carefully to the speech of one who pleads. Don't stop the person from telling you everything that they had planned to tell you. A person in distress wants to pour out his or her heart, even more than they want their case to be won. If you are one who stops a person who is

pleading, that person will say "why does he reject my plea?" Of course not all that one pleads for can be granted, but a good hearing soothes the heart. The means for getting a true and clear explanation is to listen with kindness.

18. If you want friendship to endure in the house that you enter, the house of a master, of a brother or of a friend, then in whatever place you enter beware of approaching the women there. Unhappy is the place where this is done. Unwelcome is he who intrudes on them. A thousand men are turned away from their good because of a short moment that is like a dream, and then that moment is followed by death that comes from having known that dream. Anyone who encourages you to take advantage of the situation gives you poor advice. When you go to do it, your heart says no. If you are one who fails through the lust of women, then no affair of yours can prosper.

19. If you want to have perfect conduct, to be free from every evil, then above all guard against the vice of greed. Greed is a grievous sickness that has no cure. There is no treatment for it. It embroils fathers, mothers and the brothers of the mother. It parts the wife from the husband. Greed is a compound of all the evils it is a bundle of all hateful things. That person endures whose rule is rightness, who walks a straight line, for that person will leave a legacy by such behavior. On the other hand, the greedy has no tomb.

20. Do not be greedy in the division of things. Do not covet more than your share. Don't be greedy towards your relatives. A mild person has a greater claim than the harsh one. Poor is the person who forgets his relatives. He is deprived of their company. Even a little bit of what is wanted will turn a quarreler into a friendly person.

21. When you prosper and establish your home, love your wife with ardor. Then fill her belly and clothe her back. Caress her. Give her ointments to soothe her body. Fulfill her wishes for as long as you live. She is a fertile field for her husband. Do not be brutal. Good manners will influence her better than force. Do not contend with her in the courts. Keep her from the need to resort to outside powers. Her eye is her storm when she gazes. It is by such treatment that she will be compelled to stay in your house.

22. Help your friends with things that you have, for you have these things by the grace of God. If you fail to help your friends, one will say you have a selfish Ka. One plans for tomorrow, but you do not know what tomorrow will bring. The right soul is the soul by which one is sustained. If you do praiseworthy deeds your friends will say, "welcome" in your time of need.

**Study Question**

1. Ptahhotep is similar to which other writers/ articles in literature of maat teachings?

# 6

# THE GOSPEL OF THOMAS* (200CE)

*The Gospel of Thomas (200 CE), the writing of which is credited to Didymus Judas Thomas, the twin brother of Jesus, contains adages which are recognizable as being attributed to Jesus. it does also contain some elements of gnosticism such as the importance of Light towards which all humans should strive from this corruptible world. Some of the sayings have other meanings and so they are called the secret sayings of the living Jesus.*

These are the secret sayings which the living Jesus spoke and which Didymos Judas Thomas wrote down.

(1) And he said, "Whoever finds the interpretation of these sayings will not experience death."

(2) Jesus said, "Let him who seeks continue seeking until he finds. When he finds, he will become troubled. When he becomes troubled, he will be astonished, and he will rule over the All."

(3) Jesus said, "If those who lead you say to you, 'See, the Kingdom is in the sky,' then the birds of the sky will precede you. If they say to you, 'It is in the sea' then the fish will precede you. Rather, the Kingdom is inside of you, and it is outside of you. When you come to know yourselves, then you will become known, and you will realize that it is you who are the sons of the living Father. But if you will not know yourselves, you dwell in poverty and it is you who are that poverty."

(4) Jesus said, "The man old in days will not hesitate to ask a small child seven days old about the place of life, and he will live. For many who are first will become last, and they will become one and the same."

(5) Jesus said, "Recognize what is in your sight, and that which is hidden from you will become plain to you. For there is nothing hidden which will not become manifest."

(6) His disciples questioned him and said to him, "Do you want us to fast? How shall we pray? Shall we give alms? What diet shall we observe?"

Jesus said, "Do not tell lies, and do not do what you hate, for all things are plain in the sight of Heaven. For nothing hidden will not become manifest, and nothing covered will remain without being uncovered."

(7) Jesus said, "Blessed is the lion which becomes man when consumed by man; and cursed is the man whom the lion consumes, and the lion becomes man."

(8) And he said, "The man is like a wise fisherman who cast his net into the sea and drew it up from the sea full of small fish. Among them the wise fisherman found a fine large fish. He threw all the small fish back into the sea and chose the large fish without difficulty. Whoever has ears to hear, let him hear."

(9) Jesus said, "Now the sower went out, took a handful of seeds, and scattered them. Some fell on the road; the birds came and gathered them up. Others fell on rock, did not take root in the soil, and did not produce ears. And others fell on thorns; they choked the seeds and worms ate them. And others fell on the good soil and produced good fruit: it bore sixty per measure and a hundred and twenty per measure."

(10) Jesus said, "I have cast fire upon the world, and see, I am guarding it until it blazes."

(11) Jesus said, "This heaven will pass away, and the one above it will pass away. The dead are not alive, and the living will not die. In the

* II32, 10–51, 28. From James M. Robinson, ed., *The Nag Hammadi Library* (San Francisco: Harper & Row, 1977), pp. 118–130.

days when you consumed what is dead, you made it what is alive. When you come to dwell in the light, what will you do? On the day when you were one you became two. But when you become two, what will you do?"

(12) The disciples said to Jesus, "We know that you will depart from us. Who is to be our leader?"

Jesus said to them, "Wherever you are, you are to go to James the righteous, for whose sake heaven and earth came into being."

(13) Jesus said to his disciples, "Compare me to someone and tell me whom I am like."

Simon Peter said to him, "You are like a righteous angel."

Matthew said to him, "You are like a wise philosopher."

Thomas said to him, "Master, my mouth is wholly incapable of saying whom you are like."

Jesus said, "I am not your master. Because you have drunk, you have become intoxicated from the bubbling spring which I have measured out."

And he took him and withdrew and told him three things. When Thomas returned to his companions, they asked him, "What did Jesus say to you?"

Thomas said to them, "If I tell you one of the things which he told me, you will pick up stones and throw them at me; a fire will come out of the stones and burn you up."

(14) Jesus said to them, "If you fast, you will give rise to sin for yourselves; and if you pray, you will be condemned; and if you give alms, you will do harm to your spirits. When you go into any land and walk about in the districts, if they receive you, eat what they will set before you, and heal the sick among them. For what goes into your mouth will not defile you, but that which issues from your mouth—it is that which will defile you."

(15) Jesus said, "When you see one who was not born of woman, prostrate yourselves on your faces and worship him. That one is your Father."

(16) Jesus said, "Men think, perhaps, that it is peace which I have come to cast upon the world. They do not know that it is dissension which I have come to cast upon the earth: fire, sword, and war. For there will be five in a house: three will be against two, and two against three, the father against the son, and the son against the father. And they will stand solitary."

(17) Jesus said, "I shall give you what no eye has seen and what no ear has heard and what no hand has touched and what has never occurred to the human mind."

(18) The disciples said to Jesus, "Tell us how our end will be."

Jesus said, "Have you discovered, then, the beginning, that you look for the end? For where the beginning is, there will the end be. Blessed is he who will take his place in the beginning; he will know the end and will not experience death."

(19) Jesus said, "Blessed is he who came into being before he came into being. If you become my disciples and listen to my words, these stones will minister to you. For there are five trees for you in Paradise which remain undisturbed summer and winter and whose leaves do not fall. Whoever becomes acquainted with them will not experience death."

(20) The disciples said to Jesus, "Tell us what the Kingdom of Heaven is like."

He said to them, "It is like a mustard seed, the smallest of all seeds. But when it falls on tilled soil, it produces a great plant and becomes a shelter for birds of the sky."

(21) Mary said to Jesus, "Whom are your disciples like?"

He said, "They are like children who have settled in a field which is not theirs. When the owners of the field come, they will say, 'Let us have back our field.'

They will undress in their presence in order to let them have back their field and to give it back to them. Therefore I say to you, if the owner of a house knows that the thief is coming, he will begin his vigil before he comes and will not let him dig through into his house of his domain to carry away his goods. You, then, be on your guard against the world. Arm yourselves with great strength lest the robbers find a way to come to you, for the difficulty which you expect will surely materialize. Let there be among you a man of understanding. When the grain ripened, he came quickly with his sickle in his hand and reaped it. Whoever has ears to hear, let him hear."

(22) Jesus saw infants being suckled. He said to his disciples, "These infants being suckled are like those who enter the Kingdom."

They said to him, "Shall we then, as children, enter the Kingdom?"

Jesus said to them, "When you make the two one, and when you make the inside like the outside and the outside like the inside, and the above like the below, and when you make the male and the female one and the same, so that the male not be male nor the female; and when you fashion eyes in place of an eye, and a hand in place of a hand, and a foot in place of a foot, and a likeness in place of a likeness; then will you enter the Kingdom."

(23) Jesus said, "I shall choose you, one out of a thousand, and two out of ten thousand, and they shall stand as a single one."

(24) His disciples said to him, "Show us the place where you are, since it is necessary for us to seek it."

He said to them, "Whoever has ears, let him hear. There is light within a man of light, and he lights up the whole world. If he (or: it) does not shine, he is darkness."

(25) Jesus said, "Love your brother like your soul, guard him like the pupil of your eye."

(26) Jesus said, "You see the mote in your brother's eye, but you do not see the beam in your own eye. When you cast the beam out of your own eye, then you will see clearly to cast the mote from your brother's eye."

(27) Jesus said, "If you do not fast as regards the world, you will not find the Kingdom. If you do not observe the Sabbath as a Sabbath you will not see the Father."

(28) Jesus said, "I took my place in the midst of the world, and I appeared to them in flesh. I found all of them intoxicated; I found none of them thirsty. And my soul became afflicted for the sons of men, because they are blind in their hearts and do not have sight; for empty they came into the world, and empty too they seek to leave the world. But for the moment they are intoxicated. When they shake off their wine, then they will repent."

(29) Jesus said, "If the flesh came into being because of spirit, it is a wonder. But if spirit came into being because of the body, it is a wonder of wonders. Indeed, I am amazed at how this great wealth has made its home in this poverty."

(30) Jesus said, "Where there are three gods, they are gods. Where there are two or one, I am with him."

(31) Jesus said, "No prophet is accepted in his own village; no physician heals those who know him."

(32) Jesus said, "A city being built on a high mountain and fortified cannot fall, nor can it be hidden."

(33) Jesus said, "Preach from your housetops that which you will hear in your ear and in the other ear. For no one lights a lamp and puts it under a bushel, nor does he put it in a hidden place, but rather he sets it on a lampstand so that everyone who enters and leaves will see its light."

# OGBÈWÓNRÍ (OGBÈWÚNLÉ)

*This example of a statement from Ifa Divination Literary Corpus, which is thousands of years old, is accompanied at the left margin by the marks which would be made by the Ifa priest on the divination board in the sand laid on it. These marks result from the throwing of the cowrie shells which are duly mixed around in the hands of the priest before the actual divination takes place. The marks are then consulted to reveal which verses of the lengthy, complicated Ifa literary corpus would be applicable to the situation under consultation. Sometimes Ifa pronouncements are indirect and not easy to understand, particularly from a European standpoint. On the other hand, the exchange is quite practical, because the diviner tells the supplicant exactly what to sacrifice to which Orisa in order to accomplish the cure or objective sought. Once it has been noted that the sacrifice is acceptable to the Orisa, it is made and when it has been determined that it is accepted, which may involve another throwing of the cowrie shells, the food, if it is such, is then consumed by the supplicant and the priest, if he so desires. The soup mentioned in the next to last line is a stew in Western terms, not a thin broth. Pounded yams are like mashed white potatoes; they are not made from the orange yams we have here in the United States.*

Odù Ogbèwónrí speaks of the choice between potential husbands or wives. Sacrifice assures the correct choice and a successful partnership.

*Western observation*: A great time to capitalize, both in business and emotionally, on the client's attractiveness to others.

Ajaje li o dífá fún Koko
nigbi koko nlo se obirin Apata, nlo se obirin Akuro.
Wón niki ki ó rú: Eyelé mérin ati aso onikoko mérin.
Ó gbó ó rú.
Wón ni: Akuro ni'le Koko.
Bi orí ba san Koko o san Akuro.

Ajaje divined Ifá for Koko
when she was contemplating marrying either Apata or Akuro.
She was advised to offer a sacrifice of four pigeons and four pieces of knotted cloth.
She heard and heeded the advice.
She was told that Akuro would be her favored husband.
If Koko was successful, Akuro would be successful too.

Okiti-bamba-tiipekun-opopo li o dífá f'Olófin.
A niki o wa rúbo ki Ogbè le ye oriwiwon lodo re.
Akuko mèta, àràbà iyán méta
ati obe ni ebo.
Ó gbó ó rú.
Okiti-bamba-tiipekun-opopo divined Ifá for Olófin.

He was advised to offer sacrifice so that Ogbè would give him good companions.
Three cocks, three bowls of pounded yam,

and soup should be offered.
He performed the sacrifice.


**Study Question**

1. What system of religious divination does this
selection belong to? What people and culture
does it come from? How is the ritual
performed?

# THE BLACK SAINT MAURICE OF MAGDEBURG AND ITS HISTORICAL BACKGROUND

## *Gude Suckale-Redlefsen*

*The Black St. Maurice is well known in Europe in such places named after him as St. Moritz, the ski resort in Switzerland, by his name but not always for his ethnicity. The thirteenth century statue of him in the Magdeburg Cathedral in Germany is but one piece of evidence of the African presence in Early Europe. He is fully covered in chain mail but his face, with his African features, establishes his identity. He was an early Christian saint; Maurice followed the images of the African king, Balthazar, who worshipped at the birth of the Christ Child, and the Biblical Queen of Sheba as models which were already popular in Europe. These three figures were echoed by black virgins and other presentations of Africans in European art and life. Clearly Maurice was a powerful personage as the commander of the Theban Legion. He is honored as a Christian saint complete with legend, statuary and saints day.*

## DESCRIPTION OF THE STATUE IN MAGDEBURG

The thirteenth-century statue of St. Maurice in the cathedral of Magdeburg is the oldest surviving representation of the saint as a Moor and thus the starting point for this study (cat. no. 1). Even to spectators of today the stone figure still conveys the impression of the living presence of a warrior of unshakable constancy and watchful determination. How is this effect achieved?

The height chosen by the stonemason for his figure, approximately 150 centimeters, corresponds roughly to the actual height of a thirteenth-century knight. The armor, firmly encasing the body, faithfully reproduces the fashion of the period: a cloth undertunic hanging down in deep folds, a mail hauberk, and a sturdy leather surcoat shaped like an apron at both back and front. We see the seams, rivet heads, reinforcement straps, and buckles for fastening the garment and belt at the back. But these functional details, of practical importance when donning arms, are subordinated to the design of the armor as a whole, which is based on large cubic forms. The mufflers covering the hands are of chain mail. Likewise the head covering, the coif, which terminates in broad flaps on the chest and back.

In addition to the long sword in its sheath and the dagger belted above the right hip, the saint bore a lance in his right hand and a large shield reaching down to the ground in his left. Lance and shield and the lower part of the legs are now missing from the figure.

The arms and armor, and also the bearing, give St. Maurice the aspect of a warrior who might just be about to enter into battle. Calm, resolute, and confident, the saint gazes into the distance. He has nothing in common with the many contemporary depictions of knights in which the aristocratic pose is stressed and the arms are no more than a mere attribute of chivalry.

The relatively small opening in the closely fitting mail coif was sufficient for the Magdeburg sculptor to produce a convincing characterization of St. Maurice as an African. The facial proportions show typical alterations in comparison with European physiognomy. The thick lips are large and prominent. The broad, rounded contours of the nose are recognizable although the tip has been broken off.

The African features are emphasized by the surviving remains of the old polychromy. The skin is colored bluish black, the lips are red, and the dark pupils stand out clearly against the white of the eyeballs. The golden chain mail of the coif serves, in turn, to form a sharp contrast with the dark face. Today the traces of color are no more than a mere shadow of their original intensity, so that the figure should be imagined as painted entirely in bright colors.

A twofold function was fulfilled by painting the figure. The coloring of the face was faithful to nature and served to evoke the impression of a living presence. The choice of gold for the hauberk, on the other hand, did not correspond to reality, iron chain mail usually being represented in bluish gray tones. The precious gold framed the dark countenance with the radiance of a halo and heightened the religious connotations of the otherwise realistically depicted figure. A comparable purpose was served by the canopies and tabernaclelike structures which often surmount Gothic statues and doubtless also existed in the case of the figure of St. Maurice.

The background of this astonishing figure may be more easily understood in the light of a general survey touching upon the representation of blacks in the Middle Ages (especially in Germany), the cult of St. Maurice, and the historical situation in Magdeburg.

## THE LEGEND OF ST. MAURICE AND THE THEBAN LEGION

According to the legend Maurice was a high-ranking Roman officer in command of a legion in the third century A.D. His legion was levied in the Thebaid—not, as his name might suggest, in antique Mauretania (North Africa, Morocco). The province with its capital city of Thebes was situated on the Upper Nile in the farthest corner of the Roman Empire, today the boundary between Egypt and the Sudan. At that time the emperor Diocletian (284–305) ruled the Roman Empire in association with his coemperor Maximian. As supreme commander of the Roman army in Gaul, Maximian had crossed the Alps on a campaign against the insurgent Gauls.

Having pitched his camp at Octodurum (now Martigny in Switzerland), he exhorted his subordinates to participate in a sacrifice to the Roman gods before the battle. Maurice and his legionaries, who were baptized Christians, attempted to avoid blasphemy by moving their camp to Agaunum (Saint-Maurice-en-Valais). On being ordered to return to the rest of the army and perform the heathen sacrifice, Maurice refused. Maximian retaliated by having every tenth man of the Theban Legion executed. But even in the face of this signal example the faith of the Theban Legion remained unshaken. A second bloody punitive expedition met with just as little success. Maurice and his officers Exuperius, Candidus, and Innocent attested their willingness to submit to discipline in military affairs but continued to insist on their right to freedom of religion. Thereupon Maximian, who demanded unconditional obedience, had the rest of the Theban Legion massacred together with their commander Maurice.

The question of the historical nucleus of the legend has been much debated by hagiographers. The authenticity of the martyrdom of the Theban Legion in this place is generally doubted today. But this question has no bearing on the iconographic problems discussed in this study. The cult of St. Maurice existed—whether based on fact or not—and for us it suffices that for many centuries people believed in him and sought his protection. His saint's day is 22 September.

**Study Question**

1. In what way is Maurice considered a saint? How has he become a saint? Why is it important that we know about St. Maurice?

# THE BLACK MANIFESTO

*James Forman (1929- )*

*James Forman was born in Chicago and grew up in Mississippi with his grandmother. He was a radical leader within the Civil Rights Movement in the 1960s. He spearheaded voter registration drives in the South and served as executive director of SNCC (Student Nonviolent Coordinating Committee 1964-1966) and the chairperson of UPAC, the Unemployment and Poverty Action Council. In April of 1969 James Forman presented this essay to the National Black Economic Development conference. A few days later he interrupted the Sunday morning worship service of the prestigious Riverside Church in New York City and read this manifesto. For the most part the reaction was one of outrage. However, a few thousands of dollars were collected from some churches and religious institutions.*

*Some of Forman's works are* The Making of Black Revolutionaries *(1972) and* The Political Thoughts of James Forman *(1970).*

## INTRODUCTION: TOTAL CONTROL AS THE ONLY SOLUTION TO THE ECONOMIC PROBLEMS OF BLACK PEOPLE

Brothers and Sisters:

We have come from all over the country burning with anger and despair not only with the miserable economic plight of our people but fully aware that the racism on which the Western World was built dominates our lives. There can be no separation of the problems of racism from the problems of our economic, political, and cultural degradation. To any black man, this is clear.

But there are still some of our people who are clinging to the rhetoric of the Negro, and we must separate ourselves from these Negroes who go around the country promoting all types of schemes for black capitalism.

Ironically, some of the most militant Black Nationalists, as they call themselves, have been the first to jump on the bandwagon of black capitalism. They are pimps, black power pimps and fraudulent leaders, and the people must be educated to understand that any black man or Negro who is advocating a perpetuation of capitalism inside the United States is in fact seeking not only his ultimate destruction and death but is contributing to the continuous exploitation of black people all around the world. For it is the power of the United States Government, this racist, imperialist government, that is choking the life of all people around the world.

We are an African people. We sit back and watch the Jews in this country make Israel a powerful conservative state in the Middle East, but we are concerned actively about the plight of our brothers in Africa. We are the most advanced technological group of black people in the world, and there are many skills that could be offered to Africa. At the same time, it must be publicly stated that many African leaders are in disarray themselves, having been duped into following the lines as laid out by the western imperialist governments. Africans themselves succumbed to and are victims of the power of the United States. For instance, during the summer of 1967, as the representatives of SNCC, Howard Moore and I traveled extensively in Tanzania and Zambia. We talked to high, very high, government officials. We told them there were many black people in the United States who were willing to come and work in Africa. All these government officials, who were part of the leadership in their respective governments, said they wanted us to send as many skilled people as we could contact. But this program never came into fruition, and we do not know the exact reasons, for I assure you that we talked and were committed to making this a successful program. It is our guess that the United States put the squeeze on these countries, for such a program directed by SNCC would have been too dangerous to the international prestige of the United States. It is also possible that some of the wild statements by some black leaders frightened the Africans.

In Africa today there is a great suspicion of black people in this country. This is a correct suspicion since most of the Negroes who have left the States for work in Africa usually work for the Central Intelligence Agency (CIA) or the State Department. But the respect for us as a people continues to mount, and the day will come when we can return to our homeland as brothers and sisters. But we should not think of going back to Africa today, for we are located in a strategic position. We live inside the United States, which is the most barbaric country in the world, and we have a chance to help bring this government down.

Time is short, and we do not have much time and it is time we stop mincing words. Caution is fine, but no oppressed people ever gained their liberation until they were ready to fight, to use whatever means necessary, including the use of force and power of the gun to bring down the colonizer.

We have heard the rhetoric, but we have not heard the rhetoric which says that black people in this country must understand that we are the vanguard force. We shall liberate all the people in the United States, and we will be instrumental in the liberation of colored people the world around. We must understand this point very clearly so that we are not trapped into diversionary and reactionary movements. Any class analysis of the United States shows very clearly that black people are the most oppressed group of people inside the United States. We have suffered the most from racism and exploitation, cultural degradation and lack of political power. It follows from the laws of revolution that the most oppressed will make the revolution, but we are not talking about just making the revolution. All the parties on the left who consider themselves revolutionary will say that blacks are the vanguard, but we are saying that not only are we the vanguard, but we must assume leadership, total control, and we must exercise the humanity which is inherent in us. We are the most humane people within the United States. We have suffered and we understand suffering. Our hearts go out to the Vietnamese, for we know what it is to suffer under the domination of racist America. Our hearts, our soul and all the compassion we can mount go out to our brothers in Africa, Santo Domingo, Latin America and Asia who are being tricked by the power structure of the United States which is dominating the world today. These ruthless, barbaric men have systematically tried to kill all people and organizations opposed to

its imperialism. We no longer can just get by with the use of the word "capitalism" to describe the United States, for it is an imperial power sending money, missionaries and the army throughout the world to protect this government and the few rich whites who control it. General Motors and all the major auto industries are operating in South Africa, yet the white dominated leadership of the United Auto Workers sees no relationship to the exploitation of the black people in South Africa and the exploitation of black people in the United States. If they understand it, they certainly do not put it into practice, which is the actual test. We as black people must be concerned with the total conditions of all black people in the world.

But while we talk of revolution, which will be an armed confrontation and long years of sustained guerrilla warfare inside this country, we must also talk of the type of world we want to live in. We must commit ourselves to a society where the total means of production are taken from the rich and placed into the hands of the state for the welfare of all the people. This is what we mean when we say total control. And we mean that black people who have suffered the most from exploitation and racism must move to protect their black interest by assuming leadership inside of the United States of everything that exists. The time has ceased when we are second in command and the white boy stands on top. This is especially true of the welfare agencies in this country, but it is not enough to say that a black man is on top. He must be committed to building the new society, to taking the wealth away from the rich people, such as General Motors, Ford, Chrysler, the DuPonts, the Rockefellers, the Mellons, and all the other rich white exploiters and racists who run this world.

Where do we begin? We have already started. We started the moment we were brought to this country. In fact, we started on the shores of Africa, for we have always resisted attempts to make us slaves, and now we must resist the attempts to make us capitalists. It is in the financial interest of the United States to make us capitalist, for this will be the same line as that of integration into the mainstream of American life. Therefore, brothers and sisters, there is no need to fall into the trap that we have to get an ideology, we HAVE an ideology. Our fight is against racism, capitalism and imperialism, and we are dedicated to building a socialist society inside the United States where the total means of production and distribution are in the hands of the State, and that must be led by black people, by revolutionary blacks who are concerned about the total humanity of this world. And, therefore, we obviously are different from some of those who seek a black nation in the United States, for there is no way for that nation to be viable if in fact the United

States remains in the hands of white racists. Then too, let us deal with some arguments that we should share power with whites. We say that there must be a revolutionary black vanguard, and that white people in this country must be willing to accept black leadership, for that is the only protection that black people have to protect ourselves from racism rising again in this country.

Racism in the United States is so pervasive in the mentality of whites that only an armed, well-disciplined, black-controlled government can insure the stamping out of racism in this country. And that is why we plead with black people not to be talking about a few crumbs, a few thousand dollars for this cooperative, or a thousand dollars which splits black people into fighting over the dollar. That is the intention of the government. We say . . . think in terms of total control of the United States. Prepare ourselves to seize state power. Do not hedge, for time is short, and all around the world the forces of liberation are directing their attacks against the United States. It is a powerful country, but that power is not greater than that of black people. We work the chief industries in this country, and could cripple the economy while the brothers fought guerrilla warfare in the streets. This will take some long range planning, but whether it happens in a thousand years is of no consequence. It cannot happen unless we start. How then is all of this related to this conference?

First of all, this conference is called by a set of religious people, Christians, who have been involved in the exploitation and rape of black people since the country was founded. The missionary goes hand in hand with the power of the states. We must begin seizing power wherever we are, and we must say to the planners of this conference that you are no longer in charge. We the people who have assembled here thank you for getting us here, but we are going to assume power over the conference and determine from this moment, on the direction which we want it to go. We are not saying that the conference was planned badly. The staff of the conference has worked hard and his done a magnificent job in bringing all of us together, and we must include them in the new membership which must surface from this point on. The conference is now the property of the people who are assembled here. This we proclaim as fact and not rhetoric, and there are demands that we are going to make and we insist that the planners of this conference help us implement them.

We maintain we have the revolutionary right to do this. We have the same rights, if you will, as the Christians had in going into Africa and raping our Motherland and bringing us away from our continent of peace and into this hostile and alien environment where we have been living in perpetual warfare since 1619.

Our seizure of power at this confernce is based on a program, and our program is contained in the following Manifesto:

We the black people assembled in Detroit, Michigan, for the National Black Economic Development Conference are fully aware that we have been forced to come together because racist white America has exploited our resources, our minds, our bodies, our labor. For centuries we have been forced to live as colonized people inside the United States, victimized by the most vicious, racist system in the world. We have helped to build the most industrial country in the world.

We are therefore demanding of the white Christian churches and Jewish synagogues, which are part and parcel of the system of capitalism, that they begin to pay reparations to black people in this country. We are demanding $500,000,000 from the Christian white churches and the Jewish synagogues. This total comes to 15 dollars per nigger. This is a low estimate for we maintain there are probably more than 30,000,000 black people in this country. $15 a nigger is not a large sum of money and we know that the churches and synagogues have a tremendous wealth, and its membership, white America, has profited and still exploits black people. We are also not unaware that the exploitation of colored peoples around the world is aided and abetted by the white Christian churches and synagogues. This demand for $500,000,000 is not an idle resolution or empty words. Fifteen dollars for every black brother and sister in the United States is only a beginning of the reparations due us as people who have been exploited and degraded, brutalized, killed and persecuted. Underneath all of this exploitation, the racism of this country has produced a psychological effect upon us that we are beginning to shake off. We are no longer afraid to demand our full rights a people in this decadent society.

We are demanding $500,000,000 to be spent in the following way:

1. We call for the establishment of a Southern land bank to help our brothers and sisters who have to leave their land because of racist pressure on people who want to establish cooperative farms, but who have no funds. We have seen too many farmers evicted from their homes because they have dared to defy the white racism of this country. We need money for land. We must fight for massive sums of money for this Southern Land Bank. We call for $200,000,000 to implement this program.

2. We call for the establishment of four major publishing and printing industries in the United

States to be funded with ten million dollars each. These publishing houses are to be located in Detroit, Atlanta, Los Angeles, and New York. They will help to generate capital for further cooperative investments in the black community, provide jobs and an alternative to the white-dominated and controlled printing field.

3. We call for the establishment of four of the most advanced scientific and futuristic audio—visual networks to be located in Detroit, Chicago, Cleveland, and Washington, D.C. These TV networks will provide an alternative to the racist propaganda that fills the current television networks. Each of these TV networks will be funded by ten million dollars each.

4. We call for a research skills center which will provide research on the problems of black people. This center must be funded with no less than 30 million dollars.

5. We call for the establishment of a training center for the teaching of skills in community organization, photography, movie making, television making and repair, radio building and repair and all other skills needed in communication. This training center shall be funded with no less than ten million dollars.

6. We recognize the role of the National Welfare Rights Organization and we intend to work with them. We call for ten million dollars to assist in the organization of welfare recipients. We want to organize the welfare workers in this country so that they may demand more money from the government and better administration of the welfare system of this country.

7. We call for $20,000,000 to establish a National Black Labor Strike and Defense Fund. This is necessary for the protection of black workers and their families who are fighting racist working conditions in this country.

*8. We call for the establishment of the International Black Appeal (IBA). This International Black Appeal will be funded with no less than $20,000,000. The IBA is charged with producing more capital for the establishment of cooperative businesses in the United States and in Africa, our Motherland. The International Black Appeal is one of the most important demands that we are making for we know that it can generate and raise funds throughout the United States and help our African brothers.

Tile IBA is charged with three functions and shall be headed by James Forman:

(a) Raising money for the program of the National Black Economic Development Conference

(b) The development of cooperatives in African countries and support of African Liberation movements.

(c) Establishment of a Black Anti-Defamation League which will protect our African image.

9. We call for the establishment of a Black University to be funded with $130,000,000 to be located in the South. Negotiations are presently under way with a Southern University.

10. We demand that IFCO allocate all unused funds in the planning budget to implement the demands of this conference.

In order to win our demands, we are aware that we will have to have massive support, therefore:

(1) We call upon all black people throughout the United States to consider themselves as members of the National Black Economic Development Conference and to act in unity to help force the racist white Christian churches and Jewish synagogues to implement these demands.

(2) We call upon all the concerned black people across the country to contact black workers, black women, black students and the black unemployed, community groups, welfare organization, teacher organizations, church leaders and organizations explaining how these demands are vital to the black community of the U.S.

Pressure by whatever means necessary should be applied to the white power structure of the racist Christian churches and Jewish synagogues. All black people should act boldly in confronting our white oppressors and demanding this modest reparation of 15 dollars per black man.

(3) Delegates and members of the National Black Economic Development Conference are urged to call press conferences in the cities and to attempt to get as many black organizations as possible to support the demands of the conference. The quick use of the press in the local areas will heighten the tension and these demands must be attempted to be won in a short period of time, although we are prepared for protracted and long-range struggle.

(4) We call for the total disruption of selected church-sponsored agencies operating anywhere in the U.S. and the world. Black workers, black women, black students, and the black unemployed are encouraged to seize the offices, telephones, and printing apparatus of all church-sponsored agencies and to hold these in trusteeship until our demands are met.

(5) We call upon all delegates and members of the National Black Economic Development Conference to stage sit-in demonstrations at selected black and white churches. This is not to be interpreted as a continuation of the sit-in movement of the early sixties but we know that active confrontation inside white churches is possible and will strengthen the possibility of meeting our demands. Such confrontation can take the form of reading the Black Manifesto instead of a sermon or passing it out to church members. The principle of self-defense should be applied if attacked.

(6) On May 4, 1969, or a date thereafter, depending upon local conditions, we call upon black people to commence the disruption of the racist churches and synagogues throughout the United States.

(7) We call upon IFCO to serve as a central staff to coordinate the mandate of the conference and to reproduce and distribute en masse literature, leaflets, news items, press releases, and other material.

(8) We call upon all delegates to find within the white community those forces which will work under the leadership of blacks to implement these demands by whatever means necessary. By taking such actions, white Americans will demonstrate concretely that they are willing to fight the white skin privilege and the white supremacy and racism which has forced us as black people to make these demands.

(9) We call upon all white Christians and Jews to practice patience, tolerance, understanding, and nonviolence as they have encouraged, advised, and demanded that we as black people should do throughout our entire enforced slavery in the United States. The true test of their faith and belief in the Cross and the words of the prophets will certainly be put to a test as we seek legitimate and extremely modest reparations for our role in developing the industrial base of the Western world through our slave labor. But we are no longer slaves, we are men and women, proud of our African heritage, determined to have our dignity.

(10) We are so proud of our African heritage and realize concretely that our struggle is not only to make revolution in the United States, but to protect our brothers and sisters in Africa and to help them rid themselves of racism, capitalism, and imperialism by whatever means necessary, including armed struggle. We are and must be willing to fight the defamation of our African image wherever it rears its ugly head. We are therefore charging the Steering Committee to create a Black Anti-Defamation League to be funded by money raised from the International Black Appeal.

(11) We fully recognize that revolution in the United States and Africa, our Motherland, is more than a one-dimensional operation. It will require the total integration of the political, economic, and military components and therefore, we call upon all our brothers and sisters who have acquired training and expertise in the fields of engineering, electronics, research, community organization, physics, biology, chemistry, mathematics, medicine, military science, and warfare to assist the National Black Economic Development Conference in the implementation of its program.

(12) To implement these demands we must have a fearless leadership. We must have a leadership which is willing to battle the church establishment to implement these demands. To win our demands we will have to declare war on the white Christian churches and synagogues and this means we may have to fight the total government structure of this country. Let no one here think that these demands will be met by our mere stating of them. For the sake of the churches and synagogues, we hope that they have the wisdom to understand that these demands are modest and reasonable. But if the white Christians and Jews are not willing to meet our demands through peace and good will, then we declare war and we are prepared to fight by whatever means necessary. We are, therefore, proposing the election of the following Steering Committee:

| | |
|---|---|
| Lucius Walker | Mark Comfort |
| Renny Freeman | Earl Allen |
| Luke Tripp | Robert Browne |
| Howard Fuller | Vincent Harding |
| James Forman | Mike Hamlin |
| John Watson | Len Holt |
| Dan Aldridge | Peter Bernard |
| John Williams | Michael Wright |
| Ken Cockrel | Muhammad Kenyatta |
| Chuck Wooten | Mel Jackson |
| Fannie Lou Hamer | Howard Moore |
| Julian Bond | Harold Holmes |

Brothers and sisters, we no longer are shuffling our feet and scratching our heads. We are tall, black and proud.

And we say to the white Christian churches and Jewish synagogues, to the government of this country, and to all the white racist imperialists who compose it, there is only one thing left that you can do to further degrade black people and that is to kill us. But we have been dying too long for this country. We have died in every war. We are dying in Vietnam today fighting the wrong enemy.

The new black man wants to live and to live means that we must not become static or merely believe in self-defense. We must boldly go out and attack the white Western world at its power centers. The white Christian churches are another form of government in this country and they are used by the government of this country to exploit the people of Latin America, Asia, and Africa, but the day is soon coming to an end. Therefore, brothers and sisters, the demands we make upon the white Christian churches and the Jewish synagogues are small demands. They represent 15 dollars per black person in these United States. We can legitimately demand this from the church power structure. We must demand more from the United States Government.

But to win our demands from the church which is linked up with the United States Government, we must not forget that it will ultimately be by force and power that we will win.

We are not threatening the churches. We are saying that we know the churches came with the military might of the colonizers and have been sustained by the military might of the colonizers. Hence, if the churches in colonial territories were established by military might, we know deep within our hearts that we must be prepared to use force to get our demands. We are not saying that this is the road we want to take. It is not, but let us be very clear that we are not opposed to force and we are not opposed to violence. We were captured in Africa by violence. We were kept in bondage and political servitude and forced to work as slaves by the military machinery and the Christian church working hand in hand.

We recognize that in issuing this manifesto we must prepare for a long range educational campaign in all communities of this country, but we know that the Christian churches have contributed to our oppression in white America. We do not intend to abuse our black brothers and sisters in black churches who have uncritically accepted Christianity. We want them to understand how the racist white Christian church with its hypocritical declara-

tions and doctrines of brotherhood has abused our trust and faith. An attack on the religious beliefs of black people is not our major objective, even though we know that we were not Christians when we were brought to this country, but that Christianity was used to help enslave us. Our objective in issuing this Manifesto is to force the racist white Christian church to begin the payment of reparations which are due to all black people, not only by the Church but also by private business and the U.S. government. We see this focus on the Christian church as an effort around which all black people can unite.

Our demands are negotiable, but they cannot be minimized; they can only be increased and the church is asked to come up with larger sums of money than we are asking. Our slogans are:

ALL ROADS MUST LEAD TO REVOLUTION

UNITE WITH WHOMEVER YOU CAN UNITE

NEUTRALIZE WHEREVER POSSIBLE

FIGHT OUR ENEMIES RELENTLESSLY

VICTORY TO THE PEOPLE

LIFE AND GOOD HEALTH TO MANKIND

RESISTANCE TO DOMINATION BY THE WHITE CHRISTIAN CHURCHES AND THE JEWISH SYNAGOGUES

REVOLUTIONARY BLACK POWER

WE SHALL WIN WITHOUT A DOUBT

Study Questions

1. What are the politics of James Forman? How does he view capitalism?

2. What is his critique of America? Is his critique accurate and fair? Explain.

3. Why does he call upon churches an synagogues to pay reparations?

4. How does he plan to use the reparations money? Does his spending plan seem reasonable? Why or why not?

5. How do you think Forman feels about black churches?

6. What do you think of Forman's tactics? Are they effective? Explain.

# EXCERPT FROM *JEWS AND BLACKS*

### Michael Lerner and Cornel West

*Cornel West was born in Tulsa, Oklahoma and raised in a black working class neighborhood near Sacramento, California. He is a graduate of Harvard and Princeton Universities. He is currently a Full Professor of Afro-American Studies and Philosophy of Religion at Harvard University. His works include* The American Evasion of Philosophy *(1989),* Race Matters *(1993) and* Jews and Blacks: Let the Healing Begin *(1995 with Michael Lerner).*

*Michael Lerner is the editor of* Tikkun Magazine *which has been described as the "Bible of the Jewish Left." He has authored many books including* Jewish Renewal: A Path to Healing and Transformation.

*West and Lerner have chosen to sit down together and try to hammer away at the essential issues that ripped apart what was once a morally and historically meaningful relationship between Blacks and Jews. The result is a compilation of several years of taped dialogue and discussion that touches on several issues of concern such as cultural identity, Zionism, Black Nationalism, economic conflicts, and a shared crises of leadership.*

## Introduction - Cornel West

Why are Blacks and Jews in the United States the most unique and fascinating people in modern times? Why have both groups contributed so disproportionately to the richness and vitality in American life? Can we honestly imagine what twentieth-century American democracy would be like without the past and present doings and sufferings of Blacks and Jews? What forms will progressive politics take, if any, with escalating tensions between these two historically liberal groups?

When historians look back on the emergence, development, and decline of American civilization, they obviously will note its distinctive feature - constitutional democracy and precious liberties (with its class, gender, and especially racial constraints), material prosperity, technological ingenuity, ethnic and regional diversity, market-driven yet romantic popular culture, relative lack of historical consciousness, and an obsession with progress in the future.

Both Jews and Blacks are a pariah people - a people who had to make and remake themselves as outsiders on the margins of American society and culture. Both groups assumed that the status quo was unjust and therefore found strategies to survive and thrive against the odds. Both groups defined themselves as a people deeply shaped by America but never fully a part of America. Both groups appealed to biblical texts and relied on communal bonds to sustain themselves - texts that put a premium on justice, mercy, and solidarity with the downtrodden, and bonds shot through with a deep distrust, suspicion, even paranoia, toward the powerful and privileged. Both groups have been hated and despised peoples who find it difficult, if not impossible, to fully overcome group insecurity and anxiety as well as truly be and love themselves as individuals as a people. Wearing the masks, enduring petty put-downs, and coping with subtle insults remains an everyday challenge for most Blacks and some Jews in America.

Both groups are the most modern of modern people in that they have created new and novel ways of life, innovative and improvisational modes of being in the world. Their entrée into modernity as degraded Others - dishonored slaves (Blacks) and devalued non-Christians (Jews) - forced them to hammer out the most un-American yet modern of products - tragicomic dispositions toward reality that put sadness, sorrow, and suffering at the center of their plights and predicaments. This tragicomic character of the Black and Jewish experiences in modernity - coupled with a nagging moral conscience owing to undeniable histories of underdog status and unusual slavery-to-freedom narratives in authoritative texts - haunts both groups.

And what Blacks and Jews have done with their intelligence, imagination, and ingenuity is astounding. Twentieth-century America - a century that begins only a generation after the emancipation of penniless, illiterate, enslaved Africans and the massive influx of poor Eastern European Jewish immigrants - is unimaginable without the creative breakthroughs and monumental contributions of Blacks and Jews. At the very highest levels of achievement, we have Louis Armstrong and Aaron Copland, Duke Ellington and Leonard Bernstein, John Coltrane and George Gershwin, Sarah Vaughan and Irving Berlin, Toni Morrison and Saul Bellow, W. E. B. Du Bois and Hannah Arendt, Romare Bearden and Jackson Pollock, August Wilson and Arthur Miller, Paul Robeson and Pete Seeger, Ralph Ellison and Irving Howe, Kathleen Battle and Beverly Sills, Richard Pryor and Lenny Bruce, Willie Mays and Sandy Koufax, Andre Watts and Itzhak Perlman, Jacob Lawrence and Mark Rothko, Baby face (Kenneth Edmonds) and Carole King, Thurgood Marshall and Louis Brandeis, Marvin Gaye and Bob Dylan, James Baldwin and Norman Mailer, Lorraine Hansberry and Neil Simon, Aretha Franklin and Barbra Streisand, Billy Strayhorn and Stephen Sondheim. This short and incomplete list of towering Black and Jewish figures is neither an act of providence nor a mere accident. Rather it is the result of tremendous talent, discipline, and energy of two ostracized groups who disproportionately shape the cultural life of this country.

Furthermore, Jewish power and influence - though rarely wielded in a monolithic manner - in the garment industry, show business, medical and legal profession, journalism, and the academy - has had a major impact on the shaping of American life. We are reminded of the fundamental centrality of learning in Jewish life when we realize that as of 1989, of fifty American Nobel Laureates in the medical sciences - such as biochemistry and physiology - seventeen were Jews.

This latter point - the matter of relative Jewish zeal in business and education - is a delicate one. It does not meant that Jews are innately smarter than others or that they are involved in some secret conspiracy to control the banks and newspapers, as implied by the anti-Semitic remarks of General George Brown, Chairman of the Joint Chiefs of Staff, in a lecture at Duke University in 1974. Instead these realities reflect the dominant Jewish ways of gaining access to resources, status, and power against anti-Semitic exclusions in other spheres and over three thousand years of autonomous institution-building based on self-help and self-development around literary and mathematical skills.

African-Americans also have a rich history of business enterprise and scientific achievements - yet the entrepreneurial ethic has been set back by racist attacks (nearly two-thirds of those lynched at the turn of the century were businessmen), and exclusion from significant access to capital and credit, weak communal bonds to sustain business efforts, underfunded Black schools and colleges that downplay independent business efforts, and vicious stereotypes that undercut motivation to study math and natural sciences.

?In fact, the fundamental differences between Blacks and Jews in America have been the vast impact of slavery and Jim Crow on limiting the Black quest for self-confidence in literary and scientific matters, and the containment of most Black folk in rural and agrarian areas until World War II, where access to literacy was difficult. In stark contrast, American Jews have always been primarily an urban people trying to find safe niches in industrial (and anti-Semitic) America, who fall back on strong and long traditions of independent institution-building. In this regard, the experiences of Blacks and Jews have been qualitatively different in a deeply racist and more mildly anti-Semitic America.

Yet, ironically, Jews and Blacks have been linked in a kind of symbiotic relation with each other. Whether they are allies or antagonists, they are locked into an inescapable embrace principally owing to their dominant status of degraded Others, given the racist and Christian character of the American past and present. First, because anti-Black and anti-Jewish waves are an omnipresent threat in this country. Second, because their support of progressive politics cast them as potential threats to the status quo in their critical and dissenting roles. And third, because both groups not only have a profound fascination with each other but also because they have much at stake in their own collective identities as a pariah and "chosen" people - be it in covenant with a God that "chooses" to side with the underdog or against a nation that "chooses" to treat them unequally or unkindly.

When Michael Lerner - from whom I've learned so much and come to love so dearly - and I began our dialogue, we knew we had to build upon the rich legacies of Martin Luther King, Jr., and Abraham Joshua Heschel. We had to cast our exchange in such a way that we highlighted moral ideals and existential realities bigger and better than both Black and Jewish interests. We had to examine what it means to be human as Jews and Blacks and how this relates to keeping alive the best of a precious yet precarious experiment in democracy. We also had to examine the ways in which we could revitalize progressive politics in the light of prophetic traditions in the Black and Jewish heritages. This is why our Black-Jewish dialogue - much like relevant, Black-Brown, Jewish-Asian or Black-Red dialogue - is but an instance of the human struggle for freedom and democracy. And any such struggle is predicated on the democratic faith that we everyday people can critically examine our individual and collective pasts, honestly confront our difficult present, and imaginatively project an all-embracing moral vision for the future. Our courageous foremothers and forefathers as well as our innocent children and grandchildren deserve nothing less.

## INTRODUCTION - ML

One of the greatest pleasures of my life in the past six years have been the numerous occasions in which Cornel West and I have holed ourselves away from our respective worlds and spent full days, and on one occasion a full week, talking and recording our conversations. The dialogue contained in this book represents only a fraction of the wide range of philosophical, political, religious, and personal issues that we touched on. We got to know each other's lives, sources of joy and fear, emotional realities, and range of intellectual interests. We read each other's books and articles, we hung out with each other's families, and we grew increasingly excited about the other. In the process, I not only came to deeply respect Cornel's incredible intellect but to love him.

Something deep and profound happened to both of us in the course of our dialogue. Though we started with many common assumptions, we had many areas of tension and disagreements. Often these took the form of disagreements about specific interpretations of a current reality - e.g., interpreting Israel's role in the world, or the role that Jews were playing in a particular election, or what Jesse Jackson's most recent statements meant. Over the years, as this dialogue grew, we reflected on contemporary events as they were happening. The transcripts of that whole dialogue would have been five times as long as what we are actually presenting in this book, and would have represented views that we no longer hold, because we kept changing what we were thinking as the dialogue continued.

Once we were able to fully express and explore the tension points and differences in perceptions between us, we often found common ground, and each of us changed our perceptions and the public statements we were making - in part because of these dialogues. That we had not reached total convergence was highlighted by a photograph printed in the New York Times on June 13, 1994, showing Cornel and I in heated argument outside the NAACP - sponsored National Black Summit which I was picketing (in protest of the inclusion in that meeting of the Minister Frarrakhan) and Cornel was attending. But the CNN footage was equally significant - filming the warm embrace that we gave each other before we started to argue.

Many Jews have the perception that it is not so easy to involve Blacks in a dialogue aimed at healing the rifts between Blacks and Jews. Apart from the ministers and community relations personnel, Jews report that they often find it hard to attract Blacks to participate in on-going dialogues on this topic. They sometimes report feeling that there's more interest in healing the relationship among Jews than among Blacks.

To the extent that this is true, the following explanations are sometimes proffered: that many Blacks face immediate economic oppression and are more concerned to change those circumstances than to reconcile with a group that they see as being economically advantaged (though this won't quite explain the difficulties Jews have in attracting middle-class Blacks); that many Blacks see Jews as whites (and hence don't see any need to work on some special relationship with them); and that in the post-Holocaust years Blacks have seen Jews trying to rob from them their identity as "the most oppressed group" and may find it more difficult to reconcile with a group to whom they are in most respects so close, a kind of sibling rivalry.

I do not profess to know whether this Jewish perception is true. But to the extent that it is true, we are hoping that the appearance of this dialogue might encourage others in both communities to renew their efforts to create local dialogues of their own. This dialogue is not meant to be a solution or final "answer" to the problems we explore, but an invitation to others to join us in the dialogue, to expand it broadly, to add points that we may have missed, and to help in the process of reconciliation and repair. Let the healing begin! That is not just our title; it is our fervent appeal to both communities.

Yet I do think it important to state why this issue resonates so deeply for Jews. It is not merely a survival issue. Though at one point in this dialogue I play with various paranoid fantasies of what might happen to Jews in America should Black anti-Semitism become a deeper and more pervasive reality, and though I genuinely worry about the way that America's crisis of meaning may lead to a dramatic resurgence of xenophobic nationalism and anti-Semitism, I don't believe that this quite explains why the Black-Jewish issue is so central for many liberal and progressive Jews.

For Jews in the modern world, the central question is the nature of Jewish identity. We do not have a distinctive skin color, and in the multicultural bouquet of modern America it's quite possible for many Jews to leave their Jewishness behind, fully assimilate into the American secular mainstream, and risk very little. For those who choose to remain identified as Jews, the questions of "Why remain Jewish?" and "What constitutes our identity as Jews - what does it mean to be a Jew?" become central, even burning issues on the individual and psychological level.

In Jewish Renewal (Putnam, 1994) I describe the growing number of Jews who are turning back to the Jewish tradition and finding within it a radical understanding of the nature of Jewish identity and Jewish destiny. Jewish identity as constituted by the Torah tradition consists of being a witness of God as the force in the universe that makes possible the transformation of that which is to that which ought to be.

Though the "natural attitude" toward existence is that everything is fixed and set, that the world is as it must be and little can be changed, the Jewish attitude is that the world is not a timeless and fixed entity but a created being that is sustained every day by the intention of its Creator. Moreover, human beings are created in the image of God, and charged to be partners with God in the process of changing the world from that which is to that which ought to be. Jewish destiny is to be part of the vanguard that brings this understanding to the world, that becomes a light to the nations precisely because it proclaims this possibility, and to be involved in the healing and transformation process.

The goal of this transformation is to rectify the oppression of the powerless. We were slaves. So now that we are free, our task is to spread that freedom, and to identify with the powerless. The most frequently repeated injunctions of Torah are variations on the following theme: "When you come into your land, do not oppress the stranger. Remember that you were strangers in the land of Egypt."

The very fact of needing such an injunction is a realistic recognition on the part of Torah that there

will be a tendency to oppress the stranger. As Freud was to point out thousands of year later, there is in most human beings a "repetition compulsion," a tendency to act out on others that which was done to us.

Yet the exciting proclamation of Torah is that we don't have to do this, that the chain of violence and cruelty can be broken, that we can identify with the oppressed and recognize that they, too, are created in the image of God and deserve the same dignity that we deserve.

God is the force in the universe that makes possible that transcendence of the repetition compulsion and that ability to recognize the Other as the potential embodiment of self-constituting, free, conscious, creative, and loving being. Moreover, the Torah tells us that if we are to stay in touch with the God energy within ourselves, we need to be able to recognize the Other's needs as our own needs. Hence, the Torah commandment: "ve-ahavta la-ger" ("Thou shalt love the stranger").

This was a revolutionary message, not only for the ancient world, but for the medieval and modern world as well. Most systems of oppression thrive on convincing both the oppressed and those who benefit from the oppression that the way things are is natural, fixed, inevitable, and unchangeable.

No wonder, then, that ruling elites have always hated the Jews, worried about their passion for social justice, and done their best to portray them as "weird" and "untrustworthy" and "manipulators" whom everyone else would do best to avoid or distrust. No wonder, too, if Jews, faced with the resulting hostility and oppression, have often tried to play down the revolutionary message of their tradition, temper it from within, and, ever since the Hellenist oppression following Alexander's conquest of Judea in the fourth century before the common era, to make Judaism more a "religion" like other religions, less a revolutionary and trans- formative way of life.

No wonder, also, if it became hard to see "the Other" in the humane terms mandated by Torah when the others with whom you were likely to come into contact had more social power than the Jews (who, after the destruction of the Temple, were always the strangers in someone else's land) and treated Jews with disrespect if not outright murderous hatred. Goyim-bashing became part of the defensive armoring of the Jewish people, and Blacks were just another of the many groups of non-Jews that might potentially turn on us at any moment.

Yet as the trauma of our suffering and past oppression began to recede, many Jews were able to recognize that their new safety, particularly in the United States, conferred on us a new responsibility. Not only were we beneficiaries of American abundance (bought by Americans at the cost of genociding American Indians and then enslaving millions of Africans and killing millions more in the process), we were also less likely to become the primary victimized Other in the U.S. precisely because that role was already filled by African-Americans. That might have made Jews enthusiastically embrace mainstream American racism, to justify to ourselves our own fortune. But given the legacy of Torah and the way it has helped us interpret our own history, we instead began to identify with the struggles of American Blacks.

If that identification has withered somewhat in the past decades, the fault lies not only with the attractions and allures of the dominant ethos of selfishness, but also with the way Jews have perceived that some Blacks seemed to be repudiating our interests, seeing us as indistinguishable from whites, forgetting the commitments and sacrifices Jews had made to the Black struggle, and in other ways pushing us away.

Yet liberal Jews cannot deny either the upsurge of political and cultural conservatism in some sectors of the Jewish world, often disproportionately represented among those who are affiliated with Jewish establishment organizations.

This conservative turn has not been followed by most Jews. Jews remain more likely to vote for liberal candidates and to support liberal and progressive social change programs than most other sectors of the population. But the intellectual foundation of this attachment to caring for others is being severely eroded, not only by the attractions of "fitting in" to contemporary American materialism and its culture of narcissism but also by tendencies within the more religious sectors of the population to interpret Jewish ethical obligations as applying primarily to fellow Jews, and hence to conveniently find a way of retaining all the ritual trappings of Judaism while abandoning its most challenging obligations to recognize God in each other. Even injunctions about caring for "the stranger" get reinterpreted to mean "those who have converted to Judaism" or "the resident alien who agrees to live by Jewish laws." The God of transformation, the Possibility of Possibility, becomes a contained entity that one worships on Shabbat and at home, but that does not interfere with the fervent and morally unrestricted pursuit of power and wealth in the economic marketplace.

Such a Judaism, however, stripped of its revolutionary message, no longer a witness to the possibility of transcendence, and has lost its attraction to many younger Jews. Not ready to abandon their Jewishness, suspecting that there are deep treasures built into the cultural and religious and philosophical heritage of the Jewish people, these younger Jews are deeply troubled by the way Judaism is defined by the Jewish establishment.

If Jewishness is about something more than lox and bagels and gefilte fish, it has to be about bringing a message to the world. And turning back to Torah, we find that message in the task of the Jewish people to become testifiers to the possibility of breaking the chain of violence and cruelty and establishing a world based on justice, love, caring, and recognition of the God within each other.

Yet all these flowery words seem empty if Jews ignore that we live in a society where African-Americans are being systemically demeaned, where racism continues to flourish, and where economic oppression yields degradation and daily suffering. It becomes immediately obvious that this reality poses an immediate demand on the Jewish people: to challenge those who believe that the suffering cannot or should not be alleviated, to join in the struggles to change all those societal institutions that perpetuate poverty and racism and to connect with the oppressed in a way that recognizes their fundamental humanity and fundamental similarity with us, our sisterhood and brotherhood with them. To do this in a way that is not condescending, that does not assume that we are "morally higher" or "better," but rather out of a deep recognition of God's presence in each human being, is our challenge.

If Judaism cannot recognize the God within those who have previously been treated as "demeaned Other," it has no future. This is a moment when we are celebrating the steps taken by the State of Israel to recognize that the Palestinian people have the same right to national self-determination and dignity as the Jews. In the American Jewish community that same struggle has taken place in the efforts to overthrow patriarchal aspects of Jewish life and Jewish religious practice. Both of these are central struggles, and both are connected to the equally pressing task of overcoming the racism and economic oppression that is the dirty little not-so-secret reality of American life.

To put this simply: if Jews can turn their backs on the suffering of Blacks, they become like the American majority. They would be no worse than anyone else. But in so doing, they would be embracing a worldview that is indistinguishable from the rest of American life - so in that case, why bother to stay Jewish, with all the attendant hassles, risks, and separations from others? It is only if Jews can stay connected to our task as witnesses to God's presence and hence as witnesses to the possibility of transformation of the ethos of selfishness to the ethos of caring (what I call "a Politics of Meaning") that retaining one's Jewishness has a substantive point.

So for Jews, the relationship with Blacks is not a "nice feel good" kind of thing - it speaks to our fundamental identity as a people. If we turn away, as some Jews want to do, and say, "It's no longer in our interests to be so involved and to make financial sacrifices through supporting candidates who want to redistribute our tax monies to the poor," we are not just sacrificing the best interest of African-Americans, we are simultaneously undermining the center of our being as Jews. The very way of thinking that leads some Jews to turn their backs on Black suffering is a way of thinking which creates a Jewish world which will be abandoned by future generations of Jews. So healing our relationship to Blacks is part of overcoming the distortions in the Jewish world and reclaiming a Judaism that is most deeply authentic with Jewish roots and Jewish destiny and hence most deeply connected to God.

No wonder, then, that this relationship has special importance to Jews. The centrality of this issue, and our desire to let the healing begin, is a sign of Jewish spiritual health. But healing the relationship is only a part of the task, a first step in the process of healing American society itself so that racism and poverty may, with God's help and with our willingness to make the necessary economic and political changes, be quickly eliminated.

The electoral victory of the Right in 1994 gave even greater urgency to the task of healing the rifts between Blacks and Jews. Seventy-eight percent of Jews voted Democratic in 1994, a higher percentage than any other ethnic group except African-Americans. Jews and Blacks are the backbone of the liberal progressive forces in the U.S. If we cannot heal the tensions between us, there is little hope of stemming the national flow of energy toward despair, cynicism, and selfishness that produces the climate in which the Right replaces our legitimate hunger for community with a xenophobic nationalism and fear of immigrants and those with

different lifestyles, diverts our desire for mutual recognition into anger at others who supposedly are getting the recognition we have been denied, and channels our fears about our ability to sustain loving relationships into anger at gays, feminists, and liberals who are blamed for undermining families. Anyone who does not wish to live in a society dominated by the values of the Christian Right, the Rush Limbaughs, and the Newt Gingriches has a stake in helping us repair and heal the tensions between Blacks and Jews. So the issues raised here should be of urgent concern to many who are not part of either community. I welcome their involvement with us and their support. What happens between Blacks and Jews will have consequences for all of us.

## Study Questions

1. What similarities and differences between Jews and Blacks does Cornel West highlight? What are their unique contributions to American society and culture?

2. How do both West and Lerner talk about the relationships between Blacks and Jews? What do both groups think of each other?

3. What factors have led to a historical alliance between the two groups? Why has this alliance been weakened in recent years?

4. On what does Lerner base his Jewish identity? What is there about Jewish identity and Black identity that makes a Black-Jewish alliance possible?

5. Why do these authors think a Black-Jewish alliance is important today? What role do they see for such an alliance in American politics? How important do you think this alliance is?

6. How big a problem is Black anti-Semitism and Jewish anti-Black racism? Explain.

# EDUCATION

# EXCERPT FROM PEDAGOGY OF THE OPPRESSED

*Paulo Freire (1921-1997)*

*Freire was born in Recife, a port city of north-eastern Brazil. His parents were middle class but suffered financial reverses so severe during the Great Depression that Freire learned what it is to go hungry. It was in childhood that he determined to dedicate his life to the struggle against hunger.*

*Freires most widely recognized work is* Pedagogy of the Oppressed *(1970), a call to a revolutionary education that reflected a partnership between student and teacher and took into account the conditions of students lives. In it, he argues that education is the path to permanent liberation and consists of two stages. The first stage is that by which people become aware of their oppression and through praxis transform that state. The second stage builds upon the first and is a permanent process of liberating cultural action. This early work remains the best introduction to Freires critique of education and the consequent pedagogy of liberation which he first developed in Chile. The book, which sold over 600,000 copies worldwide, has become a tool for educational betterment for many politically and socially disenfranchised groups and is required reading in education and social studies courses around the world.*

While the problem of humanization has always, from an axiological point of view, been humankind's central problem, it now takes on the character of an inescapable concern. Concern for humanization leads at once to the recognition of dehumanization, not only as an ontological possibility but as an historical reality. And as an indi-vidual perceives the extent of dehumanization, he or she may ask if humanization is a viable possibility. Within history, in concrete, objective contexts, both humanization and dehumanization are possibilities for a person as an uncompleted being conscious of their incompletion.

But while both humanization and dehumanization are real alternatives, only the first is the people's vocation. This vocation is constantly negated, yet it is affirmed by that very negation. It is thwarted by injustice, exploitation, oppression, and the violence of the oppressors; it is affirmed by the yearning of the oppressed for freedom and justice, and by their struggle to recover their lost humanity.

Dehumanization, which marks not only those whose humanity has been stolen, but also (though in a different way) those who have stolen it, is a *distortion* of the vocation of becoming more fully human. This distortion occurs within history; but it is not an historical vocation. Indeed, to admit of dehumanization as an historical vocation would lead either to cynicism or total despair. The struggle for humanization, for the emancipation of labor, for the overcoming of alienation, for the affirmation of men and women as persons would be meaningless. This struggle is possible only because dehumanization, although a concrete historical fact, is *not* a given destiny but the result of an unjust order that engenders violence in the oppressors, which in turn dehumanizes the oppressed

Because it is a distortion of being more fully human, sooner or later being less human leads the oppressed to struggle against those who made them so. In order for this struggle to have meaning, the oppressed must not, in seeking to regain their humanity (which is a way to create it), become in turn oppressors of the oppressors, but rather restorers of the humanity of both.

This, then, is the great humanistic and historical task of the oppressed: to liberate themselves and their oppressors as well. The oppressors, who oppress, exploit, and rape by virtue of their power, cannot find in this power the strength to liberate either the oppressed or themselves. Only power that springs from the weakness of the oppressed will be sufficiently strong to free both. Any attempt to "soften" the power of the oppressor in deference to the weakness of the oppressed almost always manifests itself in the form of false generosity; indeed, the attempt never goes beyond this. In order to have the continued opportunity to express their "generosity," the oppressors must perpetuate injustice as well. An unjust social order is the permanent fount of this "generosity," which is nourished by death, despair, and poverty. That is why the dispensers of false generosity become desperate at the slightest threat to its source.

True generosity consists precisely in fighting to destroy the causes which nourish false charity. False charity constrains the fearful and subdued, the "rejects of life," to extend their trembling hands. True generosity lies in striving so that these hands—whether of individuals or entire peoples—need be extended less and less in supplication, so that more and more they become human hands which work and, working, transform the world.

This lesson and this apprenticeship must come, however, from the oppressed themselves and from those who are truly solidary with them. As individuals or as peoples, by fighting for the restoration of their humanity they will be attempting the restoration of true generosity. Who are better prepared than the oppressed to understand the terrible significance of an oppressive society? Who suffer the effects of oppression more than the oppressed? Who can better understand the necessity of liberation? They will not gain this liberation by chance but through the praxis of their quest for it, through their recognition of the necessity to fight for it. And this fight, because of the purpose given it by the oppressed, will actually constitute an act of love opposing the lovelessness which lies at the heart of the oppressors' violence, lovelessness even when clothed in false generosity.

But almost always, during the initial stage of the struggle, the oppressed, instead of striving for liberation, tend themselves to become oppressors, or "sub-oppressors." The very structure of their thought has been conditioned by the contradictions of the concrete, existential situation by which they were shaped. Their ideal is to be men; but for them, to be men is to be oppressors. This is their model of humanity. This phenomenon derives from the fact that the oppressed, at a certain moment of their existential experience, adopt an attitude of "adhesion" to the oppressor. Under these circumstances they cannot "consider" him sufficiently clearly to objectivize him—to discover him "outside" themselves. This does not necessarily mean that the oppressed are unaware that they are downtrodden. But their perception of themselves as oppressed is impaired by their submersion in the reality of oppression. At this level, their perception of themselves as opposites of the oppressor does not yet signify engagement in a struggle to overcome the contradiction; the one pole aspires not to liberation, but to identification with its opposite pole.

In this situation the oppressed do not see the "new man" as the person to be born from the resolution of this contradiction, as oppression gives way to liberation. For them, the new man or woman themselves become oppressors. Their vision of the new man or woman is individualistic; because of their identification with the oppressor, they have no consciousness of themselves as persons or as members of an oppressed class. It is not to become free that they want agrarian reform, but in order to acquire land and thus become landowners—or, more precisely, bosses over other workers. It is a rare peasant who once "promoted" to overseer, does not become more of a tyrant towards his former comrades than the owner himself. This is because the context of the peasant's situation, that is, oppression, remains unchanged. In this example, the overseer, in order to make sure of his job, must be as tough as the owner—and more so. Thus is illustrated our previous assertion that during the initial stage of their struggle the oppressed find in the oppressor their model of "manhood."

Even revolution, which transforms a concrete situation of oppression by establishing the process of liberation, must confront this phenomenon. Many of the oppressed who directly or indirectly participate in revolution intend—conditioned by the myths of the old order—to make it their private revolution. The shadow of their former oppressor is still cast over them.

The "fear of freedom" which afflicts the oppressed, a fear which may equally well lead them to desire the role of oppressor or bind them to the role of oppressed, should be examined. One of the basic elements of the relationship between oppressor and oppressed is *prescription*. Every prescription represents the imposition of one individual's choice upon another, transforming the consciousness of the person prescribed to into one that conforms with the prescriber's consciousness. Thus, the behavior of the oppressed is a prescribed behavior, following as it does the guidelines of the oppressor.

The oppressed, having internalized the image of the oppressor and adopted his guidelines, are fearful of freedom. Freedom would require them to eject this image and replace it with autonomy and responsibility. Freedom is acquired by conquest, not by gift. It must be pursued constantly and responsibly. Freedom is not an ideal located outside of man; nor is it an idea which becomes myth. It is rather the indispensable condition for the quest for human completion.

To surmount the situation of oppression, people must first critically recognize its causes, so that through transforming action they can create a new situation, one which makes possible the pursuit of a fuller humanity. But the struggle to be more fully human has already begun in the authentic struggle to transform the situation. Although the situation of oppression is a dehumanized and dehumanizing totality affecting both the oppressors and those whom they oppress, it is the latter who must, from their stifled humanity, wage for both the struggle for a fuller humanity; the oppressor, who is himself dehumanized because he dehumanizes others, is unable to lead this struggle.

However, the oppressed, who have adapted to the structure of domination in which they are immersed, and have become resigned to it, are inhibited from waging the struggle for freedom so long as they feel incapable of running the risks it requires. Moreover, their struggle for freedom threatens not only the oppressor, but also their own oppressed comrades who are fearful of still greater repression. When they discover within themselves the yearning to be free, they perceive that this yearning can be transformed into reality only when the same yearning is aroused in their comrades. But while dominated by the fear of freedom they refuse to appeal to others, or to listen to the appeals of others, or even to the appeals of their own conscience. They prefer gregariousness to authentic comradeship; they prefer the security of conformity with their state of unfreedom to the creative communion produced by freedom and even the very pursuit of freedom.

The oppressed suffer from the duality which has established itself in their innermost being. They discover that without freedom they cannot exist authentically. Yet, although they desire authentic existence, they fear it. They are at one and the same time themselves and the oppressor whose consciousness they have internalized. The conflict lies in the choice between being wholly themselves or being divided; between ejecting the oppressor within or not ejecting them; between human solidarity or alienation; between following prescriptions or having choices; between being spectators or actors; between acting or having the illusion of acting through the action of the oppressors; between speaking out or being silent, castrated in their power to create and re-create, in their power to transform the world. This is the tragic dilemma of the oppressed which their education must take into account.

This book will present some aspects of what the writer has termed the pedagogy of the oppressed, a pedagogy which must be forged *with*, not *for*, the oppressed (whether individuals or peoples) in the incessant struggle to regain their humanity. This pedagogy makes oppression and its causes objects of reflection by the oppressed and from that reflection will come their necessary engagement in the struggle for their liberation. And in the struggle this pedagogy will be made and remade.

The central problem is this: How can the oppressed, as divided, unauthentic beings, participate in developing the pedagogy of their liberation? Only as they discover themselves to be "hosts" of the oppressor can they contribute to the midwifery of their liberating pedagogy. As long as they live in the duality in which *to be* is *to be like*, and *to be like* is *to be like the oppressor*, this contribution is impossible. The pedagogy of the oppressed is an instrument for their critical discovery that both they and their oppressors are manifestations of dehumanization. Liberation is thus a childbirth, and a painful one. The man or woman who emerges is a new person, viable only as the oppressor—oppressed contradiction is superseded by the humanization of all people. Or to put it another way, the solution of this contradiction is born in the labor which brings into the world this new being: no longer oppressor nor longer oppressed, but human in the process of achieving freedom.

This solution cannot be achieved in idealistic terms. In order for the oppressed to be able to wage the struggle for their liberation, they must perceive the reality of oppression not as a closed world from which there is no exit, but as a limiting situation which they can transform. This perception is a necessary but not a sufficient condition for liberation; it must become the motivating force for liberating action. Nor does the discovery by the oppressed that they exist in dialectical relationship to the oppressor, as his antithesis—that without them the oppressor could not exist—in itself constitute liberation. The oppressed can overcome the contradiction in which they are caught only when this perception enlists them in the struggle to free themselves.

The same is true with respect to the individual oppressor as a person. Discovering himself to be an oppressor may cause considerable anguish, but it does not necessarily lead to solidarity with the oppressed. Rationalizing his guilt through paternalistic treatment of the oppressed, all the while holding them fast in a position of dependence, will not do. Solidarity requires that one enter into the situation of those with whom one is solidary; it is a radical posture. If what characterizes the oppressed is their subordination to the consciousness of the master, as Hegel affirms, true solidarity with the oppressed means fighting at their side to transform the objective reality which has made them these "beings for another." The oppressor is solidary with the oppressed only when he stops regarding the oppressed as an abstract category and sees them as persons who have been unjustly dealt with, deprived of their voice, cheated in the sale of their labor— when he stops making pious, sentimental, and individualistic gestures and risks an act of love. True solidarity is found only in the plenitude of this act of love, in its existentiality, in its praxis. To affirm that men and women are persons and as persons should be free, and yet to do nothing tangible to make this affirmation a reality, is a farce.

Since it is a concrete situation that the oppressor—oppressed contradiction is established, the resolution of this contradiction must be *objectively* verifiable. Hence, the radical requirement— both for the individual who discovers himself or herself to be an oppressor and for the oppressed that the concrete situation which begets oppression must be transformed.

To present this radical demand for the objective transformation of reality, to combat subjectivist immobility which would divert the recognition of oppression into patient waiting for oppression to disappear by itself, is not to dismiss the role of subjectivity in the struggle to change structures. On the contrary, one cannot conceive of objectivity without subjectivity. Neither can exist without the other, nor can they be dichotomized. The separation of objectivity from subjectivity, the denial of the latter when analyzing reality or acting upon it, is objectivism. On the other hand, the denial of objectivity in analysis or action, resulting in a subjectivism which leads to solipsistic positions, denies action itself by denying objective reality. Neither objectivism nor subjectivism, nor yet psychologism is propounded here, but rather subjectivity and objectivity in constant dialectical relationship.

To deny the importance of subjectivity in the process of transforming the world and history is naive and simplistic. It is to admit the impossible: a world without people. This objectivistic position is as ingenuous as that of subjectivism, which postulates people without a world. World and human

beings do not exist apart from each other, they exist in constant interaction. Marx does not espouse such a dichotomy, nor does any other critical, realistic thinker. What Marx criticized and scientifically destroyed was not subjectivity, but subjectivism and psychologism. Just as objective social reality exists not by chance, but as the product of human action, so it is not transformed by chance. If humankind produce social reality (which in the "inversion of the praxis" turns back upon them and conditions them), then transforming that reality is an historical task, a task for humanity.

Reality which becomes oppressive results in the contradistinction of men as oppressors and oppressed. The latter, whose task it is to struggle for their liberation together with those who show true solidarity, must acquire a critical awareness of oppression through the praxis of this struggle. One of the gravest obstacles to the achievement of liberation is that oppressive reality absorbs those within it and thereby acts to submerge human beings' consciousness. Functionally, oppression is domesticating. To no longer be prey to its force, one must emerge from it and turn upon it. This can be done only by means of the praxis: reflection and action upon the world in order to transform it.

*Hay que hacer al opresión real todavía mas opresiva añadiendo a aquella la conciéncia de la opresión haciendo la infamia todavía mas infamante, al pregonarla.*

Making "real oppression more oppressive still by adding to it the realization of oppression" corresponds to the dialectical relation between the subjective and the objective. Only in this interdependence is an authentic praxis possible, without which it is impossible to resolve the oppressor—oppressed contradiction. To achieve this goal, the oppressed must confront reality critically, simultaneously objectifying and acting upon that reality. A mere perception of reality not followed by this critical intervention will not lead to a transformation of objective reality—precisely because it is not a true perception. This is the case of a purely subjectivist perception by someone who forsakes objective reality and creates a false substitute.

A different type of false perception occurs when a change in objective reality would threaten the individual or class interests of the perceiver. In the first instance, there is no critical intervention in reality because that reality is fictitious; there is none in the second instance because intervention would contradict the class interests of the perceiver. In the latter case the tendency of the perceiver is to behave "neurotically." The fact exists; but both the fact and what may result from it may be prejudicial to the person. Thus it becomes necessary, not precisely to deny the fact, but to "see it differently." This rationalization as a defense mechanism coincides in the end with subjectivism. A fact which is not denied but whose truths are rationalized loses its objective base. It ceases to be concrete and becomes a myth created in defense of the class of the perceiver.

Herein lies one of the reasons for the prohibitions and the difficulties designed to dissuade the people from critical intervention in reality. The oppressor knows full well that this intervention would not be to his interest. What is to his interest is for the people to continue in a state of submersion, impotent in the face of oppressive reality. Of relevance here is Lukács' warning to the revolutionary party:

> . . . il doit, pour employer les mots de Marx, expliquer aux masses leur propre action non seulement afin d'assurer la continuite des experiences révolutionnaires du prolétariat, mais aussi d'activer consciemment le développement ultérieur de ces expériences.

In affirming this necessity, Lukács is unquestionably posing the problem of critical intervention. "To explain to the masses their own action" is to clarify and illuminate that action, both regarding its relationship to the objective facts by which it was prompted, and regarding its purposes. The more the people unveil this challenging reality which is to be the object of their transforming action, the more critically they enter that reality. In this way they are "consciously activating the subsequent development of their experiences." There would be no human action if there were no objective reality, no world to be the "not I" of the person and to challenge them; just as there would be no human action if humankind were not a "project," if he or she were not able to transcend himself or herself, if one were not able to perceive reality and understand it in order to transform it.

In dialectical thought, world and action are intimately interdependent. But action is human only when it is not merely an occupation but also a preoccupation, that is, when it is not dichotomized from reflection. Reflection, which is essential to action, is implicit in Lukács requirement of "explaining to the masses their own action," just as it is implicit in the purpose he attributes to this explanation: that of "consciously activating the subsequent development of experience."

For us, however, the requirement is seen not in terms of explaining to, but rather dialoguing with the people about their actions. In any event, no reality transforms itself, and the duty which Lukács ascribes to the revolutionary party of "explaining to the masses their own action" coincides with our affirmation of the need for the critical intervention of the people in reality through the praxis. The pedagogy of the oppressed, which is the pedagogy of people engaged in the fight for their own liberation, has its roots here. And those who recognize, or begin to recognize, themselves as oppressed must be among the developers of this pedagogy. No pedagogy which is truly liberating can remain distant from the oppressed by treating them as unfortunates and by presenting for their emulation models from among the oppressors. The oppressed must be their own example in the struggle for their redemption.

The pedagogy of the oppressed, animated by authentic, humanist (not humanitarian) generosity, presents itself as a pedagogy of humankind. Pedagogy which begins with the egoistic interests of the oppressors (an egoism cloaked in the false generosity of paternalism) and makes of the oppressed the objects of its humanitarianism, itself maintains and embodies oppression. It is an instrument of dehumanization. This is why, as we affirmed earlier, the pedagogy of the oppressed cannot be developed or practiced by the oppressors. It would be a contradiction in terms if the oppressors not only defended but actually implemented a liberating education.

But if the implementation of a liberating education requires political power and the oppressed have none, how then is it possible to carry out the pedagogy of the oppressed prior to the revolution? This is a question of great importance. One aspect of the reply is to be found in the distinction between *systematic education*, which can only be changed by political power, and *educational projects*, which should be carried out *with* the oppressed in the process of organizing them.

The pedagogy of the oppressed, as a humanist and libertarian pedagogy, has two distinct stages. In the first, the oppressed unveil the world of oppression and through the praxis commit themselves to its transformation. In the second stage, in which the reality of oppression has already been transformed, this pedagogy ceases to belong to the oppressed and becomes a pedagogy of all people in the process of permanent liberation. In both stages, it is always through action in depth that the culture of domination is culturally confronted. In the first stage this confrontation occurs through the change in the way the oppressed perceive the world of oppression; in the second stage, through the expulsion of the myths created and developed in the old order, which like specters haunt the new structure emerging from the revolutionary transformation.

The pedagogy of the first stage must deal with the problem of the oppressed consciousness and the oppressor consciousness, the problem of men and women who oppress and men and women who suffer oppression. It must take into account their behavior, their view of the world, and their ethics. A particular problem is the duality of the oppressed: they are contradictory, divided beings, shaped by and existing in a concrete situation of oppression and violence.

Any situation in which "A" objectively exploits "B" or hinders his and her pursuit of self-affirmation as a responsible person is one of oppression. Such a situation in itself constitutes violence, even when sweetened by false generosity, because it interferes with the individual's ontological and historical vocation to be more fully human. With the establishment of a relationship of oppression, violence has *already* begun. Never in history has violence been initiated by the oppressed. How could they be the initiators, if they themselves are the result of violence? How could they be the sponsors of something whose objective inauguration called forth their existence as oppressed? There would be no oppressed had there been no prior situation of violence to establish their subjugation.

Violence is initiated by those who oppress, who exploit, who fail to recognize others as persons—not by those who are oppressed, exploited, and unrecognized. It is not the unloved who initiate disaffection, but those who cannot love because they love only themselves. It is not the helpless, subject to terror, who initiate terror, but the violent, who with their power create the concrete situation which begets the "rejects of life." It is not the tyrannized who initiate despotism, but the tyrants. It is not the despised who initiate hatred but those who despise. It is not those whose humanity is denied them who negate humankind, but those who denied that humanity (thus negating their own as well). Force is used not by those who have become weak under the preponderance of the strong, but by the strong who have emasculated them.

For the oppressors, however, it is always the oppressed (whom they obviously never call "the oppressed" but—depending on whether they are fellow countrymen or not-- "those people" or "the blind and envious masses" or "savages" or "natives" or "subversives") who are disaffected, who are "violent," "barbaric," "wicked," or "ferocious" when they react to the violence of the oppressors.

Yet it is—paradoxical though it may seem—precisely in the response of the oppressed to the violence of their oppressors that a gesture of love may be found. Consciously or unconsciously, the act of rebellion by the oppressed (an act which is always, or nearly always, as violent as the initial violence of the oppressors) can initiate love. Whereas the violence of the oppressors prevents the oppressed from being fully human, the response of the latter to this violence is grounded in the desire to pursue the right to be human. As the oppressors dehumanize others and violate their rights, they themselves also become dehumanized. As the oppressed, fighting to be human, take away the oppressors' power to dominate and suppress, they restore to the oppressors the humanity they had lost in the exercise of oppression.

It is only the oppressed who, by freeing themselves, can free their oppressors. The latter, as an oppressive class, can free neither others nor themselves. It is therefore essential that the oppressed wage the struggle to resolve the contradiction in which they are caught; and the contradiction will be resolved by the appearance of the new man: neither oppressor nor oppressed, but man in the process of liberation. If the goal of the oppressed is to become fully human, they will not achieve their goal by merely reversing the terms of the contradiction, by simply changing poles.

This may seem simplistic; it is not. Resolution of the oppressor—oppressed contradiction indeed implies the disappearance of the oppressors as a dominant class. However, the restraints imposed by the former oppressed on their oppressors, so that the latter cannot reassume their former position, do not constitute *oppression*. An act is oppressive only when it prevents people from being more fully human. Accordingly, these necessary restraints do not *in themselves* signify that yesterday's oppressed have become today's oppressors. Acts which prevent the restoration of the oppressive regime cannot be compared with those which create and maintain it, cannot be compared with those by which a few men and women deny the majority their right to be human.

However, the moment the new regime hardens into a dominating "bureaucracy" the humanist dimension of the struggle is lost and it is no longer possible to speak of liberation. Hence our insistence that the authentic solution of the oppressor—oppressed contradiction does not lie in a mere reversal of position, in moving from one pole to the other. Nor does it lie in the replacement of the former oppressors with new ones who continue to subjugate the oppressed—all in the name of their liberation.

But even when the contradiction is resolved authentically by a new situation established by the liberated laborers, the former oppressors do not feel liberated. On the contrary, they genuinely consider themselves to be oppressed. Conditioned by the experience of oppressing others, any situation other than their former seems to them like oppression. Formerly, they could eat, dress, wear shoes, be educated, travel, and hear Beethoven; while millions did not eat, had no clothes or shoes, neither studied nor traveled, much less listened to Beethoven. Any restriction on this way of life, in the name of the rights of the community, appears to the former oppressors as a profound violation of their individual rights—although they had no respect for the millions who suffered and died of hunger, pain, sorrow, and despair. For the oppressors, "human beings" refers only to themselves; other people are "things." For the oppressors, there exists only one right: their right to live in peace, over against the right, not always even recognized, but simply conceded, of the oppressed to survival. And they make this concession only because the existence of the oppressed is necessary to their own existence.

This behavior, this way of understanding the world and people (which necessarily makes the oppressors resist the installation of a new regime) is explained by their experience as a dominant class. Once a situation of violence and oppression has been established, it engenders an entire way of life and behavior for those caught up in it—oppressors and oppressed alike. Both are submerged in this situation, and both bear the marks of oppression. Analysis of existential situations of oppression reveals that their inception lay in an act of violence —initiated by those with power. This violence, as a process, is perpetuated from generation to generation of oppressors, who become its heirs and are shaped in its climate. This climate creates in the oppressor a strongly possessive consciousness— possessive of the world and of men and women. Apart from direct, concrete, material possession of the world and of people, the oppressor consciousness could not understand itself—could not even exist. Fromm said of this consciousness that, without such possession, "it would lose contact with the world." The oppressor consciousness tends to transform everything surrounding it into an object of its domination. The earth, property, production, the creations of people, people themselves, time—everything is reduced to the status of objects at its disposal.

In their unrestrained eagerness to possess, the oppressors develop the conviction that it is possible for them to transform everything into objects of their purchasing power; hence their strictly materialistic concept of existence. Money is the measure of all things, and profit the primary goal. For the oppressors, what is worthwhile is to have more — always more — even at the cost of the oppressed having less or having nothing. For them, *to be is to have* and to be the class of the "haves."

As beneficiaries of a situation of oppression, the oppressors cannot perceive that if *having* is a condition of *being*, it is a necessary condition for all women and men. This is why their generosity is false. Humanity is a "thing," and they possess it as an exclusive right, as inherited property. To the oppressor consciousness, the humanization of the "others," of the people, appears not as the pursuit of full humanity, but as subversion.

The oppressors do not perceive their monopoly on *having more* as a privilege which dehumanizes others and themselves. They cannot see that, in the egoistic pursuit of *having* as a possessing class, they suffocate in their own possessions and no longer *are*; they merely *have*. For them, *having* more is an inalienable right, a right they acquired through their own "effort," with their "courage to take risks." If others do not have more, it is because they are incompetent and lazy, and worst of all is their unjustifiable ingratitude towards the "generous gestures" of the dominant class. Precisely because they are "ungrateful" and "envious," the oppressed are regarded as potential enemies who must be watched.

It could not be otherwise. If the humanization of the oppressed signifies subversion, so also does their freedom; hence the necessity for constant control. And the more the oppressors control the oppressed, the more they change them into apparently inanimate "things." This tendency of the oppressor consciousness to "in-animate" everything and everyone it encounters, in its eagerness to possess, unquestionably corresponds with a tendency to sadism.

> *The pleasure in complete domination over another person (or other animate creature) is the very essence of the sadistic drive. Another way of formulating the same thought is to say that the aim of sadism is to transform a man into a thing, something animate into something inanimate, since by complete and absolute control the living loses one essential quality of life—freedom.*

Sadistic love is a perverted love—a love of death, not of life. One of the characteristics of the oppressor consciousness and its necrophilic view of the world is thus sadism. As the oppressor consciousness, in order to dominate, tries to deter the drive to search, the restlessness, and the creative power which characterize life, it kills life. More and more, the oppressors are using science and technology as unquestionably powerful instruments for their purpose: the maintenance of the oppressive order through manipulation and repression. The oppressed, as objects, as "things," have no purposes except those their oppressors prescribe for them.

Given the preceding context, another issue of indubitable importance arises: the fact that certain members of the oppressor class join the oppressed in their struggle for liberation, thus moving from one pole of the contradiction to the other. Theirs is a fundamental role, and has been so throughout the history of this struggle. It happens, however, that as they cease to be exploiters or indifferent spectators or simply the heirs of exploitation and move to the side of the exploited, they almost always bring with them the marks of their origin: their prejudices and their deformations, which include a lack of confidence in the people's ability to think, to want, and to know. Accordingly, these adherents to the people's cause constantly run the risk of falling into a type of generosity as malefic as that of the oppressors. The generosity of the oppressors is nourished by an unjust order, which must be maintained in order to justify that generosity. Our converts, on the other hand, truly desire to transform the unjust order; but because of their background they believe that they must be the executors of the transformation. They talk about the people, but they do not trust them; and trusting the people is the indispensable precondition for revolutionary change. A real humanist can be identified more by his trust in the people, which engages him in their struggle, than by a thousand actions in their favor without that trust.

Those who authentically commit themselves to the people must re-examine themselves constantly. This conversion is so radical as not to allow of ambiguous behavior. To affirm this commitment but to consider oneself the proprietor of revolutionary wisdom—which must then be given to (or imposed) the people—is to retain the old ways. The man or woman who proclaims devotion to the cause of liberation yet is unable to enter into *communion* with the people, whom he or she continues to regard as totally ignorant, is grievously self-deceived. The convert who approaches the people but feels alarm at each step they take, each doubt they express, and each suggestion they offer, and attempts to impose his "status," remains nostalgic towards his origins.

Conversion to the people requires a profound rebirth. Those who undergo it must take on a new form of existence; they can no longer remain as they were. Only through comradeship with the oppressed can the converts understand their characteristic ways of living and behaving, which in diverse moments reflect the structure of domination. One of these characteristics is the previously mentioned existential duality of the oppressed, who are at the same time themselves and the oppressor whose image they have internalized. Accordingly, until they concretely "discover" their oppressor and in turn

their own consciousness, they nearly always express fatalistic attitudes towards their situation.

*The peasant begins to get courage to overcome his dependence when he realizes that he is dependent. Until then, he goes along with the boss and says "What can I do? I'm only a peasant."*

When superficially analyzed, this fatalism is sometimes interpreted as a docility that is a trait of national character. Fatalism in the guise of docility is the fruit of an historical and sociological situation, not an essential characteristic of a people's behavior. It almost always is related to the power of destiny or fate or fortune—inevitable forces—or to a distorted view of God. Under the sway of magic and myth, the oppressed (especially the peasants, who are almost submerged in nature) see their suffering, the fruit of exploitation, as the will of God—as if God were the creator of this "organized disorder."

Submerged in reality, the oppressed cannot perceive clearly the "order" which serves the interests of the oppressors whose image they have internalized. Chafing under the restrictions of this order, they often manifest a type of horizontal violence, striking out at their own comrades for the pettiest reasons.

*The colonized man will first manifest this aggressiveness which has been deposited in his bones against his own people. This is the period when the niggers beat each other up, and the police and magistrates do not know which way to turn when faced with the astonishing waves of crime in North Africa. . . . While the settler or the policeman has the right the livelong day to strike the native, to insult him and to make him crawl to them, you will see the native reaching for his knife at the slightest hostile or aggressive glance cast on him by another native; for the last resort of the native is to defend his personality vis-à-vis his brother.*

It is possible that in this behavior they are once more manifesting their duality. Because the oppressor exists within their oppressed comrades, when they attack those comrades they are indirectly attacking the oppressor as well.

On the other hand, at a certain point in their existential experience the oppressed feel an irresistible attraction towards the oppressors and their way of life. Sharing this way of life becomes an overpowering aspiration. In their alienation, the oppressed want at any cost to resemble the oppressors, to imitate them, to follow them. This phenomenon is especially prevalent in the middle-class oppressed, who yearn to be equal to the "eminent" men and women of the upper class. Albert Memmi, in an exceptional analysis of the "colonized mentality," refers to the contempt he felt towards the colonizer, mixed with "passionate" attraction towards him.

> *How could the colonizer look after his workers while periodically gunning down a crowd of colonized? How could the colonized deny himself so cruelly yet make such excessive demands? How could he hate the colonizers and yet admire them so passionately? (I too felt this admiration in spite of myself.)*

Self-depreciation is another characteristic of the oppressed, which derives from their internalization of the opinion the oppressors hold of them. So often do they hear that they are good for nothing, know nothing and are incapable of learning anything—that they are sick, lazy, and unproductive—that in the end they become convinced of their own unfitness.

> *The peasant feels inferior to the boss because the boss seems to be the only one who knows things and is able to run things.*

They call themselves ignorant and say the "professor" is the one who has knowledge and to whom they should listen. The criteria of knowledge imposed upon them are the conventional ones. "Why don't you," said a peasant participating in a culture circle, "explain the pictures first? That way it'll take less time and won't give us a headache."

Almost never do they realize that they, too, "know things" they have learned in their relations with the world and with other women and men. Given the circumstances which have produced their duality, it is only natural that they distrust themselves.

Not infrequently, peasants in educational projects begin to discuss a generative theme in a lively manner, then stop suddenly and say to the educator: "Excuse us, we ought to keep quiet and let you talk. You are the one who knows, we don't know anything." They often insist that there is no difference between them and the animals; when they do admit a difference, it favors the animals. "They are freer than we are."

It is striking, however, to observe how this self-depreciation changes with the first changes in the situation of oppression. I heard a peasant leader say in an *asentamiento* meeting, "They used to say we were unproductive because we were lazy and drunkards. All lies. Now that we are respected as men, we're going to show everyone that we were never drunkards or lazy. We were exploited!"

As long as their ambiguity persists, the oppressed are reluctant to resist, and totally lack confidence in themselves. They have a diffuse, magical belief in the invulnerability and power of the oppressor. The magical force of the landowner's power holds particular sway in the rural areas. A sociologist friend of mine tells of a group of armed peasants in a Latin American country who recently took over a latifundium. For tactical reasons, they planned to hold the landowner as a hostage. But not one peasant had the courage to guard him; his very presence was terrifying. It is also possible that the act of opposing the boss provoked guilt feelings. In truth, the boss was "inside" them.

The oppressed must see examples of the vulnerability of the oppressor so that a contrary conviction can begin to grow within them. Until this occurs, they will continue disheartened, fearful, and beaten. As long as the oppressed remain unaware of the causes of their condition, they fatalistically "accept" their exploitation. Further, they are apt to react in a passive and alienated manner when confronted with the necessity to struggle for their freedom and self-affirmation. Little by little, however, they tend to try out forms of rebellious action. In working towards liberation, one must neither lose sight of this passivity nor overlook the moment of awakening.

Within their unauthentic view of the world and of themselves, the oppressed feel like "things" owned by the oppressor. For the latter, *to be* is *to have*, almost always at the expense of those who have nothing. For the oppressed, at a certain point in their existential experience, *to be* is not to resemble the oppressor, but *to be under* him, to depend on him. Accordingly, the oppressed are emotionally dependent.

> *The peasant is a dependent. He can't say what he wants. Before he discovers his dependence, he suffers. He lets off steam at home, where he shouts at his children, beats them, and despairs. He complains about his wife and thinks everything is dreadful. He doesn't let off steam with the boss because he thinks the boss is a superior being. Lots of times, the peasant gives vent to his sorrows by drinking.*

This total emotional dependence can lead the oppressed to what Fromm calls necrophilic behavior: the destruction of life—their own or that of their oppressed fellows.

It is only when the oppressed find the oppressor out and become involved in the organized struggle for their liberation that they begin to believe in themselves. This discovery cannot be purely intellectual but must involve action; nor can it be limited to mere activism, but must include serious reflection: only then will it be a praxis.

Critical and liberating dialogue, which presupposes action, must be carried on with the oppressed at whatever the stage of their struggle for liberation. The content of that dialogue can and should vary in accordance with historical conditions and the level at which the oppressed perceive reality. But to substitute monologue, slogans, and communiqués for dialogue is to attempt to liberate the oppressed with the instruments of domestication. Attempting to liberate the oppressed without their reflective participation in the act of liberation is to treat them as objects which must be saved from a burning building; it is to lead them into the populist pitfall and transform them into masses which can be manipulated.

At all stages of their liberation, the oppressed must see themselves as women and men engaged in the ontological and historical vocation of becoming more fully human. Reflection and action become imperative when one does not erroneously attempt to dichotomize the content of humanity from its historical forms.

The insistence that the oppressed engage in reflection on their concrete situation is not a call to armchair revolution. On the contrary, reflection — true reflection — leads to action. On the other hand, when the situation calls for action, that action will constitute an authentic praxis only if its consequences become the object of critical reflection. In this sense, the praxis is the new *raison d'être* of the oppressed; and the revolution, which inaugurates the historical moment of this *raison d'être*, is not viable apart from their concomitant conscious involvement. Otherwise, action is pure activism.

To achieve this praxis, however, it is necessary to trust in the oppressed and in their ability to reason. Whoever lacks this trust will fail to initiate (or will abandon) dialogue, reflection, and communication, and will fall into using slogans, communiqués, monologues, and instructions. Superficial conversions to the cause of liberation carry this danger.

Political action on the side of the oppressed must be pedagogical action in the authentic sense of the word and, therefore, action *with* the oppressed. Those who work for liberation must not take advantage of the emotional dependence of the oppressed—dependence that is the fruit of the concrete situation of domination which surrounds them and which engendered their unauthentic view of the world. Using their dependence to create still greater dependence is an oppressor tactic.

Libertarian action must recognize this dependence as a weak point and must attempt through reflection and action to transform it into independence. However, not even the best-intentioned leadership can bestow independence as a gift. The liberation of the oppressed is a liberation of women and men, not things. Accordingly, while no one liberates himself by his own efforts alone, neither is he liberated by others. Liberation, a human phenomenon, cannot be achieved by semihumans. Any attempt to treat people as semihumans only dehumanizes them. When people are already dehumanized, due to the oppression they suffer, the process of their liberation must not employ the methods of dehumanization.

The correct method for a revolutionary leadership to employ in the task of liberation is, therefore, not "libertarian propaganda." Nor can the leadership merely "implant" in the oppressed a belief in freedom, thus thinking to win their trust. The correct method lies in dialogue. The conviction of the oppressed that they must fight for their liberation is not a gift bestowed by the revolutionary leadership, but the result of their own *conscientizacão*.

The revolutionary leaders must realize that their own conviction of the necessity for struggle (an indispensable dimension of revolutionary wisdom) was not given to them by anyone else—if it is authentic. This conviction cannot be packaged and sold; it is reached, rather, by means of a totality of reflection and action. Only the reader's own involvement in reality, within an historical situation, led them to criticize this situation and to wish to change it.

Likewise, the oppressed (who do not commit themselves to the struggle unless they are convinced, and who, if they do not make such a commitment, withhold the indispensable conditions for this struggle) must reach this conviction as Subjects, not as objects. They also must intervene critically in the situation which surrounds them and whose mark they bear; propaganda cannot achieve this. While the conviction of the necessity for struggle (without which the struggle is unfeasible) is indispensable to the revolutionary leadership (indeed, it was this conviction which constituted that leadership), it is also necessary for the oppressed. It is necessary, that is, unless one intends to carry out the transformation *for* the oppressed rather than *with* them. It is my belief that only the latter form of transformation is valid.

The object in presenting these considerations is to defend the eminently pedagogical character of the revolution. The revolutionary leaders of every epoch who have affirmed that the oppressed must accept the struggle for their liberation—an obvious point—have also thereby implicitly recognized the pedagogical aspect of this struggle. Many of these leaders, however (perhaps due to natural and understandable biases against pedagogy), have ended up using the "educational" methods employed by the oppressor. They deny pedagogical action in the liberation process, but they use propaganda to convince.

It is essential for the oppressed to realize that when they accept the struggle for humanization they also accept, from that moment, their total responsibility for the struggle. They must realize that they are fighting not merely for freedom from hunger, but for

> ... *freedom to create and to construct, to wonder and to venture. Such freedom requires that the individual be active and responsible, not a slave or a well-fed cog in the machine.... It is not enough that men are not slaves; if social conditions further the existence of automatons, the result will not be love of life, but love of death.*

The oppressed, who have been shaped by the death-affirming climate of oppression, must find through their struggle the way to life-affirming humanization, which does not lie *simply* in having more to eat (although it does involve having more to eat and cannot fail to include this aspect). The oppressed have been destroyed precisely because their situation has reduced them to things. In order to regain their humanity they must cease to be things and fight as men and women. This is a radical requirement. They cannot enter the struggle as objects in order *later* to become human beings.

The struggle begins with men's recognition that they have been destroyed. Propaganda, management, manipulation—all arms of domination—cannot be the instruments of their rehumanization. The only effective instrument is a humanizing pedagogy in which the revolutionary leadership establishes a permanent relationship of dialogue with the oppressed. In a humanizing pedagogy the method ceases to be an instrument which the teachers (in this instance, the revolutionary leadership) can manipulate the students (in this instance, the oppressed), because it expresses the consciousness of the students themselves.

> *The method is, in fact, the external form of consciousness manifest in acts, which takes on the fundamental property of consciousness—its intentionality. The essence of consciousness is being with the world, and this behavior is permanent and unavoidable. Accordingly, consciousness is in essence a 'way towards' something apart from itself, outside itself, which surrounds it and which it apprehends by means of its ideational capacity. Consciousness is thus by definition a method, in the most general sense of the word.*

A revolutionary leadership must accordingly practice *co-intentional* education. Teachers and students (leadership and people), co-intent on reality, are both Subjects not only in the task of unveiling that reality, and thereby coming to know it critically, but in the task of re-creating that knowledge. As they attain this knowledge of reality through common reflection and action, they discover themselves as its permanent recreators. In this way, the presence of the oppressed in the struggle for their liberation will be what it should be: not pseudo—participation, but committed involvement.

Study Questions

1. Define humanization and dehumanization. How are these concepts connected to pedagogy?

2. How does dehumanization connect both to the oppressor and the oppressed?

3. Why is he critical of "false charity"? Can we see current examples? What do you think he is nervous about?

4. Why is it important to define oppression as violence? Why do oppressors sometimes feel that they are oppressed?

5. What is objectification? Why is it dangerous?

# A REVOLUTION OF VALUES

## The Promise Of Multicultural Change

### *bell hooks*

*bell hooks is now Distinguished Professor of English at City College and the Graduate Center at CUNY. She is a cultural critic, feminist theorist, and public intellectual who has published numerous books, including* Ain't I Woman: Black Women and Feminism, *and* Feminist Theory from Margin to Center. *This selection comes from her book* Teaching to Transgress (1994), *which analyzes the practice of teaching as a tool for liberation.*

Two summers ago I attended my twentieth high school reunion. It was a last-minute decision. I had just finished a new book. Whenever I finish a work, I always feel lost, as though a steady anchor has been taken away and there is no sure ground under my feet. During the time between ending one project and beginning another, I always have a crisis of meaning. I begin to wonder what my life is all about and what I have been put on this earth to do. It is as though immersed in a project I lose all sense of myself and must then, when the work is done, rediscover who I am and where I am going. When I heard that the reunion was happening, it seemed just the experience to bring me back to myself, to help in the process of rediscovery. Never having attended any of the past reunions, I did not know what to expect. I did know that this one would be different. For the first time we were about to have a racially integrated reunion. In past years, reunions had always been segregated. White folks had their reunion on their side of town and black folks had a separate reunion.

None of us was sure what an integrated reunion would be like. Those periods in our adolescent lives of racial desegregation had been full of hostility, rage, conflict, and loss. We black kids had been angry that we had to leave our beloved all-black high school, Crispus Attucks, and be bussed halfway cross town to integrate white schools. We had to make the journey and thus bear the responsibility of making desegregation a reality. We had to give up the familiar and enter a world that seemed cold and strange, not our world, not our school. We were certainly on the margin, no longer at the center, and it hurt. It was such an unhappy time. I still remember my rage that we had to awaken an hour early so that we could be bussed to school before the white students arrived. We were made to sit in the gymnasium and wait. It was believed that this practice would prevent outbreaks of conflict and hostility since it removed the possibility of social contact before classes began. Yet, once again, the burden of this transition was placed on us. The white school was desegregated, but in the classroom, in the cafeteria, and in most social spaces racial apartheid prevailed. Black and white students who considered ourselves progressive rebelled against the unspoken racial taboos meant to sustain white supremacy and racial apartheid even in the face of desegregation. The white folks never seemed to understand that our parents were no more eager for us to socialize with them than they were to socialize with us. Those of us who wanted to make racial equality a reality in every area of our life were threats to the social order. We were proud of ourselves, proud of our willingness to transgress the rules, proud to be courageous.

Part of a small integrated clique of smart kids who considered ourselves "artists," we believed we were destined to create outlaw culture where we would live as Bohemians forever free; we were certain of our radicalness. Days before the reunion, I was overwhelmed by memories and shocked to discover that our gestures of defiance had been nowhere near as daring as they had seemed at the time. Mostly, they were acts of resistance that did not truly challenge the status quo. One of my best buddies during that time was white and male. He had an old gray Volvo that I loved to ride in. Every now and then he would give me a ride home from school if I missed the bus—an action which angered and disturbed those who saw us. Friendship across racial lines was bad enough, but across gender it was unheard of and dangerous. (One day, we found out just how dangerous when grown white men in a car tried to run us off the road.) Ken's parents were religious. Their faith compelled them to live out a belief in racial justice. They were among the first white folks in our community to invite black folks to come to their house, to eat at their table, to worship together with them. As one of Ken's best buddies, I was welcome in their house. After hours of discussion and debate about possible dangers, my parents agreed that I could go there for a meal. It was my first time eating together with white people. I was 16 years old. I felt then as though we were making history, that we were living the dream of democracy, creating a culture where equality, love, justice, and peace would shape America's destiny.

After graduation, I lost touch with Ken even though he always had a warm place in my memory. I thought of him when meeting and interacting with liberal white folks who believed that having a black friend meant that they were not racist, who sincerely believed that they were doing us a favor by extending offers of friendly contact for which they felt they should be rewarded. I thought of him during years of watching white folks play at unlearning racism but walking away when they encountered obstacles, rejection, conflict, pain. Our high school friendship had been forged not because we were black and white but because we shared a similar take on reality. Racial difference meant that we had to struggle to claim the integrity of that bonding. We had no illusions. We knew there would be obstacles, conflict, and pain. In white supremacist capitalist patriarchy—words we never used then—we knew we would have to pay a price for this friendship, that we would need to possess the courage to stand up for our belief in democracy, in racial justice, in the transformative power of love. We valued the bond between us enough to meet the challenge.

Days before the reunion, remembering the sweetness of that friendship, I felt humbled by the knowledge of what we give up when we are young, believing that we will find something just as good or better someday, only to discover that not to be so. I wondered just how it could be that Ken and I had ever lost contact with one another. Along the way I had not found white folks who understood the depth and complexity of racial injustice, and who were as willing to practice the art of living a nonracist life, as folks were then. In my adult life I have seen few white folks who are really willing to go the distance to create a world of racial equality— white folks willing to take risks, to be courageous, to live against the grain. I went to the reunion hoping that I would have a chance to see Ken face-to-face, to tell him how much I cherished all that we had shared, to tell him—in words which I never dared to say to any white person back then—simply that I loved him.

Remembering this past, I am most struck by our passionate commitment to a vision of social transformation rooted in the fundamental belief in a radically democratic idea of freedom and justice for all. Our notions of social change were not fancy. There was no elaborate postmodern political theory shaping our actions. We were simply trying to change the way we went about our everyday lives so that our values and habits of being would reflect our commitment to freedom. Our major concern then was ending racism. Today, as I witness the rise in white supremacy, the growing social and economic apartheid that separates white and black, the haves and the have-nots, men and women, I have placed alongside the struggle to end racism a commitment to ending sexism and sexist oppression, to eradicating systems of class exploitation. Aware that we are living in a culture of domination, I ask myself now, as I did more than twenty years ago, what values and habits of being reflect my/our commitment to freedom.

In retrospect, I see that in the last twenty years I have encountered many folks who say they are committed to freedom and justice for all even though the way they live, the values and habits of being they institutionalize daily, in public and private rituals, help maintain the culture of domination, help create an unfree world. In the book *Where Do We Go From Here? Chaos or Community*, Martin Luther King, Jr. told the citizens of this nation, with prophetic insight, that we would be unable to go forward if we did not experience a "true revolution of values." He assured us that

> the stability of the large world house which is ours will involve a revolution of values to accompany the scientific and freedom revolutions engulfing the earth. We must rapidly begin the shift from a "thing"-oriented society to a "person"-oriented society. When machines and computers, profit motives and property rights are considered more important than people, the giant triplets of racism, materialism and militarism are incapable of being conquered. A civilization can flounder as readily in the face of

*moral and spiritual bankruptcy as it can through financial bankruptcy.*

Today, we live in the midst of that floundering. We live in chaos, uncertain about the possibility of building and sustaining community. The public figures who speak the most to us about a return to old-fashioned values embody the evils King describes. They are most committed to maintaining systems of domination—racism, sexism, class exploitation, and imperialism. They promote a perverse vision of freedom that makes it synonymous with materialism. They teach us to believe that domination is "natural," that it is right for the strong to rule over the weak, the powerful over the powerless. What amazes me is that so many people claim not to embrace these values and yet our collective rejection of them cannot be complete since they prevail in our daily lives.

These days, I am compelled to consider what forces keep us from moving forward, from having that revolution of values that would enable us to live differently. King taught us to understand that if "we are to have peace on earth" that "our loyalties must transcend our race, our tribe, our class, and our nation." Long before the word "multiculturalism" became fashionable, he encouraged us to "develop a world perspective." Yet, what we are witnessing today in our everyday life is not an eagerness on the part of neighbors and strangers to develop a world perspective but a return to narrow nationalism, isolationisms, and xenophobia. These shifts are usually explained in New Right and neoconservative terms as attempts to bring order to the chaos, to return to an (idealized) past. The notion of family evoked in these discussions is one in which sexist roles are upheld as stabilizing traditions. Nor surprisingly, this vision of family life is coupled with a notion of security that suggests we are always most safe with people of our same group, race, class, religion, and so on. No matter how many statistics on domestic violence, homicide, rape, and child abuse indicate that, in fact, the idealized patriarchal family is not a "safe" space, that those of us who experience any form of assault are more likely to be victimized by those who are like us rather than by some mysterious strange outsiders, these conservative myths persist. It is apparent that one of the primary reasons we have not experienced a revolution of values is that a culture of domination necessarily promotes addiction to lying and denial.

That lying takes the presumably innocent form of many white people (and even some black folks) suggesting that racism does not exist anymore, and that conditions of social equality are solidly in place that would enable any black person who works

hard to achieve economic self-sufficiency. Forget about the fact that capitalism requires the existence of a mass underclass of surplus labor. Lying takes the form of mass media creating the myth that feminist movement has completely transformed society, so much so that the politics of patriarchal power have been inverted and that men, particularly white men, just like emasculated black men, have become the victims of dominating women. So, it goes, all men (especially black men) must pull together (as in the Clarence Thomas hearings) to support and reaffirm patriarchal domination. Add to this the widely held assumptions that blacks, other minorities, and white women are taking jobs from white men, and that people are poor and unemployed because they want to be, and it becomes most evident that part of our contemporary crisis is created by a lack of meaningful access to truth. That is to say, individuals are not just presented untruths, but are told them in a manner that enables most effective communication. When this collective cultural consumption of and attachment to misinformation is coupled with the layers of lying individuals do in their personal lives, our capacity to face reality is severely diminished as is our will to intervene and change unjust circumstances.

If we examine critically the traditional role of the university in the pursuit of truth and the sharing of knowledge and information, it is painfully clear that biases that uphold and maintain white supremacy, imperialism, sexism, and racism have distorted education so that it is no longer about the practice of freedom. The call for a recognition of cultural diversity, a rethinking of ways of knowing, a deconstruction of old epistemologies and the concomitant demand that there be a transformation in our classrooms, in how we teach and what we teach has been a necessary revolution—one that seeks to restore life to a corrupt and dying academy.

When everyone first began to speak about cultural diversity, it was exciting. For those of us on the margins (people of color, folks from working class backgrounds, gays, and lesbians, and so on) who had always felt ambivalent about our presence in institutions where knowledge was shared in ways that re-inscribed colonialism and domination, it was thrilling to think that the vision of justice and democracy that was at the very heart of civil rights movement would be realized in the academy. At last, there was the possibility of a learning community, a place where difference could be acknowledged, where we would finally all understand, accept, and affirm that our ways of knowing are forged in history and relations of power. Finally, we were all going to break through collective academic denial and acknowledge that the education most of us had received and were giving was not and is never politically neutral. Though it was evident that change would not be immediate, there was tremendous hope that this process we had set in motion would lead to a fulfillment of the dream of education as the practice of freedom.

Many of our colleagues were initially reluctant participants in this change. Many folks found that as they tried to respect "cultural diversity" they had to confront the limitations of their training and knowledge as well as a possible loss of "authority." Indeed, exposing certain truths and biases in the classroom often created chaos and confusion. The idea that the classroom should always be a "safe," harmonious place was challenged. It was hard for individuals to fully grasp the idea that recognition of difference might also require of us a willingness to see the classroom change, to allow for shifts in relations between students. A lot of people panicked. What they saw happening was not the comforting "melting pot" idea of cultural diversity, the rainbow coalition where we would all be grouped together in our difference, but everyone wearing the same have-a-nice-day smile. This was the stuff of colonizing fantasy, a perversion of the progressive vision of cultural diversity. Critiquing this longing in a recent interview, "Critical Multiculturalism and Democratic Schooling" (in the *International Journal of Educational Reform*), Peter McLaren asserted:

> *Diversity that somehow constitutes itself as a harmonious ensemble of benign cultural spheres is a conservative and liberal model of multiculturalism that, in my mind, deserves to be jettisoned because, when we try to make culture in undisturbed space of harmony and agreement where social relations exist within cultural forms of uninterrupted accords we subscribe to a form of social amnesia in which we forget that all knowledge is forged in histories that are played out in the field of social antagonisms.*

Many professors lacked strategies to deal with antagonisms in the classroom. When this fear joined with the refusal to change that characterized the stance of an old (predominantly white male) guard it created a space for disempowered collective backlash.

All of a sudden, professors who had taken issues of multiculturalism and cultural diversity seriously were backtracking, expressing doubts, casting votes in directions that would restore biased traditions or prohibit changes in faculty and curricula that were to bring diversity of representation and perspective. Joining forces with the old guard, previously open professors condoned tactics (ostracization, belittlement, and so on) used by senior colleagues to dissuade junior faculty members from making paradigm shifts that would lead to change. In one of my Toni Morrison seminars, as we went around our circle voicing critical reflections on Morrison's language, a sort of classically white, blondish, J. Crew coed shared that one of her other English professors, an older white man (whose name none of us wanted her to mention), confided that he was so pleased to find a student still interested in reading literature—words—the language of texts and "not that race and gender stuff." Somewhat amused by the assumption he had made about her, she was disturbed by his conviction that conventional ways of critically approaching a novel could not coexist in classrooms that also offered new perspectives.

I then shared with the class my experience of being at a Halloween party. A new white male colleague, with whom I was chatting for the first time, went on a tirade at the mere mention of my Toni Morrison seminar, emphasizing that *Song of Solomon* was a weak rewrite of Hemingway's *For Whom the Bell Tolls*. Passionately full of disgust for Morrison he, being a Hemingway scholar, seemed to be sharing the often-heard concern that black women writers/thinkers are just poor imitations of "great" white men. Not wanting at that moment to launch into Unlearning Colonialism, Divesting of Racism and Sexism 101, I opted for the strategy taught to me by that in-denial-of-institutionalized-patriarch, self-help book *Women Who Love Too Much*. I just said, "Oh!" Later, I assured him that I would read *For Whom the Bell Tolls* again to see if I would make the same connection. Both these seemingly trivial incidents reveal how deep-seated is the fear that any de-centering of Western civilizations, of the white male canon, is really an act of cultural genocide.

Some folks think that everyone who supports cultural diversity wants to replace one dictatorship of knowing with another, changing one set way of thinking for another. This is perhaps the gravest misperception of cultural diversity. Even though there are those overly zealous among us who hope to replace one set of absolutes with another, simply changing content, this perspective does not accurately represent progressive visions of the way commitment to cultural diversity can constructively transform the academy. In all cultural revolutions there are periods of chaos and confusion, times when grave mistakes are made. If we fear mistakes, doing things wrongly, constantly evaluating ourselves, we will never make the academy a culturally diverse place where scholars and the curricula address every dimension of that difference.

As backlash swells, as budgets are cut, as jobs become even more scarce, many of the few progressive interventions that were made to change the academy, to create an open climate for cultural diversity are in danger of being undermined or eliminated. These threats should not be ignored. Nor should our collective commitment to cultural diversity change because we have not yet devised and implemented perfect strategies for them. To create a culturally diverse academy we must commit ourselves fully. Learning from other movements for social change, from civil rights and feminist liberation efforts, we must accept the protracted nature of our struggle and be willing to remain both patient and vigilant. To commit ourselves to the work of transforming the academy so that it will be a place where cultural diversity informs every aspect of our learning, we must embrace struggle and sacrifice. We cannot be easily discouraged. We cannot despair when there is conflict. Our solidarity must be affirmed by shared belief in a spirit of intellectual openness that celebrates diversity, welcomes dissent, and rejoices in collective dedication to truth.

Drawing strength from the life and work of Martin Luther King, Jr., I am often reminded of his profound inner struggle when he felt called by his religious beliefs to oppose the war in Vietnam. Fearful of alienating conservative bourgeois supporters, and of alienating the black church, King meditated on a passage from Romans, chapter 12, verse 2, which reminded him of the necessity of dissent, challenge and change: "Be not conformed to this world but be ye transformed by the renewal of your minds." All of us in the academy and in the culture as a whole are called to renew our minds if we are to transform educational institutions—and society—so that the way we live, teach, and work can reflect our joy in cultural diversity, our passion for justice and our love of freedom.

## Study Questions

1. While hooks does not use the language of humanization and dehumanization, her goals for education are similar. What parallels do you see here?

2. Why does she emphasize values? Why is everyday life so important, according to hooks?

3. What is "a revolution of values"? What does she see holding us back? Name some myths she discusses specifically.

4. What does she mean by a "culture of domination"? What do you think about her analysis?

5. What is the role of the university? Why does she focus on higher education in particular? Can education ever be politically neutral?

# FROM SOCIAL CLASS AND THE HIDDEN CURRICULUM OF WORK

## Jean Anyon

*Jean Anyon is chair of the Education Department at Rutgers University. To write this essay, she observed five elementary schools over the course of a full school year to examine the way that class impacts teaching methods. While most people are aware that resources are distributed unevenly among schools, she investigates the way that teaching practices themselves differ according to class. This essay first appeared in the* Journal of Education *in 1980.*

Scholars in political economy and the sociology of knowledge have recently argued that public schools in complex industrial societies like our own make available different types of educational experience and curriculum knowledge to students in different social classes. Bowles and Gintis[1] for example, have argued that students in different social-class backgrounds are rewarded for classroom behaviors that correspond to personality traits allegedly rewarded in the different occupational strata—the working classes for docility and obedience, the managerial classes for initiative and personal assertiveness. Basil Bernstein, Pierre Bourdieu, and Michael W. Apple,[2] focusing on school knowledge, have argued that knowledge and skills leading to social power and regard (medical, legal, managerial) are made available to the advantaged social groups but are withheld from the working classes, to whom a more "practical" curriculum is offered (manual skills, clerical knowledge). While there has been considerable argumentation of these points regarding education in England, France, and North America, there has been little or no attempt to investigate these ideas empirically in elementary or secondary schools and classrooms in this country.[3]

This article offers tentative empirical support (and qualification) of the above arguments by providing illustrative examples of differences in student work in classrooms in contrasting social class communities. The examples were gathered as part of an ethnographical[4] study of curricular pedagogical, and pupil evaluation practices in five elementary schools. The article attempts a theoretical contribution as well and assesses student work in the light of a theoretical approach to social-class analysis. . . . It will be suggested that there is a "hidden curriculum" in schoolwork that has profound implications for the theory—and consequence—of everyday activity in education. . . .

## THE SAMPLE OF SCHOOLS

. . . The social-class designation of each of the five schools will be identified, and the income, occupation, and other relevant available social characteristics of the students and their parents will be described. The first three schools are in a medium-sized city district in northern New Jersey, and the other two are in a nearby New Jersey suburb.

The first two schools I will call *working-class schools.* Most of the parents have blue-collar jobs. Less than a third of the fathers are skilled, while the majority are in unskilled or semiskilled jobs. During the period of the study (1978–1979), approximately 15 percent of the fathers were unemployed. The large majority (85 percent) of the families are white. The following occupations are typical: platform, storeroom, and stockroom workers; foundrymen, pipe welders, and boilermakers; semiskilled and unskilled assemblyline operatives; gas station attendants, auto mechanics, maintenance workers, and security guards. Less than 30 percent of the women work, some part-time and some full-time, on assembly lines, in storerooms and stockrooms, as waitresses, barmaids, or sales clerks. Of the fifth-grade parents, none of the wives of the skilled workers had jobs. Approximately 15 percent of the families in each school are at or below the federal "poverty" level;[5] most of the rest of the family incomes are at or below $ 12,000, except some of the skilled workers whose incomes are higher. The incomes of the majority of the families in these two schools (at or below $12,000) are typical of 38.6 percent of the families in the United States.[6]

The third school is called the *middle-class school*, although because of neighborhood residence patterns, the population is a mixture of several social classes. The parents' occupations can be divided into three groups: a small group of blue-collar "rich," who are skilled, well-paid workers such as printers, carpenters, plumbers, and construction workers. The second group is composed of parents in working-class and middle-class white-collar-jobs; women in office jobs, technicians, supervisors in industry, and parents employed by the city (such as firemen, policemen, and several of the school's teachers). The third group is composed of occupations such as personnel directors in local firms, accountants, "middle management," and a few small capitalists (owners of shops in the area). The children of several local doctors attend this school. Most family incomes are between $13,000 and $25,000, with a few higher. This income range is typical of 38.9 percent of the families in the United States.[7]

The fourth school has a parent population that is at the upper income level of the upper middle class and is predominantly professional. This school will be called the *affluent professional school*. Typical jobs are: cardiologist, interior designer, corporate lawyer or engineer, executive in advertising or television. There are some families who are not as affluent as the majority (the family of the superintendent of the district's schools, and the one or two families in which the fathers are skilled workers). In addition, a few of the families are more affluent than the majority and can be classified in the capitalist class (a partner in a prestigious Wall Street stock brokerage firm). Approximately 90 percent of the children in this school are white. Most family incomes are between $40,000 and $80,000. This income span represents approximately 7 percent of the families in the United States.[8]

In the fifth school the majority of the families belong to the capitalist class. This school will be called the *executive elite* school because most of the fathers are top executives (for example, presidents and vice-presidents) in major United States-based multinational corporations —for example, AT&T, RCA, Citibank, American Express, U.S. Steel. A sizable group of fathers are top executives in financial firms on Wall Street. There are also a number of fathers who list their occupations as "general counsel" to a particular corporation, and these corporations are also among the large multinationals. Many of the mothers do volunteer work in the Junior League, Junior fortnightly, or other service groups; some are intricately involved in town politics; and some are themselves in well-paid occupations. There are no minority children in the school. Almost all the family incomes are over $100,000, with some in the $500,000 range. The incomes in this school represent less than 1 percent of the families in the United States.[9]

Since each of the five schools is only one instance of elementary education in a particular social class context, I will not generalize beyond the sample. However the examples of schoolwork which follow will suggest characteristics of education in each social setting that appear to have theoretical and social significance and to be worth investigation in a larger number of schools. . . .

## THE WORKING-CLASS SCHOOLS

In the two working-class schools, work is following the steps of a procedure. The procedure is usually mechanical involving rote behavior and very little decision making or choice. The teachers rarely explain why the work is being assigned, how it might connect to other assignments, or what the idea is that lies behind the procedure or gives it coherence and perhaps meaning or significance. Available textbooks are not always used, and the teachers often prepare their own dittos or put work examples on the board. Most of the rules regarding work are designations of what the children are to do; the rules are steps to follow. These steps are told to the children by the teachers and are often written on the board. The children are usually told to copy the steps as notes. These notes are to be studied. Work is often evaluated not according to whether it is right or wrong but according to whether the children followed the right steps.

The following examples illustrate these points. In math, when two-digit division was introduced, the teacher in one school gave a four-minute lecture on what the terms are called (which number is the divisor, dividend, quotient, and remainder). The children were told to copy these names in their note-books. Then the teacher told them the steps to follow to do the problems, saying, "This is how you do them." The teacher listed the steps on the board, and they appeared several days later as a chart hung in the middle of the front wall: "Divide, Multiply, Subtract, Bring Down." The children often did examples of two-digit division. When the teacher went over the examples with them, he told them what the procedure was for each problem, rarely asking them to conceptualize or explain it them-selves: "Three into twenty-two is seven; do your subtraction and one is left over." During the week that two-digit division was introduced (or at any other time), the investigator did not observe any discussion of the idea of grouping involved in division, any use of manipulables, or any attempt to relate two-digit division to any other mathematical process. Nor was there any attempt to relate the steps to an actual or possible thought process of the children. The observer did not hear the terms dividend, quotient, and so on, used again. The math teacher in the other working-class school followed similar procedures regarding two-digit division and at one point her class seemed confused. She said, "You're confusing yourselves. You're tensing up. Remember, when you do this, it's the same steps over and over again—and that's the way division always is." Several weeks later, after a test, a group of her children "still didn't get it," and she made no attempt to explain the concept of dividing things into groups or to give them manipulables for their own investigation. Rather, she went over the steps with them again and told them that they "needed more practice."

In other areas of math, work is also carrying out often unexplained fragmented procedures. For example, one of the teachers led the children through a series of steps to make a 1-inch grid on their paper *without* telling them that they were making a 1-inch grid or that it would be used to study scale. She said, "Take your ruler. Put it across the top. Make a mark at every number. Then move your ruler down to the bottom. No, put it across the bottom. Now make a mark on top of every number. Now draw a line from . . ." At this point a girl said that she had a faster way to do it and the teacher said, "No, you don't; you don't even know what I'm making yet. Do it this way or it's wrong." After they had made the lines up and down and across, the teacher told them she wanted them to make a figure by connecting some dots and to measure that, using the scale of 1 inch equals 1 mile. Then they were to cut it out. She said, "Don't cut it until I check it."

In both working-class schools, work in language arts is mechanics of punctuation (commas,

periods, question marks, exclamation points), capi-talization, and the four kinds of sentences. One teacher explained to me, "Simple punctuation is all they'll ever use." Regarding punctuation, either a teacher or a ditto stated the rules for where, for example, to put commas. The investigator heard no classroom discussion of the aural context of punctu-ation (which, of course, is what gives each mark its meaning). Nor did the investigator hear any statement or inference that placing a punctuation mark could be a decision-making process, depending, for example, on one's intended meaning. Rather, the children were told to follow the rules. Language arts did not involve creative writing. There were several writing assignments throughout the year, but in each instance the children were given a ditto, and they wrote answers to questions on the sheet. For example, they wrote their "autobiog-raphy" by answering such questions as "Where were you born?" "What is your favorite animal?" on a sheet entitled "All About Me."

In one of the working-class schools, the class had a science period several times a week. On the three occasions observed, the children were not called upon to set up experiments or to give expla-nations for facts or concepts. Rather, on each occasion the teacher told them in his own words what the book said. The children copied the teacher's sentences from the board. Each day that preceded the day they were to do a science exper-iment, the teacher told them to copy the directions from the book for the procedure they would carry out the next day and to study the list at home that night. The day after each experiment, the teacher went over what they had "found" (they did the experiments as a class, and each was actually a class demonstration led by the teacher). Then the teacher wrote what they "found" on the board, and the children copied that in their notebooks. Once or twice a year there are science projects. The project is chosen and assigned by the teacher from a box of 3-by-5-inch cards. On the card the teacher has written the question to be answered, the books to use, and how much to write. Explaining the cards to the observer, the teacher said, "It tells them exactly what to do, or they couldn't do it."

Social studies in the working-class schools is also largely mechanical work that was given little explanation or connection to larger contexts. In one school, for example, although there was a book available, social studies work was to copy the teacher's notes from the board. Several times a week for a period of several months the children copied these notes. The fifth grades in the district were to study United States history. The teacher used a booklet she had purchased called "The Fabulous Fifty States." Each day she put information from the booklet in outline form on the board and the children copied it. The type of information did not vary: the name of the state, its abbreviation, state capital, nickname of the state, its main products, main business, and a "Fabulous Fact" ("Idaho grew twenty-seven billion potatoes in one year. That's enough potatoes for each man, woman, and . . ."). As the children finished copying the sentences, the teacher erased them and wrote more. Children would occasionally go to the front to pull down the wall map in order to locate the states they were copying, and the teacher did not dissuade them. But the observer never saw her refer to the map: nor did the observer ever hear her make other than perfunctory remarks concerning the information the children were copying. Occasionally the children colored in a ditto and cut it out to make a stand-up figure (representing, for example, a man roping a cow in the Southwest). These were referred to by the teacher as their social studies "projects."

Rote behavior was often called for in classroom work. When going over math and language arts skills sheets, for example, as the teacher asked for the answer to each problem, he fired the questions rapidly, staccato, and the scene reminded the observer of a sergeant drilling recruits: above all the questions demanded that you stay at attention: "The next one? What do I put here? . . . Here? Give us the next." Or "How many commas in this sentence? Where do I put them . . . The next one?"

The four fifth-grade teachers observed in the working-class schools attempted to control classroom time and space by making decisions without consulting the children and without explaining the basis for their decisions. The teacher's control thus often seemed capricious. Teachers, for instance, very often ignored the bells to switch classes—deciding among themselves to keep the children after the period was officially over to continue with the work or for disciplinary reasons or so they, the teachers, could stand in the hall and talk. There were no clocks in the rooms in either school, and the children often asked, "What period is this?" "When do we go to gym?" The children had no access to materials. These were handed out by teachers and closely guarded. Things in the room "belonged" to the teacher: "Bob, bring me my garbage can." The teachers continually gave the children orders. Only three times did the investigator hear a teacher in either working-class school preface a directive with an unsarcastic "please," or "let's" or "would you." Instead, the teachers said, "Shut up," "Shut your mouth," "Open your books," "Throw your gum away—if you want to rot your teeth, do it on your own time." Teachers made every effort to control the movement of the children, and often shouted, "Why are you out of you seat??!!" If the children got permission to leave the room, they had to take a written pass with the date and time . . .

## MIDDLE-CLASS SCHOOL

In the middle-class school, work is getting the right answer. If one accumulates enough right answers, one gets a good grade. One must follow the directions in order to get the right answers, but the directions often call for some figuring, some choice, some decision making. For example, the children must often figure out by themselves what the directions ask them to do and how to get the answer: what do you do first, second, and perhaps third? Answers are usually found in books or by listening to the teacher. Answers are usually words, sentences, numbers, or facts and dates; one writes them on paper, and one should be neat. Answers must be given in the right order, and one cannot make them up.

The following activities are illustrative. Math involves some choice: one may do two-digit division the long way or the short way, and there are some math problems that can be done "in your head." When the teacher explains how to do two-digit division, there is recognition that a cognitive process is involved; she gives you several ways and says. "I want to make sure you understand what you're doing—so you get it right"; and, when they go over the homework, she asks the *children* to tell how they did the problem and what answer they got.

In social studies the daily work is to read the assigned pages in the textbook and to answer the teacher's questions. The questions are almost always designed to check on whether the students have read the assignment and understood it: who did so and so: what happened after that; when did it happen, where, and sometimes, why did it happen? The answers are in the book and in one's understanding of the book; the teacher's hints when one doesn't know the answers are to "read it again" or to look at the picture or at the rest of the paragraph. One is to search for the answer in the "context," in what is given.

Language arts is "simple grammar, what they need for everyday life." The language arts teacher says, "They should learn to speak properly, to write business letters and thank-you letters, and to understand what nouns and verbs and simple subjects are." Here, as well, actual work is to choose the right answers to understand what is given. The teacher often says, "Please read the next sentence and then I'll question you about it." One teacher said in some exasperation to a boy who was fooling around in class, "If you don't know the answers to the questions I ask, then you can't stay in this *class*!

[pause] You *never* know the answers to the questions I ask, and it's not fair to me—and certainly not to you!"

Most lessons are based on the textbook. This does not involve a critical perspective on what is given there. For example, a critical perspective in social studies is perceived as dangerous by these teachers because it may lead to controversial topics; the parents might complain. The children, however, are often curious, especially in social studies. Their questions are tolerated and usually answered perfunctorily. But after a few minutes the teacher will say, "All right we're not going any farther. Please open your social studies workbook." While the teachers spend a lot of time explaining and expanding on what the textbooks say, there is little attempt to analyze how or why things happen, or to give thought to how pieces of a culture, or, say, a system of numbers or elements of a language fit together or can be analyzed. What has happened in the past and what exists now may not be equitable or fair, but (shrug) that is the way things are and one does not confront such matters in school. For example, in social studies after a child is called on to read a passage about the pilgrims, the teacher summarizes the paragraph and then says, "So you can see how strict they were about everything." A child asks. "Why?" "Well, because they felt that if you weren't busy, you'd get into trouble." Another child asks, "Is it true that they burned women at the stake?" The teacher says, "Yes, if a woman did anything strange, they hanged them. [sic] What would a woman do, do you think, to make them burn them? [sic] See if you can come up with better answers than my other [social studies] class." Several children offer suggestions, to which the teacher nods but does not comment. Then she says, "Okay, good," and calls on the next child to read.

Work tasks do not usually request creativity. Serious attention is rarely given in school work on *how* the children develop or express their own feelings and ideas, either linguistically or in graphic form. On the occasions when creativity or self-expression is requested, it is peripheral to the main activity or it is "enrichment" or for fun. During a lesson on what similes are, for example, the teacher explains what they are, puts several on the board, gives some other examples herself, and then asks the children if they can "make some up." She calls on three children who give similes, two of which are actually in the book they have open before them. The teacher does not comment on this and then asks several others to choose similes from the list of phrases in the book. Several do so correctly, and she says. "Oh good! You are picking them out! See how good we are?" Their homework is to pick out the rest of the similes from the list.

Creativity is not often requested in social studies and science projects, either. Social studies projects, for example, are given with directions to "find information on your topic" and write it up. The children are not supposed to copy but to "put it in your own words." Although a number of the projects subsequently went beyond the teacher's direction to find information and had quite expressive covers and inside illustrations, the teacher's evaluative comments had to do with the amount of information, whether they had "copied," and if their work was neat.

The style of control of the three fifth-grade teachers observed in this school varied from somewhat easygoing to strict, but in contrast to the working-class schools, the teachers' decisions were usually based on external rules and regulations—for example, on criteria that were known or available to the children. Thus, the teachers always honor the bells for changing classes, and they usually evaluate children's work by what is in the textbooks and answer booklets.

There is little excitement in schoolwork for the children, and the assignments are perceived as having little to do with their interests and feelings. As one child said, what you do is "store facts up in your head like cold storage—until you need it later for a test or your job." Thus, doing well is important because there are thought to be *other*, likely rewards: a good job or college.[10]

## AFFLUENT PROFESSIONAL SCHOOL

In the affluent professional school, work is creative activity carried out independently. The students are continually asked to express and apply ideas and concepts. Work involves individual thought and expressiveness, expansion and illustration of ideas, and choice of appropriate method and material. (The class is not considered an open classroom, and the principal explained that because of the large number of discipline problems in the fifth grade this year they did not departmentalize. The teacher who agreed to take part in the study said she is "more structured" this year than she usually is.) The products of work in this class are often written stories, editorials and essays, or representations of ideas in mural, graph, or craft form. The products of work should not be like everybody else's and should show individuality. They should exhibit good design, and (this is important) they must also fit empirical reality. Moreover, one's work should attempt to interpret or "make sense" of reality. The relatively few rules to be followed regarding work are usually criteria for, or limits on, individual activity. One's product is usually evaluated for the quality of its expression and for the appropriateness of its conception to the task. In many cases, one's own satisfaction with the product is an important criterion for its evaluation. When right answers are called for, as in commercial materials like SRA (Science Research Associates) and math it is important that the children decide on an answer as a result of thinking about the idea involved in what they're being asked to do. Teacher's hints are to "think about it some more."

The following activities are illustrative. The class takes home a sheet requesting each child's parents to fill in the number of cars they have, the number of television sets, refrigerators, games, or rooms in the house, and so on. Each child is to figure the average number of a type of possession owned by the fifth grade. Each child must compile the "data" from all the sheets. A calculator is available in the classroom to do the mechanics of finding the average. Some children decide to send sheets to the fourth grade families for comparison. Their work should be "verified" by a classmate before it is handed in.

Each child and his or her family has made a geoboard. The teacher asks the class to get their geoboards from the side cabinet, to take a handful of rubber bands, and then to listen to what she would like them to do. She says, "I would like you to design a figure and then find the perimeter and area. When you have it, check with your neighbor. After you've done that, please transfer it to graph paper and tomorrow I'll ask you to make up a question about it for someone. When you hand it in, please let me know whose it is and who verified it. Then I have something else for you to do that's really fun. [pause] Find the average number of chocolate chips in three cookies. I'll give you three cookies, and you'll have to *eat* your way through, I'm afraid!" Then she goes around the room and gives help, suggestions, praise, and admonitions that they are getting noisy. They work sitting, or standing up at their desks at benches in the back, or on the floor. A child hands the teacher his paper and she comments, "I'm not accepting this paper. Do a better design." To another child she says, "That's fantastic! But you'll never find the area. Why don't you draw a figure inside [the big one] and subtract to get the area?"

The school district requires the fifth grade to study ancient civilization (in particular, Egypt, Athens, and Sumer). In this classroom, the emphasis is on illustrating and re-creating the culture of the people of ancient times. The following are typical activities: the children made an 8mm film on Egypt which one of the parents edited. A girl in the class wrote the script and the class acted it out. They put the sound on themselves. They read stories of those

days. They wrote essays and stories depicting the lives of the people and the societal and occupational divisions. They chose from a list of projects, all of which involved graphic representations of ideas: for example, "Make a mural depicting the division of labor in Egyptian society."

Each child wrote and exchanged a letter in hieroglyphics with a fifth grader in another class and they also exchanged stories they wrote in cuneiform. They made a scroll and singed the edges so it looked authentic. They each chose an occupation and made an Egyptian plaque representing that occupation simulating the appropriate Egyptian design. They carved their design on a cylinder of wax, pressed the wax into clay, and then baked the clay. Although one girl did not choose an occupation but carved instead a series of gods and slaves, the teacher said, "That's all right, Amber, it's beautiful." As they were working the teacher said, "Don't cut into your clay until you're satisfied with your design."

Social studies also involves almost daily presentation by the children of some event from the news. The teacher's questions ask the children to expand what they say, to give more details, and to be more specific. Occasionally she adds some remarks to help them see connections between events.

The emphasis on expressing and illustrating ideas in social studies is accompanied in language arts by an emphasis on creative writing. Each child wrote a rebus story for a first grader whom they had interviewed to see what kind of story the child liked best. They wrote editorials on pending decisions by the school board and radio plays, some of which were read over the school intercom from the office and one of which was performed in the auditorium. There is no language arts textbook because, the teacher said, "The principal wants us to be creative." There is not much grammar, but there is punctuation. One morning when the observer arrived, the class was doing a punctuation ditto. The teacher later apologized for using the ditto. "It's just for review," she said. "I don't teach punctuation that way. We use their language." The ditto had three unambiguous rules for where to put commas in a sentence. As the teacher was going around to help the children with the ditto, she repeated several times. "Where you put commas depends on how you say the sentence; it depends on the situation and what you want to say." Several weeks later the observer saw another punctuation activity. The teacher had printed a five-paragraph story on an oak tag and then cut it into phrases. She read the whole story to the class from the book, then passed out the phrases. The group had to decide how the phrases could best be put together again. (They arranged the phrases on the floor.) The point was not to replicate the story, although that was not irrelevant, but to "decide what you think the best way is." Punctuation marks on cardboard pieces were then handed out and the children discussed and then decided what mark was best at each place they thought one was needed. At the end of each paragraph the teacher asked. "Are you satisfied with the way the paragraphs are now? Read it to yourself and see how it sounds." Then she read the original story again and they compared the two.

Describing her goals in science to the investigator, the teacher said. "We use ESS (Elementary Science Study). It's very good because it gives a hands-on experience—so they can make *sense* out of it. It doesn't matter whether it [what they find] is right or wrong. I bring them together and there's value in discussing their ideas."

The products of work in this class are often highly valued by the children and the teacher. In fact, this was the only school in which the investigator was not allowed to take original pieces of the children's work for her files. If the work was small enough, however, and was on paper, the investigator could duplicate it on the copying machine in the office.

The teacher's attempt to control the class involves constant negotiation. She does not give direct orders unless she is angry because the children have been too noisy. Normally, she tries to get them to foresee the consequences of their actions and to decide accordingly. For example, lining them up to go see a play written by the sixth graders, she says, "I presume you're lined up by someone with whom you want to sit. I hope you're lined up by someone you won't get in trouble with . . . "

One of the few rules governing the children's movement is that no more than three children may be out of the room at once. There is a school rule that anyone can go to the library at any time to get a book. In the fifth grade I observed, they sign their name on the chalkboard and leave. There are no passes. Finally, the children have a fair amount of officially sanctioned say over what happens in class. For example, they often negotiate what work is to be done. If the teacher wants to move on to the next subject, but the children say they are not ready, they want to work on their present projects some more, she very often lets them do it.

## EXECUTIVE ELITE SCHOOL

In the executive elite school, work is developing one's analytical intellectual powers. Children are continually asked to reason through a problem, to produce intellectual products that are both logically sound and of top academic quality. A primary goal of thought is to conceptualize rules by which elements may fit together in systems and then to apply these rules in solving a problem. Schoolwork helps one to achieve, to excel, to prepare for life.

The following are illustrative. The math teacher teaches area and perimeter by having the children derive formulas for each. First she helps them, through discussion at the board, to arrive at A = W x L as a formula (not *the* formula) for area. After discussing several, she says, "Can anyone make up a formula for perimeter? Can you figure that out yourselves? [pause] Knowing what we know, can we think of a formula?" She works out three children's suggestions at the board, saying to two, "Yes, that's a good one," and then asks the class if they can think of any more. No one volunteers. To prod them, she says, "If you use rules and good reasoning, you get many ways. Chris, can you think up a formula?"

She discusses two-digit division with the children as a decision-making process. Presenting a new type of problem to them, she asks, "What's the *first* decision you'd make if presented with this kind of example? What is the first thing you'd *think*? Craig?" Craig says, "To find my first partial quotient." She responds, "Yes, that would be your first decision. How would you do that?" Craig explains, and then the teacher says, "OK, we'll see how that works for you." The class tries his way. Subsequently, she comments on the merits and shortcomings of several other children's decisions. Later she tells the investigator that her goals in math are to develop their reasoning and mathematical thinking and that, unfortunately, there's no time for manipulables.

While right answers are important in math, they are not "given" by the book or by the teacher but may be challenged by the children. Going over some problems in late September the teacher says, "Raise your hand if you do not agree." A child says, "I don't agree with sixty-four." The teacher responds, "OK, there's a question about sixty-four [to class] Please check it. Owen, they're disagreeing with you. Kristen, they're checking yours." The teacher emphasized this repeatedly during September and October with statements like "Don't be afraid to say you disagree. In the last [math] class, somebody disagreed, and they were right. Before you disagree, check yours, and if you still think we're wrong, then we'll check it out." By Thanksgiving, the children did not often speak in terms of right and wrong math problems but of whether they agreed with the answer that had been given.

There are complicated math mimeos with many word problems. Whenever they go over the examples, they discuss how each child has set up the problem. The children must explain it precisely. On one occasion the teacher said, I'm more—just as interested in *how* you set up the problem as in what answer you find. If you set up a problem in a good way, the answer is *easy* to find.

Social studies work is most often reading and discussion of concepts and independent research. There are only occasional artistic, expressive, or illustrative projects. Ancient Athens and Sumer are, rather, societies to analyze. The following questions are typical of those that guide the children's independent research. "What mistakes did Pericles make after the war?" "What mistakes did the citizens of Athens make?" "What are the elements of a civilization?" "How did Greece build an economic empire?" "Compare the way Athens chose its leaders with the way we choose ours." Occasionally the children are asked to make up sample questions for their social studies tests. On an occasion when the investigator was present, the social studies teacher rejected a child's question by saying, "that's just fact. If I asked you that question on a test, you'd complain it was just memory! Good questions ask for concepts."

In social studies—but also in reading, science, and health—the teachers initiate classroom discussions of current social issues and problems. These discussions occurred on every one of the investigator's visits and a teacher told me. "These children's opinions are important—it's important that they learn to reason things through." The classroom discussions always struck the observer as quite realistic and analytical, dealing with concrete social issues like the following: "Why do workers strike?" "Is that right or wrong?" "Why do we have inflation, and what can be done to stop it?" "Why do companies put chemicals in food when the natural ingredients are available?" and so on. Usually the children did not have to be prodded to give their opinions. In fact, their statements and the interchanges between them struck the observer as quite sophisticated conceptually and verbally and well-informed. Occasionally the teachers would prod with statements such as, "Even if you don't know [the answers], if you think logically about it, you can figure it out. And I'm asking you [these] questions to help you think this through."

Language arts emphasizes language as a complex system, one that should be mastered. The children are asked to diagram sentences of complex grammatical construction, to memorize irregular verb conjugations (he lay, he has lain, and so on . . . ), and to use the proper participles, conjunc-

tions, and interjections in their speech. The teacher (the same one who teaches social studies) told then, "It is not enough to get these right on tests: you must use what you learn [in grammar classes] in your written and oral work. I will grade you on that."

Most writing assignments are either research reports and essays for social studies or experiment analyses and write-ups for science. There is only an occasional story or other "creative writing" assignment. On the occasion observed by the investigator (the writing of a Halloween story), the points the teacher stressed in preparing the children to write involved the structural aspects of a story rather than the expression of feelings or other ideas. The teacher showed them a filmstrip, "The Seven Parts of a Story," and lectured them on plot development, mood, setting, character development, consistency, and the use of a logical or appropriate ending. The stories they subsequently wrote were, in fact, well-structured, but many were also personal and expressive. The teacher's evaluative comments, however, did not refer to the expressiveness or artistry but were all directed toward whether they had "developed" the story well.

Language arts work also involved a large amount of practice in presentation of the self and in managing situations where the child was expected to be in charge. For example, there was a series of assignments in which each child had to be a "student teacher." The child had to plan a lesson in grammar, outlining, punctuation, or other language arts topics and explain the concept to the class. Each child was to prepare a worksheet or game and a homework assignment as well. After each presentation, the teacher and other children gave a critical appraisal of the "student teacher's" performance. Their criteria were: whether the student spoke clearly, whether the lesson was interesting, whether the student made any mistakes, and whether he or she kept control of the class. On an occasion when a child did not maintain control, the teacher said, "When you're up there, you have authority and you have to use it. I'll back you up. . . . "

The executive elite school is the only school where bells do not demarcate the periods of time. The two fifth-grade teachers were very strict about changing classes on schedule, however, as specific plans for each session had been made. The teachers attempted to keep tight control over the children during lessons, and the children were sometimes flippant, boisterous, and occasionally rude. However, the children may be brought into line by reminding them that "It is up to you." "You must control yourself." "You are responsible for your work." "You must set your own priorities." One teacher told a child. "You are the only driver of your car—and only you can regulate your speed." A new teacher complained to the observer that she had thought "these children" would have more control.

While strict attention to the lesson at hand is required, the teachers make relatively little attempt to regulate the movement of the children at other times. For example, except for the kindergartners the children in this school do not have to wait for the bell to ring in the morning; they may go to their classroom when they arrive at school. Fifth graders often came early to read, to finish work, or to catch up. After the first two months of school, the fifth-grade teachers did not line the children up to change classes or to go to gym, and so on, but, when the children were ready and quiet, they were told they could go—sometimes without the teachers.

In the classroom, the children could get materials when they needed them and took what they needed from closets and from the teacher's desk. They were in charge of the office at lunchtime. During class they did not have to sign out or ask permission to leave the room; they just got up and left. Because of the pressure to get work done, however, they did not leave the room very often. The teachers were very polite to the children, and the investigator heard no sarcasm, no nasty remarks, and few direct orders. The teachers never called the children "honey" or "dear" but always called them by name. The teachers were expected to be available before school, after school, and for part of their lunchtime to provide extra help if needed. . . .

The foregoing analysis of differences in schoolwork in contrasting social class contexts suggests the following conclusion: the "hidden curriculum" of schoolwork is tacit preparation for relating to the process of production in a particular way. Differing curricular, pedagogical, and pupil evaluation practices emphasize different cognitive and behavioral skills in each social setting and thus contribute to the development in the children of certain potential relationships to physical and symbolic capital,[11] to authority, and to the process of work. School experience, in the sample of schools discussed here, differed qualitatively by social class. These differences may not only contribute to the development in the children in each social class of certain types of economically significant relationships and not others but would thereby help to *reproduce* this system of relation in society. In the contribution to the reproduction of unequal social relations lies a theoretical meaning and social consequence of classroom practice.

The identification of different emphases in classrooms in a sample of contrasting social class contexts implies that further research should be conducted in a large number of schools to investigate the types of work tasks and interactions in each to see if they differ in the ways discussed here and to see if similar potential relationships are uncovered. Such research could have as a product the further elucidation of complex but not readily apparent connections between everyday activity in schools and classrooms and the unequal structure of economic relationships in which we work and live.

## ENDNOTES

1. S. Bowles and H. Gintis, *Schooling in Capitalist America: Educational Reform and the Contradictions of Economic Life* (New York: Basic Books, 1976). [Author's note]

2. B. Bernstein, *Class, Codes and Control, Vol. 3. Towards a Theory of Educational Transmission*, 2d ed. (London: Routledge & Kegan Paul, 1977); P. Bourdieu and J. Passeron, Reproduction in Education, Society and Culture (Beverly Hills, Calif.: Sage, 1977); M. W. Apple, *Ideology and Curriculum* (Boston: Routledge Kegan Paul, 1979). [Author's note]

3. But see, in a related vein, M. W. Apple and N. King, "What Do Schools Teach?" *Curriculum Inquiry* 6 (1977): 341–58; R. C. Rist, The Urban School: A Factory for Failure (Cambridge, Mass.: MIT Press, 1973). [Author's note]

4. *Ethnographical*: based on an anthropological study of cultures or subcultures—the "cultures" in this case being the five schools observed.

5. The U.S. Bureau of the Census defines poverty for a nonfarm family of four as a yearly income of $6,191 a year or less. U.S. Bureau of the Census, *Statistical Abstract of the United States*: 1978 (Washington, D.C.: U.S. Government Printing Office, 1978), p. 465, table 754. [Author's note]

6. U.S. Bureau of the Census, "Money Income in 1977 of Families and Persons in the United States," *Current Population Reports* Series P-60 no. 118 (Washington, D.C.: U.S. Government Printing Office, 1979), p. 2, table A. [Author's note]

7. Ibid. [Author's note]

8. This figure is an estimate. According to the Bureau of the Census, only 2.6 percent of families in the United States have money income of $50,000 or over. U.S. Bureau of the Census, *Current Population Reports* Series P-60. For figures on income at these higher levels, see J. D. Smith and S. Franklin, "The Concentration of Personal Wealth, 1922–1969," *American Economic Review.*, 64 (1974): 162-67. [Author's note]

9. Smith and Franklin, "The Concentration of Personal Wealth."[Author's note]

10. A dominant feeling, expressed directly and indirectly by teachers in this school, was boredom with their work. They did, however, in contrast to the working-class schools, almost always carry out lessons during class times.[Author's note]

11. *Physical and symbolic capital*: elsewhere Anyon defines *capital* as "property that is used to produce profit, interest, or rent"; she defines *symbolic capital* as the knowledge and skills that "may yield social and cultural power."

## Study Questions

1. Name and characterize the four basic categories of school that Anyon studies. How do these characteristics reflect issues of class?

2. She refers to these schools as transmitting "symbolic capital." What does she mean and why is it often overlooked?

3. This study took place thirty years ago; how have things changed since then?

4. In terms of these categories, which of these schools do you attend? If you got to choose, which would you want to attend? Why?

5. How do Anyon's claims relate to ideas about American society and the "American Dream"? What is the role of education in America?

# THE MULTICULTURAL WARS

*Hazel V. Carby*

*Hazel V. Carby is a professor of English and Afro-American Studies at Yale University. She is the author of* Reconstructuring Womanhood: The Emergence of the Afro-American Woman Novelist, *a prize-winning study of African-American women writers.*

As a black intellectual, I am both intrigued and horrified by the contradictory nature of the black presence in North American universities. We are, as students, as teachers, and as cultural producers, simultaneously visibly present in, and starkly absent from, university life. Although it costs approximately $20,000 a year to attend Yale and approximately $50,000 a year to reside in a New York jail, black males are being incarcerated at unprecedented rates. The press and the culture industry, having "discovered" the black woman writer for the first time in the seventies, are now finding it increasingly profitable to market narratives of the lives of successful black men. Articles about black males who have "made it" are no longer found only in the entertainment or sports sections of national newspapers: musicians and basketball stars have been joined by film directors and academics in the pages of our Sunday magazines.

In particular, the very existence of black male professors seems to fascinate the *New York Times.* On April 1, 1990, the *Times* ran a cover story entitled "Henry Louis Gates, Jr.: Black Studies' New Star." Stanley Fish, chair of the English Department at Duke University, patronizingly described Professor Gates's professional success as "entrepreneurial P.T. Barnumism." Adam Begley, the author of the story, concludes that with "a phone in his Mercedes-Benz, a literary agent in New York and an impressive network of contacts in the academy, publishing and the arts, [Professor Gates] seems more like a mogul than a scholar."[1] The *Times* article is, at best, ambivalent toward its black

subject and frequently adopts such an incisive tone of ridicule that one wonders if the newspaper's editorial staff consciously decided to create an April 1 cartoon of black studies as a ship of fools. A much more serious, considered, and sober article about Cornel West appeared in the same magazine, describing him as "Princeton's Public Intellectual."[2]

In stark contrast to the attention paid to individual black professors is the glaring absence of any equivalent publicity about the paltry presence of nonwhite ladder faculty in universities: 4.1 percent are Black, 3.8 percent are Asian, 1.3 percent are Latino, and 0.4 percent are Native American.[3] Derrick Bell, a professor at the Harvard Law School, has argued that

> *A widespread assumption exists that there is an irreconcilable conflict between achieving diversity in law school faculties and maintaining academic excellence. . . . It serves as the primary reason why most college and university faculties across the nation remain all-white and mostly-male almost four decades after the law barred them from continuing their long-practiced policies of excluding minorities and women because of their race and sex without regard to their academic qualifications.*[4]

These "contentions" Bell maintains "are simultaneously racially insulting and arrogantly wrong": They are insulting because they insinuate that the old rules of racial segregation rightly correlated color with intellectual inferiority. They are arrogant in that they assume that all of those with upper-class-based qualifications are by definition exemplary scholars and teachers.[5]

Bell continues by stressing that "minorities who achieve are deemed exceptions," whereas those "who fail are deemed painful proof that we must adhere to hiring standards that subsidize the well-placed members of our society while penalizing those, white as well as black, from disadvantaged backgrounds."[6] That more than ninety percent of all faculty members across the nation are white is a scandal but is not, apparently, a cause for journalistic outrage or newspaper headlines.

The percentage of black students in college populations has steadily decreased throughout the last decade, as has the number of B.A.s awarded to black students, even though the absolute number of bachelor's degrees awarded has been increasing nationally. In graduate schools, the proportion of American graduate students who are black is decreasing and the proportion of doctorates awarded to black people is also in significant decline. The number of tenured black professors has increased slightly, but the number of untenured black appointees is decreasing.[7] Clearly, if the black student population continues to decline at the undergraduate and graduate levels, the current black intellectual presence in academia, small as it is, will not be reproduced.

During the past two years, debate about the inclusion of people from a variety of ethnic, national, and class backgrounds as appropriate subjects for educational study and research has become focused on what is now commonly referred to as the multicultural curriculum. Multiculturalism appears as a controversial issue at all levels of the national educational system; the debate is not confined to universities. Despite the apparent uniformity of the issues being fought over in these multicultural wars of position, there are, in fact, significantly different interests in play and at stake as these battles take place regionally and in the public and private spheres of education. However, it is important to recognize that even though this debate is differently inflected at different levels, all aspects constitute a debate about contemporary meanings of race in North America. Indeed, I would argue that multiculturalism is one of the current code words for race—a code just as effective as the word "drugs" or the phrase "inner—city violence" at creating a common—sense awareness that race is, indeed, the subject being evoked.

Since the fall of 1990, we have witnessed a barrage of journalistic attacks on the concept of multiculturalism and attempts to institute multicultural curricula. These reports have either implicitly or explicitly acknowledged multiculturalism as a discourse about race, and many have frequently asserted that there are close and disturbing links between multiculturalism, affirmative action, and threats to freedom of speech guaranteed by the first amendment.

In common-sense terms, affirmative action is no longer referenced by the media as a necessary corrective social policy but as a social problem that itself needs correction. The press's perceptions of the threats to freedom of speech and expression have shaped a moral panic about allegedly terroristic attempts to institute "politically correct" thought and behavior. Indeed, this danger is thought to be so real that it has elicited condemnation from President Bush himself. It is as if the historical contradictions between the original Constitution, which sanctioned slavery, and the fourteenth and fifteenth amendments, have returned to haunt us yet again—only to be dispelled by a form of executive exorcism.

The fundamental contradictions of a society structured by racial inequality from its founding moment have been shaped in the 1990s by an administration in Washington that is not only unsympathetic toward any demands for civil rights but also blatantly antagonistic to such demands. If we also consider the moral panics about affirmative action, antisexist and antiracist codes of behavior, and multiculturalism in the pages of numerous journals like *Time, Newsweek,* the *Atlantic Quarterly,* the *New Republic,* the *Chronicle of Higher Education,* the *Boston Globe,* and the *New York Times,* it would appear as if liberal, as well as conservative, opposition to increasing cultural and ethnic diversity in higher education is becoming entrenched.[8]

For those of us who recognize the need for transformations in our educational systems and in the ways in which we organize fields of knowledge, it is frequently dismaying to consider what is sometimes thought to constitute change in educational policy and practice. Departments and programs in many private universities, for example, will proudly point to an "integrated" curriculum while being unable to point to an integrated student body—except in the photographs in their student handbooks, photographs that contrive to demonstrate "diversity" by self-consciously including the pitiful handful of black/Latino/Asian/Chicano/ and perhaps even fewer American Indian students on campus. As Nicolaus Mills has argued in his survey of 1990 college publications, the contemporary college view book presents an idealized world in which the dominant code word is "diversity."[9]

*"Diversity is the hallmark of the Harvard Radliffe experience," the first sentence in the Harvard University register declares. "Diversity is the virtual core of University life," the University of Michigan bulletin announces. "Diversity is rooted deeply in the liberal arts tradition and is key to our educational philosophy," Connecticut College insists.*

*"Duke's 5,800 undergraduates come from regions which are truly diverse," the Duke University bulletin declares. "Stanford values a class that is both ethnically and economically diverse," the Stanford University bulletin notes. Brown University says, "When asked to describe the undergraduate life at The College—and particularly their first strongest impression of Brown as freshmen-students consistently bring up the same topic: the diversity of the student body."*[10]

In this context, Mills concludes, diversity means that "a college is doing its best to abolish the idea that it caters to middle-class whites."[11]

The various cultural and political presences of black women in universities provide particularly good examples of the contradictions embedded in the various curricular practices that occur under the aegis of "diversity." On many campuses, coalitions of marginalized and nonmarginalized women, students, and professors have formed alliances to ensure the inclusion of the histories of black women, and other previously excluded categories of women, in the university curriculum. But the result has been a patchwork of success and spectacular failure. Clearly, the syllabi of some courses, particularly within women's studies and African-American studies programs, have been transformed, and the demand for the establishment of programs in ethnic studies is both vocal and assertive. However, changes too frequently amount only to the inclusion of one or two new books in an already established syllabus rather than a reconsideration of the basic conceptual structure of a course.

Within women's studies programs, and within some literature departments, black women writers have been used and, I would argue, abused as cultural and political icons. In spite of the fact that the writing of black women is extraordinarily diverse, complex, and multifaceted, feminist theory has frequently used and abused this material to produce an essential black female subject for its own consumption, a black female subject that represents a single dimension-either the long-suffering or the triumphantly noble aspect of a black community throughout history. Because this black female subject has to carry the burden of representing what is otherwise significantly absent in the curriculum, issues of complexity disappear under the pressure of the demand to give meaning to blackness.

Certainly, we can see how the black female subject has become very profitable for the culture industry. The Harper Collins reprinting of all the previously published books of Zora Neale Hurston, for example, has been an extraordinarily profitable publishing enterprise based primarily on sales within an academic market.[12] We need to ask why black women, or other women who are non-white, are needed as cultural and political icons by the white middle class at this particular moment? What cultural and political need is being expressed, and what role is the black female subject being reduced to play? I would argue that it is necessary to recognize the contradictions between elevating the black female subject to the status of major text within multiculturalism and failing to lead students toward an integrated society, between making the black female a subject in the classroom and failing to integrate university student and faculty bodies on a national scale. Instead of recognizing these contradictions, the black female subject is frequently the means by which many middle-class white students and faculty cleanse their souls and rid themselves of the guilt of living in a society that is still rigidly segregated. Black cultural texts have become fictional substitutes for the lack of any sustained social or political relationships with black people in a society that has retained many of its historical practices of apartheid in housing and schooling.

The cultural, political, and social complexity of black people is consistently denied in those strands of feminist and multicultural theory that emphasize "difference" and use it to mark social, cultural, and political differences as if they were unbridgeable human divisions.[13] This theoretical emphasis on the recognition of difference, of otherness, requires us to ask, different from and for whom? In practice, in the classroom, black texts have been used to focus on the complexity of response in the (white) reader/student's construction of self in relation to a (black) perceived "other." In the motivation of that response, the text has been reduced to a tool. The theoretical paradigm of difference is obsessed with the construction of identities rather than relations of power and domination[14] and, in practice, concentrates on the effect of this difference on a (white) norm. Proponents of multiculturalism and feminist theorists have to interrogate some of their basic and unspoken assumptions: to what extent are fantasized black female and male subjects invented, primarily, to make the white middle class feel better about itself? And at what point do theories of "difference," as they inform academic practices, become totally compatible with, rather than threat to, the rigid frameworks of segregation and ghettoization at work throughout our society?

We need to recognize that we live in a society in which systems of dominance and subordination are structured through processes of racialization that continuously interact with all other forces of socialization. Theoretically, we should be arguing that everyone in this social order has been constructed in our political imagination as a racialized subject. In this sense, it is important to think about the invention of the category of whiteness as well as that of blackness and, consequently, to make visible what is rendered invisible when viewed as the normative state of existence: the (white) point in space from which we tend to identify difference.

If, instead, we situated all North American peoples as racialized subjects of our political imagination, we would see that processes of racialization are determining to all our work. But processes of racialization, when they are mentioned at all in multicultural debate, are discussed as if they were the sole concern of those particular groups perceived to be racialized subjects. Because the politics of difference work with concepts of individual identity, rather than structures of inequality and exploitation, processes of racialization are marginalized and given symbolic and political meaning only when the subjects are black.

My argument for the centrality of the concept of race is not the same as the assertion from within the politics of difference, that everyone has an ethnicity. I am not arguing for pluralistic research paradigms or for a politics of pluralism, the result of much work on ethnicity. But, I am arguing for an educational politics that would reveal the structures of power relations at work in the racialization of our social order.

As a final exercise in thinking about the ways the black female subject has been addressed and, to a great extent, invented within the curricular practices designed to increase "diversity," I would like to question the marginalization of the concept of race in the phrase "women of color." This phrase carries a series of complex meanings. Historically, it has its origin in the need of subordinated, marginalized, and exploited groups of women to find common ground with each other, and in the assertion of their desire to establish a system of alliances as "women of color." But what happens when this phrase is then taken up and inserted into the language of difference and diversity? Does "women of color" have other meanings inflected by theories of difference and diversity? I know we are all supposed to be familiar with who is being evoked by this term, but do we honestly think that some people lack color? Do white women and men have no color? What does it mean socially, politically, and culturally not to have color? Are those without color not implicated in a society structured in dominance by race? Are those without color outside of the hierarchy of social relations and not racialized? Are only the so-called colored to be the subjects of a specialized discourse of difference? And, most

important, do existing power relations remain intact and unchallenged by this discourse?

We need to ask ourselves some serious questions about our culture and our politics. Is the emphasis on cultural diversity making invisible the politics of race in this increasingly segregated nation, and is the language of cultural diversity a convenient substitute for the political action needed to desegregate? In considering a response, we would be wise to remember Malcolm X's words: "There is nothing that the white man will do to bring about true, sincere citizenship or civil rights recognition for black people in this country . . . They will always talk it but they won't practice it."[15]

While the attention of faculty and administrators has been directed toward increasing the representation of different social groups in the curriculum or the college handbook, few alliances have been forged with forces across this society that will significantly halt and reverse the declining numbers of black, working-class, and poor people among university student bodies and faculty.

From one perspective, academic language in the decade of the eighties appeared to be at odds with the growing conservatism of the Reagan years. It seemed, at times, as if life in the academy was dominated by questions about the monolithic (and monoethnic) nature of courses in Western civilization; about texts that constituted all white and male literary and historical "canons"; and about issues of "diversity" and "difference." Students on campuses all over the country formed movements that condemned apartheid in South Africa and vigorously worked to persuade university administrations to divest their economic holdings in that country. However, we have to confront the fact that the white middle and upper classes in this country, from which these students predominantly come, have, simultaneously, sustained and supported apartheid-like structures that maintain segregation in housing and education in the United States. Comparisons with South African apartheid are a part of the language of black American daily life: the Bronx becomes "New York's Johannesburg"; Chicago is called "Joberg by the Lake"; and the Minneapolis Star Tribune is known by black politicians as the "Johannesburg Times."[16]

In Connecticut, the state where I live and work, the state constitution provides for free public elementary and secondary schools and specifically states that "No person shall be subjected to Segregation or Discrimination because of Religion, Race, Color, Ancestry or National Origin."[17] According to a recent report, there are 450,000 children at school in Connecticut, and one out of every four is non-white. But eight out of ten so-called minority students "are concentrated in ten percent of the school districts. By the year 2000, minority enrollments in Hartford, Bridgeport, and New Haven public schools will be approaching one hundred percent."[18]

Such systems of segregation ensure that the black working class and the urban poor will not encroach on the privileged territory of the white middle and upper classes or into the institutions that are the gatekeepers and providers of legitimated access to power, universities included. The integration that has occurred has been primarily on the grounds of class assimilation, and affirmative action has become an important mechanism for advancing a very limited number of black people into the middle class. The admissions practices at Harvard University, discussed in a recent report on affirmative action, are a good example: Harvard has sought to avoid the problem [of attrition] by ensuring that most of its black students come from middle-class families and predominantly white schools. As an admissions officer explained, "It is right for Harvard and better for the students, because there is better adjustment and less desperate alienation."[19]

Because entry into the professions is a major port of entry into the middle class, universities have been important and contested sites within which to accomplish the transformation of the previously outcast into an acceptable body for integration. The social and political consciousness of the undergraduate population currently enrolled in universities has been formed entirely during the Reagan and Bush years, and the disparity between the groups which have benefited from, and those that have been radically disadvantaged by, the social policies of conservatism is stark. Public systems of education in particular regions have had to respond rather differently from overwhelmingly white private or public universities to questions of diversity and difference.

The New York City educational system, for example, has a population of students, in some schools and colleges, where the so-called minority groups are overwhelmingly in the majority and where issues of difference and diversity are not theoretical playthings at odds with the context in which teaching occurs. New York public schools, which seem to have the most radically diverse and transformed curriculum in the country, find that this curriculum is now under vigorous attack by the New York regents. At the same time, it is precisely the state and city educational systems that have a majority population of black and Hispanic students that are disastrously underfunded. The withdrawal of federal financing and, now, the drastic decline in

state and city financing will soon decimate what is left of the promise of the city's schools and colleges.

Meanwhile, in the universities with money, the National Association of Scholars, its friends and allies, and the media campaign against curricular reform have had significant effects in shifting the general climate against educational reform and against affirmative action. Not the least of these effects is the example of the $20 million donation to Yale University for the promotion of scholarship in Western civilization, a donation that was only one of four equivalent donations from the same family within one year. No equivalent donation has ever been made to institute courses in non-Western civilizations that I have been able to find, but I can imagine the difference to the New Haven public school system an injection of $80 million might make.[20] In the public sphere, the most recent presidential educational initiative seeks to replace federal funding of the public schools with corporate funding. One has to ask, will this mean corporate control of the curriculum as well?

In the post-civil rights era, then, one has to wonder at the massive resources being mobilized in opposition to programs or courses that focus on non-white or ethnically diverse topics and issues. One wonders, too, about the strength of the opposition to affirmative action, when social mobility has been gained by so few black people, and black entry into the so-called mainstream has been on the grounds of middle-class acceptability and not the end of segregation. Perhaps it is not too cynical to speculate that the South African government has learned a significant lesson by watching the example of the United States in the last two decades: some of the most important aspects of an apartheid system can be retained without having to maintain rigid apartheid legislation. It is in this social, political, and economic context that I feel it is appropriate and important to question the disparity between the vigor of debates about the inclusion of black subjects on a syllabus and the almost total silence about, and utter disregard for, the material conditions of most black people.

From the vantage point of the academy, it is obvious that the publishing explosion of the fiction of black women has been a major influence in the development of the multicultural curriculum, and I have tried to point to the ways in which the texts of black women and men sit uneasily in a discourse that seems to act as a substitute for the political activity of desegregation. But it is also evident that in white suburban libraries, bookstores, and supermarkets an ever-increasing number of narratives of black lives are easily available. The retention of segregated neighborhoods and public schools and the apartheid—like structures of black inner-city versus white suburban life mean that those who read these texts lack the opportunity to grow up in any equitable way with each other.

Indeed, those same readers are part of the white suburban constituency that refuses to support the building of affordable housing in its affluent suburbs, aggressively opposes the bussing of children from the inner city into its neighborhood schools, and would fight to the death to prevent its children from being bused into the urban blight that is the norm for black children. For white suburbia, as well as for white middle-class students in universities, these texts are becoming a way of gaining knowledge of the other," a knowledge that appears to satisfy and replace the desire to challenge existing frameworks of segregation. Have we, as a society, successfully eliminated the need for achieving integration through political agitation for civil rights and opted instead for knowing each other through cultural texts?

## ENDNOTES

1. Adam Begley, "Henry Lousis Gates, Jr.: Black Studies' New Star," *New York Times Magazine*, April 1, 1990, 24-27.

2. Robert S. Boynton, "Princeton's Public Intellectual," *New Tork Times Magazine*, September 15, 1991, 39, 43, 49.

3. These figures are from the American Council on Education, Office of Minority Concerns, "Seventh Annual Status Report on Minorities in Higher Education," Table 13, as quoted in "Recruitment and Retention of Minority Group Members on the Faculty at Yale," the report of a committee chaired by Judith Rodin, Yale University, 1.

In the national Research Council's report *A Common Destiny,* the outlook for black faculty is gloomy: "Figures for 1997–1983 show a drop of 6.2 percent in the number of full-time black faculty at public four-year institutions and of 11.3 percent at private institutions. Black underrepresentation is greatest at elite universities and at two-year colleges. There is little prospect for growth in black representation in light of the declines in both the percentage of blacks going on to college and the percentage pursuing graduate and professional degrees." Gerald David Jaynes and Robin M. Williams, eds., *A Common Destiny: Blacks and American Society,* National Research Council, (Washington, D.C.: National Academy Press, 1989), 375.

4. Derrick Bell, "Why We Need More Black Professors in Law School," *Boston Sunday Globe*, April 28, 1991, A1.

5. Ibid.

6. Ibid.

7. "Recruitment and Retention of Minority Group Members on the Faculty at Yale," 1.

8. A number of articles in the national and local press have been extremely critical of what is called the "hegemony of

the politically correct" and described attempts to transform the canon as "liberal fascism" or terrorism. See, for example, *New York Times*, October 28, 1990, 1, 4; New York Times, December 9, 1990, 5; *Chronicle of Higher Education*, November 28, 1990, A5. An issue of <u>Newsweek</u> even went so far as to inscribe the words "Thought Police" on stone on its cover: December 24, 1990, 48–55. In contrast, the *Boston Globe Magazine* ran a much more sympathetic account of multiculturalism as a phenomenon of the "melting pot," entitled "The New World." However, it concluded with a negative article on multicultural education, "Too Many Have Let Enthusiasm Outrun Reason," by Kenneth Jackson: October 13, 1991, 27–32.

9. Nicolaus Mills, "The Endless Autumn," *The Nation*, April 16, 1990, 529–531.

10. Ibid.

11. Ibid.

12. Presumably influenced by the possibility of sharing some of the massive profits realized by the publishing industry through marketing the black female subject, film distribution companies have recently begun to vigorously market films about black women to university professors for course use. See Hazel V. Carby, "In Body, and Spirit: Representing Black Women Musicians," *Black Music Research Journal* 11 (Fall 1911), 177–192.

13. I would like to thank Paul Gilroy for the many conversations we have had on this issue. His influence upon my thinking has been profound.

14. See Elizabeth Weed, "Introduction: Terms of Reference" in *Coming to Terms: Feminism, Theory, Politics*, ed. Elizabeth Weed (London: Routledge, 1989), xvii.

15. Video interview with Malcolm X, from an installation by David Hammons at the New Museum (1989), as quoted in Maurice Berger, "Are Art Museums Racist?" *Art in America* (September 1990), 69–77.

16. John Matisonn, reporting for National Public Radio's "All Things Considered, Weekend Edition," February 2, 1991, Transcript, 21.

17. Constitution of the State of Connecticut 1965, as quoted on the PBS special "Schools in Black and White," produced and written by Vivian Eison and Andrea Haas Hubbell, broadcast September 4, 1991.

18. Ibid.

19. Andrew Hacker, "Affirmative Action: The New Look," *The New York Review*, October 12, 1989, 64.

20. Giving this extraordinary amount of money, $80 million, to an already well-endowed institution needs to be measured against initiatives to support inner-city schools by using black churches as sites for supplemental educational classes and activities. The Association for the Advancement of Science has spent $800,000 over a period of four years for educational programs in eight hundred churches in seventeen cities. The largest donation by a private foundation for church-based educational programs seems to be $2.3 million spread among nine cities from the Carnegie Foundation. See *New York Times*, August 7, 1991, A1.

Study Questions

1. Why do conservatives criticize multiculturalism? How does Carby respond to their critique?

2. What is Carby's basic criticism of multiculturalism, especially in terms of the position of African-American women?

3. She criticizes the phrase "women of color." What are her objections to this phrase?

4. What does she believe about assimilation? What is the difference between integration and assimilation?

5. Are any of her critiques about multiculturalism applicable to the curricula at your institution? Why or why not?

# CULTURAL LITERACY AND THE SCHOOLS

*E. D. Hirsch, Jr.*

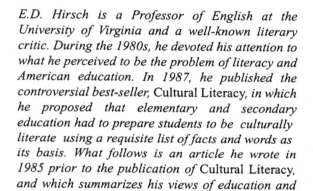

*E.D. Hirsch is a Professor of English at the University of Virginia and a well-known literary critic. During the 1980s, he devoted his attention to what he perceived to be the problem of literacy and American education. In 1987, he published the controversial best-seller,* Cultural Literacy, *in which he proposed that elementary and secondary education had to prepare students to be culturally literate using a requisite list of facts and words as its basis. What follows is an article he wrote in 1985 prior to the publication of* Cultural Literacy, *and which summarizes his views of education and literacy.*

Let me begin with a picture of what I mean by true literacy. It is good to start with our national educational goals, because unless we can agree upon our goals, we cannot deal forthrightly with the political and ideological issues that public education must always entail. Let me depict our educational goal as a social one, using the unforgettable vision of Martin Luther King, Jr. in his speech "I Have a Dream." Those of you who heard that speech or teach it will know what I am thinking. King had a vision in which the children of former slave owners sit down at the table of equality with the children of former slaves, a vision of an America where men and women deal with each other as equals and judge each other on their character rather than their origins. King had a dream of a classless society. To help us share his dream, he quoted from our most traditional texts, from Jefferson, the Bible, and patriotic and religious songs. We all know those traditional passages and songs. King reminded us that his dream has been shared and cherished by all Americans of good will.

The dream of Thomas Jefferson and Martin Luther King, Jr. carries a very specific educational implication in the modern world: No modern society can think of becoming a classless society except on the basis of universal literacy. Never mind for the moment the various utilitarian and humanistic arguments in favor of literacy. I am considering now an even more basic principle that sponsored our Jeffersonian system of public education in the first place. It is the principle that people in a democracy can be left free to think and decide things for themselves because they can all communicate with each other. Universal communication is the canvas for King's vision as well as Jefferson's. And universal communication is possible in our modern world only on the basis of universal literacy. Americans must be able to talk to each other not just in person or by telephone but across time and space through reading and writing. We can add to that traditional democratic imperative to literacy the well-known economic imperative that has been brought by the technological age. Today, only someone who reads well can adjust to changes in technology and the job market or can participate in our cultural and political life. From these very elementary considerations, it is obvious that genuine literacy must be a paramount and minimal goal of a high school education.

But what, more specifically, does that goal mean for the curriculum? That depends on what we mean by literacy. I would define literacy in this way: To be truly literate, a high school graduate must be able to grasp the meaning of written materials in any field or subject, provided that those materials are addressed to a general reader. High school graduates should be able to read serious newspapers, for instance. Remember what Jefferson said about reading newspapers:

*Were it left to me to decide whether we should have a government without newspapers, or newspapers without a government, I should not hesitate a moment to prefer the latter. But I should mean that every man should receive those papers and be capable of reading them.*

That last comment of Jefferson's is often omitted. But it is the crucial one. Every American should be able to read serious books, newspapers, and articles addressed to the general reader. And our high school graduates should also be able to convey information in writing to a general readership. Universal literacy means that every citizen must be able to give as well as receive written information.

Literacy in this fundamental sense requires not just technical proficiency but also "cultural literacy." What I mean by this term may become clear in a provisional way as I describe a recent experience.

A few years ago, I was conducting some experiments at the University of Virginia to measure the effectiveness of a piece of writing when it is read by ordinary audiences. We were measuring the actual effects of writing rather than mere opinions of its quality. Our readers in the experiment (who were mainly university students) performed just as we expected them to as long as we kept the topics simple and familiar. Then, one memorable day we transferred our experiments from the university to a community college, and my complacency about adult literacy was forever shattered. This community college was located in Richmond, Virginia, and the irony of the location will appear in a moment. Our first experiments went well, because we began by giving the students a paper to read on the topic of friendship. When reading about friendship, these young men and women showed themselves to be, on the average, just as literate as university students. The evidence showed that, based on the usual criteria of speed and accurate recall, the community college and university groups were equally skilled readers. But that evidence changed with the next piece of writing we asked them to read. It was a comparison of the characters of Ulysses S. Grant and Robert E. Lee, and the students' performance on that task was, to be blunt, illiterate. Our results showed that Grant and Lee were simply not familiar names to these young adults in the capital of the Confederacy. The students' speed and recall declined because they had to continually backtrack through the unfamiliar material to test out different hypotheses about what was meant or referred to.

Shortly after that disorienting experience, I discovered that Professor Richard Anderson of the Center for Reading Research at the University of Illinois and other researchers in psycholinguistics had reached firm conclusions about the importance of background knowledge in reading. For instance, in one experiment, Anderson and his colleagues discovered that an otherwise literate audience in India could not properly read a simple text about an American wedding. But, by the same token, an otherwise literate audience in America could not properly read a simple text about an Indian wedding. Why not? Structurally speaking, the texts were similar and the audiences were similar. It wasn't a matter of vocabulary or phonics or word recognition; it was a matter of cultural literacy. Anderson and others showed that to read a text with understanding one needs to have the background knowledge that the author has tacitly assumed the reader to have. This tacit knowledge is fundamental to literacy.

What these experiments demonstrate is that the idea that reading is a general, transferable skill unrelated to subject matter is essentially wrong, containing only the following grain of truth. Reading is a general skill only with regard to its rather elementary aspects, those involving phonics, parsing strategies, guessing strategies, eye habits, and so on. While these elementary skills are important, normally endowed students, once they acquire the rudiments, need not be continually drilled in them. Such skills are always being used, and every reading task will automatically exercise, improve, and automate them. With that single elementary exception, then, the usual picture of reading as a general skill is wrong. Reading skill varies from task to task, because reading skill depends on specific background knowledge.

To illustrate the dependency of literacy on cultural literacy, I shall quote a recent snippet from *The Washington Post*:

> *A federal appeals panel today upheld an order barring foreclosure on a Missouri farm, saying that U.S. Agriculture Secretary John R. Block has reneged on his responsibilities to some debt—ridden farmers. The appeals panel directed the USDA to create a system of processing loan deferments and of publicizing them as it said Congress had intended. The panel said that it is the responsibility of the agriculture secretary to carry our this intent "not as a private banker, but as a public broker."*

Imagine that item being read by persons who have been trained to read but are as culturally illiterate as were my community college students. They might possibly know words like foreclosure, but they would surely not understand the text as a whole. Who gave the order that the federal panel upheld? What is a federal appeals panel? Even if culturally illiterate readers bothered to look up individual words, they would not have much idea of the reality being referred to. Nor, in reading other texts, would they understand references to such things as, say, the equal protection clause or Robert E. Lee, no matter how well they could read a text on friendship. But a truly literate American does understand references to the equal protection of the laws and Robert E. Lee and newspaper reports like the one I just quoted. As a practical matter, newspaper reporters and writers of books cannot possibly provide detailed background information on every occasion. Think, if they did, how much added information would be needed even in the short item that I quoted from *The Washington Post*. Every sentence would need a dozen sentences of explanation! And each of those sentences would need a dozen more.

Writers work with an idea of what their audiences can be expected to know. They assume, they must assume, a "common reader" who knows the things that are known by other literate persons in the culture.

When I say that these writers must assume such background knowledge, I am affirming a fact about language use that sociolinguists and psycholinguists have known for twenty years: The explicit words of a text are just the tip of the iceberg in a linguistic transaction. In order to understand even the surface of a text, a reader must have the sort of background knowledge that was assumed, for example, in *The Washington Post* report that I quoted.

To understand that paragraph, literate readers would know in the backs of their minds that the American legal system allows a judgment at a lower level to be reversed at a higher level. They would know that a judge can tell the executive branch what it can or cannot do to farmers and other citizens, and they would know a lot more that is relevant. But none of their knowledge would have to be highly detailed. They wouldn't need to know, for instance, whether an appeals panel is the final level before the Supreme Court. In general, readers need to share a cloudy but still accurate sense of the *realities* that are being referred to in a piece of writing. This allows them to make the necessary associations.

Besides this topic—determined knowledge, the reader needs to know less explicit and less topic—defined matters, such as culturally shared attitudes, values, conventions, and connotations that the writer assumes the reader to have. The writer cannot start from ground zero, even in a children's reader designed for the first grade. The subtlety and complexity of written communication is directly dependent upon a shared background.

To an ill-informed adult who is unaware of what literate persons are expected to know, the assumption by writers that their readers possess cultural literacy could be regarded as a conspiracy of the literate against the illiterate for the purpose of keeping them out of the club. Although newspaper reporters, writers of books, and the framers of the verbal SAT necessarily make assumptions about the things literate persons know, no one ever announces what that body of information is. So, although we Americans object to pronouncements about what we all should know, there is a body of information that literate people *do* know. And this creates a kind of silent, *de facto* dictating from on high about the things adults should know in order to be truly literate.

Our silence about the explicit contents of cultural literacy leads to the following result, observable in the sociology of the verbal SAT. This exam is chiefly a vocabulary test, which, except for its omission of proper names and other concrete information, constitutes a test of cultural literacy. Hence, when young people from deprived backgrounds ask how they can acquire the abilities tested on the verbal SAT, they are told, quite correctly under present circumstances, that the only way to acquire that knowledge is through wide reading in many domains over many years. That is advice that deprived students already in high school are not in a position to take. Thus there remains a strong correlation between the verbal SAT score and socioeconomic status. Students from middle-class and upper-middle-class backgrounds get their knowledge for the verbal SAT not just from reading, but through the pores, from talk at home and social chitchat.

What follows from this situation goes to the heart of the school curriculum. It means nothing less than the whole conceptual basis of the curriculum as inculcating skills independently of specific content has been wrong—and not just a little wrong, but fundamentally so. The influence of this mistaken educational formalism upon our policies has been, in my opinion, a chief cause of our educational failures in the domain of literacy.

The skills orientation to education has assumed that the particular contents of the curriculum can be arbitrary.

Any good content will develop the skill of reading, but on the contrary, the information that is taken for granted between literate people is not arbitrary. Although quite fuzzy at the edges, this information is known to be central by every truly literate person in our culture. I stress *our* literate culture, because the information shared by literate Americans is different from the information shared by literate

Germans or Russians. Literacy in every nation depends on a specifically national literate culture.

Of course, no literate national culture makes absolute sense. Although Shakespeare might be better than Racine in absolute terms, we don't tell the French that they should abandon Racine for Shakespeare. For purposes of national education in America or France, neither Shakespeare nor Racine could be replaced in their respective cultures as necessary background knowledge for literacy and communication. Although we may admire our traditional culture for its own sake, it is mainly for these instrumental reasons (that is, to achieve true literacy and widescale communication) that our central traditional materials must continue to be taught and learned.

If our high school graduates are to be literate, our school curriculum must ensure, at a minimum, that students acquire those facts of cultural literacy that are requisite to true literacy. To accomplish this, the school curriculum needs significant improvement, particularly in grades K through ten. By *improvement*, I do not suggest that it must be completely overhauled. And I do not say that we need what is usually meant by the term "core curriculum." The proposal to introduce a substantial core curriculum in literature whereby every child reads *Silas Marner, Julius Caesar*, and *A Tale of Two Cities* is, I think, lacking in appropriate subtlety. A core of shared information must indeed be learned. But the means by which it is conveyed may vary a good deal. The destination is one, but the routes are many. No educational reform can succeed if it fails to keep students and teachers motivated and interested. Different pupils require different materials, and so do different teachers. For that reason alone, we need to keep diversity and local judgment at the heart of the curriculum. But we also need to be sure that our students get the ABCs of knowledge in the earlier grades. How, then, can we keep a desirable flexibility in the curriculum and also ensure that our students get the core knowledge they need in order to become literate Americans?

In broaching a solution to this problem, let me make a distinction between two kinds of knowledge taught in school. The two kinds are both necessary, but they are quite distinct. I call them "extensive" and "intensive" knowledge. I'll describe extensive knowledge first. It tends to be broad, but superficial. It is often learned by rote. It is mainly enumerative. It consists of atomic facts and categories. It does not put things together. It's the kind of knowledge possessed by the Major General in Gilbert and Sullivan's *Pirates of Penzance*.

I am the very model of a modern Major General,
I've information vegetable, animal, and mineral,

I know the kings of England, and I quote the fights historical,
From Marathon to Waterloo in order categorical;
I'm very well acquainted too with matters mathematical,
I understand equations, both the simple and quadradical,
About binomial theorem I'm teeming with a lot o' news
With many cheerful facts about the square of the hypotenuse.

This was comic because these cheerful facts were *all* the Major General knew, and they offered him no help in military strategy. Everybody in his audience also knew those same facts, which were part of the intellectual baggage that every schoolboy acquired in nineteenth-century Britain. It was clear to Gilbert and Sullivan's audience that this knowledge was just a lot of isolated, schoolboy facts that the Major General couldn't put together in any useful way.

Understanding how to put things together is the contribution of *intensive* study. Suppose that instead of just being able to list the fights historical, the Major General wanted to learn something about war and strategy. To gain that knowledge, he would have to study at least a battle or two in some detail. Yet it might not greatly matter which battle he studied carefully. It could be the battle of Austerlitz or the battle of Waterloo. But in order to gain a coherent idea of nineteenth-century warfare, General Stanley would have needed to study specific examples of warfare. Thereafter, any new fact about it that he encountered could be grafted upon or accommodated to the model—idea that he had gained from, say, the battle of Austerlitz. To generalize from this illustration, if we want to make isolated facts fit together in some coherent way, we must acquire models of how they do so from detailed, intensive study and experience.

The school curriculum should foster this intensive learning as much as possible. Indeed, it should be the chief substance of the school curriculum, particularly in the later grades. At the same time, intensive study is also the most flexible part of the school curriculum. For building mental models, it doesn't greatly matter whether the Shakespeare play read in ninth grade is *Macbeth* or *Julius Caesar*. What does matter is whether our idea of Shakespeare is formed on an actual, concrete experience of a Shakespearian play. Such intensive learning is necessary, because the mental model we get from the detailed study of an example lets us connect our atomic facts together and build a coherent picture of reality. On the other hand, since the chief function of intensive study is to get examples for such models, our choice of examples can vary with circumstances and should depend on students' knowledge and interest. That is why a lock-step core curriculum is both unnecessary and undesirable for the intensive part of the curriculum. On the other hand, there is a limit to the flexibility of the intensive curriculum. A play by Neil Simon or George Chapman is no effective substitute for a play by Shakespeare.

Although we must gain intensive knowledge to make coherent sense out of facts, we must also gain a store of particular, widely shared background facts in order to make sense of what we read. This extensive part of the curriculum, the part that is crucial to shared knowledge and literacy, has been neglected.

The best time to get this extensive background information is before tenth grade, and the earlier the better. In early grades, children are fascinated by straightforward information. Our official modern distaste for old-fashioned memorization and rote learning seems more pious than realistic. Young children are eager to master the materials essential for adult life, and if they believe in the materials they will proudly soak them up like sponges and never forget them. There is a tremendous weight of human tradition across many cultures to support this view. At about age thirteen, young Catholics get confirmed, having memorized the materials they must know in adult life. At the same age, young Jews get bar mitzvahed. At around the same age, young tribal boys and girls must show that they have mastered the rites of passage into the tribe.

There are good reasons why these universal traditions of early acculturation should have come into being. They correspond to something that seems almost biological in its appropriateness and necessity. Human beings function in the world only by becoming members of a culture. The human species survives through social and cultural organizations, not through instinct. Young children have an urge to become acculturated into the adult world by learning the facts of the tribe long before they can make sense out of them.

But in neglecting the extensive part of the school curriculum, we have forsaken the responsibility that rests with the adult members of any tribe. For many decades, we have followed educational theories and ideologies that have now turned out to be inadequate. We have forgotten the acculturative responsibilities of the earlier grades. In a larger historical perspective, we can see that we lost touch with our earlier educational traditions, and, as a consequence, whole generations of schoolchildren lost touch with earlier traditions of our national culture. But those decades did not and could not signal a permanent change in American education, because the failure to include schoolchildren in our literate traditions is in conflict with some of the root purposes of national education.

A lot of us are beginning to recognize our earlier mistakes. That is one of the meanings of the current educational reform movement. We are beginning to see that educational formalism—the idea that we can teach reading and writing as formal skills only—is not sound and has not worked. We have also seen the superficiality of believing that a literate nation can abandon its traditions and remake its literate culture from scratch according to some new ideology. That is a mistake not in moral terms, but in practical terms. When the national languages were fixed in the eighteenth century, some of the cultural baggage that went with each language also became fixed. The two elements, language and cultural baggage, cannot be disentangled. If one believes in literacy, one must also believe in *cultural* literacy.

A great deal is at stake in understanding and acting on these truths as soon as possible. For most children, the opportunity of acquiring cultural literacy, once lost in the early grades, is lost for good. That is most likely to be true with children of parents who have not themselves mastered the literate national culture. To deprive these children of cultural literacy in the early grades is to deprive most of them forever. By contrast, children from literate families may get at home what the schools have failed to provide. It is the neediest, therefore, who suffer most from out failure to live up to our educational responsibility to teach the traditional extensive curriculum.

What are the specific contents of that extensive curriculum? Let me be quite specific about goals, even if not about the contents of each grade level. I said that the extensive curriculum consists of broad, often superficial information that is taken for granted in writings directed to a mature general reader. American readers are assumed to know vaguely ho the following pre-1865 people were (I give just the briefest beginning of an alphabetical list, stopping with H.): John Adams, Benedict Arnold, Daniel Boone, John Brown, Aaron Burr, John C. Calhoun, Henry Clay, James Fenimore Cooper, Lord Cornwallis, Davy Crockett, Emily Dickinson, Stephen A. Douglas, Frederick Douglass, Jonathan Edwards, Ralph Waldo Emerson, Benjamin Franklin, Robert Fulton, Ulysses S. Grant, Alexander Hamilton, and Nathaniel Hawthorne. Most of us know rather little about most of these names, but that little is of crucial importance because it enables writers to assume a foundation from which they can treat in detail whatever they wish to focus upon.

Here is another alphabetical list: Antarctic Ocean, Arctic Ocean, Atlantic Ocean, Baltic Sea, Black Sea, Caribbean Sea, Gulf of Mexico, North Sea, Pacific Ocean, Red Sea. It has a companion list:

Alps, Appalachians, Himalayas, Rocky Mountains, Mt. Everest, Mt. Vesuvius, the Matterhorn. Because writers mention these things without explanation, readers need to have them as part of their intellectual baggage.

Another category is the large realm of allusion that belongs to our literary and mythic heritage. These traditional myths enable writers to say complex things compactly and to use emotive and ironic values of allusion. Here is a sampling of such taken-for-granted materials from the literature that one often gets in childhood: Adam and Eve, Cain and Abel, Jack and Jill, Little Jack Horner, Cinderella, Jack and the Beanstalk, Mary Had a Little Lamb, The Night Before Christmas, Peter Pan, Pinocchio, The Princes and the Pea.

Here are some patriotic songs that are generally known: The Battle Hymn of the Republic; Columbia, the Gem of the Ocean; My Country, 'Tis of Thee; America the Beautiful; The Star-Spangled Banner; This Land Is Your Land; Yankee Doodle.

At random I will add (alphabetically) such personages as Achilles, Adonis, Aeneas, Agamemnon, Antigone, and Apollo. Not to mention Robin Hood, Paul Bunyan, Satan, Sleeping Beauty, Sodom and Gemorrah, the Ten Commandments, and Tweedledum and Tweedledee.

Obviously you don't expect me to give the whole list of cultural literacy here. But perhaps it would surprise you to learn that I could do so if I had the time and you had the patience. In fact, such a list was compiled, after much consultation, by a historian, a natural scientist, and myself. It represents background knowledge that people need to have by the time they graduate high school. Although the list is 131 pages long, it could be cut down by about a third for the pre-tenth-grade age group. Perhaps its most important feature is its limited character. It represents a specific, finite body of superficial knowledge, which, if taught to youngsters in the context of a good intensive curriculum, would enable them to understand serious materials directed to a general reader.

Any such list is of course open to objections like the following: Why aren't there more women on the list? Why isn't there more representation of Chicano culture? Doesn't your list simply certify and perpetuate the existing WASP, establishment culture? Must this status quo, traditional material be the only method of achieving universal literacy? Won't this return to traditional materials make our culture even more static, dull and monolithic than it already is?

My reply is that the various movements that have been resisting such cultural dominance have been working reasonably effectively and will continue to do so. Also, as Catherine Stimpson, the well-known feminist literary critic and former editor of the feminist journal *Signs*, recently observed, we must distinguish between people who are actively trying to change our literate culture and those who are trying to make a useful dictionary of its current structure. Unless the two functions are kept separate, the dictionary makers like me, who are trying to make a serviceable list, will lose their credibility and usefulness.

Stimpson's shrewd observation describes a situation that teachers always find themselves in. Although we are citizens who want to work for social and political ends, such as a more pluralistic culture, we are also professionals whose personal politics must stop at the classroom door. In our roles as teachers, we have an obligation to be descriptive lexicographers, to tell our students what they currently need in order to be literate. If we disapprove of the current literate culture and want to change some of its elements, we should pursue outside the classroom the sort of cultural politics that Catherine Stimpson pursues. But until we succeed in changing the literate culture, we must not misinform our students by pretending that its contents are just what we wish them to be. Of course, we also have an obligation to explain to our students why it is, for example, that a pre-1865 list of Americans whom a culturally literate person might be expected to know of would not include many blacks. The content of a society's cultural literacy bears witness to its sins as well as its successes.

I mentioned feminism as an example of cultural change because it has succeeded in altering our collective usages. It has made us self-conscious about gender words and gender attitudes. Similarly, the civil rights movement succeeded in changing our usages in such ways as effectively removing the word "nigger" from the English language—a beneficent change, indeed! This kind of change goes on all the time, for both good and ill. As a result, the content of cultural literacy is always changing, as is obvious to everyone in the case of such words as DNA and *software*.

What may not be obvious is that the *central* content of cultural literacy has not changed very much in the last hundred years. What changes is at the periphery, not at the center. These days, writers can assume their readers know who Gerald Ford is, but thirty years from now they probably won't make that assumption. On the other hand, thirty years from now writers will continue to assume that George Washington could not tell a lie and that Scrooge hated Christmas. Of course, no single item of cultural literacy has any importance by itself. But the bulk of such items, taken together, are as important as anything we teach.

In the technological age, Washington and the Cherry Tree, and Scrooge and Christmas, the fights historical, the oceans geographical, the beings animalculus, and all the other shared materials of literate culture have become more, not less, important. The more we become computerized, the more we need not just shared scientific knowledge but also shared fairy tales, Greek myths, historical images, and so on. Let me explain this paradox. The more specialized and technical our civilization becomes, the harder it is for nonspecialists to participate in the decisions that deeply affect their lives. The growing power of the technological class will create, according to experts, more and more distance between the rest of us and the ruling cadre of technicians who control the systems. The technicians with their arcane specialties will not be able to communicate with us, nor we with them. This contradicts the basic principles of democracy and must not be allowed to happen.

The only antidote to this problem of specialization was put forward many centuries ago by Cicero. He said that each of us should be trained to communicate our special knowledge to the rest of our society in the language of ordinary people. That this Ciceronian ideal *can* be achieved is proven by those literate scientists who are able to write for a general literate public. But such a literate culture can only be achieved if all of us, including technicians, share enough traditional background material to enable complex communication to occur.

In conclusion, I want to stress again that the only skills that train for life are those knowledge-based activities that continue specifically to be used in life. Reading and writing, of course, continue to be used. Everyone knows they are absolutely central to productive membership in our society and to the ability to acquire new knowledge-based skills when needed. Reading and writing at the high levels required for such future flexibility are skills that are based on a large, complex system of world knowledge that I have called cultural literacy. Imparting this knowledge to our students, through the study of the humanities and the sciences, is the chief responsibility of our educational system.

Our schools have not imparted these essential facts and words, because in recent times we have not been willing as a nation to decide what the essential facts and words are. Despite our national virtues of diversity and pluralism, our failure to decide upon the core content of cultural literacy has created a positive barrier to adult literacy in this country, and thus to full citizenship and full acculturation into our

society. We Americans need to be decisive and explicit about the background information that a citizen should know in order to be literate in the 1980s. Access to this democratic literate culture is not only a proper goal of our curriculum but is also the only possible way of realizing the dream of Jefferson and King.

## Study Questions

1. What does Hirsch mean by the phrase "cultural literacy"? How does he propose to solve the problem of literacy in America? What do you think of his proposal?

2. What is universal communication? Why is it significant, according to Hirsch?

3. He anticipates criticism from those who are in favor of muticulturalism. How would they criticize his position? How would he respond?

4. Do you think there is an implicit canon of knowledge in the U.S.? What is included? Who decides what is included? Can we ever move away from the canon altogether?

5. How do recent changes in technology impact his desire for cultural literacy?

# 6

# NOBODY MEAN MORE TO ME THAN YOU* AND THE FUTURE LIFE OF WILLIE JORDAN

*June Jordan*

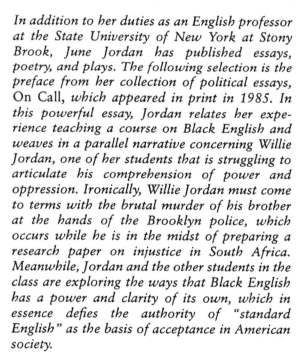

*In addition to her duties as an English professor at the State University of New York at Stony Brook, June Jordan has published essays, poetry, and plays. The following selection is the preface from her collection of political essays, On Call, which appeared in print in 1985. In this powerful essay, Jordan relates her experience teaching a course on Black English and weaves in a parallel narrative concerning Willie Jordan, one of her students that is struggling to articulate his comprehension of power and oppression. Ironically, Willie Jordan must come to terms with the brutal murder of his brother at the hands of the Brooklyn police, which occurs while he is in the midst of preparing a research paper on injustice in South Africa. Meanwhile, Jordan and the other students in the class are exploring the ways that Black English has a power and clarity of its own, which in essence defies the authority of "standard English" as the basis of acceptance in American society.*

Black English is not exactly a linguistic buffalo; as children, most of the thirty-five million Afro-Americans living here depend on this language for our discovery of the world. But then we approach our maturity inside a larger social body that will not

---

* Black English aphorisms crafted by Monica Morris, a junior at S.U.N.Y., Stony Brook, October 1984.

support our efforts to become anything other than the clones of those who are neither our mothers nor our fathers. We begin to grow up in a house where every true mirror shows us the face of somebody who does not belong there, whose walk and whose talk will never look or sound "right," because that house was meant to shelter a family that is alien and hostile to us. As we learn our way around this environment, either we hide our original word habits, or we completely surrender our own voice, hoping to please those who will never respect anyone different from themselves: Black English is not exactly a linguistic buffalo, but we should understand its status as an endangered species, as a perishing, irreplaceable system of community intelligence, or we should expect its extinction, and, along with that, the extinguishing of much that constitutes our own proud, and singular, identity.

What we casually call "English," less and less defers to England and its "gentlemen." "English" is no longer a specific matter of geography or an element of class privilege; more than thirty-three countries use this tool as a means of "intranational communication." Countries as disparate as Zimbabwe and Malaysia, or Israel and Uganda, use it as their non-native currency of convenience. Obviously, this tool, this "English," cannot function inside thirty-three discrete societies on the basis of rules and values absolutely determined somewhere else, in a thirty-fourth other country, for example.

In addition to that staggering congerie of non-native users of English, there are five countries, or

313

333,746,000 people, for whom this thing called "English" serves as a native tongue.[1] Approximately 10 percent of these native speakers of "English" are Afro-American citizens of the U.S.A. I cite these numbers and varieties of human beings dependent on "English" in order, quickly, to suggest how strange and how tenuous is any concept of "Standard English." Obviously, numerous forms of English now operate inside a natural, an uncontrollable, continuum of development. I would suppose "the standard" for English in Malaysia is not the same as "the standard" in Zimbabwe. I know that standard forms of English for Black people in this country do not copy that of Whites. And, in fact, the structural differences between these two kinds of English have intensified, becoming more Black, or less White, despite the expected homogenizing effects of television[2] and other mass media.

Nonetheless, White standards of English persist, supreme and unquestioned, in these United States. Despite our multi-lingual population, and despite the deepening Black and White cleavage within that conglomerate, White standards control our official and popular judgments of verbal proficiency and correct, or incorrect, language skills, including speech. In contrast to India, where at least fourteen languages co-exist as legitimate Indian languages, in contrast to Nicaragua, where all citizens are legally entitled to formal school instruction in their regional or tribal languages, compulsory education in America compels accommodation to exclusively White forms of "English." White English, in America, is "Standard English."

This story begins two years ago. I was teaching a new course, "In Search of the Invisible Black Woman," and my rather large class seemed evenly divided among young Black women and men. Five or six White students also sat in attendance. With unexpected speed and enthusiasm we had moved through historical narration of the 19th century to literature by and about Black women, in the 20th. I then assigned the first forty pages of Alice Walker's *The Color Purple,* and I came, eagerly, to class that morning:

"So!" I exclaimed, aloud. "What did you think? How did you like it?"

The students studied their hands, or the floor. There was no response. The tense, resistant feeling in the room fairly astounded me.

At last, one student, a young woman still not meeting my eyes, muttered something in my direction:

"What did you say?" I prompted her.

"Why she have them talk so funny. It don't sound right."

"You mean the language?"

Another student lifted his head: "It don't look right, neither. I couldn't hardly read it."

At this, several students dumped on the book. Just about unanimously, their criticisms targeted the language. I listened to what they wanted to say and silently marvelled at the similarities between their casual speech patterns and Alice Walker's written version of Black English.

But I decided against pointing to these identical traits of syntax, I wanted not to make them self-conscious about their own spoken language—not while they clearly felt it was "wrong." Instead I decided to swallow my astonishment. Here was a negative Black reaction to a prize-winning accomplishment of Black literature that White readers across the country had selected as a best seller. Black rejection was aimed at the one irreducibly Black element of Walker's work: the language—Celie's Black English. I wrote the opening lines of *The Color Purple* on the blackboard and asked the students to help me translate these sentences into Standard English:

*You better not never tell nobody but God. It'd kill your mommy.*

Dear God,

I am fourteen years old. I have always been a good girl. Maybe you can give me a sign letting me know what is happening to me.

Last spring after Little Lucious come I heard them fussing. He was pulling on her arm. She say it too soon, Fonso. I aint well. Finally he leave her alone. A week go by, he pulling on her arm again. She say, Naw, I ain't gonna. Can't you see I'm already half dead, an all of the children. [3]

Our process of translation exploded with hilarity and even hysterical, shocked laughter: The Black writer, Alice Walker, knew what she was doing! If rudimentary criteria for good fiction include the manipulation of language so that the syntax and diction of sentences will tell you the identity of speakers, the probable age and sex and class of speakers, and even the locale—urban/rural/southern/western—then Walker had written, perfectly. This is the translation into Standard English that our class produced:

*Absolutely, one should never confide in anybody besides God. Your secrets could prove devastating to your mother.*

Dear God,

I am fourteen years old. I have always been good. But now, could you help me to understand what is happening to me?

Last spring, after my little brother, Lucious, was born, I heard my parents fighting. My father kept pulling at my mother's arm. But she told him, "It's too soon for sex, Alfonso. I am still not feeling well." Finally, my father left her alone. A week went by, and then he began bothering my mother, again: Pulling her arm. She told him, "No, I won't! Can't you see I'm already exhausted from all of these children?

(Our favorite line was "It's too soon for sex, Alfonso.")

Once we could stop laughing, once we could stop our exponentially wild improvisations on the theme of Translated Black English, the students pushed to explain their own negative first reactions to their spoken language on the printed page. I thought it was probably akin to the shock of seeing yourself in a photograph for the first time. Most of the students had never before seen a written facsimile of the way they talk. None of the students had ever learned how to read and write their own verbal system of communication: Black English. Alternatively, this fact began to baffle or else bemuse and then infuriate my students. Why not? Was it too late? Could they learn how to do it, now? And, ultimately, the final test question, the one testing my sincerity: Could I teach them? Because I had never taught anyone Black English and, as far as I knew, no one, anywhere in the United States, had ever offered such a course, the best I could say was "I'll try."

He looked like a wrestler.

He sat dead center in the packed room and, every time our eyes met, he quickly nodded his head as though anxious to reassure, and encourage me.

Short, with strikingly broad shoulders and long arms, he spoke with a surprisingly high, soft voice that matched the soft bright movement of his eyes. His name was Willie Jordan. He would have seemed even more unlikely in the context of Contemporary Women's Poetry, except that ten or twelve other Black men were taking the course, as well. Still, Willie was conspicuous. His extreme fitness, the muscular density of his presence underscored the riveted, gentle attention that he gave to anything anyone said. Generally, he did not join the loud and rowdy dialogue flying back and forth, but there could be no doubt about his interest in our discussions. And, when he stood to present an argument he'd prepared, overnight, that nervous smile of his

vanished and an irregular stammering replaced it, as he spoke with visceral sincerity, word by word.

That was how I met Willie Jordan. It was in between "In Search of the Invisible Black Women" and "The Art of Black English." I was waiting for departmental approval and I supposed that Willie might be, so to speak, killing time until he, too, could study Black English. But Willie really did want to explore contemporary women's poetry and, to that end, volunteered for extra research and never missed a class.

Towards the end of that semester, Willie approached me for an independent study project on South Africa. It would commence the next semester. I thought Willie's writing needed the kind of improvement only intense practice will yield. I knew his intelligence was outstanding. But he'd wholeheartedly opted for "standard English" at a rather late age, and the results were stilted and frequently polysyllabic, simply for the sake of having more syllables. Willie's unnatural formality of language seemed to me consistent with the formality of his research into South African apartheid. As he projected his studies, he would have little time, indeed, for newspapers. Instead, more than 90 percent of his research would mean saturation in strictly historical, if not archival, material. I was certainly interested. It would be tricky to guide him into a more confident and spontaneous relationship both with language and apartheid. It was going to be wonderful to see what happened when he could catch up with himself, entirely, and talk back to the world.

September, 1984: Breezy fall weather and much excitement! My class, "The Art of Black English," was full to the limit of the fire laws. And in Independent Study, Willie Jordan showed up weekly, fifteen minutes early for each of our sessions. I was pretty happy to be teaching, altogether!

I remember an early class when a young brother, replete with his ever-present porkpie hat, raised his hand and then told us that most of what he'd heard was "all right" except it was "too clean." "The brothers on the street," he continued, "they mix it up more. Like 'fuck' and 'motherfuck.' Or like "shit." He waited. I waited. Then all of us laughed a good while, and we got into a brawl about "correct" and "realistic" Black English that led to Rule 1.

Rule 1: *Black English is about a whole lot more than mothafuckin.*

As a criterion, we decided, "realistic" could take you anywhere you want to go. Artful places, Angry places. Eloquent and sweetalkin places. Polemical places. Church. And the local Bar & Grill.

We were checking out a language, not a mood or a scene or one guy's forgettable mouthing off.

It was hard. For most of the students, learning Black English required a fallback to patterns and rhythms of speech that many of their parents had beaten out of them. I mean beaten. And, in a majority of cases, correct Black English could be achieved only by striving for incorrect Standard English, something they were still pushing at, quite uncertainly. This state of affairs led to Rule 2.

Rule 2: *If it's wrong in Standard English it's probably right in Black English, or, at least, you're hot.*

It was hard. Roommates and family members ridiculed their studies, or remained incredulous, "You studying that shit? At school?" But we were beginning to feel the companionship of pioneers. And we decided that we needed another rule that would establish each one of us as equally important to our success. This was Rule 3.

Rule 3: *If it don't sound like something that come out somebody mouth then it don't sound right. If it don't sound right then it ain't hardly right. Period.*

This rule produced two weeks of compositions in which the students agonizingly tried to spell the sound of the Black English sentence they wanted to convey. But Black English is, preeminently, an oral/spoken means of communication. And spelling don't talk. So we needed Rule 4.

Rule 4: *Forget about the spelling. Let the syntax carry you.*

Once we arrived at Rule 4 we started to fly, because syntax, the structure of an idea, leads you to the world view of the speaker and reveals her values. The syntax of a sentence equals the structure of your consciousness. If we insisted that the language of Black English adheres to a distinctive Black syntax, then we were postulating a profound difference between White and Black people, per se. Was it a difference to prize or to obliterate?

There are three qualities of Black English—the presence of life, voice, and clarity—that intensify to a distinctive Black value system that we became excited about and self-consciously tried to maintain.

1. Black English has been produced by a pre-technocratic, if not anti-technological, culture. More, our culture has been constantly threatened by annihilation or, at least, the swallowed blurring of assimilation. Therefore, our language is a system constructed by people constantly needing to insist that we exist, that we are present. Our language devolves from a culture that abhors all abstraction, or anything tending to obscure or delete the fact of the human being who is here and now/the truth of the person who is speaking or listening. Consequently, *there is no passive voice construction possible in Black English*. For example, you cannot say, "Black English is being eliminated." You must say, instead, "White people eliminating Black English." The assumption of the presence of life governs all of Black English. Therefore, overwhelmingly, *all action takes place in the language of the present indicative*. And every sentence assumes the living and active participation of at least two human beings, the speaker and the listener.

2. A primary consequence of the person-centered values of Black English is the delivery of voice. If you speak or write Black English, your ideas will necessarily possess that otherwise elusive attribute, *voice*.

3. One main benefit following from the person-centered values of Black English is that of *clarity*. If your idea, your sentence, assumes the presence of at least two living and active people, you will make it understandable, because the motivation behind every sentence is the wish to say something real, to somebody real.

As the weeks piled up, translation from Standard English into Black English or vice versa occupied a hefty part of our course work.

Standard English (hereafter S.E.): "In considering the idea of studying Black English those questioned suggested—"

(What's the subject? Where's the person? Is anybody alive in here, in that idea?)

Black English (hereafter B.E.): "I been asking people what you think about somebody studying Black English and they answer me like this:"

But there were interesting limits. You cannot "translate" instances of Standard English preoccupied with abstraction or with nothing/nobody evidently alive, into Black English. That would warp the language into uses antithetical to the guiding perspective of its community of users. Rather you must first change those Standard English sentences, themselves, into ideas consistent with the person-centered assumptions of Black English.

## GUIDELINES FOR BLACK ENGLISH

1. Minimal number of words for every idea: This is the source for the aphoristic and/or poetic force of the language; eliminate every possible word.

2.    Clarity: If the sentence is not clear it's not Black English.

3.    Eliminate use of the verb *to be* whenever possible. This leads to the deployment of more descriptive and, therefore, more precise verbs.

4.    Use *be* or *been* only when you want to describe a chronic, ongoing state of things.

He *be* at the office, by 9. (He is always at the office by 9.)

He *been* with her since forever.

5.    Zero copula: Always eliminate the verb *to be* whenever it would combine with another verb, in Standard English.

S.E.: She is going out with him.

B.E.: She going out with him.

6.    Eliminate *do* as in:

S.E.: What do you think? What do you want?

B.E.: What you think? What you want?

Rules number 3, 4, 5, and 6 provide for the use of the minimal number of verbs per idea and, therefore, greater accuracy in the choice of verb.

7.    In general, if you wish to say something really positive, try to formulate the idea using emphatic negative structure.

S.E.: He's fabulous.

B.E.: He bad.

8.    Use double or triple negatives for dramatic emphasis.

S.E.: Tina Turner sings out of this world.

B.E.: Ain nobody sing like Tina.

9.    Never use the *ed* suffix to indicate the past tense of a verb.

S.E.: She closed the door.

B.E.: She close the door. Or, she have close the door.

10. Regardless of intentional verb time, only use the third person singular, present indicative, for use of the verb *to have*, as an auxiliary.

S.E.: He had his wallet then he lost it.

B.E.: He have him wallet then he lose it.

S.E.: We had seen that movie.

B.E.: We seen that movie. Or, we have see that movie.

11. Observe a minimal inflection of verbs. Particularly, never change from the first person singular forms to the third person singular.

S.E.: Present Tense Forms: He goes to the store.

B.E.: He go to the store.

S.E.: Past Tense Forms: He went to the store.

B.E.: He go to the store. Or, he gone to the store. Or, he been to the store.

12. The possessive case scarcely ever appears in Black English. Never use an apostrophe ('s) construction. If you wander into a possessive case component of an idea, then keep logically consistent: *ours, his, theirs, mines*. But, most likely, if you bump into such a component, you have wandered outside the underlying world view of Black English.

S.E.: He will take their car tomorrow.

B.E.: He taking they car tomorrow.

13. Plurality: Logical consistency, continued: If the modifier indicates plurality then the noun remains in the singular case.

S.E.: He ate twelve doughnuts.

B.E.: He eat twelve doughnut.

S.E.: She has many books.

B.E.: She have many book.

14. Listen for, or invent, special Black English forms of the past tense, such as: "He losted it. That what she felted." If they are clear and readily understood, then use them.

15. Do not hesitate to play with words, sometimes inventing them: e.g. "astropotomous" means huge like a hippo plus astronomical and, therefore, signifies real big.

16. In Black English, unless you keenly want to underscore the past tense nature of an action, stay in the present tense and rely on the overall context of your ideas for the conveyance of time and sequence.

17. Never use the suffix *-ly* form of an adverb in Black English.

S.E.: The rain came down rather quickly.

B.E.: The rain come down pretty quick.

18. Never use the indefinite article an in Black English.

S.E.: He wanted to ride an elephant.

B.E.: He wanted to ride him a elephant.

19. Invariant syntax: in correct Black English it is possible to formulate an imperative, an interrogative, and a simple declarative idea with the same syntax:

B.E.: You going to the store?

You going to the store.

You going to the store!

Where was Willie Jordan? We'd reached the mid-term of the semester. Students had formulated Black English guidelines, by consensus, and they were now writing with remarkable beauty, purpose, and enjoyment:

*I ain hardly speakin for everybody but myself so understan that.*

—Kim Parks

Samples from student writings:

Janie have a great big ole hole inside her. Tea Cake the only thing that fit that hole. . . .

That pear tree beautiful to Janie, especial when bees fiddlin with the blossomin pear there growin large and lovely. But personal speakin, the love she get from starin at that tree ain the love what starin back at her in them relationship. (Monica Morris)

Love a big theme in, *They Eye Was Watching God*. Love show people new corners inside theyself. It pull out good stuff and stuff back bad stuff . . . Joe worship the doing uh his own hand and need other people to worship him too. But he ain't think about Janie that she a person and ought to live like anybody common do. Queen life not for Janie. (Monica Morris)

In both life and writin, Black womens have varietous experience of love that be cold like a iceberg or fiery like a inferno. Passion got for the other partner involve, man or women, seem as shallow, ankle-deep water or the most profoundest abyss. (Constance Evans)

Family love another bond that ain't never break under no pressure. (Constance Evans)

You know it really cold/When the friend you/ Always get out the fire/Act like they don't know you/When you in the beat. (Constance Evans)

Big classroom discussion bout love at this time. I never take no class where us have any long arguin for and against for two or three day. New to me and great. I find the class time talkin a million time more interesting than detail bout the book. (Kathy Esseks)

As these examples suggest, Black English no longer limited the students, in any way. In fact, one of them, Philip Garfield, would shortly "translate" a pivotal scene from Ibsen's *A Doll's House*, as his final term paper.

NORA: I didn't gived no shit. I thinked you a asshole back then, too, you make it so hard for me save mines husband life.

KROGSTAD: Girl, it clear you ain't any idea what you done. You done exact what I once done, and I losed my reputation over it.

NORA: You asks me believe you once act brave save you wife life?

KROGSTAD: Law care less why you done it.

NORA: Law must suck.

KROGSTAD: Suck or no, if I wants, judge screw you wid dis paper.

NORA: No way, man. (Philip Garfield)

But where was Willie? Compulsively punctual, and always thoroughly prepared with neat typed compositions, he had disappeared. He failed to show up for our regularly scheduled conference, and I received neither a note nor a phone call of explanation. A whole week went by. I wondered if Willie had finally been captured by the extremely current happenings in South Africa: passage of a new constitution that did not enfranchise the Black majority, and militant Black South African reaction to that affront. I wondered if he'd been hurt, somewhere. I wondered if the serious workload of weekly readings and writings had overwhelmed him and changed his mind about independent study. Where was Willie Jordan?

One week after the first conference that Willie missed, he called: "Hello, Professor Jordan? This is Willie. I'm sorry I wasn't there last week. But something has come up and I'm pretty upset. I'm sorry but I really can't deal right now."

I asked Willie to drop by my office and just let me see that he was okay. He agreed to do that. When I saw him I knew something hideous had happened. Something had hurt him and scared him to the marrow. He was all agitated and stammering and terse and incoherent. At last, his sadly jumbled account let me surmise, as follows: Brooklyn police had murdered his unarmed, twenty-five-year-old brother, Reggie Jordan. Neither Willie nor his elderly parents knew what to do about it. Nobody from the press was interested. His folks had no money. Police ran his family around and around, to no point. And Reggie was really dead. And Willie wanted to fight, but he felt helpless.

With Willie's permission I began to try to secure legal counsel for the Jordan family. Unfortunately, Black victims of police violence are truly numerous, while the resources available to prosecute their killers are truly scarce. A friend of mine at the Center for Constitutional Rights estimated that just the preparatory costs for bringing the cops into court normally approaches $180,000. Unless the execution of Reggie Jordan became a major community cause for organizing and protest, his murder would simply become a statistical item.

Again, with Willie's permission, I contacted every newspaper and media person I could think of. But the Bastone feature article in *The Village Voice* was the only result from that canvassing.

Again, with Willie's permission, I presented the case to my class in Black English. We had talked about the politics of language. We had talked about love and sex and child abuse and men and women. But the murder of Reggie Jordan broke like a hurricane across the room.

There are few "issues" as endemic to Black life as police violence. Most of the students knew and respected and liked Jordan. Many of them came from the very neighborhood where the murder had occurred. All of the students had known somebody close to them who had been killed by police, or had known frightening moments of gratuitous confrontation with the cops. They wanted to do everything at once to avenge his death. Number One: They decided to compose a personal statement of condolence to Willie Jordan and his family, written in Black English. Number Two: They decided to compose individual messages to the police, in Black English. These should be prefaced by an explanatory paragraph composed by the entire group. Number Three: These individual messages, with their lead paragraph, should be sent to *Newsday*.

The morning after we agreed on these objectives, one of the young women students appeared with an unidentified visitor, who sat through the class, smiling in a peculiar, comfortable way.

Now we had to make more tactical decisions. Because we wanted the messages published, and because we thought it imperative that our outrage be known by the police, the tactical question was this: Should the opening, group paragraph be written in Black English or Standard English?

I have seldom been privy to a discussion with so much heart at the dead beat of it. I will never forget the eloquence, the sudden haltings of speech, the fierce struggle against tears, the furious throwaway, and useless explosions that this question elicited.

That one question contained several others, each of them extraordinarily painful to even contemplate. How best to serve the memory of Reggie Jordan? Should we use the language of the killer—Standard English—in order to make our ideas acceptable to those controlling the killers? But wouldn't what we had to say be rejected, summarily, if we said it in our own language, the language of the victim, Reggie Jordan? But if we thought to express ourselves by abandoning our language wouldn't that mean our suicide on top of Reggie's murder? But if we expressed ourselves in our own language wouldn't that be suicidal to the wish to communicate with those who, evidently, did not give a damn about us/Reggie/police violence in the Black community?

At the end of one of the longest, most difficult hours of my own life, the students voted, unanimously, to preface their individual messages with a paragraph composed in the language of Reggie Jordan. *"At least we don't give up nothing else. At least we stick to the truth: Be who we been. And stay all the way with Reggie."*

It was heartbreaking to proceed, from that point. Everyone in the room realized that our decision in favor of Black English had doomed our writings, even as the distinctive reality of our Black lives always has doomed our efforts to "be who we been" in his country.

I went to the blackboard and took down this paragraph dictated by the class:

YOU COPS!

WE THE BROTHER AND SISTER OF WILLIE JORDAN, A FELLOW STONY BROOK STUDENT WHO THE BROTHER OF THE DEAD REGGIE JORDAN. REGGIE, LIKE MANY BROTHER AND SISTER, HE A VICTIM OF BRUTAL RACIST POLICE, OCTOBER 25, 1984. US APPALL, FED UP, BECAUSE THAT ANOTHER SENSELESS DEATH WHAT OCCUR IN OUR COMMUNITY. THIS WHAT WE FEEL, THIS, FROM OUR HEART, FOR WE AIN'T STAYIN' SILENT NO MORE.

With the completion of this introduction, nobody said anything. I asked for comments. At this invitation, the unidentified visitor, a young Black man, ceaselessly smiling, raised his hand. He was, it so happens, a rookie cop. He had just joined the force in September and, he said, he thought he should clarify a few things. So he came forward and sprawled easily into a posture of barroom, or fireside, nostalgia:

"See," Officer Charles enlightened us, "Most times when you out on the street and something come down you do one of two things. Over-react or under-react. Now, if you under-react then you can get yourself kilt. And if you over-react then maybe you kill somebody. Fortunately it's about nine times out of ten and you will over-react. So the brother got kilt. And I'm sorry about that, believe me. But what you have to understand is what kilt him: Over-reaction. That's all. Now you talk about Black people and White police but see, now, I'm a cop myself. And (big smile) I'm Black. And just a couple months ago I was on the other side. But it's the same for me. You a cop, you the ultimate authority: the Ultimate Authority. And you on the street, most of the time you can only do one of two things: over-react or under-react. That's all it is with the brother. Over-reaction. Didn't have nothing to do with race."

That morning Officer Charles had the good fortune to escape without being boiled alive. But barely. And I remember the pride of his smile when I read about the fate of Black policemen and other collaborators, in South Africa. I remember him, and I remember the shock and palpable feeling of shame that filled the room. It was as though that foolish, and deadly, young man had just relieved himself of his foolish, and deadly, explanation, face to face with the grief of Reggie Jordan's father and Reggie Jordan's mother. Class ended quietly. I copied the paragraph from the blackboard, collected the individual messages and left to type them up.

*Newsday* rejected the piece.

*The Village Voice* could not find room in their "Letters" section to print the individual messages from the students to the police.

None of the TV news reporters picked up the story.

Nobody raised $180,000 to prosecute the murder of Reggie Jordan. Reggie Jordan is really dead.

I asked Willie Jordan to write an essay pulling together everything important to him from that semester. He was still deeply beside himself with frustration and amazement and loss. This is what he wrote, unedited, and in its entirety:

Throughout the course of this semester I have been researching the effects of oppression and exploitation along racial lines in South Africa and its neighboring countries. I have become aware of South African police brutalization of native Africans beyond the extent of the law, even though the laws themselves are catalyst affliction upon Black men, women and children. Many Africans die each year as a result of the

deliberate use of police force to protect the white power structure.

Social control agents in South Africa, such as policemen, are also used to force compliance among citizens through both overt and covert tactics. It is not uncommon to find bold-faced coercion and cold-blooded killings of Blacks by South African police for undetermined and/or inadequate reasons. Perhaps the truth is that the only reasons for this heinous treatment of Blacks rests in racial differences. We should also understand that what is conveyed through the media is not always accurate and may sometimes be construed as the tip of the iceberg at best.

I recently received a painful reminder that racism, poverty, and the abuse of power are global problems which are by no means unique to South Africa. On October 25, 1984 at approximately 3:00 p.m. my brother, Mr. Reginald Jordan, was shot and killed by two New York City policemen from the 75th precinct in the East New York section of Brooklyn. His life ended at the age of twenty-five. Even up to this current point in time the Police Department has failed to provide my family, which consists of five brothers, eight sisters, and two parents, with a plausible reason for Reggie's death. Out of the many stories that were given to my family by the Police Department, not one of them seems to hold water. In fact, I honestly believe that the Police Department's assessment of my brother's murder is nothing short of ABSOLUTE BULLSHIT, and thus far no evidence had been produced to alter perception of the situation.

Furthermore, I believe that one of three cases may have occurred in this incident. First, Reggie's death may have been the desired outcome of the police officer's action, in which case the killing was premeditated. Or, it was a case of mistaken identity, which clarifies the fact that the two officers who killed my brother and their commanding parties are all grossly incompetent. Or, both of the above cases are correct, i.e., Reggie's murderers intended to kill him and the Police Department behaved insubordinately.

Part of the argument of the officers who shot Reggie was that he had attacked one of them and took his gun. This was their major claim. They also said that only one of them had actually shot Reggie. The facts, however, speak, for themselves. According to the Death Certificate and autopsy report, Reggie was shot eight times from point-blank range. The Doctor who performed the autopsy told me himself that two bullets entered the side of my brother's head, four bullets were sprayed into his back, and two bullets struck him in the back of his legs. It is obvious that unnecesary force was used by the police and that it is extremely difficult to shoot someone in his back when he is attacking or approaching you.

After experiencing a situation like this and researching South Africa I believe that to a large degree, justice may only exist as rhetoric. I find it difficult to talk of true justice when the oppresion of my people both at home and abroad attests to the fact that inequality and injustice are serious problems whereby Blacks and Third World people are perpetually short-changed by society. Something has to be done about the way in which this world is set up. Although it is a difficult task, we do have the power to make a change.

Willie J. Jordan, Jr.<br>EGL 487, Section 58, November 14, 1984

It is my privilege to dedicate this book to the future life of Willie J. Jordan, Jr., August 8, 1985.

## ENDNOTES

1. *English is Spreading, But What Is English*? A Presentation by Professor S. N. Sridhar, Department of Linguistics, S.U.N.Y., Stony Brook, April 9, 1985: Dean's Convocation Among the Disciplines.

2. *New York Times*, March 15, 1985, Section One, p. 14: Report on Study by Linguists at the University of Pennsylvania.

3. Alice Walker. *The Color Purple* (New York: Harcourt Brace Jovanovich, 1982), p. 11.

## Study Questions

1. How do you think Jordan would respond to Hirsch's concept of cultural literacy?

2. What argument is she making about Black English? Why is it so important? What is the connection between language and identity?

3. What did you think of the specific rules she sets out for Black English? Have they changed since this piece was written?

4. Why does she then go on to tell the story of Willie Jordan? How does it connect to the first half of the essay?

5. What do you think about the dilemma they face about whether to use standard English or Black English in their letter to the police? Would it have made a difference?

# OMOLUWABI

## The Fundamental Basis Of Yoruba Traditional Education

### Timothy A. Awoniye

*The Europeans may have thought that the Yoruba in Nigeria had no education as such before they came to establish churches and schools. In fact, the Yoruba have such a complex, sophisticated language that it takes well into middle age to begin to master all its subtleties. Traditional methods of education may include showing how to do things but it also includes a rich verbal flow of enculturation directed at the children by the parens beginning with naming. A system of values is inculcated by less formal means than those offered by European style schooling but it is effective in that the learning of the language and appropriate behavior in the culture is virtually a lifelong endeavor. Like the Chinese Confucians, the Yoruba valur filial piety and all its ramifications for the family. The Yoruba proverb states, "Proverbs are the Horses of Speech." Clearly good speech is highly esteemed and relied upon to bring wisdom.*

Thus it seems that it is both the objective and content of education that should be criticized. This point has been emphasized by Ivan D. Illich, a principal antagonist of the school system in his book *Deschooling Society*—when he writes in the chapter 'Why we must disestablish school' that

*Many students, especially those who are poor, intuitively know what the schools do for them. They school them to confuse process and substance . . . The pupil is thereby 'schooled' to confuse teaching with learning, grade advancement with education, a diploma with competence, and fluency with the ability to say*

*something new. . . . Medical treatment is mistaken for health care, social work for the improvement of community life, police protection for safety, military poise for national security, the rat race for productive work.*

The crucial implication is that it was not realized early enough in the Nigerian educational system that, in the words of Sekou Toure,

*man's social behavior and economic activities are directly conditioned by the quality of his intellectual, moral, political and physical education.*

*[Yet] if education does not help the pupil to understand this world, fit (him) into the community, and awake to awareness of a man's duties to himself and his country, the teacher's efforts are pointless.* (sic)

The implication is obvious: theoretical knowledge without any foundation in the culture of the people becomes a sham. In other words,

*We should be acquiring theoretical knowledge in vain, if we ignored the conditions of our own existence and the real world we are living in.* (sic)

In effect, many schooled Nigerians, including the Yorùbá educated elite did not appreciate that education is:

*the culture which each generation purposely gives to those who are to be its successors, in order to qualify them for at least keeping up, and if possible for raising, the level of improvement which has been attained.*

The resultant effect is that many schooled Yorùbá are members of two 'worlds' of culture (the traditional and the European cultures) but citizens of neither. He becomes a man of two 'worlds' who lives a life saturated in ignorance and superstition at home but lives in the office a different life in which all the gadgets and refinements of the machine age give the impression that he is a modern man. This is a false life based on a false education because 'the elements of European civilization are *not* fully integrated and harmonized with indigenous African culture.'

Formal education becomes a mechanical thing for the pupils without any impact on his life and living. Certificates replace instruction; knowledge becomes mistaken for character. The case was stated by the Banjo Commission which was appointed for the purpose of reviewing the Educational System in Western Nigeria. It reported:

*There was very little sign of a development of lively curiousity and a desire to know about the immediate environment and the world outside. One got the impression that pupils were just sponges imbibing knowledge not understood or digested, for the sole purpose of 'regurgitating' it for examination which would give them certificates, and a right to a life of ease, big cars, and comfort.*

The obvious truth is that, in the words of Malinowski, 'education is bigger than schooling.' one is therefore not surprised when Shaw declared that schooling has interrupted his education. In effect education is what remains when everything learnt at school has been forgotten. In other words, we learn not in the school but in life.

The implication is that we cannot properly educate the child outside his cultural environment. It seems we have failed to learn a lesson from the Southern Sotho proverb in South Africa which states that

*If a man does away with his traditional way of living, and throws away his good customs, he had better first make certain that he has something of value to replace them.*

Possibly we have been so excessively 'schooled' that we have our vision blurred as regards the immense potentialities which are embedded in the Yorùbá traditional education. Yet, Gelfand, like many others has warned that

*many people nowadays like to eulogize our Western civilization to the detriment of all others,* *and forget that other less developed communities may be able to teach us something, too.*

That the African traditional society has something to offer educational theory and practice is brought out lucidly in its traditional educational pattern through a combination of precepts and oral literature. By oral Literature, we mean, rich corpora of texts as are derivable from folklore, proverbs, poems, songs, and so on, presented in spoken form for the purpose of informing and influencing the behaviour of one another in a speech community.

The principles of Yorùbá Education are based on the concept of Omoluabi. The end-product of education is to make an individual an Omoluabi. To be an Omoluabi is to be of good character in all its ramifications. Good character, in the Yoruba sense, includes respect for old age, loyalty to one's parents and local traditions, honesty in all public and private dealings, devotion to duty, readiness to assist the needy and the infirm, sympathy, sociability, courage, an itching desire for work and many other desirable qualities. In essence, the main idea of Yorùbá Education has always been to foster good character in the individual and to make him a useful member of the community. Traditional education, therefore, embraces character—building as well as the development of physical aptitudes, the acquisition of those moral qualities felt to be an integral part of manhood, and the acquisition of the knowledge and techniques needed by all men if they are to take an active part in social life in its various forms.

The way in which each human infant is transformed into the finished adult and into the complicated individual of his community is not a monopoly of any society. Education in the Yorùbá culture is life-long process; the whole society is the 'school.'

The traditional education in the Yorùbá Society, if one may be arbitrary, begins in the womb. Pregnancy is a visible indication of a new life. Motherhood is a source of pride and joy in Yorùbá culture. Once pregnancy is effected, the society, conscious of its responsibility, starts to give guidance on what the pregnant women should eat, how she should sleep, when she should not walk, and so on. All these precautions are taken so that nothing adverse affects the child. The society is of the opinion that the pregnant mother has a responsibility imposed on her in regard to the unborn baby. Hence she is regularly greeted:

Iyá arúgbó.
E kú ìkúnra o.
Orí yíò wálè láyò o.
A ó gbòóhùn ìyá
A ó gnòóhùn omo o.

The old woman (so addressed because of the strains of pregnancy),

You are greeted on these strains of pregnancy.

The head (of the child) will come down safely.

We will hear the cry of the mother;

We will hear the cry of the baby.

The birth of the child is greeted with enthusiasm:

Iyá ikókó,
Báríkà o.
Olórun yíò bá wa wò ó.
Olórun yíò se lómo
Olórun yíò kà á kún wa.

Mother of the little being,
Congratulations.
May God care for the new-born baby.
May God make the baby a true child.
May God count the baby with us.

The importance of children to the Yorùbá society is perhaps the basis of the love and tenderness with which the child is treated. His future education is based on recognising his worth as an individual. The Yorùbá say:

Omo ni ìgbèhìn olà.
Omo lará, omo lèye.
Bí a bú ni léhìn bá ò gbó,
Omo eni a wí fún 'ni.
Kí là tún n fowó rà tí ó lékè omo?
Iná kú, ó feérú bojú;
Ogèdè kú ó fomo rè rópò.
Bí aládìlí kò sí nílé.
Omo ní n jógún ebu:
Omo ni yíó jogún ewà lódò wa.

The child is the end-product of wealth.

The child is a thing of fashion; a thing of beauty.

If one is insulted when one is away from home,

It is one's child that informs one.

What do we spend money to buy, greater than the child?

When fire is extinguished, it is ashes that survives it.

When the banana tree dies; it is the offshoot which survives it.

When the maker of palm-kernel oil is absent from home.

It is the child that inherits the factory.

It is the child that will inherit our beauty.

Consequently, the naming ceremony is both spiritual as well as educative. The child is initiated into his culture and his unforeseen future is particularly blessed. The child is expected to honour his name; and to avoid anything that will tarnish it:

Orúko ìsomo ní í bá omo kalé.

The name one bears sticks to one till death.

The ceremony is solemn, but the message is clear:

Orúko tí a fún o yíò mó o lórí.

You will successfully bear this name which we give you for life.

(Lit. 'This name we give you will stick to your head')

The name given to the child is therefore meaningful, showing the status and the circumstances at the time of birth. But the link with his lineage is preserved, for before he could understand, the mother constantly reminds him, through the recitation of praise poetry, of the lineage to which he belongs. These poems remind him of his noble ancestry and motivate him to higher ideals.

As the child develops, all efforts are made to give him an opportunity for all-round development. From the first day, his cries are interpreted with psychological precision. While he is being bathed, his parts of the body are stretched. He is thrown up and caught many times to develop his courage early. Many traditional parents now wonder about what comes from the physical education in schools when they see children brought up in the modern way who could not walk a mile on foot.

The mother-child relationship becomes a source of training. The child is loved; he is cuddled. The warmth of motherhood is enjoyed by the child all life. The psychological impact of carrying the baby on the back still needs to be investigated. But one thing is certain: it shows mother-child relationship. It is the modern method of the 'carry-cot' and 'push chair' system which baffles her. In the traditional pattern, when the child cries, the mother bursts into dancing and singing to influence the behaviour of the child:

Bó ó kú o, màá raso fún o.
Bó ó kú o, màá rèwù oyè.
Bó ó kú o, màá règbá orùn.
Gbogbo re màá wá fí somo lóge.
Erú mo rà lá a pòn ó ká o.
Omo mi o, kúrú bebe kúbe.

My child, if you do not die, I will buy clothes for you.

If you do not die, I will buy you kingly wears.

If you do not die, I will buy you necklaces of beads.

All of these things for your beauty.

And the slaves I have bought will carry you about.

My child, my true child, kúrú bebe kúbe.

Such relationships are to have significant effect on the social behaviour of the child in future. As Freud has warned, many of the adults' behaviour have their roots in childhood,

As regards sanitation and health care, the mother continues to emphasize the principles of health education early. To avoid bed-wetting, when the child is to urinate the mother makes the sound sh, sh, or ks, ks to teach the child that he must urinate outside the bed/mat. When the child grows up, if he is still bed-wetting, his colleagues react to this. They deride him in songs such as the following:

Suúlé, tòólé.
Fìgó nùdí.
Baálé jeun tán kò palè mó.
Sú sù sú.

You stool in the house; you urinate in the house.
You use a broken bottle as toilet paper.
The head of the family finished eating but did not clear the refuse.
Shame! shame!! shame!!!

The message is obvious, he must henceforth obey the rules of sanitation.

In physical development, he is encouraged as a toddler. If he is either a late-developer, or just to encourage him in his efforts to walk, the mother sings as he encourages him to take some faulty steps:

Tèèté o, tèèté o.
Kò yóko, kò yódo,
Omo olórò tinrìje eyin awó.
Kómo gbón o.
Kómo rìn o.
Kómo gbábúrò kékeré o.

Gently, gently.

He is not going to the farm, he is not going to the brook.

He is the son of a wealthy person that eats eggs.

The child should be wise.

The child should walk.

The child should have another little brother.

His linguistic development is not left uncared for. Through reinforcements, examples and precepts, the child is gradually initiated into his linguistic community. Particular attention is paid to difficult Yorùbá phonemes. For instance, tongue—twisters are specially created to make the child sharp in his speech. After all 'Omo tf yíò bá jé ásámú, kékeré ní ó tinse enu sámúsámú (A child who is going to be sharp will be clear and precise in his speech from youth.) Furthermore, the Yorùbá expect an educated man to think deeply and quickly and be able to provide suitable answers and challenges during arguments and conversations without loss of humour, but in clear and intelligible language. The formal school has something to learn from the logic and diplomacy of the Yorùbá. The purpose of the tongue-twisters therefore is speech training, Consider the following:

(1) Múra rélá, o lè lóra rélá ojo (phonemes 'l' and 'r').

(Be quick to cut the okro, you are too slow in cutting the okro)

(2) Òpòlopò olópolo kò mò pé òpòló lópòlo lópòlopò (phonemes ' ', 'kp' and 'l')

(Many intelligent people do not know that frogs have a lot of Intelligence)

(3) Adìe funfun má funfun ní funfun kú funfun mó (phonemes 'f' and 'u').

(The white-feathered chicken, do not continue to exhibit all sorts of whiteness)

(4) Mo pàdàbà lábà alábà, mo bá alábà làbà,n ò fálábà ládàbá je.

(phonemes 'a', 'd', 'b' and 'l'

(I kill West African Red-eyed turtle dove in a hut of someone. I found the owner of the hut in his hut, but I do not share my turtle dove with the owner of the hut.)

(5) Òrìsà jé là máà jé n té; Òrisa máà jé n té jé n là (phonemes 'j', 't' and 'e').

(Oh Gods, let me be wealthy but not disgraced, do not let me be disgraced, let me be wealthy).

(6) Òké gbókèé gòpe, ó kòpe tán kò rókèé lórope mó (phonemes 'gb', 'g', 'k' and 'p').

(Oke climbed the palm tree with a large bag, but after tapping the palm tree, he could not see the large bag on the palm tree again).

His linguistic development is encouraged pari pasu, with intelligence. His knowledge of numbering is extended through play-way analogies:

Ení bí ení.

Ejì bí èjí.

Eta n tagbá.

Erin wòròkò.

5  Arún n gbódó.

Efà tièlè

Eje bí eje.

Ejo ò jo mí.

Esán bí èsán.

10  Gbañgba lèwá.

One is one.

Two is two.

Three is like stinging a calabash.

Four is crooked.

5  Five is like carrying a mortal.

Six is puffed up.

Seven is seven.

Eight is not like me.

Nine is nine.

10  Ten is obvious.

He is taught to observe his environment, to know the names of plants, trees, birds, animals and so on, as well as the description of the appropriate seasons.

It is in character building that Yorùbá education is manifested in its entirety. We have earlier defined what is meant by good character in Yorùbá Education. Nothing mortifies a Yorùbá more to say that his child is 'àbíìkó' (a child that is born but not taught). A child is better àkóògbà (a child that is taught but does not learn), where the responsibility is that of the child and not his parents'. Many factors go into character-building in Yorùbá Education: honesty, morality, intelligence, knowledge, diplomacy, respect for customs, and so on.

A combination of methods is therefore employed to mould the individual into Omolúàbí. The whole society is his 'school' and the individual is guided by the unwritten norms of the society. Morality is not only taught; it is lived. Courage is not only formally taught; it is demonstrated. Endurance and devotion to duty are not only formally taught; they are exhibited. From childhood, the child is taught by examples as well as through proverbs, folk-tales, myths, direct instruction, songs, and so on, about the virtues of the society.

Folklore in particular explains the common rules and the established etiquette of daily life to the Yorùbá child. Folklore, according to Herskovits:

*performs varied functions. Myths explain the universe and . . . provide a bases for ritual and belief. Tales . . . are often regarded as an unwritten recording of tribal history. They act not only as a valuable educational device, but are equally valuable in maintaining a sense of group unity and group worth. Proverbs which with riddles have essentially old world distributions, garnish conversation with pointed allusion, help clarify an obscure reference to one deficient in worldliness, and moralise . . . Riddles divert by serving as a test of wits; they give prestige to the one who can 'pull' with sureness and ease.*

Truthfulness is in Yorùbá education. But the truthfulness is meant to be practised in both private and public lives. Stories of the consequences of lying are told to the child so that he could be guided thereby. Appropriate proverbs are literally sung into the ears of the child, motivating him through his sub-conscious mind onto the values and problems of truthfulness. He is told:

Iró pípa kì í wí pé ká má lòówó lówó;
Ilè dídà kí i wí pé ká ma dàgbá;
Sugbón ojó àtisún lebo.

Lying does not mean that one could not be rich.

Treachery does not mean you may not live to old age.

But it is the day of death (judgement) about which one should be baffled.

Bí iró sáre lógún odún;
Ojo kan lòótó yío bá a.

If a lie runs for twenty years,

It takes truth one day to catch up with it.

But he is also warned that truthfulness, though it prevails, has its agony. He is informed:

(a)  Olóòótó kì í léni.

Those who tell the truth never gain much (they may not have even a mat to sleep upon).

(b)  Otító dójà ó kùtà, owó bíntín là n ra èké.

The truth got to the market, but it was unsold; lying costs very little to buy.

Apart from truthfulness, he is taught to be hard-working. A lazy man is considered a liability to the society. A Yorùbá child is made aware very early that

Isé kò gbékún,
Ebí jàre òle

Weeping is not the answer to poverty;

A lazy man who is hungry has no one to blame but himself.

Even when he comes from a wealthy home, he is told

Agbójú lógún fi ara è fósí ta

Those who rest assured on the inheritance of their parents may succumb to poverty conseqently.

He is therefore taught that 'apá lará; ìgbónwó ni ìyekan' ('your hands are your relatives, your kith and kin are your elbows').

The going may be tough, but he is reminded that when the going is tough, only the tough gets going. He is advised:

Eni tí ó bá fé je oyin abé àpáta
Kò ní wo enu ààké.

He who wishes to eat the honey which is under the rock, should not be unduly worried about the edge of the axe. (No sweats, no sweets).

His spirit of endurance is encouraged to spread on all aspects of life including misfortunes. He should learn to endure the buffets of fortune and to bear both wealth and poverty stoically, He is told:

Igbà kí í tó lo bí òrére;
Ayé ki i tó bi òpá ìbon.

Time and seasons do not remain unchanged.

In all things, he is taught to respect elders, custom, tradition, and authority. He accepts that:

Aìfàgbà féníkan
Kò jé ayé ó gún.

Lack of respect to the constituted authority is the source of most conflicts in the world.

Socialization goes on as an integral part of a wholesome development. He is taught suitable greeting forms for appropriate occasions. He is taught to appreciate music, songs and traditional poems. The talking drum has significant social and educational value to him. Apart from socialization, the concept of omolúàbí touches on personal appearance and comportment. The Yorùbá exemplify this in the statement:

Bí a ti rín ni won n ko ni

You will be treated in the way you are met.

Perhaps most significantly, the Yorùbá education delves into issues of essential principles and contradictions of life. The Yorùbá is taught to acknowledge these principles as they touch upon the concept of man, his moral issues, fate, destiny and so on. On important issues, he is taught to reflect on how circumstances of the past may shape the conditions of the present and the hopes of the future. It is a cardinal element of Yorùbá education to honour the past before embarking on a new assignment. Thus a Yorùbá person acknowledges all precedents and all higher authorities before any undertaking:

Mo júbà.
Mo júbà Akóda,
Mo júbà Asèdá . . .
Ibàa pété owó,
Ibàa pètè esè.
Ibà àtélesè tí ò gbodò hu irun.
Ewúré wolé kó júbà, ni wón bá mú un so.
Agúntàn wolé kò júbà, ni wón bá mú un so.
Agbá tó bá wolé tí kó júbà, ó di mínú so bí eran.
Mo júbà, kí n má baà deni mímúso o.

I pay my respect and honour.
I pay my honour and respect to Akódá,
I pay my honour and respect to Asèdá.

Respect to the palm of the hand;
respect to the sole of the foot.

Respect to the sole of the foot that cannot grow hairs.

The goat enters into the house, it does not give due respect; it is tied down to a post.

The sheep enters into the house, it does not give respect; it is tied down to a post.

Even an elderly person who enters into the house and who does not offer his respects must be tied down like an animal.

I do offer respects so that I may not be tied down ('that I may not be constrained').

No major functions, ceremonies and programmes begin in the Yorùbá culture without this initial acknowledgment of precedent and authority. This way, the link between the past and the present is maintained.

Yorùbá education therefore involves the individual as well as his society. It is integrative.

Through it the individual learns to pursue his own objectives as a means to further societal interests. And when an individual transgresses against customs, steps are taken to appease the gods and get such a recalcitrant man cleansed of his misdemeanour. In other words, rites of re-integration are undertaken on his behalf.

**Study Question**

1. What can we learn from an African view of education within an African society? What are some of the principles which this author embraces in this article? Name three and show how they are the same as or different from those of our society.

# WORK AND ECONOMY

# THE COMMUNIST MANIFESTO

### Karl Marx (1818-1883)And Friedrich Engels (1820-1895)

*Karl Marx was a German economist, philosopher, and revolutionist whose writings form the basis of the body of ideas known as Marxism. While a student at the University of Berlin, the young Marx was strongly influenced by the philosophy of G.W. Hegel. In the early 1840s Marx became friends with Friedrich Engels (also a follower of the ideas of Hegel) and they collaborated on two books,* The Holy Family, *a critique of Hegelian ideas, and* The German Ideology, *in which they developed their materialistic understanding of history. They argued that human thought was determined by social and economic forces, especially those related to the means of production. In 1847 Marx moved to London where he spent much of his time studying economics and social history in the British Museum doing research for his monumental work* Das Kapital *(1867). Marx died in 1883 after years of illness before the completion of his work.*

*Engels was born in 1820 in the Rhine Province of the kingdom of Prussia. His father was a textile manufacturer. In 1838 Engels was forced by family circumstances to enter a commercial house as a clerk. Commercial affairs did not prevent Engels from pursuing his scientific and political education. In 1842 Engels moved to Manchester, England entering the service of a commercial firm of which his father was a shareholder. Here Engels studied the living conditions of factory workers through personal observation and the reading of historical docu-*ments. *He published his work in 1845 as* The Condition of the Working Class in England.

*In 1847 a London organization of workers invited Marx and Engels to prepare a program for them. It appeared in 1848 as the* Communist Manifesto. *Marx and Engel's political, social, and economic ideas continue to be influential among many scholars and social movements today.*

## BOURGEOIS AND PROLETARIANS

The history of all hitherto existing society is the history of class struggles.

Freeman and slave, patrician and plebeian, lord and serf, guild-master and journeyman, in a word, oppressor and oppressed, stood in constant opposition to one another, carried on an uninterrupted, now hidden, now open fight, a fight that each time ended, either in a revolutionary reconstitution of society at large, or in the common ruin of the contending classes.

In the earlier epochs of history, we find almost everywhere a complicated arrangement of society into various orders, a manifold gradation of social rank. In ancient Rome we have patricians, knights, plebeians, slaves; in the Middle Ages, feudal lords, vassals, guildmasters, journeymen, apprentices, serfs; in almost all of these classes, again, subordinate gradations.

The modern bourgeois society that has sprouted from the ruins of feudal society has not done away with class antagonisms. It has but established new classes, new conditions of oppression, new forms of struggle in place old ones.

Our epoch, the epoch of the bourgeoisie, possesses, however, this distinctive feature: it has simplified the class antagonisms. Society as a whole is more and more splitting up into two great hostile camps, into two great classes directly facing each other—bourgeoisie and proletariat.

From the serfs of the Middle Ages sprang the chartered Burghers of the earliest towns. From these burgesses the first elements of the bourgeoisie were developed.

The discovery of America, the rounding of the Cape, opened up fresh ground for the rising bourgeoisie. The East-Indian and Chinese markets, the colonization of America, trade with the colonies, the increase in the means of exchange and in commodities generally, gave to commerce, to navigation, to industry, an impulse never before known, and thereby, to the revolutionary element in the tottering feudal society, a rapid development.

The feudal system of industry, in which industrial production was monopolized by closed guilds, now no longer sufficed for the growing wants of the new markets. The manufacturing system took its place. The guild-masters were pushed aside by the manufacturing middle class; division of labour between the different corporate guilds vanished in the face of division of labour in each single workshop.

Meantime the markets kept ever growing, the demand ever rising. Even manufacture no longer sufficed. Thereupon, steam and machinery revolutionized industrial production. The place of manufacture was taken by the giant, modern industry, the place of the industrial middle class by industrial millionaires, the leaders of whole industrial armies, the modern bourgeois.

Modern industry has established the world market, for which the discovery of America paved the way. This market has given an immense development to commerce, to navigation, to communication by land. This development has, in its turn, reacted on the extension of industry; and in proportion as industry, commerce, navigation, railways extended, in the same proportion the bourgeoisie developed, increased its capital, and pushed into the background every class handed down from the Middle Ages.

We see, therefore, how the modern bourgeoisie is itself the product of a long course of development, of a series of revolutions in the modes of production and of exchange.

Each step in the development of the bourgeoisie was accompanied by a corresponding political advance of that class. An oppressed class under the sway of the feudal nobility, it became an armed and self-governing association in the medieval commune; here independent urban republic (as in Italy and Germany), there taxable "third estate" of the monarchy (as in France); afterwards, in the period of manufacture proper, serving either the semi-feudal or the absolute monarchy as a counterpoise against the nobility, and, in fact, cornerstone of the great monarchies in general, the bourgeoisie has at last, since the establishment of modern industry and of the world market, conquered for itself, in the modern parliamentary State, exclusive political sway. The executive of the modern State is but a committee for managing the common affairs of the whole bourgeoisie.

The bourgeoisie, historically, has played a most revolutionary part.

The bourgeoisie, wherever it has got the upper hand, has put an end to all feudal, patriarchal, idyllic relations. It has pitilessly torn asunder the motley feudal ties that bound man to his "natural superiors," and has left no other nexus between man and man than naked self-interest, than callous "cash payment." It has drowned the most heavenly ecstasies of religious fervour, of chivalrous enthusiasm, of Philistine sentimentalism in the icy water of egotistic calculation. It has resolved personal worth in exchange value and in place of the numberless indefeasible chartered freedoms has set up that single unconscionable freedom—Free Trade. In one word, for exploitation veiled by religious and political illusions it has substituted naked, shameless, direct, brutal exploitation. . . .

The need of a constantly-expanding market for its products chases the bourgeoisie over the whole surface of the globe. It must get a footing everywhere, settle everywhere, establish connections everywhere.

The bourgeoisie has through its exploitation of the world market given a cosmopolitan character to production and consumption in every country. To the great chagrin of reactionaries, it has drawn from under the feet of industry the national ground on which it stood. Old established national industries have been destroyed and are still being destroyed every day. They are dislodged by new industries, whose introduction becomes a life and death question for all civilized nations, by industries that no longer work up indigenous raw material, but raw material drawn from the remotest zones; industries whose products are consumed, not only at home, but in every quarter of the globe. In place of the old wants, satisfied by the production of the country, we find new wants, requiring for their satisfaction the products of distant lands and climes. In place of the old local and national seclusion and self-sufficiency, we have exchange in every direction, universal interdependence of nations. And as in material, so also in intellectual production. The intellectual creations of individual nations become common property. National onesidedness and narrowmindedness become more and more impossible, and from the numerous national and local literatures there arises a world literature.

The bourgeoisie, by the rapid improvement of all instruments of production, by the immensely facilitated means of communication, draws all, even the most barbarian, nations into civilization. The cheap prices of its commodities are the heavy artillery with which it batters down all Chinese walls, with which it forces the barbarians' intensely obstinate hatred of foreigners to capitulate. It compels all nations, on pain of extinction, to adopt the bourgeois mode of production; it compels them to introduce what it calls civilization into their midst, i.e., to become bourgeois themselves. In one word, it creates a world after its own image. . . .

We see then: the means of production and of exchange, on whose foundation the bourgeoisie built itself up, were generated in feudal society. At a certain stage in the development of these means of production and of exchange, the conditions under which feudal society produced and exchanged, the feudal organization of agriculture and manufacturing industry, in one word, the feudal relations of property, became no longer compatible with the already developed productive forces; they hindered production instead of promoting it; they became so many fetters. They had to be burst asunder; they were burst asunder.

Into their place stepped free competition, accompanied by a social and political constitution adapted to it, and by the economical and political sway of the bourgeois class.

A similar movement is going on before our own eyes. Modern bourgeois society with its relations of production, of exchange and of property, a society that has conjured up such gigantic means of production and of exchange, is like the sorcerer who is no longer able to control the powers of the nether world whom he has called up by his spells. For many a decade past the history of industry and commerce is but the history of the revolt of modern productive forces against modern conditions of production, against the property relations that are the conditions for the existence of the bourgeoisie and of its rule. It is enough to mention the commercial crises that by their periodical return put the existence of the entire bourgeois society on its trial, each time more threateningly. In these crises a great part, not only of the existing products, but also of the previously created productive forces, are periodically destroyed. In these crises there breaks out an epidemic that, in all earlier epochs, would

have seemed an absurdity—the epidemic of overproduction. Society suddenly finds itself put back into a state of momentary barbarism; it appears as if a famine, a universal war of devastation, had cut off the supply of every means of subsistence; industry and commerce seem to be destroyed. And why? Because there is too much civilization, too much means of subsistence, too much industry, too much commerce. The productive forces at the disposal of society no longer tend to promote bourgeois civilization and bourgeois property; on the contrary, they have become too powerful for these relations, by which they are fettered, and so soon as they overcome these fetters, they bring disorder into the whole of bourgeois society, endanger the existence of bourgeois property. The conditions of bourgeois society are too narrow to contain the wealth, created by them. And how does the bourgeoisie get over these crises? On the one hand by enforced destruction of a mass of productive forces; on the other, by the conquest of new markets, and by the more thorough exploitation of the old ones. That is to say, by paving the way for more extensive and more destructive crises, and by diminishing the means whereby crises are prevented.

The weapons with which the bourgeoisie felled feudalism to the ground are now turned against the bourgeoisie itself.

But not only has the bourgeoisie forged the weapons that bring death to itself; it has also called into existence the men who are to wield those weapons, the modern working class—the proletarians. In proportion as the bourgeoisie, i.e., capital, is developed, in the same proportion is the proletariat developed—the modern class of workers, who live only so long as they find work, and who find work only so long as their labour increases capital. These workmen, who must sell themselves piecemeal, are a commodity, like every other article of commerce, and are consequently exposed to all the vicissitudes of competition, to all the fluctuations of the market.

Owing to the extensive use of machinery and to division of labour, the work of the proletarians has lost all independent character, and, consequently, all charm for the workman. He becomes a mere appendage of the machine, and it is only the most simple, most monotonous, and most easily acquired knack, that is required of him. Hence, the cost of production of a workman is restricted, almost entirely to the means of subsistence that he requires for his maintenance, and for the propagation of his race. But the price of a commodity, and therefore also of labour is equal to its cost of production. In proportion, therefore, as the repulsiveness of the work increases, the wage decreases. Nay, more, in proportion as the use of machinery and division of labour increases, in the same proportion the burden of toil also increases, whether by prolongation of the working hours, by increase of the work exacted in a given time, or by increased speed of the machinery, etc.

Modern industry has converted the little workshop of the patriarchal master into the great factory of the industry capitalist. Masses of labourers, crowed into the factory, are organized like soldiers. As privates of the industrial army they are placed under the command of a perfect hierarchy of officers and sergeants. Not only are they slaves of the bourgeois class, and of the bourgeois State; they are daily and hourly enslaved by the machine, by the overlooker, and, above all, by the individual bourgeois manufacturer himself. The more openly this despotism proclaims gain to be its end and aim, the more petty, the more hateful and the more embittering it is.

The less the skill and exertion of strength implied in manual labour, in other words, the more modern industry becomes the more developed is the labour of men superseded by that of women. Differences of age and sex have no longer any distinctive social validity for the working class. All are instruments of labour, more or less expensive to use, according to their age and sex.

No sooner is the exploitation of the labourer by the manufacturer so far at an end that he receives his wages in cash, than he is set upon by the other portions of the bourgeoisie, the landlord, the shopkeeper, the pawnbroker, etc.

The former lower strata of the middle class— the small manufacturers, traders and persons living on small incomes, the handicraftsman and peasants—all these sink gradually into the proletariat, partly because their diminutive capital does not suffice for the scale on which modern industry is carried on and is swamped in the competition with the large capitalists, partly because their specialized skill is rendered worthless by new methods of production. Thus the proletariat is recruited from all classes of the population.

But with the development of industry the proletariat not only increases in number; it becomes concentrated in greater masses, its strength grows, and it feels that strength more. The various interests and conditions of life within the ranks of the proletariat are more and more equalized, in proportion as machinery obliterates all distinctions of labour, and nearly everywhere reduces wages to the same low level. The growing competition among the bourgeois, and the resulting commercial crises, make the wages of the workers ever more fluctuating. The

unceasing improvement of machinery, ever more rapidly developing, makes their livelihood more and more precarious; the collisions between individual workmen and individual bourgeois take more and more the character of collisions between two classes. Thereupon the workers begin to form combinations against the bourgeois; they club together in order to keep up the rate of wages; they themselves found permanent associations in order to make provision beforehand for these occasional revolts. Here and there the contest breaks out into riots. Now and then the workers are victorious, but only for a time. The real fruit of their battles lies, not in the immediate result but in the ever-expanding union of the workers. This union is helped on by the improved means of communication that are created by modern industry and that place the workers of different localities in contact with one another It was just this contact that was needed to centralize the numerous local struggles, all of the same character, into one national struggle between classes. But every class struggle is a political struggle. And that union, to attain which the Burghers of the Middle Ages, with their miserable highways, required centuries, the modern proletarians, thanks to railways, achieve in a few years.

This organization of the proletarians into a class, and consequently into a political part, is continually being upset again by the competition between the workers themselves. But it ever rises up again, stronger, firmer, mightier. It compels legislative recognition of particular interests of the workers, by taking advantage of the divisions among the bourgeoisie itself. Thus the ten-hours' bill in England was carried.

Altogether, collisions between the classes of the old society further in many ways the course of development of the proletariat. The bourgeoisie finds itself involved in a constant battle. At first with the aristocracy; later on, with those portions of the bourgeoisie itself, whose interests have become antagonistic to the progress of industry; at all times with the bourgeoisie of foreign countries. In all these battles it sees itself compelled to appeal to the proletariat, to ask for its help, and thus, to drag it into the political arena. The bourgeoisie itself therefore, supplies the proletariat with its own elements of political and general education, in other words, it furnishes the proletariat with weapons for fighting the bourgeoisie.

Further, as we have already seen, entire sections of the ruling classes are, by the advance of industry, precipitated into the proletariat, or are at least threatened in their conditions of existence. These also supply the proletariat with fresh elements of enlightenment and progress.

Finally, in times when the class struggle nears the decisive hour, the process of dissolution going on within the ruling class, in fact within the whole range of old society, assumes such a violent, glaring character, that a small section of the ruling class cuts itself adrift, and joins the revolutionary class, the class that holds the future in its hands. Just as, therefore, at an earlier period, a section of the nobility went over to the bourgeoisie, so now a portion of the bourgeoisie goes over to the proletariat, and in particular, a portion of the bourgeois ideologists who have raised themselves to the level of comprehending theoretically the historical movement as a whole.

Of all the classes that stand face to face with the bourgeoisie today, the proletariat alone is a really revolutionary class. The other classes decay and finally disappear in the face of modern industry; the proletariat is its special and essential product.

The lower middle class, the small manufacturer, the shopkeeper, the artisan, the peasant, all these fight against the bourgeoisie, to save from extinction their existence as fractions of the middle class. They are therefore not revolutionary, but conservative. Nay, more, they are reactionary, for they try to roll back the wheel of history. If by chance they are revolutionary, they are so only in view of their impending transfer into the proletariat; they thus defend not their present, but their future interests; they desert their own standpoint to place themselves at that of the proletariat.

The "dangerous class," the social scum, that passively rotting mass thrown off by the lowest layers of old society, may, here and there, be swept into the movement by a proletarian revolution; its condition of life, however, prepare it far more for the part of a bribed tool of reactionary intrigue.

In the conditions of the proletariat, those of old society at large are already virtually swamped. The proletarian is without property; his relation to his wife and children has no longer anything in common with the bourgeois family relations; modern industrial labour, modern subjection to capital, the same in England as in France, in America as in Germany, has stripped him of every trace of national character. Law, morality, religion, are to him so many bourgeois prejudices, behind which lurk in ambush just as many bourgeois interests.

All the preceding classes that got the upper hand sought to fortify their already-acquired status by subjecting society at large to their conditions of appropriation. The proletarians cannot become masters of the productive forces of society except by abolishing their own previous mode of appropriation, and thereby also every other previous mode of appropriation. They have nothing of their own to secure and to fortify; their mission is to destroy all previous securities for, and insurances of, individual property.

All previous historical movements were movements of minorities, or in the interest of minorities. The proletarian movement is the self-conscious, independent movement of the immense majority, in the interest of the immense majority. The proletariat, the lowest stratum of our present society, cannot stir, cannot raise itself up, without the whole superincumbent strata of official society being sprung into the air.

Though not in substance, yet in form, the struggle of the proletariat with the bourgeoisie is at first a national struggle. The proletariat of each country must, of course, first of all settle matters with its own bourgeoisie.

In depicting the most general phases that make up the development of the proletariat, we traced the more or less veiled civil war, raging within existing society, up to the point where that war breaks out into open revolution, and where the violent overthrow of the bourgeoisie lays the foundation for the sway of the proletariat.

Hitherto, every form of society has been based, as we have already seen, on the antagonism of oppressing and oppressed classes. But in order to oppress a class, certain conditions must be assured to it under which it can, at least, continue its slavish existence. The serf, in the period of serfdom, raised himself to membership in the commune, just as the petty bourgeois, under the yoke of feudal absolutism, managed to develop into a bourgeois. The modern labourer, on the contrary, instead of rising with the progress of industry, sinks deeper and deeper below the conditions of existence of his own class. He becomes a pauper, and pauperism develops more rapidly than population and wealth. And here it becomes evident that the bourgeoisie is unfit to rule because it is incompetent to assure an existence to its slave within his slavery, because it cannot help letting him sink into such a state that it has to feed him, instead of being fed by him. Society can no longer live under this bourgeoisie; in other words, its existence is no longer compatible with society.

The essential condition for the existence and for the sway of the bourgeois class is the accumulation of wealth in the hands of private individuals, the formation and augmentation of capital; the condition for capital is wage-labour. Wage-labour rests exclusively on competition between the labourers. The advance of industry, whose involuntary promoter is the bourgeoisie, replaces the isolation of the labourers, due to competition, by their revolutionary combination, due to association. The development of modern industry, therefore, cuts from under the feet of the bourgeoisie the very foundation on which it produces and appropriates products. What the bourgeoisie therefore produces, above all, are its own grave-diggers. Its fall and the victory of the proletariat are equally inevitable.

## Study Questions

1. Who are the bourgeois and proletariat and what is their relationship to each other?

2. How do Marx and Engels describe the characteristics of a capitalistic society? How has capitalism grown and changed since this piece was written?

3. How do the authors describe the life of the proletariat? What is their relationship to their work?

4. Why do Marx and Engels say that only the proletariat alone is a revolutionary class? What do they mean by the term "class"?

5. What is "communism" and "socialism"? Why do Americans have such a negative reaction to these concepts? Which of the authors' ideas are most troublesome? Explain.

# CAPITALISM AND DEMOCRACY

## Ira Katznelson And Mark Kesselman

*Ira Katznelson is the Ruggles Professor of Political Science and History at Columbia University. His books include* Black Men, White Cities, 1973 *and* Working Class Formation *(co-edited with Pierre Birnbaum) 1995. Mark Kesselman is also a professor of Political Science at Columbia. This essay comes from their book their The Politics of Power (1987). In this essay, they examine, the ways in which capitalism imposes structural limits on democracy, in order to raise the question of whether capitalism an democracy can co-exist.*

The United States is the world's oldest political democracy. All adult American citizens today have the right to vote. The party system invites political participation, and parties compete actively to win the support of the electorate. Interest groups lobby to defend the interests of their members. Newspapers and television provide regular reports of government activities, debate the wisdom of government policies, and expose wrongdoing by high government officials. In few countries is political debate as open, free, and extensive.

A democracy, like that of the United States, is composed of rules that tell who can govern and make laws and under what procedures they may do so. Compared to those in nondemocratic societies, public authorities are accessible and responsive. Rule is not arbitrary. Citizens are protected by rights and by laws, and they are invited into the political process as participants. Government is accountable to the people, who, in the last resort, are considered to be sovereign.

Is democracy to be judged only by formal procedures? What shall we make of uneven voting, the unequal distribution of reading skills, large divergences in the earnings and social class position of the population, and of the impact of monied interests on elections and the political process? More generally, to what extent is popular sovereignty possible in a society organized within a capitalist framework? In such societies, the divisions between those who privately own the means to produce goods and services have disproportionate power, not only because they have more money, but because governments must act in ways that promote the prosperity of private firms. In a capitalist society, the well-being of everyone for jobs and income depends on the investment decisions and the profits of private firms.

One consequence is that many political issues, including the very desirability of an economic system based on private property, are not debated in public. Further, many issues of manifestly public concern, such as where new automobile or computer plants will be built, are decided privately. The result is a contraction of public politics. The principle of majority rule, the very centerpiece of representative democracy, thus applies only to a limited sphere of questions and decisions. Just as it is frequently argued that the separation of economic from political power is beneficial for democracy, for it prevents the concentration of power in the hands of a single elite, so we may ask what the implications are for democratic citizenship when many key issues are not considered to be appropriate issues for public discussion and decision.

Further, the actions of business in pursuit of profit—indeed, the routine operation of a capitalist economic system—generate inequalities of wealth and income. In the United States, the pattern of income distribution has remained virtually unchanged in this century. In 1910, the top fifth of income earners received 46 percent of the national income; today, the richest fifth's share is still over 40 percent. The share of the bottom fifth, moreover, has actually declined from over eight percent in 1910 to just over five percent today.

This pattern of inequality in income is tied directly to even greater disparities in the distribution of wealth—ownership of corporate stock, businesses, homes and property, cash reserves, government and corporate bonds and retirement funds. Roughly 20 percent of personal wealth in the United States is owned by one-third of one percent of the population; the richest one percent own over 28 percent of the wealth; and the top 10 percent of Americans own over half (56 percent). The bottom 10 percent actually owe more than they own.

This basic structure underpins the complexity of everyday life in the United States. Although Americans have diverse ethnic and racial backgrounds, work in different kinds of jobs, live in different places, and hold widely different political opinions, all are part of the class structure and are affected by it. Capitalist production interpenetrates virtually every aspect of American society, including the place of racial minorities and women, the quality of city neighborhoods, and the political choices made by government officials and citizens. . . .

The connections between capitalism and democracy raise the most interesting and pressing questions about political life in all the advanced industrial societies of Western Europe and North America. Indeed, the central questions confronting modern social theory and political philosophy for the past century have been about the tensions inherent in societies that are simultaneously capitalist and democratic. The political content of debate in most of these countries has been shaped principally by these questions. Even when these questions are not openly on the agenda, the relationship between capitalism—which routinely generates inequalities in life condition—and democracy—which posits equal rights and responsibilities for all citizens—affects major features of political life. In the United States, it is impossible to understand the politics of power—and powerlessness—without attention to these concerns, because American society is both the most capitalist and one of the most procedurally democratic of all the countries of the West.

## STANDARDS OF DEMOCRACY

In 1961, political scientist Robert Dahl published an influential study of politics in New Haven, Connecticut. By commonly accepted standards, he argued, the city was a democracy, since virtually all its adult citizens were legally entitled to vote, their votes were honestly counted, and "two political parties contest elections, offer rival slates of candidates, and thus present the voters with at least some outward show of choice." Although the city's

residents were legally equal at the ballot box, they were substantively unequal. Economic inequality in New Haven contrasted sharply with its formal political equality. Fewer than one-sixteenth of the taxpayers owned one-third of the city's property. In the wealthiest ward, one family out of four had an income three times the city average; the majority of the families in the poorest ward earned under $2,000 per year. Only one out of thirty adults in the poorest ward had attended college, as contrasted to nearly half of those in the richest ward.[1]

Is the combination of legal equality and class inequality democratic? Dahl put the question this way, "In a system where nearly every adult may vote but where knowledge, wealth, social position, access to officials, and other resources are unequally distributed, who actually governs? . . . How does a 'democratic' system work amid inequality of resources?"[2] He placed quotation marks around the term *democratic* because its meaning in this situation is unclear. Should a democratic system be measured only by legal standards of equality, such as fair and open election procedures, or should it be measured by substantive standards, according to the control and distribution of resources? What, in short, is the relationship of capitalism and democracy?

## PROCEDURAL DEMOCRACY: STRUCTURE IGNORED

In his study of New Haven, Dahl argued that, rather than one elite group making political decisions, different elite groups determined policy in different issue areas, such as urban renewal, public education, and the nomination of candidates for office. In each area, however, there was a wide disparity between the ability of politically and economically powerful people and average citizens to make decisions. As a result of such disparities, Dahl noted, New Haven was "a long way from achieving the goal of political equality advocated by the philosophers of democracy and incorporated into the creed of democracy and equality practically every American professes to uphold."[3]

Nevertheless, he concluded that "New Haven is an example of a democratic system, warts and all."[4] Dahl never resolved the problem of capitalist inequalities in a "democratic" system. Rather, he reached his conclusion by assessing democracy only according to the procedural test (Can citizens vote? Do they have a choice between candidates? Are elections honest and conducted freely?). The structure of society and class inequalities are ignored.

This approach has dominated much recent thinking about democracy. . . . The most influential twentieth-century discussion of the relationship of capitalism and democracy is by Joseph Schumpeter in *Capitalism, Socialism,* and *Democracy.* Schumpeter defines democracy wholly in procedural terms. Even though we reject his proposed standard of democracy, it is important to review his arguments here because his work underpins the way that most American social scientists think about democracy and because the issues he raises are basic to the elaboration of the approach to democracy we propose. . . .

Schumpeter began his discussion by rejecting the "classical view of democracy," which held that democracy exists when the people decide issues in the interest of the common good of all. This view assumed that there exists a "common good"—that all the members of the political system share basic interests. Since all members of the polity share these interests, it is possible to talk of the "the people" who actually make decisions—either directly by themselves or indirectly through representatives whose job it is to accurately reflect the "common good."

Schumpeter powerfully questioned the existences of these assumed entities in a capitalist society. He wrote, "There is . . . no such thing as a uniquely determined common good that all people could agree on or be made to agree on by the force of rational argument."[5] A "common good" does not exist in societies characterized by basic structural inequalities because of the absence of shared interests. So long as patterns of inequality persist, it is impossible to speak of a "common good," since the good of some depends on the subordination of others.

Hence it is also impossible to speak of "the people," for when members of a society have different interests, there is no single, natural direction their will can take. Rather, "the people" are divided into groups that reflect the unequal distribution of power. Schumpeter thus concluded that "both the pillars of the classical doctrine inevitably crumble into dust."

Because he found the classical approach to democracy out of touch with reality, Schumpeter proposed that we accept "another theory which is much truer to life and at the same time salvages much of what sponsors of the democratic method really mean by this term."

Whereas the classical doctrine saw democracy as a set of institutional arrangements for reaching decisions to realize the people's common good, Schumpeter viewed democracy as "that institutional arrangement for arriving at political decisions in which individuals acquire the power to decide by means of a competitive struggle for the people's vote." Democracy thus becomes a set of rules for

choosing, by election, among competing political leaders; the substance of what is decided by those selected is only secondary. Schumpeter's alternative to the classical doctrine of democracy is also rooted in a profound distrust of the governed. Indeed, for Schumpeter, it is best that political elites, not "the people," make decisions, because the people are incompetent:

> *The typical citizen drops down to a lower level of mental performance as soon as he enters the political field. He argues and analyzes in a way which he would readily recognize as infantile within the sphere of his real interests. He becomes a primitive again.*[6]

For Schumpeter, and for the vast majority of American social scientists who have accepted his approach, a political system is democratic when citizens are provided with an opportunity to vote either for the political leaders in office or for a set of competing leaders who wish to get into office. Democracy is seen as a method, a set of formal procedures by which citizens can select among a limited number of alternative sets of leaders.

The role of voters in this conception resembles the role of consumers in a market economy. Much as consumers choose among competing products packaged by business people, so voters choose among competing candidates packaged by political parties. "The psycho-technics of party management and party advertising," Schumpeter wrote, "slogans and marching tunes, are not accessories. They are of the essence of politics."[7] Since neither major party challenges the basic structure of capitalist inequality, the act of choice, a legal right, replaces the substance of choice at the heart of democratic theory.

This purely procedural definition of democracy has become an ideological tool of social control. Those who benefit most from the capitalist social structure may maintain, since citizens can choose their leaders, that they have little cause for grievance. The system, by definition, is open and democratic. Those with complaints can express them in the next election. In this way, the procedural approach to democracy requires and promotes a relatively passive citizenry.

"Democracy" emerges from Schumpter's discussion without its cutting edge. The classical view of democracy, however flawed by its reliance on the concepts of "common good" and "the people," was concerned fundamentally with the substance of political decision making and the rule of the many against the powerful few. For this reason, democracy commanded far from universal acceptance. The emasculation of the term by

Schumpeter has made it far more acceptable to dominant interests. Democracy is not a standard against which existing practice can be measured critically but is rather an uncritical, incomplete description of present electoral arrangements. Not surprisingly, almost all those who define democracy in wholly procedural terms find that there is no clash between democracy and capitalist inequality.

In rejecting the classical definition of democracy, Schumpeter had three alternatives. The first was to abandon the term *democracy* altogether as hopelessly utopian. The second, which he opted for, was to retain the term but redefine it to conform to existing realities. The third alternative, which we support, was to maintain the term *democracy* as a yardstick against which to measure and test reality. Thus, in a preliminary way, we define *democracy* as a *situation in which all citizens have relatively equal chances to influence and control the making of decisions that affect them.*

This alternative recognizes that although formal democratic procedures are essential to democracy, they do not guarantee it. For democracy approached this way does not depend simply on a set of rules, important though rules may be, but on the nature of the social structure within which the rules of procedural democracy operate.

Broadly, we may distinguish [two] different, though related, approaches to our definition of democracy. The first stresses popular participation in decision making; [and] the second, the representation of interests. . . . Let us examine each of these approaches in turn.

## THE IMPORTANCE AND LIMITS OF DIRECT PARTICIPATION

Citizen participation in decision making has traditionally been regarded as the centerpiece of democracy. Convincing arguments for a participatory form of democracy were put forward by Jean Jacques Rousseau, an eighteenth-century French philosopher. His influential political theory hinged on the direct experience of political participation. For Rousseau, participation has objective and subjective components. The objective component is that citizens exercise control by participating in decision making; the subjective component is that, because they feel they have been able to participate authentically in the making of decisions that affect them, citizens come to identify with the decisions taken and develop feelings of loyalty to the society. In addition, citizens learn to participate effectively. As social theorist Carole Pateman put it in her interpretation of Rousseau's *The Social Contract*, "the more the individual citizen participates, the better

he is able to do so. . . . He learns to be a public as well as a private citizen."[8]

One of the by-products of authentic participation is that citizens learn to identify and interpret their own interests accurately and need not depend on the interpretations of others. Conversely, if participation is inauthentic, if individuals are given the feeling of participating in decision making but are not accorded the power to actually control the decision-making process, the inevitable short-term result is that they are prevented from arriving at an accurate perception of their interests. Though eighteenth-century New England town meetings were examples of direct democracy, many were dominated by a small elite who controlled the agenda and often successfully manipulated the group discussions. The key issue is thus not whether people participate in the political system but what the terms of their participation are.

In the past twenty years, many organizations—including communes, antiwar protest groups, and women's-rights groups—have been founded on classical, Rousseauian democratic principles. They reject the formal procedural approach to democracy and run themselves, instead, as participatory democracies. Their members have self-consciously sought to create open, democratic communities in which all members participate directly in decision making. For many political activists, this kind of direct democracy provides a model for how democracy should be practiced in American society as a whole.

The leap from the small group to the society, however, is impossible to make. The program of participatory groups, including face-to-face unanimous decision making and absolute equality of status and power, is actually based on principles of friendship. As political scientist Jane Mansbridge notes,

*friendship is an equal relation, it does not grow or maintain itself well at a distance, and its expression is in unanimity. . . . As participatory democracies grow from groups of fairly close acquaintances to associations of strangers, friendship can no longer serve as the basis of organization. Distrust replaces trust, and the natural equality, directness, and unanimity of friendship are transformed into rigid rules whose major purpose becomes the prevention of coercion and the protection of the individual.[9]*

In small groups where people know each other intimately and are present voluntarily, the principles of direct, unanimous democracy may work to produce a natural, organic consensus of the group's will. Beyond such small groups, however, consensus is likely to be the result of manipulation, since shared values and mutual respect can develop only in situations where group members share interests. Small groups may constitute a "people" with a "common good," but as Schumpeter demonstrated, these entities in a capitalist society are fictions on a larger scale.

If democracy is to be used as a yardstick to assess both what exists and what is possible, the direct-participation approach is ruled out, because society as a whole does not provide the "friendship" basis that direct democracy requires. Hence a second approach to our definition of democracy argues the crucial issue is not whether people participate directly, but whether all groups of the capitalist social structure and their interests achieve political *representation*.

## REPRESENTATIVE DEMOCRACY

There are four dimensions of representative democracy that provide us with an immediately useful yardstick against which to test present realities. The first is *procedures*. It is essential in a democracy that individuals and groups be able to make their views known and fairly select their leaders and public officials. Hence, civil liberties are essential. Free speech, free assembly, and freedom of the press are basic aspects of procedural representation. When these procedural guarantees are suppressed, it is extraordinarily difficult for people to formulate and express their interests.

The electoral mechanisms available to citizens for selecting their representatives are also an important factor in procedural representation. How wide is the electorate? How is party competition organized? What, in short, are the rules of the electoral process? As we have seen, electoral choice is at the heart of the formal procedural standard of democracy developed by Schumpeter.

But, unlike those who advocate procedural democracy, we believe that it is a mistake to limit the discussion of procedures of representation to elections. Rather, we must consider the nature of all of the rules that determine whether an individual or group has access to the political system and whether that access is likely to have an effect on decision making. Thus the traditionally narrow focus of issues raised about the procedures of representation must be widened. Are workers permitted to join unions? How are congressional committee chairmen selected? How does an elected mayor exercise control over nonelected city bureaucrats? To whom and how is a school system's personnel formally accountable? How are key foreign-policy decision makers chosen? How, if at all, are they formally held accountable? What are the procedures for representation in areas such as the space program, where expertise is available only to a few? Who selects the experts and to whom are they accountable? What are the procedures of leadership selection in interest groups (unions, farmers' organizations, professional associations)?

The list could easily be extended. The procedural dimension of representative democracy depends not only on equitable electoral procedures but more broadly on the mechanisms of access, influence, and accountability in government and in organizations that claim to represent the interests of their constituents. It is essential that the "rules of the game" ensure that the line that divides representatives and represented not harden and that access to ruling positions be open to all and not limited by racial, class, sexual, or other forms of discrimination.

Let us briefly consider a historical example. In the early 1900s, the Democratic party Tammany Hall machine dominated politics in New York City. During this period, most of the city's population consisted of European immigrants and their children. Because the populations of ethnic neighborhoods were relatively homogenous, the ethnic groups gained control over the Tammany political clubs in their area. Blacks, however, were excluded from these organizations. They participated in party affairs through a citywide organization called the United Colored Democracy, whose leaders were selected by the white leaders of Tammany Hall, not by other blacks. Not surprisingly, studies of political patronage in the period indicate that blacks did the least well of all the groups in the city in securing political jobs; and the jobs they did get were the least desirable." [10]

Thus both the blacks from the South and the white ethnics from Europe joined the Democratic party, but on very different procedural terms. Although both groups could vote, the differences blacks experienced in the rules of access to the Democratic party severely limited their chances of reaping the rewards of municipal patronage.

The second dimension of representation is *personnel*. Irrespective of the way in which representatives have been selected, those who govern may or may not accurately reflect the demographic characteristics of class, race, ethnicity, sex, and geography of those they formally represent. During the Cuban missile crisis of 1962, for example, which was resolved when the Soviet Union removed its offensive missiles from Cuba after an American blockade of the island had been imposed, fewer than twenty individuals made the decisions that, by their own account, might have resulted in 150,000,000 casualties. The executive committee of the National Security Council met regularly in the two-week period of crisis to recommend courses of action to President Kennedy. Almost all of the council's members were Protestant, all were white, male, and wealthy. They included an investment banker, four corporation lawyers, a former automobile company president, and a number of multimillionaires.

In this instance, a very small group of men, hardly representative of the population as a whole, had the power to make decisions of the highest consequences. Judged by the personnel dimension of representation, the absence of democracy in this case is beyond doubt. The demographic representativeness of those who make political decisions is not important just in order to fulfill abstract numerical quotas of representation. Rather, the personnel dimension of representation is important because the more demographically representative a political system is, the more likely it is that the interests of the basic groups of the social structure will be adequately and substantively represented. It is highly unlikely, for example, that a group of business leaders will accurately represent the interests of workers or that the interests of blacks will be best represented by whites. This might occasionally be the case, but group members are much more likely to represent their own interests than those of their structural antagonists. It is not surprising, therefore, that workers in unions earn better wages than those whose wage levels are entrusted to the discretion of their employers; nor is it surprising that Southern blacks have been treated more equitably by police since the passage of the Voting Rights Act of 1965 than they had been when they had to depend on the goodwill of the white community.

To represent group interests adequately, representatives must also fulfill the dimensions of *consciousness*—they must be aware of and responsive to their constituents' concerns. In this respect, subordinates often find it much more difficult than the privileged to achieve representation of their interests, since those with more resources tend to perceive their interests more accurately than subordinates. The privileged are also in a better position to put pressure on their representatives than those who are politically powerless. Thus representation concerns not only *who* rules but also the *uses* to which power is put by those who rule. The first two dimensions of representation—procedures and personnel—refer to the first of these two issues. But the dimension of consciousness asks how representatives see the interests of their constituents and how they act on behalf of these interests. To satisfy the requirements of representative democracy, those who formally represent the population must use the power conferred by their positions to promote the interests of the represented.

But even where the first three dimensions of representation are satisfied, political democracy cannot be said to exist. The last dimension that must be realized is *effectiveness*—the ability of representatives to produce the results they desire. A system cannot be democratically representative if its effectiveness is distributed very unequally among representatives. For example, given the fact that most congressional legislation is decided by the various committees, it would be difficult to argue that Polish working-class citizens who select a Polish working-class representative will be democratically represented if the representative is placed on committees irrelevant to their concerns.

Thus representative democracy is achieved only when all four dimensions are satisfied: when leaders are selected by regular procedures that are open to all people and all groups have relatively equal access to the political system; when representatives reflect the demographic composition of the population as a whole; when they are conscious of and responsive to their constituents' interests; and when they can effectively act on behalf of those interests.

## ENDNOTES

1. Robert Dahl, *Who Governs? Democracy and Power in an American City* (New Haven, Conn., 1961), pp. 3–4. [Author's note]

2. *Ibid.*, pp. 1, 3. [Author's note]

3. *Ibid.*, p. 86. [Author's note]

4. *Ibid.*, p. 311. [Author's note]

5. Joseph Schumpeter, *Capitalism, Socialism, and Democracy* (New York 1942). p. 251. [Author's note]

6. *Ibid.*, p. 262. [Author's note]

7. *Ibid.*, p. 283. [Author's note]

8. Carole Pateman, *Participation and Democratic Theory* (Cambridge, Mass., 1970), p. 25 [Author's note]

9. Jane Mansbridge, "*The Limits of Friendship*," unpublished manuscript, pp. 1–2. [Author's note]

10. Ira Katznelson, *Black Men, White Cities* (New York, 1973), chapter 5. [Author's note]

**Study Questions**

1. Why is the title of this piece significant? Does capitalism necessarily promote values that limit democracy?

2. What is the difference between legal standards of equality and substantive standards? Katznelson and Kesselman imply that we should strive toward substantive standards in the U.S. Do you agree?

3. Do you think voters have become consumers in our culture?

4. What is representative democracy? What are the four dimensions? How is it different from participatory democracy?

5. Using these four standards as goals, where are we now? Where are we going?

# GOOD-BYE TO THE WORK ETHIC

## Barbara Ehrenreich

*Barbara Ehrenreich writes essays of social criticism which have appeared in* The New York Times, The Nation, Atlantic, New Republic, Mother Jones, *and* Ms. *She is probably best-known for a collection of essays entitled* Fear of Falling, *her study of the lifestyles of the middle class. The following essay is taken from her 1990 collection,* the Worst Years of Our Lives: Irreverent Notes from a Decade of Greed, *in which she satirizes life during the 1980s.*

The media have just buried the last yuppie, a pathetic creature who had not heard the news that the great pendulum of public consciousness has just swung from Greed to Compassion and from Tex-Mex to meatballs. Folks are already lining up outside the mausoleum bearing the many items he had hoped to take with him, including a quart bottle of raspberry vinegar and the Cliff Notes for *The Wealth of Nations*. I too, have brought something to throw onto the funeral pyre—the very essence of yupdom, its creed and its meaning. Not the passion for money, not even the lust for tiny vegetables, but the *work ethic*.

Yes, I realize how important the work ethic is. I understand that it occupies the position, in the American constellation of values, once held by motherhood and Girl Scout cookies. But yuppies took it too far; they *abused* it.

In fact, one of the reasons they only lived for three years (1984–87) was that they never rested, *never* took the time to chew between bites or gaze soulfully past their computer screens. What's worse, the mere rumor that someone—anyone—was not holding up his or her end of the work ethic was enough to send them into tantrums. They blamed lazy workers for the Decline of Productivity. They blamed lazy welfare mothers for the Budget Deficit. Their idea of utopia (as once laid out in that journal of higher yup thought, the *New Republic*) was the "Work Ethic State": no free lunches, no handouts, and too bad for all the miscreants and losers who refuse to fight their way up to the poverty level by working eighty hours a week at Wendy's.

Personally, I have nothing against work, particularly when performed, quietly and unobtrusively, by someone else. I just don't happen to think it's an appropriate subject for an "ethic." As a general rule, when something gets elevated to apple-pie status in the hierarchy of American values, you have to suspect that its actual *monetary* value is skidding toward zero.

Take motherhood: nobody ever thought of putting it on a moral pedestal until some brash feminists pointed out, about a century ago, that the pay is lousy and the career ladder nonexistent. Same thing with work: would we be so reverent about the "work ethic" if it wasn't for the fact that the average working stiff's hourly pay is shrinking, year by year, toward the price of a local phone call?

In fact, let us set the record straight: the work ethic is not a "traditional value." It is a johnny-come-lately value, along with thin thighs and nonsmoking hotel rooms. In ancient times, work was considered a disgrace inflicted on those who had failed to amass a nest egg through imperial conquest or other forms of organized looting. Only serfs, slaves, and women worked. The yuppies of ancient Athens—which we all know was a perfect cornucopia of "traditional values"—passed their time rubbing their bodies with olive oil and discussing the Good, the True, and the Beautiful.

The work ethic came along a couple of millennia later, in the form of Puritanism—the idea that the amount of self-denial you endured in this life was a good measure of the amount of fun awaiting you in the next. But the work ethic only got off the ground with the Industrial Revolution and the arrival of the factory system. This was—let us be honest about it—simply a scheme for extending the benefits of the slave system into the age of emancipation.

Under the new system (aka capitalism in this part of the world), huge numbers of people had to be convinced to work extra hard, at pitifully low wages, so that the employing class would not have to work at all. Overnight, with the help of a great number of preachers and other well-rested propagandists, work was upgraded from an indignity to an "ethic."

But there was a catch: the aptly named *working class* came to resent the resting class. There followed riots, revolutions, graffiti. Quickly, the word went out from the robber barons to the swelling middle class of lawyers, financial consultants, plant managers, and other forerunners of the yuppie: Look busy! Don't go home until the proles have punched out! Make 'em think *we're* doing the work and that they're lucky to be able to hang around and help out!

The lawyers, managers, etc., were only too happy to comply, for as the perennially clever John Kenneth Galbraith once pointed out, they themselves comprised a "new leisure class" within industrial society. Of course, they "work," but only under the most pleasant air-conditioned, centrally heated, and fully carpeted conditions, and then only in a sitting position. It was in their own interest to convince the working class that what looks like lounging requires intense but invisible effort.

The yuppies, when they came along, had to look more righteously busy than anyone, for the simple reason that they did nothing at all. Workwise, that is. They did not sow, neither did they reap, but rather sat around pushing money through their modems in

games known as "corporate takeover" and "international currency speculation." Hence their rage at anyone who actually works—the "unproductive" American worker, or the woman attempting to raise a family on welfare benefits set below the average yuppie's monthly health spa fee.

So let us replace their cruel and empty slogan-"Go for it!"—with the cry that lies deep in every true worker's heart: "Gimme a break." What this nation needs is not the work ethic, but a *job* ethic: If it needs doing—highways repaired, babies changed, fields plowed—let's get it done. Otherwise, take five. Listen to some New Wave music, have a serious conversation with a three-year-old, write a poem, look at the sky. Let the yuppies Rest in Peace; the rest of us deserve a break.

## Study Questions

1. What does the term "yuppie" mean? What are some of the characteristics of yuppies or some of the values they hold? Do these notions of yuppies describe reality or are they stereotypes?

2. Define "the work ethic." How is this idea related to the "American Dream" or ideas about what it means to be an American? Where did this concept come from? How has its meaning changed over time?

3. What is the tone of this piece? Is Ehrenreich trying to be serious or humorous? Explain.

4. How does Ehrenreich's understanding of work compare to the discussion of work in Marx?

5. What does Ehrenreich mean by the phrase "job ethic"? How is this different from the "work ethic"?

# 4

# THE OVERWORKED AMERICAN

*Juliet B. Schor*

*Juliet B. Schor is an economist who argues that Americans work longer, and less productive, hours than ever before. Specifically, Schor sees a direct correlation between the increase in work hours and the decline of American family relations.*

In the last twenty years the amount of time Americans have spent at their jobs has risen steadily. Each year the change is small, amounting to about nine hours, or slightly more than one additional day of work. In any given year, such a small increment has probably been imperceptible. But the accumulated increase over two decades is substantial. When surveyed, Americans report that they have only sixteen and a half hours of leisure a week, after the obligations of job and household are taken care of. Working hours are already longer than they were forty years ago. If present trends continue, by the end of the century Americans will be spending as much time at their jobs as they did back in the nineteen twenties.

The rise of worktime was unexpected. For nearly a hundred years, hours had been declining. When this decline abruptly ended in the late 1940s, it marked the beginning of a new era in worktime. But the change was barely noticed. Equally surprising, but also hardly recognized, has been the deviation from Western Europe. After progressing in tandem for nearly a century, the United States veered off into a trajectory of declining leisure, while in Europe work has been disappearing. Forty years later, the differences are large. U.S. manufacturing employees currently work 320 more hours — the equivalent of over two months—than their counterparts in West Germany or France.

The decline in Americans' leisure time is in sharp contrast to the potential provided by the growth of productivity. Productivity measures the goods and services that result from each hour worked. When productivity rises, a worker can either produce the current output in less time, or remain at work the same number of hours and produce more. Every time productivity increases, we are presented with the possibility of either more free time or more money. That's the productivity dividend.

Since 1948, productivity has failed to rise in only five years. The level of productivity of the U.S. worker has more than doubled. In other words, we could now produce our 1948 standard of living (measured in terms of marketed goods and services) in less than half the time it took in that year. We actually could have chosen the four-hour day. Or a working year of six months. Or, *every worker in the United States could now be taking every other year off from work—with pay.* Incredible as it may sound, this is just the simple arithmetic of productivity growth in operation.

But between 1948 and the present we did not use any of the productivity dividend to reduce hours. In the first two decades after 1948, productivity grew rapidly, at about 3 percent a year. During that period, worktime did not fall appreciably. Annual hours per labor force participant fell only slightly. And on a per-capita (rather than a labor force) basis, they even rose a bit. Since then, productivity growth has been lower, but still positive, averaging just over 1 percent a year. Yet hours have risen steadily for two decades. In 1990, the average American owns and consumes more than twice as much as he or she did in 1948, but also has less free time.

How did this happen? Why has leisure been such a conspicuous casualty of prosperity? In part, the answer lies in the difference between the markets for consumer products and free time. Consider the former, the legendary American market. It is a veritable consumer's paradise, offering a dazzling array of products varying in style, design, quality, price, and country of origin. The consumer is treated to

GM versus Toyota, Kenmore versus GE, Sony, or Magnavox, the Apple versus the IBM. We've got Calvin Klein, Anne Klein, Liz Claiborne, and Levi-Strauss; McDonald's, Burger King, and Colonel Sanders. Marketing experts and advertisers spend vast sums of money to make these choices appealing—even irresistible. And they have been successful. In cross-country comparisons, Americans have been found to spend more time shopping than anyone else. They also spend a higher fraction of the money they earn. And with the explosion of consumer debt, many are now spending what they haven't earned.

After four decades of this shopping spree, the American standard of living embodies a level of material comfort unprecedented in human history. The American home is more spacious and luxurious than the dwellings of any other nation. Food is cheap and abundant. The typical family owns a fantastic array of household and consumer appliances: we have machines to wash our clothes and dishes, mow our lawns, and blow away our snow. On a per-person basis, yearly income is nearly $22,000 a year—or sixty-five times the average income of half the world's population.

On the other hand, the "market" for free time hardly even exists in America. With few exceptions, employers (the sellers) don't offer the chance to trade off income gains for a shorter work day or the occasional sabbatical. They just pass on income, in the form of annual pay raises or bonuses, or, if granting increased vacation or personal days, usually do so unilaterally. Employees rarely have the chance to exercise an actual choice about how they will spend their productivity dividend. The closest substitute for a "market in leisure" is the travel and other leisure industries that advertise products to occupy our free time. But this indirect effect has been weak, as consumers crowd increasingly expensive leisure spending into smaller periods of time.

Nor has society provided a forum for deliberate choice. The growth of worktime did not occur as a result of public debate. There has been little attention from government, academia, or civic organizations. For the most part, the issue has been off the agenda, a nonchoice, a hidden trade off. It was not always so. As early as 1791, when Philadelphia carpenters went on strike for the ten-hour day, there was public awareness about hours of work. Throughout the nineteenth century, and well into the twentieth, the reduction of worktime was one of the nation's most pressing social issues. Employers and workers fought about the length of the working day, social activists delivered lectures, academics wrote treatises, courts handed down decisions, and government legislated hours of work. Through the Depression, hours remained a major social preoccu-

pation. Today these debates and conflicts are long forgotten. Since the 1930s, the choice between work and leisure has hardly been a choice at all, at least in any conscious sense.

In its starkest terms, my argument is this: Key incentive structures of capitalist economies contain biases toward long working hours. As a result of these incentives, the development of capitalism led to the growth of what I call "long hour jobs." The eventual recovery of leisure came about because trade unions and social reformers waged a protracted struggle for shorter hours. Some time between the Depression and the end of the Second World War, that struggle collapsed. As the inevitable pressures toward long hours reasserted themselves, U.S. workers experienced a new decline that now, at the century's end, has created a crisis of leisure time. I am aware that these are strong claims which overturn most of what we have been taught to believe about the way our economy works. . . .

Ironically, the tendency of capitalism to expand work is often associated with a growth in joblessness. In recent years, as a majority have taken on the extra month of work, nearly one-fifth of all participants in the labor force are unable to secure as many hours as they want or need to make ends meet. While many employees are subjected to mandatory overtime and are suffering from overwork, their co-workers are put on involuntary part-time. In the context of my story, these irrationalities seem to make sense. The rational, and humane, solution—reducing hours to spread the work—has practically been ruled out of court.

In speaking of "long hour jobs" exclusively in terms of the capitalist marketplace, I do not mean to overlook those women who perform their labor in the privacy of their own homes. Until the late nineteenth century, large numbers of single and married women did participate in the market economy, either in farm labor or through various entrepreneurial activities (taking in boarders, sewing at home, and so on). By the twentieth century, however, a significant percentage of married women, particularly white women, spent all their time outside the market nexus, as full-time "domestic laborers," providing goods and, increasingly, services for their families. And they, too, have worked at "long hour jobs."

Studies of household labor beginning in the 1910s and continuing through to the 1970s show that the amount of time a full-time housewife devoted to her work remained virtually unchanged for over fifty years-despite dramatic changes in household technology. As homes, like factories, were "industrialized," refrigerators, laundry machines, vacuum cleaners, and microwaves took up residence in the American domicile. Ready-made clothes and processed food supplanted the home-produced variety. Yet with all these labor-saving innovations, no labor has been saved. Instead, housework expanded to fill the available time. Norms of cleanliness rose. Standards of mothering grew more rigorous. Cooking and baking became more complicated. At the same time, a variety of cheaper and more efficient ways of providing household services failed in the market, and housewives continued to do their own.

The stability of housewives' hours was due to a particular bias in the incentives of what we may term the "labor market for housewives." Just as the capitalist labor market contains structural biases toward long hours, so too has the housewife's situation. . . . And in neither case has technology automatically saved labor. It has taken women's exodus from the home itself to reduce their household labor. As women entered paid employment, they cut back their hours of domestic work significantly—but not by enough to keep their total working time unchanged. According to my estimates, when a woman takes a paying job, her schedule expands by at least twenty hours a week. The overwork that plagues many Americans, especially married women, springs from a combination of full-time male jobs, the expansion of housework to fill the available hours, and the growth of employment among married women.

However scarce academic research on the rising workload may be, what we do know suggests it has contributed to a variety of social problems. For example, work is implicated in the dramatic rise of "stress." Thirty percent of adults say that they experience high stress nearly every day; even higher numbers report high stress once or twice a week. A third of the population says that they are rushed to do the things they have to do—up from a quarter in 1965. Stress-related diseases have exploded, especially among women, and jobs are a major factor. Workers' compensation claims related to stress tripled during just the first half of the 1980s. Other evidence also suggests a rise in the demands placed on employees on the job. According to a recent review of existing findings, Americans are literally working themselves to death—as jobs contribute to heart disease, hypertension, gastric problems, depression, exhaustion, and a variety of other ailments. Surprisingly, the high-powered jobs are not the most dangerous. The most stressful workplaces are the "electronic sweatshops" and assembly lines where a demanding pace is coupled with virtually no individual discretion.

Sleep has become another casualty of modern life. According to sleep researchers, studies point to a "sleep deficit" among Americans, a majority of whom are currently getting between 60 and 90 minutes less a night than they should for optimum health and performance. The number of people showing up at sleep disorder clinics with serious problems has skyrocketed in the last decade. Shiftwork, long working hours, the growth of a global economy (with its attendant continent-hopping and twenty-four-hour business culture), and the accelerating pace of life have all contributed to sleep deprivation. If you need an alarm clock, the experts warn, you're probably sleeping too little.

The juggling act between job and family is another problem area. Half the population now says they have too little time for their families. The problem is particularly acute for women: in one study, half of all employed mothers reported it caused either "a lot" or an "extreme" level of stress. The same proportion feel that "when I'm at home I try to make up to my family for being away at work, and as a result I rarely have any time for myself." This stress has placed tremendous burdens on marriages. Two-earner couples have less time together, which researchers have found reduces the happiness and satisfaction of a marriage. These couples often just don't have enough time to talk to each other. And growing numbers of husbands and wives are like ships passing in the night, working sequential schedules to manage their child care. Among young parents, the prevalence of at least one partner working outside regular daytime hours is now close to one half. But this "solution" is hardly a happy one. According to one parent. "I work 11–7 to accommodate my family—to eliminate the need for baby-sitters. However, the stress on myself is tremendous."

A decade of research by Berkeley sociologist Arlie Hochschild suggests that many marriages where women are doing the "second shift" are close to the breaking point. When job, children, and marriage have to be attended to, it's often the marriage that is neglected. The failure of many men to do their share at home creates further problems. A twenty-six-year-old legal secretary in California reports that her husband "does no cooking, no washing, no anything else. How do I feel? Furious. If our marriage ends, it will be on this issue. And it just might."

Serious as these problems are the most alarming development may be the effect of the work explosion on the care of children. According to economist Sylvia Hewlett, "child neglect has become endemic to our society." A major problem is that children are increasingly left alone, to fend for themselves while their parents are at work. Nationwide, estimates of children in "self"—or, more accurately, "no"—care range up to seven million. Local studies have found figures of up to one-third of children caring for themselves. At least half a million preschoolers are thought to be left at home part of each day. One 911 operator reports large numbers of frightened callers: "It's not uncommon to hear from a child of six or seven who has been left in charge of even younger siblings."

Even when parents are at home, overwork may leave them with limited time, attention, or energy for their children. One working parent noted, "My child has severe emotional problems because I am too tired to listen to him. It is not quality time; it's bad quantity time that's destroying my family." Economist Victor Fuchs has found that between 1960 and 1986, the time parents actually had available to be with children fell ten hours a week for whites and twelve for blacks. Hewlett links the "parenting deficit" to a variety of problems plaguing the country's youth: poor performance in school, mental problems, drug and alcohol use, and teen suicide. According to another expert, kids are being "cheated out of childhood.... There is a sense that adults don't care about them."

Of course, there's more going on here than lack of time. Child neglect, marital distress, sleep deprivation and stress-related illnesses all have other causes. But the growth of work has exacerbated each of these social ailments. Only by understanding why we work as much as we do, and how the demands of work affect family life, can we hope to solve these problems.

The past forty years should provide a warning. They have brought us nothing in the way of leisure time and a saner pace of life. The bias of the system is strongly toward the status quo. But time poverty is straining the social fabric. Continued growth threatens environmental balance, and gender equality requires new work patterns. Despite these obstacles, I am hopeful. By understanding how we came to be caught up in the cycle of work-and-spend, perhaps we can regain a reasonable balance between work and leisure.

## Study Questions

1. Do you agree with the author that Americans are overworked? How much work is too much? How much leisure time should we have?

2. Why haven't the gains in productivity in the past decades been translated into greater leisure time for American workers? How does capitalism have a bias toward the "long hour jobs"?

3. Do you find it surprising that modern "labor saving" appliances in the home have NOT resulted in less time devoted to housework over the last fifty years? Why is it that we spend more time shopping than ever before? Is this a bad thing? Why or why not?

4. What social problems does the author claim are made worse because of long work hours? Can you think of any more?

5. How does Barbara Ehrenreich's analysis of the work ethic add to Schor's discussion?

6. Do the same factors that lead to being overworked in the job market also affect college students? Are you overworked? Do you have enough leisure time? Why or why not?

7. If you had a choice between a job that allowed for a "comfortable" lifestyle working forty hours a week versus a job that paid twice as much for working sixty hours a week, which would you choose? Why?

# MURDER, INC.

## *Robert Sherrill*

*Robert Sherrill, who was born in Georgia, has worked as a journalist and editor. He lives in Washington, D. C. and is a contributing editor to* The Nation. *His books include* Military Justice is to Justice as Military Music is to Music *(1970), and* The Oil Follies of 1970-1980: How the Petroleum Industry stole the Show (And Much More Besides) *(1983). This essay investigates corporate responsibility in terms of their role in selling products they know are harmful or fatal to human beings.*

There are something over fifteen hundred men and women on the death rows of America. Given the social context in which they operated, one might reasonably assume that they were sentenced to be executed not because they are murderers but because they were inefficient. Using guns and knives and the usual footpad paraphernalia, they dispatched only a few more than their own number. Had they used asbestos, mislabeled pharmaceutical drugs and devices, defective autos, and illegally used and illegally disposed chemicals, they could have killed, crippled, and tortured many thousands of people. And they could have done it without very much fuss.

Corporate criminals, as we all know, live charmed lives. Not until 1978 had a corporation ever been indicted for murder (Ford Motor Company, which was acquitted), and not until 1985 had corporate executives ever been brought to trial for murder because of the lethal mischief done by their company.

The executives who made history last year were the president, plant manager, and plant foreman of Film Recovery Systems Corporation, a ratty little silver-rendering operation in Elm Grove Village outside Chicago. The silver was recovered by cooking used X-ray films in vats of boiling cyanide. Film Recovery hired mostly illegal immigrants, who were afraid to protest working conditions so foul that they made employees vomit and faint. The illegals were preferred also because they couldn't read much English and would not be spooked by written warnings on the drums of cyanide. To make doubly sure that fright wouldn't drive workers away, management had the skull-and-cross-bones signs scraped off the drums. Although the antidote for cyanide poisoning is cheap and easy to obtain, Film Recovery Systems didn't keep any on hand.

So it came to pass that Stefan Golab, a sixty-one-year-old illegal immigrant from Poland, took too hefty a lungful of cyanide fumes and died. Charged with murder on the grounds that they had created such unsafe working conditions as to bring about "a strong probability of death and great bodily harm," the three officials were convicted and sentenced to twenty-five years in prison.

Will executives at other villainous corporations be similarly charged and convicted? Don't bet on it. In this instance the law was applied so properly, so rightly, so common-sensically that one would be foolish to expect such usage to appear again soon. It was a sort of Halley's Comet of Justice.

The idea of treating corporate murderers as just plain murderers strikes many people as excessive. Some lawyers who cautiously approved the conviction in principle said they were afraid it would confuse people generally because a bald murder charge is usually associated with a bullet in the gut or an ice pick in the neck, and nice people would have a hard time adapting the charge to the way things are sometimes accomplished in the front office. Speaking for this timid viewpoint, Alan Derschowitz, Harvard's celebrated criminal law specialist, said he thought the Film Recovery case showed we need a new category of crime. "We should have one that specifically reflects our condemnation of this sort of behavior," he said, "without necessarily assimilating it into the most heinous forms of murder" - as if the St. Valentine's Day massacre were any more heinous than Bhopal.

During the trial, the Illinois prosecutor accused the defendants of "callousness, disregard of human lives, and exposing people to dangerous products all for the sake of profits." No wonder the verdict has been so modestly praised. If that's enough to rate a murder charge, our whole commercial system is at risk. If it were to become the rule, we could look forward to a lineup of accused corporate executives extending out the courthouse and around the block several times. Since there is not statute of limitations on murder, prosecutors would be obliged to charge those executives at Firestone who, a few years back, allegedly killed and injured no telling how many people by flooding the market with ten million tires they knew to be defective; and the executives at Ford who sent the Pinto into circulation knowing its gas tank was so poorly designed that a rear-end collision could turn the car into a fire trap (several dozen men, women, and children were burned alive). From the pharmaceutical fraternity would come such as D. William Shedden, former vice-president and chief medical officer for Eli Lilly Research Laboratories, who recently pleaded guilty to fifteen criminal counts relating to the marketing of Oraflex, an arthritis drug that the Food and Drug Administration says has been "possibly" linked to forty-nine deaths in the United States and several hundred abroad, not to mention the hundreds who have suffered nonfatal liver and kidney failure. Seems as how the folks at Lilly, when they sought approval from the FDA, forgot to mention that the drug was already known to have killed at least twenty-eight people in Europe. (Shedden was fined $15,000; Lilly, which earned $3.1 billion in 1984, was fined $25,000). And let's be sure to save an early murder indictment for those three sly dogs at SmithKline Beckman Corporation who whizzed their product, Selacryn, through the FDA without mentioning that it had caused severe liver damage in some patients in France. False labels were used to peddle it in this

country, where it has been linked to thirty-six deaths and five hundred cases of liver and kidney damage.

Now comes a ripple of books that, were there any justice, would put a dozen or so hangdog executives in the dock. Three of the books made particularly persuasive cases. Paul Brodeur's *Outrageous Misconduct: The Asbestos Industry on Trial* (Pantheon) is an account of how the largest manufacturer of asbestos products, Manville Corporation (previously known as Johns-Manville Corporation), and other asbestos companies committed over the years what one plaintiff's attorney called "the greatest mass murder in history," which is possibly true if one means industrial mass murder, not political. People who regularly inhale asbestos fibers are likely to die, or at least be crippled, from the lung disease called asbestosis or the even worse (at least it sounds worse) mesothelioma. It sometimes takes twenty or thirty years for asbestosis to appear, so a measure of the slaughter from it is somewhat vague. But the best experts in the field, which means Dr. Irving J. Selikoff and his staff at the Mount Sinai Hospital in New York City, estimate that aside from the many thousands who have died from asbestos disease in the past, there will be between eight and ten thousand deaths from asbestos-related cancer each year for the next twenty years. These deaths are not accidental. Manville et al. knew exactly what they were doing. Brodeur's book is mainly an account of how the asbestos companies, though they claimed to be ignorant of the deadly quality of their product until a study by Dr. Selikoff was released in 1964, had for forty years known about, and had suppressed or disregarded, hundreds of studies that clearly showed what asbestos was doing to the people who inhaled it. Did the companies even care what was happening? Typically, at a Manville asbestos mine in Canada, company doctors found that of seven hundred and eight workers, only four - who had worked there less than four years - had normal lungs. Those who were dying of asbestosis were not told of their ailment.

The other two books, Susan Perry and Jim Dawson's *Nightmare: Women and the Dalkon Shield* (Macmillan) and Morton Mintz's *At Any Cost: Corporate Greed, Women and the Dalkon Shield* (Pantheon), remind me of what Dr. Jules Amthor said to my favorite detective: "I'm in a very sensitive profession, Mr. Marlowe. I'm a quack." The murderous quackery of the Dalkon Shield, an intrauterine device, was committed by A. H. Robins, a company that should have stuck to making Chap Stick and Sergeant's Flea & Tick Collars, and left birth-control gadgets to those who knew how to make them properly. These two books should convince anyone, I think, that compared to the fellows at A. H. Robins, the Film Recovery exec-

MURDER, INC.                                                                    355

utives were pikers when it came to showing disregard for human lives for the sake of profits. Profits were plentiful, that's for sure. A. H. Robins sold more than 4.5 million Dalkon Shields worldwide (2.8 million in the United States) for $4.35 each; not bad for a device that cost only twenty-five cents to produce. The death count among women who wore the shield still isn't complete; the last I heard it was twenty. But wearers of the shield also have reported stillbirths, babies with major congenital defects, punctured uteri, forced hysterectomies, sterilization from infection, and various tortures and illnesses by the thousands - some generous portion, we many presume, of the 9,230 lawsuits that A. H. Robins has settled out of court. And as both books make clear, the company launched the Dalkon Shield fully aware of the shield's dangers, sold it with false advertising, kept on selling it for several years after the company knew what its consumers were going through, and pulled a complicated cover-up of guilt.

Dershowitz is right in one respect: corporate murderers are not like your typical killer on death row. Corporate murderers do not set out to kill. There's no profit in that. They are simply willing to accept a certain amount of death and physical torment among their workers and customers as a sometimes necessary byproduct of the free enterprise system. Mintz has uncovered a dandy quote from history to illustrate this attitude. When it was suggested to Alfred P. Sloan, Jr., president of General Motors circa 1930, that he should have safety glass installed in Chevrolets, he refused with the explanation, "Accidents or no accidents, my concern in this matter is a matter of profit and loss."

The Sloan spirit is everywhere. Brodeur quotes from a deposition of Charles H. Roemer, once a prominent New Jersey attorney who handled legal matters for the Union Asbestos and Rubber Company. Roemer reveals that around 1942, when Union Asbestos discovered a lot of its workers coming down with asbestos disease, he and some of Union Asbestos's top officials went to Johns-Manville and asked Vandiver Brown, Manville's attorney, and Lewis Brown, president of Manville, if their physical examination program had turned up similar results. According to Roemer, Vandiver Brown said, in effect, Sure, our X-rays show many of our workers have that disease, but we don't tell them they are sick because if we did, they would stop working and sue us. Roemer recalled asking, "Mr. Brown, do you mean to tell me you would let them work until they dropped dead?" and Brown answering, "Yes, we save a lot of money that way."

Saving money, along with making money, was obviously the paramount objective of A. H. Robins,

too. This was evident from the beginning, when Robins officials learned - *six months before marketing the device nationally* - that the Dalkon Shield multifilament tail had a wicking tendency and could carry potentially deadly bacteria into the uterus. Did the company hold up marketing the shield until it could be further tested and made safe? No, no. That would have meant a delay, for one thing, in recovering the $750,000 they had paid the shield's investors. Though Robins knew it was putting its customers in great jeopardy, it hustled the shield into the market with promotional claims that it was "safe" and "superior" to all other intrauterine devices; and never, during the four years the shield was on the market, did A. H. Robins conduct wicking studies of the string. The shield's promotional literature, by the way, was a classic example of phony drugstore hype. A. H. Robins claimed the shield kept the pregnancy rate at 1.1 percent; the company was well aware that the shield allowed at least a 5 percent pregnancy rate, one of the most slipshod in the birth-control business. A. H. Robins also advertised that the device could be easily inserted in "even the most sensitive woman," although in fact many doctors, before inserting the shield, had to give patients an anesthetic, and many women were in pain for months.

Not long after the shield went on the market, Wayne Crowder, one of the few heroes in this sorry tale, a quality-control engineer at Chap Stick, which manufactured many of the shields for its parent firm, rejected 10,000 of them because he was convinced the strings could wick bacteria. His boss overruled him with the remark, "Your conscience doesn't pay your salary." Crowder also suggested a method for stopping the wicking, but his technique was rejected because it would have cost an extra five cents per device. Crowder kept on complaining (he would ultimately be fired as an irritant) and he finally stirred Daniel French, president of Chap Stick, to convey Crowder's criticism to the home office. French was told to mind his own business and not worry about the safety of the shield, which prompted him to go into the corporate softshoe routine he knew would please. He wrote A. H. Robins: "It is not the intention of Chap Stick Company to attempt any unauthorized improvements in the Dalkon Shield. My only interest in the Dalkon Shield is to produce it at the lowest possible price, and therefore, increase Robin's gross profit level."

Of course, when thousands of women began dying, screaming, cursing, and suing, it gets a little difficult to pretend that all is well with one's product, but for more than a decade A. H. Robins did its best, never recalling the gadget, never sending a warning to doctors about possible deadly side effects, and continuing to the last - continuing right up to the present even after losing hundreds of millions of dollars in lawsuits - to argue that the shield is just hunky-dory. The A. H. Robins school spirit was beautifully capsulated by one of its officials who told the National Observer, "But after all, we are in business to sell the thing, to make a profit. I don't mean we're trying to go out and sell products that are going to be dangerous, fatal, or what have you. But you don't put all the bad things in big headlines."

Where is the corporate executive who will not savor the easy insouciance of 'or what have you"?

One of the more fascinating characteristics of corporate murderers is the way these fellows cover up their dirty work. They are really quite bold and successful in their deviousness. When one considers how many top officials there are at places like Manville and Robins, and when one assumes (obviously naively) among the lot of them surely there must be at least one or two with a functioning conscience, the completeness of their cover-ups is indeed impressive. Which isn't to say that their techniques are very sophisticated. They simply lie, or hide or burn the incriminating material. When the litigation flood began to break over Manville Corporation in the late 1960's, the asbestos gang began thwarting their victims' attorneys by claiming certain Manville executives couldn't give depositions because they were dead (when they were very much alive), by refusing to produce documents ordered by the court, and by denying that certain documents existed when in fact they did. A. H. Robins was just as expert at that sort of thing. According to Mintz, "Thousands of documents sought by lawyers for victims of the Dalkon Shield sank from sight in suspicious circumstances. A few were hidden for a decade in a home basement in Tulsa, Oklahoma. Other records were destroyed, some admittedly in a city dump in Columbus, Indiana, and some allegedly in an A. H. Robins furnace. And despite court orders, the company did not produce truckloads of documents for judicial rulings on whether the women's lawyers could see the papers."

A. H. Robin's most notorious effort at a cover-up ultimately failed, thanks to one Roger Tuttle, a classic example of what can happened when the worm turns.

Tuttle was an attorney for A. H. Robins in the early 1970's. He says that immediately after the company lost its first Dalkon Shield lawsuit, his superiors ordered him (they deny it) to search through the company's files and burn every document that he thought might be used against A.

H. Robins in future lawsuits - documents that, in Tuttle's words, indicated "knowledge and complicity, if any, of top officials in what at that stage of the game appeared to be a grim situation." Unfortunately for the company, Tuttle did not fully obey orders. He took possession of some of the juiciest documents and kept them. Just why he rebelled isn't clear. Perhaps it was because Tuttle, a plain little guy who admits he isn't the smartest attorney in the world, was tired of having his employers push him around, which they often did. He says he did it because he was ashamed that "I personally lacked the courage" to challenge the order and "I wanted some sop for my own conscience as an attorney." Whatever his motivation, Tuttle sat on the purloined files for nearly ten years. He moved on to other jobs, finally winding up, a born-again Christian, on the Oral Roberts University law faculty. Watching the Dalkon Shields trials from afar, troubled by the plaintiffs' inability to cope with A. H. Robins's cover-up, Tuttle finally decided to step forward and provide the material their attorneys needed for the big breakthrough.

A lucky windfall like that is the only way victims can overcome the tremendous imbalance in legal firepower. In the way they muster defense, corporate murderers bear no resemblance to the broken down, half-nuts, penniless drifters on death row, dozens of whom have no attorney at all. Corporate killers are like the Mafia in the way they come to court with a phalanx of attorneys. They are fronted by the best, or at least the best known. Griffin Bell, President Carter's Attorney General, has been one of A. H. Robin's attorneys.

There are two other significant differences between corporate killers and the habitués of death rows. In the first place, the latter generally did not murder as part of doing business, except for the relatively few who killed coincidental to a holdup. They did not murder to protect their rackets or territory, as the Mafia does, and they did not murder to exploit a patent or to increase production of sales, as corporate murderers do. One judge accused A. H. Robins officials of taking "the bottom line as your guiding beacon and the low road as your route." Killing for the bottom line has probably not sent a single murderer to death row anywhere. In the second place, most of the men and women on death row were lonely murderers. No part of society supported what they did. But just as the Mafia can commit murder with impunity only because it has the cooperation of police and prosecutors, so too corporate murderers benefit from the collusion of respectable professions, particularly doctors (who, for a price, keep quiet), and insurance companies (who, to help Manville, did not reveal what their actuarial tables told about the risks to asbestos workers; and, for Robins, worked actively backstage to conceal the Dalkon Shield's menace to public health), and government agencies who are supposed to protect public health but look the other way.

It was an old, and in its way valid, excuse that Film Recovery's officials gave the court: "We are just operating like other plants, and none of the government health and safety inspectors who dropped around - neither the Elm Grove Village Public Health Department nor the Environmental Protection Agency - told us we shouldn't be letting our workers stick their heads in vats of boiling cyanide." They were probably telling the truth. That's the way health and safety regulators have usually operated.

Brodeur tells us that a veritable parade of government inspectors marched through the Pittsburgh Corning asbestos plant in Tyler, Texas, over a period of six and a half years without warning the workers that the asbestos dust levels were more than twenty times the maximum recommended for health safety. One Department of Labor official later admitted he had not worn a respirator when inspecting the plant because he did not want to excite the workers in asking questions about their health. Though the Public Health Service several times measured the fallout of asbestos dust, never did it warn the workers that the stuff was eating up their lungs. Finally things got so bad at Tyler that federal inspectors, forced to bring charges against the owners for appalling infractions of health standards, recommended that they be fined $210. Today the men and women who worked in that plant (since closed) are dying of lung cancer at a rate five times greater than the national average.

There is one more significant difference between the people on death row and the corporate murders: the former sometimes say they are sorry; the latter never do. Midway through 1985, Texas executed Charles Milton, thirty-four, because when he stuck up a liquor store the owner and his wife wrestled Milton for the gun, it went off, and the woman died. Shortly before the state killed him with poison, Milton said, "I am sorry Mrs. Denton was killed in the struggle over the gun." There. He said it. It wasn't much, but he said it. And that's more than the folks at Manville have ever said about the thousands of people killed with asbestos. When it comes to feeling no remorse, A. H. Robins doesn't take a back seat to anybody. In a famous courtroom confrontation between Federal Judge Miles W. Lord and three A. H. Robins officials, including company president E. Claiborne Robins, Jr., Judge Lord asked them to read silently to themselves a long reprimand

of their actions. The most scathing passage, quoted both by Mintz and by Perry and Dawson was this:

*Today as you sit here attempting to once more to extricate yourselves from the legal consequences of your acts, none of you has faced up to the fact that more than 9,000 women [the figure two years ago (in 1984)] have made claims that they gave up part of their womanhood so that your company might prosper. It is alleged that others gave their lives so you might so prosper. And there stand behind them legions more who have been injured but who had not sought relief in the courts of this land...*

*If one poor young man were by some act of his - without authority or consent - to inflict such damage upon one woman, he would be jailed for a good portion of the rest of his life. And yet your company, without warning to women, invaded their bodies by the millions and caused them injuries by the thousands. And when the time came for these women to make their claims against your company, you attacked their characters. You inquired into their sexual practices and into the identity of their sex partners. You exposed these women - and ruined families and reputations and careers - in order to intimidate those who would raise their voices against you. You introduced issues that had no relationship whatsoever to the fact that you planted in the bodies of these women instruments of death, of mutilation, of disease.*

Judge Lord admitted that he did not have the power to make them recall the shield but he begged them to do it on their own: "You've got lives out there, people, women, wives, moms, and some who will never be moms...You are the corporate conscience. Please, in the name of humanity, lift your eyes above the bottom line."

It was a pretty stirring piece of writing (later, when Judge Lord got so pissed off he read it aloud, they say half the courtroom was in tears), and the judge asked them if it had had any impact on them.

Looking sulky, they just stared at him and said nothing.

A few weeks later, at A. H. Robins's annual meeting, E. Claiborne Robins, Jr., dismissed Lord's speech as a "poisonous attack." The company did not recall the shield for another eight months.

Giving deposition for 1984, Ernest L. Bender, Jr., senior vice-president for corporate planning and development, was asked if he had ever heard an officer or employee say he or she was "sorry or remorseful about any infection that's been suffered by any Dalkon Shield wearer." He answered, "I've never heard anyone make such remarks because I've never heard anyone that said the Dalkon Shield was the cause."

What punishment is fitting for these fellows?

If they are murderers, why not the death sentence? Polls show that eight-four percent of Americans favor the death penalty, but half think the penalty is unfairly applied. Let's restore their faith by applying justice equally and poetically. In Georgia recently it took the state two 2,080 volts spaced over nineteen minutes to kill a black man who murdered during a burglary. How fitting it would be to use the same sort of defective electric chair to execute, for example, auto manufacturers and tire manufacturers who knowingly kill people with defective merchandise. In Texas recently it took the state executioners forty minutes to administer the lethal poison to a drifter who had killed a woman. Could anything be more appropriate than to tie down drug and device manufacturers who have killed many women and let slow-witted executioners poke around their bodies for an hour or so, looking for just the right blood vessel to transport the poison? At a recent Mississippi execution, the prisoner's protracted gasping for breath became such an ugly spectacle that prison authorities, in a strange burst of decorum, ordered witnesses out of the death chamber. That sort of execution for Manville executives who specialized in spreading long-term asphyxiation over thousands of lives would certainly be appropriate.

But these things will never happen. For all our popular declarations of democracy, most Americans are such forelock-tugging toadies that they would be horrified to see, say, Henry Ford II occupying the same electric chair that cooked black, penniless Alpha Otis Stephens.

Nor will we incarcerate many corporate murderers. Though some of us with a mean streak may enjoy fantasizing the reception that our fat-assed corporate killers would get from some of their cellmates in America's more interesting prisons I like to think of the pious chaps from A. H. Robins spending time in Tennessee's notorious Brushy Mountain Prison that is not going to happen very often either, the precedent of Film Recovery to the contrary notwithstanding. The Film Recovery trio had the misfortune of working for a crappy little corporation that has since gone defunct. Judges will not be so stern with killers from giant corporations.

So long as we have any army of crassly aggressive plaintiff attorneys to rely on, however, there is always the hope that we can smite the corporations and the men who run them with a punishment they probably fear worse than death or loss of freedom: to wit, massive loss of profits.

Pamela C. Van Duyn, whose use of the Dalkon Shield at the age of twenty-six destroyed one Fallopian tube and critically damaged the other (her childbearing chances are virtually nil), says: "As far as I'm concerned, the last dime that is in Claiborne Robins's pocket ought to be paid over to all the people that have suffered." Author Brodeur dreams of an even broader financial punishment for the industry he hates:

When I was a young man, out of college in 1953, I went into the Army Counterintelligence Corps and went to Germany, where I saw one of the death camps, Dachau. And I saw what the occupational army had done to Dachau. They had razed it, left the chimneys standing, and the barbed wire as a monument - quite the same way the Romans left Carthage. What I would do with some of these companies that are nothing more or less than killing grounds would be to sell their assets totally, reimburse the victims, and leave the walls as a reminder just the way Dachau was that a law-abiding and decent society will not tolerate this kind of conduct.

He added, "I know perfectly well that this is not going to happen in the private enterprise system."

How right he is. The laws, the court system, federal and state legislatures, most of the press, the unions most of the establishment is opposed to applying the final financial solution to killer corporations.

As it became evident that juries were inclined to agree with Mrs. Van Duyn's proposal to wring plenty of money from A. H. Robins, the corporation in 1985 sought protection under Chapter 11 of the Federal Bankruptcy Code. It was a sleazy legal trick they had picked up from Manville Corporation, which had declared bankruptcy in August 1982. Although both corporations had lost hundreds of millions in court fights, neither was actually in financial trouble. Indeed, at the time it copped out under Chapter 11, Manville was the nation's 181st largest corporation and had assets of more than $2 billion. Bankruptcy was a transparent ploy - or, as plaintiff attorneys put it, a fraudulent abuse and perversion of the bankruptcy laws - but with the connivance of the federal courts it is a ploy that has worked. Not a penny has been paid to the victims of either corporation since they declared bankruptcy, and the 16,500 pending lawsuits against Manville and the 5,000 lawsuits pending against A. H. Robins (those figures are climbing every day) have been frozen.

Meanwhile, companies are not even mildly chastised. Quite the contrary. Most major newspapers have said nothing about Manville's malevolent cover-up but have clucked sympathetically over its courtroom defeats. The New York Times editorially seemed to deplore the financial problems of the asbestos industry almost as much as it deplored the industry's massacre of workers: "Asbestos is a tragedy, most of all for the victims and their families but also for the companies, which are being made to pay the price for decisions made long ago." Senator Gary Hart, whose home state, Colorado, is corporate headquarters for Manville, pitched in with legislation that would lift financial penalty from the asbestos companies and dump it on the taxpayers. And in Richmond, Virginia, corporate headquarters for the makers of Dalkon Shield, civic leaders threw a banquet for E. Claiborne Robins, Sr. The president of the University of Virginia assured Robins that "Your example will cast its shadow into eternity, as the sands of time carry the indelible footprint of your good works. We applaud you for always exhibiting a steadfast and devoted concern for your fellow man. Truly, the Lord has chosen you as one of His most essential instruments."

After similar encomiums from other community leaders, the top man behind the marketing of the Dalkon Shield was given the Great American Tradition Award.

## Study Questions

1. Regarding the 1,500 men and women on death row in America, Sherrill says, "Given the social context in which they operated, one might reasonably assume that they were sentenced to be executed not because they are murderers but because they were inefficient." In what ways, if any, is he right? In what ways, if any, is he wrong?

2. How would you describe Sherrill's tone? Can you locate specific diction and phrasing that contribute to the tone of this essay? Is the tone effective in persuading you that Sherrill is justified in making his argument about corporate killers?

3. Why does Sherrill entitle his essay, "Murder, Inc."? What is the literary reference of this title - and why is it significant?

4. Have you ever been cheated by or injured by a company? What happened? How did it make you feel? What was your response?

5. Sherrill focuses particularly on three instances of corporate greed and criminality: Film Recovery Systems Corporation, A. H. Robins, and Manville Corporation. Much of his evidence comes from books published recently on the latter two corporations. Is Sherrill's strategy here a good one? What was his purpose, do you think, in focusing on a few corporations? Do you find his account persuasive, or do you think Sherrill has basically done a hatchet job on these corporations?

# STATE AND NATIONALISM

# ON LIBERTY (1859)

## *John Stuart Mill (1806-1873)*

*John Stuart Mill was one of the foremost British proponents of liberalism during the nineteenth century. He was a champion of individual rights, particularly those for women (On The Subjection of Women). In this treatise On Liberty (1859) the basis of his argument is that in the past, the monarchy often imposed their power at the expense of common people, making it a necessity for them to gain liberty by limiting such power. However, he says now that democracy has replaced monarchy, there exists the danger of denying liberty to individuals whether through what he terms as "acts of public authority" or through utilizing more subtle means of morals and social pressure, which he terms as "collective opinion."*

The aim, therefore, of patriots was to set limits to the power which the ruler should be suffered[1] to exercise over the community; and this limitation was what they meant by liberty. It was attempted in two ways. First, by obtaining a recognition of certain immunities, called political liberties or rights, which it was to be regarded as a breach of duty in the ruler to infringe; and which if he did infringe, specific resistance, or general rebellion, was held to be justifiable. A second, and generally a later expedient, was the establishment of constitutional checks, by which the consent of the community, or of a body of some sort, supposed to represent its interests, was made a necessary condition to some of the more important acts of the governing power. To the first of these modes of limitation, the ruling power, in most European countries, was compelled, more or less, to submit. It was not so with the second; and, to attain this, or when already in some degree possessed, to attain it more completely, became everywhere the principal object of the lovers of liberty. And so long as mankind were content to combat one enemy by another, and to be ruled by a master, on condition of being guaranteed more or less efficaciously against his tyranny, they did not carry their aspirations beyond this point.

A time, however, came, in the progress of human affairs, when men ceased to think it a necessity of nature that their governors should be an independent power, opposed in interest to themselves. It appeared to them much better that the various magistrates of the State should be their tenants or delegates, revocable at their pleasure. In that way alone, it seemed, could they have complete security that the powers of government would never be abused to their disadvantage. By degrees this new demand for elective and temporary rulers became the prominent object of the exertions of the popular party, wherever any such party existed; and superseded, to a considerable extent, the previous efforts to limit the power of rulers. As the struggle proceeded for making the ruling power emanate from the periodical choice of the ruled, some persons began to think that too much importance had been attached to the limitation of the power itself. *That* (it might seem) was a resource against riders whose interests were habitually opposed to those of the people. What was now wanted was, that the rulers should be identified with the people; that their interest and will should be the interest and will of the nation. The nation did not need to be protected against its own will. There was no fear of its tyrannizing over itself. Let the rulers be effectually responsible to it, promptly removable by it, and it could afford to trust them with power of which it could itself dictate the use to he made. Their power was but the nations own power, concentrated, and in a form convenient for exercise. This mode of thought, or rather perhaps of feeling, was common among the last generation of

European liberalism, in the Continental section of which it still apparently predominates. . . .[2]

In time, however, a democratic republic came to occupy a large portion of the earths surface, and made itself felt as one of the most powerful members of the community of nations; and elective and responsible government became subject to the observations and criticisms which wait upon a great existing fact. It was now perceived that such phrases as "self-government," and "the power of the people over themselves," do not express the true state of the case. The "people who exercise the power are not always the same people with those over whom it is exercised; and the "self-government" spoken of is not the government of each by himself, but of each by all the rest. The will of the people, moreover, practically means the will of the most numerous or the most active *part* of the people; the majority, or those who succeed in making themselves accepted as the majority; the people, consequently *may* desire to oppress a part of their number; and precautions are as much needed against this as against any other abuse of power. The limitation, therefore, of the power of government over individuals loses none of its importance when the holders of power are regularly accountable to the community, that is, to the strongest party therein. This view of things, recommending itself equally to the intelligence of thinkers and to the inclination of those important classes in European society to whose real or supposed interests democracy is adverse, has had no difficulty in establishing itself, and in political speculations "the tyranny of the majority" is now generally included among the evils against which society requires to be on its guard.

Like other tyrannies, the tyranny of the majority was at first, and is still vulgarly, held in dread, chiefly as operating through the acts of the public authorities. But reflecting,[3] persons perceived that when society is itself the tyrant—society collectively over the separate individuals who compose it—its means of tyrannizing are not restricted to the acts which it may do by the hands of its political functionaries. Society can and does execute its own mandates: and if it issues wrong mandates instead of right, or any mandates at all in things with which it ought not to meddle, it practices a social tyranny more formidable than many kinds of political

oppression, since, though not usually upheld by such extreme penalties, it leaves fewer means of escape, penetrating much more deeply into the details of life, and enslaving the soul itself. Protection, therefore, against the tyranny of the magistrate is not enough; there needs protection also against the tyranny of the prevailing opinion and feeling; against the tendency of society to impose, by other means than civil penalties, its own ideas and practices as rules of conduct on those who dissent from them; to fetter the development, and, if possible, prevent the formation, of any individuality not in harmony with its ways, and compel all characters to fashion themselves upon the model of its own. There is a limit to the legitimate interference of collective opinion with individual independence: and to find that limit, and maintain it against encroachment, is as indispensable to a good condition of human affairs, as protection against political despotism.

## ENDNOTES

1. Allowed.
2. Mill was writing in 1859.
3. Thoughtful.

### Study Questions

1. What does Mills mean by "tyranny of the majority"?

2. What are some of the inconsistencies of democracy that you have observed in present day society?

3. According to Mills, what should the relationship of he individual and society be? How should power be shared between them?

# ON THE DUTY OF CIVIL DISOBEDIENCE

## Henry David Thoreau (1817-1862)

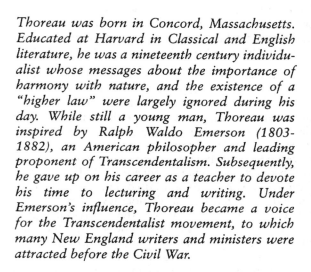

*Thoreau was born in Concord, Massachusetts. Educated at Harvard in Classical and English literature, he was a nineteenth century individualist whose messages about the importance of harmony with nature, and the existence of a "higher law" were largely ignored during his day. While still a young man, Thoreau was inspired by Ralph Waldo Emerson (1803-1882), an American philosopher and leading proponent of Transcendentalism. Subsequently, he gave up on his career as a teacher to devote his time to lecturing and writing. Under Emerson's influence, Thoreau became a voice for the Transcendentalist movement, to which many New England writers and ministers were attracted before the Civil War.*

*In March 1845, Thoreau left Concord to live at Walden Pond, where he built a small cabin and lived simply for two years. Walden Pond, or Life in the Woods, is an account of his experience and his most famous work. Unfortunately, Thoreau did not achieve literary fame during his lifetime, and much of his works about the natural world were not discovered until years after his death. Many contemporary nature writers consider Thoreau to be the forefather of the environmental movement because of his deep engagement with and reverence for the natural world.*

*The excerpt below is an outgrowth of reflections written by Thoreau concerning an incident* *that occurred in 1846 when he was jailed for one night after he refused to pay his tax. In order to avoid public embarrassment, a member of his family came forward and paid the tax, much to his consternation.*

Unjust laws exist: shall we be content to obey them, or shall we endeavor to amend them, and obey them until we have succeeded, or shall we transgress them at once? Men generally, under such a government as this, think that they ought to wait until they have persuaded the majority to alter them. They think that, if they should resist, the remedy would be worse than the evil. But it is the fault of the government itself that the remedy *is* worse than the evil. *It* makes it worse. Why is it not more apt to anticipate and provide for reform? Why does it not cherish its wise minority? Why does it cry and resist before it is hurt? Why does it not encourage its citizens to be on the alert to point out its faults, and *do* better than it would have them? Why does it always crucify Christ, and excommunicate Copernicus and Luther, and pronounce Washington and Franklin rebels?

One would think, that a deliberate and practical denial of its authority was the only offence never contemplated by government; else, why has it not assigned its definite, its suitable and proportionate penalty? If a man who has no property refuses but once to earn nine shillings for the State, he is put in prison for a period unlimited by any law that I know, and determined only by the discretion of those who placed him there: but if he should steal ninety times nine shillings from the State, he is soon permitted to go at large again.

If the injustice is part of the necessary friction of the machine of government, let it go, let it go: perchance it will wear smooth,—certainly the machine will wear out. If the injustice has a spring, or a pulley, or a rope, or a crank, exclusively for itself, then perhaps you may consider whether the remedy will not be worse than the evil; but if it is of such a nature that it requires you to be the agent of injustice to another, then, I say, break the law. Let your life be a counter friction to stop the machine. What I have to do is to see, at any rate, that I do not lend myself to the wrong which I condemn.

As for adopting the ways which the State has provided for remedying the evil, I know not of such ways. They take too much time, and a man's life will be gone. I have other affairs to attend to. I came into this world, not chiefly to make this a good place to live in, but to live in it, be it good or bad. A man has not every thing to do, but something; and because he cannot do *every thing*, it is not necessary that he should do *something* wrong. It is not my business to be petitioning the governor or the legislature any more than it is theirs to petition me; and, if they should not hear my petition, what should I do then? But in this case the State has provided no way: its very Constitution is the evil. This may seem to be harsh and stubborn and conciliatory but it is to treat with the utmost kindness and unconsideration the only spirit that can appreciate or deserves it. So is all change for the better, like birth and death which convulse the body.

I do not hesitate to say, that those who call themselves abolitionists should at once effectually withdraw their support, both in person and property, from the government of Massachusetts, and not wait till they constitute a majority of one, before they suffer the right to prevail through them. I think that it is enough if they have God on their side, without waiting for that other one. Moreover, any man more right than his neighbors, constitutes a majority of one already . . .

They who know of no purer sources of truth, who have traced up its stream no higher, stand, and wisely stand, by the Bible and the Constitution, and drink at it there with reverence and humility; but they who behold where it comes trickling into this lake or that pool, gird up their loins once more, and continue their pilgrimage toward its fountain-head.

No man with a genius for legislation has appeared in America. They are rare in the history of the world. There are orators, politicians, and eloquent men, by the thousand; but the speaker has not yet opened his mouth to speak, who is capable of settling the much-vexed questions of the day. We love eloquence for its own sake, and not for any truth which it may utter, or any heroism it may inspire. Our legislators have not yet learned the comparative value of free-trade and of freedom, of union, and of rectitude, to a nation. They have no genius or talent for comparatively humble questions of taxation and finance, commerce and manufactures and agriculture. If we were left solely to the wordy wit of legislators in Congress for our guidance, uncorrected by the seasonable experience and the effectual complaints of the people, America would not long retain her rank among the nations. For eighteen hundred years, though perchance I have no right to say it, the New Testament has been written; yet where is the legislator who has wisdom and practical talent enough to avail himself of the light which it sheds on the science of legislation?

The authority of government, even such as I am willing to submit to,—for I will cheerfully obey those who know and can do better than I, and in many things even those who neither know nor can do so well,—is still an impure one: to be strictly just, it must have the sanction and consent of the governed. It can have no pure right over my person and property but what I concede to it. The progress from an absolute to a limited monarchy, from a limited monarchy to a democracy, is a progress toward a true respect for the individual. Is a democracy, such as we know it, the last improvement possible in government? Is it not possible to take a step further towards recognizing and organizing the rights of man? There will never be a really free and enlightened State, until the State comes to recognize the individual as a higher and independent power, from which all its own power and authority are derived, and treats him accordingly. I please myself with imagining a State at last which can afford to be just to all men, and to treat the individual with respect as a neighbor; which even would not think it inconsistent with its own repose, if a few were to live aloof from it, not meddling with it, nor embraced by it, who fulfilled all the duties of neighbors and fellow-men. A State which bore this kind of fruit, and suffered it to drop off as fast as it ripened, would prepare the way for a still more perfect and glorious State, which also I have imagined, but not yet anywhere seen.

**Study Questions**

1. How does Thoreau justify his civil disobedience?

2. How much authority does Thoreau believe should be given to the government and to individuals?

3. How does he characterize the Ideal State? Does he believe such a State exists or ever existed?

# 3

# THE DECLARATION OF INDEPENDENCE AS ADOPTED BY CONGRESS

*In Congress July 4, 1776*

When in the Course of human events, it becomes necessary for one people to dissolve the political bands which have connected them with another, and to assume among the powers of the earth, the separate and equal station to which the Laws of Nature and of Nature's God entitle them, a decent respect to the opinions of mankind requires that they should declare the causes which impel them to the separation. We hold these truths to be self-evident, that all men are created equal, that they are endowed by their Creator with certain unalienable Rights, that among these are Life, Liberty and the pursuit of Happiness. That to secure these rights, Governments are instituted among Men, deriving their just powers from the consent of the governed, That whenever any Form of Government becomes destructive of these ends, it is the Right of the People to alter or to abolish it, and to institute new Government, laying its foundation on such principles and organizing its powers in such form, as to them shall seem most likely to effect their Safety and Happiness. Prudence, indeed, will dictate that Governments long established should not be changed for light and transient causes; and accordingly all experience hath shown, that mankind are more disposed to suffer, while evils are sufferable, than to right themselves by abolishing the forms to which they are accustomed. But when a long train of abuses and usurpations, pursuing invariably the same Object evinces a design to reduce them under absolute Despotism, it is their right, it is their duty, to throw off such Government, and to provide new Guards for their future security. Such has been the patient sufferance of these Colonies; and such is now the necessity which constrains them to alter their former Systems of Government. The history of

the present King of Great Britain is a history of repeated injuries and usurpations, all having in direct object the establishment of an absolute Tyranny over these States. To prove this, let Facts be submitted to a candid world. He has refused his Assent to Laws, the most wholesome and necessary for the public good. He has forbidden his Governors to pass Laws of immediate and pressing importance, unless suspended in their operation till his Assent should be obtained; and when so suspended, he has utterly neglected to attend to them. He has refused to pass other Laws for the accommodation of large districts of people, unless those people would relinquish the right of Representation in the Legislature, a right inestimable to them and formidable to tyrants only. He has called together legislative bodies at places unusual, uncomfortable, and distant from the depository of their public Records, for the sole purpose of fatiguing them into compliance with his measures. He has dissolved Representative Houses repeatedly, for opposing with manly firmness his invasions on the rights of the people. He has refused for a long time, after such dissolutions, to cause others to be elected; whereby the Legislative powers, incapable of Annihilation, have returned to the People at large for their exercise; the State remaining in the mean time exposed to all the dangers of invasion from without, and convulsions within. He has endeavoured to prevent the population of these States; for that purpose obstructing the Laws for Naturalization of Foreigners; refusing to pass others to encourage their migrations hither, and raising the conditions of new Appropriations of Lands. He has obstructed the Administration of justice, by refusing his Assent to Laws for establishing judiciary powers. He has made Judges dependent on his Will alone, for the tenure of their offices, and the amount and payment of their salaries. He has erected a multitude of New Offices, and sent hither swarms of Officers to harrass our people, and eat out their substance. He has kept among us, in times of peace, standing Armies without the Consent of our legislatures. He has affected to render the Military independent of and superior to the Civil power. He has combined with others to subject us to a jurisdiction foreign to our constitution, and unacknowledged by our laws; giving his Assent to their Acts of pretended Legislation: For Quartering large bodies of armed troops among us: For protecting them, by a mock Trial, from punishment for any Murders which they should commit on the Inhabitants of these States: For cutting off our Trade with all parts of the world: For imposing Taxes on us without our Consent: For depriving us in many cases of the benefits of Trial by Jury: For transporting us beyond Seas to be tried for pretended offences: For abolishing the free System of English Laws in a neighbouring Province, establishing therein an Arbitrary government, and enlarging its Boundaries so as to render it at once an example and fit instrument for introducing the same absolute rule into these Colonies: For taking away our Charters, abolishing our most valuable Laws, and altering fundamentally the Forms of our Governments: For suspending our own Legislatures, and declaring themselves invested with power to legislate for us in all cases whatsoever. He has abdicated Government here, by declaring us out of his Protection and waging War against us. He has plundered our seas, ravaged our Coasts, burnt our towns, and destroyed the Lives of our people. He is at this time transporting large Armies of foreign Mercenaries to complot the works of death, desolation and tyranny, already begun with circumstances of Cruelty & perfidy scarcely paralleled in the most barbarous ages, and totally unworthy the Head of a civilized nation. He has constrained our fellow Citizens taken Captive on the high Seas to bear Arms against their Country, to become the executioners of their friends and Brethren, or to fall themselves by their Hands. He has excited domestic insurrections amongst us, and has endeavoured to bring on the inhabitants of our frontiers, the merciless Indian Savages, whose known rule of warfare, is an undistinguished destruction of all ages, sexes and conditions. In every stage of these Oppressions We have Petitioned for Redress in the most humble terms: Our repeated Petitions have been answered only by repeated injury. A Prince, whose character is thus marked by every act which may define a Tyrant, is unfit to be the ruler of a free people. Nor have We been wanting in attentions to our Brittish brethren. We have warned them from time to time of attempts by their legislature to extend an unwarrantable jurisdiction over us. We have reminded them of the circumstances of our emigration and settlement here. We have appealed to their native justice and magnanimity, and we have conjured them by the ties of our common kindred to disavow these usurpations, which, would inevitably interrupt our connections and correspondence. They too have been deaf to the voice of justice and of consanguinity. We must, therefore, acquiesce in the necessity, which denounces our Separation, and hold them, as we hold the rest of mankind, Enemies in War, in Peace Friends.

We, therefore, the Representatives of the united States of America, in General Congress, Assembled, appealing to the Supreme judge of the world for the rectitude of our intentions, do, in the Name, and by Authority of the good People of these Colonies, solemnly publish and declare, That these United Colonies are, and of Right ought to be Free and Independent States; that they are Absolved from all Allegiance to the British Crown, and that all political connection between them and the State of Great Britain, is and ought to be totally dissolved; and that as Free and Independent States, they have full Power to levy War, conclude Peace, contract Alliances, establish Commerce, and to do all other Acts and Things which Independent States may of right do. And for the support of this Declaration, with a firm reliance on the protection of divine Providence, we mutually pledge to each other our Lives, our Fortunes and our sacred Honor.

## Study Questions

1. What reasons are given for the adoption of this document?

2. What justification is given for declaring independence?

3. What complaints does the declaration make against the King of Great Britain?

4. How does the declaration talk about individual rights? Did those who adopted this document believe in equal rights for all? Explain.

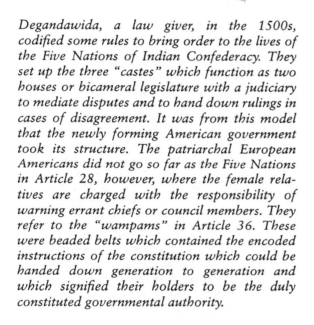

# CONSTITUTION OF THE IROQUOIS FEDERATION

## *Degandawida (Mohawk)*

*Degandawida, a law giver, in the 1500s, codified some rules to bring order to the lives of the Five Nations of Indian Confederacy. They set up the three "castes" which function as two houses or bicameral legislature with a judiciary to mediate disputes and to hand down rulings in cases of disagreement. It was from this model that the newly forming American government took its structure. The patriarchal European Americans did not go so far as the Five Nations in Article 28, however, where the female relatives are charged with the responsibility of warning errant chiefs or council members. They refer to the "wampams" in Article 36. These were beaded belts which contained the encoded instructions of the constitution which could be handed down generation to generation and which signified their holders to be the duly constituted governmental authority.*

[Although the Iroquois federation was founded about 1500, the constitution was not put into writing until after 1850. This version was inscribed by Seth Newhouse, a Seneca, in 1880.]

## CONSTITUTION OF THE FIVE NATIONS INDIAN CONFEDERACY.

This is wisdom and justice of the part of the Great Spirit to create and raise chiefs, give and establish unchangeable laws, rules and customs between the Five Nation Indians, viz the Mohawks, Oneidas, Onondagas, Cayugas and Senecas and the other nations of Indians here in North America. The object of these laws is to establish peace between the numeras nations of Indians, hostility will be done away with, for the preservation and protection of life, property and liberty.

Laws, rules and customs as follows:

1.   And the number of chiefs in this confederation of the five Nation Indians are fifty in number, no more and no less. They are the ones to arrange, to legislate and to look after the affairs of their people.[*]

2.   And the Mohawks, an Indian Nation, forms a part of the body of this Five Nation Indians confederation, and their representatives in this confederation is nine chiefs.

3.   And the Oneidas, an Indian Nation, forms a party of the body of this Five Nation Indians confederation, and their representatives in this confederation is nine chiefs.

4.   And the Onondagas, an Indian Nation, form a part of the body of this Five Nation Indians confederation, and their representatives in this confederation is fourteen chiefs.

5.   And the Cayugas, an Indian Nation, forms a part of the body of this Five Nation Indians confederation, and their representatives in this confederation is ten chiefs.

6.   And the Senecas, an Indian Nation, forms a part of the body of this Five Nation Indians confederation, and their representatives in this confederation is eight chiefs.

---

[*] These fifty include the long dead Degandawida and Hiawatha who are supposed to be present in spirit. Their places have never been filled by living men.

From Thomas R. Henry, *Wilderness Messiah: The Story of Hiawatha and the Iroquois* (New York, 1955), Appendix 2.

7. And when the Five Nation Indians confederation chiefs assemble to hold a council, the council shall be duly opened and, closed by the Onondaga chiefs, the Firekeepers. They will offer thanks to the Great Spirit that dwells in heaven above: the source and ruler of our lives, and it is him that sends daily blessings upon us, our daily wants and daily health, and they will then declare the council open for the transaction of business, and give decisions of all that is done in the council.

8. And there are three totems or castes of the Mohawk Nation viz. the Tortoise, the Wolf and the Bear; each has 3 head chiefs, 9 in all. The chiefs of the Tortoise and Wolf castes are the council by themselves, and the chiefs of the Bear castes are to listen and watch the progress of the council or discussion of the two castes; and if they see any error they are to correct them, and explain, where they are wrong; and when they decide with the sanction of the Bear castes then their speaker will refer the matter to the other side of the council fire, to the second combination chiefs, viz The Oneidas and Cayugas.

9. And the council of the five Nations shall not be opened, until all of the three castes of the Mohawk chiefs are present; and if they are not all present it shall be legal for them to transact the business of the council if all the three totems have one or more representatives present, and if not it shall not be legal except in small matters; for all the three castes of the Mohawk chiefs must be present to be called a full council.

10. And the business of the council of the Five Nation Indians is transacted by two combination of chiefs; viz first the Mohawks and Senecas, and second the Oneidas and Cayugas.

11. And when a case or proposition is introduced in the council of the five nations, the Mohawk chiefs with the Senecas shall first consider the matter, and whatever the decision may be; then the speaker will refer the matter to the other side of the council fire; to the second combination chiefs, the Oneidas and Cayugas, for their consideration, and if they all agree unanimously then the speaker of the council shall refer the matter to the Fire keepers; and it is then their duty to sanction it; and their speaker will then pronounce the case as passed in council.

12. And if a dissention arises between the two combination chiefs in council, and they agree to refer the matter to the Fire keepers to decide, then the Fire keepers shall decide which of the two or more propositions is most advantageous to their people, and their decision is final.

13. And when any case or proposition has passed unanimously between the two combination chiefs, and the case or proposition is then referred to the Fire keepers for their sanction: and if the Fire keepers see that the case or proposition is such that it will be injurious and not to the advantage of their people, then they will refer the case or proposition back to the Mohawk chiefs, and point out where it would be injurious to the people and then they will reconsider the case. When it is right the case is then referred again to the Fire keepers and then they will pass it.

14. And when there is a case, proposition, or any subject before the council of the Five Nation Indians, no chief or chiefs has any right to stand up to speak without permission from the council, and if he has anything to say by way of explanation, he can do so in a low tone to the combined chiefs whereof he is a member.

15. And when anything is under the consideration of the council, they must agree unanimously if possible before it is referred to the other side of the council fire, to the second combination chiefs; otherwise it would be illegal so to do by one or more chiefs, unless sanction[ed] by the rest of the combined chiefs of which he or they is a member.

16. The speaker of the council of the Five Nations council shall be appointed from time to time when it is necessary, by the first combined chiefs Viz the Mohawks and Senecas during the day or days when the council is in session.

17. And the duty of the speaker of the council as aforesaid is to order the Fire keepers to open and close the council, and to address the council when necessary and to refer cases propositions etc. to the second combined chiefs and to the Fire keepers, and to proclaim a sanctioned cases, or anything when passed by the council.

18. A speaker of the Fire keepers shall be chosen from time to time, as occasion shall require; by the Onondaga chiefs themselves.

19. The speaker of the Second Combined Chiefs appointment, shall be on the same condition as the speaker of the Fire keepers.

20. Each of the Principal chiefs has one war chief and a runner, and should war break out then the office of the principal chief ceases during the war; then the war chiefs will take their places and council for the Five Nations till

the end of the war; then the office will cease and the principal chiefs shall resume their places and their duties as before.

21. And if the Principal chief desires to have anything to do with the war, this he can do by giving up the emblem which he received by his relatives when he was first made chief.

22. And the duty of the messenger or runner is to carry tidings from place to place by Order of the Five Nation Indians confederation session, or by his superior chiefs.

23. And if the Principal chief does fail in his judgement in the Five Nation Indians confederation council of course the duty of his war chief is to assist him, and he is bound to listen.

24. And the duty of the Head Principal Chief of the Onondagas, Ododarho, is to keep the Five Nation Indians confederation council fire clean all around, that no dust or dirt is to be seen. There is a long wing of a bird, and a stick is placed by his side, and he will take the long wing and sweep or dust the dirt away from the council fire, and if he sees any creeping creature crawling towards the Five Nation Indians council fire he will take the stick and pitch the crawling creature away from the fire, and his cousin chiefs of the Onondagas will act with him at all times, and the crawling creature signifies any case or proposition or subject brought before the Five Nation Indians council which would be ruinous and injurious to their people, and they are to reject anything which on the nature would be ruinous and injurious and not to the advantage of their people, and they are to consider first by themselves during the council, and then call the attention of the council to the fact, case or proposition, and the council are not to receive it after it had been rejected by the council.

25. And the Fire Keepers of the Five Nation Indians confederation council the Onondaga principal chiefs are combined together by themselves expressly to open and close the Five Nation Indians confederation council and to sanction, and decide any case, proposition, subject, point or points, when it is referred to them and all the chiefs must be present during the session, an agree unanimously, for one or two or more chiefs to sanction, and to give decision is illegal if the rest of their cousin chiefs are present and the council shall not be organized if the Onondaga chief of chiefs are not present to open and close the council, but he or they shall not sanction, or give decision on any

case, proposition, subject, point or points till all the rest of their cousin chiefs shall be present.

26. The duty of the two head Seneca chiefs, Viz, Ke non keri dawi and De yo nin ho hakarawen, who are stationed at the door of the Five Nations Indians confederation session, is to watch and if they see any crawling creature entering in the session they will disallow to enter in the session; Crawling creature signifies any case of proposition which brought before the session would be ruinous, or injourious to the people; and also if they see stranger near the door they will bring the stranger in their session and ask what is their message have they with them.

27. And if any one of the Five Nation Indians confederation chiefs should die, and there being no member in the caste fit for the office to succeed him; then the chiefs of the Five Nation Indians shall take the emblem of chieftainship and put it in another family of the same caste as the deceased chief; until such time as they shall have a member qualified for the office, then the emblem of chieftainship shall be restored to the said family; on the female side.

28. And if the principal chief or chiefs of the Five Nation Indians confederation, disregards the constitution of the Five Nation Indians, then his female relatives will come to him and warn him or they to come back, and walk according to this constitution; if he or they disregards the warning after the first and second warnings, then she will refer the matter to the war chief, and the war chief will now say to him, so you did not listen to her warnings, now it is just where the bright noonday sun stands, an its before that sun's brightness I now discharge you as a chief an I now disposses you of the office of chieftainship. I now give her the chieftainship for she is the proprietor, and as I have now discharged you as a chief, so you are no longer a chief you will now go where you want it to go, an you will now go alone, an the rest of the people will not go with you for we know not of what kind of a spirit has got in you, and as the Great Spirit could not handle sin therefore he could not come to take you out of the prespice in the place of destruction, and you will never be restored again to the place you did occupy once. Then the war chief will notify the Five Nation Indians confederation of his dismissal and they will sanction it.

29. Kariwhiyho, the good message is the love of the Great Spirit, the Supreme Being, now this Kariwhiyho is the surrounding guard of the Five Nation Indians confederation principal chiefs, an this Kariwhiyho it loves all alike the

members of the Five Nation Indians confederation, and other nations of Indians that are
attached to it by an through customary way of
treaties, an if the Five Nation Indians confederation principal chiefs were to submit to laws
and regulations made by other people, or course
he or they the chief or chiefs are now gone
through outside the boundary of the Kari-
whiyhos surrounding guard, but their chieftainship fell of from their heads, an it remains
inside the Five Nation Indians confederation,
and he or they are now gone outside of the
Kariwhiyho's surrounding guard alone without
his or their chieftainship, the emblem of his or
their chieftainship, their authority an honour.

30. And there is Five arrows bound together.
This is the symbol of Union, Power, Honour,
and Dominion of the Five Nation Indians
confederation, an if one of the Five arrows was
to be taken out then the remainder is easily
broken asunder. This signifies if one of the Five
Nations were to emigrate to a distant country of
course they now withdrawn from the confederation therefore the Power of the Five Nation
Indians confederation decreased.

31. Adodarho, the head chief of the Ononadagas or fire keepers, it is them are entrusted
the care of the Five Nation Indians confederation council fire, and if there is any business to
be transacted, they will send a messenger to the
head chief of the Fire Keepers Adodarho; and
state the nature of the business to him. Then
Adodarho will call his cousin chiefs together
and hold a council by themselves and consider
the matter, and if they find that the matter is
worth the consideration of the council of the
Five Nations, then Adodarho will send a
messenger and notify the rest of the chiefs of the
five nations to assemble at their council house,
or wherever their residence where the council
fire is keept, and its smoke assends up perpetually to the sky, this it signifies that other Indian
Nations are allies to the Five Nation Indians
confederation, and as an imperial council fire,
and when the chiefs assemble together and the
council fire opened according to their rules, then
the Fire Keepers will announce to the council
the nature business for which they came
together to consider.

32. And when the Five Nation Indian chief dies,
the council will be adjourned ten days if it is in
session, and if it is not in session it will not be
summoned before the ten days expire; and if the
three Brothers, Viz; Mohawks, Ononadagas
and Senecas, should lose one by death of their
number, then the four brothers Ya dat he wah,

Oneidas and Cayugas, shall come to the residence of the deceased chief on the tenth day and
comfort and cheer up their spirits again and if it
is to Ya dat ha wah that loses one of their
number then the three Brothers will perform the
ceremony according to their customs by passing
a certain number of strings of wampum, and
diring the ceremony is in progress, a successor
must be pointed out to them; then the female
relatives of the deceased chief shall select one
out of kindreds fit for the office of a chief, and if
they are not ready, then they will postpone it till
another time, and when they are ready; all the
chiefs will assemble together to perform a long
ceremony of what is called Oka yon donts hera
to install the new chief or chiefs.

33. Yoh he do da oe, this is the title of a chief,
and it is a peculiar way of how he becomes chief
when a warrior assists the chiefs in their
councils and otherwise, and he is found to be a
wise councilor in war and peace, and of sober
habits trustworthy and honest, then the chiefs
will place him among the rest of the chiefs; as a
chief and proclaim in their council, that such a
one has become what is called Wa ka dine dot
he se he now becomes a chief. And also if a
warrior do exploits that will tend to the
advantage and interest of his people, he also
will become Yo ne do da oe amongst them as
well, so his class of chiefs are not of the same
order as the principle chiefs; for when he
departs this life no one is to take his place or
succeed him, and if he does wrong in their
councils he could not be put out of the council,
but he will not be allowed any more to speak in
their council, and if he resign his office no one is
able to prevent him.

34. And if the Five Nation Indian confederation
chief die, then his comrades will send a
messenger to notify the rest of the confederate
chiefs to attend his funeral.

35. And when the Five Nation Indians confederation chief get sick, and as he is now
approaching unto death, then his female relatives, or his comarade chiefs will come and
disposses him the emblem of his chieftainship.

36. And you can create an install a new chief or
chiefs when you will hear my words again, and
the way that you will hear my words again is
when you will read the wampams, for its the
wampams that talls all my Laws, Rules,
Customs, which I gave you the Five Nation
Indians, on this occasion you can create and
install a new chief in the first combined chiefs,
the second and the third as well.

37. And when one is made chief his skin are said to be seven Ni yo roe ka ra ke (each of the seven is six inches) in thickness and they were made so when they were made a chief or chiefs; this symbolizes, that when they are in council and engaged in their duties they will not willingly offend, and they are not easily to be offended, and they are not to take offence in any thing that might be said in council against them; but to go one calmly, and of a good conscience to deliberate whatever is before them to council.

38. The title of the Five Nation Indians confederation principal chiefs are Lords, and this title was from the beginning when the confederation first established.

39. And if any of the chiefs resign his office as a chief, he shall tell his Brother chiefs, and if he selects one to take his place and be a chief instead, and his Brother chiefs accepts his resignation, and one to fill his place, but he will not be made a chief, until sanctioned by his female relatives.

40. The Great Spirit the Supreme Being has chosen to Mohawk Nation as head in this confederation, for it is with them that the confederation originated. Therefore if the Mohawk chiefs disallow anything, or protest any case or proposition that is brought before the council it shall not be lawful for the council to pass it, for he hath chosen them to be the leader of this confederation government, and all the affairs of the Five Nation Indians, and others that are united with them are in their hands; and he hath given the Mohawk chiefs a calm and tender hearts towards their people, and if any difficulty arise amongst them the people the chiefs in council will settle it for them.

## Study Questions

1. According to this constitution, how do you understand their concept of justice?

2. What are the parallels and similarities to our constitution? How does that reflect differences and similarities in our cultural values?

3. What role do women play in their culture? How would you compare that to ours?

4. What kinds of checks and balances do you see here? Why is unanimity so important?

# THE "DECLARATION OF SENTIMENTS" (1848)

## Seneca Falls Convention

*In 1848, a group of women gathered in Seneca Falls, New York "to discuss the social, civil and religious condition and rights of woman." The convention was organized by Elizabeth Cady Stanton and Lucretia Mott, who had met in London in 1840 as delegates to the World Anti-Slavery Society where they were denied a place on the floor with the rest of the female delegates. At that time women were not allowed to speak in public, one of many "rights" women did not share with men. Mott and Cady Stanton left the hall and began to talk about the lack of women's rights in general, and they determined that a forum was needed where women could discuss how they could secure the same rights as men. The Seneca Falls Convention took place eight years later, and is considered the birthplace of the women's movement.*

*At Seneca Falls, Elizabeth Cady Stanton would present the Declaration of Sentiments and Resolutions, based on the American Declaration of Independence. Included in the demands in the declaration were equality with men before the law, in education and employment.*

When, in the course of human events, it becomes necessary for one portion of the family of man to assume among the people of the earth a position different from that which they have hitherto occupied, but one to which the laws of nature and of nature's God entitle them, a decent respect to the opinions of mankind requires that they should declare the causes that impel them to such a course.

We hold these truths to be self-evident: that all men and women are created equal; that they are endowed by their Creator with certain inalienable rights; that among these are life, liberty, and the pursuit of happiness; that to secure these rights governments are instituted, deriving their just powers from the consent of the governed. Whenever any form of government becomes destructive of these ends, it is the right of those who suffer from it to refuse allegiance to it, and to insist upon the institution of a new government, laying its foundation on such principles, and organizing its powers in such form, as to them shall seem most likely to effect their safety and happiness. Prudence, indeed, will dictate that governments long established should not be changed for light and transient causes; and accordingly all experience hath shown that mankind are more disposed to suffer, while evils are sufferable, than to right themselves by abolishing the forms to which they were accustomed. But when a long train of abuses and usurpations, pursuing invariably the same object, evinces a design to reduce them under absolute despotism, it is their duty to throw off such government, and to provide new guards for their future security. Such has been the patient sufferance of the women under this government, and such is now the necessity which constrains them to demand the equal situation to which they are entitled.

The history of mankind is a history of repeated injuries and usurpations on the part of man toward woman, having in direct object the establishment of an absolute tyranny over her. To prove this, let facts be submitted to a candid world.

He has never permitted her to exercise her inalienable right to the elective franchise.

He has compelled her to submit to laws, in the formation of which she had no voice.

He has withheld from her rights which are given to the most ignorant and degraded men—both natives and foreigners.

Having deprived her of this first right of a citizen, the elective franchise, thereby leaving her without representation in the halls of legislation, he has oppressed her on all sides.

He has made her, if married, in the eye of the law, civilly dead.

He has taken from her all right in property, even to the wages she earns.

He has made her, morally, an irresponsible being, as she can commit many crimes with immunity, provided they be done in the presence of her husband. In the covenant of marriage, she is compelled to promise obedience to her husband, he becoming, to all intents and purposes, her master—the law giving him power to deprive her of her liberty, and to administer chastisement.

He has so framed the laws of divorce, as to what shall be the proper causes, and in case of separation, to whom the guardianship of the children shall be given, as to be wholly regardless of the happiness of women—the law, in all cases, going upon a false supposition of the supremacy of man, and giving all power into his hands.

After depriving her of all rights as a married woman, if single, and the owner of property, he has taxed her to support a government which recognizes her only when her property can be made profitable to it.

He has monopolized nearly all the profitable employments, and from those she is permitted to follow, she receives but a scanty remuneration. He closes against her all the avenues to wealth and distinction which he considers most honorable to himself. As a teacher of theology, medicine, or law, she is not known.

He has denied her the facilities for obtaining a thorough education, all colleges being closed against her.

He allows her in Church, as well as State, but a subordinate position, claiming Apostolic authority for her exclusion from the ministry, and, with some exceptions, from any public participation in the affairs of the Church.

He has created a false public sentiment by giving to the world a different code of morals for men and women, by which moral delinquencies which exclude women from society, are not only tolerated, but deemed of little account in man.

He has usurped the prerogative of Jehovah himself, claiming it as his right to assign for her a sphere of action, when that belongs to her conscience and to her God.

He has endeavored, in every way that he could, to destroy her confidence in her own powers, to lessen her self-respect, and to make her willing to lead a dependent and abject life.

Now, in view of this entire disfranchisement of one-half the people of this country, their social and religious degradation—in view of the unjust laws above mentioned, and because women do feel themselves aggrieved, oppressed, and fraudulently deprived of their most sacred rights, we insist that they have immediate admission to all the rights and privileges which belong to them as citizens of the United States.

In entering upon the great work before us, we anticipate no small amount of misconception, misrepresentation, and ridicule; but we shall use every instrumentality within our power to effect our object. We shall employ agents, circulate tracts, petition the State and National legislatures, and endeavor to enlist the pulpit and the press in our behalf. We hope this Convention will be followed by a series of Conventions embracing every part of the country.

**Study Questions**

1. Compare the Declaration of Sentiments with the Declaration of Independence. Why is the language of the women's declaration similar to that of the Declaration of Independence?

2. How does the Declaration of Sentiments both endorse and critique the Declaration of Independence?

3. Which of the "injuries" or rights denied do you think are the most significant? How have women's rights changed since this was written?

# 6

# WHAT WE WANT, WHAT WE BELIEVE

## The Black Panthers

*In 1966 two young blacks from Oakland, California, Huey Newton and Bobby Seale, organized the Black Panther Party, taking its name from the SNCC organized political party in Lowndes County, Mississippi. These Black Panthers sought a militant community-based organization to deal with the problems in northern ghettoes. Their platform, "What We Want, What We Believe," took an aggressive stand against the problems of northern black life.*

1. We want freedom. We want power to determine the destiny of our Black Community.

We believe that black people will not be free until we are able to determine our destiny.

2. We want full employment for our people.

We believe that the federal government is responsible and obligated to give every man employment or a guaranteed income. We believe that if the white American businessmen will not give full employment, then the means of production should be taken from the businessmen and placed in the community so that the people of the community can organize and employ all of its people and give a high standard of living.

3. We want an end to the robbery by the CAPITALIST of our Black Community.

We believe that this racist government has robbed us and now we are demanding the overdue debt of forty acres and two mules. Forty acres and two mules was promised 100 years ago as restitution for slave labor and mass murder of black people. We will accept the payment in currency which will be distributed to our many communities. The Germans are now aiding the Jews in Israel for the genocide of the Jewish people. The Germans murdered six million Jews. The American racist has taken part in the slaughter of over fifty million black people; therefore, we feel that this is a modest demand that we make.

4. We want decent housing, fit for shelter of human beings.

We believe that if the white landlords will not give decent housing to our black community, then the housing and the land should be made into cooperatives so that our community, with government-aid, can build and make decent housing for its people.

5. We want education for our people that exposes the true nature of this decadent American society. We want education that teaches us our true history and our role in the present-day society.

We believe in an educational system that will give to our people a knowledge of self. If a man does not have knowledge of himself and his position in society and the world, then he has little chance to relate to anything else.

6. We want all black men to be exempt from military service.

We believe that Black people should not be forced to fight in the military service to defend a racist government that does not protect us. We will not fight and kill other people of color in the world who, like black people, are being victimized by the white racist government of America. We will protect ourselves from the force and violence of the racist police and the racist military, by whatever means necessary.

7. We want an immediate end to POLICE BRUTALITY and MURDER of black people.

We believe we can end police brutality in our black community by organizing black self-defense groups that are dedicated to defending our black community from racist police oppression and brutality. The Second Amendment to the Constitution of the United States gives a right to bear arms. We, therefore, believe that all back people should arm themselves for self-defense.

8. We want freedom for all black men held in federal, state, county, and city prisons and jails.

We believe that all black people should be released from the many jails and prisons because they have not received a fair and impartial trial.

9. We want all black people when brought to trial to be tried in court by a jury of their peer group or people from their black communities, as defined by the Constitution of the United States.

We believe that the courts should follow the United States Constitution so that black people will receive fair trials. The 14th Amendment of the U.S. Constitution gives a man a right to be tried by his peer group. A peer is a person from a similar economic, social, religious, geographical, environmental, historical and racial background. To do this the court will be forced to select a jury from the black community from which the black defendant came. We have been, and are being tried by all-white juries that have no understanding of the "average reasoning man" of the black community.

10. We want land, bread, housing, education, clothing, justice, and peace. And as our major political objective, a United Nations supervised plebiscite to be held throughout the black colony in which only black colonial subjects will be allowed to participate, for the purpose of determining the will of black people as to their national destiny.

When, in the course of human events, it becomes necessary for one people to dissolve the political bands which have connected them with another, and to assume, among the powers of the earth, the separate and equal station to which the laws of nature and nature's God entitle them, a decent respect to the opinions of mankind requires that they should declare the causes which impel them to the separation.

We hold these truths to be self-evident, that all men are created equal; that they are endowed by their Creator with certain unalienable rights; that among these are life, liberty, and the pursuit of happiness. That, to secure these rights, governments are instituted among men, deriving their just powers from the consent of the governed: that, whenever any form of government becomes destructive of these ends, it is the right of the people to alter or to abolish it, and to institute a new government, laying its foundation on such principles, and organizing its powers in such form, as to them shall seem most likely to effect their safety and happiness. Prudence, indeed, well dictate that governments long established should not be changed for light and transient causes; and, accordingly, all experience hath shown, that mankind are more disposed to suffer, while evils are sufferable, than to right themselves by abolishing the forms to which they are accustomed. But, when a long train of abuses and usurpations, pursing invariably the same object, evinces a design to reduce them under absolute despotism, it is their right, it is their duty, to throw off such government, and to provide new guards for their future security.

**Study Questions**

1. Why does Black Nationalism become so significant after the mid-sixties?

2. Why do the Black Panthers utilize the language of the Declaration of Independence to support their demands?

3. Analyze their specific goals. Which are the most challenging to dominant American culture and why?

4. Which of these goals do you think have been achieved? Which do you think will never happen?

# THE LAWS

*Maxine Hong Kingston*

*Maxine Hong Kingston was born in 1940 to Chinese immigrant parents. She is the author of* The Woman Warrior: Memoirs of a Girlhood Among Ghosts *(1976),* China Men *(1980), and* Tripmaster Monkey: His Fake Book *(1988). The* Woman Warrior *won the National Book Critics Award in 1976; she wrote both* The Woman Warrior *and* China Men *as companion pieces, to describe the experiences of female and male immigrants to the U.S. In this essay, taken from* China Men, *she describes the history of legal oppression suffered by these immigrants.*

*The United States of America and the Emperor of China cordially recognize the inherent and inalienable right of man to change his home and allegiance, and also the mutual advantage of the free migration and emigration of their citizens and subjects respectively from the one country to the other for purposes of curiosity, of trade, or as permanent residents. Article V OF THE BURLINGAME TREATY, SIGNED IN WASHINGTON, D. C., JULY 28, 1868, AND IN PEKING, NOVEMBER 23, 1869*

*The First Years*: 1868, the year of the Burlingame Treaty, was the year 40,000 miners of Chinese ancestry were Driven Out. The Fourteenth Amendment, adopted in that same year, said that as naturalized Americans have the same rights as native-born Americans, but in 1870 the Nationality Act specified that only "free whites" and "African aliens" were allowed to apply for naturalization. Chinese were not white; this had been established legally in 1854 when Chan Young unsuccessfully applied for citizenship in Federal District Court in San Francisco and was turned down on grounds of race. (He would have been illegal one way or another anyway; the Emperor of China did not give permission for any of his subjects to leave China until 1859.) Debating the Nationality Act, Congressmen declared that America would be a nation of "Nordic fiber."

1878: California held a Constitutional Convention to settle "the Chinese problem." Of the 152 delegates, 35 were not American citizens but Europeans. The resulting constitution, voted into existence by a majority party of Working Men and Grangers, prohibited Chinese from entering California. New state laws empowered cities and counties to confine them within specified areas or to throw them out completely. Ship owners and captains were to be fined and jailed for hiring or transporting them. (This provision was so little respected that the American merchant marine relied heavily on Chinese seamen from the Civil War years to World War I.) "Mongolians, Indians, and Negroes" were barred from attending public schools. The only California fishermen forced to pay fishing and shellfish taxes were the Chinese, who had brought shrimp nets from China and started the shrimp, abalone, and lobster industries. (The taxes were payable monthly.) Those Chinese over eighteen who were not already paying a miner's tax had to say a "police tax," to cover the extra policing their presence required. Though the Chinese were filling and leveeing the San Joaquin Delta for thirteen cents a square yard, building the richest agricultural land in the world, they were prohibited from owning land or real estate. They could not apply for business licenses. Employers could be fined and jailed for hiring them. No Chinese could be hired by state, county, or municipal governments for public works. No "Chinese or Mongolian or Indian" could testify in court "either for or against a white man."

381

At this time San Francisco supplemented the anti-Chinese state laws with some of its own: a queue tax, a "cubic air ordinance" requiring that every residence have so many cubic feet of air per inhabitant, a pole law prohibiting the use of carrying baskets on poles, cigar taxes, shoe taxes, and laundry taxes.

Federal courts declared some of the state and city laws unconstitutional, and occasionally citizens of a county or city repealed an especially punitive ordinance on the grounds that it was wrong to invite the Chinese to come to the United States and then deny them a livelihood. The repealed laws were often reenacted in another form.

*1880*: The Burlingame Treaty was modified. Instead of being free, the immigration of Chinese laborers to the United States would be "reasonably limited." In return (so as not to bring about limits on American entry into China), the American government promised to protect Chinese from lynchings.

*1881*: The Burlingame Treaty was suspended for a period of twenty years. (Since 1881 there has been no freedom of travel between China and the United States). In protest against this suspension and against the refusal to admit Chinese boys to U. S. Army and Naval academies, China ordered scholars studying in the United States to return home. The act suspending the treaty did have two favorable provisions: all Chinese already resident in the United States in 1882 could stay; and they were permitted to leave and reenter with a Certificate of Return.

*1882*: Encouraged by fanatical lobbying from California, the U.S. Congress passed the first Chinese Exclusion Act. It banned the entrance of Chinese laborers, both skilled and unskilled, for ten years. Anyone unqualified for citizenship could not come in—and by the terms of the Nationality Act of 1870, Chinese were not qualified for citizenship. Some merchants and scholars were granted temporary visas.

*1884*: Congress refined the Exclusion Act with an Act to Amend an Act. This raised fines and sentences and further defined "merchants" to exclude "hucksters, peddlers, or those engaged in taking, draying, or otherwise preserving shell or other fish for home consumption or exportation."

*1888*: The Scott Act, passed by Congress, again forbade the entry of Chinese laborers. It also declared that Certificates of Return were void, Twenty thousand Chinese were trapped outside the United States with now-useless re-entry permits. Six hundred returning travelers were turned back at American ports. A Chinese ambassador, humiliated by immigration officers, killed himself. The law decreed that Certificates of Residence had to be shown on demand. Any Chinese caught without one was deported.

*1889*: Chinese pooled money to fight the various Exclusion Acts in the Courts. They rarely won. In *Chae Chan Ping v. The United States*, Chae Chan Ping argued for the validity of his Certificate of Return. The Supreme Court ruled against him, saying that "regardless of the existence of a prior treaty," a race "that will not assimilate with us" could be excluded when deemed "dangerous to . . . peace and security. . . . It matters not in what form aggression and encroachment come, whether from the foreign nation acting in its national character or from vast hordes of its people crowding in upon us." Moreover said the Court, "sojourners" should not "claim surprise" that any Certificates of Return obtained prior to 1882 were "held at the will of the government, revocable at any time, at its pleasure."

*1892*: The Geary Act extended the 1882 Exclusion Act for another ten years. It also decreed that Chinese caught illegally in the United States be deported after one year of hard labor.

Chinese Americans formed the Equal Rights League and the Native Sons of the Golden State in order to fight disenfranchisement bills. Chinese Americans demanded the right to have their citizenship confirmed before traveling abroad.

*1893*: In *Yue Ting v. The United States*, the U. S. Supreme Court ruled that Congress had the right to expel members of a race who "continue to be aliens, having taken no steps toward becoming citizens, and incapable of becoming such under the naturalization laws." This applied only to Chinese; no other race or nationality was excluded from applying for citizenship.

*1896*: A victory. In *Yick Wo v. Hopkins*, the U. S. Supreme Court overturned San Francisco safety ordinances, saying that they were indeed designed to harass laundrymen of Chinese ancestry.

*1898*: Another victory. The Supreme Court decision in *The United States v. Wong Kim Ark* stated that a person born in the United States to Chinese parents is an American. This decision has never been reversed or changed, and it is the law on which most Americans of Chinese ancestry base their citizenship today.

*1900*: Deciding *The United States v. Mrs. Cue Lim*, the Supreme Court ruled that wives and children of treaty merchants—citizens of China, aliens traveling on visas—were allowed to come to the United States.

*1904:* The Chinese Exclusion Acts were extended indefinitely, and made to cover Hawaii and the Philippines as well as the continental United States. The question of exclusion was not debated in Congress; instead, the measure passed as a rider on a routine appropriations bill. China boycotted American goods in protest.

*1906:* The San Francisco Board of Education ordered that all Chinese, Japanese, and Korean children be segregated in an Oriental school. President Roosevelt, responding to a protest from the Japanese government, persuaded the Board of Education to allow Japanese to attend white schools.

*1917:* Congress voted that immigrants over sixteen years of age be required to pass an English reading test.

*1924:* An Immigration Act passed by Congress specifically excluded "Chinese women, wives, and prostitutes." Any American who married a Chinese woman lost his citizenship; any Chinese man who married an American woman caused her to lose her citizenship. Many states had also instituted antimiscegenation laws. A Supreme Court case called *Chang Chan et al. v. John D. Nagle* tested the law against wives; Chang Chan et al. lost. For the first time, the 1924 Immigration Act distinguished between two kind of "aliens": "immigrants" were admitted as permanent residents with the opportunity to become citizens eventually; the rest—scholars, merchants, ministers, and tourists—were admitted on a temporary basis and were not eligible for citizenship. The number of persons allowed in the category of immigrant was set by law at one-sixth of one percent of the total population of that ancestry in the United States as of the 1920 census. The 1920 Census had the lowest count of ethnic Chinese in this country since 1860. As a result, only 105 Chinese immigrants were permitted each year.

In *Cheuno Sumchee v. Nagle*, the Supreme Court once again confirmed the right of treaty merchants to bring their wives to the United States. This was a right that continued to be denied to Chinese Americans.

*1938:* A Presidential proclamation lifted restriction on immigration for Chinese and nationals of a few other Asian countries. The Chinese were still ineligible for citizenship, and the quota was "100."

*1943:* The United States and China signed a treaty of alliance against the Japanese, and Congress repealed the Exclusion Act of 1882. Immigration continued to be limited to the 1924 quota of 105,

however, and the Immigration and Nationalization Service claimed to be unable to find even that many qualified Chinese. A "Chinese" was defined is anyone with more than 50 percent Chinese blood, regardless of citizenship or country of residence. At this time Japanese invaders were killing Chinese civilians in vast numbers; it is estimated that more than 10 million died. Chinese immigration into the United States did not rise.

*1946:* Congress passed the War Bride Act, enabling soldiers to bring Japanese and European wives home, then enacted a separate law allowing the wives and children of Chinese Americans to apply for entry as "non-quota immigrants." Only now did the ethnic Chinese population in the United States begin to approach the level of seventy years previous. When the first Exclusion Act was passed in 1882, there were some 107,000 Chinese here. The Acts and the Driving Out steadily reduced the number to fever than 70,000 in the 1920s.)

*1948:* The Refugee Act passed by Congress this year applied only to Europeans. A separate Displaced Persons Act provided that for a limited time—1948 to 1954—ethnic Chinese already living in the United States could apply for citizenship. During the postwar period about 10,000 Chinese were permitted to enter the country, under individual private bills passed by Congress. Confidence men, like the Citizenship Judges of old, defrauded hopeful Chinese by promising to acquire one of these bills for $1,500.

*1950:* After the Chinese Communist government took over in 1949, the United States passed a series of Refugee Relief Acts and a Refugee Escapee Act expanding the number of "non-quota immigrants" allowed in. As a condition of entry, the Internal Security Act provided that these refugees swear they were not Communists. (Several hundred "subversives or anarchists" of various races were subsequently deported; some were naturalized citizens who were "denaturalized" beforehand.)

*1952:* The Immigration and Nationality Act denied admission to "subversive and undesirable aliens" and made it simpler to deport "those already in the country." Another provision of this act was that for the first time Chinese women were allowed to immigrate under the same conditions as men.

*1954:* Ruling on *Mao v. Brownell*, the Supreme Court upheld laws forbidding Chinese Americans to send money to relatives in China. Before the Communist Revolution, there were no such restrictions in effect; Chinese Americans sent $70 million during World War II. Nor could they send money or gifts through CARE, UNESCO, or church organizations, which provided only for non-Communist countries.

*1957*: The Refugee Relief Act of 1953 expired in 1956 and was followed by the Act of 1957, which provided for the distribution of 18,000 visas that had remained unused.

*1959*: Close relatives, including parents, were allowed to enter.

*1960*: A "Fair Share Refugee Act" allowed certain refugees from Communist and Middle Eastern countries to enter. Close to 20,000 people who were "persecuted because of race, religion, or political beliefs" immigrated before this act was repealed in 1965, when a new act allowed the conditional entry of 10,200 refugees annually.

*1962*: A Presidential directive allowed several thousand "parolees" to enter the United States from Hong Kong. Relatives of citizens and resident aliens were eligible. President Kennedy gave Congress a special message on immigration saying, "It is time to correct the mistakes of the past."

*1965*: A new Immigration and Nationality Act changed the old quota system so that "national origin" no longer means "race" but "country of birth." Instead of being based on a percentage of existing ethnic populations in the United States, quotas were reallocated to countries—20,000 each. But this did not mean that 20,000 Chinese immediately could or did come to the United States. Most prospective immigrants were in Hong Kong, a British colony. Colonies received 1 percent of the mother country's allotment: only 200. "Immediate relatives," the children, spouses, and parents of citizens, however, could enter without numerical limitations. Also not reckoned within the quota limitations were legal residents returning from a visit abroad.

*1968*: Amendments to the Immigration and Nationality Act provided that immigrants not be allocated by race or nation but by hemispheres, with 120,000 permitted to enter from the Western Hemi-

sphere and 170,000 from the Eastern Hemisphere. This act limits immigration from the Western Hemisphere for the first time in history. The 20,000-per-country quota remained in effect for the Eastern Hemisphere, no per-country limitation for the Western Hemisphere.

*1976*: The Immigration and Nationality Act Amendments, also called the Western Hemisphere Bill, equalized the provisions of law regulating immigration from the two hemispheres. The House Committee on the judiciary in its report on this legislation stated, "This constitutes an essential first step in a projected long-term reform of U. S. Immigration law." The 20,000-per-country limit was extended to the Western Hemisphere. The limitation on colonies was raised from 200 to 600.

*1978*: The separate quotas for the two hemispheres were replaced by a worldwide numerical limitation on immigration of 290,000 annually. On the basis of the "immediate relatives" clause, about 22,000 Chinese enter legally each year, and the rate is increasing. There are also special quotas in effect for Southeast Asian refugees, most of whom are of Chinese ancestry. In the last decade, the ethnic Chinese population of the United States has doubled. The 1980 census may show a million or more.

## Study Questions

1. What kinds of restrictive laws are directed at Chinese-Americans?

2. Compare this essay to the Declaration of Independence. What does this essay suggest about the principles put forth in the Declaration?

3. How does the government justify these exclusionary laws? What kinds of arguments do they use?

4. How have things changed today?

# FIVE MYTHS ABOUT IMMI-GRATION

## David Cole

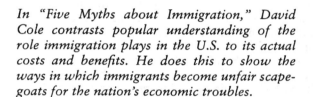

*In "Five Myths about Immigration," David Cole contrasts popular understanding of the role immigration plays in the U.S. to its actual costs and benefits. He does this to show the ways in which immigrants become unfair scapegoats for the nation's economic troubles.*

For a brief period in the mid-nineteenth century, a new political movement captured the passions of the American public. Fittingly labeled the "Know-Nothings," their unifying theme was nativism. They liked to call themselves "Native Americans," although they had no sympathy for people we call Native Americans today. And they pinned every problem in American society on immigrants. As one Know-Nothing wrote in 1856: "Four fifths of the beggary and three-fifths of the crime spring from our foreign population; more than half the public charities, more than half the prisons and almshouses, more than half the police and the cost of administering criminal justice are for foreigners."

At the time, the greatest influx of immigrants was from Ireland, where the potato famine had struck, and Germany, which was in political and economic turmoil. Anti-alien and anti-Catholic sentiments were the order of the day, especially in New York and Massachusetts, which received the brunt of the wave of immigrants, many of whom were dirt-poor and uneducated. Politicians were quick to exploit the sentiment: There's nothing like a scapegoat to forge an alliance.

I am especially sensitive to this history: My forebears were among those dirt-poor Irish Catholics who arrived in the 1860s. Fortunately for them, and me, the Know-Nothing movement fizzled within fifteen years. But its pilot light kept burning, and is turned up whenever the American public begins to feel vulnerable and in need of an enemy.

Although they go by different names today, the Know-Nothings have returned. As in the 1850s, the movement is strongest where immigrants are most concentrated: California and Florida. The objects of prejudice are of course no longer Irish Catholics and Germans; 140 years later, "they" have become "us." The new "they" because it seems "we" must always have a "they" are Latin Americans (most recently, Cubans), Haitians and Arab Americans, among others.

But just as in the 1850s, passion, misinformation and shortsighted fear often substitute for reason, fairness and human dignity in today's immigration debates. In the interest of advancing beyond know-nothingism, let's look at five current myths that distort public debate and government policy relating to immigrants.

I. America is being overrun with immigrants. In one sense, of course, this is true, but in that sense it has been true since Christopher Columbus arrived. Except for the real Native Americans, we are a nation of immigrants.

It is not true, however, that the first-generation immigrant share of our population is growing. As of 1990, foreign-born people made up only 8 percent of the population, as compared with a figure of about 15 percent from 1870 to 1920. Between 70 and 80 percent of those who immigrate every year are refugees or immediate relatives of U.S. citizens.

Much of the anti-immigrant fervor is directed against the undocumented, but they make up only 13 percent of all immigrants residing in the United States, and only 1 percent of the American population. Contrary to popular belief, most such aliens do not cross the border illegally but enter legally and remain after their student or visitor visa expires. Thus, building a wall at the border, no matter how high, will not solve the problem.

II. Immigrants take jobs from U.S. citizens. There is virtually no evidence to support this view, probably the most widespread misunderstanding about immigrants. As documented by a 1994 A.C.L.U. Immigrants' Rights Project report, numerous studies have found that immigrants actually create more jobs than they fill. The jobs immigrants take are of course easier to see, but immigrants are often highly productive, run their own businesses and employ both immigrants and citizens. One study found that Mexican immigration to Los Angeles County between 1970 and 1980 was responsible for 78,000 new jobs. Governor Mario Cuomo reports that immigrants own more than 40,000 companies in New York, which provide thousands of jobs and $3.5 billion to the state's economy every year.

III. Immigrants are a drain on society's resources. This claim fuels many of the recent efforts to cut off government benefits to immigrants. However, most studies have found that immigrants are a net benefit to the economy because, as a 1994 Urban Institute report concludes, "immigrants generate significantly more in taxes paid than they cost in services received." The Council of Economic Advisers similarly found in 1986 that "immigrants have a favorable effect on the overall standard of living."

Anti-immigrant advocates often cite studies purportedly showing the contrary, but these generally focus only on taxes and services at the local or state level. What they fail to explain is that because most taxes go to the federal government, such studies would also show a net loss when applied to U.S. citizens. At most, such figures suggest that some redistribution of federal and state monies may be appropriate; they say nothing unique about the costs of immigrants.

Some subgroups of immigrants plainly impose a net cost in the short run, principally those who have most recently arrived and have not yet "made it." California, for example, bears substantial costs for its disproportionately large undocumented population, largely because it has on average the poorest and least educated immigrants. But that has been true of every wave of immigrants that has ever reached our shores; it was as true of the Irish in the 1850s, for example, as it is of Salvadorans today. From a long-term perspective, the economic advantages of immigration are undeniable.

Some have suggested that we might save money and diminish incentives to immigrate illegally if we

denied undocumented aliens public services. In fact, undocumented immigrants are already ineligible for most social programs, with the exception of education for schoolchildren, which is constitutionally required, and benefits directly related to health and safety, such as emergency medical care and nutritional assistance to poor women, infants, and children. To deny such basic care to people in need, apart from being inhumanly callous, would probably cost us more in the long run by exacerbating health problems that we would eventually have to address.

IV. Aliens refuse to assimilate, and are depriving us of our cultural and political unity. This claim has been made about every new group of immigrants to arrive on U.S. shores. Supreme Court Justice Stephen Field wrote in 1884 that the Chinese "have remained among us a separate people, retaining their original peculiarities of dress, manners, habits, and modes of living, which are as marked as their complexion and language." Five years later, he upheld the racially based exclusion of Chinese immigrants. Similar claims have been made over different period of our history about Catholics, Jews, Italians, Eastern Europeans and Latin Americans.

In most instances, such claims are simply not true; "American culture" has been created, defined and revised by persons who for the most part are descended from immigrants once seen as anti-assimilationists. Descendants of the Irish Catholics, for example, a group once decried as separatist and alien, have become Presidents, senators and representatives (and all of these in one family, in the case of the Kennedy's). Our society exerts tremendous pressure to conform, and cultural separatism rarely survives a generation. But more important, even if this claim were true, is this a legitimate rationale for limiting immigration in a society built on the values of pluralism and tolerance?

V. Noncitizen immigrants are not entitled to constitutional rights. Our government has long declined to treat immigrants as full human beings, and nowhere is that more clear than in the realm of constitutional rights. Although the Constitution literally extends the fundamental protections in the Bill of Rights to all people, limiting to citizens only the right to vote and run for federal office, the federal government acts as if this were not the case.

In 1893 the executive branch successfully defended a statute that required Chinese laborers to establish their prior residence here by the testimony of "at least one credible white witness." The Supreme Court ruled that this law was constitutional because it was reasonable for Congress to presume that nonwhite witnesses could not be trusted.

The federal government is not much more enlightened today. In a pending case I'm handling in the Court of Appeals for the Ninth Circuit, the Clinton Administration has argued that permanent resident aliens lawfully living here should be extended no more First Amendment rights than aliens applying for first time admission from abroad that is, none. Under this view, students at a public university who are citizens may express themselves freely, but students who are not citizens can be deported for saying exactly what their classmates are constitutionally entitled to say.

Growing up, I was always taught that we will be judged by how we treat others. If we are collectively judged by how we have treated immigrants -

those who appear today to be "other" but will in a generation be "us" - we are not in very good shape.

**Study Questions**

1. Why does he articulate each of these myths?

2. How does he counteract them?

3. Why is it important that we analyze these myths?

4. Compared to the essay "The Laws," how has popular understanding of immigration changed over the years?

5. What policies or laws about immigration do you think the author would recommend?

# CIVILIZATION AND ITS DISCONTENTS

*Sigmund Freud (1856-1939)*

*Sigmund Freud was an Austrian psychologist who founded psychoanalysis (also known as "depth psychology"), the probing of the mind through the "free association" of ideas embedded in the subconscious. Freud believed that the basic nature of the human condition lay both in the continuous struggle of the individual against society, and that of the individual against the self.*

*Students will most likely connect Freud to his theory of "ego, superego, and id"-- wherein he contended that conflicting primal drives exist below the surface of human consciousness, and that these subconscious drives determine the behavior of the individual. The ego (consciousness) must negotiate the continual struggle between the id (sexuality and aggression) and the superego (conscience, or knowing the difference between right and wrong) which can result in happiness or self-destructive behavior. Freud's reasoning was contrary to the notion of his predecessors, who believed that environment is solely responsible for shaping the human consciousness.*

*The excerpt below is from Freud's 1929 book,* Civilization and Its Discontents *in which he applied his insights to the field of history. In this discourse, Freud focuses on the historical conflict between private sexual drives and the demands of civilization for cooperation. He proposes that this conflict cannot be resolved because love relationships at their height exclude all interest of other people, yet the precepts of civilization demand that all*

*members of society bond together in strong ties of friendship. The aggressive drive aggravates this conflict between sexuality and civilization.*

*During his time, one of the most powerful ideologies in existence was communism, which holds as its central premise that human nature is wholly good until corrupted by personal property (see* The Communist Manifesto*). Freud saw communism as purporting an "untenable illusion" because it taught that the abolition of private property would bring an end to ill-will and engender peaceful coexisrtence. However, for Freud, aggression is contagious and inevitable, as has been proven throughout history. Therefore, Freud ultimately concludes that it is utterly necessary to impose upon civilization ways of keeping aggressiveness and sexuality in check. While this solution inevitably makes people unhappy, it is of greater worth because it provides security for the survival of communal life.*

Psycho-analytic work has shown us that it is precisely these frustrations of sexual life which people known as neurotics cannot tolerate. The neurotic creates substitutive satisfactions for himself in his symptoms, and these either cause him suffering in themselves or become sources of suffering for him by raising difficulties in his relations with his environment and the society he belongs to. The latter fact is easy to understand; the former presents us with a new problem. But civilization demands other sacrifices besides that of sexual satisfaction.

We have treated the difficulty of cultural development as a general difficulty of development by tracing it to the inertia of the libido, to its disinclination to give up an old position for a new one. We are saying much the same thing when we derive the antithesis between civilization and sexuality from the circumstance that sexual love is a relationship between two individuals in which a third can only be superfluous or disturbing, whereas civilization depends on relationships between a considerable number of individuals. When a love-relationship is at its height there is no room left for any interest in the environment; a pair of lovers are sufficient to themselves, and do not even need the child they have in common to make them happy. In no other case does Eros so clearly betray the core of his being, his purpose of making one out of more than one; but when he has achieved this in the proverbial way through the love of two human beings, he refuses to go further.

So far, we can quite well imagine a cultural community consisting of double individuals like this, who, libidinally satisfied in themselves, are connected with one another through the bonds of common work and common interests. If this were so, civilization would not have to withdraw any energy from sexuality. But this desirable state of things does not, and never did, exist. Reality shows us that civilization is not content with the ties we have so far allowed it. It aims at binding the members of the community together in a libidinal way as well and employs every means to that end. It favours every path by which strong identifications can be established between the members of the community, and it summons up aim-inhibited libido on the largest scale so as to strengthen the communal bond by relations of friendship. In order for these aims to be fulfilled, a restriction upon sexual life is unavoidable. But we are unable to understand what the necessity is which forces civilization along this path and which causes its antagonism to sexuality. There must be some disturbing factor which we have not yet discovered.

The clue may be supplied by one of the ideal demands, as we have called them, of civilized society. It runs: 'Thou shalt love thy neighbour as thyself.' It is known throughout the world and is undoubtedly older than Christianity, which puts it forward as its proudest claim, Yet it is certainly not very old; even in historical times it was still strange to mankind. Let us adopt a naïve attitude towards it, as though we were hearing it for the first time; we shall be unable then to suppress a feeling of surprise and bewilderment. Why should we do it? What good will it do us? But, above all, how shall we achieve it? How can it be possible? My love is something valuable to me which I ought not to throw away without reflection. It imposes duties on me for whose fulfillment I must be ready to make sacrifices. If I love someone, he must deserve it

in some way (I leave out of account the use he may be to me, and also his possible significance for me as a sexual object, for neither of these two kinds of relationship comes into question where the precept to love my neighbour is concerned.) He deserves it if he is so like me in important ways that I can love myself in him; and he deserves it if he is so much more perfect than myself that I can love my ideal of my own self in him. Again, I have to love him if he is my friend's son, since the pain my friend would feel if any harm came to him would be my pain too—I should have to share it. But if he is a stranger to me and if he cannot attract me by any worth of his own or any significance that he may already have acquired for my emotional life, it will be hard for me to love him. Indeed, I should be wrong to do so, for my love is valued by all my own people as sign of my preferring them, and it is an injustice to them if I put a stranger on a par with them. But if I am to love him (with this universal love) merely because he, too, is an inhabitant of this earth, like an insect, an earth-worm or a grass-snake, then I fear that only a small modicum of my love will fall to his share—not by any possibility as much as, by the judgement of my reason, I am entitled to retain for myself. What is the point of a precept enunciated with so much solemnity if its fulfilment cannot be recommended as reasonable?

On closer inspection, I find still further difficulties. Not merely is this stranger in general unworthy of my love; I must honestly confess that he has more claim to my hostility and even my hatred. He seems not to have the least trace of love for me and shows me not the slightest consideration. If it will do him any good he has no hesitation in injuring me, nor does he ask himself whether the amount of advantage he gains bears any proportion to the extent of the harm he does to me. Indeed, he need not even obtain an advantage; if he can satisfy any sort of desire by it, he thinks nothing of jeering at me, insulting me, slandering me and showing his superior power; and the more secure he feels and the more helpless I am, the more certainly I can expect him to behave like this to me. If he behaves differently, if he shows me consideration and forbearance as a stranger, I am ready to treat him in the same way, in any case and quite apart from any precept. Indeed, if this grandiose commandment had run 'Love thy neighbour as they neighbor loves thee', I should not take exception to it. And there is a second commandment, which seems to me even more incomprehensible and arouses still stronger opposition in me. It is 'Love thine enemies'. If I think it over, however, I see that I am wrong in treating it as a greater imposition. At bottom it is the same thing. . . .

The existence of this inclination to aggression, which we can detect in ourselves and justly assume to be present in others, is the factor which disturbs our relations with our neighbour and which forces civilization into such a high expenditure [of energy]. In consequence of this primary mutual hostility of human beings, civilized society is perpetually threatened with disintegration. The interest of work in common would not hold it together; instinctual passions are stronger than reasonable interests. Civilization has to use its utmost efforts in order to set limits to man's aggressive instincts and to hold the manifestations of them in check by psychical reaction-formations. Hence, therefore, the use of methods intended to incite people into identifications and aim-inhibited relationships of love, hence the restriction upon sexual life, and hence too the ideal's commandment to love one's neighbour as oneself—a commandment which is really justified by the fact that nothing else runs so strongly counter to the original nature of man. In spite of every effort, these endeavours of civilization have not so far achieved very much. It hopes to prevent the crudest excesses of brutal violence by itself assuming the right to use violence against criminals, but the law is not able to lay hold of the more cautious and refined manifestations of human aggressiveness. The time comes when each one of us has to give up as illusions the expectations which, in his youth, he pinned upon his fellow-men, and when he may learn how much difficulty and pain has been added to his life by their ill-will. At the same time, it would be unfair to reproach civilization with trying to eliminate strife and competition from human activity. These things are undoubtedly indispensable. But opposition is not necessarily enmity; it is merely misused and made an *occasion* for enmity.

The communists believe that they have found the path to deliverance from our evils. According to them, man is wholly good and is well-disposed to his neighbour; but the institution of private property has corrupted his nature. The ownership of private wealth gives the individual power, and with it the temptation to ill-treat his neighbour; while the man who is excluded from possession is bound to rebel in hostility against his oppressor. If private property were abolished, all wealth held in common, and everyone allowed to share in the enjoyment of it, in-will and hostility would disappear among men. Since everyone's needs would be satisfied, no one would have any reason to regard another as his enemy; all would willingly undertake the work that was necessary I have no concern with any economic criticisms of the communist system; I cannot enquire into whether the abolition of private property is expedient or advantageous. But I am able to recognize that the psychological premises on which the system is based are an untenable illusion. In abolishing private property we deprive the human

love of aggression of one of its instruments, certainly a strong one, though certainly not the strongest; but we have in no way altered the differences in power and influence which are misused by aggressiveness, nor have we altered anything in its nature. Aggressiveness was not created by property. It reigned almost without limit in primitive times, when property was still very scanty, and it already shows itself in the nursery almost before property has given up its primal, anal form; it forms the basis of every relation of affection and love among people (with the single exception, perhaps, of the mother's relation to her male child). If we do away with personal rights over material wealth, there still remains prerogative in the field of sexual relationships, which is bound to become the source of the strongest dislike and the most violent hostility among men who in other respects are on an equal footing. If we were to remove this factor, too, by allowing complete freedom of sexual life and thus abolishing the family, the germ-cell of civilization, we cannot, it is true, easily foresee what new paths the development of civilization could take; but one thing we can expect, and that is that this indestructible feature of human nature will follow it there.

It is clearly not easy for men to give up the satisfaction of this inclination to aggression. They do not feel comfortable without it. The advantage which a comparatively small cultural group offers of allowing this instinct an outlet in the form of hostility against intruders is not to be despised. It is always possible to bind together a considerable number of people in love, so long as there are other people left over to receive the manifestations of their aggressiveness. I once discussed the phenomenon that it is precisely communities with adjoining territories, and related to each other in other ways as well, who are engaged in constant feuds and in ridiculing each other—like the Spaniards and Portuguese, for instance, the North Germans and South Germans, the English and Scotch, and so on. I gave this phenomenon the name of 'the narcissism of minor differences', a name which does not do much to explain it. We can now see that it is a convenient and relatively harmless satisfaction of the inclination to aggression, by means of which cohesion between the members of the community is made easier. In this respect the Jewish people, scattered everywhere, have rendered most useful services to the civilizations of the countries that have been their hosts; but unfortunately all the massacres of the Jews in the Middle Ages did not suffice to make that period more peaceful and secure for their Christian fellows. When once the Apostle Paul had posited universal love between men as the foundation of his Christian community extreme intolerance on the part of Christendom towards those who remained outside it became the inevitable consequence. To the Romans, who had not founded their communal life as a State upon love, religious intolerance was something foreign, although with them religion was a concern of the State and the State was permeated by religion. Neither was it an unaccountable chance that the dream of a Germanic world dominion called for anti-semitism as its complement, and it is intelligible that the attempt to establish a new, communist civilization in Russia should find its psychological support in the persecution of the bourgeois. One only wonders, with concern, what the Soviets will do after they have wiped out their bourgeois.

If civilization imposes such great sacrifices not only on man's sexuality but on his aggressivity, we can understand better why it is hard for him to be happy in that civilization. In fact, primitive man was better off in knowing no restrictions of instinct. To counterbalance this, his prospects of enjoying this happiness for any length of time were very slender. Civilized man has exchanged a portion of his possibilities of happiness for a portion of security. We must not forget, however, that in the primal family only the head of it enjoyed this instinctual freedom; the rest lived in slavish suppression. In that primal period of civilization, the contrast between a minority who enjoyed the advantages of civilization and a majority who were robbed of those advantages was, therefore, carried to extremes. As regards the primitive peoples who exist today, careful researches have shown that their instinctual life is by no means to be envied for its freedom. It is subject to restrictions of a different kind but perhaps of greater severity than those attaching to modern civilized man.

When we justly find fault with the present state of our civilization for so inadequately fulfilling our demands for a plan of life that shall make us happy, and for allowing the existence of so much suffering which could probably be avoided—when, with unsparing criticism, we try to uncover the roots of its imperfection, we are undoubtedly exercising a proper right and are not showing ourselves enemies of civilization. We may expect gradually to carry through such alterations in our civilization as will better satisfy our needs and will escape our criticisms. But perhaps we may also familiarize ourselves with the idea that there are difficulties attaching to the nature of civilization which will not yield to any attempt at reform. Over and above the tasks of restricting the instincts, which we are prepared for there forces itself on our notice the danger of a state of things which might be termed 'the psychological poverty of groups'. This danger is most threatening where the bonds of a society are chiefly constituted by the identification of its members with one another, while individuals of the leader type do not acquire the importance that should fall to them in the formation of a group. The present cultural state of America would give us a good opportunity for studying the damage to civilization which is thus to be feared. But I shall avoid the temptation of entering upon a critique of American civilization; I do not wish to give an impression of wanting myself to employ American methods.

### Study Question

1. In the final paragraph of this excerpt, Freud sees a potential problem inherent in America's success in forging a "collective identity." What potential problem does he see and do you think he is accurate?

# RACISM AND CULTURE

## Frantz Fanon (1925-1961

*Frantz Fanon was born in the French colony of Martinique to a middle-class family. He left Martinique in 1943, after volunteering to fight with the Free French in World War II; he remained in France after the war to study medicine and psychiatry on scholarship in Lyon.*

*Frantz Fanon is best recognized as the author of two powerful statements of anti-colonial revolutionary thought,* Black Skin, White Masks *(1952) and* The Wretched of the Earth *(1961), works which made him a prominent contributor to black American revolutionary political thought and action during the 1960s. Fanon draws on his medical and psychological training to advance the understanding that racism generates a destructive social mechanism that blinds the black man to his subjection to a universalized white norm an alienates his consciousness. To this end, a racist culture hinders psychological health in the black man.*

*The essay below is taken from an address he delivered in Paris before the first Congress of Negro Writers and Artists, which took place in 1956.*

The unilaterally decreed normative value of certain cultures deserves our careful attention. One of the paradoxes immediately encountered is the rebound of egocentric, sociocentric definitions.

There is first affirmed the existence of human groups having no culture; then of a hierarchy of cultures; and finally, the concept of cultural relativity.

We have here the whole range from overall negation to singular and specific recognition. It is precisely this fragmented and bloody history that we must sketch on the level of cultural anthropology.

There are, we must say, certain constellations of institutions, established by particular men, in the framework of precise geographical areas, which at a given moment have undergone a direct and sudden assault of different cultural patterns. The technical, generally advanced development of the social group that has thus appeared enables it to set up an organized domination. The enterprise of deculturation turns out to be the negative of a more gigantic work of economic, and even biological, enslavement.

The doctrine of cultural hierarchy is thus but one aspect of a systematized hierarchization implacably pursued.

The modern theory of the absence of cortical integration of colonial peoples is the anatomicpsychological counterpart of this doctrine. The apparation of racism is not fundamentally determining. Racism is not the whole but the most visible, the most day-to-day and, not to mince matters, the crudest element of a given structure.

To study the relations of racism and culture is to raise the question of their reciprocal action. If culture is the combination of motor and mental behavior patterns arising from the encounter of man with nature and with his fellow-man, it can be said that racism is indeed a cultural element. There are thus cultures with racism and cultures without racism.

This precise cultural element, however, has not become encysted. Racism has not managed to harden. It has had to renew itself, to adapt itself, to change its appearance. It has had to undergo the, fate of the cultural whole that informed it.

The vulgar, primitive, over-simple racism purported to find in biology—the Scriptures having proved insufficient—the material basis of the doctrine. It would be tedious to recall, the efforts then undertaken: the comparative form of the skulls, the quantity and the configuration of the folds of the brain, the characteristics of the cell layers of the cortex, the dimensions of the vertebrae, the microscopic appearance of the epiderm, etc. . . .

Intellectual and emotional primitivism appeared as a banal consequence, a recognition of existence.

Such affirmations, crude and massive, give way to a more refined argument. Here and there, however, an occasional relapse is to be noted. Thus the "emotional instability of the Negro," the "subcritical integration of the Arab," "the quasi-generic culpability of the Jew" are data that one comes upon among a few contemporary writers. The monograph by J. Carothers, for example, sponsored by the World Health Organization, invokes "scientific arguments" in support of a physiological lobotomy of the African Negro.

These old-fashioned positions tend in any case to disappear. This racism that aspires to be rational, individual, genotypically and phenotypically determined, becomes transformed into cultural racism. The object of racism is no longer the individual man but a certain form of existing. At the extreme, such terms as "message" and "cultural style" are resorted to. "Occidental values" oddly blend with the already famous appeal to the fight of the "cross against the crescent."

The morphological equation, to be sure, has not totally disappeared, but events of the past thirty years have shaken the most solidly anchored convictions, upset the checkerboard, restructured a great number of relationships.

The memory of Nazism, the common wretchedness of different men, the common enslavement of extensive social groups, the apparition of "European colonies," in other words the institution of a colonial system in the very heart of Europe, the growing awareness of workers in the colonizing and racist countries, the evolution of techniques, all this has deeply modified the problem and the manner of approaching it.

We must look for the consequences of this racism on the cultural level.

Racism, as we have seen, is only one element of a vaster whole: that of the systematized oppression of a people. How does an oppressing people behave? Here we rediscover constants.

We witness the destruction of cultural values, of ways of life. Language, dress, techniques, are devalorized. How can one account for this constant? Psychologists, who tend to explain everything by movements of the psyche, claim to discover this behavior on the level of contacts between individuals: the criticism of an original hat, of a way of speaking, of walking. . . .

Such attempts deliberately leave out of account the special character of the colonial situation. In reality the nations that undertake a colonial war have no concern for the confrontation of cultures. War is a gigantic business and every approach must be governed by this datum. The enslavement, in the strictest sense, of the native population is the prime necessity.

For this its systems of reference have to be broken. Expropriation, spoliation, raids, objective murder, are matched by the sacking of cultural patterns, or at least condition such sacking. The social panorama is destructured; values are flouted, crushed, emptied.

The lines of force, having crumpled, no longer give direction. In their stead a new system of values is imposed, not proposed but affirmed, by the heavy weight of cannons and sabers.

The setting up of the colonial system does not of itself bring about the death of the native culture. Historic observation reveals, on the contrary, that the aim sought is rather a continued agony than a total disappearance of the preexisting culture. This culture, once living and open to the future, becomes closed, fixed in the colonial status, caught in the yoke of oppression. Both present and mummified, it testifies against its members. It defines them in fact without appeal. The cultural mummification leads to a mummification of individual thinking. The apathy so universally noted among colonial peoples is but the logical consequence of this operation. The reproach of inertia constantly directed at "the native" is utterly dishonest. As though it were possible for a man to evolve otherwise than within the framework of a culture that recognizes him and that he decides to assume.

Thus we witness the setting tip of archaic, inert institutions, functioning under the oppressor's supervision and patterned like a caricature of formerly fertile institutions.

These bodies appear to embody respect for tradition, the cultural specificities, the personality of the subjugated people. This pseudorespect in fact is tantamount to the most utter contempt, to the most elaborate sadism. The characteristic of a culture is to be open, permeated by spontaneous, generous, fertile lines of force. The appointment of "reliable men" to execute certain gestures is a deception that deceives no one. Thus the Kabyle *djemaas* named by the French authority are not recognized by the natives. They are matched by another *djemaa* democratically elected. And naturally the second as a rule dictates to the first what his conduct should be.

The constantly affirmed concern with "respecting the culture of the native populations" accordingly does not signify taking into consideration the values borne by the culture, incarnated by men. Rather, this behavior betrays a determination to objectify, to confine, to imprison, to harden. Phrases such as "I know them," "that's the way they are," show this maximum objectification successfully achieved. I can think of gestures and thoughts that define these men.

Exoticism is one of the forms of this simplification. It allows no cultural confrontation. There is on the one hand a culture in which qualities of dynamism, of growth, of depth can be recognized. As against this, we find characteristics, curiosities, things, never a structure.

Thus in an initial phase the occupant establishes his domination, massively affirms his superiority. The social group, militarily and economically subjugated, is dehumanized in accordance with a polydimensional method.

Exploitation, tortures, raids, racism, collective liquidations, rational oppression take turns at different levels in order literally to make of the native an object in the hands of the occupying nation.

This object man, without means of existing, without a *raison d'être*, is broken in the very depth of his substance. The desire to live, to continue, becomes more and more indecisive, more and more phantomlike. It is at this stage that the well-known guilt complex appears. In his first novels, Wright [American writer] gives a very detailed description of it.

Progressively, however, the evolution of techniques of production, the industrialization, limited though it is, of the subjugated countries, the increasingly necessary existence of collaborators, impose a new attitude upon the occupant. The complexity of the means of production, the evolution of economic relations inevitably involving the evolution of ideologies, unbalance the system. Vulgar racism in its biological form corresponds to the period of crude exploitation of man's arms and legs. The perfecting of the means of production inevitably brings about the camouflage of the techniques by which man is exploited, hence of the forms of racism.

It is therefore not as a result of the evolution of people's minds that racism loses its virulence. No inner revolution can explain this necessity for racism to seek more subtle forms to evolve. On all sides men become free, putting an end to the lethargy to which oppression and racism had condemned them.

In the very heart of the "civilized nations" the workers finally discover that the exploitation of man, at the root of a system, assumes different faces. At this stage racism no longer dares appear without disguise. It is unsure of itself. In an ever greater number of circumstances the racist takes to cover. He who claimed to "sense," to "see through" those others, finds himself to be a target, looked at, judged. The racist's purpose has become a purpose haunted by bad conscience. He can find salvation only in a passion-driven commitment such as is found in certain psychoses. And having defined the symptomatology of such passion-charged deliria is not the least of Professor Baruk's merits.

Racism is never a super-added element discovered by chance in the course of the investigation of the cultural data of a group. The social constellation, the cultural whole, are deeply modified by the existence of racism.

It is a common saying nowadays that racism is a plague of humanity. But we must not content ourselves with such a phrase. We must tirelessly look for the repercussions of racism at all levels of sociability. The importance of the racist problem in contemporary American literature is significant. The Negro in motion pictures, the Negro and folklore, the Jew and children's stories, the Jew in the café are inexhaustible themes.

Racism, to come back to America, haunts and vitiates American culture. And this dialectical gangrene is exacerbated by the coming to awareness and the determination of millions of Negroes and Jews to fight this racism by which they are victimized.

This passion-charged, irrational, groundless phase, when one examines it, reveals a frightful visage. The movement of groups, the liberation, in certain parts of the world, of men previously kept down, make for a more and more precarious equilibrium. Rather unexpectedly, the racist group points accusingly to a manifestation of racism among the oppressed. The "intellectual primitivism" of the period of exploitation gives way to the "medieval, in fact prehistoric fanaticism" of the period of the liberation.

For a time it looked as though racism had disappeared. This soul-soothing, unreal impression was simply the consequence of the evolution of forms of exploitation. Psychologists spoke of a prejudice having become unconscious. The truth is that the rigor of the system made the daily affirmation of a superiority superfluous. The need to appeal to various degrees of approval and support, to the native's cooperation, modified relations in a less crude, more subtle, more "cultivated" direction. It was not rare, in fact, to see a "democratic and humane" ideology at this state. The commercial undertaking of enslavement, of cultural destruction, progressively gave way to a verbal mystification.

The interesting thing about this evolution is that racism was taken as a topic of meditation, sometimes even as a publicity technique.

Thus the blues—"the black slave lament"—was offered up for the admiration of the oppressors. This modicum of stylized oppression is the exploiter's and the racist's rightful due. Without oppression and without racism you have no blues. The end of racism would sound the knell of great Negro music. . . .

As the all-too-famous Toynbee might say, the blues are the slave's response to the challenge of oppression.

Still today, for many men, even colored, Armstrong's music has a real meaning only in this perspective.

Racism bloats and disfigures the face of the culture that practices it. Literature, the plastic arts, songs for shopgirls, proverbs, habits, patterns, whether they set out to attack it or to vulgarize it, restore racism. This means that a social group, a country, a civilization, cannot be unconsciously racist.

We say once again that racism is not an accidental discovery. It is not a hidden, dissimulated element. No superhuman efforts are needed to bring it out.

Racism stares one in the face for it so happens that it belongs in a characteristic whole: that of the shameless exploitation of one group of men by another which has reached a higher stage of technical development. This is why military and economic oppression generally precedes, makes possible, and legitimizes racism.

The habit of considering racism as a mental quirk, as a psychological flaw, must be abandoned.

But the men who are a prey to racism, the enslaved, exploited, weakened social group—how do they behave? What are their defense mechanisms?

What attitudes do we discover here?

In an initial phase we have seen the occupying power legitimizing its domination by scientific arguments, the "inferior race" being denied on the basis of race. Because no other solution is left it, the racialized social group tries to imitate the oppressor and thereby to deracialize itself. The "inferior race" denies itself as a different race. It shares with the "superior race" the convictions, doctrines, and other attitudes concerning it.

Having witnessed the liquidation of its systems of reference, the collapse of its cultural patterns, the native can only recognize with the occupant that "God is not on his side." The oppressor, through the inclusive and frightening character of his authority, manages to impose on the native new ways of seeing, and in particular a pejorative judgment with respect to his original forms of existing.

This event, which is commonly designated as alienation, is naturally very important. It is found in the official texts under the name of assimilation.

Now this alienation is never wholly successful. Whether or not it is because the oppressor quantitatively and qualitatively limits the evolution, unforeseen, disparate phenomena manifest themselves.

The inferiorized group had admitted, since the force of reasoning was implacable, that its misfortunes resulted directly from its racial and cultural characteristics.

Guilt and inferiority are the usual consequences of this dialectic. The oppressed then tries to escape these, on the one hand by proclaiming his total and unconditional adoption of the new cultural models, and on the other, by pronouncing an irreversible condemnation of his own cultural style.

Yet the necessity that the oppressor encounters at a given point to dissimulate the forms of exploitation does not lead to the disappearance of this exploitation. The more elaborate, less crude economic relations require a daily coating, but the alienation at this level remains frightful.

Having judged, condemned, abandoned his cultural forms, his language, his food habits, his sexual behavior, his way of sitting down, of resting, of laughing, of enjoying himself, the oppressed *flings himself* upon the imposed culture with the desperation of a drowning man.

Developing his technical knowledge in contact with more and more perfected machines, entering into the dynamic circuit of industrial production, meeting men from remote regions in the framework of the concentration of capital, that is to say, on the job, discovering the assembly line, the team, production "time," in other words yield per hour, the oppressed is shocked to find that he continues to be the object of racism and contempt.

It is at this level that racism is treated as a question of persons. "There are a few hopeless racists, but you must admit that on the whole the population likes. . . . "

With time all this will disappear.

This is the country where there is the least amount of race prejudice . . .

Films on race prejudice, poems on race prejudice, messages on race prejudice. . . .

Spectacular and futile condemnations of race prejudice. In reality, a colonial country is a racist country. If in England, in Belgium, or in France, despite the democratic principles affirmed by these respective nations, there are still racists, it is these racists who, in their opposition to the country as a whole, are logically consistent.

It is not possible to enslave men without logically making them inferior through and through. And racism is only the emotional, affective, sometimes intellectual explanation of this inferiorization.

The racist in a culture with racism is therefore normal. He has achieved a perfect harmony of economic relations and ideology. The idea that one forms of man, to be sure, is never totally dependent on economic relations, in other words—and this must not be forgotten—on relations existing historically and geographically among men and groups. An ever greater number of members belonging to racist societies are taking a position. They are dedicating themselves to a world in which racism would be impossible. But everyone is not up to this kind of objectivity, this abstraction, this solemn commitment. One cannot with impunity require of a man that he be against "the prejudices of his group.

And, we repeat, every colonialist group is racist.

"Acculturized" and deculturized at one and the same time, the oppressed continues to come up against racism. He finds this sequel illogical, what he has left behind him inexplicable, without motive, incorrect. His knowledge, the appropriation of precise and complicated techniques, sometimes his intellectual superiority as compared to a greater number of racists, lead him to qualify the racist world as passion-charged. He perceives that the racist atmosphere impregnates all the elements of the social life. The sense of an overwhelming injustice is correspondingly very strong. Forgetting racism as a consequence, one concentrates on racism as cause. Campaigns of deintoxication are

launched. Appeal is made to the sense of humanity, to love, to respect for the supreme values. . . .

Race prejudice in fact obeys a flawless logic. A country that lives, draws its substance from the exploitation of other peoples, makes those peoples inferior. Race prejudice applied to those peoples is normal.

Racism is therefore not a constant of the human spirit.

It is, as we have seen, a disposition fitting into a well-defined system. And anti-Jewish prejudice is not different from anti-Negro prejudice. A society has race prejudice or it has not. There are no degrees of prejudice. One cannot say that a given country is racist but that lynchings or extermination camps are not to be found there. The truth is that all that and still other things exist on the horizon. These virtualities, these latencies circulate, carried by the life-stream of psychoaffective, economic relations. . . .

Discovering the futility of his alienation, his progressive deprivation, the inferiorized individual, after this phase of deculturation, of extraneousness, comes back to his original positions.

This culture, abandoned, sloughed off, rejected, despised, becomes for the inferiorized an object of passionate attachment. There is a very marked kind of overvaluation that is psychologically closely linked to the craving for forgiveness.

But behind this simplifying analysis there is indeed the intuition experienced by the inferiorized of having discovered a spontaneous truth. This is a psychological datum that is part of the texture of History and of Truth.

Because the inferiorized rediscovers a style that had once been devalorized, what he does is in fact to cultivate culture. Such a caricature of cultural existence would indicate, if it were necessary, that culture must be lived, and cannot be fragmented. It cannot be had piecemeal.

Yet the oppressed goes into ecstasies over each rediscovery. The wonder is permanent. Having formerly emigrated from his culture, the native today explores it with ardor. It is a continual honeymoon. Formerly inferiorized, he is now in a state of grace.

Not with impunity, however, does one undergo domination. The culture of the enslaved people is sclerosed, dying. No life any longer circulates in it. Or more precisely, the only existing life is dissimulated. The population that normally assumes here and there a few fragments of life, which continues to attach dynamic meanings to institutions, is an anonymous population. In a colonial system these are the traditionalists.

The former emigré, by the sudden ambiguity of his behavior, causes consternation. To the anonymity of the traditionalist he opposes a vehement and aggressive exhibitionism.

The state of grace and aggressiveness are the two constants found at this stage. Aggressiveness being the passion-charged mechanism making it possible to escape the sting of paradox.

Because the former emigré is in possession of precise techniques, because his level of action is in the framework of relations that are already complex, these rediscoveries assume an irrational aspect. There is an hiatus, a discrepancy between intellectual development, technical appropriation, highly differentiated modes of thinking and of logic, on the one hand, and a "simple pure" emotional basis on the other. . . .

Rediscovering tradition, living it as a defense mechanism, as a symbol purity, of salvation, the decultured individual leaves the impression that the mediation takes vengeance by substantializing itself. This falling back on archaic positions having no relation to technical development is paradoxical. The institutions thus valorized no longer correspond to the elaborate methods of action already mastered.

The culture put into capsules, which has vegetated since the foreign domination, is revalorized. It is not reconceived, grasped anew, dynamized from within. It is shouted. And this headlong, unstructured, verbal revalorization conceals paradoxical attitudes.

It is at this point that the incorrigible character of the inferiorized is brought out for mention. Arab doctors sleep on the ground, spit all over the place, etc. . . .

Negro intellectuals consult a sorcerer before making a decision, etc. . . .

"Collaborating" intellectuals try to justify their new attitude. The customs, traditions, beliefs, formerly denied and passed over in silence are violently valorized and affirmed.

Tradition is no longer scoffed at by the group. The group no longer runs away from itself. The sense of the past is rediscovered, the worship of ancestors resumed. . . .

The past, becoming henceforth a constellation of values, becomes identified with the Truth.

This rediscovery, this absolute valorization almost in defiance of reality objectively indefensible, assumes an incomparable and subjective importance. On emerging from these passionate espousals, the native will have decided, "with full knowledge of what is involved," to fight all forms of exploitation and of alienation of man.

At this same time, the occupant, on the other hand, multiplies appeals to assimilation, then to integration, to community.

The native's hand-to-hand struggle with his culture is too solemn, too abrupt an operation to tolerate the slightest slip-up. No neologism can mask the new certainty: the plunge into the chasm of the past is the condition and the source of freedom.

The logical end of this will to struggle is the total liberation of the national territory. In order to achieve this liberation, the inferiorized man brings all his resources into play, all his acquisitions, the old and the new, his own and those of the occupant.

The struggle is at once total, absolute. But then race prejudice is hardly found to appear.

At the time of imposing his domination, in order to justify slavery, the oppressor had invoked scientific argument. There is nothing of the kind here.

A people that undertakes a struggle for liberation rarely legitimizes race prejudice. Even in the course of acute periods of insurrectional armed struggle one never witnesses the recourse to biological justifications.

The struggle of the inferiorized is situated on a markedly more human level. The perspectives are radically new. The opposition is the henceforth classical one of the struggles of conquest and of liberation.

In the course of struggle the dominating nation tries to revive racist arguments but the elaboration of racism proves more and more ineffective. There is talk of fanaticism, of primitive attitudes in the face of death, but once again the now crumbling mechanism no longer responds. Those who were once unbudgeable, the constitutional cowards, the timid, the eternally inferiorized, stiffen and emerge bristling.

The occupant is bewildered.

The end of race prejudice begins with a sudden incomprehension.

The occupant's spasmed and rigid culture, now liberated, opens at last to the culture of people who have really become brothers. The two cultures can affront each other, enrich each other.

In conclusion, universality resides in this decision to recognize and accept the reciprocal relativism of different cultures, once the colonial status is irreversibly excluded.

## Study Questions

1. How does Fanon define racism? What is its relationship to culture?

2. What is exoticism? What role does it play in Fanon's analysis?

3. Identify the methods of colonization used upon oppressed peoples, and their effects upon the individual. What does Fanon say about internalized oppression?

4. What connection(s) does Fanon draw between people of African and Jewish descent?

5. Provide examples of Fanon's theories of racism and culture that you see are evident in present-day American society. Do not restrict yourself to the African-American experience.

# THE ROSETTA STONE

## E. A. Budge (1857-1934)

*These selections from E. A. Budge's* The Rosetta Stone *(1929) serve to introduce various aspects of the writing on the stone and its value to the modern world. (1) We see a list of the young Pharaoh Ptolemy V's (205-180 BCE) benefactions to the country and people, no doubt administered by a prime minister or guardian. The benefits are to restore order and confidence after the disruptions of war. (2) This list is followed by an example in hieroglyphs and English of the gifts bestowed. (3) Then a brief gloss of the cartouche of Cleopatra which was one of the first translations made in the long process of breaking the code of the Stone. (4) An example of how a Greek name, Alexander, would be represented in hieroglyphs. Many such cartouches are being made in silver and gold for non Egyptians today. These brief examples demonstrate how the translations were begun to give us the key to unlock the mysteries of Egyptian civilizations which were, up to that point, considered incomprehensible and part of a dead civilization.*

In 1799, Napoleon's troops discovered the Rosetta Stone buried in sand in Egypt near the town, Rashid and may have stood in the temple there. Up to that time the significance of the Egyptian hieroglyphs had been lost. The Rosetta Stone was a key to unlock that mystery because the same text, some of which is described here, was inscribed in Greek (a known language) and Egyptian. It took several scholars, the eminent being Champollion, thirty years to fully translate the text. That translation opened up our knowledge of

Egyptian religion and language and launched extensive scholarship of Egyptian culture. The following selections help us to understand the decree itself, a word-for-symbol translation of some of the text, about Ptolemy V (203-181 BCE), and how an hieroglyphic name inscription is constructed. The presence of Greek as well as the Egyptian can be explained since Ptolemy was part of the dynasty begun by Alexander's general, Ptolemy, who was part of Alexander's Greek troops.

### THE ROSETTA STONE

The Decree summarizes the benefactions which Ptolemy V had bestowed upon the priesthoods, and upon the soldiers and sailors and civilians of Egypt, and orders an augmentation of the honors to be paid to the king as a token of their gratitude. The opening lines contain the date, and describe the assembling of priesthoods at Memphis, and then follows the list of the king's benefactions, which include:

1. Gifts of corn and money to the temples.

2. Gifts to the officers and men in the King's Army.

3. The remission of taxes to increase the comfort and prosperity of all classes.

4. The withdrawal of claims to arrears of taxes.

5. The release of offenders who had been in prison for a long time.

6. The restoration to the temples of sacrosanct lands and revenues.

7. The reduction of the taxes paid by the priests.

8. The abolition of the obligation of the priests to visit Alexandria annually.

9. The abolition of the press-gang for the Navy.

10. The remission of two-thirds of the tax on the byssus due from the temples to the king.

11. The restoration of peace and order throughout Egypt, and of the ceremonies connected with the worship of the gods.

12. The forgiveness of those who had rebelled, and the granting to them of permission to return to their homes, and to resume possession of their lands and property.

13. The formation of an Army and a Navy to defend Egypt at the King's expense.

14. The siege and capture of the City of Lyco-polis which had been fortified by the rebels.

15. The punishment of the ringleaders of the rebellion against Ptolemy IV Philopator, the father of the King. Some of the rebels were impaled at Memphis.

16. The remission of the contributions of corn and money due to the King from the temples, and of the tax on byssus.

17. The remission of the tax of one artaba per arura of land, and one jar of wine per arura of the vineyard.

18. The endowment of the temples of Apis and Mnevis and the other sacred animals, and payment of all charges connected with their burials, and the maintenance of their cults.

19. The maintenance of cults of the gods throughout Upper and Lower Egypt.

Among the royal names and titles which he studied were the following:—

[THE ENDOWMENTS OF APIS, MNEVIS, AND THE OTHER SACRED ANIMALS MADE BY PTOLEMY V]

*àritu-nef* *àakhu* *uru* *en* *Ḥap* *Merur* *ḥà*
He made {endow-ments} great of Apis [and] Mnevis and

R 3 *àuiu* *neb* *àakhu* *em* *heru* *er*
sacred animal every, endowments more than

*àri-sen* *en* *tep-àu* *àb-f* *àq* *her*
had made they [his] ancestors. {His heart (i.e. mind)} {went (i.e. occupying itself)} with

*sekheru(?)-sen* *em* *at (?)* *neb* *erṭa* *nef* *khet*
their plans (or, affairs) at moment every. He gave thing

*nebt* *djàr-sen*
every [which] they needed

I. CLEOPATRA .—
The Greek text of the Philae Obelisk made it certain that this cartouche contained the name of Cleopatra. YOUNG had shown that = R or L, = A, = U or O, = P, = R, and that was always added at the end of a female proper name. The two letters of unknown value were ⊿ and ⌒, and their position in the cartouche showed that they must represent K and T.

Let us assume that a king of some foreign country came to visit the king of EGYPT in predynastic times, and that the royal scribe of the day wished to record the event, and to preserve in writing the names of the foreign king and his country. To do this he would have to write down two series of pictures, the sounds of which, as words, would reproduce the sounds of the foreign names, without reference to the objects which these sounds represented. This also was the case when Egyptian hieroglyphs were concerned. Alexander, a Macedonian, became king of EGYPT, and the Eygptian scribes reproduced his name:

A—L—K—S—A—N—T—R—S.

**Study Question**

1. What is the significance of the Rosetta Stone? Why is it important for historians, linguists, world Africans and others to know of it and to understand its meaning? When and where was it discovered? How did its text correlate with other texts? Where were those texts found?

# 12

# SUNDIATA

*The first Emperor of Mali, West Africa was Sundiata (Sonjara, Sunjata, etc.) who is still celebrated today as a great culture hero whose story is still being told orally in a call-and-response style. This passage from the Johnson translation (1980) is an example of the original manner in which the griot told the epic and the audience supported the telling just as the preachers in African-American churches preach with replies coming from the congregation. Without that interaction, the griot and the preacher fail in their purpose to inspire and communicate. The West African origins of the African-American sermon in West African secular storytelling sessions is clear.*

He went to slay Nyani Mansa
Saying he was but running the dogs    Reply: That's the Truth!
Tura Magan with the army marched on.   Reply: Indeed
He slayed the Sanumu King
Saying he was but running the dogs.   Reply: Indeed

*Sundiata is acting as though the battle, slaying and final victory was only a hunting expedition; in the following selection, he is nonchalant about these considerable accomplishments. The cola (Kola) nuts offered to the triumphant marchers are symbols of hospitality and welcome. They contain a stimulant substance and are used for that purpose by today's African businessmen just as Americans drink coffee to keep alert. The Niane novelistic redaction of the Sundiata Epic ends with statesmanlike activity on Sundiata's part as he distributes the lands he had won in battle back to their original rulers who then swear loyalty to him thus constructing the new Malian Empire by the strong, effective*

*combination of conquest and diplomacy. (Niane 77-81)*

The villages of Mali gave Maghan Sundiata an unprecedented welcome. At normal times a traveller on foot can cover the distance from A-ba to Niani with only two halts, but Sogolon's son with his army took three days. The road to Mali from the river was flanked by a double human hedge. Flocking from every corner of Mali, all the inhabitants were resolved to see their saviour from close up. The women of Mali tried to create a sensation and they did not fail. At the entrance to each village they had carpeted the road with their multi-coloured pagnes so that Sundiata's horse would not so much as dirty its feet on entering their village. At the village exits the children, holding leafy branches in their hands, greeted Djata with cries of 'Wassa, Wassa, Ayé'.

Sundiata was leading the van. He had donned his costume of a hunter king—a plain smock, skin-tight trousers and his bow slung across his back. At his side Balla Fasséké was still wearing his festive garments gleaming with gold. Between Djata's general staff and the army Sosso Balla had been placed, amid his father's fetishes. But his hands were no longer tied. As at Ka-ba, abuse was everywhere heaped upon him and the prisoner did not dare look up at the hostile crowd. Some people, always ready to feel sympathy, were saying among themselves:

'How few things good fortune prizes!'

'Yes, the day you are fortunate is also the day when you are the most unfortunate, for in good fortune you cannot imagine what suffering is.'

The troops were marching along singing the 'Hymn to the Bow,' which the crowd took up. New songs flew from mouth to mouth. Young women offered the soldiers cool water and cola nuts. And so the triumphal march across Mali ended outside Niani, Sundiata's city.

It was a ruined town which was beginning to be rebuilt by its inhabitants. A part of the ramparts had been destroyed and the charred walls still bore the marks of the fire. From the top of the hill Djata looked on Niani, which looked like a dead city. He saw the plain of Sounkarani, and he also saw the site of the young baobab tree. The survivors of the catastrophe were standing in rows on the Mali road. The children were waving branches, a few young women were singing, but the adults were mute.

'Rejoice,' said Balla Fasséké to Sundiata, 'for your part you will have the bliss of rebuilding Niani, the city of your fathers, but nevermore will anyone rebuild Sosso out of its ruins. Men will lose recollection of the very site of Soumaoro's city.

With Sundiata peace and happiness entered Niani. Lovingly Sogolon's son had his native city rebuilt. He restored in the ancient style his father's old enclosure where he had grown up. People came from all the villages of Mali to settle in Niani. The walls had to be destroyed to enlarge the town, and new quarters were built for each kin group in the enormous army.

Sundiata had left his brother Manding Bory at Bagadou-Djeliba on the river. He was Sundiata's Kankoro Sigui, that is to say, viceroy. Manding Bory bad looked after all the conquered countries. When reconstruction of the capital was finished he went to wage war in the south in order to frighten the forest peoples. He received an embassy from the country of Sangaran where a few Kondé clans had settled, and although these latter had not been represented at Kouroukan Fougan, Sundiata granted his alliance and they were placed on the same footing as the Kondés of the land of Do.

After a year Sundiata held a new assembly at Niani, but this one was the assembly of dignitaries and kings of the empire. The kings and notables of all the tribes came to Niani. The kings spoke of their administration and the dignitaries talked of their kings. Fakoli, the nephew of Soumaoro, having proved himself too independent, had to flee to evade the Mansa's anger. His lands were confiscated and the taxes of Sosso were payed directly into the granaries of Niani. In this way, every year, Sundiata gathered about him all the kings and notables; so justice prevailed everywhere, for the kings were afraid of being denounced at Niani.

Djata's justice spared nobody. He followed the very word of God. He protected the weak against the strong and people would make journeys lasting several days to come and demand justice of him.

Under his sun the upright man was rewarded and the wicked one punished.

In their new-found peace the villages knew prosperity again, for with Sundiata happiness had come into everyone's home. Vast fields of millet, rice, cotton, indigo and fonio surrounded the villages. Whoever worked always had something to live on. Each year long caravans carried the taxes in kind to Niani.

You could go from village to village without fearing brigands. A thief would have his right hand chopped off and if he stole again he would be put to the sword.

New villages and new towns sprang up in Mali and elsewhere. 'Dyulas,' or traders, became numerous and during the reign of Sundiata the world knew happiness.

There are some kings who are powerful through their military strength. Everybody trembles before them, but when they die nothing but ill is spoken of them. Others do neither good nor ill and when they die they are forgotten. Others are feared because they have power, but they know how to use it and they are loved because they love justice. Sundiata belonged to this group. He was feared, but loved as well. He was the father of Mali and gave the world peace. After him the world has not seen a greater conqueror, for be was the seventh and last conqueror. He had made the capital of an empire out of his father's village, and Niani became the navel of the earth. In the most distant lands Niani was talked of and foreigners said, 'Travellers from Mali can tell lies with impunity,' for Mali was a remote country for many peoples.

The griots, fine talkers that they were, used to boast of Niani and Mali saying: 'If you want salt, go to Niani, for Niani is the camping place of the Sahel caravans. If you want gold, go to Niani, for Bouré, Bambougou and Wagadou work for Niani. If you want fine cloth; go to Niani, for the Mecca road passes by Niani. If you want fish, go to Niani, for it is there that the fishermen of Maouti and Djenné come to sell their catches. If you want meat, go to Niani, the country of the great hunters, and the land of the ox and the sheep. If you want to see an army, go to Niani, for it there that the united forces of Mali are to be found. If you want to see a great king, go to Niani, for it is there that the son of Sogolon lives, the man with two names.'

This is what the master of the spoken word used to sing.

I must mention Kita among the great cities of the empire, the city of holy water which became the second capital of the Keitas. I shall mention vanished Tabon, the iron-gated city. I shall not forget Do, nor Kri, the motherland of Sogolon, the buffalo woman. I shall also cite Koukouba, Bataniba and Kambasiga, towns of the sofas. I shall mention the town of Diaghan, Mema, the town of hospitality, and Wagadou, where the descendants of Alexander the Great used to reign. How many heaped-up ruins, how many vanished cities! How many wildernesses peopled by the spirits of great kings! The silk-cotton trees and baobabs that you see in Mali are the only traces of extinct cities.

## ETERNAL MALI

How many piled-up ruins, how much buried splendor! But all the deeds I have spoken of took place long ago and they all had Mali as their background. Kings have succeeded kings, but Mali has always remained the same.

Mali keeps its secrets jealously. There are things which the uninitiated will never know, for the griots, their depositaries, will never betray them. Maghan Sundiata, the last conqueror on earth, lies not far from Niani-Niani at Balandougou, the weir town.

After him many kings and many Mansas reigned over Mali and other towns sprang up and disappeared. Hajji Mansa Moussa, of illustrious memory, beloved of God, built houses at Mecca for pilgrims coming from Mali, but the towns which he founded have all disappeared, Karanina, Bouroun-Kouna—nothing more remains of these towns. Other kings carried Mali far beyond Djata's frontiers, for example Mansa Samanka and Fadima Moussa, but none of them came near Djata.

Maghan Sundiata was unique. In his own time no one equalled him and after him no one had the ambition to surpass him. He left his mark on Mali for all time and his taboos still guide men in their conduct.

## Study Questions

1. By what three methods did Sundiata become Emperor?

2 How is the epic normally transmitted to the people?

3. In what historic era is the Sundiata epic placed?

4. What is an epithet? What is an ideophone? ive example of each of those in Sundiata.

5. Give examples of the oral lore of the Mandeng society.

# SOCIAL CHANGE

# LIFE OF HEKTOR

*Homer (sixth century BCE)*

Hektor and His Family from the *Iliad*

*These scenes from the* Iliad, *an epic cast in elevated language featuring heroic Greek men attacking the great city of Troy, actually show Hektor, the Trojan champion, scion of the house of Priam, interacting with his family. His brother, Paris or Alexandros, has abducted Helen who was living a privileged life as the wife of Menelaus, one of the Atreides brothers. Since the abduction, during the ten years the Greeks have been fighting the war (1200 BCE). Under the leadership of his brother, Agamemnon, Paris has been living with Helen in the Palace at Troy. Hektor is impatient with his somewhat feckless brother who is not taking his place in the battle line. Helen asks Hektor to rest but he refuses, citing his responsibility to the troops battling outside. He instructs his mother to sacrifice the best woven cloths to Athena and has an intimate family visit with his wife and son. We see Hektor as a responsible family man; the fact that he is killed by the brilliant, fast-running Achilles shows us an anti-war bias on the author's part. All the realistically portrayed scenes of battle and slaughter notwithstanding, we readers realize that, in the end, war is violently destructive, tears families apart, and lays waste the constructive civilization which has been built up.*

Now, when Hektor reached the Skaian Gates
daughters and wives of Trojans rushed to greet him
with questions about friends, sons, husbands,
    brothers.
"Pray to the gods!" he said to each in turn,

as grief awaited many. He walked on
and into Priam's palace, fair and still,
made all of ashlar, with bright colonnades.
Inside were fifty rooms of polished stone
one by another, where the sons of Priam
slept beside their wives; apart from these
across an inner court were twelve rooms more
all in one line, of polished stone, where slept
the sons-in-law of Priam and their wives.
Approaching these, he met his gentle mother
going in with Laódike, most beautiful
of all her daughters. Both hands clasping his,
she looked at him and said:

                "Why have you come
from battle, child? Those fiends, the Akhaians,
    fighting
around the town, have worn you out; you come
to climb our Rock and lift your palms to Zeus
Wait, and I'll serve you honeyed wine.
First you may offer up a drop to Zeus,
to the immortal gods, then slake your thirst
Wine will restore a man when he is weary
as you are, fighting to defend your own."

Hektor answered he, his helmet flashing:

"No, my dear mother, ladle me no wine;
You'd make my nerve go slack: I'd lose my edge.
May I tip wine to Zeus with hands unwashed?
I fear to—a bespattered man, and bloody,
may not address the lord of gloomy cloud.
No, it is you I wish would bring together
our older women, with offerings, and go visit
the temple of Athêna, Hope of Soldiers.
Pick out a robe, most lovely and luxurious,
most to your liking in the women's hall;
place it upon Athêna's knees; assure her
a sacrifice of heifers, twelve young ones
ungoaded ever in their lives, if in her mercy
relenting toward our town, our wives and
    children,
she keeps Diomêdês out of holy Troy.

He is a wild beast now in combat and pursuit.
Make your way to her shrine, visit Athêna,
Hope of Soldiers.
                                    As for me, I go
for Paris, to arouse him, if he listens.
If only earth would swallow him here and now
What an affliction the Olympian
brought up for us in him—a curse for Priam
and Priam's children! Could I see that man
dwindle into Deaths night, I'd feel my soul
relieved of its distress"

So Hektor spoke, and she walked slowly on
into the mégaron. She called her maids,
who then assembled women from the city.
But Hékabê went down to the low chamber
fragrant with cedar, where the robes were kept,
embroidered work by women of Sidonia
Aléxandros had brought, that time he sailed
and ravished Helen, princess, pearl of kings.
Hékabê lifted out her loveliest robe,
most ample, most luxurious in brocade,
and glittering like starlight under all.
This offering she carried to Athêna
with a long line of women in her train.
On the Akrópolis, Athêna's shrine
was opened for them by Theanô, stately
daughter of Kisseus, wife to Antênor,
and chosen priestess of Athêna. Now
all crying loud stretched out their arms in
        prayer,
while Theanô with grace took up the robe
to place it on fair-haired Athêna's knees.
She made petition then to Zeus's daughter:
                                    "Lady,
excellent goddess, towering friend of Troy,
smash Diomêdês lance-haft! Throw him hard
below the Skaian Gates, before our eyes!
Upon this altar we'll make offering
of twelve young heifers never scarred!
Only show mercy to our town,
mercy to Trojan men, their wives and children."

These were Theanô's prayers, her vain prayers.
Pallas Athêna turned away her head.

During the supplication at the shrine,
Hektor approached the beautiful house Aléx-
        andros
himself had made, with men who in that time
were master-builders in the land of Troy.
Bedchamber, hall, and court, in the upper town,
they built for him near Priam's hall and
        Hektor's.
Now Hektor dear to Zeus went in, his hand
gripping a spear eleven forearms long,
whose bronze head shone before him in the air
as shone, around the neck, a golden ring.
He found his brother in the bedchamber

handling a magnificent cuirass and shield
and pulling at his bent-horn bow, while Helen
among her household women sat nearby,
directing needlecraft and splendid weaving.
At sight of him, to shame him, Hektor said:
"Unquiet soul, why be aggrieved in private?
Our troops are dying out there where they fight
around our city, under our high walls.
The hue and cry of war, because of you,
comes in like surf upon this town.
You'd be at odds with any other man
you might see quitting your accursed war.
Up; into action, before torches thrown
make the town flare!"

                            And shining like a god
Aléxandros replied:

                            "Ah, Hektor,
this call to order is no more than just.
So let me tell you something: hear me out.
No pettishness, resentment toward the Trojans,
kept me in this bedchamber so long,
but rather my desire, on being routed,
to taste grief to the full
                            In her sweet way
my lady rouses me to fight again-
and I myself consider it better so.
Victory falls to one man, then another.
Wait, while I put on the wargod's gear,
or else go back; I'll follow, sure to find you."

For answer, Hektor in his shining helm
said not a word, but in low tones
enticing Helen murmured:

                            "Brother dear—
dear to a whore, a nightmare of a woman!
That day my mother gave me to the world
I wish a hurricane blast had torn me away
to wild mountains, or into tumbling sea
to be washed under by a breaking wave,
before these evil clays could come!-or granted
terrible years were in the gods! design,
I wish I had had a good man for a lover
who knew the sharp tongues and just rage of
        men.
This one—his heart's unsound, and always will
        be,
and he will win what he deserves. Come here
and rest upon this couch with me, dear brother.
You are the one afflicted most
by harlotry in me and by his madness,
our portion, all of misery, given by Zeus
that we may live in song for men to come."

Great Hektor shook his head, his helmet
        flashing, and said:
                            "No, Helen, offer me no rest;
I know you are fond of me. I cannot rest.

Time presses, and I grow impatient now
to lend a hand to Trojans in the field
who feel a gap when I am gone. Your part
can be to urge him-let him feel the urgency
to join me in the city. He has time:
I must go home to visit my own people,
my own dear wife and my small son. Who
    knows
if I shall be reprieved again to see them,
or beaten down under Akhaian blows
as the immortals will."

                    He turned away
and quickly entered his own hall, but found
Princess Andrómakhê was not at home.
With one nursemaid and her small child, she
    stood
upon the tower of Ilion, in tears,
bemoaning what she saw.
              Now Hektor halted
upon his threshold, calling to the maids:

"Tell me at once, and clearly, please,
my lady Andrómakhê, where has she gone?
To see my sisters, or my brothers' wives?
Or to Athêna's temple? Ladies of Troy
are there to make petition to the goddess."

The busy mistress of the larder answered:

"Hektor, to put it clearly as you ask,
she did not go to see your sisters, nor
your brothers' wives, nor to Athêna's shrine
where others are petitioning the goddess.
Up to the great square tower of Ilion
she took her way, because she heard our men
were spent in battle by Akhaian power.
In haste, like a madwoman, to the wall
she went, and Nurse went too, carrying the
    child."

At this word Hektor whirled and left his hall,
taking the same path he had come by,
along byways, walled lanes, all through the
    town
until he reached the Skaian Cates, whereby
before long he would issue on the field.
There his warm heartd lady
came to meet him, running: Andrómakhê,
whose father, Eëtíôn, once had ruled
the land under Mount Plakos, dark with forest,
at Thebe under Plakos-lord and king
of the Kilikians. Hektor was her lord now,
head to foot in bronze; and now she joined him.
Behind her came her maid, who held the child
against her breast, a rosy baby still,
Hektoridês, the world's delight, as fresh
as a pure shining star. Skamándrios
his father named him; other men would say
Ast´yanax, "Lord of the Lower Town,"

as Hektor singlehanded guarded Troy.
How brilliantly the warrior smiled, in silence,
his eyes upon the child! Andrómakhê
rested against him, shook away a tear,
and pressed his hand in both her own, to say:

"Oh, my wild one, your bravery will be
your own undoing! No pity for our child,
poor little one, or me in my sad lot—
soon to be deprived of you! soon, soon
Akhaians as one man will set upon you
and cut you down! Better for me, without you,
to take cold earth for mantle. No more comfort,
no other warmth, after you meet your doom,
but heartbreak only. Father is dead, and
    Mother.
My father great Akhilleus killed when he
besieged and plundered Thêbê, our high town,
citadel of Kilikians. He killed him,
but, reverent at last in this, did not
despoil him. Body, gear, and weapons forged
so handsomely, he burned, and heaped a
    barrow
over the ashes. Elms were planted round
by mountain-nymphs of him who bears the
    stormcloud.
Then seven brothers that I had at home
in one day entered Death's dark place.
    Akhilleus,
prince and powerful runner, killed all seven
amid their shambling cattle and silvery sheep.
Mother, who had been queen of wooded Plakos,
he brought with other winnings home, and
    freed her,
taking no end of ransom. Artemis
the Huntress shot her in her father's house.
Father and mother—I have none but you,
nor brother, Hektor; lover none but you!
Be mercifull Stay here upon the tower!
Do not bereave your child and widow me!
Draw up your troops by the wild figtree; that
    way
the city lies most open, men most easily
could swarm the wall where it is low:
three times, at least, their best men tried it there
in company of the two called Aías, with
Idómeneus, the Atreidai, Diomêdês—
    whether someone who had it from oracles
had told them, or their own hearts urged them on."

Great Hektor in his shimmering helmet
    answered:

"Lady, these many things beset my mind
no less than yours. But I should die of shame
before our Trojan men and noblewomen
if like a coward I avoided battle,
nor am I moved to. Long ago I learned
how to be brave, how to go forward always

and to contend for honor, Father's and mine.
Honor—for in my heart and soul I know
a day will come when ancient Ilion falls,
when Priam and the folk of Priam perish.
Not by the Trojans' anguish on that day
am I so overborne in mind-the pain
of Hékabê herself, or Priam king,
or of my brothers, many and valorous,
who will have fallen in dust before our enemies-
as by your own grief, when some armed
        Akhaian
takes you in tears, your free life stripped away.
Before another woman's loom in Argos
it may be you will pass, or at Messêis
or Hypereiê fountain, carrying water,
against your will—iron constraint upon you.
And seeing you in tears, a man may say:
'There is the wife of Hektor, who fought best
of Trojan horsemen when they fought at Troy.'
So he may say—and you will ache again
for one man who could keep you out of
        bondage.
Let me be hidden dark down in my grave
before I hear your cry or know you captive!"

As he said this, Hektor held out his arms
to take his baby. But the child squirmed round
on the nurse's bosom and began to wail,
terrified by his father's great war helm-
the flashing bronze, the crest with horsehair
        plume
tossed like a living thing at every nod.
His father began laughing, and his mother
laughed as well. Then from his handsome head
Hektor lifted off his helm and bent
to place it, bright with sunlight, on the ground.
When he had kissed his child and swung him
        high
to dandle him, he said this prayer:

                                    "O Zeus
and all immortals, may this child, my son,
become like me a prince among the Trojans.
Let him be strong and brave and rule in power
at Ilion; then someday men will say
'This fellow is far better than his father!'
seeing him home from war, and in his arms
the bloodstained gear of some tall warrior slain-
making his mother proud."

                            After this prayer,
into his dear wife's arms he gave his baby,
whom on her fragrant breast
she held and cherished, laughing through her
        tears.
Hektor pitied her now. Caressing her,
he said:

            "Unquiet soul, do not be too distressed
by thoughts of me. You know no man
        dispatches me
into the undergloom against my fate;
no mortal, either, can escape his fate,
coward or brave man, once he comes to be.
Go home, attend to your own handiwork
at loom and spindle, and command the maids
to busy themselves, too. As for the war,
that is for men, all who were born at Ilion,
to put their minds on—most of all for me."

He stooped now to recover his plumed helm
as she, his dear wife, drew away, her head
turned and her eyes upon him, brimming tears.
She made her way in haste then to the ordered
house of Hektor and rejoined her maids,
moving them all to weep at sight of her.
In Hektor's home they mourned him, living still
but not, they feared, again to leave the war
or be delivered from Akhaian fury.

**Study Question**

1. What does this section of the *Iliad* show us about
Hektor? Given the scenes from Hektor's family
life, what do you think the author is saying
about war?

# 2

# THE EFFECTS OF ATOMIC BOMBS ON HIROSHIMA AND NAGASAKI

*On August 6, 1945, the United States dropped the atomic bomb on the city of Hiroshima in Japan. Shortly thereafter, a second atomic bomb was dropped on Nagasaki. The destruction of these two cities and its aftermath are described below.*

## INTRODUCTION

The available facts about the power of the atomic bomb as a military weapon lie in the story of what it did at Hiroshima and Nagasaki. Many of these facts have been published, in official and unofficial form, but mingled with distortions or errors. The United States Strategic Bombing Survey, therefore, in partial fulfillment of the mission for which it was established, has put together in these pages a fairly full account of just what the atomic bombs did at Hiroshima and Nagasaki. Together with an explanation of how the bomb achieved these effects, this report states the extent and nature of the damage, the casualties, and the political repercussions from the two attacks. The basis is the observation, measurement, and analysis of the Survey's investigators. The conjecture that is necessary for understanding of the complex phenomena and for applying the findings to the problems of defense of the United States is clearly labelled.

When the atomic bombs fell, the United States Strategic Bombing Survey was completing a study of the effects of strategic bombing on Germany's ability and will to resist. A similar study of the effects of strategic bombing on Japan was being planned. The news of the dropping of the atomic bomb gave a new urgency to this project, for a study of the air war against Japan clearly involved new weapons and new possibilities of concentration of attack that might qualify or even change the conclu-

sions and recommendations of the Survey as to the effectiveness of air power. The directors of the Survey, therefore, decided to examine exhaustively the effects of the atomic bombs, in order that the full impact on Japan and the implications of their results could be confidently analyzed. Teams of experts were selected to study the scenes of the bombings from the special points of emphasis of physical damage, civilian defense, morale, casualties, community life, utilities and transportation, various industries, and the general economic and political repercussions. In all, more than 110 men—engineers, architects, fire experts, economists, doctors, photographers, draftsmen—participated in the field study at each city, over a period of 10 weeks from October to December, 1945. Their detailed studies are now being published.

## THE EFFECTS OF THE ATOMIC BOMBINGS

### THE ATTACKS AND DAMAGE

1. *The attacks.* A single atomic bomb, the first weapon of its type ever used against a target, exploded over the city of Hiroshima at 0815 on the morning of 6 August 1945. Most of the industrial workers had already reported to work, but many workers were enroute and nearly all the school children and some industrial employees were at work in the open on the program of building removal to provide firebreaks and disperse valuables to the country. The attack came 45 minutes after the "all clear" had been sounded from a previous alert. Because of the lack of warning and the populace's indifference to small groups of planes, the explosion came as an almost complete surprise, and the people had not taken shelter. Many were caught in the open, and most of the rest in flimsily constructed homes or commercial establishments.

The bomb exploded slightly northwest of the center of the city. Because of this accuracy and the flat terrain and circular shape of the city, Hiroshima was uniformly and extensively devastated. Practically the entire densely or moderately built-up portion of the city was leveled by blast and swept by fire. A "fire-storm," a phenomenon which has occurred infrequently in other conflagrations, developed in Hiroshima: fires springing up almost simultaneously over the wide flat area around the center of the city drew in air from all directions. The inrush of air easily overcame the natural ground wind, which had a velocity of only about 5 miles per hour. The "fire-wind" attained a maximum velocity of 30 to 40 miles per hour 2 or 3 hours after the explosion. The "fire-wind" and the symmetry of the built-up center of the city gave a toughly circular shape to the 4.4 square miles which were almost completely burned out.

The surprise, the collapse of many buildings, and the conflagration contributed to an unprecedented casualty rate. Seventy to eighty thousand people were killed, or missing and presumed dead, and an equal number were injured. . . .

At Nagasaki, 3 days *later*, the city was scarcely more prepared, though vague references to the Hiroshima disaster had appeared in the newspaper of 8 August. From the Nagasaki Prefectural Report on the bombing, something of the shock of the explosion can be inferred:

*The day was clear with not very much wind— an ordinary midsummer's day. The strain of continuous air attack on the city's population and the severity of the summer had vitiated enthusiastic air raid precautions. Previously, a general alert had been sounded at 0748, with a raid alert at 0750; this was canceled at 0830, and the alertness of the people was dissipated by a great feeling of relief.*

The city remained on the warning alert, but when two B-29s were again sighted coming in the raid signal was not given immediately; the bomb was dropped at 1102 and the raid signal was given a few minutes later, at 1109. Thus only about 400 people were in the city's tunnel shelters, which were adequate for about 30 percent of the population.

*When the atomic bomb exploded, an intense flash was observed first, as though a large amount of magnesium had been ignited, and the scene grew hazy with white smoke. At the same time at the center of the explosion, and a short while later in other areas, a tremendous roaring sound was heard and a crushing blast wave and intense heat were felt. The people of Nagasaki,*

*even those who lived on the outer edge of the blast, all felt as though they had sustained a direct hit, and the whole city suffered damage such as would have resulted from direct hits everywhere by ordinary bombs.*

*The zero area, where the damage was most severe, was almost completely wiped out and for a short while after the explosion no reports came out of that area. People who were in comparatively damaged areas reported their condition under the impression that they had received a direct hit. If such a great amount of damage could be wreaked by a near miss, then the power of the atomic bomb is unbelievably great.*

In Nagasaki, no fire-storm arose, and the uneven terrain of the city confined the maximum intensity of damage to the valley over which the bomb exploded. The area of nearly complete devastation was thus much smaller; only about 1.8 square miles. Casualties were lower also; between 35,000 and 40,000 were killed, and about the same number injured. People in the tunnel shelters escaped injury, unless exposed in the entrance shaft.

Hiroshima before the war was the seventh largest city in Japan, with a population of over 340,000, and was the principal administrative and commercial center of the southwestern part of the country. As the headquarters of the Second Army and of the Chugoku Regional Army, it was one of the most important military command stations in Japan, the site of one of the largest military supply depots, and the foremost military shipping point for both troops and supplies. Its shipping activities had virtually ceased by the time of the attack, however, because of sinkings and the mining of the Inland Sea. It had been relatively unimportant industrially before the war, ranking only twelfth, but during the war new plants were built that increased its significance. These factories were not concentrated, but spread over the outskirts of the city; this location, we shall see, accounts for the slight industrial damage.

The impact of the atomic bomb shattered the normal fabric of community life and disrupted the organizations for handling the disaster. In the 30 percent of the population killed and the additional 30 percent, seriously injured were included corresponding proportions of the civic authorities and rescue groups. A mass flight from the city took place, as persons sought safety from the conflagration and a place for shelter and food. Within 24 hours, however, people were streaming back by the thousands in search of relatives and friends and to determine the extent of their property loss. Road blocks had to be set up along all routes leading into the city, to keep curious and unauthorized people out. The bulk of the dehoused population found refuge in the surrounding countryside; within the city the food supply was short and shelter virtually nonexistent.

On 7 August, the commander of the Second Army assumed general command of the counter-measures, and all military units and facilities in the area were mobilized for relief purposes. Army buildings on the periphery of the city provided shelter and emergency hospital space, and dispersed Army supplies supplemented the slight amounts of food and clothing that had escaped destruction. The need far exceeded what could be made available. Surviving civilians assisted; although casualties in both groups had been heavy, 190 policemen and over 2,000 members of the Civilian Defense Corps reported for duty on 7 August.

The status of medical facilities and personnel dramatically illustrates the difficulties facing authorities. Of more than 200 doctors in Hiroshima before the attack, over 90 percent were casualties and only about 30 physicians were able to perform their normal duties a month after the raid. Out of 1,780 nurses, 1,654 were killed or injured. Though some stocks of supplies had been dispersed, many were destroyed. Only three out of 45 civilian hospitals could be used, and two large Army hospitals were rendered unusable. Those within 3,000 feet of ground zero were totally destroyed, and the mortality rate of the occupants was practically 100 percent. Two large hospitals of reinforced concrete construction were located 4,900 feet from ground zero. The basic structures remained erect but there was such severe interior damage that neither was able to resume operation as a hospital for some time and the casualty rate was approximately 90 percent, due primarily to falling plaster, flying glass, and fire. Hospitals and clinics beyond 7,000 feet, though often remaining standing, were badly damaged and contained many casualties from flying glass or other missiles.

With such elimination of facilities and personnel, the lack of care and rescue activities at the time of the disaster is understandable; still, the eyewitness account of Father Siemes shows how this lack of first-aid contributed to the seriousness of casualties. At the improvised first-aid stations, he reports:

> ... Iodine is applied to the wounds but they are left uncleansed. Neither ointment nor other therapeutic agents are available. Those that have been brought in are laid on the floor and no one can give them any further care. What could one do when all means are lacking? Among the passersby, there are many who are uninjured. In a purposeless, insensate manner,

> distraught by the magnitude of the disaster, most of them rush by and none conceives the thought of organizing help on his own initiative. They are concerned only with the welfare of their own families—in the official aid stations and hospitals, a good third or half of those that had been brought in died. They lay about there almost without care, and a very high percentage succumbed. Everything was lacking, doctors, assistants, dressings, drugs, etc ...

Effective medical help had to be sent in from the outside, and arrived only after a considerable delay.

Fire-fighting and rescue units were equally stripped of men and equipment. Father Siemes reports that 30 hours elapsed before any organized rescue parties were observed. In Hiroshima, only 16 pieces of fire-fighting equipment were available for fighting the conflagration, three of them borrowed. However, it is unlikely that any public fire department in the world, even without damage to equipment or casualties to personnel, could have prevented development of a conflagration in Hiroshima, or combatted it with success at more than a few locations along its perimeter. The total fire damage would not have been much different.

When the atomic bomb fell, Nagasaki was comparatively intact. Because the most intense destruction was confined to the Urukami Valley, the impact of the bomb on the city as a whole was less shattering than at Hiroshima. In addition, no fire-storm occurred; indeed, a shift in wind direction helped control the fires. Medical personnel and facilities were hard-hit, however. Over 80 percent of the city's hospital beds and the Medical College were located within 3,000 feet of the center of the explosion, and were completely gutted by fire; buildings of wooden construction were destroyed by fire and blast. The mortality rate in this group of buildings was between 75 and 80 percent. Exact casualty figures for medical personnel are unknown, but the city seems to have fared better than Hiroshima: 120 doctors were at work on 1 November, about one-half of the preraid roster. Casualties were undoubtedly high: 600 out of 850 medical students at the Nagasaki Medical College were killed and most of the others injured; and of the 20 faculty members, 12 were killed and 4 others injured.

The city's repair facilities were completely disorganized by the atomic bomb, so that with the single exception of shutting off water to the affected areas no repairs were made to roads, bridges, water mains, or transportation installations by city forces. The prefecture took full responsibility for such restoration as was accomplished, delegating to the scattered city help the task of assisting in relief of victims. There were only 3 survivors of 115 employees of the street car company, and as late as the middle of November 1945 no cars were running. A week after the explosion, the water works officials made an effort to supply water to persons attempting to live in the bombedout areas, but the leakage was so great that the effort was abandoned. It fell to the prefecture, therefore, to institute recovery measures even in those streets normally the responsibility of the city. Of the entire public works construction group covering the Nagasaki city area, only three members appeared for work and a week was required to locate and notify other survivors. On the morning of 10 August, police rescue units and workers from the Kawaminami shipbuilding works began the imperative task of clearing the Omura-Nagasaki pike, which was impassable for 8,000 feet. A path 6 1/2 feet wide was cleared despite the intense heat from smouldering fires, and by 15 August had been widened to permit two-way traffic. No trucks, only rakes and shovels, were available for clearing the streets, which were filled with tile, bricks, stone, corrugated iron, machinery, plaster, and stucco. Street areas affected by blast and not by fire were littered with wood. Throughout the devastated area, all wounded had to be carried by stretcher, since no motor vehicles were able to proceed through the cluttered streets for several days. The plan for debris removal required clearance of a few streets leading to the main highway; but there were frequent delays caused by the heat of smouldering fires and by calls for relief work. The debris was simply raked and shoveled off the streets. By 20 August the job was considered complete. The streets were not materially damaged by the bomb nor were the surface or the abutments of the concrete bridges, but many of the wooden bridges were totally or partially destroyed by fire.

Under the circumstances—fire, flight of entire families, destruction of official records, mass cremation—identification of dead and the accurate count of casualties was impossible. As at Hiroshima, the season of the year made rapid disposal of bodies imperative, and mass cremation and mass burial were resorted to in the days immediately after the attack. Despite the absence of sanitary measures, no epidemics broke out here. The dysentery rate rose from 25 per 100,000 to 125 per 100,000. A census taken on 1 November 1945 found a population of 142,700 in the city.

At Nagasaki, the scale of destruction was greater than at Hiroshima, though the actual area destroyed was smaller because of the terrain and the point of fall of the bomb. The Nagasaki Prefectural Report described vividly the impress of the bomb on the city and its inhabitants:

*Within a radius of 1 kilometer from ground zero, men and animals died almost instantaneously from the tremendous blast pressure and heat; houses and other structures were smashed, crushed and scattered; and fires broke out. The strong complex steel members of the structures of the Mitsubishi Steel Works were bent and twisted like jelly and the roofs of the reinforced concrete National Schools were crumpled and collapsed, indicating a force beyond imagination. Trees of all sizes lost their branches or were uprooted or broken off at the trunk.*

*Outside a radius of 1 kilometer and within a radius of 2 kilometers from ground zero, some men and animals died instantly from the great blast and heat, but the great majority were seriously or superficially injured. Houses and other structures were completely destroyed while fires broke out everywhere. Trees were uprooted and withered by the heat.*

*Outside a radius of 2 kilometers and within a radius of 4 kilometers from ground zero, men and animals suffered various degrees of injury from window glass and other fragments scattered about by the blast and many were burned by the intense heat. Dwelling and other structures were half damaged by blast.*

*Outside a radius of 4 kilometers and within a radius of 8 kilometers from ground zero, living creatures were injured by materials blown about by the blast; the majority were only superficially wounded. Houses were half or only partially damaged.*

While the conflagration with its uniformly burnt-out area caught the attention of Hiroshima, the blast effects, with their resemblance to the aftermath of a hurricane, were most striking at Nagasaki. Concrete buildings had their sides facing the blast stove in like boxes. Long lines of steel-framed factory sheds, over a mile from ground zero, leaned their skeletons away from the explosion. Blast resistant objects such as telephone poles leaned away from the center of the explosion; on the surrounding hills trees were blown down within considerable areas. Although there was no general conflagration, fires contributed to the total damage in nearly all concrete structures. Evidence of primary fire is more frequent than at Hiroshima.

GENERAL EFFECTS

1. *Casualties.* The most striking result of the atomic bombs was the great number of casualties. The exact number of dead and injured will never be known because of the confusion after the explosions. Persons unaccounted for might have been burned beyond recognition in the falling buildings,

disposed of in one of the mass cremations of the first week of recovery, or driven out of the city to die or recover without any record remaining. No sure count of even the preraid population existed. Because of the decline in activity in the two port cities, the constant threat of incendiary raids, and the formal evacuation programs of the Government, an unknown number of the inhabitants had either drifted away from the cities or been removed according to plan. In this uncertain situation, estimates of casualties have generally ranged between 100,000 and 180,000 for Hiroshima, and between 50,000 and 100,000 for Nagasaki. The Survey believes the dead at Hiroshima to have been between 70,000 and 80,000 with an equal number injured; at Nagasaki over 35,000 dead and somewhat more than that injured seems the most plausible estimate.

Most of the immediate casualties did not differ from those caused by incendiary or high-explosive raids. The outstanding difference was the presence of radiation effects, which became unmistakable about a week after the bombing. At the time of impact, however, the causes of death and injury were flash burns, secondary effects of blast and falling debris, and burns from blazing buildings. No records are available that give the relative importance of the various types of injury, especially for those who died immediately after the explosion. Indeed, many of these people undoubtedly died several times over, theoretically, since each was subjected to several injuries, any one of which would have been fatal.

*Radiation disease.* The radiation effects upon survivors resulted from the gamma rays liberated by the fission process rather than from induced radioactivity or the lingering radio-activity of deposits of primary fission products. Both at Nagasaki and at Hiroshima, pockets of radio-activity have been detected where fission products were directly deposited, but the degree of activity in these areas was insufficient to produce casualties. Similarly, induced radio-activity from the interaction of neutrons with matter caused no authenticated fatalities. But the effects of gamma rays—here used in a general sense to include all penetrating high-frequency radiations and neutrons that caused injury—are well established, even though the Allies had no observers in the affected areas for several weeks after the explosions.

Our understanding of radiation casualties is not complete. In part the deficiency is in our basic knowledge of how radiation effects animal tissue.

According to the Japanese, those individuals very near the center of the explosion but not affected by flash burns or secondary injuries became

ill within 2 or 3 days. Bloody diarrhea followed, and the victims expired, some within 2 to 3 days after the onset and the majority within a week. Autopsies showed remarkable changes in the blood picture—almost complete absence of white blood cells, and deterioration of bone marrow. Mucous membranes of the throat, lungs, stomach, and the intestines showed acute inflammation.

The majority of the radiation cases, who were at greater distances, did not show severe symptoms until 1 to 4 weeks after the explosion, though many felt weak and listless on the following day. After a day or two of mild nausea and vomiting, the appetite improved and the person felt quite well until symptoms reappeared at a later date. In the opinion of some Japanese physicians, those who rested or subjected themselves to less physical exertion showed a longer delay before the onset of subsequent symptoms. The first signs of recurrence were loss of appetite, lassitude, and general discomfort. Inflammation of the gums, mouth, and pharynx appeared next. Within 12 to 48 hours, fever became evident. In many instances it reached only 100° Fahrenheit and remained for only a few days. In other cases, the temperature went as high as 104° or 106° Fahrenheit. The degree of fever apparently had a direct relation to the degree of exposure to radiation. Once developed, the fever was usually well sustained, and in those cases terminating fatally it continued high until the end. If the fever subsided, the patient usually showed a rapid disappearance of other symptoms and soon regained his feeling of good health. The other symptoms commonly seen were shortage of white corpuscles, loss of hair, inflammation and gangrene of the gums, inflammation of the mouth and pharynx, ulceration of the lower gastro-intestinal tract, small livid spots (petechiae) resulting from escape of blood into the tissues of the skin or mucous membrane, and larger hemorrhages of gums, nose and skin.

Loss of hair usually began about 2 weeks after the bomb explosion, though in a few instances it is reported to have begun as early as 4 to 5 days afterward. The areas were involved in the following order of frequency with variations depending on the degree of exposure: scalp, armpits, beard, pubic region, and eyebrows. Complete baldness was rare. Microscopic study of the body areas involved has shown atrophy of the hair follicles. In those patients who survived after 2 months, however, the hair has commenced to regrow. An interesting but unconfirmed report has it that loss of the hair was less marked in persons with grey hair than in those with dark hair. . . .

The effects of the bomb on pregnant women are marked, however. Of women in various stages of pregnancy who were within 3,000 feet of ground zero, all known cases have had miscarriages. Even up to 6,500 feet they have had miscarriages or premature infants who died shortly after birth. In the group between 6,500 and 10,000 feet, about one-third have given birth to apparently normal children. Two months after the explosion, the city's total incidence of miscarriages, abortions, and premature birth was 27 percent as compared with a normal rate of 6 percent. Since other factors than radiation contributed to this increased rate, a period of years will be required to learn the ultimate effects of mass radiation upon reproduction.

Treatment of victims by the Japanese was limited by the lack of medical supplies and facilities. Their therapy consisted of small amounts of vitamins, liver extract, and an occasional blood transfusion. Allied doctors used penicillin and plasma with beneficial effects. Liver extract seemed to benefit the few patients on whom it was used: It was given in small frequent doses when available. A large percentage of the cases died of secondary disease, such as septic bronchopneumonia or tuberculosis, as a result of lowered resistance. Deaths from radiation began about a week after exposure and reached a peak in 3 to 4 weeks. They had practically ceased to occur after 7 to 8 weeks.

Unfortunately, no exact definition of the killing power of radiation can yet be given, nor a satisfactory account of the sort and thickness of concrete or earth that will shield people. From the definitive report of the Joint Commission will come more nearly accurate statements on these matters. In the meanwhile the awesome lethal effects of the atomic bomb and the insidious additional peril of the gamma rays speak for themselves.

2. *Morale.* As might be expected, the primary reaction to the bomb was fear—uncontrolled terror, strengthened by the sheer horror of the destruction and suffering witnessed and experienced by the survivors. Between one-half and two-thirds of those interviewed in the Hiroshima and Nagasaki areas confessed having such reactions, not just for the moment but for some time. As two survivors put it:

*Whenever a plane was seen after that, people would rush into their shelters; they went in and out so much that they did not have time to eat. They were so nervous they could not work.*

*After the atomic bomb fell, I just couldn't stay home. I would cook, but while cooking I would always be watching out and worrying whether an atomic bomb would fall near me.*

The behavior of the living immediately after the bombings, as described earlier, clearly shows the state of shock that hindered rescue efforts. A Nagasaki survivor illustrates succinctly the mood of survivors:

*All I saw was the flash and I felt my body get warm and then I saw everything flying around. My grandmother was hit on the head by a flying piece of roof and she was bleeding. . . . I became hysterical seeing my grandmother bleeding and we just ran around without knowing what to do.*

*I was working at the office. I was talking to a friend at the window. I saw the whole city in a red flame, then I ducked. The pieces of the glass hit my back and face. My dress was torn off by the glass. Then I got up and ran to the mountain where the good shelter was.*

The two typical impulses were these: Aimless, even hysterical activity or flight from the city to shelter and food.

**Study Questions**

1. After reading this selection, what is your understanding of inhumanity in the world?

2. Research the events that led up to the decision to drop the atomic bomb on Hiroshima and Nagasaki. Do you think the United States was justified in this decision? Why?

3. What role do you think race and culture played in the decision to drop the atomic bomb.

# WHEN HEAVEN AND EARTH CHANGED PLACES

*Le Ly Hayslip*

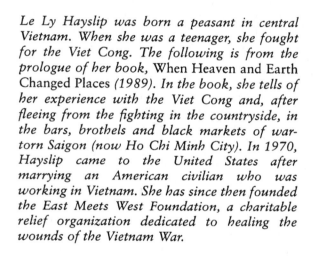

*Le Ly Hayslip was born a peasant in central Vietnam. When she was a teenager, she fought for the Viet Cong. The following is from the prologue of her book,* When Heaven and Earth Changed Places *(1989). In the book, she tells of her experience with the Viet Cong and, after fleeing from the fighting in the countryside, in the bars, brothels and black markets of war-torn Saigon (now Ho Chi Minh City). In 1970, Hayslip came to the United States after marrying an American civilian who was working in Vietnam. She has since then founded the East Meets West Foundation, a charitable relief organization dedicated to healing the wounds of the Vietnam War.*

Everything I knew about the war I learned as a teenaged girl from the North Vietnamese cadre leaders in the swamps outside Ky La. During these midnight meetings, we peasants assumed everything we heard was true because what the Viet Cong said matched, in one way or another, the beliefs we already had.

The first lesson we learned about the new "American" war was why the Viet Cong was formed and why we should support it. Because this lesson came on the heels of our war with the French (which began in 1946 and lasted, on and off, for eight years), what the cadre leaders told us seemed to be self-evident.

First, we were taught that Vietnam was *con rong chau tien*—a sovereign nation which had been held in thrall by Western imperialists for over a century. That all nations had a right to determine their own destiny also seemed beyond dispute, since we farmers subsisted by our own hands and felt we owed nothing to anyone but god and our ancestors for the right to live as we saw fit. Even the Chinese, who had made their own disastrous attempt to rule Vietnam in centuries past, had learned a painful lesson about our country's zeal for independence. "Vietnam," went the saying that summarized their experience, "is nobody's lapdog."

Second, the cadres told us that the division of Vietnam into North and South in 1954 was nothing more than a ploy by the defeated French and their Western allies, mainly the United States, to preserve what influence they could in our country.

"*Chia doi dat nuoc?*" the Viet Cong asked, "Why should outsiders divide the land and tell some people to go north and others south? If Vietnam were truly for the Vietnamese, wouldn't we choose for ourselves what kind of government our people wanted? A nation cannot have *two* governments," they said, "any more than a family can have two fathers."

Because those who favored America quickly occupied the seats of power formerly held by the French, and because the North remained pretty much on its own, the choice of which side best represented independence was, for us, a foregone conclusion. In fact, the Viet Cong usually ended our indoctrination sessions with a song that played on our worst fears:

Americans come to kill our people,
Follow America, and kill your relatives!
The smart bird flies before it's caught.
The smart person comes home before Tet.
Follow us, and you'll always have a family.
Follow America, and you'll always be alone!

After these initial "lessons," the cadre leaders introduced us to the two Vietnamese leaders who personified each view—the opposite poles of our tiny world. On the South pole was President Ngo Dinh Diem, America's staunch ally, who was Catholic like the French. Although he was idolized by many who said he was a great humanitarian and patriot, his religion alone was enough to make him suspicious to Buddhists on the Central Coast. The loyalty we showed him, consequently, was more duty to a landlord than love for a founding father. Here is a song the Republican schoolteachers made us learn to praise the Southern president:

> In stormy seas, Vietnam's boat rolls and pitches.
> Still we must row; our President's hand upon
>     the helm.
> The ship of state plows through heavy seas,
> Holding fast its course to democracy.
> Our President is celebrated from Europe to
>     Asia,
> He is the image of philanthropy and love.
> He has sacrificed himself for our happiness.
> He fights for liberty in the land of the Viet.
> Everyone loves him earnestly, and behind him
>     we will march
> Down the street of freedom, lined with fresh
>     flowers,
> The flag of liberty crackling above our heads!

In the North, on the other pole, was Ho Chi Minh, whom we were encouraged to call *Bac Ho*—Uncle Ho—the way we would refer to a trusted family friend. We knew nothing of his past beyond stories of his compassion and his love for our troubled country—the independence of which, we were told, he had made the mission of his life.

Given the gulf between these leaders, the choice of whom we should support again seemed obvious. The cadre leaders encouraged our natural prejudices (fear of outsiders and love of our ancestors) with stirring songs and tender stories about Uncle Ho in which the Communist leader and our ancient heroes seemed to inhabit one congenial world. Like an unbroken thread, the path from our ancestors and legends seemed to lead inevitably to the Northern leader—then past him to a future of harmony and peace.

But to achieve that independence, Ho said, we must wage total war. His cadremen cried out "We must hold together and oppose the American empire. There is nothing better than freedom, independence, and happiness!"

To us, these ideas seemed as obvious as everything else we had heard. *Freedom* meant a Vietnam free of colonial domination. *Independence* meant one Vietnamese people—not two countries, North and South—determining its own destiny. *Happiness* meant plenty of food and an end to war—the ability, we assumed, to live our lives in accordance with our ancient ways. We wondered: how can the Southerners oppose these wonderful things? The answer the Viet Cong gave us was that the Republicans prized Yankee dollars more than the blood of their brothers and sisters. We did not think to question with our hearts what our minds told us must be true.

Although most of us thought we knew what the Viet Cong meant by freedom, independence, and happiness, a few of us dared to ask what life the Northerners promised when the war was over. The answer was always the same: "Uncle Ho promises that after our victory, the Communist state will look after your rights and interests. Your highest interest, of course, is the independence of our fatherland and the freedom of our people. Our greatest right is the right to determine our own future as a state." This always brought storms of applause from the villagers because most people remembered what life was like under the French.

Nonetheless, despite our vocal support, the Viet Cong never took our loyalty for granted. They rallied and rewarded and lectured us sternly, as the situation demanded, while the Republicans assumed we would be loyal because we lived south of a line some diplomats had drawn on a map. Even when things were at their worst—when the allied forces devastated the countryside and the Viet Cong themselves resorted to terror to make us act the way they wanted—the villagers clung to the vision the Communists had drummed into us. When the Republicans put us in jail, we had the image of, "Communist freedom"—freedom from war—to see us through. When the Viet Cong executed a relative, we convinced ourselves that it was necessary to bring "Communist happiness"—peace in the village—a little closer. Because the Viet Cong encouraged us to voice our basic human feelings through patriotic songs, the tortured, self-imposed silence we endured around Republicans only made us hate the government more. Even on those occasions when the Republicans tried to help us, we saw their favors as a trick or sign of weakness. Thus, even as we accepted their kindness, we despised the Republicans for it.

As the war gathered steam in the 1960s, every villager found his or her little world expanded—usually for the worse. The steady parade of troops through Ky La meant new opportunities for us to fall victim to outsiders. Catholic Republicans spurned and mistreated Buddhists for worshiping their ancestors. City boys taunted and cheated the country bumpkins" while Vietnamese servicemen from other provinces made fun of our funny accents and strange ways. When the tactics on both sides got so rough that people were in danger no matter which side they favored, our sisters fled to the cities where they learned about liquor, drugs, adultery, materialism, and disrespect for their ancestors. More than one village father died inside when a "stranger from Saigon" returned in place of the daughter he had raised.

In contrast to this, the Viet Cong were, for the most part, our neighbors. Even though our cadre leaders had been trained in Hanoi, they had all been born on the Central Coast. They did not insult us for our manners and speech because they had been raised exactly like us. Where the Republicans came into the village overburdened with American equipment designed for a different war, the Viet Cong made do with what they had and seldom wasted their best ammunition—the goodwill of the people. The cadremen pointed out to us that where the Republicans wore medals, the Viet Cong wore rags and never gave up the fight. "Where the Republicans pillage, rape, and plunder," they said, "we preserve your houses, crops, and family"; for they knew that it was only by these resources—our food for rations, our homes for hiding, our sons and brothers for recruits—that they were able to keep the field.

Of course, the Viet Cong cadremen, like the Republicans, had no desire (or ability, most of them) to paint a fairer picture. For them, there could be no larger reason for Americans fighting the war than imperialist aggression. Because we peasants knew nothing about the United States, we could not stop to think how absurd it would be for so large and wealthy a nation to covet our poor little country for its rice fields, swamps, and pagodas. Because our only exposure to politics had been through the French colonial government (and before that, the rule of Vietnamese kings), we had no concept of democracy. For us, "Western culture" meant bars, brothels, black markets, and *xa hoi van minh*— bewildering machines—most of them destructive. We couldn't imagine that life in the capitalist world was anything other than a frantic, alien terror. Because, as peasants, we defined "politics" as something other people did someplace else, it had no relevance to our daily lives—except as a source of endless trouble. As a consequence, we overlooked the power that lay in our hands: our power to achieve virtually anything we wanted if only we acted together. The Viet Cong and the North, on the other hand, always recognized and respected this strength.

We children also knew that our ancestral spirits demanded we resist the outsiders. Our parents told us

of the misery they had suffered from the invading Japanese ("small death," our neighbors called them) in World War II, and from the French, who returned in 1946. These soldiers destroyed our crops, killed our livestock, burned our houses, raped our women, and tortured or put to death anyone who opposed them—as well as many who did not. Now, the souls of all those people who had been mercilessly killed had come back to haunt Ky La—demanding revenge against the invaders. This we children believed with all our hearts. After all, we had been taught from birth that ghosts were simply people we could not see.

There was only one way to remove this curse. Uncle Ho had urged the poor to take up arms so that everyone might be guaranteed a little land on which to cultivate some rice. Because nearly everyone in Central Vietnam was a farmer, and because farmers must have land, almost everyone went to war: with a rifle or a hoe; with vigilance to give the alarm; with food and shelter for our fighters; or, if one was too little for anything else, with flowers and songs to cheer them up. Everything we knew commanded us to fight. Our ancestors called us to war. Our myths and legends called us to war. Our parents' teachings called us to war. Uncle Ho's cadre called us to war. Even President Diem had called us to fight for the very thing we now believe he was betraying—an independent Vietnam. Should an obedient child be less than an ox and refuse to do her duty?

And so the war began and became an insatiable dragon that roared around Ky La. By the time I turned thirteen, that dragon had swallowed me up.

## Study Questions

1. At the end of Hayslip's selection, she says, "And so the war began and became an insatiable dragon that roared around Ky La. By the time I turned thirteen, that dragon had swallowed me up." How does Hayslip attempt to explain the origins of the Vietnam War in the countryside and why peasants fought for the Viet Cong?

2. The Vietnam War was a cross-cultural encounter between the Americans and the Vietnamese. Hayslip offers the perspective of Vietnamese villagers on the arrival of "Western culture" in their country. What can you learn about the nature and meaning of the war by taking this perspective into account?

# REPORT

## Donald Barthelme

*Donald Barthelme was a writer and Professor of Creative Writing at the University of Houston. He also was in the Army in Korea and Japan, which provides some of the impetus for this story, published in 1968 at the beginning of the Vietnam War. His works include several collections of short stories, and the novels* Snow White *(1967) and* The Dead Father *(1975).*

Our group is against the war. But the war goes on. I was sent to Cleveland to talk to the engineers. The engineers were meeting in Cleveland. I was supposed to persuade them not to do what they are going to do. I took United's 4:45 from LaGuardia arriving in Cleveland at 6:13. Cleveland is dark blue at that hour. I went directly to the motel, where the engineers were meeting. Hundreds of engineers attended the Cleveland meeting. I noticed many fractures among the engineers, bandages, traction. I noticed what appeared to be fracture of the carpal scaphoid in six examples. I noticed numerous fractures of the humeral shaft, of the os calcis of the pelvic girdle. I noticed a high incidence of clay-shoveller's fracture. I could not account for these fractures. The engineers were making calculations, taking measurements, sketching on the black board, drinking beer, throwing bread, buttonholing employers, hurling glasses into the fireplace. They were friendly.

They were friendly. They were full of love and information. The chief engineer wore shades. Patella in Monk's traction, clamshell fracture by the look of it. He was standing in a slum of beer bottles and microphone cable. "Have some of this chicken a la Isambard Kingdom Brunel[1] the Great Ingineer," he said. "And declare who you are and what we can do for you. What is your line, distinguished guest?"

[1] 19th century British engineer.

"Software," I said. "In every sense. I am here representing a small group of interested parties. We are interested in your thing, which seems to be functioning. In the midst of so much dysfunction, function is interesting. Other people's things don't seem to be working. The State Department's thing doesn't seem to be working. The U.N.'s thing doesn't seem to be working. The democratic left's thing doesn't seem to be working. Buddha's thing -"

"Ask us anything about our thing, which seems to be working," the chief engineer said. "We will open our hearts and heads to you, Software Man, because we want to be understood and loved by the great lay public, and have our marvels appreciated by the public, for which we daily unsung produce tons of new marvels each more life-enhancing than the last. Ask us anything. Do you want to know about evaporated thin-film metallurgy? Monolithic and hybrid integrated-circuit processes? The algebra of inequalities? Optimization theory? Complex high-speed micro-miniature closed and open loop systems? Fixed variable mathematical cost searches? Epitaxial deposition of semiconductor materials. Gross interfaced space gropes? We also have specialists in the cukooflower, the doctorfish, and the dumdum bullet as these relate to aspects of today's expanding technology, and they do in the damnedest ways."

I spoke to him then about the war. I said the same things people always say when they speak against the war. I said that the war was wrong. I said that large countries should not burn down small countries. I said that the government had made a series of errors. I said that these errors once small and forgivable were now immense and unforgivable. I said that the government was attempting to conceal its original errors under layers of new errors. I said that the government was sick with

error, giddy with it. I said that ten thousand of our
soldiers had already been killed in pursuit of the
government's errors. I said that tens of thousands of
the enemy's soldiers and civilians had been killed
because of various errors, ours and theirs. I said that
we are responsible for errors made in our name. I
said that the government should not be allowed to
make additional errors.

"Yes, yes," the chief engineer said, "there is
doubtless much truth in what you say, but we can't
possibly *lose* the war, can we? And stopping is
losing, isn't it? The war regarded as a process,
stopping regarded as an abort? We don't know *how*
to lose a war. That skill is not among our skills. Our
array smashes their array, that is what we know.
That is the process. That is what is."

"But let's not have any more of this dispir-
iting downbeat counterproductive talk. I have a few
new marvels here I'd like to discuss with you just
briefly. A few new marvels that are just about ready
to be gaped at by the admiring layman. Consider for
instance the area of realtime online computer-
controlled wish evaporation. Wish evaporation is
going to be crucial in meeting the rising expectations
of the world's peoples, which are as you know rising
entirely too fast."

I noticed then distributed about the room a
great many transverse fractures of the ulna. "The
development of the pseudo-ruminant stomach for
underdeveloped peoples," he went on, "is one of
our interesting things you should be interested in.
With the pseudoruminant stomach they can chew
cuds, that is to say, eat grass. Blue is the most
popular color worldwide and for that reason we are
working with certain strains of your native
Kentucky *Poa pratensis*, or bluegrass, as the staple
input for the p/r stomach cycle, which would also
give a shot in the arm to our balance-of-payments
thing don't you know..." I noticed about me then a
great number of metatarsal fractures in banjo
splints. "The kangaroo initiative...eight hundred
thousand harvested last year...highest percentage of
edible protein of any herbivore yet studied..."

"Have new kangaroos been planted?"

The engineer looked at me.

"I intuit your hatred and jealousy of our
thing," he said. "The ineffectual always hate our
thing and speak of it as anti-human, which is not at
all a meaningful way to speak of our thing. Nothing
mechanical is alien to me," he said (amber spots
making bursts of light in his shades), "because I am
human, in a sense, and if I think it up, then 'it' is
human too, whatever 'it' may be. Let me tell you,
Software Man, we have been damned forbearing in

the matter of this little war you declare yourself to
be interested in. Function is the cry, and our thing is
functioning like crazy. There are things we could do
that we have not done. Steps we could take that we
have not taken. These steps are, regarded in a
certain light, the light of our enlightened self-
interest, quite justifiable steps. We could, of course,
get irritated. We could, of course, *lose patience*.

"We could, of course, release thousands
upon thousands of self-powered crawling-along-the-
ground lengths of titanium wire eighteen inches long
with diameter of .0005 centimeters (that is to say,
invisible) which, scenting an enemy, climb up his
trouser leg and wrap themselves around his neck.
We have developed those. They are within our capabilities. We could, of course, release in the arena of
the upper air our new improved pufferfish toxin
which precipitates an identity crisis. No special technical problems there. That is almost laughably easy.
We could, of course, place up to two million
maggots in their rice within twenty-four hours. The
maggots are ready, massed in secret staging areas in
Alabama. We have hypodermic darts capable of pie-
balding the enemy's pigmentation. We have rots,
blights, and rusts capable of attacking his alphabet.
Those are dandies. We have a hut-shrinking
chemical which penetrates the fibers of the bamboo,
causing it, the hut, to strangle its occupants. This
operates only after 10 p.m., when people are
sleeping. Their mathematics are at the mercy of a
suppurating surd we have invented. We have a
family of fishes trained to attack their fishes. We
have the deadly testicle-destroying telegram. The
cable companies are cooperating. We have a green
substance, that, well, I'd rather not talk about. We
have a secret word that, if pronounced, produces
multiple fractures in all living things in an area the
size of four football fields."

"That's why -"

"Yes. Some damned fool couldn't keep his
mouth shut. The point is that the whole structure of
enemy life is within our power to *rend, violate,
devour, and crush*. But that's not the interesting
thing."

"You recount these possibilities with
uncommon relish."

"Yes I realize that there is too much relish
here. But you must realize that these capabilities
represent in and of themselves highly technical and
complex and interesting problems and hurdles on
which our boys have expended many thousands of
hours of hard work and brilliance. And that the
effects are often grossly exaggerated by the irresponsible victims. And that the whole thing represents a

fantastic series of triumphs for the multi-disciplined problem-solving team concept."

"I appreciate that."

"We could unleash all this technology at once. You can imagine what would happen then. But that's not the interesting thing."

"What is the interesting thing?"

"The interesting thing is that we have a moral sense. It is on punched cards, perhaps the most advanced and sensitive moral sense the world has ever known."

"Because it is on punched cards?"

"It considers all considerations in endless and subtle detail," he said.

"It even quibbles. With this great new moral tool, how can we go wrong? I confidently predict that, although we *could* employ all this splendid new weaponry I've been telling you about, *we're not going to do it*."

"We're not going to do it?"

I took United's 5:44 from Cleveland arriving at Newark at 7:19. New Jersey is bright pink at that hour. Living things move about the surface of New Jersey at that hour molesting each other only in traditional ways. I made my report to the group. I stressed the friendliness of the engineers. I said, It's all right. I said, We have a moral sense. I said, *We're not going to do it.* They didn't believe me.

## Study Questions

1. What does this article say about the relationship between technology and war?

2. What is the tone of this story? is the author serious or humorous? Explain.

3. What attitudes toward war do the characters express? Do you see any examples of these attitudes in the American public today? Explain.

4. This story was first published during the Vietnam War. What is this story saying about this war specifically and war in general?

5. How do the characters understand morality? What is their morality? What is the morality of war?

# NONVIOLENCE AND SOCIAL CHANGE (1967)

## Martin Luther King, Jr. (1929-1968)

*Martin Luther King, Jr. is one of the world's best-known advocates of non-violent social change strategies. While his roots were in the African-American Baptist tradition, he drew from many cultural sources including the ideas of Ghandi and the Boston school of philosophy known as personalism. He graduated from Morehouse College and Boston university. In 1955 while pastor of the Dexter Avenue Baptist Church in Montgomery, Alabama, he helped launch the Civil Rights Movement by becoming a leader of the boycott of the segregated city busses of Montgomery. King expanded this protest movement in 1957 when he and other black ministers formed the Southern Christian Leadership Conference (SCLC).*

*His early efforts concentrated on ending segregation and obtaining voting rights for African-Americans. This excerpt comes from a radio lecture he gave for the Canadian Broadcasting Corporation in 1967 and included in the book, (The Trumpet of Conscience 1967). In these essays his critique of American society has deepened and enlarged. In this period of his life he spoke out against the Vietnam War and against the very social and economic structures of America. He was assassinated on April 4, 1968, while seeking to assist a garbage worker's strike in Memphis.*

There is nothing wrong with a traffic law which says you have to stop for a red light. But when a fire is raging, the fire truck goes right through that red light, and normal traffic had better get out of its way. Or, when a man is bleeding to death, the ambulance goes through those red lights at top speed.

There is a fire raging now for the Negroes and the poor of this society. They are living in tragic conditions because of the terrible economic injustices that keep them locked in as an "underclass," as the sociologists are now calling it. Disinherited people all over the world are bleeding to death from deep social and economic wounds. They need brigades of ambulance drivers who will have to ignore the red lights of present system until the emergency is solved.

Massive civil disobedience is a strategy for social change which is at least as forceful as an ambulance with its siren on full. In the past ten years, nonviolent civil disobedience has made a great deal of history, especially in the Southern United States. When we and the Southern Christian Leadership Conference went to Birmingham, Alabama, in 1963, we had decided to take action on the matter of integrated public accommodations. We went knowing that the Civil Rights Commission had written powerful documents calling for change, calling for the very rights we were demanding. But nobody did anything about the Commission's report. Nothing was done until we acted on these very issues, and demonstrated before the court of world opinion the urgent need for change. It was the same story with voting rights. The Civil Rights Commission, three years before we went to Selma, had recommended the changes we started marching for, but nothing was done until, in 1965, we created a crisis the nation couldn't ignore. Without violence, we totally disrupted the system, the life style of Birmingham, and then of Selma, with their unjust and unconstitutional laws. Our Birmingham struggle came to its dramatic climax when some 3,500 demonstrators virtually filled every jail in that city and surrounding communities, and some 4,000 more continued to march and demonstrate nonviolently. The city knew then in terms that were crystal-clear that Birmingham could no longer continue to function until the demands of the Negro community were met. The same kind of dramatic crisis was created in Selma two years later. The result on the national scene was the Civil Rights Bill and the Voting Rights Act, as President and Congress responded to the drama and the creative tension generated by the carefully planned demonstrations.

Of course, by now it is obvious that new laws are not enough. The emergency we now face is economic, and it is a desperate and worsening situation. For the 35 million poor people in America—not even to mention, just yet, the poor in the other nations—there is a kind of strangulation in the air. In our society it is murder, psychologically, to deprive a man of a job or an income. You are in substance saying to that man that he has no right to exist. You are in a real way depriving him of life, liberty, and the pursuit of happiness, denying in his case the very creed of his society. Now, millions of people are being strangled that way. The problem is international in scope. And it is getting worse, as the gap between the poor and the "affluent society" increases.

The question that now divides the people who want radically to change that situation is: can a program of nonviolence—even if it envisions massive civil disobedience—realistically expect to deal with such an enormous, entrenched evil?

First of all, will nonviolence work, psychologically, after the summer of 1967? Many people feel that nonviolence as a strategy for social change was cremated in the flames of the urban riots of the last two years. They tell us that Negroes have only now begun to find their true manhood in violence; that the riots prove not only that Negroes hate whites, but that, compulsively, they must destroy them.

This blood-lust interpretation ignores one of the most striking features of the city riots. Violent they certainly were. But the violence, to a startling degree, was focused against property rather than against people. There were very few cases of injury to persons, and the vast majority of the rioters were not involved at all in attacking people. The much publicized "death toll" that marked the riots, and the many injuries, were overwhelmingly inflicted on the rioters by the military. It is clear that the riots were exacerbated by police action that was designed to injure or even to kill people. As for the snipers, no account of the riots claims that more than one or two dozen people were involved in sniping. From the facts, an unmistakable pattern emerges: a

handful of Negroes used gunfire substantially to intimidate, not to kill; and all of the other participants had a different target—property.

I am aware that there are many who wince at a distinction between property and persons—who hold both sacrosanct. My views are not so rigid. A life is sacred. Property is intended to serve life, and no matter how much we surround it with rights and respect, it has no personal being. It is part of the earth man walks on; it is not man.

The focus on property in the 1967 riots is not accidental. It has a message; it is saying something.

If hostility to whites were ever going to dominate a Negro's attitude and reach murderous proportions, surely it would be during a riot. But this rare opportunity for bloodletting was sublimated into arson, or turned into a kind of stormy carnival of free-merchandise distribution. Why did the rioters avoid personal attacks? The explanation cannot be fear of retribution, because the physical risks incurred in the attacks on property were no less than for personal assaults. The military forces were treating acts of petty larceny as equal to murder. Far more rioters took chances with their own lives, in their attacks on property, than threatened the life of anyone else. Why were they so violent with property then? Because property represents the white power structure, which they were attacking and trying to destroy. A curious proof of the symbolic aspect of the looting for some who took part in it is the fact that, after the riots, police received hundreds of calls from Negroes trying to return merchandise they had taken. Those people wanted the experience of taking, of redressing the power imbalance that property represents. Possession, afterward, was secondary.

A deeper level of hostility came out in arson, which was far more dangerous than the looting. But it, too, was a demonstration and a warning. It was directed against symbols of exploitation, and it was designed to express the depth of anger in the community.

What does this restraint in the summer riots mean for our future strategy?

If one can find a core of nonviolence toward persons, even during the riots when emotions were exploding, it means that nonviolence should not be written off for the future as a force in Negro life. Many people believe that the urban Negro is too angry and too sophisticated to be nonviolent. Those same people dismiss the nonviolent marches in the South and try to describe them as processions of pious, elderly ladies. The fact is that in all the marches we have organized some men of very violent tendencies have been involved. It was routine for us to collect hundreds of knives from our own ranks before the demonstrations, in case of momentary weakness. And in Chicago last year we saw some of the most violent individuals accepting nonviolent discipline. Day after day during those Chicago marches I walked in our lines and I never saw anyone retaliate with violence. There were lots of provocations, not only the screaming white hoodlums lining the sidewalks, but also groups of Negro militants talking about guerrilla warfare. We had some gang leaders and members marching with us. I remember walking with the Blackstone Rangers while bottles were flying from the sidelines, and I saw their noses being broken and blood flowing from their wounds; and I saw them continue and not retaliate, not one of them, with violence. I am convinced that even very violent temperaments can be channeled through nonviolent discipline, if the movement is moving, if they can act constructively and express through an effective channel their very legitimate anger.

But even if nonviolence can be valid, psychologically, for the protesters who want change, is it going to be effective, strategically, against a government and a status quo that have so far resisted this summer's demands on the grounds that "we must not reward the rioters"? Far from rewarding the rioters, far from even giving a hearing to their just and urgent demands, the administration has ignored its responsibility for the causes of the riots, and instead has used the negative aspects of them to justify continued inaction on the underlying issues. The administration's only concrete response was to initiate a study and call for a day of prayer. As a minister, I take prayer too seriously to use it as an excuse for avoiding work and responsibility. When a government commands more wealth and power than has ever been known in the history of the world, and offers no more than this, it is worse than blind, it is provocative. It is paradoxical but fair to say that Negro terrorism is incited less on ghetto street corners than in the halls of Congress.

I intended to show that nonviolence will be effective, but not until it has achieved the massive dimensions, the disciplined planning, and the intense commitment of a sustained, direct-action movement of civil disobedience on the national scale.

The dispossessed of this nation—the poor, both white and Negro—live in a cruelly unjust society. They must organize a revolution against that injustice, not against the lives of the persons who are their fellow citizens, but against the structures through which the society is refusing to take means which have been called for, and which are at hand, to lift the load of poverty.

The only real revolutionary, people say, is a man who has nothing to lose. There are millions of poor people in this country who have very little, or even nothing, to lose. If they can be helped to take action together, they will do so with a freedom and a power that will be a new and unsettling force in our complacent national life. Beginning in the New Year, we will be recruiting three thousand of the poorest citizens from ten different urban and rural areas to initiate and lead a sustained, massive, direct-action movement in Washington. Those who choose to join this initial three thousand, this nonviolent army, this "freedom church" of the poor, will work with us for three months to develop nonviolent action skills. Then we will move on Washington, determined to stay there until the legislative and executive branches of the government take serious and adequate action on jobs and income. A delegation of poor people can walk into a high official's office with a carefully, collectively prepared list of demands. (If you're poor, if you're unemployed anyway, you can choose to stay in Washington as long as the struggle needs you.) And if that official says, "But Congress would have to approve this," or, "But the President would have to be consulted on that," you can say, "All right, we'll wait." And you can settle down in his office for as long a stay as necessary. If you are, let's say, from rural Mississippi, and have never had medical attention, and your children are undernourished and unhealthy, you can take those little children into the Washington hospitals and stay with them there until the medical workers cope with their needs, and in showing it your children you will have shown this country a sight that will make it stop in its busy tracks and think hard about what it has done. The many people who will come and join this three thousand, from all groups in the country's life, will play a supportive role, deciding to be poor for a time along with the dispossessed who are asking for their right to jobs or income—jobs, income, the demolition of slums, and the rebuilding by the people who live there of new communities in their place; in fact, a new economic deal for the poor.

Why camp in Washington to demand these things? Because only the federal Congress and administration can decide to use the billions of dollars we need for a real war on poverty. We need, not a new law, but a massive, new national program. This Congress has done nothing to help such measures, and plenty to hinder them. Why should Congress care about our dying cities? It is still dominated by senior representatives of the rural South, who still unite in an obstructive coalition with unprogressive Northerners to prevent public funds from going where they are socially needed. We broke that coalition in 1963 and 1964, when the

Civil Rights and Voting Rights laws were passed. We need to break it again by the size and force of our movement, and the best place to do that is before the eyes and inside the buildings of these same Congressmen. The people of this country, if not the Congressmen, are ready for a serious economic attack on slums and unemployment, as two recent polls by Lou Harris have revealed. So we have to make Congress ready to act on the plight of the poor. We will prod and sensitize the legislators, the administrators, and all the wielders of power until they have faced this utterly imperative need.

I have said that the problem, the crisis we face, is international in scope. In fact, it is inseparable from an international emergency which involves the poor, the dispossessed, and the exploited of the whole world.

Can a nonviolent, direct-action movement find application on the international level, to confront economic and political problems? I believe it can. It is clear to me that the next stage of the movement is to become international. National movements within the developed countries—forces that focus on London, or Paris, or Washington, or Ottawa— must help to make it politically feasible for their governments to undertake the kind of massive aid that the developing countries need if they are to break the chains of poverty. We in the West must bear in mind that the poor countries are poor primarily because we have exploited them through political or economic colonialism. Americans in particular must help their nation repent of her modern economic imperialism.

But movements in our countries alone will not be enough. In Latin America, for example, national reform movements have almost despaired of nonviolent methods; many young men, even many priests, have joined guerrilla movements, in the hills. So many of Latin America's problems have roots in the United States of America that we need to form a solid, united movement, nonviolently conceived and carried through, so that pressure can be brought to bear on the capital and government power structures concerned, from both sides of the problem at once. I think that may be the only hope for a nonviolent

solution in Latin America today; and one of the most powerful expressions of nonviolence may come out of that international coalition of socially aware forces, operating outside governmental frameworks.

Even entrenched problems like the South African Government and its racial policies could be tackled on this level. If just two countries, Britain and the United States, could be persuaded to end all economic interaction with the South African regime, they could bring that government to its knees in a relatively short time. Theoretically, the British and American governments could make that kind of decision; almost every corporation in both countries has economic ties with its government which it could not afford to do without. In practice, such a decision would represent such a major reordering of priorities that we should not expect that any movement could bring it about in one year or two. Indeed, although it is obvious that nonviolent movements for social change must internationalize, because of the interlocking nature of the problems they all face, and because otherwise those problems will breed war, we have hardly begun to build the skills and the strategy, or even the commitment, to planetize our movement for social justice.

In a world facing the revolt of ragged and hungry masses of God's children; in a world torn between the tensions of East and West, white and colored, individualists and collectivists; in a world whose cultural and spiritual power lags so far behind her technological capabilities that we live each day on the verge of nuclear co-annihilation; in this world, nonviolence is no longer an option for intellectual analysis, it is an imperative for action.

### Study Question

1. How does King inform and instruct his readers while at the same time defending his actions? Provide examples of the effectiveness of King's argument.

# 6

# YOM HASHOAH, YOM YERUSHALAYIM: A MEDITATION

*Irena Klepfisz*

*Irene Klepfisz currently teaches Women's Studies at Barnard College. She is a Jewish lesbian poet and activist who has written several books, including* A Few Words in the Mother Tongue *(1990). The essay comes from her 1990 book,* Dreams of an Insomniac: Jewish Feminism Essays, Speeches, and Diatribes. *In this essay, she discusses her visits to Jerusalem and her commitment to ending the hostility between Israel and Palestine.*

In the winter of 1984-85 I traveled with Melanie Kaye/Kantrowitz to Israel and a lot of my confusion abated. Our trip had a specific purpose: to find material from progressive Israeli women for a book we were co-editing, *The Tribe of Dina: A Jewish Women's Anthology.* Melanie and I made contact with Israeli activists, met Israeli lesbians, visited the West Bank. The situation at that time was very bleak, worse than we had imagined. We had expected to find a strong, energetic Left movement. But the recent Israeli elections had placed Meier Kahane in the Knesset, and Labor and Likud had been forced into a paralyzing coalition. We found most people were depressed, frustrated, unclear what direction to take. We paid tribute to the Holocaust by visiting *Yad Vashem* and later learned of the bitter anger of the Sephardim about the way the Holocaust of European Jews was memorialized and the oppression of Arab Jews ignored. I was particularly impressed with this as I listened to Sephardic women describe their experiences and their treatment by Ashkenazis. On the West Bank we found, not surprisingly, Palestinians living in Palestinian cities. Hebron, Ramallah, Bir Zeit—how could anyone claim these were Jewish territories?

The Jewish settlements, surrounded by barbed wire, seemed bizarre, out of place. Though I had understood the politics of this long before, the trip made the politics more concrete.

Despite this, I came back more knowledgeable, more solidly grounded in my belief that it was possible to be strongly Jewish identified, to believe in the necessity of the State of Israel, and to fight for Palestinian rights. The activists that I met gave me confidence that a peace movement existed, that many Israelis wanted the establishment of a Palestinian state and that they needed American Jewish support. I also felt a new, strong connection to Israeli activists, particularly the feminists and lesbians. The trip was a turning point in my commitment to the issue of peace in Israel and in Palestine. I had moved very far from that night at Womanbooks.

The 1984 trip was not my first. I had been to Israel in 1963. I stayed with my friend Pearl, whom I had met when she was studying in the States. Like me, Pearl was born in Poland and was a child survivor of the Holocaust. Pearl had once told me that when her family first settled in Israel, they were given a house, and that for weeks, perhaps months, after they moved in, a Palestinian woman would come and sit on the steps and weep. It had been her home.

Pearl's story brings the Holocaust again to the forefront in dealing with Israeli politics. Jewish survivors and Palestinians who are stateless press against each other although I would wish them to become disentangled; the powerful lessons each evokes and teaches me remain intertwined.

I was particularly conscious of this in 1987 when I attended the International Women Writers Conference in Jerusalem. Toward the end of my

437

Israeli activists, particularly the feminists and lesbians. The trip was a turning point in my commitment to the issue of peace in Israel and in Palestine. I had moved very far from that night at Womanbooks.

The 1984 trip was not my first. I had been to Israel in 1963. I stayed with my friend Pearl, whom I had met when she was studying in the States. Like me, Pearl was born in Poland and was a child survivor of the Holocaust. Pearl had once told me that when her family first settled in Israel, they were given a house, and that for weeks, perhaps months, after they moved in, a Palestinian woman would come and sit on the steps and weep. It had been her home.

Pearl's story brings the Holocaust again to the forefront in dealing with Israeli politics. Jewish survivors and Palestinians who are stateless press against each other although I would wish them to become disentangled; the powerful lessons each evokes and teaches me remain intertwined.

I was particularly conscious of this in 1987 when I attended the International Women Writers Conference in Jerusalem. Toward the end of my stay, a group of American and Israeli Jewish writers and I met with two Palestinian women in East Jerusalem. One of them had been in Nairobi in 1985. She, like the Palestinian woman in Pearl's story, was born in a neighborhood in which one of the Israelis was living, a neighborhood now completely Jewish. During our meeting, the Palestinian women asked us to promote the cause of their people. I was deeply moved by this encounter and by the knowledge that women who had attended the Nairobi conference had been affected by it and were now trying to make contact with Jewish women. The next day I took a tour of the Jewish settlements around Jerusalem. I was shocked at their size; they were cities, fortresses. I realized for the first time that the term "settlement" was a euphemism.

This last trip took place in April, the month when Jews commemorate the Holocaust. While there, I became aware that the Israelis were already preparing to "celebrate" the twentieth anniversary of the reunification of Jerusalem. I saw the two holidays as symbolic and wanted to put them in perspective. I remembered what the Palestinian woman had said: "Write about what you see. Write what is happening to us." And I did.

### Yom Hashoah, Yom Yerushalayim (1987)

*In late April, Israeli Jews and Jews all over the world observed Yom Hashoah, the day commemorating the Holocaust, the murder of their six million.*

*As a Jewish child-survivor born in Warsaw during the war, mourning the Holocaust is an important part of my yearly cycle. Coming in the beginning of spring it reaffirms my belief that Jews need a safe homeland in a world that for centuries has proved hostile; it makes me consider once more the enormity of our loss, the irretrievability, and the moral lessons to be drawn for the present and future.*

*One of these is that the cry "Never Again!" applies not only to ourselves but to others. Never again are we Jews to be deprived of the life, culture and religion we choose to be ours; never again are any other people to be deprived of their life, culture and religion.*

*Yet as we move toward summer, as Peres and Shamir struggle for power, as peace and security for all in the Middle East remain elusive, the Israeli government prepares for another holiday on June 5, Yom Yerushalayim—the reunification of Jerusalem. That this day is designated for celebration ought to cause deep sorrow, for Yom Yerushalayim veils a reality that should be mourned—the twentieth anniversary of the Israeli military occupation of the West Bank.*

*I know that there are American Jews and allies who deny out of fear and shame the validity of the term "military occupation." Yet as hard as it is for those of us who are rooted in our Jewish communities who share a commitment to Jewish survival and a Jewish state, we need to use this term openly.*

*The Israeli military occupation is just that: the Palestinians on the West Bank are under military law, without a civil judicial system, frequently denied rights to lands on which they and their ancestors were born. Like any military occupation, the Israeli one is brutal and arbitrary. It arrests and detains without charges hundreds of "suspicious" civilians. In twenty years, it has generated over a thousand regulations, which only recently were coded, published and made available by Raja Shehadeh, the Palestinian attorney. Like in military occupation, the aim is to divest the occupied of will, collective identity, and cultural autonomy. This is done through the disruption of daily life, the control of educational institutions, and the systematic degradation of the Palestinian people. Predictably, the response and counter-response have been escalating violence and oppression.*

*One insidious example: The act of tree planting, so cherished by American Jews as a way of supporting Israeli and Jewish aspirations for nurture and stability, has been perverted. Today on the West Bank, the presence of olive trees is often considered illegal. Palestinian orchards, as well as newly-planted trees, are being uprooted and transplanted on Israeli soil. Why? If the land remains uncultivated for three years, the Israeli government can claim it. If the land sports no house, it too can be claimed; and if there is a house, the house may be bulldozed. Land on the West Bank is slowly being dragged from Palestinian control. Slowly, slowly push "them" back and back until the land is empty—as some have pretended it was from the start.*

*Need I say that this contradicts what I have always been taught were Jewish values: the sense of justice, of legal order, of respect for other human beings, the necessity for culture, roots, and self-determination? And we need to keep hold of this contradiction as we move from Yom Hashoah toward Yom Yerushalayim to remind ourselves that the six million who died were ordinary men, women, and children who simply wanted to go on with their lives and were not permitted to do so.*

*Yet it is in their name that both the U.S. and Israeli governments (for different reasons) justify current Israeli policies on the West Bank and thereby deny the decent and ordinary life that each Palestinian, like any other human being, yearns for. American Jews and non-Jews must recognize that the invocation of the Holocaust by our government does not necessarily express a concern for Jewish survival. Certainly the Iran/contra affair has proven the cynicism with which U.S. policy makers regard Israel—a puppet that carries out actions declared illegal by the Congress.*

*During a recent trip to Israel with a friend who was visiting for the first time, I saw a dramatic enactment of the way the Holocaust is pitted against the occupation. On her last afternoon, my friend was given two choices: to tour Yad Vashem, Israel's museum and research center for the Holocaust, or to tour the "settlements"—a euphemism for the stone fortresses that ring Jerusalem outside the Green Line. There was not time for both. In this instance, the forced choice between honoring and mourning our dead and acknowledging and addressing present wrongs was simply a matter of bad planning.*

*Both the American and Israeli governments present us with a similar false choice. They play upon real fear of genocide and desire for security and they press us to choose "us or them." They pretend that the military occupation on the West Bank is somehow an answer to Yad Vashem. It is not, for the last twenty years have brought neither safety nor security. Sabras, Holocaust survivors, and later refugees fleeing anti-Semitism have lost sons and daughters in the struggle to contain the Palestinians. Hardly a single Israeli Jewish family has been spared. And the violence continues.*

*Some will consider my words disloyal to Jews and to Israelis. But many Israeli Jews acknowledge*

*these things openly. In April, more than twenty thousand Israelis and Palestinians came to a peace festival in Neve Shalom, the Israeli Arab/Jewish town, to express their support of the possibility of Jews and Palestinians living in peace. In May, Arab and Jewish university students together protested discriminatory tuition charges. Most American Jews and allies ignore such realities. They ignore the very present, if splintered, peace movement in Israel made up of more than fifty Arab/Israeli and Palestinian Jewish peace organizations that are groping toward a nonviolent, political solution (a fact rarely discussed in the American media). They forget that thousands of Israelis do not want to see another generation killed or maimed, but want peace now and an end to the present occupation; they forget that many of these Israelis support self-determination for Palestinians side by side with Jews. Our loyalty should be to these Israelis and Jews, for they are the repositories of the values we call Jewish.*

*Some maintain that you can't talk to the Palestinians; they're all terrorists. Yet talks between Israelis and the PLO have been going on for years; it is only governmental hypocrisy that obscures this reality, most recently with the government choosing to press charges against Israelis who met openly with PLO representatives in Rumania.*

*I have also heard many urge the Palestinians simply to emigrate to other Arab countries. This shows ignorance of (or disrespect for) the political and cultural diversity of the Middle East. Would anyone suggest to Swedes that they resettle in Norway because it too is a Scandinavian country?*

*Other debates about Israel focus on innocence. But there has been so much violence on both sides that such debates have no meaning. The issue is no longer who is to blame, is most innocent, or has fanned the hostilities. The issue is to recognize the undeniable fact that the Israeli military has wielded power over the West Bank for the past twenty years and that it must stop.*

## THE JEWISH WOMEN'S COMMITTEE TO END THE OCCUPATION

In April 1988, exactly a year after my trip to Israel, I helped found a new political group, the Jewish Women's Committee to End the Occupation of the West Bank and Gaza. It happened like this: since the *intifada* began in December 1987, there were intensified efforts to pressure Israel to withdraw from the Territories and to recognize a Palestinian state. In February, New Jewish Agenda had staged a protest opposite the Israeli Consulate in mid-Manhattan. A short time later we heard news of Beita, where Israeli teenagers had been protected by Palestinian villagers from extremists. This did not stop the Israeli Defense Forces from blowing up houses in the village in retaliation for the death of an Israeli teenager who had been shot by her Israeli guard after he had been hit by a stone thrown by a Palestinian. Grace Paley called me and wanted to stage a vigil in protest. I was unenthusiastic. We'd hold the vigil and the next day we would read of more outrageous actions.

In analyzing my response, I realized that an ongoing vigil might be more effective because the situation was continuous. Clare Kinberg from New Jewish Agenda and Grace agreed. We were, however, unclear about the makeup of our vigil. Should it be just women, or men and women together? That week, Lil Moed, peace activist in Israel, gave a talk at Agenda's office and brought news of the work of two Israeli women's groups: Women in Black, who were holding weekly vigils in front of Shamir's house protesting Israel's actions in response to the *intifada*, and SHANI, Israeli Women's Alliance Against the Occupation. It made sense to organize an American Jewish women's vigil in solidarity with Israeli women working for peace.

That is the genesis of the Committee. We needed endorsements for the first flyer, so I began calling Jewish women in New York City. Everyone on the list was already sympathetic, so I did not hesitate to state our position: end the violence now, support an international peace conference and a two-state solution. But whenever I had to say what we were actually going to do, I would take a deep breath, for our weekly Monday night vigils were to be held at 515 Park Avenue, the offices of the Conference of Presidents of Major American Jewish organizations, an organization that claims to speak for American Jewry and always endorses Israeli government action in regard to the Occupied Territories. I knew the deep feelings most Jews—including myself—have about public criticism of other Jews even when they disagree with them.

By selecting the Conference offices as the site of the protest, we had decided that instead of pressuring Israel directly, we would pressure the established American Jewish community that promotes, justifies and supports the policies of the Israeli government. American Jews need to start dealing with their involvement with Israeli policies. Given the support American Jews extend to Israel, we cannot claim neutrality on this question.

So, within a space of six days, the Jewish Women's Committee was formed and on Monday, April 25 at 5 o'clock, the day after the first major Jewish rally protesting Israeli policies in the Occupied Territories, eleven Jewish women—a number of them lesbians—gathered in front of the offices of the Conference of Presidents. At first it all seemed just like other demonstrations. You confer with the police, establish the rules about where you stand and where you leaflet. You approach people. Some take the lavender flyer, some don't. Some Jews don't like it and crumple it in disgust. All of this was expected.

What I did not expect was the intensity with which my doubts kept surfacing. I did not doubt for one moment that the occupation in Gaza and the West Bank and the second-class status of Palestinians within the Green Line were evils to be struggled against. No extenuating circumstances could justify morally what we had witnessed during the past five months of the *intifada*—Palestinians (many of them children) killed, maimed, illegally imprisoned and tortured, their homes demolished, their schools and shops closed. Yet despite my conviction that these evils had to be stopped, I found that standing in front of a Jewish organization, publicly questioning its integrity was not easy. A number of Jews came by and asked. "Aren't you ashamed?" and I wondered if what we were doing was right. In the past, I had always felt secure in my devotion to my Jewishness, to the Jewish people; I had never felt shame. Yet standing on line those first few weeks, I felt shame over what Israel was doing and also some shame about myself. This was a sense of my Jewishness that was completely new to me.

The confusion I felt during the initial vigils was intense. But equally intense was my reaction to those Jews who insisted on referring to the Holocaust, insisted that the Holocaust precluded our taking this kind of political action. Their fears and anger were unqualified. That first day a Jewish man came up to me and said: "I wish you were buried in Poland like my parents." Other Jews also wished another Holocaust upon us. Still others said our action would only lead all Jews, including us, "back to the ovens." Over and over again, in one form or another, we were told that the vigil was not only disloyal, but a form of collaboration with contemporary and historical Nazis. We were told that to give the Palestinians a state was to give Hitler his final victory, that our behavior was desecrating the Holocaust of the 1940s and ensuring the Holocaust of the 1990s, perhaps even the 1980s. I was stunned and offended by these extreme remarks, but I did not find them ridiculous. Shame was a new feeling for me as a Jew, but, like the Jews who cursed us, fear has been my Jewish companion for as long as I can remember, and I understand its power. I soon came to recognize that the strange mixture of both shame and fear was the basis of a new aspect of my Jewishness, a mixture that brought into stark relief my feelings about Israel and about my background as a survivor.

I want to come to grips with this mixture, the shame, the fear and also the anger, for I have a lot of anger toward the Jewish community. It's a community I fight for and deeply love, but which, I remind myself, loves me only conditionally. I need to remind myself how I feared this community's rejection when I first came out as a lesbian. My being a child survivor, my family's activism in the Jewish underground during the war, my own strong attachment to Yiddish and activism in promoting *yidishkayt* and strong Jewish identity—none of these were sufficient armor against homophobia. Today I feel I have gained acceptance, but it was a tough process; I have scars and remember with bitterness many moments of pain.

The vigil brought new fears and anger to the surface. At the big April 24th Passover Peace rally I had feared the counter demonstrators and their propensity toward violence. They screamed with such venom, such hatred for others—Arabs, Palestinians, Jews who disagree with them. They were ready to send us all to gas chambers and relished the idea. These Jews deliberately evoked fear: "Think, be like us—or die!" My fear of these Jews, the militant right, is rational. They are dangerous.

But I fear not only these Jews; I fear also those kinder Jews who taught me my moral and political lessons, and this fear is more difficult to describe and explain. Do not speak ill of a Jew in public, they taught; and I have always obeyed. The command had nothing to do with social graces or pride. It was a command meant to help me get through life more safely. Publicly criticizing Jews gives fuel to the anti-Semites and endangers the Jewish community. It's a centuries-old rule for survival. Backed by the knowledge that anti-Semitism can turn into the Holocaust, the rule has even greater force for us in the post-Holocaust era than it did for our parents and grandparents. Anyone who breaks the rule places the Jewish people in danger and shows lack of respect and love for them. The response must be murderous rage. By participating in a vigil in front of the Conference of Presidents, I break the rule. I am afraid of the rage this may unleash as well as the unintended danger it might bring to Israel. After all, I might be wrong.

But the tangle of emotions does not end here, for I also fear history. I fear that I will misinterpret the present and not recognize my rightful role. This is a fear I have had all my life. Knowing that the world was passive and indifferent while six million Jews died, I have always considered passivity and indifference the worst of evils. Those who do nothing, I believe are good Germans, collaborators. I do not want to be a collaborator.

So in trying to determine the right actions for myself in regard to Israel, I too leap to the Holocaust for analogies and models, and I am trapped. On the one hand, I face the wrath of my own people; on the other, the wrath of history. I don't know how to find a balance. I want to be able to act with conscience, I want to remain part of the community. I don't know how to decide, how to feel certain and centered in my decision. These are the knots of feelings that emerged in the early days of our vigils as I listened to the remarks and arguments of passersby and staff workers from the building.

In reviewing my feelings, am I being finicky? Palestinians are dying. Israel seems ready to break apart. Jews and Israelis worry about possible civil war. Should I be spending time examining my Jewish fears? I think I should because they remind me I have not left the tribe, that I am not as far from some of those Jews who confront us on line as I would like to think. I have to understand their emotions if I ever hope to reach them. They form the bond that connects us across the great political chasm that separates us. To deal with the Israeli/Palestinian situation effectively, I need to calm their fears as much as I need to calm my own. I need to convince them of what I have to convince myself again and again. That Jews must choose and risk for peace. That we must choose justice despite our fears. That our fears are real, rooted in history, but that they cannot control us or stop us from making just choices.

## CHOICES

During the Holocaust, choice was the nightmare. Whether through direct order by a Nazi or through the tangled strategies for survival, making decisions-who to take on a journey, who to leave behind, to set out early or late—was always the nightmare.

When I was little, I asked my mother over and over: "If the Nazis made you choose between me and my father, who would you choose to be killed?" At age ten I had absorbed the full horror of the choices Jews faced—of the life-death choices. I knew the idea of the third way was myth, romance. Someone stood and pointed and said: "*Choose! Choose now or they both die!*" I was, of course, testing my mother, trying to find out how much she loved me. In my fantasy, I mistakenly thought she had power. "And if you had to choose between me and Elza," I would persist, "who would you pick?" Elza, orphaned daughter of family friends, my almost-sibling and, therefore, a rival for my mother's love "*Pick me! Pick me!*" my ten-year-old heart would beat and yearn, never fully understanding what it was I was asking, but clearly tapping the core of the Holocaust nightmare.

For most of my life, making decisions has been fraught with tensions way beyond what others regard as appropriate. I frequently experience as crisis what seems much simpler for other people. It is a psychology rooted in the past, not the present. It is something I need to watch.

Have Jews in the Diaspora and Israel permanently adopted this life/death psychology? Are we unable to see the present for what it is? Are we always looking at it through the immediate past, through the Holocaust? Is this why we do not perceive that the third way is not myth, that there *is* a third way in Israel, that there must be?'

## Study Questions

1. What is a secular Jewish identity? Why would it be significant? What does being Jewish mean to Klepfisz?

2. What role does the Holocaust play here? Why is it such a foundational aspect of contemporary Jewish identity.

3. Why does she spend so much time discussing Palestine? Why is it significant?

4. Why does she see the choice between Palestine and the Holocaust as a "false choice"?

5. Why does she focus particularly on the U.S.'s role in the Israel-Palestine conflict? What are the responses from American Jews? What is she calling for?

# POP CULTURE

# FIVE MYTHS OF CONSUMERSHIP

## *Dallas Smythe*

*Dallas Smythe was a member of the Institute of Communication Research at the University of Illinois, Urbana-Champagne. This essay first appeared in the news magazine,* The Nation, *in 1969. In this essay, he explores some of the ways in which consumption, or the desire to buy, has supplanted all other things in contemporary American life.*

Andrew Fletcher said in 1704, "I believe if a man were permitted to write all the ballads, he need not care who should make the laws of the nation." Our culture includes not only traditional forms of "high" culture such as painting and literature, but also "popular culture"—the radio and TV, the screen and theatre, pocket books, phonograph records, popular songs, pornography, both "hard" and "soft" etc. Indeed the borderline between popular culture and all consumption goods has been obliterated by Madison Avenue. For at least a generation now we in North America have become accustomed to endowing our automobiles with virility, our refrigerators with sensual pleasure, our breakfast cereals with athletic prowess, our shaving cream with the taste of lemon/lime. I argue that our popular culture is dominated today by an economic system that regards life, people and things primarily as aspects of consumption. The basic myth of our culture is that consumption is the goal of life.

Twenty years ago Harold Innis said that the purpose of institutions is to help us make the right decisions at the right time. He went on from there to say that the application of mass production to the communications industry (referring then just to print media and radio) had atomized previous institutions—the family, the church, the labor union—over the preceding eighty years. We must now recognize that the constituencies of these institutions are substantially under the control of the private government which is our privately owned economic system. This is not to say that evil men run the economic system. Or that a conspiracy has betrayed our nonbusiness institutions or taken them over. But it is to say that, pursuing its rational self-interest, the business community *as a whole* has created a situation whereby we subordinate our lives to its values. We live according to the consumption myth. How does it work?

As a society, we can look at North America as a unit, like a voluntary organization club, or a neighborhood improvement association—in that it works from an agenda that is agreed to either explicitly or implicitly. What is left off the agenda does not get considered attention. And popular culture, by filling our time with commercial actions and values, sets an agenda which gives consumption the top priority. I recall a recent advertisement in *The New York Times* which filled a full page with the message: "Buy Something." The popular culture's imperative-"Buy Something"—is the most important educational influence in North America today.

Just as a society lives by the agenda set by its popular culture, the popular culture rests on the agenda established by mass communication. The top priority for the mass media is consumption. Mass communications market mass-produced consumer goods. Without the marketing services of the communications media, the consumer goods industries—food, automobiles, drugs, etc.—could not dispose of their mass-produced products.

The mass media performs this marketing function by educating the population to be dutiful consumers. The educational process starts early. Before they can read, almost before they can talk, children are exposed to the bombardment of advertising messages on TV and radio. Skillfully engineered "point of sale" displays reinforce the educational experience when a mother shops at the supermarket with her child perched on the shopping cart, monitoring the whole operation. In this way, the child learns the importance of products. Lessons so learned are reinforced daily throughout our lives.

The explicit commercial message is thus the prime item on the commercial mass-medium agenda. Commercial announcements on TV cost much more per minute than do the entertainment programs they frame. They are engineered with great care and much experimentation by the most sophisticated techniques.

This raises an interesting question. Is the broadcast program material the product which the commercial broadcasting industry produces? The program material cannot be the chief product because it brings in no revenue from the audience to the broadcasting station. In fact in economic terms, the program material broadcast commercially is a giveaway—an inducement to the population to become viewers or listeners. The chief product of the commercial broadcasters is the audience itself. Viewers and listeners are counted by market surveys, evaluated in terms of income level, age and sex, packaged and sold to advertisers.

In saying that the program material is a giveaway, I do not mean to overlook its importance. It is in fact carefully engineered. Take *The Monkees*, for example, which was engineered as any consumer commodity is engineered. The market was researched. Other entertainers, and particularly the Beatles, were analyzed to determine what characteristics in a program would "deliver" a young audience to the advertiser. A formula was developed, and the agency or network set out to recruit the elements that would fill it. The young men who came to comprise the Monkees did not even know one another until this process was near completion. From among hundreds at auditions, each was selected because he best embodied some appeals, some myths, which would "draw" and "hold" the audience. But this was only the beginning. *The Monkees* had to be publicized, advertised. Crowds had to be created and manipulated to produce pushing and fighting for autographs. The public had to be taught to resonate

when the myth which is *The Monkees* was mentioned. At that point the broadcasters were ready to produce *the audiences* for *The Monkees* which could be sold to the advertisers.

Finally, on this point, national advertisers tell their writers just what sort of entertainment they wish to broadcast. One major advertiser of breakfast food in the United States and Canada not long ago was instructing its writers:

> *In general, the moral code of the characters in our dramas will be more or less synonymous with the moral code of the bulk of the American middle class, as it is commonly understood. There will be no material that may give offense, either directly or by inference, to any organized minority group, lodge or other organizations, institutions, residents of any state or section of the country, or a commercial organization of any sort. This will be taken to include political organizations, fraternal organizations, college and school groups, labor groups, industrial, business and professional organizations, religious orders, civic clubs, memorial and patriotic societies (Anti-Tobacco-League, for example), athletic organizations, women's groups. etc., which are in good standing.*
>
> *We will treat mention of the Civil War carefully, mindful of the sensitiveness of the South on this subject. No written material may be used that might give offense to our Canadian neighbors. . . . There will be no material for or against sharply drawn national or regional controversial issues. . . . Where it seems fitting, the characters should reflect recognition and acceptance of the world situation in their thoughts and actions, although in dealing with war, our writers should minimize the "horror" aspects. . . . Men in uniform shall not be cast as heavy villains or portrayed as engaging in any criminal activity. There will be no material on any of our programs which could in any way further the concept of business as cold, ruthless and lacking all sentiment or spiritual motivation.*

Similar instructions go out to writers from many national advertisers. If such a process took place in schools or universities we should call it indoctrination and brainwashing. It is no less brainwashing when it takes place on the instruction of private business. Commercial indoctrination educates us in the myth that consumption is a sufficient goal, a sufficient substance for life. This is the basic myth.

A second, correlative myth cultivated systematically by mass media and the private enterprise system, is that the consumer is king: that he rules the system; can always turn off the switch, is in fact free to choose among products. If there were any substance to this myth, the Madison Avenue myth makers and their platoons of consumer preference engineers would not have done their job and not earned their salaries. Unfortunately, they have done their jobs and earned their salaries, large though they may be.

A third myth grows directly out of the pivotal importance of the commercial mass media to the marketing of goods. This is that some special magic resides in "communication." When an institution, be it the family, the church, a government agency, a business organization faces any kind of internal problem, the up-to-date "sophisticated" reaction is to call the difficulty one of communication. The aura that attends the doctor, or for that matter the medicine man, now surrounds those who call them experts in communication. Possibly no single person has contributed more to this mystification than Marshall McLuhan, whose brilliant but unsystematic essays serve to confuse people and thus create the mystery which requires the services of a medicine man for practical application. The hearty welcome which McLuhan's theme, "The medium is the message," receives from advertisers, their agencies and broadcasters is not surprising. If the content of the mass media is not important, if the medium is the message, then criticism of program policy is irrelevant. "The medium is the message." whatever McLuhan means by it translates only too easily into the proposition that the act of consumership is the sufficient object of the exercise.

The fourth myth connected with the consumer system is designed to obscure the fact that the huge corporations which dominate North American economic life have preempted large chunks of the roles formerly played by other institutions. In the United States, where this myth originated, it centered on the assumption that the corporation is a legal entity and hence similar to an individual. Thurman Arnold put it this way in *The Folklore of Capitalism*:

*Since individuals are supposed to do better if left alone, this symbolism freed industrial enterprise from regulation in the interest of furthering any current morality. The laissez-faire religion based on a conception of a society composed of competing individuals, was transferred automatically to industrial organizations*

*with nationwide power and dictatorial forms of government.*

*This mythology gave the Government in Washington only a minor part to play in social organization. . . . Government in Washington was supposed to act so as to instill "confidence" in great organizations.*

One way of exposing this myth is to define government. It is any organization the final decisions of which are subject to no immediate appeal. In North America, then, there are parallel systems of government the private and the public. And in essential matters the former has the last word. President Kennedy came off second best when he tried to overrule the steel companies a few years ago and his successor learned the lesson.

The fifth myth arises out of the fourth. It is that if the public government makes decisions in matters of communications policy application, this is censorship and automatically bad, but if private government makes such decisions, all will be well. A relatively small number of such decisions, made in the operation of the mass media of communications, involves the mass production of enormous amounts of content. I suggest that the myth that public government is malevolent while private government is benevolent is insupportable, especially in the absence of democratic process in the private government's decision making.

If this analysis of the myth-making picture of our consumption-tied economy is valid, what could, what should, be done about it? This is a question which the young people who so disturb many of us have been wrestling with for some time. While there is no single explanation for the increasingly urgent protests being made by beatniks, hippies, the New Left and the Yippies, one evident basis for their behavior is that they reject the consumer-tied system as inhuman, immoral and indecent. Their studied defiance of convention in matters of dress, hair styling and domestic arrangements is a protest against the irrelevance of the pursuit of consumption on a continent and in a world where other goals should prevail.

They tell us what these problems are: stubborn pockets of poverty where the delights of consumption are bitter illusions; neglect of the right of minority groups to a cultural identity of their own; abuse of the environment by the pollution of air and water which unplanned economic system forces on us; irrational military adventures; imperial exploitation of underdeveloped by developed nations, and so on.

The young people's protests overlap those of the blacks whose concern for "soul" is also a defiance of consumership values. By their irritating even infuriating, tactics, the young people are trying to force our attention upon these problems. Before cracking down on them from position of power in the North American institutional structure, we should listen carefully to what they—the young and the blacks—are protesting.

If these protest movements do not manage to get the agenda of problems sorted out more sensibly—if the consumer society manages to absorb these rebellious people into safe establishment niches, then we shall be in trouble even deeper than we are today. We shall have proved ourselves so indoctrinated to the consumption-based life that we no longer care enough to take over our own institutions and make them serve our human needs.

Do I have a panacea—any easy solution to the problems arising from our slavery to what Erich Fromm calls the "*homo consumens*" myth? Of course not. I do feel that an essential first step toward that solution is to confront the facts honestly and, as Freud said, to face our guilt squarely. Assuming that that was done. I would say

the next step was to rub the brainwash off some traditional notions. For example, the notion of planning. Faced with the necessity of planning for survival, the people of this continent have never shrunk from it. And I mean by planning simply policy making followed by action regardless of whose toes are stepped on.

We face a seamless web of persuasion and power based on the consumption drive of North American private industry. If the people are to be masters of their own fate they must plan for cultural survival. Planning does not mean breaking the machines or denying ourselves the benefits of modern technology. The Scandinavian countries, Holland and Switzerland, have disposed of that bugaboo. Planning does mean that public decisions must be accepted even when they tell private enterprise when and where and how to invest its capital. That is the nub of the planning issue and it must be squarely faced. If we do not accept planning on those terms, we have no real proposal for putting man first and consumption second. If we do plan on those terms, the mass media and the popular culture will be obliged to cultivate myths more compatible with human dignity and human "values" than the cluster of myths surrounding the consumption which now guide our lives.

**Study Questions**

1. What is the main myth that he identifies here? Why is it significant?

2. What role does the media play in terms of perpetuating these myths?

3. Why does he distinguish between public and private? What does that have to do with consumership?

4. Why are we more willing to allow private industry to make rules than public government?

# THE MORE YOU SUBTRACT, THE MORE YOU ADD

## Cutting Girls Down to Size

### *Jean Kilbourne*

*Jean Kilbourne is a lecturer, writer, and visiting scholar at Wellesley College. She is perhaps best known for her videos, especially* Killing Us Softly: Advertising's Image of Women, *upon which the book* Deadly Persuasion (1999) *is based. In her work, she focuses on the tyranny of the beauty ideal, the obsession with thinness, the dismemberment of women's bodies, and the connection between the sexualization of children and the fear of powerful women. She has also made videos criticizing the advertising of cigarettes and alcohol.*

When I was sixteen, like almost everyone else in the world, I fell wildly in love for the first time. My feelings were so intense that now, decades later, I still dream about him from time to time. He was good for me in every way, but I also began a sinister love affair around the same time, one that nearly consumed me - my love affair with alcohol and cigarettes. As adults in a toxic culture, some of us fall in love with cars or chocolate cake or, more dangerously, drugs. But, just as we are more vulnerable to the glory and heartbreak of romantic love than we will ever be again, at no time are we more vulnerable to the seductive power of advertising and of addiction than we are in adolescence.

Adolescents are new and inexperienced consumers and such prime targets. They are in the process of learning their values and roles and developing their self-concepts. Most teenagers are sensitive to peer pressure and find it difficult to resist or even to question the dominant cultural messages perpetuated and reinforced by the media. Mass communication has made possible a kind of national peer pressure that erodes private and individual values and standards, as well as community values and standards. As Margaret Mead once said, today our children are not brought up by parents; they are brought up by the mass media.

Advertisers are aware of their role and do not hesitate to take advantage of the insecurities and anxieties of young people, usually in the guise of offering solutions. A cigarette provides a symbol of independence. A pair of designer jeans or sneakers convey status. The right perfume or beer resolves doubts about femininity or masculinity. All young are vulnerable to these messages and adolescence is a difficult time for most people, perhaps especially these days. According to the Carnegie Corporation, "Nearly half of all American adolescents are at high or moderate risk of seriously damaging their life chances." But there is a particular kind of suffering in our culture that afflicts girls.

As most of us know so well by now, when a girl enters adolescence, she faces a series of losses loss of self-confidence, loss of a sense of efficacy and ambition, and the loss of her "voice," the sense of being a unique and powerful self that she had in childhood. Girls who were active, confident, feisty at the ages of eight and nine and ten often become hesitant, insecure, self-doubting at eleven. Their self-esteem plummets. As Carol Gilligan, Mary Pipher and other social critics and psychologists have pointed out in recent years, adolescent girls in America are afflicted with a range of problems, including low self-esteem, eating disorders, binge drinking, date rape and other dating violence, teen pregnancy, and a rise in cigarette smoking. Teenage women today are engaging in far riskier health behavior in greater numbers than any prior generation.

The gap between boys and girls is closing, but this is not always for the best. According to a 1998 status report by a consortium of universities and research centers, girls have closed the gap with boys in math performance and are coming close in science. But they are also now smoking, drinking, and using drugs as often as boys their own age. And, although girls are not nearly as violent as boys, they are committing more crimes than ever before and are far more often physically attacking each other.

It is important to understand that these problems go way beyond individual psychological development and pathology. Even girls who are raised in loving homes by supportive parents grow up in a toxic cultural environment, at risk for self-mutilation, eating disorders, and addictions. The culture, both reflected and reinforced by advertising, urges girls to adopt a false self, to bury alive their real selves, to become "feminine," which means to be nice and kind and sweet, to compete with other girls for the attention of boys, and to value romantic relationships with boys above all else. Girls are put into a terrible double bind. They are supposed to repress their power, their anger, their exuberance and be simply "nice," although they also eventually must compete with men in the business world and be successful. They must be overtly sexy and attractive but essentially passive and virginal. It is not surprising that most girls experience this time as painful and confusing, especially if they are unconscious of these conflicting demands.

Of course, it is impossible to speak accurately of girls as a monolithic group. The socialization that emphasizes passivity and compliance does not apply to many African-American and Jewish girls, who are often encouraged to be assertive and outspoken, and working-class girls are usually not expected to be stars in the business world. Far from protecting these girls from eating disorders and other problems, these differences more often mean that the problems remain hidden or undiagnosed and the girls are even less likely to get help. Eating problems affect girls from African-American, Asian, Native American, Hispanic, and Latino families and from every socioeconomic background. The racism and classism that these girls experience exacerbate their problems. Sexism is by no means the only trauma they face.

We've learned a lot in recent years about the pressures on girls and the resulting problems. So much that some people think it is time to stop talking about it maybe to focus on boys or just move on. It's important to remember that this discussion of the problems of adolescent girls is very recent. In 1980, not a single chapter in the Handbook on Adolescent Psychology was devoted to girls. As with other fields in psychology, the research was done on boys and assumed to apply to girls as well. The research on girls and the discussion of their issues is long overdue and far from complete.

Of course, we must continue to pay attention to the problems of boys, as well. Two books published recently address these problems. In *Raising Cain: Protecting the Emotional Life of Boys*, Daniel Kindlon and Michael Thompson examine the "culture of cruelty" that boys live in and the "tyranny of toughness" that oppresses them. In *Real Boys: Rescuing Our Sons from the Myths of Boyhood*, psychologist William Pollock examines the ways that boys manifest their social and emotional disconnection through anger and violence. We've seen the tragic results of this in the school shootings, all by angry and alienated boys.

The truth is that the problems of boys and girls are related, and not only because girls are often the victims of these angry, violent boys and the men they become. The "emotional illiteracy" of men, as Kindlon and Thompson call it, harms boys and girls, men and women. Most of us understand that the cultural environment plays a powerful role in creating these problems. But we still have a lot to learn about the precise nature of this role and what we can do about it. How can we resist these destructive messages and images? The first step, as always, is to become as conscious of them as possible, to deconstruct them. Although I am very sympathetic to the harm done to boys by our cultural environment, the focus of my work has always been on girls and women.

Girls try to make sense of the contradictory expectations of themselves in a culture dominated by advertising. Advertising is one of the most potent messengers in a culture that can be toxic for girls' self-esteem. Indeed, if we looked only at advertising images, this would be a bleak world for females. Girls are extremely desirable to advertisers because they are new consumers, are beginning to have significant disposable income, and are developing brand loyalty that might last a lifetime. Teenage girls spend over $4 billion annually on cosmetics alone.

*Seventeen*, a magazine aimed at girls about twelve to fifteen, sells these girls to advertisers in an ad that says, "She's the one you want. She's the one we've got." The copy continues, "She pursues beauty and fashion at every turn" and concludes with, "It's more than a magazine. It's her life." In another similar ad, *Seventeen* refers to itself as a girl's "Bible." Many girls read magazines like this and take the advice seriously. Regardless of the intent of advertisers, what are the messages that girls are getting? What are they told?

Primarily girls are told by advertisers that what is most important about them is their perfume, their clothing, their bodies, their beauty. Their "essence" is their underwear. "He says the first thing he noticed about you is your great personality," says an ad featuring a very young woman in tight jeans. The copy continues, "He lies." "If this is your idea of a great catch," says an ad for a cosmetic kit from a teen magazine featuring a cute boy, "this is your tackle box." Even very little girls are offered makeup and toys like Special Night Barbie, which shows them how to dress up for a night out. Girls of all ages get the message that they must be flawlessly beautiful and, above all these days, they must be thin.

Even more destructively, they get the message that this is possible, that, with enough effort and self-sacrifice, they can achieve this ideal. Thus many girls spend enormous amounts of time and energy attempting to achieve something that is not only trivial but also completely unattainable. The glossy images of flawlessly beautiful and extremely thin women that surround us would not have the impact they do if we did not live in a culture that encourages us to believe we can and should remake our bodies into perfect commodities. These images play into the American belief of transformation and ever-new possibilities, no longer via hard work but via the purchase of the right products. As Anne Becker has pointed out, this belief is by no means universal. People in many other cultures may admire a particular body shape without seeking to emulate it. In the Western world, however, "the anxiety of no recognition ('I don't fit in') faced by the majority of spectators is more often translated into identifications ('I want to be like that') and attempts at self-alteration."

Women are especially vulnerable because our bodies have been objectified and commodified for so long. And young women are the most vulnerable, especially those who have experienced early deprivation, sexual abuse, family violence, or other trauma. Cultivating a thinner body offers some hope of control and success to a young woman with a poor self-image and overwhelming personal problems that have no easy solutions.

Although troubled young women are especially vulnerable, these messages affect all girls. A researcher at Brigham and Women's Hospital in Boston found that the more frequently girls read magazines, the more likely they were to diet and to feel that magazines influence their ideal body shape.

Nearly half reported wanting to lose weight because of magazine pictures (but only 29 percent were actually overweight). Studies at Stanford University and the University of Massachusetts found that about 70 percent of college women say they feel worse about their own looks after reading women's magazines. Another study, this one of 350 young men and women, found that a preoccupation with one's appearance takes a toll on mental health. Women scored much higher than men on what the researchers called "self-objectification." This tendency to view one's body from the outside in regarding physical attractiveness, sex appeal, measurements, and weight as more central to one's physical identity than health, strength, energy level, coordination, or fitness has many harmful effects including diminished mental performance, increased feelings of shame and anxiety, depression, sexual dysfunction, and the development of eating disorders.

These images of women seem to affect men most strikingly by influencing how they judge the real women in their lives. Male college students who viewed just one episode of Charlie's Angels, the hit television show of the 1970s that featured three beautiful women, were harsher in their evaluations of the attractiveness of potential dates than were males who had not seen the episode. In another study, male college students shown centerfolds from Playboy and Penthouse were more likely to find their own girlfriends less sexually attractive.

Adolescent girls are especially vulnerable to the obsession with thinness, for many reasons. One is the ominous peer pressure on young people. Adolescence is a time of such self-consciousness and terror of shame and humiliation. Boys are shamed for being too small, too "weak," too soft, too sensitive. And girls are shamed for being too sexual, too loud, too boisterous, too big (in any sense of the word), having too hearty an appetite. Many young women have told me that their boyfriends wanted them to lose weight. One said that her boyfriend had threatened to leave her if she didn't lose five pounds. "Why don't you leave him," I asked, "and lose 160?"

The situation is very different for men. The double standard is reflected in an ad for a low-fat pizza: "He eats a brownie...you eat a rice cake. He eats a juicy burger...you eat a low fat entrée. He eats a pizza...you eat a pizza. Finally, life is fair." Although some men develop eating problems, the predominant cultural message remains that a hearty appetite and a large size is desirable in a man, but not so in a woman.

Indeed, a 1997 television campaign targets ravenous teenage boys by offering Taco Bell as the remedy for hunger (and also linking eating with sex via the slogan "Want some?"). One commercial features a fat guy who loses his composure when he realizes his refrigerator is empty. In another, two quite heavy guys have dozed off in front of the television set and are awakened by hunger pangs, which only Taco Bell can satisfy. It is impossible to imagine this campaign aimed at teenage girls.

Normal physiological changes during adolescence result in increased body fat for women. If these normal changes are considered undesirable by the culture (and by parents and peers), this can lead to chronic anxiety and concern about weight control in young women. A ten-year-old girl wrote to *New Moon*, a feminist magazine for girls, "I was at the beach and was in my bathing suit. I have kind of fat legs, and my uncle told me I had fat legs in front of all my cousins and my cousins' friends. I was so embarrassed; I went up to my room and shut the door. When I went downstairs again, everyone started teasing me." Young women are even encouraged to worry about small fluctuations in their weight. "Sometimes what you wear to dinner may depend on what you eat for breakfast," says an ad for cereal that pictures a slinky black dress. In truth, daily and weekly and monthly fluctuations in weight are perfectly normal.

The obsession starts early. Some studies have found that from 40 to 80 percent of fourth-grade girls are dieting. Today at least one-third of twelve- to thirteen-year-old girls are actively trying to lose weight by dieting, vomiting, using laxatives, or taking diet pills. One survey found that 63 percent of high-school girls were on diets, compared with only 16 percent of men. And a survey in Massachusetts found that the single largest group of high school students considering or attempting suicide are girls who feel they are overweight. Imagine. Girls made to feel so terrible about themselves that they would rather be dead than fat. This wouldn't be happening, of course, if it weren't for our last "socially acceptable" prejudice - weightism. Fat children are ostracized and ridiculed from the moment they enter school, and fat adults, women in particular, are subjected to public contempt and scorn. This strikes terror into the hearts of all women, many of whom, unfortunately, identify with the oppressor and become vicious to themselves and each other.

No wonder it is hard to find a woman, especially a young woman, in America today who has a truly healthy attitude toward her body and toward food. Just as the disease of alcoholism is the extreme end of a continuum that includes a wide range of alcohol use and abuse, so are bulimia and anorexia the extreme results of an obsession with eating and weight control that grips many young women with serious and potentially very dangerous results. Although eating problems are often thought to result from vanity, the truth is that they, like other addictions and compulsive behavior, usually have deeper roots not only genetic predisposition and biochemical vulnerabilities, but also childhood sexual abuse.

Advertising doesn't cause eating problems, of course, any more than it causes alcoholism. Anorexia in particular is a disease with a complicated etiology, and media images probably don't play a major role. However, these images certainly contribute to the body-hatred so many young women feel and to some of the resulting eating problems, which range from bulimia to compulsive overeating to simply being obsessed with controlling one's appetite. Advertising does promote abusive and abnormal attitudes about eating, drinking, and thinness. It thus provides fertile soil for these obsessions to take root in and creates a climate of denial in which these diseases flourish.

The influence of the media is strikingly illustrated in a recent study that found a sharp rise in eating disorders among young women in Fiji soon after the introduction of television to the culture. Before television was available, there was little talk of dieting in Fiji. "You've gained weight" was a traditional compliment and "going thin" the sign of a problem. In 1995 television came to the island. Within three years, the number of teenagers at risk for eating disorders more than doubled, 74 percent of the teens in the study said they felt "too big or too fat," and 62 percent said they had dieted in the past month. Of course, this doesn't prove a direct causal link between television and eating disorders. Fiji is a culture in transition in many ways. However, it seems more than coincidental that the Fiji girls who were heavy viewers of television were 50 percent more likely to describe themselves as fat and 30 percent more likely to diet than those girls who watched television less frequently. As Ellen Goodman says, "The big success story of our entertainment industry is our ability to export insecurity: We can make any woman anywhere feel perfectly rotten about her shape."

Being obsessed about one's weight is made to seem normal and even appealing in ads for unrelated products, such as a scotch ad that features a very thin and pretty young woman looking in a mirror while her boyfriend observes her. The copy, addressed to him, says, "Listen, if you can handle 'Honey, do I look fat? You can handle this." These two are so intimate that she can share her deepest fears with him - and he can respond by chuckling at her adorable vulnerability and knocking back another scotch. And everyone who sees the ad gets the message that it is perfectly normal for all young women, including thin and attractive ones, to worry about their weight.

"Put some weight on," says a British ad featuring an extremely thin young woman but the ad is referring to her watch. She is so thin she can wear the watch on her upper arm and this is supposed to be a good thing.

Not all of this is intentional on the part of the advertisers, of course. A great deal of it is based on research and is intended to arouse anxiety and affect women's self-esteem. But some of it reflects the unconscious attitudes and beliefs of the individual advertisers, as well as what Carl Jung referred to as the "collective unconscious." Advertisers are members of the culture too and have been as thoroughly conditioned as anyone else. The magazines and the ads deliberately create and intensify anxiety about weight because it is so profitable. On a deeper level, however, they reflect cultural concerns and conflicts about women's power. Real freedom for women would change the very basis of our male-dominated society. It is not surprising that many men (and women, to be sure) fear this.

"The more you subtract, the more you add," says an ad that ran in several women's and teen magazines in 1997. Surprisingly, it is an ad for clothing, not for a diet product. Overtly, it is a statement about minimalism in fashion. However, the fact that the girl in the ad is very young and very thin reinforces another message, a message that an adolescent girl constantly gets from advertising and throughout the popular culture, the message that she should diminish herself; she should be less than she is.

On the most obvious and familiar level, this refers to her body. However, the loss, the subtraction, the cutting down to size also refers to her sense of her self, her sexuality, her need for authentic connection, and her longing for power and freedom. I certainly don't think that the creators of this particular ad had all this in mind. They're simply selling expensive clothing in an unoriginal way, by using a very young and very thin woman and an unfortunate tagline. It wouldn't be important at all were there not so many other ads that reinforce this message and did it not coincide with a cultural crisis taking place now for adolescent girls.

"We cut Judy down to size," says an ad for a health club. "Soon, you'll both be taking up less space," says an ad for a collapsible treadmill, referring both to the product and to the young woman exercising on it. The obsession with thinness is most deeply about cutting girls and women down to size. It is only a symbol, albeit a very powerful and destructive one, of tremendous fear of female power. Powerful women are seen by many people (women as well as men) as inherently destructive and dangerous. Some argue that it is men's awareness of just how powerful women can be that has created the attempts to keep women small. Indeed, thinness as an ideal has always accompanied period of greater freedom for women as soon as we got the vote, boyish flapper bodies came into vogue. No wonder there is such pressure on young women today to be thin, to shrink, to be like little girls, not to take up too much space, literally and figuratively.

At the same time there is relentless pressure on women to be small, there is also pressure on us to succeed, to achieve, to "have it all." We can be successful as long as we stay "feminine" (i.e., powerless enough not to be truly threatening). One-way to do this is to present an image of fragility, to look like a waif. This demonstrates that one is both in control and still very "feminine." One of the many double binds tormenting young women today is the need to be both sophisticated and accomplished, yet also delicate and childlike. Again, this applies mostly to middle-to-upper-class white women.

The changing roles and greater opportunities for women promised by the women's movement are trivialized, reduced to the private search for the slimmest body. In one commercial, three skinny young women dance and sing about the "taste of freedom." They are feeling free because they can now eat bread, thanks to a low-calorie version. A commercial for a fast-food chain features a very slim young woman who announces, "I have a license to eat." The salad bar and lighter fare have given her freedom to eat (as if eating for women were a privilege rather than a need). "Free yourself," says ad after ad for diet products.

You can never be too rich or too thin, girls are told. This mass delusion sells a lot of products. It also causes enormous suffering, involving girls in false quests for power and control, while deflecting attention and energy from that which might really empower them. "A declaration of independence," proclaims an ad for perfume that features an emaciated model, but in fact the quest for a body as thin as the model's becomes a prison for many women and girls.

The quest for independence can be a problem too if it leads girls to deny the importance of and need for interpersonal relationships. Girls and young women today are encouraged by the culture to achieve a very "masculine" kind of autonomy and independence, one that excludes interdependence, mutuality, and connection with others. Catherine Steiner-Adair suggests that perhaps eating disorders emerge at adolescence because it is at this point that "females experience themselves to be at a crossroads in their lives where they must shift from a relational approach to life to an autonomous one, a shift that can represent an intolerable loss when independence is associated with isolation." In this sense, she sees eating disorders as political statements, a kind of hunger strike: "Girls with eating disorders have a heightened, albeit confused, grasp of the dangerous imbalance of the culture's values, which they cannot articulate in the face of the culture's abject denial of their adolescent intuitive truth, so they tell their story with their bodies."

Most of us know by now about the damage done to girls by the tyranny of the ideal image, weightism, and the obsession with thinness. But girls get other messages too that "cut them down to size" more subtly. In ad after ad girls are urged to be "barely there" beautiful but silent. Of course, girls are not just influenced by images of other girls. They are even more powerfully attuned to images of women, because they learn from these images what is expected of them, what they are to become. And they see these images again and again in the magazines they read, even those magazines designed for teenagers, and in the commercials they watch.

"Make a statement without saying a word," says an ad for perfume. And indeed this is one of the primary messages of the culture to adolescent girls. "The essence of a look can reveal more than words," says another perfume ad, this one picturing a woman lying on her back. "More than words can say, says yet another perfume ad, and a clothing ad says, "Classic is speaking your mind (without saying a word)." An ad for lipstick says, "Watch your mouth, young lady," while the ad for nail polish says, "Let your fingers do the talking," and one for hairspray promises "hair that speaks volumes." In another ad, a young woman's turtleneck is pulled over her mouth. And an ad for a movie soundtrack features a chilling image of a young woman with her lips sewn together.

It is not only the girls themselves who see these images, of course. Their parents and teachers and doctors see them and they influence their sense of how girls should be. A 1999 study done at the University of Michigan found that, beginning in preschool, girls are told to be quiet much more often than boys. Although boys were much noisier than girls, the girls were told to speak softly or to use a "nicer" voice about three times more often. Girls were encouraged to be quiet, small, and physically constrained. The researcher concluded that one of

the consequences of this socialization is that girls grow into women afraid to speak up for themselves or to use their voices to protect themselves from a variety of dangers.

A television commercial features a very young woman lying on a bed, giggling, silly. Suddenly a male hand comes forward. His finger touches her lips and she becomes silent, her face blank. Another commercial features a very young woman, shot in black and white but with colored contact lenses. She never speaks but she touches her face and hair as a female voiceover says, "Your eyes don't just see, they also speak…Your eyes can say a lot, but they don't have to shout. They can speak softly. Let your eyes be heard…without making a sound." The commercial ends with the young woman putting her finger in her mouth.

"Score high on nonverbal skills," says a clothing ad featuring a young African-American woman, while an ad for mascara tells young women to "make up your own language." And an Italian ad feature a very thin young woman in an elegant coat sitting on a window seat. The copy says, "This woman is silent. This coat talks." Girls, seeing these images of women, are encouraged to be silent, mysterious, not to talk too much or too loudly. In many different ways, they are told, "the more you subtract, the more you add." In this kind of climate, a Buffalo jeans ad featuring a young woman screaming, "I don't have to scream for attention but I do," can seem like an improvement until we notice that she's really getting attention by unbuttoning her blouse to her navel. This is typical of the mixed messages so many ads and other forms of the media give girls. The young woman seems fierce and powerful, but she's really exposed, vulnerable.

The January 1998 cover of Seventeen highlights an article, "Do you talk too much?" On the back cover is an ad for Express mascara, which promises "high voltage volume instantly!" As if the way that girls can express themselves and turn up the volume is via their mascara. Is this harmless wordplay, or is it a sophisticated and clever marketing ploy based on research about the silencing of girls, deliberately designed to attract them with the promise of at least some form of self-expression? Advertisers certainly spend a lot of money on psychological research and focus groups. I would expect these groups to reveal, among other things, that teenage girls are angry but reticent. Certainly the cumulative effect of these images and words urging girls to express themselves only through their bodies and through products is serious and harmful.

Many ads feature girls and young women in very passive poses, limp, doll-like, sometimes acting like little girls, playing with dolls and wearing bows in their hair. One ad uses a pacifier to sell lipstick and another the image of a baby to sell Baby Doll Blush Highlight. "Lolita seems to be a comeback kid," says a fashion layout featuring a woman wearing a ridiculous hairstyle and a babydoll dress, standing with shoulders slumped and feet apart. In women's and teen magazines it is virtually impossible to tell the fashion layouts from the ads. Indeed, they exist to support each other.

As Erving Goffman pointed out in *Gender Advertisements*, we learn a great deal about the disparate power of males and females simply through the body language and poses of advertising. Women, especially young women, are generally subservient to men in ads, through both size and position. Sometimes it is as blatant as the women serving as a footrest in the ad for Think Skateboards.

Other times, it is more subtle but quite striking (once one becomes aware of it). The double-paged spread for Calvin Klein's clothing for kids conveys a world of information about the relative power of boys and girls. One of the boys seems to be in the act of speaking, expressing himself, while the girl has her hand over her mouth. Boys are generally shown in ads as active, rambunctious, while girls are more often passive and focused on their appearance. The exception to the rule involves African-American children, male and female, who are often shown in advertising as passive observers of their white playmates.

That these stereotypes continue, in spite of all the recent focus on the harm done to girls by enforced passivity, is evident in the most causal glance at parents' magazines. In the ads in the March 1999 issues of *Child and Parents*, all of the boys are active and all of the girls are passive. In *Child*, a boy plays on the jungle gym in one ad, while in another, a girl stands quietly, looking down, holding some flowers. In *Parents*, a boy rides a bike full of excitement, while a girl is happy about having put on lipstick. It's hard to believe that this is 1999 and not 1959. The more things change, the more they stay the same.

Girls are often shown as playful clowns in ads, perpetuating the attitude that girls and women are childish and cannot be taken seriously, whereas even very young men are generally portrayed as secure, powerful, and serious. People in control of their lives stand upright, alert, and ready to meet the world. In contrast, females often appear off-balance, insecure, and weak. Often our body parts

are bent, conveying unpreparedness, submissiveness, and appeasement. We exhibit what Goffman terms "licensed withdrawal" seeming to be psychologically removed, disoriented, defenseless, spaced out.

Females touch people and things delicately, we caress, whereas males grip, clench, and grasp. We cover our faces with our hair or our hands, conveying shame and embarrassment. And, no matter what happens, we keep on smiling "Just smiling the bothers away," as one ad says. This ad is particularly disturbing because the model is a young African-American woman, a member of a group that has long been encouraged to just keep smiling, no matter what. She's even wearing a kerchief, like Aunt Jemima. The cultural fear of angry women is intensified dramatically when the women are African-American.

An extreme example of the shaming and trivialization of girls and women is a recent little trend of ads featuring young women sitting on the toilet, such as the shoe ad with popular MTV star Jenny McCarthy (although the ad offended a lot of people, it also boosted sales of Candies shoes by 19 percent). Unfortunately, this phenomenon is not restricted to the United States. An Italian ad for sneakers and a British one for a magazine use the same image. Such pictures are especially humiliating to self-conscious teenagers.

Girls and young women are often presented as blank and fragile. Floating in space, adrift in a snowstorm. A Valentino clothing ad perhaps unwittingly illustrates the tragedy of adolescence for girls. It features a very young woman with her head seemingly enclosed in a glass bubble labeled "Love." Some ads and fashion layouts picture girls as mermaids or underwater as if they were drowning or lying on the ground as if washed up to shore, such as the Versace makeup ad picturing a young girl caught up in fishing nets, rope, and seashells. An ad for vodka features a woman in the water and the copy, "In a past life I was a mermaid who fell in love with an ancient mariner. I pulled him into the sea to be my husband. I didn't know he couldn't breathe underwater." Of course, she can't breathe underwater either.

Breathe underwater. As girls come of age sexually, the culture gives them impossibly contradictory messages. As the *Seventeen* ad says, "She wants to be outrageous. And accepted." Advertising slogans such as "because innocence is sexier than you think," "Purity, yes. Innocence never," and "nothing so sensual was ever so innocent" place them in a double bind. "Only something so pure could inspire such unspeakable passion," declares an ad for Jovan musk that features a white flower.

Somehow girls are supposed to be both innocent and seductive, virginal and experienced, all at the same time. As they quickly learn, this is tricky.

Females have long been divided into virgins and whores, of course. What is new is that girls are now supposed to embody both within themselves. This is symbolic of the central contradiction of the culture we must work hard and produce and achieve success and yet, at the same time, we are encouraged to live impulsively, spend a lot of money, and be constantly immediately gratified. This tension is reflected in our attitudes toward many things, including sex and eating. Girls are promised fulfillment both through being thin and through eating rich foods, just as they are promised fulfillment through being innocent and virginal and through wild and impulsive sex.

Young people, boys and girls, are surrounded by messages urging them to be sexually active. Teachers report a steady escalation of sex talk among children, starting in preschool, as our children are prematurely exposed to a barrage of sexual information and misinformation through advertising, television shows, music, and films. "You can learn more about anatomy after school," says an ad for jeans, which manages to trivialize sex, relationships, and education all in one sentence.

The consequences of all this sexual pressure on children are frightening. The average age of first sexual intercourse is about sixteen for girls and fifteen for boys. Far more disturbing is the fact that seven in ten girls who had sex before the age of fourteen and six in ten of those who had sex before the age of fifteen report having sex involuntarily. One of every ten girls under the age of twenty becomes pregnant in the United States each year, more than in any other industrialized country in the world: twice as high as in England and Wales, France and Canada, and nine times as high as in the Netherlands or Japan. And as many as one in six sexually active adolescents has a sexually transmitted disease.

Of course, advertising and the media are not solely to blame for these appalling statistics. But they are the leading source of sex education in the nation and they create a climate which encourages a very cavalier attitude toward sex. The typical teenage viewer who watches an average of three to five hours of television a days sees a minimum of two thousand sexual acts per year on television alone. There is also abundant sexual activity, of course, in music videos, books, movies, cartoons, video games, and song lyrics aimed at teenagers, almost all of it portraying sexual behavior as consequence-free and much of it exploiting women's

bodies and glamorizing sexual violence. Magazines targeting girls and young women are filled with ads and articles on how to be beautiful and sexy and appealing to boys all in service of the advertisers, of course, who sell their wares on almost every page. "How Smart Girls Flirt," "Sex to Write Home About," "15 Ways Sex Makes You Prettier," and "Are you Good in Bed?" are some of the cover stories for a teen magazine called *Jane*.

At the same time, there is rarely any accurate information about sex (the networks still refuse to run condom ads) and certainly never any emphasis on relationships or intimacy (there is hardly time in thirty seconds for the sexual encounter, let alone any development of character!). We have to fight to get sex education into our schools, and the government refuses to fund any program that doesn't insist on abstinence as the only choice suitable for young people (how quickly people forget their own adolescence). Young people learn in school and in church that sex can hurt or kill them, but not that it can bring pleasure, joy, and connection. How can they learn to say, "Yes!" In a loving and responsible way?

It is difficult to do the kind of research that would prove the effects of the media on sexual attitudes and behavior because of the perceived sensitivity of sex as a topic and because of the difficulty in finding a comparison group. However, the few existing studies consistently point to a relationship between exposure to sexual content and sexual beliefs, attitudes, and behavior. Two studies have found correlations between watching higher doses of "sexy" television and early initiation of sexual intercourse, and studies of adolescents have found that heavy television viewing is predictive of negative attitudes toward virginity. In general, key communication theories and years of research on other kinds of communications effects, such as the effect of violent images, suggest that we are indeed affected by the ubiquitous, graphic, and consequence-free depictions of sexual behavior that surround us in all forms of the mass media.

Jane Brown and her colleagues concluded from their years of research that the mass media are important sex educators for American teenagers. Other potential educators, such as parents, schools, and churches, are doing an inadequate job, and even if that were to change dramatically, the media would remain compelling teachers. Brown faults media portrayals for avoiding the "three C's" commitment, contraceptives, and consequences and concludes, "It is little wonder that adolescents find the sexual world a difficult and often confusing place and that they engage in early and unprotected sexual intercourse with multiple partners."

The emphasis for girls and women is always on being desirable, not on experiencing desire. Girls who want to be sexually active instead of simply being the objects of male desire are given only one model to follow, that of exploitive male sexuality. It seems that advertisers can't conceive of a kind of power that isn't manipulative and exploitive or a way that women can be actively sexual without being like traditional men.

Women who are "powerful" in advertising are uncommitted. They treat men like sex objects: "If I want a man to see my bra, I take him home," says an androgynous young woman. They are elusive and distant: "She is the first woman who refused to take your phone calls," says one ad. As if it were a good thing to be rude and inconsiderate. Why should any of us, male or female, be interested in someone who won't take our phone calls, who either cares so little for us or is so manipulative?

Mostly though, girls are not supposed to have sexual agency. They are supposed to be passive, swept away, overpowered. "See where it takes you," says a perfume ad featuring a couple passionately embracing. "Unleash your fantasies," says another. "A force of nature." This contributes to the strange and damaging concept of the "good girl" as the one who is swept away, unprepared for sex, versus the "bad girl" as the one who plans for sex, uses contraception, and is generally responsible. A young woman can manage to have sex and yet in some sense maintain her virginity by being "out of control," drunk, or deep in denial about the entire experience.

No wonder most teenage pregnancies occur when one or both parties is drunk. Alcohol and other mind-altering drugs permit sexual activity at the same time that they allow denial. One is almost literally not there. The next day one has an excuse. I was drunk, I was swept away. I did not choose this experience.

In adolescence girls are told that they have to give up much of what they know about relationships and intimacy if they want to attract men. Most tragically, they are told they have to give up each other. The truth is that one of the most powerful antidotes to destructive cultural messages is close and supportive female friendships. But girls are often encouraged by the culture to sacrifice their relationships with each other and to enter into hostile competition for the attention of boys and men. "What the bitch who's about to steal your man wears," says one ad. And many ads feature young women fighting or glaring at each other.

Of course, some girls do resist and rebel. Some are encouraged (by someone a loving parent, a supportive teacher) to see the cultural contradictions clearly and to break free in a healthy and positive way. Others rebel in ways that damage themselves. A young woman seems to have only two choices: She can bury her sexual self, be a "good girl," give in to what Carol Gilligan terms "the tyranny of nice and kind" (and numb the pain by overeating or starving or cutting herself or drinking heavily). Or she can become a rebel flaunt her sexuality, seduce inappropriate partners, smoke, drink flamboyantly, use other drugs. Both of these responses are self-destructive, but they begin as an attempt to survive, not to self-destruct.

Many girls become women who split themselves in two and do both have a double life, a secret life a good girl in public, out of control in private. A feminist in public, involved in an abusive relationship or lost in sadomasochistic fantasies in private. A lawyer by day, a barfly by night. Raiding the refrigerator or drinking themselves into a stupor alone in their kitchens at night, after the children are in bed, the laundry done. Doing well in school, but smoking in order to have a sexier, a cooler image. Being sexual only when drunk.

There are few healthy alternatives for girls who want to truly rebel against restrictive gender roles and stereotypes. The recent emphasis on girl power has led to some real advances for girls and young women, especially in the arenas of music and sports. But it is as often co-opted and trivialized. The Indigo Girls are good and true, but it is the Spice Girls who rule. Magazines like *New Moon*, *Hues* and *Teen Voices* offer a real alternative to the glitzy, boy-crazy, appearance-obsessed teen magazines on the newsstands, but they have to struggle for funds since they take no advertising. There are some good zines and Websites for girls on the Internet but there are also countless sites that degrade and endanger them. And Barbie continues to rake in two billion dollars a year and will soon have a postal stamp in her honor - while a doll called "Happy to be me," similar to Barbie but much more realistic and down to earth, was available for a couple of years in the mid-1990s (I bought one for my daughter) and then vanished from sight. Of course, Barbie's makers have succumbed to pressure somewhat and have remade her with a thicker waist, smaller breasts, and slimmer hips. As a result, according to Anthony Cortese, she has already lost her waitressing job at Hooter's and her boyfriend Ken has told her that he wants to start seeing other dolls.

Girls who want to escape the stereotypes are viewed with glee by advertisers who rush to offer them, as always, power via products. The emphasis in the ads is always on their sexuality, which is exploited to sell them makeup and clothes and shoes. "Lil' Kim is wearing lunch box in black," says a shoe ad featuring a bikini-clad young woman in a platinum wig stepping over a group of nuns - the ultimate bad girl, I guess, but also the ultimate sex object. A demon woman sells a perfume called Hypnotic Poison. A trio of extremely thin African-American women brandish hair appliances and products as if they were weapons and the brand is 911. A cosmetics company has a line of products called "Bad Gal." In one ad, eyeliner is shown in cartoon version as a girl is holding a dog saying, "grrrr," surely a reference to "grrrrls," a symbol these days of "girl power" (as in cybergrrrl.com, the popular Website for girls and young women). Unfortunately, *girl power* doesn't mean much if girls don't have the tools to achieve it. Without reproductive freedom and freedom of violence, *girl power* is nothing but a marketing slogan.

So, for all the attention paid to girls in recent years, what girls are offered mostly by the popular culture is a superficial toughness, an "attitude," exemplified by smoking, drinking, and engaging in casual sex all behaviors that harm themselves. In 1990 Virginia Slims offered girls a T-shirt that said, "Sugar and spice and everything nice? Get real." In 1997 Winston used the same theme in an ad featuring a tough young woman shooting pool and saying, "I'm not all sugar & spice. And neither are my smokes." As if the alternative to the feminine stereotype was sarcasm and toughness, and as if smoking was somehow an expression of one's authentic self ("get real").

Of course, the readers and viewers of these ads don't take them literally. But we do take them in another grain of sand in a slowly accumulating and vast sand pile. If we entirely enter the world of ads, imagine them to be real for a moment, we find that the sand pile has completely closed us in, and there's only one escape route buy something. "Get the power," says an ad featuring a woman showing off her biceps. "The power to clean anything," the ad continues. "Hey girls, you've got the power of control," says an ad for ....hairspray. "The possibilities are endless" (clothing). "Never lose control" (hairspray again). "You never had this much control when you were on your own." (hair gel). "Exceptional character" (a watch). "An enlightening experience" (face powder). "Inner strength" (vitamins). "Only Victor's Secret could make control so sensual" (girdles). "Stronger longer" (shampoo). Of course, the empowerment, the enlightenment, is as impossible to get through products as is anything else love, security, romance, passion. On one level, we know this. On another, we keep buying and hoping and buying.

Other ads go further and offer products as a way to rebel, to be a real individual. "Live outside the lines," says a clothing ad featuring a young woman walking out of a men's room. This kind of rebellion isn't going to rock the world. And, no surprise, the young woman is very thin and conventionally pretty. Another pretty young woman sells a brand of jeans called "Revolt." "Don't just change...revolt," says the copy, but the young woman is passive, slight, her eyes averted.

"Think for yourself," says yet another hollow-cheeked young woman, demonstrating her individuality via an expensive sweater. "Be amazing" (cosmetics). "If you're going to create electricity, use it" (watches). "If you let your spirit out, where would it go" (perfume). These women are all perfect examples of conventional "femininity," as is the young woman in a Halston perfume ad that says, "And when she was bad she wore Halston." What kind of "bad" is this?

"Nude with attitude" feature an African-American woman in a powerful pose, completely undercut by the brevity of her dress and the focus on her long legs. Her "attitude" is nothing to fear she's just another sex object. Good thing, given the fear many people have of powerful African-American women.

The British ad "For girls with plenty of balls" is insulting in ways too numerous to count, beginning with the equation of strength and courage and fiery passion with testicles. What this ad offers girls is body lotion.

Some ads do feature women who seem really angry and rebellious, but the final message is always the same. "Today, I indulge my dark side," says an ad featuring a fierce young woman tearing at what seems to be a net. "Got a problem with that?" The slogan is "be extraordinary not ordinary." The product that promises to free this girl from the net that imprisons her? Black nail polish.

Nail polish. Such a trivial solution to such an enormous dilemma. But such triviality and superficiality is common in advertising. How could it be otherwise? The solution to any problem always has to be a product. Change, transformation, is thus inevitably shallow and moronic, rather than meaningful and transcendent. These days, self-improvement seems to have more to do with calories than with character, with abdomens than with absolutes, with nail polish than with ethics.

It has not always been so, Joan Jacobs Brumberg describe this vividly in <u>The Body Project: An Intimate History of American Girls</u>

When girls in the nineteenth century thought about ways to improve themselves, they almost always focused on their internal character and how it was reflected outward in behavior. In 1892, the personal agenda of an adolescent diarist read: "Resolved, not to talk about myself or feelings. To think before speaking. To work seriously...To be dignified. Interest myself more in others." A century later, in the 1990s, American girls think very differently. In a New Year's resolution written in 1982, a girl wrote: "I will try to make myself better in every way I possibly can with the help of my budget and baby-sitting money. I will lose weight, get new lenses, already got new haircut, good makeup, new clothes and accessories."

Not that girls didn't have plenty of problems in the nineteenth century. But surely by now we should have come much further. This relentless trivialization of a girl's hopes and dreams, her expectations for herself, cuts to the quick of her soul. Just as she is entering womanhood, eager to spread her wings, to become truly sexually active, empowered, independent the culture moves in to cut her down to size.

Black nail polish isn't going to help. But it probably won't hurt either. What hurts are some of the other products offered to girls as a way to rebel and to cope especially our deadliest drugs, alcohol and nicotine. These drugs are cynically and deliberately offered by advertisers to girls as a way to numb the pain of disconnection, to maintain the illusion of some kind of relationship, to be more appealing to men, to be both "liberated" and "feminine," and, perhaps most tragically, to subvert their rebellious spirits, the very spark within that could, if not co-opted, empower them to change their lives.

## Study Questions

1. Why do advertisements target adolescents?

2. Why does she particularly focus on ads directed at young girls? What are girls taught to be by these ads? What are the consequences?

3. How does race and class impact these ads? Does her argument apply primarily to white middle-class girls?

4. Why are girls encouraged to be passive?

5. How do advertisers use sex in these sorts of ads? Why does she say it is problematic? How does it connect to actual information about sex?

# GANGSTA RAP AND AMERICAN CULTURE (1996)

## Michael Eric Dyson (1959- )

*Dyson received his Ph.D. in religion from Princeton University and is currently the* Ida B. Wells-Barnet University Professor *at DePaul University at Chicago. Dyson is an ordained Baptist minister, political activist, and cultural and social critic. The is author of* Making Malcolm: The Myth and Meaning of Malcolm X *(1994),* Race Rules: Navigating the Color Line *(1996),* Between God and Gangsta Rap: Bearing Witness to Black Culture *(1996), and* I May Not Get There With You: the True Martin Luther King, Jr. *(2000).*

The recent attacks on the entertainment industry, especially gangsta rap, by Senator Bob Dole, former Education Secretary William Bennett, and political activist C. Delores Tucker, reveal the fury that popular culture can evoke in a wide range of commentators. As a thirty-five-year-old father of a sixteen year-old son and as a professor and ordained Baptist minister who grew up in Detroit's treacherous inner city, I too am disturbed by many elements of gangsta rap. But I'm equally anguished by the way many critics have used its artists as scapegoats. How can we avoid the pitfall of unfairly attacking black youth for problems that bewitched our culture long before they gained prominence? First, we should understand what forces drove the emergence of rap. Second, we should place the debate about gangsta rap in the context of a much older debate about "negative" and "positive" black images. Finally, we should acknowledge that gangsta rap crudely exposes harmful beliefs and practices that are often maintained with deceptive civility in much of mainstream society, including many black communities.

If the fifteen-year evolution of hip-hop teaches us any thing, it's that history is made in unexpected ways by unexpected people with unexpected results. Rap is now safe from the perils of quick extinction predicted at its humble start. But its birth in the bitter belly of the '70s proved to be a Rosetta stone of black popular culture. Afros, "blunts," funk music, and carnal eruptions define a "back-in-the-day" hip-hop aesthetic. In reality, the severe '70s busted the economic boom of the '60s. The fallout was felt in restructured automobile industries and collapsed steel mills. It was extended in exported employment to foreign markets. Closer to home, there was the depletion of social services to reverse the material ruin of black life. Later, public spaces for black recreation were gutted by Reaganomics or violently transformed by lethal drug economies.

Hip-hop was born in these bleak conditions. Hip-hoppers joined pleasure and rage while turning the details of their difficult lives into craft and capital. This is the world hip-hop would come to "represent": privileged persons speaking for less visible or vocal peers. At their best, rappers shape the tortuous twists of urban fate into lyrical elegies. They represent lives swallowed by too little love or opportunity. They represent themselves and their peers with aggrandizing anthems that boast of their ingenuity and luck in surviving. The art of "representin" that is much ballyhooed in hip-hop is the witness of those left to tell the afflicted's story.

As rap expands its vision and influence, its unfavorable origins and its relentless quest to represent black youth are both a consolation and challenge to hip-hoppers. They remind rappers that history is not merely the stuff of imperial dreams from above. It isn't just the sanitizing myths of those with political power. Representing history is within reach of those who seize the opportunity to speak for themselves, to represent their own interests at all costs. Even rap's largest controversies are about representation. Hip-hop's attitudes toward women and gays continually jolt in the unvarnished malevolence they reveal. The sharp responses to rap's misogyny and homophobia signify its central role in battles over the cultural representation of other beleaguered groups. This is particularly true of gangsta rap.

While gangsta rap takes the heat for a range of social maladies from urban violence to sexual misconduct, the roots of our racial misery remain buried beneath moralizing discourse that is confused and sometimes dishonest There's no doubt that gansta rap is often sexist and that it reflects a vicious misogyny that has seized our nation with frightening intensity. It is doubly wounding for black women who are already beset by attacks from outside their communities to feel the thrust of musical daggers to their dignity from within. How painful it is for black women, many of whom have fought valiantly for black pride, to hear the dissonant chord of disdain carried in the angry epithet "bitch."

The link between the vulgar rhetorical traditions expressed in gansta rap and the economic exploitation that dominates the marketplace is real. The circulation of brutal images of black men as sexual outlaws and black females as "hos" in many gangsta rap narratives mirrors ancient stereotypes of black sexual identity. Male and female bodies are turned into commodities. Black sexual desire is stripped of redemptive uses in relationships of great affection or love.

Gangsta rappers, however, don't merely respond to the values and visions of the marketplace; they help shape them as well. The ethic of consumption that pervades our culture certainly supports the rapacious materialism shot through the narratives of gangsta rap. Such an ethic, however, does not exhaust the literal or metaphoric purposes of material wealth in gangsta culture. The imagined and real uses of money to help one's friends, family, and neighborhood occupies a prominent spot in gangsta rap lyrics and lifestyles.

Equally troubling is the glamorization of violence and the romanticization of the culture of guns that pervades gangsta rap. The recent legal troubles of Tupac Shakur. Dr. Dre, Snoop Doggy Dogg, and other gangsta rappers chastens any defense of the genre based on simplistic claims that these artists are merely performing roles that are divorced from real life. Too often for gangsta rappers, life does indeed imitate and inform art.

But gangsta rappers aren't simply caving in to the pressure of racial stereotyping and its economic rewards in a music industry hungry to exploit their artistic imaginations. According to this view gangsta rappers are easily manipulated pawns in a chess game of material dominance where their consciences are sold to the highest bidder. Or else gangsta rappers are viewed as the black face of white desire to distort the beauty of black life. Some critics even suggest that white record executives discourage the production of "positive rap" and reinforce the desire for lewd expressions packaged as cultural and racial authenticity.

But such views are flawed. The street between black artists and record companies runs both ways. Even though black artists are often ripe for the picking—and thus susceptible to exploitation by white and black record labels—many of them are quite sophisticated about the politics of cultural representation. Many gangsta rappers helped to create the genre's artistic rules. Further, they have figured out how to financially exploit sincere and sensational interest in "ghetto life." gangsta rap is no less legitimate because many "gangstas" turn out to be middle-class blacks faking home boy roots. This fact simply focuses attention on the genre's essential constructedness, its literal artifice. Much of gangsta rap makes voyeuristic whites and naive blacks think they're getting a slice of authentic ghetto life when in reality they're being served colorful exaggerations. That doesn't mean, however that the best of gangsta rappers don't provide compelling portraits of real social and economic stuffering.

Critics of gangsta rap often ignore how hip-hop has been developed without the assistance of a majority of black communities. Even "positive" or "nation-conscious" rap was initially spurned by those now calling for its revival in the face of gangsta rap's ascendancy. Long before white record executives sought to exploit transgressive sexual behavior among blacks, many of us failed to lend support to politically motivated rap. For instance, when political rap group Public Enemy was at its artistic and popular height, most of the critics of gangsta rap didn't insist on the group's prominence in black cultural politics. Instead Public Enemy and other conscientious rappers were often viewed as controversial figures whose inflammatory racial rhetoric was cause for caution or alarm. In this light, the hue and cry directed against gangsta rap by the new defenders of "legitimate" hip-hop rings false.

Also, many critics of gangsta rap seek to curtail its artistic freedom to transgress boundaries defined by racial or sexual taboo. That's because the burden of representation falls heavily on what may be termed the race artist in a far different manner than the one I've described above. The race artist stands in for black communities. She represents millions of blacks by substituting or sacrificing her desires and visions for the perceived desires and visions of the masses. Even when the race artist manages to maintain relative independence of vision, his or her work is overlaid with, and interpreted within the social and political aspirations of blacks as a whole. Why? Because of the appalling lack of redeeming or nonstereotypical representations of black life that are permitted expression in our culture.

This situation makes it difficult for blacks to affirm the value of nontraditional or transgressive artistic expressions. Instead of viewing such cultural products through critical eyes-seeing the good and the bad, the productive and destructive aspects of such art-many blacks tend to simply dismiss such work with hypercritical disdain. A suffocating standard of "legitimate" art is thus produced by the limited public availability of complex black art. Either art is seen as redemptive because it uplifts black culture and shatters stereotypical thinking about blacks or it is seen as bad because it reinforces negative perceptions of black culture.

That is too narrow a measure for the brilliance and variety of black art and cultural imagination. Black folk should surely pay attention to how black art is perceived in our culture. We must be mindful of the social conditions that shape perceptions of our cultural expressions and that stimulate the flourishing of one kind of art versus another. (After all, die-hard hip-hop fans have long criticized how gangsta rap is eagerly embraced by white record companies while "roots" hip-hop is grossly underfinanced.)

But black culture is too broad and intricate—its artistic manifestations too unpredictable and challenging—for us to be obsessed with how white folk view our culture through the lens of our art. And black life is too differentiated by class, sexual identity, gender, region, and nationality to fixate "negative" or "positive" representations of black culture. Black culture is good and bad, uplifting and depressing, edifying and stifling. All of these features should be represented in our art, should find resonant voicing in the diverse tongues of black cultural expressions.

Gangsta rappers are not the first to face the grueling double standards imposed on black artists. Throughout African-American history, creative personalities have sought to escape or enliven the role of race artist with varying degrees of success. The sharp machismo with which many gangsta rappers reject this office grates on the nerves of many traditionalists. Many critics argue that since gangsta rap is often the only means by which many white Americans come into contact with black life, its pornographic representations and brutal stereotypes of black culture are especially harmful. The

understandable but lamentable response of many critics is to condemn gangsta rap out of hand. They aim to suppress gangsta rap's troubling expressions rather than critically engage its artists and the provocative issues they address. Or the critics of gangsta rap use it for narrow political ends that fail to enlighten or better our common moral lives.

Tossing a moralizing *j'accuse* at the entertainment industry may have boosted Bob Dole's standing in the polls over the short term. It did little, however, to clarify or correct the problems to which he has drawn dramatic attention. I'm in favor of changing the moral climate of our nation. I just don't believe that attacking movies, music, and their makers is very helpful. Besides right-wing talk radio hosts wreak more havoc than a slew of violent films. They're the ones terrorist Timothy McVeigh was inspired by as he planned to bomb the Federal building in Oklahoma city.

A far more crucial task lies in getting at what's wrong with our culture and what it needs to get right. Nailing the obvious is easy. That's why Dole, along with William Bennett and C. Delores Tucker, goes after popular culture, especially gangsta rap. And the recent attempts of figures like Tucker and Dionne Warwick as well as national and local lawmakers to censor gangsta rap or to outlaw its sale to minors are surely misguided. When I testified before the U.S. Senate's Subcommittee on juvenile justice, as well as the Pennsylvania House of Representatives, I tried to make this point while acknowledging the need to responsibly confront gangsta rap's problems. Censorship of gangsta rap cannot begin to solve the problems of poor black youth. Nor will it effectively curtail their consumption of music that is already circulated through dubbed tapes and without the benefit of significant airplay.

A crucial distinction needs to be made between censorship of gangsta rap and edifying expressions of civic responsibility and community conscientiousness. The former seeks to prevent the sale of vulgar music that offends mainstream moral sensibilities by suppressing the First Amendment. The latter, however, is a more difficult but rewarding task. It seeks to oppose the expression of misogynistic and sexist sentiments in hip-hop culture through protest and pamphleteering through community activism, and through boycotts and consciousness raising.

What Dole, Bennett, and Tucker shrink from helping us understand—and what all effective public moralists must address—is why this issue now? Dole's answer is that the loss of family values is caused by the moral corruption of popular culture, and therefore we should hold rap artists, Hollywood moguls, and record executives responsible for our moral chaos. It's hard to argue with Dole on the surface, but a gentle scratch reveals that both his analysis and answer are flawed.

Too often, "family values" is a code for a narrow view of how families work, who gets to count as a legitimate domestic unit, and consequently, what values are crucial to their livelihood. Research has shown that nostalgia for the family of the past, when father knew best, ignores the widespread problems of those times, including child abuse and misogyny. Romantic portrayals of the family on television and the big screen, anchored by the myth of the Benevolent Patriarch, hindered our culture from coming to grips with its ugly domestic problems.

To be sure, there have been severe assaults on American families and their values, but they have not come mainly from Hollywood but from Washington with the dismantling of the Great Society. Cruel cuts in social programs for the neediest, redistribution of wealth to the rich, and an unprincipled conservative political campaign to demonize poor black mothers and their children have left latter-day D. W. Griffiths in the dust. Many of gangsta raps most vocal black critics (such as Tucker) fail to see how the alliances they forge with conservative white politicians such as Bennett and Dole are plagued with problems. Bennett and Dole have put up roadblocks to many legislative and political measures that would enhance the fortunes of the black poor they now claim in part to speak for. Their outcry resounds as crocodile tears from the corridors of power paved by bad faith.

Moreover many of the same conservative politicians who support the attack on gangsta rap also attack black women (from Lani Guinier to welfare mothers), affirmative action, and the redrawing of voting districts to achieve parity for black voters. The war on gangsta rap diverts attention away from the more substantive threat posed to women and blacks by many conservative politicians. gangsta rap's critics are keenly aware of the harmful effects that genre's misogyny can have on black teens. Ironically, such critics appear oblivious to how their rhetoric of absolute opposition to gangsta rap has been used to justify political attacks on poor black teens.

That doesn't mean that gratuitous violence and virulent misogyny should not be opposed. They must be identified and destroyed. I am wholly sympathetic, for instance, to sharp criticism of gangsta rap's ruinous sexism and homophobia though neither Dole, Bennett, nor Tucker have made much of the latter plague. "Fags" and "dykes" are prominent in the genre's vocabulary of rage. Critics' failure to make this an issue only reinforces invisible status of gay men and lesbians in mainstream and

black cultural institutions. Homophobia is a vicious emotion and practice that at links mainstream middle-class and black institutions to the vulgar expressions of gangsta rap. There seems to be an implicit agreement between gangsta rappers and political elites that gays, lesbians, and bisexuals basically deserve what they get.

But before we discard the genre, we should understand that gangsta rap often reaches higher than its ugliest, lowest common denominator. Misogyny, violence, materialism, and sexual transgression are not its exclusive domain. At its best, this music draws attention to complex dimensions of ghetto life ignored by many Americans. Of all the genres of hip-hop—from socially conscious rap to black nationalist expressions, from pop to hardcore—gangsta rap has most aggressively narrated the pains and possibilities, the fantasies and fears of poor black urban youth. gangsta rap is situated in the violent climes of postindustrial Los Angeles and its bordering cities. It draws its metaphoric capital in part from the mix of myth and murder that gave the Western frontier a dangerous appeal a century ago.

Gangsta rap is largely an indictment of mainstream and bourgeois black institutions by young people who do not find conventional methods of addressing personal and social calamity useful. The leaders of those institutions often castigate the excessive and romanticized violence of this music without trying to understand what precipitated its rise in the first place. In so doing, they drive a greater wedge between themselves and the youth they so desperately want to help.

If Americans really want to strike at the heart of sexism and misogyny in our communities, shouldn't we take a closer look at one crucial source of these blights: religious institutions, including the synagogue, the temple and the church? For instance the central institution of black culture, the black church, which has given hope and inspiration to millions of blacks has also given us an embarassing legacy of sexism and misogyny. Despite the great good it has achieved through a heroic tradition of emancipatory leadership, the black church continues to practice and justify *ecclesiastical apartheid*. More than 70 percent of black church members are female, yet they are generally excluded from the church's central station of power, the pulpit. And rarely are the few ordained female ministers elected pastors.

Yet black leaders, many of them ministers, excoriate rappers for their verbal sexual misconduct. It is difficult to listen to civil rights veterans deplore the hostile depiction of women in gangsta rap without mentioning the vicious sexism of the movements for racial liberation of the 1960s. And of course the problem persists in many civil rights organizations today.

Attacking figures like Snoop Doggy Dogg or Tupac Shakur—or the companies that record or distribute them is an easy out. It allows scapegoating without sophisticated moral analysis and action. While these young black males become whipping boys for sexism and misogyny, the places in our culture where these ancient traditions are nurtured and rationalized—including religious and educational institutions and the nuclear family—remain immune to forceful and just criticism.

Corporate capitalism, mindless materialism and pop culture have surely helped unravel the moral fabric of our society. But the moral condition of our nation is equally affected by political policies that harm the vulnerable and poor. It would behoove Senator Dole to examine the glass house of politics he abides in before he decides to throw stones again. If he really wants to do something about violence he should change his mind about the ban on assault weapons he seeks to repeal. That may not be as sexy or self-serving as attacking pop culture, but it might help save lives.

Gangsta rap's greatest "sin" may be that it tells the truth about practices and beliefs that rappers hold in common with the mainstream and with black elites. This music has embarrassed mainstream society and black bourgeois culture. It has forced us to confront the demands of racial repre-sentation that plague and provoke black artists. It has also exposed our polite sexism and our disregard for gay men and lesbians. We should not continue to blame gangsta rap for ills that existed long before hip-hop uttered its first syllable. Indeed gangsta rap's in-your-face style may do more to force our nation to confront crucial social problems than countless sermons or political speeches.

## Study Questions

1. How does Dyson assess rap music? What does he see as positive and negative in rap? Is his analysis fair? Do you agree with him?

2. What is his critique of conservative attacks on rap music? How does he respond to those who claim rap music is causing "moral chaos" or the destruction of "family values"?

3. What does he say about religious institutions and their criticism of rap music?

4. What do you think of his use of the term "gansta rap"? Is this an accurate or useful label for some rap music? What are the different genres of rap music? Which ones does Dyson discuss?

# THE IDEOLOGY OF MACHINES

## Computer Technology (1992)

### *Neil Postman*

*Neil Postman is Professor of Media Ecology and Chair of the Department of Culture and Communication at New York University. He has written more than 18 books including* Amusing Ourselves to Death *(1985) and* The Disappearance of Childhood. *His work concerns the impact of media and technology upon American life and culture. This excerpt is taken from his book,* Technopoly *(1992).*

That American Technopoly has now embraced the computer in the same hurried and mindless way it embraced medical technology is undeniable, was perhaps inevitable, and is certainly most unfortunate. This is not to say that the computer is a blight on the symbolic landscape; only that, like medical technology, it has usurped powers and enforced mind-sets that a fully attentive culture might have wished to deny it. Thus, an examination of the ideas embedded in computer technology is worth attempting. Others, of course, have done this, especially Joseph Weizenbaum in his great and indispensable book *Computer Power and Human Reason.* Weizenbaum, however, ran into some difficulties, as everyone else has, because of the "universality" of computers, meaning (a) that their uses are infinitely various, and (b) that computers are commonly integrated into the structure of other machines. It is, therefore, hard to isolate specific ideas promoted by computer technology. The computer, for example, is quite unlike the stethoscope, which has a limited function in a limited context. Except for safecrackers, who, I am told, use stethoscopes to hear the tumblers of lock click into place, stethoscopes are used only by doctors. But

everyone uses or is used by computers, and for purposes that seem to know no boundaries.

Putting aside such well-known functions as electronic filing, spreadsheets, and word-processing one can make a fascinating list of the innovative, even bizarre, uses of computers. I have before me a report from *The New York Times* that tells us how computers are enabling aquatic designers to create giant water slides that mimic roller coasters and eight-foot-high artificial waves. In my modest collection, I have another article about the uses of personal computers for making presentations at corporate board meetings. Another tells of how computer graphics help jurors to remember testimony better. Gregory Mazares, president of the graphics unit of Litigation Sciences, is quoted as saying, "We're a switched-on, tuned-in, visually oriented society, and jurors tend to believe what they see. This technology keeps the jury's attention by simplifying the material and by giving them little bursts of information." While Mr. Mazares is helping switched-on people to remember things Morton David, chief executive officer of Franklin Computer, is helping them find any word in the Bible with lightning speed by producing electronic Bibles (The word "lightning," by the way, appears forty–two times in the New International version and eight times in the King James version. Were you so inclined you could discover this for yourself in a matter of seconds.) This fact so dominates Mr. David's imagination that he is quoted as saying, "Our technology may have made a change as momentous as the Gutenberg invention of movable type." And then there is an article that reports a computer's use to make investment decisions, which helps you, among other things, to create "what-if' scenarios, although with how much accuracy we are not told. In *Technology Review* we find a description of how computers are used to help the police locate the addresses of callers in distress; a prophecy is made that in time police officers will have so much instantly available information about any caller that they will know how seriously to regard the caller's appeal for help.

One may well wonder if Charles Babbage had any of this in mind when he announced in 1822 (only six years after the appearance of Laënnec's stethoscope) that he had invented a machine capable of performing simple arithmetical calculations. Perhaps he did, for he never finished his invention and started work on a more ambitious machine, capable of doing more complex tasks. He abandoned that as well, and in 1833 put aside his calculator project completely in favor of a programmable machine that became the forerunner of the modern computer. His first such machine, which he characteristically never finished, was to be controlled by punch cards adopted from devices French weavers used to control thread sequences in their looms.

Babbage kept improving his programmable machine over the next thirty-seven years, each design being more complex than the last. At some point, he realized that the mechanization of numerical operations gave him the means to manipulate non-numerical symbols. It is not farfetched to say that Babbage's insight was comparable to the discovery by the Greeks in the third century B.C. of the principle of alphabetization—that is, the realization that the symbols of the alphabet could be separated from their phonetic function and used as a system for the classification, storage, and retrieval of information. In any case, armed with his insight, Babbage was able to speculate about the possibility of designing "intelligent" information machinery, though the mechanical technology of his time was inadequate to allow the fulfillment of his ideas. The computer as we know it today had to await a variety of further discoveries and inventions, including the telegraph, the telephone, and the application of Boolean algebra to relay-based circuitry, resulting in Claude Shannon's creation of digital logic circuitry. Today, when the word "computer" is used without a modifier before it, it normally refers to some version of the machine invented by John von Neumann in the 1940s. Before that the word "computer" referred to a person (similarly to the early use of the word "typewriter") who performed some kind of mechanical calculation. As calculation shifted from people to machines, so did the word, especially because of the power of von Neumann's machine.

Certainly, after the invention of the digital computer, it was abundantly clear that the computer was capable of performing functions that could in some sense be called "intelligent." In 1936, the great English mathematician Alan Turing showed that it was possible to build a machine that would, for many practical purposes, behave like a problem-solving human being. Turing claimed that he would call a machine "intelligent" if, through typed messages, it could exchange thoughts with a human being—that is, hold up its end of a conversation. In the early days of MIT's Artificial Intelligence Laboratory, Joseph Weizenbaum wrote a program called ELIZA, which showed how easy it was to meet Turing's test for intelligence. When asked a question with a proper noun in it, ELIZA's program could respond with "Why are you interested in," followed by the proper noun and a question mark. That is, it could invert statements and seek more information about one of the nouns in the statement. Thus, ELIZA acted much like a Rogerian psychologist, or at least a friendly and inexpensive therapist. Some people who used ELIZA refused to believe that they were conversing with a mere machine. Having, in effect, created a Turing machine, Weinzenbaum eventually pulled the program off the computer network and was stimulated to write *Computer Power and Human Reason*, in which, among other things, he raised questions about the research programs of those working in artificial intelligence; the assumption that whatever a computer can do, it *should* do; and the effects of computer technology on the way people construe the world—that is, the ideology of the computer, to which I now turn.

The most comprehensive idea conveyed by the computer is suggested by the title of David Bolter's book, *Turing's Man*. His title is a metaphor, of course, similar to what would be suggested by saying that from the sixteenth century until recently we were "Gutenberg's Men." Although Bolter's main practical interest in the computer is in its function as a new kind of book, he argues that it is the dominant metaphor of our age; it defines our age by suggesting a new relationship to information, to work, to power, and to nature itself. That relationship can best be described by saying that the computer redefines humans as "information processors" and nature itself as information to be processed. The fundamental metaphorical message of the computer, in short, is that we are machines—thinking machines, to be sure, but machines nonetheless. It is for this reason that the computer is the quintessential, incomparable, near perfect machine for Technopoly. It subordinates the claims of our nature, our biology, our emotions, our spirituality. The computer claims sovereignty over the whole range of human experience, and supports its claim by showing that it "thinks" better than we can. Indeed, in his almost hysterical enthusiasm for artificial intelligence, Marvin Minsky has been quoted as saying that the thinking power of silicon "brains" will be so formidable that "if we are lucky, they will keep us as pets." An even giddier remark, although more dangerous, was offered by John McCarthy, the inventor of the term "artificial intelligence." McCarthy claims that "even machines as simple as thermostats can be said to have beliefs." To the obvious question, posed by the philosopher John Searle, "What beliefs does your thermostat have?," McCarthy replied, "My thermostat has three beliefs—it's too hot in here, it's too cold in here, and it's just right in here."

What is significant about this response is that it has redefined the meaning of the word "belief." The remark rejects the view that humans have internal states of mind that are the foundation of belief and argues instead that "belief" means only what someone or something does. The remark also implies that simulating an idea is synonymous with duplicating the idea. And, most important, the remark rejects the idea that mind is a biological phenomenon.

In other words, what we have here is a case of metaphor gone mad. From the proposition that humans are in some respects like machines, we move to the proposition that humans are little else but machines and, finally, that human beings are machines. And then, inevitably, as McCarthy's remark suggests, to the proposition that machines are human beings. It follows that machines can be made that duplicate human intelligence, and thus research in the field known as artificial intelligence was inevitable. What is most significant about this line of thinking is the dangerous reductionism it represents. Human intelligence, as Weizenbaum has tried energetically to remind everyone, is not transferable. The plain fact is that humans have a unique, biologically rooted, intangible mental life which in some limited respects can be simulated by a machine but can never be duplicated. Machines cannot feel and, just as important, cannot *understand*. ELIZA can ask, "Why are you worried about your mother?," which might be exactly the question a therapist would ask. But the machine does not know what the question means or even *that* the question means. (Of course, there may be some therapists who do not know what the question means either, who ask it routinely, ritualistically, inattentively. In that case we may say they are acting like a machine.) It is meaning, not utterance, that makes mind unique. I use "meaning" here to refer to something more than the result of putting together symbols the denotations of which are commonly shared by at least two people. As I understand it, meaning also includes those things we call feelings, experiences, and sensations that do not have to be, and sometimes cannot be, put into symbols. They "mean" nonetheless. Without concrete symbols, a computer is merely a pile of junk. Although the quest for a machine that duplicates mind has ancient roots, and although digital logic circuitry has given that quest a scientific structure, artificial intelligence does not and cannot lead to a meaning-making, understanding, and feeling creature, which is what a human being is.

All of this may seem obvious enough, but the metaphor of the machine as human (or the human as machine) is sufficiently powerful to have made serious inroads in everyday language. People now commonly speak of "programming" or "deprogramming" themselves. They speak of their brains as a piece of "hard wiring," capable of "retrieving data," and it has become common to think about thinking as a mere matter of processing and decoding.

Perhaps the most chilling case of how deeply our language is absorbing the "machine as human" metaphor began on November 4, 1988, when the Computers around the ARPANET network became sluggish, filled with extraneous data, and then clogged completely. The problem spread fairly quickly to six thousand computers across the United States and overseas. The early hypothesis was that a software program had attached itself to other programs, a situation which is called (in another human-machine metaphor) a "virus." As it happened, the intruder was a self-contained program explicitly designed to disable computers, which is called a "worm." But the technically incorrect term "virus" stuck, no doubt because of its familiarity and its human connections. As Raymond Gozzi, Jr., discovered in his analysis of how the mass media described the event, newspapers noted that the computers were "infected," that the virus was "virulent" and "contagious," that attempts were made to "quarantine" the infected computers, that attempts were also being made to "sterilize" the network, and that programmers hoped to develop a "vaccine" so that computers could be "inoculated" against new attacks.

This kind of language is not merely picturesque anthropomorphism. It reflects a profound shift in perception about the relationship of computers to humans. If computers can become ill, then they can become healthy. Once healthy, they can think clearly and make decisions. The computer, it is implied, has a will, has intentions, has reasons—which means that humans are relieved of responsibility for the computer's decisions. Through a curious form of grammatical alchemy, the sentence "we use the computer to calculate" comes to mean "The computer calculates." If a computer calculates, then it may decide to miscalculate or not calculate at all. That is what bank tellers mean when they tell you that they cannot say how much money is in your checking account because "the computers are down." The implication, of course, is that no person at the bank is responsible. Computers make mistakes or get tired or become ill. Why blame people? We may call this line of thinking an "agentic shift," a term I borrow from Stanley Milgram to name the process whereby humans transfer responsibility for an outcome from themselves to a more abstract agent. When this happens, we have relinquished control, which in the case of the computer means that we may, without excessive remorse, pursue ill-advised or even inhuman goals because the computer can accomplish them or be imagined to accomplish them.

Machines of various kinds will sometimes assume a human or, more likely, a superhuman aspect. Perhaps the most absurd case I know of is in a remark a student of mine once made on a sultry summer day in a room without air conditioning. On being told the thermometer read ninety-eight degrees Fahrenheit, he replied, "No wonder it's so hot!" Nature was off the hook. If only the thermometers would behave themselves, we could be comfortable. But computers are far more "human" than thermometers or almost any other kind of technology. Unlike most machines, computers do no work; they direct work. They are, as Norbert Wiener said, the technology of "command and control" and have little value without something to control. This is why they are of such importance to bureaucracies.

Naturally, bureaucrats can be expected to embrace a technology that helps to create the illusion that decisions are not under their control. Because of its seeming intelligence and impartiality, a computer has an almost magical tendency to direct attention away from the people in charge of bureaucratic functions and toward itself, as if the computer were the true source of authority. A bureaucrat armed with a computer is the unacknowledged legislator of our age, and a terrible burden to bear. We cannot dismiss the possibility that, if Adolf Eichmann had been able to say that it was not he but a battery of computers that directed the Jews to the appropriate crematoria, he might never have been asked to answer for his actions.

Although (or perhaps because) I came to "administration" late in my academic career, I am constantly amazed at how obediently people accept explanations that begin with the words "The computer shows . . . " or "The computer has determined . . . " It is Technopoly's equivalent of the sentence "it is God's will," and the effect is roughly the same. You will not be surprised to know that I rarely resort to such humbug. But on occasion, when pressed to the wall, I have yielded. No one has as yet replied, "Garbage in, garbage out." Their defenselessness has something Kafkaesque about it. In *The Trial*, Josef K. is charged with a crime of what nature, and by whom the charge is made, he does not know. The computer turns too many of us into Josef Ks. It often functions as a kind of impersonal accuser which does not reveal, and is not required to reveal, the sources of the judgments made against us. It is apparently sufficient that the computer has pronounced. Who has put the data in, for what purpose, for whose convenience, based on what assumptions are questions left unasked.

This is the case not only in personal matters but in public decisions as well. Large institutions such as the Pentagon, the Internal Revenue Service, and multinational corporations tell us that their decisions are made on the basis of solutions generated by computers and this is usually good enough to put our minds at ease or, rather, to sleep. In any case, it constrains us from making complaints or accusations. In part for this reason, the computer has strengthened bureaucratic institutions and suppressed the impulse toward significant social change. "The arrival of the Computer Revolution and the founding of the Computer Age have been announced many times," Weizenbaum has written. "But if the triumph of a revolution is to be measured in terms of the social revision it entrained, then there has been no computer revolution."

In automating the operation of political, social, and commercial enterprises, computers may or may not have made them more efficient but they have certainly diverted attention from the question whether or not such enterprises are necessary or how they might be improved. A university, a political party, a religious denomination, a judicial proceeding, even corporate board meetings are not improved by automating their operations. They are made more imposing, more technical, perhaps more authoritative, but defects in their assumptions, ideas, and theories will remain untouched. Computer technology, in other words, has not yet come close to the printing press in its power to generate radical and substantive social, political, and religious thought. If the press was, as David Reesman called it, "the gunpowder of the mind," the computer, in its capacity to smooth over unsatisfactory institutions and ideas, is the talcum powder of the mind.

I do not wish to go as far as Weinzenbaum in saying that computers are merely ingenious devices to fulfill unimportant functions and that the computer revolution is an explosion of nonsense. Perhaps that judgment will be in need of amendment in the future, for the computer is a technology of a thousand uses—the Proteus of machines, to use Seymour Papert's phrase. One must note, for example, the use of computer-generated images in the phenomenon known as Virtual Reality. Putting on a set of miniature goggle-mounted screens, one may block out the real world and move through a simulated three dimensional world which changes its components with every movement of one's head. That Timothy Leary is an enthusiastic proponent of Virtual Reality does not suggest that there is a constructive future for this device. But who knows? Perhaps, for those who can no longer cope with the real world, Virtual Reality will provide better therapy than ELIZA.

What is clear is that, to date, computer technology has served to strengthen Technopoly's hold, to make people believe that technological innovation is synonymous with human progress. And it has done so by advancing several interconnected ideas.

It has, as already noted, amplified beyond all reason the metaphor of machines as humans and humans as machines. I do not claim, by the way, that computer technology originated this metaphor. One can detect it in medicine, too: doctors and patients have come to believe that, like a machine, a human being is made up of parts which when defective can be replaced by mechanical parts that function as the original did without impairing or even affecting any other part of the machine. Of course, to some degree that assumption works, but since a human being is in fact not a machine but a biological organism all of whose organs are interrelated and profoundly affected by mental states, the human-as-machine metaphor has serious medical limitations and can have devastating effects. Something similar may be said of the mechanistic metaphor when applied to workers. Modern industrial techniques are made possible by the idea that a machine is made of isolatable and interchangeable parts. But in organizing factories so that workers are also conceived of as isolatable and interchangeable parts, industry has engendered deep alienation and bitterness. This was the point of Charlie Chaplin's *Modern Times*, in which he tried to show the psychic damage of the metaphor carried too far. But because the computer "thinks" rather than works, its power to energize mechanistic metaphors is unparalleled and of enormous value to Technopoly, which depends on our believing that we are at our best when acting like machines, and that in significant ways machines may be trusted to act as our surrogates. Among the impli-

cations of these beliefs is a loss of confidence in human judgment and subjectivity. We have devalued the singular human capacity to see things whole in all their psychic, emotional and moral dimensions, and we have replaced this with faith in the powers of technical calculation.

Because of what computers commonly do, they place an inordinate emphasis on the technical processes of communication and offer very little in the way of substance. With the exception of the electric light, there never has been a technology that better exemplifies Marshall McLuhan's aphorism "The medium is the message." The computer is almost all process. There are, for example, no "great computerers," as there are great writers, painters, or musicians. There are "great programs" and "great programmers," but their greatness lies in their ingenuity either in simulating a human function or in creating new possibilities of calculation, speed, and volume. Of course, if J. David Bolter is right, it is possible that in the future computers will emerge as a new kind of book, expanding and enriching the tradition of writing technologies. Since printing created new forms of literature when it replaced the handwritten manuscript, it is possible that electronic writing will do the same. But for the moment, computer technology functions more as a new mode of transportation than as a new means of substantive communication. It moves information—lots of it, fast, and mostly in a calculating mode. The computer, in fact, makes possible the fulfillment of Descartes' dream of the mathematization of the world. Computers make it easy to convert facts into statistics and to translate problems into equations. And whereas this can be useful (as when the process reveals a pattern that would otherwise go unnoticed), it is diversionary and dangerous when applied indiscriminately to human affairs. So is the computer's emphasis on speed and especially its capacity to generate and store unprecedented quantities of information. In specialized contexts, the value of calculation, speed, and voluminous information may go uncontested. But the "message" of computer technology is comprehensive and domineering. The computer argues, to put it baldly, that the most serious problems confronting us at both personal and public levels require technical solutions through fast access to information otherwise unavailable. I would argue that this is, on the face of it, nonsense. Our most serious problems are not technical, nor do they arise from inadequate information. If a nuclear catastrophe occurs, it shall not be because of inadequate information. Where people are dying of starvation, it does not occur because of inadequate information. If families break up, children are mistreated, crime terrorizes a city, education is impotent, it does not happen because of inadequate information. Mathematical equations, instantaneous communication, and vast quantities of information have nothing whatever to do with any of these problems. And the computer is useless in addressing them.

And yet, because of its "universality," the computer compels respect, even devotion, and argues for a comprehensive role in all fields of human activity. Those who insist that it is foolish to deny the computer vast sovereignty are singularly devoid of what Paul Goodman once called "technological modesty"—that is, having a sense of the whole and not claiming or obtruding more than a particular function warrants. Norbert Wiener warned about lack of modesty when he remarked that, if digital computers had been in common use before the atomic bomb was invented, people would have said that the bomb could not have been invented without computers. But it was. And it is important to remind ourselves of how many things are quite possible to do without the use of computers.

Seymour Papert, for example, wishes students to be epistemologists, to think critically, and to learn how to create knowledge. In his book *Mindstorms*, he gives the impression that his computer program known as LOGO now makes this possible. But good teachers have been doing this for centuries without the benefit of LOGO. I do not say that LOGO, when used properly by a skilled teacher, will not help, but I doubt that it can do better than pencil and paper, or speech itself, when used properly by a skilled teacher.

When the Dallas Cowboys were consistently winning football championships, their success was attributed to the fact that computers were used to evaluate and select team members. During the past several years, when Dallas has been hard put to win more than a few games, not much has been said about the computers, perhaps because people have realized that computers have nothing to do with winning football games, and never did. One might say the same about writing lucid, economical, stylish prose, which has nothing to do with word processors. Although my students don't believe it, it is actually possible to write well without a processor and, I should say, to write poorly with one.

Technological immodesty is always an acute danger in Technopoly, which encourages it. Technopoly also encourages insensitivity to what skills may be lost in the acquisition of new ones. It is important to remember what can be done without computers, and it is also import important to remind ourselves of what may be lost when we do use them.

I have before me an essay by Sir Bernard Lovell, founder of Britain's Jodrell Bank Observatory, in which he claims that computers have stifled scientific creativity. After writing of his awe at the ease with which computerized operations provide amazing details of distant galaxies, Sir Bernard expresses concern that "literal-minded, narrowly focused computerized research is proving antithetical to the free exercise of that happy faculty known as serendipity—that is, the knack of achieving favorable results more or less by chance." He proceeds to give several examples of monumental but serendipitous discoveries, contends that there has been a dramatic cessation of such discoveries, and worries that computers are too narrow as filters of information and therefore may be antiserendipitous. He is, of course, not "against" computers, but is merely raising questions about their costs.

Dr. Clay Forishee, the chief FAA scientist for human performance issues, did the same when he wondered whether the automated operation of commercial aircraft has not disabled pilots from creatively responding when something goes wrong. Robert Buley, flight-standards manager of Northwest Airlines, goes further. He is quoted as saying, "If we have human operators subordinated to technology then we're going to lose creativity [in emergencies]." He is not "against" computers. he is worried about what we lose by using them.

M. Ethan Katsch, in his book *The Electronic Media and the Transformation of Law*, worries as well. He writes, "The replacement of print by computerized systems is promoted to the legal profession simply as a means to increase efficiency."' But he goes on to say that, in fact, the almost unlimited capacity of computers to store and retrieve information threatens the authority of precedent, and he adds that the threat is completely unrecognized. As he notes, "a system of precedent is unnecessary when there are very few accessible cases, and unworkable when there are too many." If this is true, or even partly true, what exactly does it mean? Will lawyers become incapable of choosing relevant precedents? Will judges be in constant confusion from "precedent overload"?

We know that doctors who rely entirely on machinery have lost skill in making diagnoses based on observation. We may well wonder what other human skills and traditions are being lost by our immersion in a computer culture. Technopolists do not worry about such things. Those who do are called technological pessimists, Jeremiahs, and worse. I rather think they are imbued with technological modesty, like King Thamus.

**Study Questions**

1. Can computers think? Do they have "intelligence"? What does Postman argue? What do you think?

2. What do the metaphors "machine as human" and "human as machine" mean? What does Postman think about them? Do you agree?

3. How does the author critique the role of computers in our society? What role does he think computers should play? What do you think?

4. Why is Postman so critical of technology? What does he think about "technological solutions" to social problems? What are the dangers of "technopoly"?

# 5

# "THE CHOKING DOBERMAN" AND ITS ANCESTORS (1984)

## "New" Urban Legends

### Jan Harald Brunvand

*Jan Harald Brunvand is Professor of English and folklore at the University of Utah and is the author of* The Study of American Folklore *(4th edition 1998). He is one of the leading folklorists in America and has published a series of works on Urban Legends that include* The Vanishing Hitchhiker *(1981),* The Mexican Pet *(1986), and* Too Good to be True *(1999). This excerpt shows how Urban Legends reflect the political and racial climate in contemporary American society.*

What is more welcome on a routine day than a new and intriguing true story or rumor told in the first person? The very opening sentence of such a story makes our ears tingle and draws our attention sharply away from the workaday world: "Did you hear about what happened to a neighbor of mine?" or "My aunt just had the most amazing experience," or "I was told by my hairdresser about this terrible thing that happened to another customer of hers."

All of us hear "urban legends," and we retell them eagerly at home or at parties, work, school, and everywhere we meet other people. The advice and opinion columns of the daily press pass on such stories too, as do some radio and television broadcasters. The media both pick up rumors and legends front the oral stream and feed them back into it again.

Is a dog biting a man not news? It is if it has the right twist. Here is a "Dog bites man" urban legend that recently got into the pages of *Woman's World* magazine (20 April 1982):

*A weird thing happened to a woman at work. She got home one afternoon and her German shepherd was in convulsions. So she rushed the dog to the vet, then raced home to get ready for a date. As she got back in the door, her phone rang. It was the vet, telling her that two human fingers had been lodged in her dog's throat. The police arrived and they all followed a bloody trail to her bedroom closet, where a young burglar huddled—moaning over his missing thumb and forefinger.*

It matters little that Philip Brennan, Jr., the author of the article in which that legend appeared as a teaser, titled his piece "Rumor Madness" and emphasized the completely untrue nature of such narratives. Hundreds of thousands of readers will have read the story, and a goodly number of them will have found it so gripping that they discussed it with or retold it to their families and friends; finally, the legend of the watchdog in convulsions began to return from whence it first came to the author's ears—back to modern American folklore.

But where did the story come from? What other familiar stories are merely legends? Who tells such stories, and why are they believed by so many tellers and listeners? It is their status as folklore, and their behavior and meaning as part of modern oral tradition, that this book about new urban legends deals with.

From the start there are problems with the idea of new urban legends in folklore. First, these "legends"—which are by definition *believed* oral

477

narratives—are not necessarily taken as literal truth by all of their tellers all of the time. Sometimes they are told, or printed, merely as jokes or (as with the *Woman's World* text) as typical examples of recent popular fallacies. Furthermore, some are really more *rumor* (plotless unverified reports) than *legend* (traditional believed story). Second, though the stories are modern, they are not just "urban" in their circulation or subject matter. They are often, but not always, city stories. Third, and most important, urban legends (as I continue to call them, following folkloristic tradition) often appear to be "new" when they begin to spread, but even the newest-sounding stories may have gone the rounds before.

A "new urban legend," then, may be merely a modern story told in a plausible manner by a credible narrator to someone who hasn't heard the story before, at least not recently enough to remember it. And this sort of thing happens to folklorists just as well as to any other folk.

No sooner had I finished *The Vanishing Hitchhiker* in 1981 than people started telling and mailing me strange and funny stories of all kinds, many of which sounded like urban legends. Some stories, people claimed, were authentic, though peculiar, real-life occurrences—and they seemed so. But these stories eventually also showed up in the supposed experiences of many other people and had the scent of legend rather than truth. An example of this is "The Stolen Specimen." Other stories were old ones not told much lately, and I had forgotten about them; these included "The Rattle in the Cadillac," "The Licked Hand," and "The Poison Dress." Still other stories turned out to be genuine instances of modern folklore that American folklorists had not taken notice of, such as "The Elephant That Sat on a VW," "The Bump in the Rug," and "The Double Theft."

The most fascinating ones I received were the stories that incorporated thoroughly up-to-date references and thus might represent actual new urban legends. Mentions in these stories of Superglue, jogging, butane cigarette lighters, automobile cruise control, and the 911 emergency telephone number all suggested the possibility of uniquely modern legends; but in most such narratives only the details proved to be new while the structures or ideas were definitely old.

The particular story that came most often to my attention shortly before *The Vanishing Hitchhiker* got into print was the one about the choking dog. It had a plot that sounded as fresh as this morning's headlines, and plenty of true believers passing it along as gospel. The story of the dog—usually a Doberman—that was choking on fingers bitten off an intruder turned out to be a fine example of a

"new" urban legend sweeping the country but its apparent newness just thinly masked much older folklore elements.

In order to expose this new legend as the old story it is, and also to demonstrate how folklore research sometimes works, I give in this chapter the history of the choking dog plot, insofar as it call be written, plus an account of my detective work that established its sources. Unlike most other new urban legends that spring up, for this one a fairly complete genealogy can be traced.

## "THE CHOKING DOBERMAN"

The earliest reliably dated complete American version of "The Choking Doberman" story that I have found introduced most of the elements that are characteristic of this new tradition. From the Phoenix, Arizona, *New Times*, 24 June 1981:

GAGGING DOG STORY BAFFLES POLICE

*It happened in Las Vegas. A woman returned from work and found her large dog, a Doberman, lying on the floor gasping for air. Concerned over the animal's welfare, she immediately loaded the pet into her car and drove him to a veterinarian.*

*The vet examined the dog but finding no reason for his breathing difficulties, announced that he'd have to perform a tracheotomy and insert tubes down the animal's throat so he could breathe. Hie explained that it wasn't anything she'd want to watch and urged the woman to go home and leave the Doberman there overnight.*

*When the woman returned home, the phone was ringing off the hook. She answered it, and was surprised to discover it was the vet. Even more surprising was his message—"Get out of the house immediately! Go to the neighbor's and call the police"*

*It seems that when the vet performed the operation, he found a very grisly reason for the dog's breathing difficulty—three human fingers were lodged in its throat. Concerned that the person belonging to the dismembered fingers might still be in the house, he phoned to warn the woman.*

*According to the story, police arrived at her house and found an unconscious intruder, sans fingers, lying in a closet.*

*New Times learned of the story from an employee of a large industrial plant in the Valley. He said he had gotten the story third hand from another employee who in turn: had heard it from a woman whose relatives in Las*

*Vegas knew the dog's owner. As of Friday, New Times was not able to nail down the identity of the Doberman's mistress.*

*According to a spokesman at the Las Vegas Sun, that paper, too, was very interested in breaking the story. Unfortunately, even though the story was all over Vegas last Thursday, the paper—and police—weren't able to dig up one shred of evidence to prove the incident ever occurred. "The police are baffled," the Sun spokesman said.*

Besides the telltale signs of a vigorous oral tradition in this news story, two details remind us of other urban traditions: one is the *suffering pet theme* (as in "The Poisoned Pussycat at the Party" and "The Pet in the Oven" legends); the second is the *urgent warning given over the telephone* (as in "The Baby-sitter and the Man Upstairs" legend). The conclusion of "The Choking Doberman" story also calls to mind not only the killer who is hidden upstairs in the baby-sitter's house, but also "The Killer in the Backseat," yet another American urban legend, in which a would-be killer lurks in the back of a woman's car. (Legends not discussed in this book appear in *The Vanishing Hitchhiker*.)

"The Choking Doberman" legend—and legend it had to be—was evidently being told all over the country during the summer of 1981, judging from newspaper accounts. The same week the Phoenix, Arizona, story was published, columnist Ron Hudspeth of the *Atlanta Journal* discussed the same story under the headline "Don't bet your life on 'gospel' truths" (25 June 1981): "A half-dozen people have called me with that story in recent weeks," Hudspeth wrote, and "each is dead serious [though] none can identify the woman involved." In Nebraska the *Lincoln Journal* ran a similar article on the Fourth of July: "Police Can't Put Finger on Story." Numerous calls had come in, both to the newspaper and the police in Lincoln, and *Journal* staff writer Toni Cook made manful efforts to follow up the fruitless leads for possible verification of "The Choking Doberman," supposedly having been told on the popular Paul Harvey radio show or learned from "reliable" informants in Iowa. Cook finally decided that he was barking up the wrong tree, that this was "the stuff of which legends are made."

Meanwhile, in the Northwest, Associated Press writer Jim Klahn in Seattle (as reported in the *Portland Oregonian*, 19 July 1981) concluded a lengthy job of research on the Doberman story by writing "It's nothing more than a transcontinental rumor—so far." He mentioned that the story had crossed his news agency's General Desk in New York months before, besides being rampant by word of mouth in his part of the country.

In August "The Choking Doberman" made the news in Florida; "You'll find this story pretty hard to swallow," read the *Tampa Bay Star* headline (19 August 1981) for an article that featured a cartoon version of the legend. The *Star* quoted a St. Petersburg Police Department spokesman as saying, "I think it started at a cocktail party where a bunch of newsmen were." Journalists, at any rate, found "The Choking Doberman" irresistible and kept coming up with witty headlines like "Reporter's Dogged Search Reveals Some Hard-bitten Truths" (*The Spectator*, Hamilton, Ontario, Canada, 1 December 1981), "Weird Story Makes Rounds" (*The Herald Palladium*, Benton Harbor and St. Joseph, Michigan, 31 December 1981), and the inevitable "Did you hear the one about . . . ?" (Los Angeles *Herald Examiner*, 3 February 1982). This L.A. version, in a column by Digby Diehl, gives a nice example of how such stories spread in different versions, and how even a seasoned journalist at first might be fooled by one:

*An astonishing story was told to me by my friend Judy Riley at a dinner party a few weeks ago. One day a woman she knew had returned to her Brentwood home from a shopping spree to discover the family dog, a German shepherd, choking and unable to breath. She rushed the dog to the veterinarian's office; the vet was so busy she was told to leave her pet for observation. When the woman returned home, her telephone was ringing; the vet was on the other end and spoke in a calm but firm tone: "Set down the receiver and run out of your house immediately. Go to a neighbor's house. I'll be right there." Puzzled, and a bit frightened, the woman followed instructions.*

*Minutes later, four police cars arrived, and hiding in the bedroom closet of the house the officers found a large, menacing burglar who was bleeding to death and terrified. The veterinarian arrived on the scene and explained to the homeowner that when he examined her dog to determine the cause of the choking, he had found three human fingers lodged in the dog's throat. He called the police and then called her.*

*Everyone at the dinner party, was stunned by Judy's story. We marveled at the veterinarian's cool; we speculated about our own dogs' ability to attack an intruder; we agreed that urban crime was coming too close for comfort. I re-told the story several times during the following week and thought no more about it until, at a party in Santa Barbara, another friend recounted almost precisely the same story about her friend in Montecito who had a boxer. Subsequently, I heard the story repeated—each time as second-hand truth—about friends in Palos Verdes, Long Island, and San Francisco.*

*Judy Riley was not lying, of course; she was passing on a bit of urban mythology as I had. And part of the power of this folklore is that at the time of the telling we believe the story to be true.*

Diehl had exactly caught the nature of urban legend transmission in this account. A trusted friend at an ordinary social gathering passes on a story in good faith that describes something that supposedly happened to a third party; listeners accept this plausible anecdote as truth and discuss its pros and cons. There is no immediate reason to question such a narrative, since it deals with current concerns, like crime, pets, police, and punishment. Only later, having by then told the story to others, might one hear a varying version and suddenly perceive it as probably apocryphal.

Actual tellings of "The Choking Doberman" in oral tradition—of which I have collected examples virtually from coast to coast—usually dramatize the dog owner's shock, especially at the point of her hearing the vet's surprising commands over the telephone. In the following selection from a version told in Louisiana, for instance, we get this imagined dialogue:

*So, she went back on home, and when she entered, the phone was ringing. And he said, "Leave your apartment immediately and call me back." And she said, "What are you talking about?" "Who is this?" And he said, "This is Dr. So-and-so, the veterinarian." He said, "Get out of that apartment. Go to another telephone. Go to a neighbor or friend or something like that." She said, "You must be out of your mind!" So he said, "Alright, if you won't leave any other way," he said, "would you like to know what was choking that dog? Two black fingers!"*

*And she panicked, and she dropped the phone, and ran over to a neighbor and called him back, and said, "Alright, I'm over at the neighbors. Did you say two black fingers"?*

*"Yes," he said. "Call the cops." So she called the cops.*

The mention of black fingers in the story, with the subsequent discovery of a black intruder hiding in the house, injects a negative racial stereotype into most oral versions of "The Choking Doberman" that is seldom mentioned in published accounts. Providing a striking example of how such themes enter urban legend tradition, a Salt Lake City man told "The Choking Doberman" to a woman in his bowling league, and she happened to be a University

of Utah folklore student who then told the story to me. The intruder, her friend said, was black; he had read all about it in the March 1982 issue of *Shooting Times* magazine. "Fine," I said to her, "Can he show us the story in the magazine?" So he gave her— and she gave *me*—a photocopy of the page from *Shooting Times*, but it was not a black man mentioned there—no definite race was either specified or implied. The storyteller just understood the story that way, and his attitude was typical, for the "black fingers" (occasionally "Mexican fingers") motif has been a standard feature of the oral tradition of this urban legend since it surfaced in the United States.

Core elements of "The Choking Doberman" remain consistent in hundreds of versions I have gathered: the dog is choking, some fingers are extracted, and an injured intruder is found. The points of variation in the story are fairly predictable: the number of fingers, the breed of dog, the race and the hiding place of the intruder, and the exact words of the characters. But widespread folk dissemination of the tradition has introduced an occasional imaginative element into the tale. Sometimes, for example, the bitten burglar leaves the house, but he is caught when he goes to a hospital for treatment; in other versions the FBI is able to trace the escaped intruder by means of fingerprints taken from his severed fingers. (Both of these variations suggest trust in law enforcement officers to get their man.) Several graphically gory versions mention blood dripping from the wheezing watchdog's mouth, or blood seeping from the intruder's hiding place. One veterinarian treating the pet warns the dog's owner, in a curious bit of unnatural natural history, that once a guard dog has tasted blood it has to be killed, since it would forever lust after more and more blood.

I heard of one version of the story in which the dog's owner at first thought the Doberman was choking on a frozen hot dog, and with this in mind we might speculate whether a phallic symbol should be understood by the consistent reference to the intruder's fingers; after all, why didn't the dog go for the throat? And, if fingers could symbolize the penis, would their severence then imply a castration motif? Supporting such a possible reading—besides sexual interpretations of other urban legends (see "The Hook" in my first book)—are related stories to be discussed later in which various male intruders (or supposed intruders) come at their female victims through (symbolic?) windows or doorways with their fingers or hands sticking in at the terrified targets first. Often the intruder is found hiding in a bedroom or a closet therein, probably suggesting that his purpose was rape. Also encouraging a sexual meaning for the legend is this version I received from a reader who heard it in the Midwest:

*A husband returned home from his bowling night and found the family's Doberman choking horribly in the bedroom while his wife was in hysterics. Reassuring her he got down on the floor to see what he could do for the dog, but noticed a trickle of blood running from under the bed. Peering under it, he discovered a half-naked man holding a handkerchief over his badly bleeding hand. His wife tearfully confessed that she and the man had been having an affair. She had always locked the bedroom door to keep Rover out, but this time she had forgotten, and the dog had entered. Apparently he had mistaken their affection for an attack upon the woman, and had sought to defend her by taking a rather sizable chunk out of his hand.*

Considering this sexy version of "The Choking Doberman," we should ponder why with the phallic reality in range this dog went so directly for the mere symbol. Maybe it was an English major at obedience school.

While published versions of "The Choking Doberman" have consistently suppressed the racial and the possible sexual overtones of the legend, with but one exception known to me they have at least clearly stated that the story is untrue—calling it rumor, legend, myth, and the like. The only unqualified firsthand report of "The Choking Doberman" I have found was published in the 10 November 1981 issue of the scandal tabloid *Globe*, printed there as the day's twenty-five-dollar prize "Liveliest Letter":

My Neighbor's Dog Fingered Intruder

*When my neighbor's only son went into the service, he gave her a sleek black dog called Tiger to keep her company.*
*One day, site was working on her old treadle sewing machine when she heard strange sounds coming from Tiger. It was as if he was gagging on something.*
*She quickly bundled him off to the vet, only a short distance away. After a brief check, the vet told my neighbor to go back home. He wanted to keep Tiger there for a few more tests and would call her later.*
*The moment she arrived home, the phone rang. It was the vet.*
*"Get out of the house," he yelled excitedly. "Come back here."*
*My neighbor was completely mystified, yet site complied with the unusual, but urgent demand.*
*Back at the vet's, she was told Tiger was fine, but, added the vet, "He had two human fingers lodged in his mouth.*

*"I've already called the police."*
*When the police later checked the house, they found a man in a severe state of shock, cowering in the closet. He had fingers missing. Apparently, he had broken in through a back window.*

*Tiger had really proved himself worthy of his name.*

—Gayla Crabtree
Lansing, Michigan

Now we have a dog with a name, plus the charming detail of "her old treadle sewing machine," and—best of all—the signed testimony of the neighbor of the victim. Our suspicions arise, however, not only from the doubtful nature of much of the "news" in publications like *Globe*, but also from the fact that a man providing the female victim with her guard dog is not an uncommon motif in the larger tradition, and it preserves the familiar cultural stereotype of protective male/helpless less female that is also projected in other American folklore.

Sometimes, for instance, a father gives his daughter the dog for protection when she goes off to college in another city alone. Or a divorcee may acquire the dog, following her lawyer's advice, shortly after she has shed her husband and is living alone again. And in one version the choking dog is discovered by a female dog-sitter who is watching over a boyfriend's Doberman while he is out of town. But these similarities to oral tradition aside, can we give any credence at all to the Gayla Crabtree/Lansing, Michigan/*Globe*/happened-to-my-neighbor version?

Conveniently, a Michigan journalist did the research on this story that a folklorist might have done. Dan Poorman, a reporter for the *Lansing State Journal*, spotted the letter in *Globe* and went in search of Gayla Crabtree and her neighbor. He quickly learned that there was no one by that name in Lansing who knew anything about the incident and no police or veterinarian reports on the case, and that rumors of such an occurrence had been floating around southern Michigan for some time. Poorman also extracted from the Globe offices in New York City the comment, "It's easy to make up a story." After some more digging, Poorman located a Lansing woman who, using the pen name Gayla Crabtree, had sent *Globe* a story she had heard in a beauty parlor, retold as her neighbor's actual experience. So much for our first-person report.

But the important question to students of folk legends is not "Are they true?" but "Why are they told?" And what do they mean? The consistent themes in variants of "The Choking Doberman" point clearly to fearful current concerns about threats of burglary and violent crimes, especially as these take place in private homes and are directed against women by men. The woman living alone is perceived, according to the legend, as a likely victim for the male intruder. As I have already suggested, this may be understood as an intended sexual assault.

The principal shock in the conclusion of the story—as in several other urban legends—comes from the fact that the intruder is discovered to be hiding right on the premises, and that he was there all the time. Inclusion of a veterinarian and of the police in the legend provides supposed validation, as does reference to friends, relatives, or neighbors who allegedly know the facts behind the case. Specific details—such as the number of fingers, the breed of dog, the dog's name, the hiding place, and so forth—all contribute to the plausibility of the story, which is, after all, no more unreasonable than many news items one reads or hears nowadays. The negative racial reference in oral versions of the story simply reflects the racism in our society in general, as it is also echoed in many versions of "The Killer in the Backseat" legend, in which the driver of the pursuing car is said to be a black man.

What about the dog in the story? Bruno Bettleheim's suggestion in *The Uses of Enchantment* (1976) that ferocious dogs in fairy tales "symbolize the violent, aggressive and destructive drives in man," might be applied to "The Choking Doberman," perhaps, only in the sense that the dog as the man's alter ego vigorously protects the woman. But let us consider further the Doberman pinscher in particular in these current stories. Dobermans (or is it Dobermen?) are traditionally used as guard dogs, sometimes trained as attack dogs, and always look rather lean, hungry, and active. The Doberman's very demeanor, then, suggests something sinister, and if it isn't specifically a Doberman in the story, it's always some large and threatening-looking dog.

Not surprisingly, the Doberman pinscher has an image problem as well as a similar role in other folk stories. Recently (28 December 1982) Ann Landers published a poignant and revealing letter that began:

> *I am a Doberman pinscher, 8 months old. My master says I am the most gentle, friendly dog he has ever had.*
>
> *Now for my problem: Everywhere we go, I hear people say, "That Doberman is friendly now, but wait three or four years. He will go berserk and rip your son's arm off." They say my brain is too big for my skull and that is why I will become vicious one day.*

This dog seems to have heard the legend that describes a young couple with a pet Doberman and a new baby; one day when they have been out briefly, leaving the dog to guard the child, they return to find that the dog in a fit of misdirected sibling rivalry has leapt into the crib (or overturned it) and killed the baby (or chewed off its legs of arms). In another legend, told to me over the telephone from Regina, Saskatchewan, a man has accidentally cut off a finger while working in his home shop; he is rushed to the hospital, where an attendant says that a surgeon might be able to reattach the finger if it is brought in right away. The man's wife hurries home, but she arrives just a moment too late: their Doberman has chewed the severed finger to bits. Or how about the Doberman left in a parked car with the window slightly open for air while the driver stops briefly to shop? Returning to the car, this dog owner, according to the story, finds a finger lying on the seat nearest the open window, while the dog is moving about in the car in an agitated manner. One recent offensive riddle-joke in oral tradition makes a racial/dog connection that is also relevant to our story: "What's brown and black and looks good on a nigger?" Answer: "A Doberman."

But our quest for the history and meaning of "The Choking Doberman" does not end on this sour note. This is only the beginning, since it turns out that several other legends—some new, some old—include many of these same themes First there is the recent apocryphal one about the ladies on the elevator in New York—or did you *believe* that one when you heard it?

## "THE ELEVATOR INCIDENT"

This new American urban legend that has been going around simultaneously with "The Choking Doberman" for the past few years also deals with frightened, isolated, white women, a supposedly threatening black man, and a dog. The strong emphasis on such themes probably shows how scared people really are, though in this story the fright is shown to be a foolish overreaction, and the black man is both genial and generous.

The story's variations and rapid spread can easily be traced through press reports and writers' accounts of' where they picked it up. Let's begin with a column by Jack Jones of the Rochester, N.Y., *Democrat and Chronicle* (5 January 1982):

> *. . . three          unidentified          Rochester women . . . recently visited New York [City]. The women were on an elevator. A black man got on the elevator with a dog.*

*The elevator door closed.*
*"Sit!" the man commanded.*
*The three women sat.*
*The man apologized and explained to the women that he was talking to his dog.*
*The women then nervously said that they were new to New York, and asked the nice man if he knew of a good restaurant.*
*The women went to the restaurant recommended by the man. They had a good meal, and called for their check. The waiter explained that the check had been paid by Reggie Jackson—the man they had met on the elevator.*

Journalist Jones of Rochester managed to get ball player Jackson, formerly of New York—now California—on the telephone. And Jackson, after delivering himself of "a depressing sound—a cross between a groan and a laugh," flatly denied the report, saying, "I've heard the story a thousand times. . . . I would never own a dog in New York. It would be cruel to have a dog in New York. Whatever you've been told isn't true."

Two days later, Bob Minzesheimer, another *Democrat and Chronicle* staff writer, revealed under the headline "Reggie's story still going strong" that columnist Frank Weikel of the *Cincinnati Enquirer* had beaten the Rochester paper to the nonstory by one day; Weikel's "metro today" column for 4 January 1982 had credited "The Elevator Incident" to "a businessman who says it was a friend of a relative." Weikel added, "The guy's been an impeccable source." Well, nobody's perfect.

On 29 January "The Editorial Notebook" column of the *New York Times* discussed the Reggie Jackson anecdote. "It's this season's quintessential New York story," writer Robert Curvin declared, "though . . . it may be next season's quintessential Los Angeles story." In the *Times* version the women were four doctors' wives from York, Pennsylvania, the black man with the Doberman rode down on their hotel elevator with them, and he paid for their breakfast rather than dinner. Curvin also referred to "a Bob Newhart story" (presumably a TV skit) in which a black man had a white dog, and his command to it was "Sit, Whitey!"

Another enterprising reporter, Leigh Montville of *The Boston Globe*, researched the same story; the column containing his results, headlined "The cold facts of a winter tale," ran on 11 February 1982, along with a photograph of Reggie Jackson in civilian clothes more or less fitting the description given by storytellers of "a giant bearded black man, wearing a cowboy hat and jeans." This time the three elderly white ladies were staying in "an exclusive Park Avenue apartment" owned by the son of one of them;

he warned them, "Never resist a mugger . . . do whatever he wants. It's better than dying."

In the conclusion of the Boston Globe story, Reggie Jackson sent champagne to their table and smiled at them from where he was dining across the room in "a fashionable hotel restaurant." Judging from Leigh Montville's summary of his sources for the story, mothers may be a major influence in spreading the legend. (Is this a mother lode of urban folklore?) The summing up:

*My mother has told me this story.*
*"It's true," she said. "I know a woman who knows a woman who was on the elevator."*
*. . . I heard two passengers on a plane to Baltimore tell the story to each other. One guy said it was his mother from Peabody who was involved, swore it was true. The other guy said his mother in Atlanta had told him the same story. She said her best friend was on the elevator.*
*. . . A sportswriter from Philadelphia told me the story. He said a woman in his office had told him the story. She said it was her mother who was on the elevator.*

Montville's and others' mothers notwithstanding, Reggie Jackson's agent, Matt Merola ("in charge of confirming and denying these Reggie rumors"), told the Boston Globe sports writer over the telephone, "I tell everyone it's true. It's it nice story, a good story, if you want it to be true, it's true. Whatever way you heard it, that's the way it happened." Then he admitted "I've had maybe 50 calls on this thing. It's been going on for six months now. . . . No, it's not true. . . . The part about his looks—he goes around town wearing jeans and a cowboy hat all the time—might fit, but the rest doesn't."

So the details of the legend don't fit Reggie Jackson, and the impeccable sources closest to the baseball superstar—plus the star himself—deny the story as it was told by the impeccable sources known to journalists. Did the story, then, die out? Of course not; instead it grew and spread. Why? Because, as Reggie's agent himself said, "It's a nice story."

Mike Harden of the *Columbus* [Ohio] Citizen-Journal fell for the story, and published it in his "One for the Road" column of 13 February 1982. Local variation: the dog is a small one, and the ladies hadn't noticed it; but again, Reggie sent them champagne. Two weeks later Harden confessed in another column that he had published it as a secondhand story, one "which thrived on the Columbus cocktail circuit the way mesquite thrives in cow flop." On 12 June Nora McCabe of the

Toronto Globe and Mail wrote about the "Three little old ladies from Hamilton [who] decided to ignore all the horror stories they'd heard about New York City"; would you believe who they met on an elevator there? Jackson himself, in Toronto with the California Angels, told reporter McCabe, "It's completely erroneous. I've heard it a thousand times—two dogs, two people, whatever. . . . It started about 2 1/2 years ago but I dunno how."

Meanwhile, back in Ohio, Steve Love of the *Akron Beacon Journal* had heard a new version: Three couples from Canton, Ohio staying in a Manhattan hotel that had a rooftop restaurant, boarded the elevator to go up for dinner, and they met boxer Larry Holmes and his huge dog in the same elevator. That's scary except that reporter Love both knew the Reggie Jackson version already (happened in Las Vegas) and also recalled the old Bob Newhart skit. (See "Last laugh belonged to fearful," 14 July 1982). Wilt Chamberlain, "Magic" Johnson, O. J. Simpson, and "Mean" Joe Greene have also been mentioned in versions of "The Elevator Incident," though Reggie Jackson still leads the league in comical elevator episodes. Besides this variation in personal names, another typical folkloristic development for the story is that sometimes there are *three* warnings to the women about dangers they face in the big city: from the travel agent, an airline stewardess, and a taxi driver.

Wherever and whenever the story sprang up, there does seem to have been a much nastier prototype of "The Elevator Incident" circulating in the Midwest some twenty years before the story was sanitized and attached to Reggie Jackson. This legend, much more graphic and sexually explicit than the current version, was collected by folklorist Xenia Cord of Indiana University at Kokomo; she heard it in Cleveland, Ohio, in the early 1960's:

> *A woman went shopping in downtown Cleveland, properly attired in dress, hat, and gloves. Although she was somewhat hesitant to go alone into the downtown area, because the black population had become more obvious and more aggressive of late, she felt that her proper attire would somehow armor her against insult. Arriving downtown, she went to the May Company, an aging but still elegant department store. She entered the ornate self-service elevator. Just as the doors began to shut, two large black men got on. Instead of facing the front of the car, they faced her and approached, forcing her to move to the back corner of the car. Slowly and deliberately they both unzipped their pants, and urinated all over her!*

If we seem in tracing "The Elevator Incident" to have moved far away from "The Choking Doberman," bear in mind that both legends draw their effects from racial stereotypes, fear of crime, and people's efforts to thwart or mollify a potential assailant. To state the similarities more directly, both legends are specifically about white women frightened by black men who they think might want to rob or even rape them. In either plot, the woman may be the wife or the mother of a husband or a son who offers helpful advice or even practical aid toward the woman's defense. (In a way, the elevator story is a bit more like "The Killer in the Backseat" legend than "The Choking Doberman," in that the black man who frightens the woman or women is really a gallant benefactor in the end.)

Besides the general symbolic and psychological affinity of "The Elevator Incident" with "The Choking Doberman," both legends situate the woman or women in a restricted space where escape may be difficult (a hallway or elevator), both may include the son's help or warning, and both may involve a dog. In *some* of the elevator stories (as in *all* of the choking-dog stories) special emphasis is put on the fingers of the black male character in the story. While it is true that simply grabbing the closing elevator door is a natural way to stop it for entry it seems odd that exactly this tiny detail is preserved in several tellings

As interesting as these two recent legends are, however, with their similar emphasis on analogous themes and details, neither one can clearly be said to be the original of the other. They seem to be coexisting independent oral-narrative traditions that deal with related material.

## Study Questions

1. What are "urban legends"? What are their characteristics? How do they get started? Why do people enjoy telling and hearing about them?

2. What do such legends tell us about our society? What does the "Choking Doberman" legend say about our society? How does it help to "explain" or articulate" issues of gender, class, and race in America?

3. How are the "Choking Doberman" and the "Elevator Incident" legends similar and how are they different?

4. Have you ever heard and/or retold an urban legend? How does one know the difference between "fact" and "urban legend"? Are the urban legends told on college campuses any different than those told in other settings? Explain.